D0935821

THE GLOBAL PARTNERSHIP

The Global Partnership

International Agencies and Economic Development

Edited by

RICHARD N. GARDNER

and

MAX F. MILLIKAN

FREDERICK A. PRAEGER, *Publishers*

New York · Washington · London

FREDERICK A. PRAEGER, *Publishers*
111 Fourth Avenue, New York, N.Y. 10003, U.S.A.
77–79 Charlotte Street, London W.1, England

Published in the United States of America in 1968
by Frederick A. Praeger, Inc., Publishers

Library of Congress Catalog Card Number: 68-16087

The essays in this volume originally appeared in a special issue
of *International Organization* entitled "The Global Partnership:
International Agencies and Economic Development," Vol. XXII, No. 1 (Winter, 1968).

PRINTED IN THE UNITED STATES OF AMERICA

PREFACE

In a world divided by deep national, ideological, and racial antagonisms the concept of a global partnership to abolish poverty has a decidedly utopian sound. Yet such a partnership is in the making and provides one of the notable victories for international cooperation in an age marked by national conflict. The essays in this volume chart the growth of this global partnership and the work of the various international agencies through which it works.

Everyone knows what international agencies have failed to do; what they have succeeded in doing is still largely unknown—and therefore needs telling. But the purpose of this volume is not to celebrate past accomplishments. It is rather to examine, in a critical and realistic way, the potentialities and the limitations of international agencies in the struggle for economic development. If the examination lends no support for unrelieved pessimism, neither does it encourage facile optimism. As these essays make clear, the efforts of rich and poor countries alike are still grossly inadequate when measured against the problem to be solved—the achievement of standards of living in the less developed countries compatible with human dignity. If the international war on poverty is to succeed, an entirely new level of effort will be needed on the part of both developed and less developed countries. How successfully international agencies can stimulate this effort and administer programs in the common interest is a vital question. The answer will do much to determine the prospects for mankind in the remaining one-third of this century.

The authors of these essays draw upon a rich vein of personal experience and scholarship in the field of multilateral cooperation for development. We have asked them to focus not only on the economic issues but also on the equally important political and administrative questions involved. We hope the result will prove useful to policymakers as well as to students of economics, political science, and international organizations.

v

We wish to express our sincere appreciation to those who have contributed to this volume and to the members of the Board of Editors of *International Organization* for their helpful suggestions. Each author's contribution is, of course, his own responsibility and does not purport to represent the views of any institution with which he may be associated.

We are also indebted to the Trustees of the World Peace Foundation for sponsoring this undertaking with a generous grant.

RICHARD N. GARDNER

MAX F. MILLIKAN

September 1967

CONTENTS

Preface. *Richard N. Gardner and Max F. Millikan*   v

An Introductory Essay. *Max F. Millikan*   1

The United Nations as an Instrument of Economic and
Social Development. *Walter M. Kotschnig*   16

The Role of Trade in Economic Development. *Isaiah Frank*   44

The General Agreement on Tariffs and Trade. *John W. Evans*   72

The United Nations Conference on Trade and Development.
Richard N. Gardner   99

The International Monetary Fund. *Edward M. Bernstein*   131

The World Bank Group. *Roy Blough*   152

Regional Development Financing. *Henry S. Bloch*   182

Multilateral Technical Assistance. *Karl Mathiasen III*   204

The Consortia Technique. *Paul N. Rosenstein-Rodan*   223

The Organization for Economic Cooperation and Development.
Goran Ohlin   231

The Nine Wise Men and the Alliance for Progress. *Raúl Sáez S.*   244

Multilateral Assistance: Possibilities and Prospects.
Frank M. Coffin   270

Private Foreign Investment and International Organizations.
Stanley D. Metzger   288

Education for Development. *Robert W. Cox*   310

Toward a World Population Program. *Richard N. Gardner*   332

International Cooperation in Food and Population. *Roger Revelle*   362

The Application of Science and Technology to Development.
Sherman E. Katz   392

Wanted: A World Development Plan. *Jan Tinbergen*   417

International Agencies and Economic Development: An Overview.
Robert E. Asher   432

Selected Bibliography   459

Index   477

THE GLOBAL PARTNERSHIP

An Introductory Essay

MAX F. MILLIKAN

THE essays in this volume are designed to throw light on the relations between two of the major novel and unique features of the current epoch of human history, features which distinguish the last quarter century from any other episode in the long record of man's efforts to deal with the problems of his society.

The first of these features is to be found in the burgeoning efforts of the last 25 years to organize world society. We can refer to this feature in shorthand as the emergence of a set of genuinely international institutions. Nothing is wholly new in this world, and the list of organizations that can lay some claim to being called international goes far back in history. But measured in any way you choose, whether by the numbers of people involved, the range of issues dealt with, or the exhaustion of the letters of the alphabet in an acronymic orgy of institution building, we have witnessed since World War II a quantum jump in our preoccupation with the problems of international organization. To believers in the urgent necessity of world government we have taken only a few tiny and uncertain steps in the direction of their target, but comparing 1968 with 1940 or 1945 the numbers and roles of international institutions have expanded explosively. Beginning with the IMF, IBRD, GATT, FAO, and the central foundations of the United Nations structure itself there has been a proliferation of agencies like UNESCO, WHO, WMO, and more recently UNCTAD and UNIDO, a multiplicity of bodies outside the UN family like OECD, LAFTA, and CIAP, numerous regional banks, and the continuation of a few older institutions like ILO and the OAS which suggest only the beginning of the long, long list.[1]

MAX F. MILLIKAN is Director of the Center for International Studies, Massachusetts Institute of Technology, Cambridge, Massachusetts.

[1] As mentioned in their respective order, the International Monetary Fund (IMF), the International Bank for Reconstruction and Development (IBRD), the General Agreement on Tariffs and Trade (GATT), the Food and Agriculture Organization (FAO), the United Nations Edu-

I

The second of the major features of our epoch upon which we are here focusing attention is the rapid growth of the concern of the whole world community with the welfare of all of its parts, and especially of its less advantaged members, of which economic performance has come to be a convenient if sometimes misleading index. We can call this for short the increasing concern with the problem of world economic and social development. Postwar improvements in the statistical record have made us all aware that in terms of economic indexes the international distribution of income is very uneven and that two-thirds of the world is very far behind the other third. For this reason this developmental concern has been very largely concentrated on the problems of the less developed countries. Again it would be incorrect to describe this as historically a completely new phenomenon. The colonialization of the nineteenth and earlier centuries, with all of its many faults, included a component of concern for what would now be called development, and this paternalistic and somewhat condescending humanitarianism was also widely reflected in private charitable and missionary activities. But until World War II such public activity as there was in this field was confined to the responsibilities which national governments accepted for the peoples coming under their direct jurisdiction.

It is remarkable that before World War II no one's list of the top priority problems of the world community would have included the economic and social development of the less developed countries. In 1968 it is inconceivable that it would be left off of anybody's list. The developed countries for their part are coming increasingly to view it both as in their national interest and as part of their world responsibility to allocate time, resources, and effort to the development problems of countries to which they have no special political ties. This is evidenced by the establishment during the past decade in virtually all of the developed countries of special ministries or other major governmental units specifically charged with the development assistance problem.[2]

For most of the less developed countries their own development has of course become since the war a priority objective of their own national policy. This by itself gives no evidence of a growing concern on their part

cational, Scientific and Cultural Organization (UNESCO), the World Health Organization (WHO), the World Meteorological Organization (WMO), the United Nations Conference on Trade and Development (UNCTAD), the United Nations Industrial Development Organization (UNIDO), the Organization for Economic Cooperation and Development (OECD), the Latin American Free Trade Association (LAFTA), the Inter-American Committee on the Alliance for Progress (CIAP), the International Labor Organization (ILO), and the Organization of American States (OAS).

[2] For an illuminating brief survey of this trend see Goran Ohlin, *Foreign Aid Policies Reconsidered* (Paris: Development Center of the Organization for Economic Cooperation and Development, 1966), Chapter II.

with development as a world problem. There are many small signs, however, that increasingly in the less developed countries the problem is
being seen less exclusively as a national and parochial one and more and
more as an issue meriting international consideration and attention. National self-interest is unquestionably and appropriately the dominant
element in the concern of the less developed countries with the world
development problem since each is dependent for capital, technical assistance, and trading opportunities on the policies of the developed world.
Nonetheless, they are beginning to take an interest in each other's problems and exhibiting some small beginnings of a willingness to accept
international responsibilities as well as international favors.

These two features of the post-World War II era, the emergence of
genuinely international institutions and the increasing concern with the
problem of world economic and social development, have many common roots but so far only limited relation to each other. They both reflect
a growing conviction that in a world where both physical and psychological distance are collapsing under the impact of the modern revolution in transportation and communications the distinctions between domestic and foreign policies are becoming less and less meaningful. New
Delhi and Tokyo are in many senses nearer New York in 1968 than was
either San Francisco or New Orleans 40 years ago. The economic, social,
intellectual, and political interdependencies among all the parts of the
world community are now so much more pervasive than they were only
yesterday that both international institutions and world development have
a wholly new meaning. The recognition of this fact is disappointingly
slow, but a look back at 1940 underlines how dramatic have been the
changes that have already taken place.

But international institutions have been built up for many reasons
other than development, and nations pursue their development activities
to only a minor extent through international institutions. To take a financial measure, only about 10 percent of the flow of development aid in
both capital and technical assistance as defined by OECD is being
channeled through multilateral institutions, and the balance is being
administered bilaterally.[3] As we will see presently, this understates the
degree to which development assistance has been multilateralized during
the past decade, but there are some very real and valid questions to which
the essays in the remainder of this volume are addressed as to whether
the emerging philosophy of world economic and social development
and the institutional arrangements made by the world community to im-

[3] See the report by Willard L. Thorp, *Development Assistance Efforts and Policies of the
Members of the Development Assistance Committee: 1966 Review* (Paris: Organization for Economic Cooperation and Development, 1966), Statistical Annex, Table 4, p. 150, and Table 11,
pp. 162–163.

plement that philosophy are in step. As a prelude to the discussion of particular functional problems and particular institutional forms in the essays to follow it might be well to review briefly some of the elements that have affected the history of the relation between international institutions and world economic development over the past ten or fifteen years. There has been an important thread of continuity in that history, but there have also been some notable evolutionary changes not all of which are fully appreciated. I would like to concentrate on three such changes.

The first relates to some changes in the ways in which some of the more important of the developed countries have perceived their interest in the development process. The second has to do with changes in the diagnosis and understanding of the problem of development both in the developed countries and in the less developed parts of the world. The third concerns changes in the nature of the institutional arrangements employed by the world community to carry out its development activities.

It is tempting to take the gross annual flow of official financial resources for economic development from the developed to the underdeveloped countries as an index of the level of acceptance by the developed countries of their world developmental responsibilities. For reasons I will explain later this index is at best misleading. What it shows for the OECD countries is a rapid rise from the average level of the early 1950's of under two billion dollars to a level of about six billion in 1961. From then until the present the level has stayed roughly constant in the neighborhood of six billion. Since the gross national products of the major developed countries have continued to rise briskly through the 1960's, their official contributions figured as a percentage of gross national product have been falling for the past few years.[4] To this must be added disbursements of Sino-Soviet bloc aid which began at around $100 million in 1956 and rose to $300 or $400 million in the early 1960's and perhaps private capital flows of two or three billion dollars a year, much of which was by oil interests. Taken as an index, this suggests rapidly mounting levels of concern during the fifties followed by at best a leveling off in the sixties or in terms of percentage of gross national products an actual decline through the early years of the Development Decade widely heralded by the UN. This corresponds with the widespread impression that, for example, in the United States there has been a marked recent disenchantment with the aid program and a tendency to retrench since the peak at the beginning of the Kennedy Administration.

[4] See *The Flow of Financial Resources to Less-Developed Countries, 1956–1963* (Paris: Organization for Economic Cooperation and Development, 1964), Table II-1, p. 18; and Thorp, *Development Assistance Efforts and Policies.*

This global statistical record, however, conceals some significant changes in the motivations of aid programs both in the United States and in Western Europe which are relevant to our present concerns. In the United States the decade of the fifties was a period of intense—some would say almost pathological—concentration on the East-West conflict and on the ideological competition with the Union of Soviet Socialist Republics, particularly in the underdeveloped countries. To a considerable extent the United States aid program was presented by the executive branch and defended by its Congressional supporters as making a major contribution to the long-run security interests of the United States through its presumed effect in inhibiting the advance of Communism in the underdeveloped world. The bulk of United States aid funds went to countries on the periphery of the Sino-Soviet bloc and especially to those with which this country had military alliances of one kind or another. Indeed in the 1950's we described all economic aid to countries with which we had such alliances as defense support. The entry of the Soviet bloc into the aid business in the mid-fifties was regarded by many in the United States as a competitive move to which we had to respond with increased aid allocations. As the popular and Congressional preoccupation with the East-West conflict subsided to somewhat more sober levels, the articulation of United States interests in economic aid underwent something of a transformation.

This was reflected in the substantial expansion of aid to Latin America in the sixties and in the elaboration of the institutional machinery of the Alliance for Progress described in more detail in Raúl Sáez' essay in this volume. Thus accompanying the leveling off of gross United States aid flows was a change in the philosophy and underlying motivation of the United States aid program which brought it much closer to the kind of program which could be multilateralized. This shift should of course not be exaggerated. There was always an element of world community responsibility in the support of the aid programs of the fifties, and those of the sixties have certainly not shed all their United States strategic and short-term political purposes. Nonetheless, there has been a real if limited shift in the mood and temper of United States aid activities symbolized in the new war on hunger and emphasis on education and health which tempers one's interpretation of changes in the aggregate aid budget.

There has been a related if somewhat more subtle change in the thinking underlying several of the larger European aid programs, notably those of France and the United Kingdom. As Goran Ohlin has pointed out,[5] the overwhelming bulk of the aid of European countries which formerly had colonial empires has gone to their former colonies. While

[5] *Foreign Aid Policies Reconsidered*, Chapter IV, pp. 81–83.

there has been no significant statistical change in this gross fact over the past decade, there is some reason to believe from government and other reports in these countries that the motivation for aid may have significantly altered. The feeling of responsibility as well as of political interest in former colonies does not die abruptly, and a good deal of the early motivation for French, British, Belgian, and Dutch aid was of this sort. As more and more of the colonial ties are broken and the traditional relationships recede further into history, one would expect this motive to wane and the amounts made available under it to decrease. The fact that the levels have been maintained in the sixties and in the case of some countries with no colonial history, like the Scandinavian countries and Austria, even markedly increased, suggests that there has been an important shift from narrowly national to somewhat more international motivations in European aid programs. Even France, whose aid levels, while the highest in Europe in per capita terms, have been most narrowly restricted to areas of special French political interest and which has been the most hesitant in accepting internationalization of aid efforts, has shown signs in the Jeanneney report and in credits to non-French territories that new directions for its aid are not impossible.

In summary, what we have been saying with respect to motivations is that among the donors there has been more of a movement toward a willingness to support aid as a constructive policy of the world community toward its less affluent members than is suggested either by the statistics of aid levels or by the increase in the use of multilateral agencies.

Let us turn now to our second set of evolutionary changes during the postwar period, those changes in our diagnosis of the fundamental nature of the problem of development. In summary, this is the story of a running battle between our growing recognition that development is a highly complex and many-faceted process requiring simultaneous action on many fronts covered by many disciplines, on the one hand, and, on the other, the human tendency to want to simplify, establish priorities, and concentrate action on one or two critical fields. This is a serious enough problem for the intellectuals whose professional business it is to provide as sophisticated a diagnosis of the barriers to modernization as modern social and natural science will permit. It is a much more serious problem for the politicians—in both developed and underdeveloped countries—who must articulate a rationale for the actions they are proposing to take which is simple enough to be widely understood and plausible enough to generate the necessary degree of popular support. In practice this has meant that both in the development programs of the less developed countries and in the aid efforts of the developed countries the emphasis has shifted about erratically from capital to technical assistance to human resources and institution building; from social overhead to steel plants to small-scale industry to agriculture to fertilizer; from national economic plans to international trading arrangements to monetary policy to implementation. The most sophisticated observers have known from the beginning that all these things were necessary and that both bilateral and multilateral institutional mechanisms were needed, but the jungle of agencies, national and international, to deal with the development problem with which we are confronted in the year 1968 has come into being in part through a historical process of successive rediscovery of each of the major elements of the developmental process, usually with a new institution resulting at each stage.

One of the early simplifications was the economist's model according to which the essence of the process of development is to be found in an increase in the rate of saving and investment in the less developed countries from the traditional levels of 5 to 8 percent to the required levels of a minimum of 12 to 15 percent. The less developed countries were described as being caught in a low-income trap in which they were too poor to reduce their consumption and increase their investment to the level necessary to escape from poverty. The simple solution to this dilemma was clearly an infusion of capital resources from outside which could be supplied either by individual donor nations or by a multilateral fund to which they would all contribute. The World Bank, which was set up very early to finance bankable projects, has come increasingly to perform this function. The provision of developmental capital to fill what has more recently been called the savings gap in the underdeveloped countries has continued to be a major element in the aid picture up to the present, though as our understanding of capital requirements has changed and enlarged there has been a proliferation of institutions devoted to meeting this need. The principal multilateral ones are described in the essays by Roy Blough and Henry Bloch in this volume. In its early days the World Bank concentrated its resources mainly on relatively large projects of a social overhead character in transportation, power, and irrigation and did not concern itself much with the internal development policies of the recipients of its loans; while the indebtedness of the underdeveloped countries was limited, it could make loans on fairly conventional banker's terms. Changes in our understanding of the role of outside capital, in the importance ascribed to self-help policies by the less developed countries, and in the mounting debt burden of those countries have led both to changes in the policies and mode of operation of the Bank itself and to the establishment of such new institutions as the International Finance Corporation (IFC), the International Development Association (IDA), and the various regional development banks described more fully in a later essay.

Another focus of attention in early development assistance activities quite different from the capital-oriented models of the economists was the notion that the top priority in development was the transfer of the knowledge, talents, and techniques responsible for the progress of the developed countries to the underdeveloped world through programs of technical assistance. This was the concept which underlay the American Point Four Program enunciated by President Harry S. Truman in 1949 and the UN's Expanded Program of Technical Assistance (EPTA) launched by that body in the following year. While there is nothing inconsistent in the functions of supplying capital and technical assistance, and perceptive discussions of the relations between the two can be found in some of the early literature, it is nonetheless true that two very different casts of characters with rather different diagnoses of the central problems of development were involved in these early efforts, and that connections between them were minimal. Each has undergone evolutionary change over the succeeding years. Within the UN structure, as Walter Kotschnig brings out in his essay, the gap was partially bridged by the establishment of the United Nations Special Fund in 1957. This was a compromise to meet the demands of the underdeveloped countries for a capital fund which the developed countries were not prepared to support financially. The Special Fund was designed to perform those kinds of technical assistance particularly relevant to placing the underdeveloped countries in a position to utilize large-scale capital resources more effectively. Thus, its main activity consisted of preinvestment surveys.

The full integration of technical assistance and capital financing activities into a coordinated development assistance system has yet to be achieved, but substantial movement in this direction has occurred with the merger of the Special Fund and the Expanded Program of Technical Assistance into the UN Development Program (UNDP) and with the growing importance of the technical assistance activities of such capital financing institutions as the World Bank Group. Karl Mathiasen describes the evolution of multilateral technical assistance in his essay.

In the late 1950's a new fashion swept the world of development analysts and had its impact on multilateral development institutions. This was the focus on human resources and institution building. Educational assistance and organizational help to institutions in the developing countries were prominent in technical assistance activities from the beginning, but new voices were raised in the late fifties saying that the most critical bottleneck to development was the absence of human skills running from simple literacy to modern technological competence and that top priority should go in development assistance to investment in human beings. This was sparked partly by a concern with economic development itself and partly by a worry over the destabilizing political consequences of patterns of education inappropriate to development needs which were producing in many of the underdeveloped countries groups of young people unsettled by education but frustrated by their inability to find productive and satisfying jobs in their societies. There was a new interest in education to which UNESCO responded and a new concern with what was called manpower planning which breathed new life into an old organization which had lost much of its prestige, the International Labor Organization. Robert Cox's essay focuses on this range of considerations. Again we have made some progress at integrating education and manpower planning with other elements of development planning, and agencies with other functions like the World Bank, FAO, and UNDP are devoting increasing attention to the educational dimensions of their problems, but we have not yet achieved an integrated systems approach.

Another strand of thinking concerned with one sort of technical assistance which blossomed in the early sixties was the more effective application of science and technology to development problems. This, as described in Sherman Katz' essay, had its kickoff in the huge 1963 UN Conference on the Application of Science and Technology for the Benefit of the Less Developed Areas (UNCSAT). Mercifully the pressures from the underdeveloped countries for the establishment of still another permanent multilateral institution devoted to this subject were resisted, and a compromise arrangement for a continuing UN committee was substituted. I do not think any knowledgeable person ever really assumed that development could be brought about by waving a scientific wand, and the conference underlined that the skillful application of science and technology to the whole range of development problems was a pervasive task for all the institutions in the development business rather than an appropriate province for a new and separate organization.

In addition to these various functional differences of emphasis there were debates from the beginning about the priority to be given to the various different sectors of each developing economy in order most effectively to promote self-sustaining economic growth. One group, given both doctrinal and financial support from the Communist countries, pointed out correctly that development was everywhere accompanied by a rapid expansion in the fraction of the labor force and of all other resources devoted to manufacturing industry. They derived from this the incorrect logical implication that policies for development should therefore be concentrated on the promotion of the manufacturing sector. There were differences of opinion within this group as to which elements of manufacturing deserved priority. The Soviet Union had emphasized in its own growth the expansion of the heavy industry complex based on steel, and this had a romantic appeal for some of the less sophisticated elements in the underdeveloped world who saw in the establishment of steel mills and aluminum plants a kind of symbolic testimony of their entry into the modern age. Other groups among the economists, pointing out that capital was the scarcest resource in the developing world and that heavy industry tended to be quite capital intensive, argued that priority should rather be placed on the consumer goods and raw materials-processing industries in the early stages, heavy machinery coming later. There was no reflection of this industrial doctrine in the early history of international organizations, and UNIDO, the United Nations Industrial Development Organization, did not make its appearance on the scene until the mid-sixties.

There was from the early days a contrary view that since the bulk of the populations of the underdeveloped world lived in rural communities and since, however rapidly industrialization took place, the bulk of the gross products of these countries would consist of agricultural activities for some time to come, the key to development was to be found in agriculture, community development, and rural uplift. Supporters of this philosophy rallied internationally around the Food and Agriculture Organization whose functions are described here in the essay by Roger Revelle. Meanwhile, a third emphasis, social overhead capital, transport, communications, and power, was bolstered by the lending policies of the International Bank, which were heavily concentrated in these fields in the early days. The population explosion discussed by Richard Gardner was too dramatic to be neglected by the early analysts but too politically sensitive to be reflected in any national or international institutional activity until quite recently.

While the more perceptive development analysts had recognized from the beginning that each of these activities has an important place in virtually every underdeveloped country, that the search for a single critical bottleneck is doomed to failure, and that in a systems problem like development excessive concentration on what are conceived to be overriding priorities is likely to be self-defeating, the interconnections and interdependencies between these various programs were only dimly perceived in practice. One reflection of that perception was the growing interest in the late 1950's and early 1960's in national economic development planning. This technique of relating the manifold parts of a development program was launched fairly early by a few of the governments of underdeveloped countries like India for a combination of political and economic reasons and was actively promoted by some elements of the international organization community, notably the Economic Commission for Latin America (ECLA) under Raúl Prebisch, at a fairly early date. By 1961 its importance was sufficiently recognized so that even the United States government began officially to encourage the preparation of national economic plans by recipients as a condition for long-term aid commitments. Technical assistance agencies began to give economic planning assistance, the country reviews of the International Bank were increasingly focused on national economic plans, and the reviewing of such plans came to be one of the functions of such international bodies as the Nine Wise Men and the Development Assistance Committee (DAC) of OECD.

As the 1960's progressed it became increasingly clear that these national planning efforts had two very serious weaknesses. The first was that the plans, being essentially national activities, could say very little about and do very little to influence the international economic environment in which each country had to operate. The second was that countries came increasingly to recognize that the gap between sophisticated plans on paper and effective implementation of the policies and programs called for in the plan was a very large one and that good planning was only a relatively small part of effective development programs.

The first of these omissions was underlined by the foreign trade and foreign exchange problems with which the underdeveloped countries increasingly found themselves confronted. Foreign trade had been a preoccupation of international organizations since League of Nations days, and one of the first postwar international organizations, the International Monetary Fund, was established to deal with international monetary problems. But these early concerns were focused very heavily on the bulk of the world's trade and finance which took place among the developed countries, and the factors relating trade and development outlined by Isaiah Frank in his essay were not emphasized in early development thinking. This emphasis in the principal postwar trade organization, GATT, as described by John Evans, was so marked as to lead the underdeveloped countries to press vigorously in the early 1960's for a new organization, UNCTAD, which would concentrate specifically on the trade and development problems of the less developed world. Richard Gardner describes the evolution of this new institution in his essay. At the same time, the older organizations like GATT and the IMF began to turn an increasing proportion of their efforts and energies toward the trade and international financing problem of the less developed countries. Edward Bernstein examines the IMF role in this process in his essay.

In the academic world the models constructed by economists to analyze development have, in the last few years, reflected an increasing recognition that what has come to be called the foreign exchange gap is a separate bottleneck distinct from the savings gap and, in many under-developed countries, more limiting. The problem for analysis is that while the savings gap can be fairly fully explored for any given country by examining relationships internal to the country's economy, with foreign aid introduced as an arbitrary exogenous feature, the foreign exchange gap can be effectively analyzed only with international models which study the interactions between the policies and programs of different countries.

This calls, as Jan Tinbergen points out in his essay, for an extension of planning from the national to the international arena in ways which have only begun to be hinted at to date. National economic planning is designed to illuminate the domestic allocation of national resources confronted by national governments. We are just beginning to think about the rational allocation by collective decision of international resources in a similar manner. Just as in mixed economies national economic planning must make estimates of the probable behavior of private buyers, sellers, and investors in order to plan effectively for public development programs, so in the international field an appraisal of the factors influencing private capital flows is a necessary part of any systematic thinking about international resource allocation. Stanley Metzger deals with this problem in his essay.

The other problem of more effective attention to everything that is involved in the implementation of development programs is not one that lends itself to international institutional solutions. The UN Committee for Development Planning appointed by the Secretary-General to review the progress of the Development Decade has been concentrating its attention on these problems of implementation but has so far done little more than to give the problem a little sharper definition.

In summary, the major characteristic of the past decade in the evolution of our perception of the nature of the economic and social development problem has been an increasingly realistic recognition both of the complexity of the problem and of the length of time necessary to make significant progress toward its solution.

The increased realization of complexity is reflected not so much in the multiplication of international institutions to deal with different aspects of development as it is in the increased awareness that each of these institutions must concern itself more and more with the interactions between its own central mission and those of many of the other agencies. The controversies of the early years over priorities to agriculture, industry, or social overhead or emphases on capital, technical assistance, or human resources are giving way slowly but surely to a heightened concern with how to make the various pieces fit together. This is well illustrated in the current excitement about the world food problem which is now seen not as a problem exclusively for FAO or the agricultural specialists but as one that is so intimately tied up with the whole problem of development that it is getting an important share of the attention of UNIDO, UNCTAD, the World Bank Group, and all the rest.

With respect to time scale it is now recognized that one decade is not, as was suggested in 1960, a long enough time period to really launch the less developed countries into self-sustaining growth, and while the accomplishments so far in the Development Decade are substantial, the Economic and Social Council (ECOSOC) of the United Nations has already taken steps to launch constructive thinking on targets and procedures for a second Development Decade, the decade of the 1970's. It is to be hoped that this greater degree of realism will lead to increasingly effective performance.

The third evolutionary change in the postwar period on which I would like to offer a few comments is the change in our perception of the institutional requirements for dealing with world economic and social development. In the late 1940's and early 1950's this problem too was greatly oversimplified. It was viewed as a simple alternative between a series of bilaterally conceived and administered aid programs, relatively unrelated to each other, on the one hand, and a single multilateral institution handling all economic development assistance in a consistent and coordinated way, on the other. We have already described one set of changes in this caricature of the problem which have come about under the impact of the explosive proliferation of both national and international institutions as one after another of the aspects of the development problem has received concentrated attention. While there is increasing concern with the coordination of the activities of all the international institutions with each other and with those of the even greater number of specialized national bodies, no serious student would now argue that a plausible solution is to merge all development assistance into one mammoth organization. The appropriate roles for national as opposed to international institutions is still a lively subject but it is seldom any longer posed as an either-or debate.

Meanwhile the subject has been complicated by the addition of another dimension of growing importance in the last few years. It is increasingly recognized that at least with respect to some problems the jump from national to world loyalties is rather too big a one to be taken in one step and that an appropriate way station is the development of a whole series of regional institutions to deal with the common problems of small groups of countries. For analytic and training purposes increasing emphasis is being put on the regional economic commissions of the United Nations, regional development banks are playing an increasing role in the supply of capital, regional trading arrangements have been launched in Europe and Latin America and are being discussed elsewhere, and an interesting set of organs for the regional review of development plans and performance has been tried in Latin America and is reported on in detail in Raúl Sáez' essay. The growth of this regional approach is parallel with the growing recognition that effective development requires not merely appropriate relations between the developed countries on the one side and the less developed on the other but also much more intimate relations between the underdeveloped countries themselves. Since the problems and characteristics of these countries vary substantially from region to region, a regional focus makes sense from an economic as well as from a political point of view.

There has, however, been a much more fundamental change in attitudes toward multilateralization than is revealed either in the growth in international institutions or in the channeling of resources directly through them. This is an increasing recognition that the problem of multilateralization is not solvable by institutional machinery alone but requires a growing recognition of common interests, the need for common criteria, and the necessity for joint commitments between donors, between donors and recipients, and between recipients themselves. There has been a multilateralization of spirit and approach to development problems which to my mind is much more significant than its institutional reflection. One form in which this has been expressed is the increasing degree of consultation and collaboration among donors both as to the requirements of recipients and as to donor's methods of operating their bilateral programs. This has been reflected, for example, in the increasing weight given by its members to the deliberations of the Development Assistance Committee of OECD described by Goran Ohlin in his essay. The World Bank has taken the lead in another series of consultative procedures through the various consortia of donors which the Bank has organized around the programs of a number of the principal recipient countries. There are limitations in these procedures which are underlined by Paul Rosenstein-Rodan in his essay on this subject, but they certainly represent a major advance over uncoordinated bilateral aid.

Finally, there was the experiment of the Nine Wise Men which was an attempt to introduce into essentially bilateral aid procedures an advisory review of Latin American development programs by a panel of experts selected primarily from the region itself. While this experiment cannot be classed as an unqualified success, it is historically a very important move in the direction of multilateralization. In addition to these attempts to put bilateral aid in an increasingly multilateral framework there has been an increasing number of projects like the Mekong River project involving a number of recipient as well as donor countries. If one were to take as one's index of multilateralization not the fraction of development assistance administered by international institutions, as is commonly done, but the fraction whose volume and character are significantly influenced by international consultation and review, the record of the 1960's so far would show much more notable progress.

The progress is still only a bare beginning. Frank Coffin in his essay analyzes the political forces in the United States and the other developed countries inhibiting and those promoting the full acceptance by the world community of responsibility for the economic and social development of all of its parts. The essays in this volume, trenchantly summarized by Robert Asher in his final overview, give an account not only of how far we have come in the short period since the end of World War II but of how much farther we have to go if we are to realize the full potential of international economic development.

The United Nations as an Instrument of Economic and Social Development

WALTER M. KOTSCHNIG

CHANGE has been the one constant in the brief but eventful history of the United Nations. Whatever its shortcomings, the UN has proved itself responsive to the turbulent forces of a dynamic age. Whether it will be able to marshal these forces, to channel them for productive ends, remains to be seen.

The changes wrought in the Organization are most clearly evident in its economic and social endeavors. In contrast with the Covenant of the League of Nations the Charter assigns an important place to economic and social matters, to "the creation of conditions of stability and well-being," and to the promotion of fundamental human rights. It assumes a close relationship between the maintenance of peace and security and the economic and social advancement of peoples. However, few, if any, founders of the United Nations anticipated that twenty years after its establishment close to 80 percent of its total resources would be devoted to economic and social programs. Nor did anyone foresee in 1945 the phenomenal increase of these resources, reaching a total of $290.8 million in 1966,[1] and their concentration on the development of the vast under-developed regions of the world. If the assessed budgets of the specialized agencies and the International Atomic Energy Agency (IAEA), but not counting the International Bank for Reconstruction and Development

WALTER M. KOTSCHNIG is United States Deputy Assistant Secretary of State, Bureau of International Organization Affairs. He has served as deputy United States representative on the Economic and Social Council of the United Nations since 1947.

[1] Assessed UN budget and voluntary contributions to United Nations Development Program (UNDP). In 1946 the total resources, in the absence of voluntary contributions, amounted to $19.3 million.

(IBRD) and related financial institutions, are added, together with the voluntary contributions to the United Nations Children's Fund (UNICEF) and the World Food Program (WFP), the total resources of the United Nations system in 1966 amounted close to $530 million.

Both in composition and in concept the United Nations as it emerged from the San Francisco United Nations Conference on International Organization was essentially an organization of the West. Its original membership of 51 States was made up of eight European states firmly wedded to traditional democratic institutions; four old British Commonwealth states; twenty Latin American countries whose leadership gloried in their "Latinidad" while, by and large, maintaining strong economic and political bonds with the United States; seven states from the Middle East, including Turkey, Iran, Iraq, Lebanon, Syria, and Egypt with their intellectual, commercial, and, to some extent, political ties with Western Europe; only three Asian countries—China, India, and the Philippines; the Union of Soviet Socialist Republics and two of its constituent republics; three additional European states—Czechoslovakia, Poland, and Yugoslavia, which were moving or being moved into the Soviet orbit although not yet beholden to Moscow; only two African states—Ethiopia and Liberia; and the United States, which emerged from the war a military colossus, an economic giant, and the leading creditor nation. The three Communist Member States aside, the leaders of this grouping of nations shared a remarkably wide basis of common thought, political tradition, and economic philosophy. The pervasive influence of the United States, its concepts, and aspirations were clearly reflected in the Charter as hammered out at Dumbarton Oaks and in San Francisco.

This, of course, does not mean that during the early years of the UN there was any lack of controversy and differences of opinion, particularly in the economic field.[2] Serious differences existed among highly developed countries of the West, such as Australia and the United Kingdom, on the one hand, and the United States, on the other, regarding commercial and foreign exchange policies and their impact on full employment. American and British ideas regarding a general liberalization of trade ran into many-sided opposition. The question of commodity agreements designed to assure to developing countries fair and equitable returns on their exports of primary commodities became an early bone of contention between developed and developing countries (or LDC's, i.e., less developed countries, as they are frequently called in contemporary jargon). The dollar gap, balance of payments, monetary stability, infla-

[2] See Williams Adams Brown, Jr., "The Inheritance of the United Nations" in Robert E. Asher and others, *The United Nations and Promotion of the General Welfare* (Washington: Brookings Institution, 1957), pp. 153–199; and Richard N. Gardner, *Sterling-Dollar Diplomacy* (Oxford: Clarendon Press, 1956).

tion, and other financial issues were recurrent and controversial themes in the Economic and Social Council (ECOSOC) and the General Assembly, as well as in the International Bank for Reconstruction and Development and the International Monetary Fund (IMF).

Whatever the differences, it is evident from the early records of the Economic and Social Council that most of the problems discussed not only involved immediate interests of the highly developed countries but tended to be viewed and "solved" in keeping with their economic and social concepts and doctrines. Debates were held within the framework of parliamentary procedures modeled on those of the democratic institutions of the Western world. There was a sustained dialogue between the proponents of opposing views and the vote was a meaningful tool of decisionmaking rather than a ready guillotine.

Western influence is clearly reflected in some of the major achievements of the first decade in the life of the UN, such as the creation of a UN system of organizations composed of the specialized agencies, old and new, tied into the United Nations by formal agreement aimed at coordinated action; the creation of functional and regional commissions; the development of effective central services such as the Statistical Office of the United Nations and a clearly articulated Department of Economic and Social Affairs in the UN Secretariat; the preparation of a long series of outstanding reports by experts which frequently resulted in policy recommendations by ECOSOC and the General Assembly, and follow-up by governments acting individually and jointly; the drafting and approval of such basic instruments as the Universal Declaration of Human Rights; and the initiation of technical assistance programs.

During this period the forward thrust of the UN was, alas, seriously blunted by two developments beyond its control. To this day it has not recovered from these setbacks. The first was the failure of UN-sponsored efforts to establish the International Trade Organization (ITO). When it became clear that the Havana Charter would not obtain the necessary ratifications, attempts were made to distribute ITO functions among various UN bodies and organizations (for instance, ECOSOC was assigned cartels and other restrictive business practices) for which they were not equipped. The General Agreement on Tariffs and Trade (GATT), operating outside the UN and only loosely connected with it, became the chosen multilateral instrument for international trade negotiations and related questions. This sharply reduced the role of the UN in trade matters, present and future, and helped create the conditions which in 1965 led to the establishment of the United Nations Conference on Trade and Development (UNCTAD).

The second adverse development was the refusal of the Soviet Union in 1948 to participate in the European Recovery Program (ERP) or to permit the countries within its orbit to share in it. To what extent UN cooperation in the Marshall Plan might have benefited that great reconstruction effort is an open question. There can be little doubt, however, that cooperation of East and West in the rebuilding of Europe would have helped to lay a firm basis for greatly expanded multilateral action within the UN framework at a later stage.

The Soviet refusal marked the beginning of the Cold War with all its tragic consequences and inhibitions on constructive endeavor in the UN. Reasoning turned into propaganda, argument into vituperation. Endless speeches on the glories of life in the Communist states contrasted with the misery of the masses in capitalist countries and the imminent collapse of the latter filled the record of almost every meeting. Statistics kept at that time show that on many occasions the two to three members who, out of the total ECOSOC membership of eighteen, represented Eastern European countries used up more than half of ECOSOC's time.

Even so the time may not have been altogether wasted. If nothing else, the "debates" did result in a measure of confrontation and a clarification of views. Basic differences in political philosophy and economic thought on such subjects as the relative merits of the public compared with the private sector, the role of trade unions in Communist and non-Communist states and the significance of freedom of information were articulated. The very excess of the propaganda and unbridled attacks on the part of the Soviet bloc minimized the impact on the members. It helped pile up an almost unbroken record of Soviet voting defeats at that period. The excesses of this period may even have contributed to the eventual shift of the Soviet Union, after the death of Joseph Stalin, toward "peaceful coexistence," which was prompted by profound changes in domestic conditions and in relations with other countries in their orbit and by the general world situation.

EMERGENCE OF NEW NATIONS: THE MEMBERSHIP EXPLOSION

Only nine new Members were admitted to the UN during the nine years from 1946 to 1954: two developed countries from Western Europe (Iceland and Sweden); six developing countries from the Middle East and Asia (Afghanistan, Thailand, Pakistan, Yemen, Burma, and Indonesia); and Israel. These accessions, while slightly increasing the voting strength of the developing countries and providing a somewhat larger audience for Soviet speeches on colonialism and the new economic imperialism of the United States, did not substantially change the power constellation in bodies such as ECOSOC or their preoccupations. The

United States initiative in 1949 proposing a greatly enlarged program of technical assistance (the Expanded Program of Technical Assistance [EPTA]) was not due to pressures in the UN but was largely a self-generated expression of practical American idealism as formulated by President Harry S. Truman in his second inaugural address. It was strongly opposed by the Soviet group, which waited until 1953 to make its first voluntary contribution and which still maintains it at the low level of about 3 percent of total voluntary contributions.

Nineteen hundred fifty-five saw more drastic changes in membership. Sixteen new Members were admitted, including four from Eastern Europe (Albania, Bulgaria, Hungary, and Rumania); six other European countries (Austria, Finland, Ireland, Italy, Portugal, and Spain); four developing countries from Asia; one Middle Eastern nation; and Libya, the first African country admitted since 1945. These additions made the Soviet group more vocal without decisively changing its voting strength and gave more resonance to the voice of Asia. That voice was heard, however, more loudly in the Trusteeship Council and the General Assembly in demanding political independence for peoples remaining under foreign rule. Pressures for more substantial financial aid to the developing countries and for improvement in their terms of trade were, however, beginning to mount.

The growth of membership during the next four years was small but foreshadowed the membership explosion of the early sixties. Only seven new Members were added between 1956 and 1959, all, with the exception of Japan, newly emerging states from Africa (Morocco, the Sudan, Tunisia, Ghana, and Guinea) and Asia (Malaysia). In 1960 alone seventeen new states were accepted for membership, all, with the exception of Cyprus, from Africa. Another 22 achieved membership by the end of 1966 (thirteen from Africa, plus Mongolia, Jamaica, Trinidad and Tobago, Kuwait, Malta, the Maldive Islands, Singapore, Barbados, and Guyana).

Tedious as this recitation of statistical data may be, it is essential to an understanding of what has happened in recent years to the United Nations and its economic and social programs. Starting out in the forties as a Western-inspired organization, it became an arena in which East and West sought to gain favor and influence with the newly emerging states of Asia and Africa. Emphasis then shifted to North-South relations or, more accurately, to the interests and concerns of the developing countries and their relations with and demands upon the states of advanced economic and social development.

By the end of 1966 the UN had 122 Members. Of these 87 were in the category of developing countries, including 37 from Africa, 24 from

Asia and the Middle East, and 24 from Latin America and the Caribbean. Malta and Cyprus complete the list. All of them are seeking and receiving development assistance from the United Nations. Most of them tend to negotiate and vote as a bloc on issues of aid and trade and other major economic and financial issues. This is particularly significant in the case of the Latin American states, which in such new UN organs as UNCTAD and the United Nations Industrial Development Organization (UNIDO) joined the developing countries of Africa and Asia in a frequently bitter confrontation with the North. The developing countries potentially have absolute control over decisionmaking since a two-thirds majority of the total membership (82 out of 122) is sufficient to carry any resolution.

The voting strength of the developing countries is in inverse ratio to their assessed contributions to the organizations. Fifty-four are assessed at the minimum rate of 0.04 percent. They thus jointly contribute only 2.16 percent of the total assessed budget of the UN. Another 28,[3] assessed at rates ranging from 0.05 to 0.36 percent, contribute another 3.51 percent of the total budget. Therefore, 82 countries, representing an absolute UN majority, provide only 5.67 percent of the assessed budget.

The above is not meant to suggest that the developing countries are not doing their part in giving financial support to an organization which spends close to 80 percent on economic and social programs primarily designed to further their development. Assessments are calculated on complicated formulas which do not favor any one group over another. Thus, the comparatively minimal contributions which the developing countries make reflect above all their lack of financial resources and their lag in economic development. The recognition that they are poor casts no aspersion upon them but is rather a challenge to the *beati possedentes.* The fact remains, however, that a vast and potentially dangerous discrepancy exists between their voting strength and their ability to contribute toward UN resources.

The impact of the new political constellation on the Organization has been profound. A new dynamism, intolerant of the past and impatient in its drive for new purposes and objectives, is evident. New priorities have been established to meet the needs and aspirations of the developing countries. There has been steady pressure to reinterpret the powers of the General Assembly and other intergovernmental bodies within the UN. The work programs in the economic and social fields have become increasingly action oriented. New organs and organizations have been created within the UN and much of the institutional pattern as estab-

---

[3] This includes Yugoslavia, which has achieved a position of leadership among the developing countries.

lished under the Charter has been changed. In a word, the UN of 1967 is radically different from the institution created in 1945. A proper understanding of the UN as it now exists and operates requires a more detailed analysis of the changes that have occurred.[4]

DECADE OF DEVELOPMENT

When President John F. Kennedy, in 1961, invited the General Assembly to designate the sixties as the United Nations Development Decade (UNDD), he spoke to the condition of the new United Nations in the making. The acceptance of his proposal not only reflected the needs and aspirations of the developing countries but gave a clear focus to all the economic and social activities of the United Nations and established "development" as *the* overriding objective.

In its resolution on the subject[5] the General Assembly set as its goal the attainment by the developing countries of "a minimum annual rate of growth of aggregate national income of 5 per cent at the end of the Decade." It emphasized the need for increasing the transfer of resources to developing countries by expressing the hope that the flow of international assistance and capital

> should be increased substantially so that it might reach as soon as possible approximately 1 per cent of the combined national incomes of the economically advanced countries.[6]

Finally, the General Assembly endorsed the United States suggestion that resources available for technical assistance through the Special Fund and the Expanded Program of Technical Assistance be increased so that their combined 1962 budgets reach the target of $150 million.

In his appraisal of the Decade in 1965 the Secretary-General brought out the true significance of UNDD:

> The launching of the Development Decade represents a new departure in international economic relations. By agreeing to co-ordinate action with a view to attaining a 5 per cent growth rate in developing countries, Governments in fact extended the concept of sustained and expanding demand from the domestic economy to the world at large. Furthermore, the adoption of a target for the transfers of resources to developing countries in terms of a proportion of the national incomes of developed countries showed that the concept of shared resources is beginning to enter the philosophy

---

[4] For an earlier study covering the impact of the growing membership on the UN up to 1965 see Harold Karan Jacobson, "The Changing United Nations," in Roger Hilsman and Robert C. Good (ed.), *Foreign Policies in the Sixties: The Issues and Instruments* (Baltimore, Md: Johns Hopkins Press, 1965).

[5] General Assembly Resolution 1710 (XVI), December 19, 1961.

[6] General Assembly Resolution 1711 (XVI), December 19, 1961.

of States in relation not simply to their own citizens but to other States as well.[7]

A year later, Philippe de Seynes, Undersecretary for Economic and Social Affairs, stated, after referring to the widespread disappointment with the poor international performance at midpoint in the Decade, that

> the concept is alive and enduring. . . . It has become a symbol of the collective responsibility of the international community for the development of the Third World. . . . It is . . . a unifying principle providing us with a dynamic and positive notion of co-ordination—something more than the traditional measures to combat duplication of effort—which enables us to merge an important part of our activities in a concerted effort.[8]

It is clear from these statements that UNDD is not designed to produce a blueprint for the millennium. It has not produced and is not expected to bring forth a definitive plan to end poverty, retardation, and desperately low levels of living everywhere in the world by a given time. It is difficult to conceive how such a plan could be achieved even in theory. Such an attempt could even be harmful for it might raise expectations not likely to be fulfilled and divert energies from programs and projects which can achieve early results and prepare the way for the attainment of long-range objectives. The UNDD concept does, however, provide an ordering principle. It gives focus and direction to the sum total of UN efforts and those of its related agencies; it releases latent energies and resources needed to achieve effective development in the territories inhabited by two-thirds of the world population; and it brings about coordinated and concerted action by national governments and within the system of United Nations organizations rather than a medley of unrelated programs and projects.

This does not, of course, mean that planning is not needed to establish realistic development targets either on the country, regional, or overall level, to clarify ways and means, to avoid false starts, to test performance, and to coordinate progress in such fields as health, education, agriculture, industry, and trade. De Seynes puts the same thought this way:

> It would not be sufficient to merely study planning methods or to produce projections which were as accurate as possible; what was much more important was to examine planning experience in concrete situations, to devise methods and criteria for assessing performance and the implementation of plans of individual countries, seeking to intensify, on the basis of quantitative data as well as qualitative judgments, the study of the main obstacles

---

[7] *The United Nations Development Decade at Mid-Point: An Appraisal by the Secretary General* (United Nations Publication Sales No: 65.I.26 [UN Document E/4071/Rev.1]) (United Nations, 1965), p. 6.

[8] "World Economic Trends" (UN Document E/L.1127, July 13, 1966), pp. 3-4.

to growth and trying to evaluate the efficiency of the policies pursued in relation to those objectives and those obstacles.[9]

Consequently, much emphasis has recently been given to providing the UN with basic planning facilities. Particular attention has been given to the work of the Committee for Development Planning which had its first session in 1966. Planning centers have also been established at the seats of the regional economic commissions.[10] There is a growing volume of studies and publications in special fields, many of which preceded the establishment of the Committee for Development Planning. Examples are *Studies in Long-Term Economic Projections for the World Economy*[11] (prepared by the Economic Projections and Programming Center in the UN Secretariat); projections for agricultural commodities up to 1970 by the Food and Agriculture Organization (FAO), which is at present preparing a monumental Indicative World Plan for Agriculture, overall and by countries; trade projections by UNCTAD; a world plan drawn up by the International Telecommunication Union (ITU) for the establishment of a coherent system of international telecommunications; the plan of the World Meteorological Organization (WMO) for the creation of the World Weather Watch with its far-reaching implications for agriculture, air transport, and so forth. As a matter of fact, most of the specialized agencies as well as the functional commissions of ECO-SOC are engaged in long-range planning, both in terms of targets and programs. There is, also, a general trend toward two-year or longer programming cycles.

While many of these studies and plans, several of which are discussed in greater detail elsewhere in this volume, are near universal in scope, practically all of them are angled to the needs and requirements of the developing countries. This orientation is seen even more clearly in the UN work programs adopted in recent years. A few representative examples can be cited by way of illustration. The use of science and technology for the benefit of the developing countries is obviously a matter of high priority. Transferal of the requisite knowledge and skills to the developing lands was the central issue in the United Nations Conference on the Application of Science and Technology for the Benefit of the Less Developed Countries (UNCSAT) in 1963. As a follow-up to this conference the Economic and Social Council created an Advisory Committee on the Application of Science and Technology to Development composed of high-level experts. This committee has been working on a

[9] *Ibid.*, p. 7.
[10] For a discussion in depth of these problems see Jan Tinbergen's essay "Wanted: A World Development Plan" elsewhere in this volume.
[11] *Studies in Long-Term Economic Projections for the World Economy: Aggregative Models* (United Nations Publication Sales No. 64.II.C.2 [UN Document E/3842]) (United Nations, 1964).

world plan in this area, has established a set of priorities tailored to the needs of the developing countries, and has recently given attention to a program for the exploration of natural resources in the less developed parts of the world. It has prepared a study on the world protein gap, evident in large parts of Africa and Asia, with specific recommendations for international action not only to feed but to provide an adequate diet for the expanding world population and avert an "impending protein crisis."[12]

On an even wider basis the United Nations itself, its Population Commission, FAO, the World Health Organization (WHO), the World Food Program, and other UN bodies are coming to grips with the crucial issue of establishing a balance between rapidly increasing populations and the resources required to sustain them. This, of course, is again primarily a problem in Asia, Africa, and Latin America. Programs to promote and assist family planning have been slow in coming, for reasons which need not be discussed here. But there are indications of an impending breakthrough. In this context there is also a discernible trend, led by the United States, away from food relief toward the promotion of sharp increases in agricultural production in the developing countries. The requirements of modern agriculture, the necessary input of fertilizers and machinery, and effective land reform in the broadest sense of the word are being stressed. While FAO holds the key to many of these problems, the recently established United Nations Industrial Development Organization is expected to render major support through the promotion of agroindustries. More will have to be said later about this organization, which, like UNCTAD, is essentially a creation of the developing countries.

In the social field the Social Commission of ECOSOC last year changed its name to the Commission for Social Development. Its ambitious plans call for concerted programs on the part of the UN and the competent specialized agencies to raise the levels of living and health, education, and welfare in the poorer countries. The Committee on Housing, Building, and Planning of the Council is also concentrating its programs on the appalling housing conditions in the developing countries, even to the neglect, as some feel, of the very real problems of housing and urban renewal in highly developed countries, including the United States.

The primacy of the interests of the developing countries has been evident also in the field of human rights. In the 21st General Assembly a majority of these countries were able to sterilize Article 1, paragraph 2, of the International Covenant on Economic, Social, and Cultural Rights and the International Covenant on Civil and Political Rights, which

---

[12] UN Document E/4343, May 25, 1967.

provides for the exercise of the right of permanent sovereignty over national resources *in accordance with principles of international law*. They proposed and voted the addition of an independent article to the effect that:

> Nothing in the present Covenant shall be interpreted as impairing the inherent right of all peoples to enjoy and utilize fully and freely their natural wealth and resources.[13]

The intent of this article is to remove obstacles to expropriation of foreign-held property or the cancellation of contracts and concessions. This type of "legislation" reflects the drive of the developing countries for "their place in the sun." It also reflects a lack of sophistication since, alas, it is bound to affect adversely the private investment climate and thus prove counterproductive.

Notwithstanding such lapses, the "operational programs," i.e., the technical assistance and preinvestment activities of the UN, gained in volume and impetus due to the pressures brought to bear by the new Members. Their accession helped to highlight their needs and meant greater pressure on the developed countries to provide additional financial assistance. Contributions to EPTA and the Special Fund, later combined in the UN Development Program (UNDP), increased from $72.4 million in 1960 to $156.9 million in 1966. Pledges to UNDP for 1967 totaled more than $172 million.

A decisive number of the new Members joined the United States and other Western states in bringing about the merger of EPTA and the Special Fund in the new UNDP in 1965 in the face of the strenuous opposition of several specialized agencies unduly concerned with their "autonomy." The merger and the creation of effective management and intergovernmental control permitted, for the first time, overall planning of the UN's largest operational program. It gave impetus to better coordination of programs and projects on the country level and greatly advanced sound administration of UN activities in the recipient countries. Thus, the operational programs and the countries benefiting from them have registered a remarkable gain in recent years.

It would be a mistake to ascribe the shift in emphasis in UN economic and social programs to the new Members from Africa and Asia alone. As a matter of record, many of the most successful initiatives antedated the new numerical majorities of the developing countries. This is true even though some of them were undoubtedly shaped by the mounting

---

[13] Article 25 of the International Covenant on Economic, Social, and Cultural Rights and Article 47 of the International Covenant on Civil and Political Rights. Both Covenants as well as the Optional Protocol to the International Covenant on Civil and Political Rights are contained in the annex to Part A of General Assembly Resolution 2200 (XXI) of December 16, 1966.

vocal clamor on the part of the developing countries for the establishment of a Special United Nations Fund for Economic Development (SUNFED) in a form unacceptable to most of the developed countries (see page 30 below).

The United States along with smaller industrialized countries such as the Netherlands and the northern tier of Europe brought about the establishment of EPTA, 1949; the International Finance Corporation (IFC), 1956, and the International Development Association (IDA), 1960, both initiated through ECOSOC; the creation of the Special Fund, 1958; and, with the help of the developing countries, the birth of UNDP. More recently, the new stress on development in the social field and the extension of the work in the field of housing were to no small degree of United States inspiration. This is a record well to be remembered in view of attempts by some LDC's, aided in varying degrees by the Communist bloc countries, to tar the United States in the UN with the brush of "economic imperialism" and "neocolonialism."

With the first UN Development Decade having less than three years to run there has been a growing sense of frustration and mounting criticism in the developing world over its shortcomings and failures. The anticipated growth rates in the LDC's have been lagging. The flow of international assistance has been well below one percent of the combined incomes of the economically advanced countries. George D. Woods of the International Bank has estimated that in order to achieve a desirable growth rate an additional $4 to $5 billion in international financial aid is needed annually. Paul G. Hoffman, UNDP Administrator, makes the figure as high as $15 billion by 1970. Inasmuch as this question is discussed in detail by Roy Blough elsewhere in this volume we will refrain from comment at this point. It is certain, however, that the gap in production, income, and levels of living between "the rich and the poor" is widening rather than closing in many cases.

This sad fact does not mean the failure of a "plan," for there has been no "plan." Growth rates have improved in a large number of developing countries.[14] Income has gone up in absolute terms on a per capita basis, except where it has remained stationary or even declined due to rapid and rampant population increase. This, unfortunately, is true of some of the poorest countries and may extend to other countries unless the rate of population growth can be substantially reduced. But there is no cause for despair. Viewed as a symbol of released energies and as an ordering

---

[14] See *Gross National Product, Growth Rates and Trend Data* (Agency for International Development, RC-W-138) (Washington, March 31, 1967). The 1960–1966 average GNP growth rates of nineteen developing countries were 5.0 or above with twelve developed countries being in the same range (United States average, 4.8). The AID study does not cover the centrally planned economies.

principle to achieve concerted action the UN Development Decade has far from failed. In the words of the Secretary-General, "The developing world, for all its frustrations, is in motion."[15] It has made some break from tradition and quite a few of even the least developed countries are learning to invest their resources in the right things. The marked shift in emphasis from industrialization per se to the modernization of agriculture is a case in point. There is reasonable hope that UNDD will go beyond being a helpful concept, a symbol, an ordering principle, and engender a new ethic of development in developing and developed countries alike.

In accordance with the requests of the General Assembly in Resolution 2218 (XXI) of December 19, 1966, and ECOSOC Resolution 1152 (XLI) of August 4, 1966, the Council Committee for Development Planning has already examined the question of preparing guidelines and proposals for the second United Nations Development Decade.[16] Looking toward the establishment of a "charter" for the second Development Decade, it proposed the setting of development targets in terms of GNP, overall and by sectors. It further proposed that the means to be employed by both the developed and the developing countries to achieve those targets should be specified. Thus, the developed countries would be expected to make specific pledges in both quantitative and qualitative terms relating to the scale and character of their aid and trade policies. There can be no doubt about the significance of this ambitious proposal. Whether it is realistic to expect advance pledges by governments covering a ten-year period is another question.

Reinterpretation of the Powers of the UN

The United Nations was not established as a legislative body. Its powers are essentially recommendatory, except for certain actions with respect to threats to the peace, breaches of the peace, and acts of aggression (Chapter VII of the Charter and Article 25); certain problems relating to the operation of the trusteeship system; questions of membership; elections to principal organs of the UN; the creation of subsidiary bodies; and budgetary questions and similar housekeeping functions, including the establishment of rules of procedure. There is nothing in the Charter which gives binding character to any "decisions" on action to be taken by Members of the Organization on economic, social, and related matters (again, with the exception of enforcement actions under Chapter VII). Article 2, paragraph 7, specifically prevents the UN from interven-

---

[15] *The United Nations Development Decade at Mid-Point*, p. 30.
[16] "Committee for Development Planning, Report on the Second Session (10–20 April 1967)" (UN Document E/4362), pp. 27–28.

ing in matters essentially within the domestic jurisdiction of Member States. Needless to say, "recommendations" by any of the principal organs of the UN carry considerable weight and call for consideration by UN Members, but they are not binding.

These limitations on the powers of the UN do not apply to the establishment of operational programs of the UN itself, the formulation of policies, rules, and regulations governing these operations, and the approval of specific programs and projects. It must be remembered, however, that participation in all the major operational activities (such as EPTA, the Special Fund, and UNICEF) is voluntary: They are financed from voluntary contributions, and there is no obligation on the part of any Member to contribute to or share in the benefits of these activities if it does not like the ground rules under which they operate. Some minor operational programs such as the Advisory Social Welfare and Human Rights Services are financed from the assessed budget by common consent. They are small and do not place substantial burdens on any Member. Attempts to escalate them and, consequently, to increase beyond the limits of common consent the financial obligations of the Members would be fraught with serious consequences and could cause a constitutional crisis.

Changes have occurred in these basic concepts as a result of the massive increase in membership during the last six years. These, however, have been "atmospheric" rather than juridical, representing differences in approach and interpretation rather than changes of the Charter. Due largely to the impatience and lack of experience or sophistication of many of the LDC's, resolutions now tend to be treated as if they were more than recommendations. Attempts are made, by way of resolutions, to "legislate" action on the part of Member governments, to prescribe new approaches and attitudes, to establish new binding "principles," or rules and regulations of international behavior. The wording of resolutions is fought over as if a new constitution were being written. Or, what is more serious, by automatic majorities the LDC's vote texts which, in their view, place "obligations" upon important minorities which have made it clear by their negative vote that they are not able or willing to accept them. The "majority" seems to care little that such "obligations" often relate to matters within the domestic jurisdiction of all Members.

A prize example of such an ill-considered attempt to "legislate" is the persistence with which the developing countries insist on the binding nature of various "principles" and recommendations in the Final Act of UNCTAD.[17] These, in their view, put an "obligation," both in terms

---

[17] *Proceedings of the United Nations Conference on Trade and Development, Geneva, 23 March–16 June 1964,* Vol. I: *Final Act and Report* (United Nations Publication Sales No: 64.II.-B.11 [UN Document E/CONF.46/141, Vol. I]) (United Nations, 1964).

of domestic legislation and international action, on the very developed countries which opposed and voted against them both in the first UN Conference on Trade and Development and in subsequent meetings of such bodies as the General Assembly and ECOSOC.

Another striking example is the "decision" in the 21st session of the General Assembly (Resolution 2186 [XXI] of December 13, 1966)

> to bring into operation the United Nations Capital Development Fund . . . as an organ of the General Assembly which shall function as an autonomous organization within the United Nations. . . .

The resolution further provides that

> expenses for administrative activities shall be borne by the regular budget of the United Nations, which shall include a separate budgetary provision for such expenses.

This resolution culminated the long drive by the developing countries, mentioned earlier, to establish a Special UN Fund for Economic Development under the direct control of the UN membership. While contributions to this fund are voluntary, the resolution makes it clear that administrative expenses are to be financed from the assessed budget. The developed countries are thus obligated to provide the lion's share of administrative expenses for a fund most of them strongly oppose. Their opposition is based primarily on a conviction that every effort ought to be made to use existing institutions such as IBRD, IFC, and, above all, IDA, as well as such newly created regional banks as the Inter-American, Asian, and African Development Banks, rather than create yet another fund which must be figured in billions rather than in millions if it is to make any real difference. It will be interesting to see what happens when the 22nd session of the General Assembly must decide how much UN Members are to be "taxed" to provide administrative support for a fund the capital resources of which may never materialize.

Even more serious is the blithe disregard frequently shown for Charter provisions. A serious instance of such disregard, affecting Chapters IX and X of the Charter,[18] has been the denial, overt or implied, by a majority of LDC's of the coordinative arrangements laid down in the Charter. These coordinative arrangements constitute the very basis of the UN system of organizations. Equally serious is their refusal to recognize the powers and functions of the Economic and Social Council in this respect. This point will require further consideration.

---

[18] Chapter IX is entitled "International Economic and Social Cooperation" and includes Articles 55–60. Chapter X is entitled "The Economic and Social Council" and includes Articles 61–72.

INSTITUTIONAL CHANGES

The developing countries have not been content with making the most of their absolute majority in the General Assembly. To buttress their position throughout the UN, particularly on the economic and social side, they waged a successful campaign in 1965 and 1966 to increase the size and radically to alter the composition of existing intergovernmental bodies and to create new bodies so organized as to assure LDC majorities. To achieve these objectives they demanded that whenever at all feasible "equitable geographic distribution" be the overriding principle in determining the composition of any intergovernmental body (even of expert committees). Other criteria, such as the ability to discharge the obligations of membership under the Charter, the availability of qualified experts, or the readiness to contribute effectively to the promotion of the general welfare, were given little weight or discarded altogether.

In mounting their drive for hegemony the new Members showed a remarkable ability to organize themselves and thus to bring about significant changes in procedures. Voting by group is, of course, part of the democratic process and has been characteristic of many votes taken in the UN since its inception. The free world countries, though naturally coalescing on a basis of common socioeconomic thought or regional interest, did not form rigid blocs. Decisions more often than not were taken by mixed majorities crossing group lines. This situation changed radically at the first UNCTAD Conference. Not only was the membership of the Conference organized along group lines (A: Afro-Asian states; B: Western European and other states; C: Latin American states; and D: Socialist states of Eastern Europe) but the Asian-African and the Latin American groups fused into the "group of 75" developing countries. Open dialogue, negotiations, and consultations between the groups to achieve common or broad consent were reduced to a minimum. Group B found itself confronted with resolutions written by the "75" and offered on a take-it-or-leave-it basis. Leadership of the "75" drifted to the more extreme and uninhibited members of the group which were able to defeat efforts of the moderates among the LDC's to maintain the dialogue and obtain common agreements. The pattern established at UNCTAD has carried over to this day. There are, however, signs of erosion and a desire for greater independence among members of the group which now numbers well into the eighties. The UNCTAD pattern certainly had a bearing on the enlargement of practically every kind of organ or body under the General Assembly and ECOSOC and it had an even greater bearing on their composition.

ECOSOC was among the first of their targets. With the arrival of close to two score members from Africa the Council came under heavy attack. It was called completely unrepresentative of the total UN membership and a tool of the "colonialists" and the vested interests of the rich. One African delegate proclaimed in public session that his chief purpose in serving on ECOSOC was to destroy it. In 1964-1965 the effectiveness of the Council was seriously impaired. A majority of the LDC's reinterpreted Chapters IX and X as vesting all responsibility for economic and social matters in the General Assembly. They denied that the Council had any real functions or power, particularly to coordinate programs and activities.

Most of the developed countries readily agreed that the Council was too small and unrepresentative of the UN's enlarged membership. As a matter of fact, as early as 1958 the Netherlands, supported by the United States, initiated a resolution in ECOSOC recommending that the Council be enlarged. The amendment of Article 61, paragraph 1, of the Charter on December 17, 1963, which raised the membership of the Council from eighteen to 27, met with general acclaim. As to composition the center of gravity shifted decisively to the developing countries. In 1967 the Council was composed of seventeen LDC's (seven from Africa; five from Asia; five from Latin America), seven Western states, including Canada and the United States, and three Socialist states of Eastern Europe. The LDC's have thus achieved a majority of seventeen out of 27 in a body which takes all votes by simple majority. There is, however, encouraging evidence that this development has lessened opposition to the Council and that it will be better able to discharge the functions assigned to it under the Charter in the future.

By the same token most of the Council's functional commissions and committees have also been enlarged from a membership varying from eighteen to 24 to a new membership varying from 27 to 32, with seats distributed to assure the LDC's built-in majorities. In such major bodies as the Commission for Social Development and the Commission on Human Rights with new memberships of 32 the LDC's constitute absolute majorities, including eight African members.

The Governing Council of UNDP, established by the General Assembly in Resolution 2029 (XX) of November 22, 1965, has 37 members elected by ECOSOC under a formula providing for

> equitable and balanced representation of the economically more developed countries on the one hand, having due regard to their contribution to the United Nations Development Programme, and of the developing countries on the other hand, taking into account the need for suitable regional representation among the latter members. . . .

This was a hard-won compromise to assure effective performance of a program moving toward an expenditure of close to $200 million a year, with the United States providing 40 percent of the funds. The formula governing the elections provides for nineteen seats for the developing countries and seventeen for the economically advanced countries. While this gives the developing countries a built-in majority, no vote has ever been taken in the Governing Council. All decisions have been taken by consensus, which is highly significant. The balance is sufficiently close to discourage tests of strength by vote. Even more telling is the fact that the advanced countries not only provide most of the funds but do so voluntarily. Their contributions could be reduced or even discontinued if unacceptable decisions were taken.

UNCTAD AND UNIDO

The developing countries consider UNCTAD *the* major organ for development. It is their greatest achievement in institution building within the UN. It reflects most clearly their determination "to take over" and to develop new patterns of trade and economic behavior tailored to further their own interests and economic growth. These facts emerge clearly in Richard N. Gardner's essay in this volume. Three points made by him require highlighting and elaboration here. They are essential to the main thread running through this discussion.

The first is the take-over in terms of votes. Composed of 55 members, the Trade and Development Board of UNCTAD is larger than any of the corresponding boards or councils of the major specialized agencies. The escalation in numbers was as much due to the desire of some of the Western European countries to be represented on the Board as to the drive of the LDC's for "equitable geographic distribution." Eighteen of its members are elected from the principal trading states and highly developed countries. Thirty-one seats are reserved for developing countries and six for the Soviet group.

Second, UNCTAD's mandate covers not only trade but also development. Reference in the Final Act to "trade-related" problems of development are little more than a cover for the claim that any aspect of development has an impact on trade and is therefore within the competence of UNCTAD. Indeed, the interrelationships between trade and development are so close as to give this claim a semblance of justification. "Development," however, is the overriding concern of the UN in all its economic and social programs and also has top priority in most of the specialized agencies and other related organizations. UNCTAD's attempt to assume the commanding position in guiding the development programs of the entire UN system of organizations is bound to lead to conflict, dislocations, and confusion of functions and responsibilities. It weakens rather than strengthens overall development efforts undertaken multilaterally. A clear and present danger thus exists that vital interests of the developing countries will be buried in jurisdictional conflicts and ill-conceived attempts at "empire building." Conflicts on shipping, insurance, and tourism as well as the respective roles of UNCTAD and GATT in the field of trade promotion have already arisen.

Third, there are serious, unresolved problems in the coordination of programs and activities for which UNCTAD claims primary responsibility. The Charter clearly and unreservedly confers responsibility for coordination upon the General Assembly and ECOSOC. Over the years these two principal UN organs have developed extensive coordination devices and machinery including formal agreements with the specialized agencies, the Administrative Committee on Coordination (ACC), the Advisory Committee on Administrative and Budgetary Questions (ACABQ), and the sessional Coordination Committee of the Economic and Social Council. UNDP, with its responsibilities for the planning, administration, and financing of the technical assistance and preinvestment program of the UN system also plays a major role in coordination. In 1966 the General Assembly's *Ad Hoc* Committee of Experts to Examine the Finances of the United Nations and the Specialized Agencies (*Ad Hoc* Committee of Fourteen) gave new impetus and guidance to effective coordination within the UN and its related agencies. Partly in response to the recommendations of the *Ad Hoc* Committee ECOSOC in 1966 reestablished its earlier Special Committee on Coordination as a greatly strengthened Committee for Program and Coordination (CPC) composed of sixteen governmental experts. To this the General Assembly added another five members, all but one from developing countries. At the Committee's session in the spring of 1967 the developing countries played a very constructive role. They were among the first to reaffirm the coordinating responsibilities of ECOSOC and the General Assembly. The Committee decided to review in depth UNCTAD and UNIDO programs, together with their financial implications, at its second session in 1968.

UNCTAD has been exceedingly reluctant to play its part within this framework of established coordination machinery. There has been a continuing trend, actively supported by key members of the UNCTAD secretariat, to bypass ECOSOC and disregard its coordinative functions as laid down in the Charter. In contrast with the secretariats of the specialized agencies the UNCTAD secretariat has taken almost no part in the labors of the Council or in the other coordinating bodies set up by the Council and/or the General Assembly. Its thrust has been to take over the work and functions of the UN and UN-related bodies such as GATT rather than to coordinate with them.

These observations are not made in a spirit of barren criticism. UNCTAD obviously is a body of major importance dealing with crucial problems of both the developing countries and the highly advanced states. Its very importance, however, makes it mandatory that UNCTAD, as a major addition to the UN structure, fit itself harmoniously into the UN system of organizations and thus give additional strength to the common drive for economic and social growth.

The story of the United Nations Industrial Development Organization is in many respects similar to that of UNCTAD. Also essentially a creation of the developing countries, its purpose is

> to promote industrial development . . . and by encouraging the mobilization of national and international resources to assist in, promote and accelerate the industrialization of the developing countries, with particular emphasis on the manufacturing sector.[19]

Like UNCTAD it is an organ of the General Assembly and "shall function as an autonomous organization within the United Nations. . . . " It has its own secretariat (to be located in Vienna) and its separate budget within the assessed budget of the UN. Unlike UNCTAD there is no provision for a periodic conference. UNIDO is governed by an Industrial Development Board (IDB) similar to UNCTAD's Trade and Development Board. The Board's 45 members are elected by the General Assembly under a formula which gives 25 seats to Africa, Asia, and Latin America; fifteen to Europe, North America, Australia, New Zealand, and Japan; and five to the Socialist states of Eastern Europe. On coordination and cooperation with UN bodies and other organizations Resolution 2152 (XXI) states that the

> Organization shall play the central role in and be responsible for reviewing and promoting the co-ordination of all activities of the United Nations system in the field of industrial development.

The resolution contains references to the functions of ECOSOC, similar to those, although somewhat more explicit, contained in the UNCTAD statute.

It is thus evident that UNIDO presents the UN with many of the same problems it faces in its relations with UNCTAD. They should prove, however, less intractable. The Organization's objectives are more limited and do not roam over the entire field of development. In the

---

[19] General Assembly Resolution 2152 (XXI), November 17, 1966. Growing out of the modest beginnings of the ECOSOC Committee for Industrial Development (CID), the Organization was established in principle by Resolution 2089 (XX), December 20, 1965.

absence of periodic conferences with a membership larger than that of the United Nations there are likely to be fewer power plays and a greater willingness to cooperate constructively with established UN organs and within the framework of the Charter. Unlike UNCTAD no pressure has so far developed for the creation of complex subsidiary machinery.

For the time being UNIDO's problems lie elsewhere. The Industrial Development Board's first session in April of 1967 revealed that the Organization is still in search of a clear-cut program. As in the old CID there continues to be an overemphasis on study, research, reports, manuals, and other paper productions which, while useful in themselves, do not build smokestacks or create effective management of industrial plants. There was a fair measure of agreement that the Organization should be more "action oriented" and should build up its operations in the field rather than at headquarters.

The Board grappled, rather inconclusively, with the problem of priorities, i.e., the type of industries most likely to advance the interests and modernization of the developing countries. Among those discussed were consumer industries which might yield early and readily visible gain in the welfare of the broad mass of people, thus providing tangible motivation for the acceleration of industrial development. Also discussed were agroindustries to permit the modernization of agriculture in the face of the impending world food crisis and export-oriented industries to help obtain the foreign exchange necessary to pay for the imports required to sustain industrialization. The Soviet group, as usual, led the parade of those urging concentration on basic capital industries. There was also discussion of the relative importance of the public as compared with the private sector and a proper balance of the two. In a more practical vein, much attention was given to furnishing truly effective technical assistance which could set in motion an organized flow of technology and know-how to the developing countries. This must include a transfer of managerial skill and financial expertise. It means assistance to countries in planning, in the formulation of requests for aid, and in the implementation and execution of projects and programs as well as a major effort of training to provide skilled manpower. UNIDO cannot itself be expected to provide the billions of dollars required to build individual plants and vast industrial complexes throughout two-thirds of the inhabited area of the globe. It must be expected, however, to create the conditions making such investment possible and attractive.

For this reason UNIDO must secure personnel of a different type from those generally found in international organizations. UNIDO will have to draw heavily in its recruiting on practitioners of industry, on proven organizers, practical technologists, and managerial talent. Such personnel will obviously have to be found primarily in the plants and establishments of industrialized countries, including those countries in the less developed parts of the world which have already gained industrial experience. This need for a certain type of personnel is likely to prove difficult to square with the principle of equitable geographic distribution, so highly cherished by the developing countries.

Another major problem faced by UNIDO is that of financing. Funds will, of course, be available from UNDP, including close to $7 million already especially pledged to UNDP for "special industrial services." The developing countries expect, furthermore, a sharp increase in the UN's assessed budget to support by 1968 a central secretariat of close to 700 persons. Above all, they are intent on the establishment of a special voluntary fund for industrial development. Indeed, they decided that a special pledging conference should be held in 1968. This fund is expected to provide investment capital. In adopting this course the developing countries are adding to the ever lengthening list of special purpose funds created on the basis of voluntary contributions. However, there is little, if any, indication that the major contributing countries will find it possible to give sustenance to the proposed fund.

As in other recent conferences the developing countries, by and large, acted as a bloc. However, there were obvious differences of opinion within the bloc and few sharp, emotion-laden confrontations between developed and developing states.

PROBLEMS AND PROSPECTS

The forced pace at which the economic sector in the United Nations has been transformed in recent years has left little time for contemplation or analysis in depth of the results achieved. There has been an unprecedented proliferation of meetings, conferences, working parties, and seminars. The stamina of those most directly involved as delegates, experts, and advisers has been tested almost beyond endurance as they rush from conference to conference, from caucus to caucus. The stacks of documentation mount steadily and few persons, if any, are conversant with all that is published. Even major countries, such as the United States, are finding it increasingly difficult to provide the manpower and expertise necessary to keep on top of all the new developments, to formulate policy, and to adequately brief their delegations. Many of the smaller countries are clearly unable to maintain informed positions on the myriad issues with which the United Nations confronts them. This fact in itself encourages rash action, often taken without benefit of formal instructions or informed judgment. It also increases an uncritical reliance by countries on the group to which they belong and look for guidance.

On the other hand, it is evident that the UN has been revitalized and is very much alive in driving to achieve its central objectives in the economic and social field. Literally thousands of programs and projects have been initiated throughout the countries of Asia, Africa, and Latin America, as well as some countries elsewhere, and they are bearing fruit. They have made substantial contributions to these countries' ability to organize themselves, individually and in cooperation with others, for the task of modernization and the achievement of higher levels of living. Progress has been made in planning, nationally, regionally, and on a worldwide basis, in the transfer of knowledge and technology, and in the creation of conditions conducive to accelerated economic and social development. To cite just one concrete example, the Administration of UNDP reported recently that by the end of 1966 31 completed Special Fund projects (feasibility studies of power and resources development, etc.) had led to capital investments of $1.6 billion. Every $1 spent on these projects by UNDP had yielded over $40 in capital investment.

Most encouraging of all is the emergence of a new type of sophisticated leadership among the developing countries. It blends the experience of the "middle states" on the scale of development and the native genius and hard work of some representatives of new countries. Many of them have benefited from educational experience abroad and are therefore equipped to help build bridges between North and South. They have acquired a remarkable grasp of the complexities of the UN system and are increasingly ready to face the realities of the economics of growth and development. They recognize that development cannot be legislated, nor cooperation with the highly developed states decreed. These new leaders show few signs of "alienation" and are ready to pursue an active dialogue with the countries of the North. They are intent on furthering cohesion among the developing countries on the move. At the same time, they recognize that there is great variety within the developing countries and that differing stages of development among them may call for a large variety of solutions. The revolution of rising expectations, on which volumes have been written during the last fifteen years, is beginning to be transformed into an evolution of shared responsibility. While by no means general, these trends hold real promise for the future of the UN and the solution of at least some of the major problems it will have to cope with during the years to come. At this stage we can only list and annotate them:

1) Many countries continue to be obsessed with voting and the need of assuring automatic majorities. However, the "consensus" procedure practiced in UNDP and the fact that it has not so far proved necessary to invoke the conciliation procedures established by UNCTAD indicate

a reverse trend. With the reopening of the dialogue between developed and developing countries which permits sustained negotiations the dangers of bloc voting are being reduced. There will, of course, always be votes in cases where there are, at least for the time being, irreconcilable differences between some groups of countries. While it would be desirable to have fewer such votes, they are useful in highlighting basic differences of position. They enable the minority to make clear its refusal to subscribe to proposals or to accept obligations which run counter to its vital interests.

2) In an interdependent world the economic development of any group of countries depends on and affects all countries. It requires a continuing review and appraisal of the performance of the world economy, giving due weight to the economic conditions of developed and developing countries alike. It requires, also, that nations harmonize their policies and actions to achieve common ends as postulated in Article 1, paragraph 4, of the Charter. These are central functions which, in broad perspective, can only be performed by central organs and call for a centralization of data and research in the UN Secretariat in New York. The Secretariat, of course, must draw heavily on the assistance of the secretariats of other UN bodies such as UNCTAD, UNIDO, the regional economic commissions, and, as appropriate, the specialized agencies.

On the intergovernmental level the General Assembly and ECOSOC are the primary organs of overall review and harmonization. The General Assembly and ECOSOC have not performed satisfactorily in this respect in the past. However, to transfer their function to some other body such as UNCTAD is no solution. What is needed is a greater concentration by the General Assembly and ECOSOC on the interrelationships of policies and action in various sectors of the world economy. The interrelationships between agriculture, industry, trade, and transport, as well as such basic factors as population growth, manpower, or the impact of science and technology on development must all be considered. As technical organizations such as UNCTAD and UNIDO become more effective within their field of competence, the General Assembly should be progressively relieved of the burden of discussing technical issues and matters of detail which take up much time and can better be dealt with elsewhere. ECOSOC can make a significant contribution to the work of the Assembly by calling attention to key problems requiring the Assembly's consideration and action.

Progress in the area of review and harmonization is, at best, likely to be slow. It will depend to what extent the General Assembly is willing to assert its authority over the technical bodies within the UN and over their secretariats. This, in turn, will depend on the degree of sophistication achieved by its members. For the moment the prospect is uncertain.

3) There must also be harmonization of programs and activities within the UN itself and with its related agencies. That means improved coordination. The difficulties which have arisen in this respect with UNCTAD will, hopefully, be resolved by making a distinction between functional or sectoral coordination on the one hand and overall coordination on the other. Overall coordination of programs and activities is clearly a function—and perhaps the most important function—of ECOSOC. A show of self-restraint by the Council itself would help it discharge this function effectively. With the ever enlarging scope of the economic and social interests and activities of the UN and its related agencies the Council should realize that it can only fulfill its task of systemwide coordination by increasingly relying on functional bodies (such as UNCTAD, UNIDO, the Commission for Social Development, and the Committee for Development Planning) to do a job of substantive coordination within those sectors of policy and activity in which they have technical competence. In other words, as far as is possible the Council must be willing to delegate coordination efforts on substantive issues. In return, these sectoral bodies and their secretariats must stop their attempts to take over the overall coordinating functions of ECOSOC. They should also cease their attempts to take over the substantive activities of other bodies and agencies rather than helping in their coordination.

The outlook in this respect is promising. There has been growing support for ECOSOC since its enlargement gave the developing countries a decisive voice. Moreover, many of these countries have of late shown an intense interest in the review, evaluation, and coordination of programs as a means of avoiding loss of scarce resources to peripheral programs and of assuring their effective use for high-priority purposes. And, as also indicated above, some of their representatives, impatient with the separatism of some of the technical agencies and bodies, have been among the most active members of the Committee for Program and Coordination which was established by ECOSOC in 1966 and enlarged on LDC initiative in the Assembly.

Some of the developing countries are on record as favoring a drastic revamping of the entire UN system of organizations. They are highly critical of such organizations as UNESCO and some other specialized agencies because of their reluctance to bring their activities into line with development plans and programs on an overall and a country basis. They are pressing for a centralization of planning and policy formulation in the General Assembly and, under its authority, of ECOSOC. This approach may become a source of serious controversy. The centralization which is envisaged would severely limit the autonomy of the technical agencies and call for basic changes in their constitutions and their relationship agreements with the United Nations. It will require real statesmanship, particularly on the part of the specialized agencies, to avoid a major conflict and to help achieve closely concerted action within the UN system of organizations as now established without a serious loss of freedom of action of its constituent parts.

4) There has been mounting criticism, first in the developed countries and lately among some of the LDC's, about the proliferation of new initiatives, institutions, and conferences. Nathaniel McKitterick protested that

> the representatives of the less developed countries are borrowing a page from past US practice and are launching initiatives over the whole panorama of UN economic and social activities without any serious regard for the real capabilities and limitations of the system.[20]

Richard Gardner warns that, "We should also beware of the tendency to think that every new proposal requires a new institution to carry it out." In his view, "The main problem is that the multiplication of agencies has proceeded to a point where it is beginning to impair the efficiency of the entire system."[21] He concludes by suggesting that perhaps a little "birth control"—or at least better "family planning"—is needed.

Unfortunately, the right "Pill" for the purpose has not yet been found. Initiatives likely to exceed the capabilities of the UN continue to be launched. Long-standing proposals for new institutions, in the social field, for instance, are periodically revived and new agencies are proposed. Divisions of existing secretariats are made into "Centers," requiring new staff and substantial funds. Responsibility lies with governments in all parts of the world which labor under the illusion that a new institution would help them solve their problems; with governments which want their country to be the home of an international agency; and, last but not least, the ambitions and ingenuity of international officials who want their own little empire or a special suite in the palace of the nations.

Whether the international community will be better able than national governments to cope with Parkinson's Law is a moot point. Major UN contributors are allergic to the steep rise in the budgets of the UN and other agencies. Quite a few of the developing countries are beginning to feel the financial pinch even though they may contribute only a small fraction of the assessed budgets of the UN organizations to which they belong. Evidence is building up that they would rather have established institutions use available resources to full effect than engage in new ventures.

[20] Nathaniel M. McKitterick, *U.S. Diplomacy in the Development Agencies of the United Nations* (Planning Pamphlet No. 122) (Washington: National Planning Association, 1965), p. 31.
[21] Richard N. Gardner (ed.), *Blueprint for Peace* (New York: McGraw-Hill, 1966), p. 9.

5) The creation of ever new machinery might also be more easily prevented if the UN Secretariat were better staffed and organized. The shifting of functions from New York Headquarters to Geneva, Vienna, and other places and the transfer of personnel to serve in the "autonomous" secretariats of UNCTAD and UNIDO have left the Department of Economic and Social Affairs weakened and in disarray. Curing this situation will require strong leadership and a major reorganization. There is indeed need for better "family planning." On the question of staffing the UN is still a long way from achieving an optimum balance between "equitable geographic distribution" and requisite competence. This problem will be gradually eased as the developing countries find it possible to release for international service thoroughly experienced and competent personnel. As time goes on, they will clearly be able to produce such personnel. This may also stimulate countries in East and West to present better candidates, who are certainly available.

6) Related to the proliferation of institutions is the problem of "special funds." Insofar as budgetary considerations may reduce or eliminate further institutional proliferation pressures are certain to mount for special purpose funds secured by voluntary contributions primarily, if not exclusively, from the affluent countries. This trend is already very much in evidence. In addition to the UN Capital Development Fund already "voted" all kinds of plans are afoot for special purpose funds inside and outside the UN system to meet the impending food crisis and increase agricultural production; to close the protein gap; to finance a worldwide survey of nonagricultural resources; to provide investment capital for UNIDO; to promote literacy, etc. There is enough talk of special pledging conferences to keep the personnel of national treasuries busy for quite some time to come.

The very number of such proposals may well prove their undoing. There is a level of tolerance which cannot be exceeded without battle fatigue overcoming such traditionally high contributors to UN institutions and programs as the United States. In some of the major European countries there is already a marked reluctance to provide additional funds. It shows in the way their contributions are leveling off, even to the United Nations Development Program. The Soviet Union and its allies, while frequently supporting the creation of new funds, have done little to give them substance.

Since some of the causes for which special purpose funds are sought have undoubted merit, better ways must be found to secure the necessary resources. Rather than establishing a multitude of ill-nourished separate funds, agreement might well be reached to build up and use UNDP as a central fund financing most of the operational programs of the UN and its related agencies. This would avoid fragmentation of resources, provide for effective management and planning, and probably command more substantial support on the part of the international community. In January 1967 the management of UNDP was given authority to accept funds-in-trust from individual contributors for specific purposes. This should make it easier for governments which so desire to shift some of their bilateral aid funds to multilateral administration.

7) The UN is not equipped nor was it ever designed to serve as an investment institution for capital financing to supplement or replace IBRD, IFC, and IDA.[22] The recent creation of the regional development banks in Latin America, Asia, and Africa is designed to fill gaps in the pattern of intergovernmental finance institutions. All these institutions combined, together with consortia, appear to offer ample machinery for channeling aid and investment capital to the developing countries. To round out the picture, the role of private investment, if encouraged, should be of major importance.

Financing is likely to be a bone of contention for years to come. It is reasonable, however, to suppose that present machinery and arrangements, if strengthened as necessary and feasible, will prevent any serious disruption within the UN and permit the Organization to concentrate on the programs and work it is best qualified to undertake.

In the light of all that has been said the conclusion is warranted that the United Nations as an instrument of economic and social development is becoming increasingly effective. In the words of Paul Hoffman[23] a global partnership is in the making.

---

[22] Many of the LDC's and some of the developed countries are urging that UNDP, with its less than $200 million per year, should be transformed into a capital investment fund. This would obviously provide only very limited resources for investment purposes. It would certainly diminish the funds desperately needed for technical assistance and preinvestment projects and might well be the beginning of the end of the most effective operational program of the UN.

[23] "Progress Report on a Global Partnership," *UN Monthly Chronicle*, March 1967 (Vol. 4, No. 3), pp. 64–73.

The Role of Trade in Economic Development

ISAIAH FRANK

THE key role of trade in the development process is widely accepted today. Two recent events, both relating to international organizations, underscore this acceptance. One was the convening in 1964 of the United Nations Conference on Trade and Development (UNCTAD) and its establishment as a permanent organ of the UN system. Under UNCTAD's aegis a continuing examination is being conducted as to ways of reshaping world trade policies in the interests of the developing countries. The other event was the adoption early the following year of a new set of articles on trade and development in the General Agreement on Tariffs and Trade (GATT). In the new articles recognition of the role of exports in economic development was established for the first time in the text of the GATT itself, and a constitutional basis was provided for GATT's many activities designed to promote the exports of developing countries. Elsewhere in this volume are essays evaluating the contributions of UNCTAD and GATT toward the promotion of development in the world's poor countries.[1] In this essay I will rather explore more generally the relation between international trade and economic development and discuss some of the problems that have arisen in the effort to make trade a more effective instrument of development.

Trade as an "engine of growth" was a concept widely applied to the experience of the nineteenth century and particularly to the temperate-zone primary producers such as Canada and Australia. But for today's less developed countries the emphasis on the key role of trade is rela-

ISAIAH FRANK is Clayton Professor of International Economics at The Johns Hopkins University School of Advanced International Studies, Washington, D.C. He was formerly United States Deputy Assistant Secretary of State for Economic Affairs.

[1] See also Isaiah Frank, "New Perspectives on Trade and Development," *Foreign Affairs,* April 1967 (Vol. 45, No. 3), pp. 520–540.

tively recent, having come to the fore early in the decade of the sixties. Prior to that time, interest tended to center on other strategic variables in the development process. Until the mid-fifties heaviest stress was laid on the problem of low savings rates and the need to channel a higher proportion of domestic output into investment.[2] The problem was typically seen as how to break the vicious circle of low per capita incomes causing low rates of savings which in turn meant inadequate investment to permit an increase in the level of income. Later, the focus shifted to the shortage of human qualities needed for effective use of physical resources. Entrepreneurship, trained "middle-level" manpower, skills of all sorts—these were seen as crucial bottlenecks setting sharp limits to the absorptive capacity for more capital.

Insofar as trade policy was concerned the fifties were an inward-looking period. During these years import substitution commended itself to many developing countries both as the surest path to industrialization and as the best way of coping with the balance-of-payments pressures that inevitably accompany the effort to force the pace of development. "Balanced growth" took precedence over specialization for export markets.

As a consequence of two developments in the latter half of the 1950's the limitations of this approach became increasingly apparent. One was the realization that the strategy of industrialization through import substitution could be pushed only so far before running into a dead end. Because of the small size of domestic markets industrialization in "watertight compartments" meant high costs and inefficiencies, and the possibilities of development along these lines were quickly exhausted. The second factor was the serious deterioration in the export performance of developing countries: The rate of increase of their export earnings declined from 4.2 percent annually in 1950–1955 to 2.9 percent in 1955–1960 with a concomitant sag in the growth of per capita income from 2.5 percent to 1.8 percent. These trends were the product of a sluggish growth in external demand for the primary products of developing countries combined with an adverse movement in their terms of trade. As the end of the fifties drew near, it became clear that the principal trade need of the developing countries was not so much the encouragement of further import substitution as the stimulation of an increase in their exports in order to pay for the imports essential to development. Only through export expansion could low-income countries overcome what came to be regarded as a constraint on growth at least equal in seriousness to the

---

[2] One of the most frequently cited formulations was that of W. Arthur Lewis:

> The central problem in the theory of economic growth is to understand the process whereby a community is converted from being a 5 percent to a 12 percent saver—with all the changes in attitudes, in institutions and in techniques which accompany this conversion.

(*The Theory of Economic Growth* [Homewood, Ill: Richard D. Irwin, 1955], p. 226.)

shortage of savings and skills, namely, the limitation on their capacity to import.

RELATION BETWEEN TRADE AND GROWTH

The new focus on export expansion is reflected in the current debate on a wide range of issues, a debate centering in UNCTAD and GATT but also involving other international organizations including the International Bank for Reconstruction and Development (IBRD), the International Monetary Fund (IMF), and the regional economic commissions of the United Nations. Among the issues under active discussion are preferences, regional economic arrangements, export diversification, "effective" versus "nominal" tariffs, buffer funds, commodity agreements, nontariff barriers, and supplementary finance to offset unexpected shortfalls that threaten to disrupt development programs.

In the preoccupation with policies to promote the trade of developing countries it is easy to lose sight of the fact that trade is not an end in itself. The goal is economic development, and trade expansion is important insofar as it conduces to that goal. If one is to evaluate problems or policies currently under discussion, it therefore seems desirable to begin with an exploration of the relationships between trade and growth.

A Statistical Overview

If one looks at a cross section of countries at a given point in time, there appears to be no discernible relationship between stage of growth as measured by per capita income and importance of foreign trade in a country's economy. There are rich countries with low ratios of exports to gross national product (United States, 4 percent) and also with high ratios (Sweden, 20 percent). At the other end of the income scale are poor countries with low export ratios (India, 5 percent) and also with high ratios (Ceylon, 21 percent).[3]

If countries are ranged according to population, however, a systematic inverse relationship emerges between size of country and foreign trade as a proportion of national income. This is not surprising. Small countries tend to be less diversified in economic resources and structure than large countries while, at any given level of per capita income, their pattern of demand tends to be the same. Consequently, much of what would be internal trade for large countries is international trade for small countries.

Turning from a cross-sectional view to the question of how foreign trade and national income are related over time, the matter becomes more speculative. As a country sheds its primitive, subsistence way of

---

[3] A study cited by Kuznets and based on data for 52 countries shows no systematic change in foreign trade ratios as one moves along the per capita income scale. (Simon Kuznets, *Six Lectures on Economic Growth* [Glencoe, Ill: Free Press, 1959], p. 96.)

life and enters the world economy, the ratio of foreign trade to national income clearly rises. But what happens as development proceeds is not so clear-cut. A common view has been that the spread of industrialization tends to reduce the importance of trade by narrowing the differences in comparative advantage as between nations, differences that were originally determined mainly by natural resource endowments. Data presented by Deutsch and Eckstein indicate that the foreign trade ratio increased during the early stages of development, reached a plateau, and then declined. But Kuznets finds no clear pattern in the change over time in the ratio of foreign trade to national income.[4]

New light has been cast on this subject by Robert Lipsey in his empirical study of long-term trends in United States foreign trade.[5] Until recently it had been accepted that there had been a substantial long-term decline in the trade-to-output ratio for the United States. Indeed, Lipsey confirms this view on the basis of current-value data for the period 1879–1960 which show steep declines in the ratios of either exports or imports to gross national product (GNP). When the time series are corrected for price changes, however, a strikingly different result emerges: Both ratios remain relatively stable over the entire period.

Lipsey's finding reflects the fact that the prices of internationally traded goods have fallen compared to the prices of domestic output as a whole. One explanation is that a large share of domestic output consists of services as well as of many "sheltered" goods such as heavy building materials which cannot readily be replaced by foreign sources of supply when domestic prices go up.

Recent explorations of interregional trade in the United States add to the weight of Lipsey's evidence against the doctrine of the declining role of foreign trade in economic development. By looking at interregional trade Richard Cooper was able to abstract from the arbitrary effect on foreign trade ratios of changes in commercial policy.[6] On the basis of incomplete evidence he concludes that although the economic structure of the regions of the United States has tended to converge over the last century, interregional trade has grown more rapidly than total output. Specialization based on economies of scale appears to have replaced specialization based on traditional differences in comparative costs. As stated by Cooper,

[4] Karl W. Deutsch and Alexander Eckstein, "National Industrialization and the Declining Share of the International Economic Sector 1890–1959," World Politics, January 1961 (Vol. 13, No. 2), pp. 267–299; and Kuznets, pp. 101–103.

[5] Robert E. Lipsey, Price and Quantity Trends in the Foreign Trade of the United States (Princeton, N.J: Princeton University Press, 1963).

[6] Richard N. Cooper, "Growth and Trade: Some Hypotheses About Long-Term Trends," Journal of Economic History, December 1964 (Vol. 24, No. 4), pp. 609–628.

If the optimum scale of output for many industries has increased faster than the size of local markets, trade will increase relative to output, even though other factors have diminished the gains from trade.[7]

What all this adds up to is that in the present state of our knowledge generalizations should be avoided as to the long-term statistical relationship between foreign trade and economic growth. Growth affects trade in many ways and they all do not operate in the same direction. Perhaps as more and improved data become available for today's developing countries, some systematic long-term relationships may be observed for groups of countries of similar economic structure. But even here skepticism is in order. After all, foreign trade and national income are aggregate variables and each is affected by many internal and external factors.[8] Rather than pursue further the search for patterns of uniformity in historical experience we turn to the question of how foreign trade affects growth.

Exports as an Earner of Foreign Exchange

The most obvious gain from exports is the access to goods from abroad provided by earnings of foreign exchange. In 1965 export receipts of developing countries amounted to over $36 billion or about three and one-half times the volume of foreign exchange accruing from economic aid and foreign investment combined.

Exports permit not only the satisfaction of a broader range of consumer demand than can be supported by the narrow structure of traditional domestic output but also provide access to the capital equipment and technology of advanced countries that are crucial to the development process. Whatever the nature of the goods imported, however, an increase in trade has the same effect on real national income as a technological innovation. The specialization dictated by comparative advantage allows a country to increase the output at its disposal with a given input of resources.

Underlying the classical doctrine of comparative costs are the assumptions of given resources and techniques, full employment, and the free mobility of factors within each country. Accordingly, trade permits a country to reallocate its resources more efficiently, but an increase in pro-

[7] *Ibid.*, p. 625.

[8] C. P. Kindleberger concludes his historical discussion of British and French experience by noting that "the relationships between foreign trade and growth are varied and complex" and that "occasionally they are remote." ("Foreign Trade and Economic Growth: Lessons from Britain and France, 1850 to 1913," *Economic History Review*, December 1961 [Second Series, Vol. 14, No. 2], pp. 289–305.) However, his effort to classify actual cases in accordance with three models in which trade acts as either a leading, balancing, or lagging sector in the economy is somewhat forced and unconvincing. (C. P. Kindleberger, *Foreign Trade and the National Economy* [New Haven, Conn: Yale University Press, 1962].)

duction for export can take place only at the cost of a decrease in production for the home market. However, in his "vent for surplus" theory Adam Smith recognized that for poor countries some of the assumptions might not apply. Unemployment and factor immobility in certain occupations may mean in effect that surplus capacity can respond to increased foreign demand at virtually no sacrifice of production for the domestic market. In such a case the country's comparative advantage may be viewed as in part a reflection of the immobility of human and capital resources.[9]

Suggesting a similar strand of thought are recent discussions of the "resource gap" which must be filled if less developed countries are to achieve certain target rates of growth. It is sometimes put forth that the gap can be filled by either increased aid (or foreign investment) or increased exports since both provide command over resources from abroad. But unless one assumes that the increase in exports is achieved through the absorption into production of previously unemployed (or underemployed) resources, trade and aid cannot be viewed as equivalent alternatives for acquiring additional resources. External capital clearly adds to total resources. Assuming no unemployment, exports merely permit the conversion of domestic resources into foreign resources. Theoretically, they add to total resources only to the extent of the gains from the allocation effects of increased trade. Since gap projections commonly assume a one-for-one substitutability of exports for external capital, it follows that the existence of idle resources in developing countries is taken for granted.

The analogy with Smith's vent-for-surplus doctrine should not, however, be pushed too far. Smith assumed that the surplus labor and land were already in the export sector and that they could not be readily shifted to other uses. Gap projections, on the other hand, are predicated on some degree of resource mobility since their time perspective is generally long enough for substantial social and economic transformation. The main point, though, is that over and above any benefits via a fuller exploitation of comparative advantage increased trade can add to total output through the utilization of previously unemployed resources; and in the present situation of much of the less developed world this may be the more important contribution. For example, in Latin America urban unemployment and underemployment have been growing at an alarming rate. The urgency of the drive to industrialize and to improve access for exports of manufactured products can be explained in part by the need to absorb these human resources in productive activity.

[9] See H. Myint, "The 'Classical Theory' of International Trade and the Underdeveloped Countries," *Economic Journal*, June 1958 (Vol. 68, No. 270), pp. 317–337.

For a number of countries, especially those beyond the early stages of development, the effective constraint on growth is not a shortage of domestic savings nor of imported capital equipment but rather a shortage of imported raw materials and intermediate products needed to operate existing plant. Due to a sluggishness in transforming resources released from domestic consumption into either increased exports or import substitutes countries in this category, e.g., India, Turkey, Chile, and Brazil, have been under severe balance-of-payments pressures. It is not uncommon to see industrial plants in developing countries operating at a fraction of capacity because foreign exchange simply was not available for the importation of essential materials. Meanwhile, the foreign exchange for equipment associated with new plant construction may be fully provided because of the tendency of most foreign aid givers to tie their assistance to capital projects. Under these circumstances increased exports have a crucial role in a strategy of development. By permitting a country to break the bottlenecks on the side of imported materials they bring into play idle human and capital resources. For developing countries experiencing severe balance-of-payments stringencies, therefore, the payoff on increased exports in terms of greater domestic output may be some multiple of the value of the imports they finance.

As an earner of foreign exchange exports make possible one further contribution worth separate mention. By financing imports they provide a check on domestic monopoly or at least help in preventing its inefficiencies from getting too far out of hand. The competition-inducing effects of trade are often cited in relation to advanced industrialized countries, rarely in relation to less developed countries.[10] Presumably, this is due to the general acceptance of the case for infant industry protection. But there is wide recognition today that such protection can be carried too far and that the domestic monopoly problem may be particularly acute for newly developing countries with their limited markets for manufactured goods. More import competition may be the best way of inducing cost reductions and improvements in the quality of goods, but it is often dependent on an increase in export earnings. To the extent that UNCTAD and GATT stimulate the adoption of policies to improve the foreign exchange earnings of developing countries they make a contribution to overcoming the monopoly problem that should not be overlooked.

Focus of Attraction for Foreign Capital

Export growth and foreign investment often go hand in hand. A powerful force behind the movement of foreign capital in the latter part

[10] A noteworthy exception is Gottfried Haberler. See his *International Trade and Economic Development* (Cairo: National Bank of Egypt, 1959), p. 14.

of the nineteenth century was the demand in Europe for the primary products of the overseas areas. Trade and investment were particularly closely tied in the classic pattern of British economic relations with the "regions of recent settlement," i.e., Canada, Argentina, Uruguay, South Africa, Australia, and New Zealand. Foreign capital was attracted not only to the export sector itself but also to other commercial and industrial activities and to public utilities. In the period 1880–1913 railroads were in fact the single most important outlet for British overseas investment, accounting for 40 percent of the total.[11] On all these investments, however, the transfer abroad of interest and dividends and the repayment of principal was facilitated by the buoyancy of export markets for the food and raw materials of the overseas areas.

Even today the predominant pattern of United States private investments in less developed countries reflects a preference for primary products for which the markets are overwhelmingly external. By the end of 1965 United States direct investments in the developing world as a whole amounted to $15,119 million. Of this total, $8,322 million or 55 percent was in mining and smelting and in petroleum. In Latin America, however, there has been a distinct shift recently toward United States investment in manufacturing for the local market, much of it centered in the four large or relatively high per capita income countries of Brazil, Argentina, Mexico, and Venezuela. If Latin America is excluded, the proportion of the remaining United States direct investment in developing countries that is concentrated in mining, smelting, and petroleum rises to 72 percent.[12]

If a developing country is relatively small in population and toward the lower end of the scale in per capita income, foreign investment in manufacturing is unlikely to take place except where the country is part of a broader regional free trade arrangement. Small domestic markets are no deterrent, however, to foreign investment in primary materials for export. Moreover, the problem of effecting the transfer of income is automatically facilitated since foreign investment earnings and export receipts will tend to fluctuate together.[13] An indigenous raw material base is certainly not a

[11] Sir Arthur Salter, *Foreign Investment* (Essays in International Finance No. 12) (Princeton, N.J: International Finance Section, Department of Economics, Princeton University, February 1951).

[12] $3,534 million out of a total of $5,748 million. Data are from United States Department of Commerce, Office of Business Economics, *Survey of Current Business*, September 1966 (Vol. 46, No. 9).

[13] S. Shahid Husain, "Export Fluctuations and Debt Servicing Problems: Relationship between the Fluctuations in Export Earnings and Direct Investment Income Payments—A Statistical Test," Essay I in Volume III of Dragoslav Avramovic and others, *Economic Growth and External Debt* (Baltimore, Md: Johns Hopkins Press, 1964), pp. 119–124. Husain also points out that in developing countries where foreign capital has moved into industries producing for the local market the stimulus to growth "has been accompanied by an increase in the short-run rigidities in the balance of payments. . . ." (*Ibid.*, p. 124.)

prerequisite for development. Bue it can be an enormous advantage in the early stages as a magnet for attracting foreign capital without which economic advance is likely to be slower and more painful.

Over the last couple of decades foreign investment in raw materials has been strongly attacked as exploitative and as leading to lopsided "enclave economies" rather than inducing widely shared growth throughout the country.[14] Surely, the broadly diffused benefits that accompanied foreign investment in primary production in the "regions of recent settlement" were often lacking in Southeast Asia, Africa, and Latin America where highly developed extractive activities geared to export markets have coexisted with backwardness and stagnation in the rest of the economy.

The contribution of foreign capital to development depends, however, not only on the automatic spillover effect of the investment in stimulating other sectors of the economy. It depends also on the share of the increase in real income resulting from the investment which remains in the local economy and the way this increase is mobilized for broader development purposes. Whether, for example, foreign investment in Libyan oil leads to development will depend partly on the share of oil revenues accruing to the Libyan government through royalties and taxes and on how these resources are applied in a broad effort to build a more diversified, growing economy. Singer[15] may have been right that the automatic stimulus to development resulting from investment in manufacturing is stronger than in extractive industries oriented to export markets. But I suspect that the bargaining power of a low-income country in negotiating the terms on which the foreign investment can take place is greater in extractive industries.

The Singer thesis evolved against a historical pattern of colonial or quasi-colonial relationships. Local governments could hardly have been expected to adopt and enforce those tax and other policies which would have maximized the contribution of foreign investment to the overall development of their economies. Today, with politically independent governments actively committed to promoting development, the situation is quite different. There is an increasing awareness of the potential contribution of private foreign investment even in extractive industries and of the delicate balance of conditions and policies necessary both to attract such investment and to maximize its general contribution to development.

Although trade and foreign investment are mutually supporting, the major international trade organizations have generally not attempted to

---

[14] One of the earliest and most forceful expositions of this point of view is in H. W. Singer, "The Distribution of Gains Between Investing and Borrowing Countries," *American Economic Review*, May 1950 (Vol. 40, No. 2), pp. 473–485.

[15] *Ibid.*

deal with policies in the field of private foreign investment. GATT's terms of reference are too restrictive: It inherited the commercial policy provisions of the abortive Havana Charter for an International Trade Organization (ITO) but not its provisions on foreign investment. As far as UNCTAD is concerned, there is a widespread feeling that, given the composition of that body, the risk is too great that discussion of this politically sensitive subject would degenerate into ideological polemics. But other organizations have been concerned with increasing the flow of private capital to developing countries through measures to improve the investment climate. The World Bank has established a Convention for the Settlement of Investment Disputes, and the Organization for Economic Cooperation and Development (OECD) has been considering a Convention for the Protection of Private Property and a Multilateral Investment Guarantee Scheme.

Escape from Domestic Market Limitations

Economies of scale underlie much of modern industry. In freeing production from the limitations imposed by small domestic markets exports make a vital contribution to the development process. Fifty developing countries have populations of less than five million and 75 have less than fifteen million. It is difficult to conceive of industrialization in any meaningful sense for them except on the basis of the wider markets provided by exports.

It is rare, however, to find investment in manufacturing initially undertaken primarily for the export market. Notwithstanding such special cases as Hong Kong and Puerto Rico, the typical pattern is first to establish a base in the home market through a policy of protection against import competition. Various factors account for this sequence. First is greater familiarity with the precise character of demand in the home market, a factor of particular importance when a new product is being introduced and when numerous adaptations are required as the market is tested.[16] Second, primary reliance on exports is generally regarded as too risky since access to foreign markets can be closed off at any time. The current restrictions in advanced countries on imports of cotton textiles are a case in point. And third, in fields where capital costs are high, so that marginal and average costs diverge substantially, export dumping is common. In such cases competition in export markets may be possible only if subsidized through higher prices charged in a protected home market.

The dangers inherent in a policy of industrialization through high protection are well-known. The infant industry may never grow up. Be-

---

[16] See Staffan B. Linder, *An Essay on Trade and Transformation* (New York: John Wiley & Sons, 1961), pp. 87–93. Also see William W. Lockwood, *The Economic Development of Japan* (Princeton, N.J.: Princeton University Press, 1954), Chapters 6 and 7.

sides protection from foreign competition the local manufacturer often enjoys considerable insulation from domestic competition because the limited home market offers little inducement for more than one firm to enter the field. Even where there are several firms, close family and social ties commonly lead to collusive practices. The result is inefficient, high-cost production geared to a small upper-class market at prices completely ruling out the possibility of competing successfully in export markets.

It may appear, therefore, that less developed countries, particularly those small and poor in natural resources, are caught in a trap which prevents escape from the limitations of their domestic markets through the export route. The problem is how to manage the transition from import substitution to export promotion. One solution that has captured the imagination of leaders of developing countries is the regional approach in which protection on a regional scale takes the place of national protection. Regional integration can take many forms ranging from the mutual removal by member countries of restrictions on trade in individual products or sectors to more comprehensive arrangements such as free trade areas, customs unions, or common markets. Regardless of the scheme's coverage, however, the basic objective is to widen the market so that the benefits of competition and scale can be reaped even during the early phases of establishing an industry when protection may be necessary. With appropriate policies the regional market should develop at a later stage into a base for exports of manufactured products to advanced countries.

Both UNCTAD and GATT have devoted a good deal of attention to the possibilities of expanding trade among the developing countries themselves through regional arrangements, and significant progress has been made toward this goal, particularly in Latin America. But the developing countries see their main escape from the limitations of domestic markets in increasing exports of manufactured products to the huge markets of the advanced countries. Toward this end they seek preferential access to those markets, an issue that seems certain to loom large in any trade negotiations in the foreseeable future. Even if granted, however, preferences would simply mean improved terms of access for the exports of developing countries but would in themselves provide no assurance that advantage could be taken of the new opportunities. Just as important, but thus far regretfully outside the purview of GATT and UNCTAD, are the economic policies of the developing countries themselves and their effect upon the capacity to produce and export manufactured products at prices acceptable in world markets.[17]

[17] For an elaboration of this point in respect to UNCTAD see Isaiah Frank, *Foreign Affairs*, Vol. 45, No. 3, pp. 536–540.

Stimulant of Economic Activity

Rapidly expanding exports may stimulate growth by inducing complementary investment throughout the economy. If the stimulus is powerful enough, exports may become an "engine of growth" or a "leading sector" in the development process. Hirschman[18] has used the expression "backward linkages" to describe the inducements to supply through domestic production the inputs needed in the expanding sector (e.g., fertilizer for food production) and "forward linkages" to describe the inducements to use the outputs of the expanding sector in new activities (e.g., food processing).

Although the necessary impetus for such linkages can in theory be supplied either by exports or by production for the home market, there is a minimum critical level below which the stimulus is unlikely to work. It is precisely in permitting production to pierce this level that exports can become a "leading sector." Rostow cites this phenomenon in connection with the British textile industry:

> From its modern beginnings, but notably from the 1780's forward, a very high proportion of total cotton-textile output was directed abroad, reaching 60% by the 1820's. The evolution of this industry was a more massive fact, with wide secondary repercussions, than if it were simply supplying the domestic market. Industrial enterprise on this scale had secondary reactions on the development of urban areas, the demand for coal, iron and machinery, the demand for working capital and ultimately the demand for cheap transport, which powerfully stimulated industrial development in other directions.[19]

There are also times when the spillover effect of exports may be peculiarly associated with the character as well as the scale of foreign demand. Lockwood's account of the Japanese trade in silk yarn provides a good illustration:

> To satisfy the demands of American weaving and hosiery mills for uniform, high-grade yarns, however, it was necessary to improve the quality of the product, from the silkworm egg on through to the bale of silk. In sericulture this meant the introduction of scientific methods of breeding and disease control; in reeling it stimulated the shift to large filatures equipped with machinery; in marketing it led to large-scale organization in the collection and sale of cocoons and raw silk. . . . Clearly the foreign market afforded the chief impetus to technological change in this instance. . . . And it exerted steady pressure in favor of the application of science, machinery, and modern business enterprise.[20]

[18] Albert O. Hirschman, *The Strategy of Economic Development* (New Haven, Conn: Yale University Press, 1958), Chapter 6.

[19] W. W. Rostow, *The Stages of Economic Growth* (London: Cambridge University Press, 1961), pp. 54-55.

[20] Lockwood, pp. 338-339.

The concept of foreign trade as an engine of growth rests not only on specific technical linkages of the Hirschman type but also on the more general multiplier effects of expanding exports on income, employment, and investment. A particularly close association has been displayed between rapid export growth and rapid increases in gross national product for the smaller among developing countries (Israel, Jordan, Iraq, Trinidad, and Jamaica) where market dimensions set sharp limits to development via the alternative route of import substitution.[21]

Thus, in addition to its role of providing foreign exchange to meet import requirements for growth there are other ways that foreign trade contributes to development—as a magnet for attracting foreign capital, an escape from the limitations of small domestic markets, and a spur to overall investment. It is the combined impact of all of these that lends support to the notion of exports as an engine of growth.

THE CURRENT TRADE PROBLEMS OF THE DEVELOPING COUNTRIES

Exports may have provided the spark for the engine of growth in the nineteenth century and may well be playing a similar role in some cases today. But, by and large, developing countries would be satisfied if exports performed efficiently the lesser and more passive role of providing the fuel for continuing growth in the form of steadily increasing supplies of foreign exchange.

In long-term historical perspective recent export trends may not seem discouraging. Almost 90 percent of the exports of developing countries consist of primary products. Since the end of World War II the physical volume of these exports has grown at rates at least equal to the trend that prevailed from the mid-1870's to World War I, when exports of primary goods stimulated the rapid growth of the "regions of recent settlement." And the postwar growth has been in marked contrast to the stagnation of the interwar period. Even the relative prices of primary products in terms of the prices of manufactures have on the average been far higher than during the interwar years and probably not lower than the average of the several decades prior to World War I.[22]

The trouble with this historical approach is that it ignores the changes

---

[21] John Pincus, *Trade, Aid and Development* (New York: McGraw-Hill, 1967), p. 74. Pincus' figures relate to the period 1950–1952 to 1961–1964. Exports are also assigned a key role in Lamfalussy's analysis of the differential growth performances of the United Kingdom and the countries of the European Economic Community (EEC) in the period of 1953–1961. Indeed, he regards the faster growth of the Six as export led and as centering on the effect of exports on savings and investment. (A. Lamfalussy, *The United Kingdom and the Six* [Homewood, Ill: Richard D. Irwin, 1963], p. 111.)

[22] International Bank for Reconstruction and Development, *The Commodity Problem* (Washington, 1964, mimeographed), Annex 1, Charts 2 and 3.

in the international environment against which the present and prospective export situation of developing countries must be assessed. As long as the poorer countries of the world are determined to force the pace of development through conscious policies the relevant question is not whether their trade prospects are as favorable as in the past when such goals did not exist. It is, instead, whether they are such as to lend support to or act as a constraint on a country's own development efforts.

The Trade Gap

Because of the integral relationship between rates of growth and the import requirements of developing countries attention has recently focused on the concept of the "trade gap," the gap between the need for imports to sustain a given development effort and the export earnings likely to be available to finance the imports.

In preparation for the first UNCTAD Conference in 1964 the UN Secretariat calculated the trade gap of the developing countries for 1970 on the assumption of a target growth rate of 5 percent, a figure set out as one of the goals of the Development Decade.[23] According to the UN, unless certain basic changes in policy were adopted, the trade deficit of the developing countries would rise from an observed level of $1.5 billion in 1960 to $11 billion in 1970. Moreover, they would experience a $9 billion deficit on invisible account, i.e., net payments for freight, insurance, interest, dividends, etc. The total current balance-of-payments deficit of $20 billion was presented as a measure of the foreign exchange shortage that would have to be met principally through changes in trade policies leading to higher exports or through increased capital flows via aid and private investment.

The UN estimate rested on an extrapolation of past trends in certain broad aggregates of the balance of payments of developing countries. Subsequently, a number of more detailed calculations[24] were made yielding much lower gaps; the most elaborate projection was that of Bela Balassa whose range of gap estimates centered around $12 billion. These wide variations are not surprising. Since the estimates represent the differences between such large aggregates as imports and exports, small percentage variations in projecting the aggregates can lead to large percentage variations in the gap.

Regardless of the precise figure, however, low-income countries believe

[23] *World Economic Survey, 1963* (United Nations Publication Sales No: 64.II.C.1 [UN Document E/3908]) (United Nations, 1964), Vol. I: *Trade and Development: Trends, Needs and Policies*, pp. 29–41.

[24] Bela Balassa, *Trade Prospects for Developing Countries* (Homewood, Ill: Richard D. Irwin, 1964). See also Alfred Maizels, *Industrial Growth and World Trade* (Cambridge: Cambridge University Press, 1963); and United States Agency for International Development, *Development Policies and Assistance Requirements* (Washington, December 1964, mimeographed).

that their prospects for future growth will be seriously constrained by shortages of foreign exchange. The anticipated shortage is, of course, a reflection of expectations concerning the behavior of all items in the balance of payments—the trade account, the service account, and net private capital movements, with foreign aid viewed as a balancing item. But the spotlight in recent years has centered on problems and policies in the field of trade.

Imports

The key variables determining import requirements are the growth objectives of the developing countries and their income elasticity of demand for imports (the ratio between the percentage change in imports and the percentage change in income).

Although a 5 percent growth rate has commanded general acceptance as an overall target, there is much less consensus as to the likely behavior of imports in relation to the growth of GNP. The UN study assumes that the rise in imports between 1960 and 1970 would be 15 percent greater than the increase in domestic output. Balassa, on the other hand, projects different elasticities for each of his four regions; when weighted by GNP, however, they average slightly less than unity for developing countries as a whole.

The argument for a greater-than-unity income elasticity for imports rests on the higher investment coefficient associated with more rapid growth rates and the higher import content of investment goods than of consumption goods. The import content of gross domestic capital formation varies widely as between developing countries but there is a concentration around a range of 40–45 percent. By contrast, the median value of imports of consumption goods and raw materials as a proportion of total consumption is only about 20 percent.[25]

But can the import-increasing effects of higher investment be offset by curtailing imports for consumption? The fact that capital goods imports (machinery and transport equipment) make up only about one-third of the developing countries' total imports underscores such a possibility.[26] Rapid development, however, is not always consistent with a high degree of compressibility of imports other than capital goods. That shortages of raw materials and intermediate products have often been the operative bottleneck to increases in output of developing countries has already been noted. Moreover, in Africa and elsewhere the role of imported consumption goods can be quite important in providing incentives for farmers to earn cash by shifting from subsistence to the market economy.

[25] Avramovic, pp. 137, 139.
[26] World Economic Survey, 1963, Vol. I, p. 37.

Nevertheless, I am inclined to agree with Hla Myint who in a recent article called attention to a greater flexibility of developing countries' import requirements than is commonly assumed in trade gap projections:

> The assumption that the imported capital goods and other inputs are required in rigidly fixed proportions with domestic inputs is plausible only when we confine ourselves to the import-substituting industries in the modern sector, based on imported technology and requiring machinery and other components of production which cannot be easily supplied from domestic production. But once we have learned to take into account the wider import-substituting possibilities through the expansion of domestic agriculture, and in some countries the expansion of smaller-scale industries using local materials and techniques, this assumption becomes less plausible. After all, the output of the modern manufacturing sector contributes to a relatively small proportion of the total domestic output of an underdeveloped country. Even if the aim of the development policy is to increase this proportion, there still seem to be possibilities of making the overall import requirements for the expansion of the domestic economy as a whole more flexible through substitutive relationships with the much larger domestic sector, where the import requirements of output expansion are more flexible.[27]

New light has been shed on the possible *future* course of the relation between imports and growth in a recent UN study of plans of developing countries as they existed in the mid-sixties.[28] Using a group of 24 countries for which data were available, the UN compared past elasticities of merchandise imports with the elasticities specified or implied in the plans. For all but four countries imports in the past (generally during the fifties) grew at a faster rate than the corresponding increase in gross domestic product (elasticities higher than one). But this past relation has not been reflected in the import targets which most countries have adopted in their current plans. In the great majority of cases lower import elasticities are projected, and in two-thirds of the countries the elasticities are lower than one.

Seeking to explain this change, the UN finds that it cannot be ascribed to a shift in domestic requirements away from investment with its high import requirement. On the contrary, the plans typically call for an increasing share of investment in total expenditure and an offsetting re-

[27] Hla Myint, "The 'Widening Trade Gap' of the Developing Countries: A Critical View," an unpublished paper prepared at the Yale Growth Center, November 1965, pp. 8–9. In the light of Myint's reference to import-substitution possibilities through the expansion of domestic agriculture it is interesting to note that the percentage increase in food imports into developing countries between 1953 and 1960 exactly paralleled the rate of increase of imports of machinery and transport equipment.

[28] *World Economic Survey, 1964* (United Nations Publication Sales No: 65.II.C.1 [UN Document E/4046/Rev.1]) (United Nations, 1965), Part I: *Development Plans: Appraisal of Targets and Progress in Developing Countries*, Chapter 4.

duction in consumption. Rather, the main explanation is the assumption that import-substituting production would sharply expand in consumer goods as well as in raw materials and intermediate products. And, as Myint suggests, a major element in the low targets for consumer goods imports is the planned increase in the substitution of domestic food production for imports.

The results of the UN study must be viewed with caution, however. For one thing, some countries not included in it experienced low income elasticities of import demand during the fifties (e.g., Brazil, 0.6 percent) and may well have reached the limit of import substitution possibilities consistent with high growth rates. More important, import figures included in current plans have generally not been worked out in detail and have often been determined as residuals. "Import targets," the UN points out, "have tended to be treated flexibly as a means of reconciling over-all growth targets with the estimates of foreign exchange receipts."[29] Taking these considerations into account, it seems imprudent to assume that, over the longer term, import requirements of developing countries can lag much behind the growth of domestic output.

Although low-income countries may have some flexibility in planning their requirements for commodity imports, they have little leeway regarding certain other major needs for foreign exchange, notably debt service. According to the UN, payments of interest and amortization on public and publicly guaranteed debt rose from $1.8 billion in 1960 to $3.1 billion in 1964. In addition to the increase in contractual debt service there has been a marked rise in net investment income payments in the form of dividends and branch profits of foreign investment—from $2.1 billion in 1960 to $3.0 billion in 1964.[30] It is the anticipation of a rapid increase in the *totality* of foreign exchange needs (in the face of a leveling off of financial assistance from abroad) that has impelled developing countries to continue to focus attention on ways of improving their long-run export prospects.

Exports

Whatever the uncertainty as to import requirements for growth, the prevailing view at the first UNCTAD Conference was one of pessimism as to the export prospects of developing countries. The pessimism grew out of the 1950–1962 experience when their exports grew at an average rate of only 3.4 percent, compared with 8 percent for the industrialized countries. This lag resulted partly from the slow growth in the physical

[29] *Ibid.*, p. 81.
[30] "Review of International Trade and Development 1966, Part One, Trends in International Trade and Development" (UN Document TD/B/82/Add.1, July 20, 1966), p. 58.

volume of exports and partly from the decline in prices that was concentrated in the latter part of the fifties. From 1956 to 1962 the situation became particularly acute. Fortunately, the volume of foreign aid rose substantially and served as a major offset to the sluggish increase of exchange receipts through foreign trade.

With the leveling off in the flow of aid in the sixties, however, developing countries have had to rely entirely on an increase in export earnings to finance their expanding requirements for foreign exchange. In the first half of the decade their export situation improved considerably. Responsible for much of the improvement was the accelerated growth in their principal markets, the advanced countries. But divergent long-term trends in particular commodity markets persisted, with the most rapid increases recorded in exports of petroleum and in manufactures, both being concentrated in a limited group of countries. Apart from these two categories, exports from developing countries in 1960–1965 grew at the modest rate of 4 percent, agricultural raw materials showing the slowest growth. Looking to the future, the UN projects a continuation of the pattern of growth rates by commodity groups that prevailed in the past, with the most serious problems confronting countries heavily dependent on traditional agricultural exports.[31]

Several forces of a long-run nature adversely affect market prospects for exports of primary commodities to the developed world. Except for countries at very low income levels, the demand for food grows at a slower rate than increases of income. While some "superior" food products such as fruit, vegetables, and meat face relatively buoyant market prospects, they are unlikely to bulk large enough in the exports of less developed countries to offset the lag in other food exports. For example, the market for coffee is characterized by low income elasticities of demand, whereas grains, sugar, and fats and oils encounter high protection in the advanced countries.

Industrial raw materials are also subject to forces limiting the growth of demand. As per capita incomes rise in the rich countries, the proportion of personal outlays on services, compared with physical goods, increases. In the decade 1954–1964, for instance, this proportion rose from 36 percent to 41 percent in the United States. Within the category of industries producing physical goods the input of raw materials has been declining steadily per unit of output, e.g., electrolytic tin plating or the use of transistors in place of radio tubes. Moreover, competition from synthetics exerts constant pressure on the market for many natural products. In the period 1953–1955 to 1963–1965 the use of man-made fibers

[31] *UNCTAD Commodity Survey 1966* (United Nations Publication Sales No: 67.II.D.9 [UN Document TD/B/C.1/23/Rev.1]) (United Nations, 1967), Chapter 4.

as a proportion of all apparel fibers rose from 26 percent by weight to 39 percent; the share of synthetic rubber in world rubber consumption went up from 38 percent to 62 percent.[32] Plastics substitute for metals, synthetics for leather in handbags and shoes, paper for jute in manufacturing.

Substitution trends are not simply reflections of technological possibilities but a direct function of price relationships. To the extent that price movements make the natural products more competitive the trends will be moderated. By the same token, substitution trends will be accentuated by commodity agreements which raise the prices of natural raw materials. In any case, the prospects for increases in demand for agricultural raw materials are much less favorable than those for metals and minerals where substitution has operated with less force.

Before turning to the supply side of the equation it is worth recalling how far our perspective has changed in the last decade and a half. In the early 1950's the Paley Commission was established to inquire into the "adequacy of materials, chiefly industrial materials, to meet the needs of the free world in the years ahead." The problem was conceived as one of

> soaring demands, shrinking resources, the consequent pressure toward rising real costs . . . , the ultimate threat of an arrest or decline in the standard of living.[33]

Contrast this with current thinking. The prevailing view is that while for brief periods it may be difficult to adjust supply to rising demand, over the longer run many primary products are subject to supply responses that are excessively high.

For most newly emerging countries the expansion of traditional primary commodity exports is virtually the only means of acquiring the resources needed for mounting a development program. Given the rudimentary state of the domestic economy, to shift into new lines of primary production or to invest in manufacturing is only a minor possibility in the short run. Moreover, small producers do not commonly concern themselves individually with the effect of marginal output on price. Where government plans and programs affect investment in primary materials, they are typically prepared in isolation from those of other developing countries. As was the case when African countries emerged as sizable coffee exporters, the result is likely to be sharp increases in output, severe competition among developing countries, and pressures on prices. For some products these pressures are aggravated by the arti-

---

[32] *Ibid.*, Chapter 1.

[33] The President's Materials Policy Commission, *Resources for Freedom,* 5 vols. (Washington: United States Government Printing Office, 1962), Vol. I, p. 1.

ficial stimulation of output in advanced countries through protective devices. In many basic materials, therefore, the supply problem is not, as conceived by the Paley Commission, how to meet rising world demand but how to do so without adversely affecting the earning capacity and growth prospects of the developing countries.

To meet the problem UNCTAD called for three major approaches: eliminate protection and other measures in advanced countries which artificially reduce import demand for primary products, e.g., sugar; establish international agreements for the purpose of shoring up raw material prices; and encourage the establishment of domestic manufacturing not only to substitute for imports but also to supplement foreign exchange earnings from traditional exports with earnings from the export of manufactured products.

The current plans of most developing countries include targets for diversifying exports. Although major export commodities will remain dominant for the plan period, a reduction is typically projected in the share of export staples in total exports. To some extent the diversification reflects the introduction of new primary products or an expansion in the share of minor primary products. But for the most part it is expected to take the form of an increase in the share of manufactures and semi-manufactures including more processing of food and raw materials.[34]

In stressing exports of manufactures as the main long-run solution to their trade problem the developing countries are not turning their backs on the dictates of comparative advantage. Rather, they are implicitly accepting the distinction drawn by Nurkse in his Wicksell Lectures between "established" and "incremental" comparative advantage in traditional exports:

> To the extent that external demand for such products is growing there is even a *prima facie* case for expanding the traditional exports. It is to make use of growing resources which cannot with comparative advantage be absorbed by expansion in the traditional sectors that industrialization becomes really necessary. We therefore envisage industrial activities, whether for export or home use, as being set up on top of the existing export sectors, so long as in these sectors a country still enjoys a high "established" comparative advantage even though, as a consequence of sluggish expansion of external demand, its "incremental" comparative advantage in these lines may be low.[35]

In short, "incremental" comparative advantage takes account of the adverse effects on prices and earnings of increases is the output of products, the demand for which is growing slowly.

[34] *World Economic Survey, 1964,* Part I, p. 75.

[35] Ragnar Nurkse, *Patterns of Trade and Development* (New York: Oxford University Press, 1961), p. 36.

Terms of Trade

The long-term trade problem of developing countries is sometimes expressed not so much as a growing gap between anticipated export proceeds and import requirements but rather as a secular tendency for the prices of developing countries' exports to deteriorate relative to the prices of their imports. This tendency is presumed to result mainly from two causes: the disparity between the slow growth of import demand in advanced countries for primary products and the more rapid growth of less developed countries' import demand for industrial products; and the disparity between the monopolistic conditions characterizing markets for industrial products and the competitiveness of markets for primary products.

Empirically, the evidence for declining terms of trade is weak. Over the medium term the trend is highly dependent on the initial and terminal years chosen. According to UN indexes[36] the terms of trade of developing countries improved between 1948 and 1965, import prices declining by 10 percent and export prices declining by only 4 percent. However, if the starting point is taken as 1951, a year when commodity markets were affected by the Korean War boom, the situation is dramatically reversed. "Normal" years are difficult to choose: Export price trends vary widely by commodity and country and what is normal for some may be abnormal for others.

Over the longer run changes in overall terms of trade of developing countries become even less meaningful because of the conceptual and statistical difficulties in constructing valid indexes, particularly of import prices. The composition of manufactured imports changes substantially over long periods and such products are subject to significant quality changes that are hard to take into account in price indexes. In any case, Lipsey's recent statistical investigation concludes, on the basis of data going back to the 1870's and 1880's, that there is little empirical support for the doctrine of long-term declining terms of trade for developing countries.[37]

Conventional measures of the terms of trade focus entirely on changes in prices of exports relative to prices of imports. Such "commodity" or "barter" terms of trade indexes reveal nothing about what has been happening to the volume of exports which, together with changes in the barter terms of trade, determine a country's capacity to import. Yet it is the capacity of the developing countries to import in relation to their

[36] The figures refer to UN indexes constructed by combining country indexes. (International Monetary Fund, *International Financial Statistics,* Supplement to 1965–1966 Issues; and February 1967 [Vol. 20, No. 2].)

[37] Lipsey, p. 17.

import requirements that was pinpointed by UNCTAD as the emerging strategic constraint on development.

Nor do conventional measures give a satisfactory indication of the real costs of imports to the developing countries. The real costs are dependent not only on movements in the relative prices of exported and imported goods but also on productivity changes in the exporting country. If the inputs of labor and other factors required to produce a unit of exports decline to a greater extent than the decline in export prices relative to import prices, then in a real sense the terms of trade have improved.

There is no argument with the proposition that for some periods some less developed countries have experienced deteriorating terms of trade and that such trends have had harmful effects on development. But the debate becomes sterile when such propositions, specific as to time and place, are expanded into universal and inexorable laws of economic behavior. Even where deteriorating terms of trade have occurred, they tell only a partial story of how countries have fared in their ability to finance development. As for the future course of the terms of trade it will depend not only on disparities in the growth of demand for imports as between developing and industrial countries but also on responses on the side of supply. Hopefully, with improved national planning, more diversification, and a greater willingness to consider international commodity control agreements where appropriate conditions of supply in the future may bring about more favorable price trends from the point of view of the developing countries.

Export Instability

Related to, but conceptually different from, long-term export trends is the problem of short-term fluctuations in the prices and volume of exports of developing countries. The concept of export instability refers to movements around a long-term trend which are likely to be reversed in the short term, say a year or two. While it is the underlying trend which is clearly the developing world's main concern, much of the literature on the foreign trade problems of developing countries centers on the phenomenon of instability.

Instability in export markets may affect the trend itself, and the degree of interaction will depend on the frequency, amplitude, and duration of the short-term deviations around the trend. On the demand side, for example, price instability in raw materials may intensify the consumer's preference for synthetic substitutes with more stable prices.[38] And on the supply side the speculative aspects of growing export crops may deter

---

[38] The need to protect against fluctuations through carrying excessive inventories or through hedging operations imposes a cost on the user of primary products.

the farmer's willingness to move into such crops even where market prospects are buoyant. The two types of problems are often further linked in policies designed to cope with them. Commodity agreements avowedly directed to moderating instability are almost invariably set up as a means of increasing the export earnings of primary producers in the long run.

The orthodox view on export instability can be found in many UN publications[39] as well as in most of the academic literature on economic development since World War II. Essentially, the thesis runs in the following terms:

1) Exports of developing countries consist overwhelmingly of primary materials, with one or two typically making up the bulk of the exports of individual countries.

2) Both the supply and demand for primary materials are characterized by a high degree of instability. Producers, particularly in agriculture, are able to exercise little control over output. They are vulnerable to the hazards of weather, pests, and disease, and, in the case of tree crops, such as coffee and cocoa, current output will reflect decisions taken several years earlier when market conditions may have been quite different. Minerals may be less subject to uncontrolled output variations, but they, as well as agricultural raw materials, are exposed to wide fluctuations in demand originating in the business cycles of advanced countries.

3) In the short run the price elasticity of both the supply of and demand for primary materials is generally low. The long gestation period for such crops as rubber, hard fibers, coffee, cocoa, and tea means a lag of several years in the response of output to price. But even for annual crops, once planting has taken place, the output effect of a change in price will be delayed for many months since it is likely to have its impact only on next year's harvest. While the price elasticity of supply in the case of minerals is, on the whole, higher than in agriculture, it too is low as compared with manufacturing because of high overhead costs and the heavy expenses entailed in closing down and starting up operations. In any case, for both minerals and agricultural products the response of *demand* to changes in price is unquestionably sluggish. The demand for raw materials depends on the demand for the finished product. Since their cost is only a small fraction of the cost of the final product (tin in a tin can, raw cotton in a shirt), changes in the price of the raw ma-

---

[39] See, for example, *Commodity Trade and Economic Development* (United Nations Publication Sales No: 1954.II.B.1 [UN Document E/2519, November 25, 1963]) (United Nations, 1954); *International Compensation for Fluctuations in Commodity Trade* (United Nations Publication Sales No: 61.II.D.3 [UN Document E/3447, April 1961]) (United Nations, 1961); and *Proceedings of the United Nations Conference on Trade and Development, Geneva, 23 March–16 June 1964* (hereinafter cited as *UNCTAD Proceedings*), Vol. III: *Commodity Trade* (United Nations Publication Sales No: 64.II.B.13 [UN Document E/CONF.46/141, Vol. III]) (United Nations, 1964).

terials will not significantly affect the price of the product nor therefore the volume of demand. As for food, price elasticities may be substantial for "superior" foods such as meat, dairy products, or fruit, but for basic staples the response of demand to changes in price is minimal.

4) Low price elasticities combined with uncontrolled changes in supply and demand, such as those mentioned in 2) above, mean magnified fluctuations in price and therefore sharp swings in export proceeds.

5) Through their impact on domestic incomes, savings, tax revenue, and the capacity to import, export fluctuations adversely affect the ability to plan and carry out investment programs and thus seriously retard the growth of developing countries.

Unfortunately, much discussion has been clouded by imprecision as to the meaning of export instability or by a tendency to move without warning from one concept to another. First, if export instability is defined in terms of fluctuations around an underlying trend, it clearly is important, in measuring instability, to eliminate the trend and to specify what formula has been used for this purpose. At the first UNCTAD, measures of instability were presented which were based on average year-to-year changes over the period 1950–1961 uncorrected for trend.[40] On this basis a high but constant rate of increase would appear as a high degree of instability. But if trend were eliminated, the same pattern would yield zero instability. The method used in eliminating trend also makes a difference. For example, during 1948–1958 export proceeds of primary exporting countries fluctuated on the average 12 percent when the trend line was established by the least-squares method but only 8 percent when a five-year moving average was used.[41]

Second, it is necessary to specify whether the export instability relates to prices, quantities, or proceeds. For those commodities where changes in the quantity of exports reflect primarily changes in supply conditions rather than responses to changes in demand price fluctuations tend to have a moderating effect on fluctuations in export earnings. In general, this was the pattern in the period 1955–1961.[42] It may well be that the postwar success in moderating business cycles in advanced countries implies that for the future demand-induced variations in export volume will diminish so that fluctuations in quantity and price will tend increasingly to offset each other, thereby mitigating instability in export earnings.[43]

[40] *UNCTAD Proceedings,* Vol. III, p. 85.

[41] Raymond F. Mikesell, "International Commodity Stabilization Schemes and the Export Problems of Developing Countries," *American Economic Review,* May 1963 (Vol. 53, No. 2), p. 76.

[42] *UNCTAD Proceedings,* Vol. III, p. 86.

[43] The need to be explicit as to the distinction between the behavior of export prices and proceeds is illustrated by a comparison of the results of the investigations by Michaely and Massell. One of Michaely's major conclusions is a close association between commodity concentration and the amplitude of fluctuations of a country's export prices. Massell, however, finds only a tenuous

Third, the effects of instability in export proceeds tend to get confused with the consequences of an inadequate level of foreign exchange earnings. This is understandable particularly when the fluctuations are superimposed on a declining trend in export proceeds. Yet the effects of export instability relate not to the adequacy of earnings, whatever their level, but to the consequences of receiving them in uncertain annual amounts rather than in a steady (or steadily increasing or decreasing) stream over time. The fact that commodity stabilization agreements have proved so difficult to negotiate has led one expert to question whether exporters and importers are willing to pay a substantial premium for stabilization.[44]

This impression is broadly consistent with the results of a recent comprehensive study of export instability by MacBean.[45] On the basis of empirical analysis he concludes that for less developed countries as a whole the seriousness of the problem of instability of export earnings has been greatly overstated. The average level of instability has not been much greater for poor than for rich countries, and it is strongly correlated neither with the proportion of primary products in total exports nor with the commodity concentration of exports. For individual countries where a high degree of instability has occurred it has been due not simply to concentration on primary products per se but to specialization in a particular product such as rubber or jute which is peculiarly subject to wide variability in demand and supply. On the whole, moreover, the substantial instability experienced by these countries was due primarily not to fluctuations in demand arising from changes in business activity in advanced countries but to supply variations induced by local causes such as weather, political strife, or national economic policies. MacBean also finds little evidence to show that changes in income or investment in developing countries are closely related to fluctuations in export earnings. Although conceding that the growth of *individual* countries might well be inhibited by export instability, he finds no support for this association as a general proposition.

The policy implications drawn by MacBean are broad indeed. For those countries where instability of export earnings does pose serious problems national stabilization measures may be indicated. The character of the measures would depend on the particular object of stabilization,

relationship between instability of export earnings and commodity concentration. These results are not mutually inconsistent but they clearly illustrate the necessity of being quite explicit as to what one means by "instability of exports." (Michael Michaely, *Concentration in International Trade* [Amsterdam: North Holland Company, 1962]; and B. F. Massell, "Export Concentration and Fluctuations in Export Earnings: A Cross-Sectional Analysis," *American Economic Review,* March 1964 [Vol. 54, No. 3], pp. 47–63.)

[44] Gerda Blau, "International Commodity Arrangements and Policies," *UNCTAD Proceedings,* Vol. III, p. 142.

[45] Alasdair I. MacBean, *Export Instability and Economic Development* (Cambridge, Mass: Harvard University Press, 1966).

whether producer prices or incomes on the one hand or total investment or the national income on the other. MacBean is skeptical, however, of the more elaborate national schemes on grounds of both cost and questionable efficacy. As for action on the international plane, he also has a strong distaste for conventional approaches including commodity agreements which tend to be complex and exceedingly difficult to negotiate and police. MacBean's preference is rather for a simple extension of existing access to liquidity for developing countries such as is embodied in the IMF's facility for the compensatory financing of export shortfalls.

Although MacBean's findings have been widely accepted in recent writings on the commodity problem,[46] it is too soon to consign to oblivion some of the basic propositions of the orthodox school. MacBean's method consists essentially of correlations using both cross-country data and time-series analyses. Some of the conceptual and methodological limitations of MacBean's approach are discussed in a searching paper by R. M. Sundrum in which a number of alternative measures of export instability are presented lending support to the conventional view.[47]

A word of caution is also in order about the scope of MacBean's study. The investigation is strictly focused on short-term fluctuations in export earnings around an underlying trend. It does not purport to deal with the adequacy of the level or the rate of increase of export earnings as reflected in the trend itself, a subject which was the point of departure for the main debate at UNCTAD. Nor is the study addressed to the uncertainty of the trend and the disruptive consequences for development of unpredictable and persistent adverse movements in export earnings. The latter problem is regarded as serious by the staff of the World Bank and is the object of its pending proposal for supplementary finance.

A Note on International Organizations

I have tried to delineate the contribution of foreign trade to economic development and to place in perspective some of the principal trade problems faced by the developing countries. By way of conclusion a brief word is in order about GATT and UNCTAD, the major international organizations attempting to deal with these problems. Since GATT and UNCTAD are each the subject of separate essays in this volume, I will limit myself to some observations on the relation between the two.

GATT's early approach to economic development was a reflection of

[46] See, for example, Harry G. Johnson, *Economic Policies Toward Less Developed Countries* (Washington: Brookings Institution, 1967), pp. 143–144; and Pincus, *Trade, Aid and Development*, p. 285.

[47] R. M. Sundrum, "The Measurement of Export Instability," a preliminary unpublished paper prepared for the International Bank, June 9, 1967.

the tendency until about the mid-1950's to think of development largely
in terms of a closed economy. Under the impact of the Economic Commission for Latin America (ECLA) import substitution was widely regarded as the main path to industrialization, and comparatively little
attention was given to the need to stimulate exports. As a result the focus
of GATT's interest in development was to assure that the obligations of
Contracting Parties to reduce trade barriers or to limit their use would
not impede the freedom of low-income countries to protect their infant
industries. This was the rationale of the original Article 18 of the GATT
and the subsequent revision adopted in 1955 which further loosened the
constraints on developing countries against the imposition of import
restrictions considered necessary to advance their growth.

Responding in the late fifties to the new conception of the developing
world's trade problems in terms of the need for export expansion, GATT
was handicapped by the broad exceptions from its rules for agriculture
and by the techniques of tariff bargaining which it had evolved over the
years. The inability of the developing countries to offer "reciprocity" or
to qualify as the "principal supplier" of a commodity often meant that
some products of interest to them fell outside the scope of negotiations.
Nonetheless, through the application of the most-favored-nation clause
they did become incidental beneficiaries of important tariff concessions
negotiated among advanced countries.

Toward the late fifties GATT devoted an increasing share of its activities to expanding the trade of the less developed countries without demanding reciprocity on their part. Its efforts culminated in the adoption
in 1961 of a comprehensive "program of action" directed at reducing or
eliminating barriers encountered in the markets of advanced countries.
But progress was slow. And there was a tendency to blame GATT as an
organization rather than to regard the situation as indicating primarily
the reluctance of GATT members to alter their policies.

Under these circumstances UNCTAD was launched in 1964 as a new
organization dedicated to exerting pressure on the advanced countries to
adapt their policies to the needs of the developing countries. But UNC-
TAD's frame of reference has been far broader than that of GATT. The
removal of trade barriers, whether on a most-favored-nation or preferential basis, is only one of its concerns. In addition, UNCTAD sponsors
commodity agreements designed both to shore up the prices of primary
product exports over the long run and to moderate their short-term
fluctuations. It also has promoted various financial mechanisms to offset
export instability and to provide protection against unanticipated but
persistent adverse export movements which threaten to disrupt development programs.

In strictly institutional terms UNCTAD may appear to be treading on the established jurisdiction of other organizations. Apart from the sponsorship of commodity agreements where it has a clear field, UNCTAD's other programs impinge on the activities of GATT, the IMF, and IBRD. Improved access to the markets of advanced countries will undoubtedly need to be negotiated through GATT where the formal commitments on tariff and quota treatment have been adopted. UNCTAD's proposed liberalization of the compensatory financing of export fluctuations has been incorporated into the IMF facility. And preventing the disruption of development programs by persistent adverse export movements has been a matter for study by the World Bank.

But the role of UNCTAD has been to bring together in one place the consideration of all these closely related matters and to act as a center of initiative and pressure for new approaches to solving the growth problems of the low-income countries. In this role it has already achieved a good measure of success, and the fact that established organizations are the vehicles for carrying out some of the new policies does not detract from UNCTAD's substantial achievements.

The General Agreement on Tariffs and Trade

John W. Evans

INTRODUCTION

Among the features that distinguish the General Agreement on Tariffs and Trade (GATT) from other international organizations concerned with the trade of less developed countries are two that are especially significant. GATT is the only interregional organization in which the undertakings by members take the form of contractual commitments. It is also an organization that is concerned with trade not only between developed and less developed countries but within these two groups as well. The question can be raised, however, as to whether an organization so constituted and oriented is suited to the task of facilitating the export earnings of the less developed countries or whether, on the contrary, a more specialized body, devoted exclusively to that task, is likely to achieve better results.

In this inquiry it will be taken as given that an increase in the export earnings of less developed countries will, in general, help to promote their economic development. It will also be assumed that the removal of trade barriers by developed countries, though it will not in itself provide an assurance of such increased export earnings, is a prerequisite to their maximization.

A good starting point may be to look at the way in which the less developed countries themselves customarily view the accomplishments of GATT on their behalf. The conclusion they most frequently express is derogatory, ranging from the view that GATT has done much less for them than was both desirable and possible to the unqualified denial that

Since this essay was written, John W. Evans has joined the staff of the Office of the President's Special Representative for Trade Negotiations as Assistant Special Representative for Commercial Policy. The views expressed are his own and not those of the United States government.

it has accomplished anything of benefit to their trade. These public expressions, of course, are in part designed to inspire the developed countries to greater endeavor. But they also reflect a measure of disillusionment that, at least until very recently, has been widespread and genuine. There are reasons, unrelated to objective measurement, why these countries from the beginning have tended to discount the present and potential usefulness of GATT as an instrument for furthering their development:

1) The initiative for the formation of GATT was taken by developed countries, and they played the dominant role in drawing up its rules and procedures. Moreover, the leaders among these were, first, the richest and most powerful of all, the United States, and then, the colonial powers of Western Europe. It is not surprising that countries too new or too poor to have acquired interests and responsibilities beyond their own borders should have assumed that such an initiative by their wealthier neighbors must have been designed primarily for the purpose of preserving their own privileged status.

2) The text of the original GATT avoided distinctions between members based on their degree of economic development and applied much the same rules to both the weaker and the stronger partners.

3) As the first multilateral instrument arising out of the United States Trade Agreements Program, with its emphasis on reciprocal bargaining, there was reason to assume that any benefits to be obtained under the GATT must be paid for; and the underdeveloped countries were convinced that their own bargaining power was inadequate to extract concession of value from the others.

4) The apprehensions aroused by these circumstances were reinforced by the concrete trading results obtained by the less developed countries during the first few years of GATT's life. Due, in part, to the deterioration in their terms of trade after the close of the Korean War the growth in their export earnings was disappointingly small, and they tended to attribute this to the failure of GATT to open up new export opportunities.

The GATT and the ITO Charter

It is a fact that the original GATT rules ignored the special export problems of less developed countries. But this omission was due in important measure to the preoccupation of the less developed countries themselves with import substitution rather than export expansion as the true road to economic development.

The GATT was drawn up at Geneva during the 1947 session of the Preparatory Committee of the United Nations Conference on Trade and Employment as the document that would give contractual force to the tariff concessions negotiated at that meeting between 23 governments, including nine that fitted clearly into the "less developed" category.[1] Most of its provisions were expected to be replaced later by those of the Havana Charter for an International Trade Organization (ITO). Meanwhile, following the pattern of the prewar bilateral trade agreements of the United States, the GATT rules were focused on safeguarding the tariff concessions, i.e., reductions or bindings, negotiated between its signatories. It did contain, however, some important extensions of the traditional rules, reflecting postwar conditions and the special preoccupations of the founders. Among these, the less developed countries obtained some recognition of their special needs. But two peculiarities of the Article that embodied this recognition (Article XVIII[2]) are significant.

First, the special facilities accorded to a contracting party in the interest of its economic development were paralleled by identical facilities for any contracting party in the interest of its postwar reconstruction. They were legally available not only to Brazil and Burma but also to France and the United Kingdom. Still under the influence of the tradition of reciprocal trade agreements, the drafters went to some lengths to avoid making any formal distinction between different classes of members.

Secondly, Article XVIII was concerned exclusively with the circumstances that would justify a country—presumably underdeveloped or unreconstructed—in imposing import barriers not otherwise permitted under the Agreement. In its emphasis on the dangers rather than the benefits of trade to economic development and reconstruction it reflected the prevailing fear of unrestrained competition with the United States on the part of not only Asia and Latin America but Europe as well.

When, a few months after the close of the Geneva conference, 56 countries met to agree on a Charter for ITO, this negative approach to trade, especially among the greatly enlarged contingent of less developed countries,[3] persisted. Now representing a majority of 32, they insisted on, and obtained, many changes in the Geneva draft of the Charter. But instead of using their influence to make it more difficult for developed countries to evade their commitments, they threw their weight, in general, with

[1] Brazil, Burma, Ceylon, Chile, Cuba, India, Lebanon, Pakistan, and Syria. Throughout this essay the category of less developed countries does not include any country of Europe, Rhodesia, Israel, or Yugoslavia.

[2] Article XVIII, in its 1947 version, provided that less developed countries and countries engaged in postwar reconstruction could be released from the relevant obligations of the GATT in order to provide special protection to "particular industries" but only in accordance with specified criteria and procedures. Different criteria and procedures were specified for dealing with requests for release from the obligation not to increase tariffs that had been "bound" and the obligation not to use quantitative restrictions (quotas) for protecting a domestic industry against competition.

[3] The nine listed in note 1 above plus Afghanistan, Argentina, Bolivia, Colombia, Costa Rica, the Dominican Republic, Ecuador, Egypt, El Salvador, Guatemala, Haiti, Indonesia, Iran, Iraq, Liberia, Mexico, Nicaragua, Panama, Peru, the Philippines, Transjordan, Uruguay, and Venezuela.

those that wished to weaken those commitments. Their opposition extended even to the most-favored-nation (MFN) clause on which most of the benefits they could hope to derive from the GATT necessarily depended.

> The most violent controversies at the conference and the most protracted ones were those evoked by issues raised in the name of economic development. . . . The underdeveloped countries attacked the Geneva draft at several points. They challenged the commitment to negotiate for the reduction of tariffs. They objected to a provision which enabled parties to the GATT to determine whether this commitment had been fulfilled. They sought freedom to set up new preferential systems, impose import quotas, and employ other restrictive devices without prior approval. And they proposed that a semi-autonomous economic development committee be established within the trade organization for the purpose of facilitating these escapes.[4]

At the end of the Havana Conference the ITO Charter, as signed by 53 countries, was as deficient as the GATT in any provision directed expressly toward encouraging the exports of less developed countries. The counterpart of Article XVIII had been somewhat revised to increase its ease of use, and economic development had been explicitly or implicitly recognized in two new chapters: one that would have permitted the formation of regional preferential areas among less developed countries and one that empowered the organization to sponsor international commodity stabilization agreements. The GATT was amended at the end of the Havana Conference to incorporate the changes that had been made in the provisions already contained in the General Agreement. But, in the expectation that the Charter itself would soon come into force, these new chapters, not being directly related to the defense of negotiated tariff concessions, were omitted.

The failure of the United States to ratify the Havana Charter destroyed any chance it might have had of acceptance by others. But, unexpectedly, the GATT survived. Although at times handicapped by its status as an executive agreement[5] rather than a treaty, it has become an organization in all but name and has developed procedures over time that have enabled it to perform most of the more important functions that had been contemplated for ITO. But until 1966 the only legal commitments of the Contracting Parties directed toward the economic development of underdeveloped countries were those of Article XVIII, designed to facilitate the use by those countries of restrictions against imports.

---

[4] Clair Wilcox, *A Charter for World Trade* (New York: Macmillan, 1949), pp. 48–49.

[5] United States administrations have continued their participation in GATT under the President's executive powers, supplemented by the authority delegated in the 1945 extension of the Trade Agreements Act and its successor acts.

Tariff Negotiations

Given the GATT emphasis on the negotiation of reciprocal benefits, it is easy to understand the early misgivings of underdeveloped countries. More explanation, however, is needed for the fact that those misgivings have persisted during most of the two ensuing decades. In 1965 a spokesman for one of the largest of the less developed contracting parties, looking back over the record until then, said:

> The developing countries of course had had no bargaining power, politically or economically. The rule of reciprocity has required them to give a matching concession, but clearly they were not in a position to give any. While over the last fifteen years, tariffs on industrial products of interest to industrial nations have been gradually brought down, those on products of interest to developing countries have remained at a high level.[6]

No one has made an empirical study to determine the extent to which the developed countries in GATT have held their less developed partners to the principle of reciprocity in tariff negotiations. The sheer volume of labor that would be involved in a statistical analysis of all the thousands of tariff concessions that have been granted in the five GATT negotiating conferences before the Kennedy Round is sufficient to discourage the most ambitious student. But there are conceptual difficulties as well. Because any tariff concession granted to one contracting party by another is required to be generalized to all contracting parties, the normal procedure in tariff negotiations in the past has been to concede a tariff reduction or binding only as the result of a bargain struck with the "principal supplier" of the product. There are but a relatively small number of products of which a less developed country is the principal supplier. But in many cases one or more such countries have been substantial beneficiaries of tariff reductions negotiated between two developed countries. Should these indirect concessions be taken into account? Consider another problem. In the early GATT negotiations especially, many less developed countries, now independent, were represented by the governments of their respective metropoles. The tariff concessions obtained on their behalf may have been extracted in exchange for concessions in the tariff of the colony or in exchange for a concession by the metropole itself. What sort of allowance should be made in the negotiating balance sheet for this sort of reciprocity? Most difficult to deal with is the fact that the perceived value of a tariff concession at the time it is negotiated involves judgments as to its probable effect on trade that are not subject to statistical measurement.

---

[6] Ambassador K. B. Lall of India at the Seventh World Conference of the Society for International Development.

It is possible, however, to test empirically the generalization that the developed countries have not granted meaningful tariff concessions on products of interest to underdeveloped countries. The following sample makes no pretense to being scientifically selected. Its choice has been dictated by the fact that only the United States has published comprehensive analyses of its tariff negotiations and that even this country has done so only once in sufficient detail for our purpose, i.e., in 1948, after the conclusion of the Geneva negotiations. Fortunately for the significance of the sample, the tariff negotiations conducted in 1947 were much more important than any of those that followed, up to the Kennedy Round. And the trade affected by negotiations on the United States tariff constituted a very significant part of the total trade involved in the 1947 negotiations. Not only was the trade of the United States about 25 percent of all trade conducted by the participants, but the American market was one of the few at that time in which improved trade opportunities resulting from tariff reductions were not likely to be nullified in whole or in part by quantitative restrictions.

The United States Tariff Commission published in 1949 an analysis of the results of United States tariff negotiations[7] showing, for all "principal" dutiable articles (i.e., those that were imported into the United States in amounts of $500,000 or more in 1939), the tariff concessions granted by the United States both at Geneva and in previous bilateral negotiations, together with the value of imports from the leading suppliers to the United States market. If we designate as "less developed country items" all those articles of which a less developed country was the principal supplier to the United States or on which a tariff concession was negotiated directly with a less developed country, we find the following results. Of the 246 principal articles in the United States Tariff Classification (omitting preferential rates applied only to Cuba) 53 were less developed country items. Of these the tariffs on 21, or 40 percent, were reduced at Geneva, and the tariff on fourteen items, or 26 percent of the total, was reduced by the full 50 percent permitted by the law.

Some of these reductions might be discounted on the grounds that they were of principal benefit to American processors of the raw material involved, such as manganese ore, bauxite, raw wool (of a type principally supplied by Uruguay), and zinc ores, though imports of a number of these directly competed with the output of domestic producers. But tariff reductions were also granted on processed products and simple manufactures, such as mica films and splittings, zinc metal, shelled Brazil

[7] United States Tariff Commission, *Operation of the Trade Agreements Program, June 1934–April 1948* (Washington: United States Government Printing Office, 1949), Part III, Tables 33, 34, 35, and 36.

nuts, burlaps, and jute bags. Geneva concessions included not only tariff reductions but the binding of reductions that had been granted to one or more countries in previous bilateral tariff negotiations. If these are included in the tally, 65 percent of the less developed country items were the subject of concessions.

A large measure of caution is needed in interpreting these results. A small proportion of the world's less developed areas were represented at the Geneva negotiations, even when those territories that were represented by their metropoles are included. Also, since the statistics are based on actual trade in 1939, they make no allowance for those products in which less developed countries may at a later date have acquired an export interest or export potential.

Before leaving this Tariff Commission study it may be of interest to look at the effect of post-Geneva negotiations on the items we have been examining.[8] I am, therefore, especially indebted to John Howard of the United States Tariff Commission for providing me with the 1966 rates on the articles classified above as less developed country items. The reductions that have taken place since 1947 are largely the result of negotiations in which the President's authority to reduce tariffs was much less generous than that available for the first GATT tariff negotiations. Nevertheless, of the 53 less developed country items examined the tariffs on three have been removed entirely and those on two others have been temporarily suspended. The 1966 rates (*ad valorem* equivalents in the case of five items involving compound rates) represent reductions to below the 1948 level in 23 cases, of which seven were reductions of more than 50 percent. The tariffs on three items have been increased by termination of an earlier bilateral trade agreement. It should be noted that some of the tariff changes included above result from the reclassification of the United States tariff and not from negotiations.

A more subjective list of products of export interest to the less developed countries, but one that may be more relevant to future trade prospects, has been compiled by Committee III of GATT, based primarily on information supplied by the less developed contracting parties themselves. Unfortunately, because of differences in classification and coverage it has not been feasible to determine what proportion of the products on the Committee III list were the subject of tariff concessions at Geneva. But it is possible to determine with less chance of error whether a tariff reduction granted at Geneva affected a product falling *within* one or more of the product categories in the Committee III list and thus to obtain a further test of whether the concessions granted were biased against

---

[8] Direct comparison is rendered difficult by the more or less total revision of United States tariff classifications since 1962.

products of interest to less developed countries. Of the 170 tariff positions on which reductions were granted by the United States at Geneva in 1947, 52 appear to be included in the Committee III list, among them a number of those recorded above as "less developed country items" but also many of which a developed country was the principal supplier, including ferromanganese, wood manufactures, cotton gloves, linen towels, cotton netting, essential oils, jute lining fabrics, silk fabrics, leather, and various leather manufactures.

These facts, of course, even if they were more complete, would not refute the contention that the less developed countries lack tariff bargaining power. But, given the absence of bargaining power, the fact that substantial direct concessions were received suggests that concessions, at least by the United States, were granted to less developed countries without the requirement of strict reciprocity. This impression is strengthened by an analysis of the rather scanty facts that are available. The Tariff Commission study cited above[9] reveals that the less developed countries granting tariff concessions to the United States in 1947 imported from it less than $14 million of the products affected. A precisely comparable figure for the other side of the bargain is not available, but United States imports from the less developed country negotiator or principal supplier of the products subject to United States concessions (excluding products of which less than $500,000 was imported) amounted to more than $45 million.[10]

A final fact worth noting is the manner in which the most-favored-nation clause has provided the underdeveloped countries with a partial substitute for bargaining power. Because of the requirement that any concessions be generalized to all contracting parties, products of interest to a less developed country have sometimes been omitted from a negotiation because the principal supplier was not a participant. But it has meant in other cases that less developed countries could stand on the sidelines while developed countries negotiated between themselves concessions from which their less developed partners reaped some of the benefits. For example, of the concessions granted by the United States at Geneva and recorded in the Tariff Commission report referred to above there were 23 items, other than those designated above as "less developed country items," on which a concession by the United States was initially negotiated with another developed country but where one or more less developed countries were among the five leading exporters to the United States.

This tentative excursion into the forest of past tariff negotiations does

---

[9] *Ibid.*, Part IV, Table 7.
[10] *Ibid.*, Part IV, Table 33.

not tell us as much as it would be desirable to know. But it at least shows that there are trees where others have said there were none. And it suggests that those who have concluded that the process of tariff negotiation has not resulted in benefits to less developed countries would be much nearer the truth if they rested their case on a more demonstrable fact; the growth in the exports of those countries has been alarmingly slow, given the goal of rapid economic development. In seeking an explanation for this failure it is not necessary to jump to the conclusion that the tariff negotiating mechanism is to blame. The many hurdles that need to be surmounted by less developed countries before export opportunities can be translated into increased trade are too well-known to need exposition here.

Before leaving the subject of tariff reductions it may be well to emphasize that these facts have been presented not for the purpose of building an argument against the need for doing much more in the tariff field. Rather, the purpose has been to dispel some myths that have grown up around the whole subject so that future action can be directed to overcoming real rather than imaginary obstacles.

Dispensations from the GATT Rules

The escape hatch in the GATT for "economic reconstruction and development" was never used by a developed country. And, with one notable exception, it was rarely used by a less developed country. In 1949, following the procedures of Article XVIII, Ceylon applied for and was granted "releases" permitting it to impose quota limitations for specified periods on imports of a long list of simple manufactures under the provisions of its Industrial Products Act. In response to further applications these releases were later extended and supplemented to cover other products. In no case was a request by Ceylon denied by the Contracting Parties though the representatives of that country obtained little pleasure from the laborious sessions in which successive working parties struggled to satisfy themselves that the criteria of Article XVIII had been met. The only other less developed countries invoking the Article before its amendment in 1956 were Cuba and Haiti. The Haiti release was later judged by the Contracting Parties to have been unnecessary on the ground that the restriction involved was permissible under the General Agreement without special dispensation. The United Kingdom, too, applied for a release on behalf of its territory, Northern Rhodesia, but withdrew the application, after encountering opposition, because of the injury that would accrue to the trade of another less developed territory, the Belgian Congo.[11]

[11] The details of these cases, including the factors taken into account, are set forth in General Agreement on Tariffs and Trade, *Basic Instruments and Selected Documents*, Vol. II: *Decisions, Declarations, Resolutions, Rulings and Reports* (Geneva, May 1952); and First, Second, Third, and Fourth Supplements (Geneva, various dates).

In 1956 Article XVIII was amended to increase the ease with which it could be used for economic development and to eliminate the possibility of its application to postwar reconstruction. But, with the exception of a new section providing an easy escape for less developed countries in balance-of-payments difficulties, no country other than Ceylon and Cuba made use of its provisions.

The restraint exercised by the less developed countries in their use of the right to take extraordinary protective action under Article XVIII does not provide an index to the frequency with which they have resorted to special measures. Other roads were usually open to them. For example, the right to use quantitative restrictions for balance-of-payments reasons, with incidental protective effect, has been available to virtually all less developed countries throughout the life of GATT. And when, as has frequently been the case, a less developed country has found it expedient to apply an import restriction other than the quantitative limitations permitted for a country in balance-of-payments difficulties, it has proved not too arduous to obtain from the Contracting Parties a waiver of its obligation by the required two-thirds majority. Neither developed nor less developed countries have been reticent in seeking waivers though requests by the former have often encountered stiff resistance. Of the 39 successful requests for waivers from 1949 to 1963, including extensions of earlier waivers, 24 involved dispensations granted directly to less developed countries or granted to developed countries for the benefit of their less developed territories or former territories. Most of the waivers granted directly to less developed countries were designed to permit the use of surcharges on imports for balance-of-payments reasons or the temporary increase of bound duties, pending renegotiation. The indirect waivers were in all cases designed to permit the continued use of tariff preferences for the benefit of former dependent territories or territories for which a developed country had assumed special responsibilities.

Enforcement of Obligations

The emphasis placed in recent international meetings on special measures to stimulate the exports of less developed countries has tended to obscure the importance to those exports of the more conventional activities of GATT directed to obtaining compliance with the rules of the Agreement. There will be space here for only a few highlights.

Customarily, the Contracting Parties enforce the Agreement by persuasion, backed by a judicious use of confrontation, euphemistically called "consultation." When these tactics fail, a contracting party that considers itself injured may file a complaint to the effect that a benefit it had a right to expect under the Agreement has been nullified or impaired. If the consultation that ensues does not result in a satisfactory settlement, the Contracting Parties may, if they agree with the plaintiff, authorize it to withdraw such benefits to the trade of the offending party as they consider appropriate. It is of some interest that the first important test case under this provision (Article XXIII) was brought by a less developed country, Chile, against Australia. The Chilean complaint arose out of the discontinuance by the Australian government of a subsidy on the importation of natural nitrates while it continued to subsidize competitive domestic synthetic fertilizers. Chile complained that the discriminatory application of the subsidy, permitted by the GATT rules, impaired the value of the tariff concession granted by Australia in 1947. A working party agreed with Chile, and Australia discontinued the subsidy. It was clear in this case that Australia conceded not so much because of the fear of retaliatory action by Chile as because of its desire to maintain its record of compliance with the spirit of the Agreement. But one of the concerns of the less developed contracting parties has been that they lack the bargaining power to force favorable action under Article XXIII in a case where a developed country is unwilling to act voluntarily. This fear is not without some foundation. But it serves to underline a point made earlier, namely, that less developed countries have not typically been required to pay for the benefits they have received by reciprocal concessions of comparable value. If they had, of course, the threat of withdrawal of such a concession would provide bargaining power.

The only case in which a less developed country was the defendant in a complaint case arose out of the imposition by Brazil of "discriminatory" internal taxes on a number of products on which it had previously granted tariff bindings. The item "Brazilian internal taxes" appeared repeatedly on the agenda of GATT sessions beginning in 1950. At one session the Contracting Parties passed a resolution calling the attention of members to their right to "invoke Article XXIII," that is, to take retaliatory action, against Brazil, but none did so; the case was closed in 1956 when Brazil announced the repeal of the offending taxes.

The most serious problem of enforcement the Contracting Parties have faced has been the difficulty of persuading members to dismantle their quantitative import restrictions when those restrictions were no longer justified by balance-of-payments difficulties. The pressures that have been exerted to this end have been directed almost exclusively against developed countries, and less developed countries have made common cause with other contracting parties in their demands for compliance with the terms of the Agreement. The results, while usually overdue, have been considerable. With the important exception of cotton textiles, the only sector in which a substantial body of quantitative import restrictions is still maintained by developed countries on products exported by less developed countries is the perennially embattled sector of temperate zone agricultural products, a sector of interest to more developed than less developed countries.

The role of less developed contracting parties in the rather timid efforts of the Contracting Parties to enforce the GATT rule[12] governing the formation of customs unions and free trade areas has been ambivalent. Many of them have joined other contracting parties in attacking certain aspects of the European Economic Community (EEC), as embodied in the Treaty of Rome, especially the provisions for the extension of preferences to the former African territories of France. The Contracting Parties left the issue unresolved and the EEC in possession of the field. But the precedent, thus established, of noninterference in efforts at regional integration has been applied without favor, the same tolerance being shown toward agreements in Latin America and Africa that fail to meet the GATT criteria. Even the arrangements in Central America and East Africa, which come the closest to conforming to the intent of the GATT exception, fail to provide for full free trade in accordance with a fixed schedule. The rest range from areas involving the exchange of selected preferences to those based only on expressions of initial determination to integrate economically at some unstated time in the future.

Perhaps the clearest case in which the less developed contracting parties have been deprived of benefits accorded to them under the GATT is that of cotton textiles. The Long-Term Arrangement Regarding International Trade in Cotton Textiles, while not sanctioned by any provision of the Agreement, was negotiated within the GATT framework on the initiative of the United States. Under it exporting countries "voluntarily" limit their exports to those countries that demand such action on the ground that their domestic markets are being disrupted by excessive imports. In the absence of such voluntary limitation the importing country may enforce these limits by quantitative controls. The Arrangement provides for a modest rate of expansion of trade but at a rate substantially slower than might have occurred in its absence. The Cotton Textile Arrangement was subscribed to by most less developed contracting parties exporting cotton textiles only because they were persuaded that the alternative would be still less attractive, namely, that those importing countries then maintaining quotas in contravention of the Agreement would continue to do so without further liberalization and that the United States would initiate similar restrictions. It is difficult to say to what extent lack

[12] Article XXIV of the GATT exempts from the basic requirement of nondiscrimination: a completed customs union or free trade area and an "interim agreement" to achieve such a union or area "within a reasonable length of time" according to a plan and schedule that is not disapproved by the Contracting Parties.

of bargaining power was responsible for the plight of the underdeveloped textile exporters, especially since Japan shares their uncomfortable position. The Arrangement serves, nevertheless, as the clearest demonstration of one of the problems facing less developed countries if they make very rapid progress in developing exports of labor intensive manufactured goods.

THE PROGRAM FOR THE EXPANSION OF TRADE

As early as 1954 and repeatedly in the next few years annual progress reports prepared by the GATT Secretariat underlined the widening gap between the trade expansion being achieved by developed countries and that by less developed countries. In 1957 the twelfth session of the Contracting Parties engaged a panel of experts[13] to make a survey of significant trends in world trade. The panel was instructed to consider, among other things, "the failure of the trade of less-developed countries to develop as rapidly as that of industrialized countries." The report of the panel, the so-called "Haberler Report,"[14] marked a turning point in GATT history. The report confirmed the findings of the GATT Secretariat. It did not find any general tendency toward discrimination against the exports of less developed countries per se, but it did identify many factors, including trade barriers and unfavorable price trends, that impeded the growth of the export earnings of those countries in the sectors of foodstuffs and industrial raw materials and provided the impetus for a wide-ranging search for novel methods of improving those earnings. The first fruit of the Haberler Report was the decision of the Contracting Parties in November 1958 to launch a program directed toward an expansion of international trade and, *inter alia,* toward "maintaining and expanding the export earnings of the less-developed countries."

The institutional structure erected by the Contracting Parties in carrying out this program is too elaborate to describe here. But a summary of the methods that have been and are being pursued will give some idea of the complexity of the problems to be solved and the difficulties involved in overcoming them.

Fact Finding. The Contracting Parties have engaged in studies to identify the products in which the less developed countries have an actual or potential comparative advantage and the tariff and nontariff barriers of other countries that interfere with the exploitation of those advantages.

Coordination of Development Plans with Trade Opportunities. The Secretariat and working groups have worked with the governments of

---

[13] Roberto de Oliveira Campos, Gottfried Haberler, James Meade, and Jan Tinbergen.
[14] General Agreement on Tariffs and Trade, *Trends in International Trade: A Report by a Panel of Experts* (Geneva, October 1958).

selected less developed countries in the analysis of their programs for economic development in order to identify the most promising export products and to define the actions required both by those countries and by importing countries to make their development possible.

Market Facts and Analysis. The Contracting Parties have established a Trade Information and Trade Advisory Service, which conducts a clearinghouse for trade information and marketing techniques.

Technical Assistance and Education. An in-service training program has been established for officials of less developed countries; and upon request expert teams from developed countries have been sent to advise governments concerning the development of their export markets.

Reduction of Trade Barriers. By systematic exhortation and confrontation of individual members the Contracting Parties have attempted to accelerate the process of reducing or eliminating by unilateral action those trade barriers that may restrict imports from less developed countries. Special emphasis has been placed on the removal of residual quantitative restrictions, the elimination of nontariff barriers, including those maintained legally under the GATT, the elimination of both customs duties and internal taxes on tropical products, and the inclusion in Kennedy Round reductions of products of potential export interest to less developed countries.

The New "Part IV"

The drive of the GATT Contracting Parties to stimulate the exports of less developed countries reached a climax in 1964 when they wrote into the Agreement a new section (Part IV), which entered into force in 1966. This action brought to an end the period during which the GATT contained neither textual recognition of the role of exports in economic development nor a constitutional framework for many of the activities in which the Contracting Parties had been engaged since the Haberler Report.

There was little dissent from the view that the General Agreement should be amended to give a high priority to the development of the exports of less developed countries. But there were fundamental differences of view as to how this purpose should be translated into firm commitments, differences not only between the developed and the less developed countries but within the two groups. Among the proposals made by one or more of the less developed countries were demands that the developed countries bind themselves: not to increase any barrier to the importation of products of particular interest to less developed countries; to "take immediate steps" for the reduction and elimination of such barriers; to take similar action concerning internal taxes that impede consumption of those products; to eliminate differentials in tariffs between raw materials and processed products; to "take full account of the need" to improve the prices of products exported by less developed countries in relation to the prices of products imported by them; in tariff negotiations, to give priority to reducing tariffs on products of interest to the less developed countries without reciprocal action on their part; to grant less developed countries tariff preferences on imports of manufactured products; and to stabilize the prices of primary products "at remunerative levels" through international commodity arrangements.[15]

As the agreed text emerged, most though not all of these proposals survived, in qualified form. The developed contracting parties agreed "except when compelling reasons . . . make it impossible" to freeze against increase existing import barriers and internal taxes and to "accord high priority" to their reduction and elimination and to the reduction of tariff differentials between raw materials and processed goods. They agreed to procedures calling for reports, complaints, and confrontation of individual contracting parties in order to make these commitments as effective as possible.[16] They agreed that the Contracting Parties acting jointly (i.e., as an organization) *might* promote arrangements for achieving "stable, equitable and remunerative" commodity prices, *should* collaborate with any UN institution that might be formed as a result of the United Nations Conference on Trade and Development (UNCTAD), and *should* collaborate with governments and international organizations in coordinating trade and aid relationships.[17] They also accepted as a contractual commitment the pledge they had made earlier in a ministerial resolution, i.e., not to expect reciprocity from less developed countries in tariff negotiations.[18]

A case can be made that the amendment of the GATT did little more than codify trends already apparent and give legal shape to norms that had been accepted in practice by most developed countries as essential to the orderly development of the new countries. But it served a useful purpose both in establishing more explicit bench marks against which further progress could be measured and in defining more clearly the areas on which more work was needed.

The two most insistent demands of the less developed countries on

[15] General Agreement on Tariffs and Trade, Committee on the Legal and Institutional Framework, *Proposed Chapter on Trade and Development: Comparative Provisions of Five Submissions* (Geneva, February 24, 1964).

[16] Part IV, Article XXXVII, of the Agreement, contained in General Agreement on Tariffs and Trade, *Basic Instruments and Selected Documents*, Thirteenth Supplement: *Decisions, Reports, etc., of the Second Special Session and the Twenty-second Session* (Geneva, July 1965), pp. 4–6.

[17] Article XXXVIII, in *ibid.*, pp. 6–7.

[18] Article XXXVI, in *ibid.*, p. 4.

which no consensus emerged were that the developed countries should grant tariff preferences to less developed countries and that they sponsor international commodity arrangements designed not merely to stabilize fluctuating commodity prices but to prevent or reverse longer-term adverse trends in those prices.

Preferences

The preference proposal was an issue over which both the developed countries and the less developed countries were divided among themselves. Most of the former, with a few exceptions including that of the United States, declared that they agreed with the idea of preferences "in principle." But the majority held widely differing views as to the conditions under which preferences should be granted. Although in recent debates in GATT the less developed countries have presented a united front in their demands for preferences, a fundamental conflict of interest among them has persisted in private and is likely to emerge into the open if agreement among the developed countries should permit the debate to move from the level of generalization to the details of implementation. The African countries now enjoying preferential access to EEC markets are aware that they would probably lose markets if the preferences they enjoy should be extended to all less developed countries. More generally, there is a divergence of outlook among less developed countries depending upon their relative size and on the stage they have already reached in the development of manufacturing industries. The least developed among them see little likelihood of gain to them from generalized preferences under which they would have to compete on equal terms with India or with Brazil.

In spite of the complexity of the problem there seems to be a growing belief that there must be some circumstances in which a departure from the strict rule of nondiscrimination would be of benefit to the exports of less developed countries at least for a limited period of time during which those export industries in which these countries have a potential comparative advantage may achieve the ability to compete with their more established counterparts in developed countries. The search for agreement as to the circumstances in which preferences should be sanctioned is being pursued outside GATT, but if any agreement in principle should be reached among the principal protagonists, it could not, without impairing the usefulness of GATT, be translated into action unless ratified by the Contracting Parties as an acceptable departure from the GATT rules.

Actions Taken Under Part IV

Part IV of the GATT entered into force on June 27, 1966, with respect to those contracting parties that had accepted it. By the end of 1966, 51 countries had formally accepted the new commitments, and nine others had subscribed to a declaration providing for their *de facto* application pending formal ratification. The latter included the member states of the EEC with the exception of France. All the other developed countries in GATT, including the United States, the United Kingdom, Japan, Canada, and the Nordic European Free Trade Association (EFTA) countries had accepted definitively.

The Contracting Parties have conducted two reviews of the operation of these new provisions. A quantitative appraisal of the actions reported by individual countries for these reviews would be too great an undertaking for this study. In the removal of quantitative restrictions, especially, even to name the items affected would occupy several pages. But progress in the unilateral reduction or elimination of tariffs and internal taxes has also been significant.

The following examples, from the reports of some of the key developed countries, are illustrative. The EEC extended earlier duty suspensions affecting tea, tropical hardwoods, a number of spices, and other tropical products. Japan, "in advance implementation of its offers in the Kennedy Round," suspended duties on coffee and cocoa beans and halved its excise taxes on coffee and cocoa powder. These suspensions were in addition to similar action taken earlier on tropical woods and nonferrous metals. The United Kingdom announced the removal of duties on shelled almonds and sisal and the suspension of duties on tea and tropical hardwoods. And the United States announced the initial or renewed suspension of duties on copper, bauxite, nickel, graphite, tropical hardwoods, certain tropical fibers, copra, palm nuts and kernels and palm oil.

RESULTS OF THE KENNEDY ROUND

Although the undertakings of the developed contracting parties in Part IV were not conditioned on simultaneous action by all of them, it was evident from the outset that their performance was likely to be severely limited except as part of a general movement. Thus, the Kennedy Round of tariff negotiations presented the first real test of their ability to turn promises into action.

The Kennedy Round not only achieved deeper tariff cuts than any previous negotiation but affected a very much larger segment of world trade than any of its predecessors, and this would seem to be equally true of the benefits it brought to the participating less developed countries. In its preliminary summary the GATT Secretariat found that the long list of items that had been specified by the less developed countries as of special export interest to them received, on the whole, treatment comparable to that accorded by the industrialized countries to all the positions in their tariffs. The tariff was cut in half on about 50 percent, unweighted, of the less developed country list. Five percent of the list was affected by reductions ranging from just over half the tariff to total elimination, and reductions of less than half were granted on 26 percent of the list, leaving 21 percent of the list on which no reductions were made.[19]

Unfortunately for the interpretation of these results, many of the products listed by the less developed countries are of more potential than actual interest to them, the bulk of the world exports in these products being supplied by developed countries.[20] Statistics prepared by the United States delegation, however, based on actual trade with those countries, show more clearly that the less developed countries did, in fact, enjoy solid benefit from the "no reciprocity" rule. The United States granted tariff concessions on products accounting in 1964 for $570 million of imports from the nine actively participating less developed countries. For three-quarters of this, one of these countries was the "principal supplier." From them the United States received concessions on $205 million of trade. But almost all ($550 million) of the United States concessions represented tariff reductions, and 96 percent of those reductions were of 50 percent or more. In contrast, all but $20 million of the concessions granted by the "nine" consisted of the "binding" of existing rates and only about 3 percent of the actual tariff reductions were cuts of as much as half. It is clear that the United States did not demand reciprocity from the less developed countries. And while similar figures are not yet available to show the balance of concessions exchanged by other developed countries with their less developed partners, all available evidence suggests that none of them demanded reciprocity in those exchanges.

The sector in which the greatest hope had been held for the total elimination of tariffs by the industrial countries had been that of "tropical products," in which less developed countries have a near monopoly. But

[19] "GATT Trade Negotiations: Brief Summary of Results," GATT Press Release GATT/992, June 30, 1967.

[20] Similar results, however, are revealed in a GATT analysis, prepared after this essay was completed, based on actual less developed country trade. This study (GATT Documents COM TD/48, October 19, 1967, and COM TD/48/Add.1, October 26, 1967) gives the distribution of Kennedy Round concessions as they affect less developed country exports (1964) in selected product groups (tropical products, processed foods, nonferrous metals, cotton yarn and fabrics, clothing, other textiles, and leather and manufactures) to six major industrialized participants (the EEC, Japan, Sweden, Switzerland, the United Kingdom, and the United States). Forty-five percent of this trade was admitted duty free before the Kennedy Round. Of the dutiable trade covered, tariffs on 60 percent were reduced or eliminated, over 40 percent being subject to tariff cuts of 50 percent or more.

the GATT Secretariat reported that only 39 percent of dutiable imports in that sector—many imports already enjoyed free entry—benefited from any tariff reduction.[21] As shown above, the principal impediment to more important results came from the less developed countries themselves or, rather, from those of them that already enjoyed preferential access to the markets of industrialized countries. The European Economic Community cited their obligations to the African countries associated with them in the Yaoundé Convention of Association as the reason it could do very little in the field of tropical products. This in turn inhibited action by others. In the case of the United States it affected the legal right of the President to proclaim tariff eliminations under the "tropical products authority" of the Trade Expansion Act.

Two other major impediments helped limit the benefits of the Kennedy Round to the developing countries. The disappointment of those few among them that depend on the exports of temperate zone agricultural products, such as Argentina and Uruguay, was a reflection of the meager overall results obtained in that sector; their chagrin was shared by other agricultural exporters such as Australia, New Zealand, and the United States. Argentina, however, suffered a special disappointment when the beef concession it had negotiated with the delegation of the Community was vetoed by France in the closing hours of the conference, presumably in response to the violent protests of farmers in Brittany.

Temperate agriculture aside, the most serious loss of potential benefits to less developed countries resulted from the demand of industrialized countries for "reciprocity" from their *developed* partners. Too often, a developed country achieved the desired balance by the withdrawal of a previous offer concerning a product of which another developed country was the principal supplier—a process which secondary suppliers, whether developed or not, were in no position to prevent.

While the Kennedy Round was only a qualified success from the point of view of the less developed countries, it was nonetheless a major accomplishment and brought much greater potential benefit to their export trade than any previous tariff negotiation. Their public reaction to the results, however, was predictable. At the closing meeting of the conference the developing countries that had participated read a joint statement that made no reference to the positive results but catalogued the benefits they had hoped for but had not received:

> elimination of duties on products of particular export interest to developing countries, tropical products, commodity agreements, compensation for loss of preferences and removal of non-tariff barriers.[22]

[21] "GATT Trade Negotiations: Brief Summary of Results," GATT Press Release GATT/992, June 30, 1967.

[22] "Joint Statement by the Developing Participating Countries in the Kennedy Round Negotiations," GATT Press Release GATT/994, June 30, 1967.

THE TASKS REMAINING

Exports from the less developed countries to the rest of the world increased in volume at an annual rate of about 6 percent from 1960–1965 and in value by about 6.4 percent. The increase in volume was about 50 percent greater than the projections prepared by the United Nations for the Development Decade.[23] But these relatively favorable overall results conceal wide differences as between regions and between countries in the same region. Taking 1959-1960 as 100, an index of export earnings in 1964-1965 shows such contrasts as 167 for Bolivia against 101 for Ghana and 186 for Paraguay compared with 115 for Brazil.[24] Furthermore, the overall results would be more impressive if they had not been achieved during a period when the value of total world trade was increasing still more rapidly. From 1960 to 1965 the share of underdeveloped areas in world exports fell from 21.8 percent to 19.9 percent,[25] continuing the decline, though at a gentler rate, that had been noted by the GATT Secretariat in the early 1950's.

This relative decline, of course, should be interpreted with caution. What is needed is progress in absolute terms, not in an abstract statistical concept. It is also evident that trade results are not in themselves a measure of the changes that have taken place in trade barriers. But after these allowances have been made, the developed countries cannot afford to be complacent at the failure of the exports of underdeveloped countries to grow more rapidly so long as there is a reasonable chance that they are being prevented from doing so by remaining barriers.

Even in the field of the "traditional" exports of less developed countries the Contracting Parties have gone only part way toward reaching the agreed objective of free trade. Even after the Kennedy Round, revenue duties or internal taxes remain on some tropical products, especially those, such as cane sugar and tropical vegetable oils, that compete with temperate zone agricultural products. Impediments to the agricultural exports of temperate zone developing countries are both more formidable and more intractable, being inseparable from the protection maintained by developed countries against each other. Worthwhile progress toward their removal can probably occur only in association with a general move by the developed countries toward the restoration of competition as the regulator of agricultural production and trade.

The area in which there is the greatest room for trade liberalization of potential value to most underdeveloped countries is that of industrial

---

[23] General Agreement on Tariffs and Trade, *International Trade 1965* (Geneva, 1966), pp. 12–13.

[24] *Ibid.,* p. 27.

[25] *Ibid.,* p. 2.

products. Within the limits imposed by existing standards of nondiscrimination in international trade the pace of progress in this sector will be determined by the speed with which developed countries reduce their MFN duties and remove those quantitative restrictions that are applied to imports from all sources. But in one significant segment of the industrial sector it should be feasible for the developed countries to act more quickly, that is, by the removal of those tariff differentials that render it unprofitable for less developed countries to process for export the raw materials they produce.

As has frequently been demonstrated in recent studies[26] the fact that most developed countries charge higher tariff rates on materials imported in processed form than in unprocessed form results in "effective rates" of protection for processors in the importing country that are often much higher than appears from the nominal tariff protection for the completed product. Similar demonstrations[27] purporting to show that effective rates are also "relatively high" on manufactured goods of export interest to less developed countries are less convincing, but in the field of early processing the reduction of tariff rates on the processed product designed to bring the effective protection at least down to the existing nominal rate should encourage further industrial development in a sector in which some less developed countries possess a natural advantage because of their ability to produce the raw material at competitive prices.

Another useful step that could be taken independently of the removal of trade barriers on a broader front would be to provide the less developed countries with a more effective guarantee that those industrial exports they do succeed in developing will not be excluded from world markets on grounds of market disruption. But the fear of "low wage" imports will be difficult to overcome if the exports of those countries are likely to be directed toward a single export market. It is unlikely, therefore, that any developed country will forswear protection of its labor-intensive industries except in the context of a concerted movement by all the major importing countries. In spite, therefore, of what has been said above about the Cotton Textile Arrangement it may well be that it could provide a practical vehicle for achieving general liberalization of cotton textile trade if its professed aim of "orderly expansion" of trade should become the actual aim of all its signatories.

There are no industrial products of importance that are not produced for export by some developed country. Therefore, no country can now eliminate tariffs on manufactured goods for the benefit of the developing

---

[26] See, for example, Harry G. Johnson, *Economic Policies Toward Less Developed Countries* (Washington: Brookings Institution, 1967), pp. 96–104.

[27] *Ibid.*, p. 96.

industries of poorer countries without simultaneously opening its markets to unrestrained competition from developed countries. It is this problem that has given rise to the demands of less developed countries that the most-favored-nation clause be suspended on their behalf. The complex of issues involved in the proposal that preferences be granted by developed countries to underdeveloped countries cannot be dealt with here. But one aspect of the problem does deserve emphasis. The less developed countries would be the heaviest losers from a general breakdown of the MFN principle. If a compromise can be found that will reconcile the differences of view concerning preferences so as to make it possible for less developed countries to develop their manufactured exports more rapidly, it is of importance to them that this not be accomplished by destroying the value of the most-favored-nation clause. It should be made explicit in any agreement that preferences are exceptional and temporary so as to avoid the loss of a safeguard vital both to world trade in general and to the trading interests of the underdeveloped countries themselves.

Trade Between the Less Developed Countries

The explicit commitments of the new Part IV of the GATT engage only the developed contracting parties. In its negotiation the less developed countries repulsed efforts to obtain their adherence to comparable undertakings toward each other. The final text does, however, include an agreement by them to take

> appropriate action . . . for the benefit of the trade of other less-developed contracting parties, in so far as such action is consistent with their individual present and future development. . . . [28]

The difficulty that was encountered in reaching agreement on this provision is illustrative of the more general inability of GATT, at least up to now, to influence the commercial policies of the less developed countries themselves. In any complete solution to the interrelated problems of trade and development these policies cannot be overlooked. It is entirely possible for a less developed country to impede both it own development and that of other less developed countries by an effort to protect all of its potential producers against competition. The Contracting Parties should be able to help their less developed members in the adoption of policies that would avoid that danger, but before this can be done it will be necessary, perhaps as the result of action under the new GATT commitments, to convince them that concern with their economic decisions is motivated by interest in their welfare and not by zeal for the enforcement of liberal trading principles.

[28] Article XXXVIII, contained in GATT, *Basic Instruments and Selected Documents,* Thirteenth Supplement, p. 7.

INSTITUTIONAL CONSIDERATIONS

If the kind of action that should be taken is clear, the question remains: Are the less developed countries most likely to achieve their ends through participation in GATT or in a body exclusively devoted to their needs? The answer must lie in the nature of the action needed and the categories of countries from which action is required. In the elimination of trade barriers it is clear that the decisions required must be taken by the governments of the developed countries acting in accordance with their constitutional processes and their judgments of their national interests. The role that can be performed by an international organization is not to replace those judgments or processes but to influence them. To accomplish this it must achieve agreement among nations similarly placed to take parallel action.

An organization, to be capable of inducing governments to take concerted action, must meet certain minimum tests. It must include in its membership the countries that are expected to participate in the desired act. Those members must recognize its competence in the relevant field of action. And its constitutional structure and procedures must provide adequate opportunity for members requesting action to present their demands.

The membership of GATT includes all the developed countries that rely primarily on the price mechanism, that is, all those countries in which assurance of the right to compete freely would bring concrete benefits to the trade of less developed countries. Only Czechoslovakia and Poland among the members of the Eastern European trading bloc are contracting parties. But market access commitments by countries with totally managed economies are not meaningful. In any event, the posture of the Union of Soviet Socialist Republics and its Eastern European neighbors in UNCTAD did not suggest that the presence of those countries in GATT would add appreciably to its contribution to the trade problems of less developed countries. The most urgent need is to bring about parallel action by developed countries that are members of the competitive world trading system, and for this purpose the present membership of GATT is complete.

By March 1967 the less developed country membership in GATT had grown to 44 out of a total of 71 contracting parties. In addition, four less developed countries were provisional members and ten others participated under special arrangements or applied the Agreement *de facto,* pending formal accession. But a substantial number of less developed countries remain outside GATT. While the newly independent countries of Africa have almost all taken advantage of the easy terms of entry accorded to former dependent territories, a number of less developed countries with a longer history of independence have continued to abstain. Among the Central American countries only Nicaragua is a participant in GATT. In South America, Venezuela, Colombia, Ecuador, Bolivia, and Paraguay are absent. In other continents the abstentions include: Liberia and Ethiopia; the countries of North Africa except Tunisia and the United Arab Republic; all of the Middle East except Israel; and in Southeast Asia, Laos, Thailand, the Philippines, and the two Vietnams.

The less developed countries appear to be divided in their judgment as to whether their interests would be promoted or endangered by GATT membership. But almost all the larger among them (Mexico is the most notable exception) are active participants. This may suggest that some of the smaller countries have taken too seriously criticisms of GATT voiced by others in the heat of debate and have been persuaded that the price of admission to GATT is too high for a poor country to pay. If so, the new provisions of Chapter IV of the GATT may in time allay their fears and induce them to accede if encouraged to do so by such influential participants as Argentina, Brazil, Chile, Nigeria, Ghana, the United Arab Republic, India, and Pakistan. Even without the inclusion of these missing less developed countries, however, the forces of economic development are well represented, quantitatively and qualitatively.

Finally, the unique advantage of GATT as a forum for dealing with the trade problems of less developed countries is the fact that the developed countries from which action is required recognize its competence in the field of trade. The industrialized contracting parties have for nearly two decades looked to GATT as the focal point for the negotiation and coordination of their commercial policy objectives except those involved in regional integration. More importantly, this coordination has, for the most part, been effected not by the passage of resolutions but by the exchange of precise commitments and by consultation on specific trade problems. Concrete achievements on behalf of less developed countries have been furthered by the practice among developed contracting parties of regarding their collective commitments to those countries as obligations undertaken toward the Contracting Parties as a whole.

Commodity Problems

While the competence and effectiveness of GATT in the field of trade policy suggests that it is the most useful forum for the less developed countries to use in pressing their trade claims, many of their other economic objectives can be more appropriately pursued in other organizations. GATT has either no useful role, or at best an auxiliary role, in effecting the transfer of income from developed to less developed countries by such devices as grants, low-interest financing, or compensation for unfavorable movements in the terms of trade.

Paragraph (h) of Article XX of the GATT provides an exception to the GATT rules in favor of commodity agreements that are not disapproved by the Contracting Parties. By giving their tacit approval the Contracting Parties have thus facilitated all the commodity agreements concluded since 1947. The new Part IV of the GATT, however, provides for more affirmative action by the Contracting Parties, "where appropriate." It remains to be seen whether any country will bring this provision into play by asking GATT to sponsor a commodity conference. If not, and if past experience is a guide, other international organizations will probably continue to serve as a focal point for the establishment of commodity study groups and negotiating conferences. In the Kennedy Round, however, it was considered expedient to conduct some part of the bargaining by sectors, with the countries principally interested as exporters or importers attemping to arrive at global agreements that go beyond simply the exchange of tariff concessions. Especially in the case of agricultural commodities these sector negotiations attempted to deal with the broader subjects of production policy and price maintenance. If this experiment should be repeated in later negotiations, the fields of trade agreements and of commodity stabilization agreements may so overlap as to require that both be pursued through a single organization, or, if not, that the Contracting Parties play a more active role in the negotiation of commodity agreements.

Voting Power and Its Consequences

Article XXV of the GATT provides that each Contracting Party shall be entitled to have one vote "at all meetings of the Contracting Parties." If we assume that the interests of developed and less developed countries are respectively monolithic and always opposed, the effect of the unit vote is potentially explosive. The less developed members, accounting for 15 percent of free world exports, can outvote by a wide margin developed country members doing about 80 percent of that trade. Constitutionally, they could block any action desired by the developed contracting parties and could pass any resolution they themselves wished. The danger that this situation could represent to the less developed countries themselves, however, has been averted both by their own restraint and by the force of the GATT tradition against reaching substantive decisions by vote. The organization owes its survival to the fact that from its beginning its members have realized the futility of attempting to impose obligations on a minority, even where the voting majority also possessed the balance of trading and bargaining power. A group holding the preponderance of ballot power but lacking the other attributes of power would exploit its voting strength only at serious risk both to the life of the organization and to the accomplishment of its own purposes.

One important category of decisions in which a formal vote cannot constitutionally be avoided arises when the Contracting Parties are asked to relieve an individual contracting party of one of its obligations by a waiver. The temptation of less developed countries to use their power to block waivers, for bargaining purposes, must have been difficult to resist. On at least one occasion, in fact, this bargaining weapon has been brandished. When the United States and Canada petitioned the Contracting Parties for a waiver to permit them to establish a partial free trade area in automobiles and parts, the most vigorous opposition came from the representative of a country with no export interest in automobiles, Jamaica. But the weapon of potential veto was returned to its scabbard and the waiver granted.

The less developed countries have found that in GATT their preponderant vote may and does permit them to press their claims with confidence and to exert powerful influence on the direction and emphasis of the activities of the organization. But they have not attempted to use their majority vote to seize control. They have stopped short of action that would destroy the organization. But why should they draw back from that destruction? Why have they chosen to preserve an institution in which their voting power cannot be profitably exploited? The answer would seem to be that they have understood their need for an organization they cannot control. They must realize that great trading powers are not likely to implement obligations they have not freely accepted. Resolutions voted by a majority over their objections may give momentary satisfaction but pay no dividends. Compromise resolutions accepted *faute de mieux* are not much better. The best chance the less developed countries have of obtaining actual, as opposed to verbal, benefits is through an organization where no hint of coercion by ballot can arise. If no such organization were in existence, they would be wise to seek its creation.

To put the discussion of the last few paragraphs in a sentence, GATT has for the less developed countries at least the negative advantage that the governments of developed countries will not be predisposed to ignore decisions arrived at within its framework. Fortunately, there have been many signs in the last few years that the developed contracting parties do consider it to be in their interest to induce each other to act on behalf of the less developed members. It seems likely, therefore, that the supposed distinction between a GATT operated for the benefit of its developed members and one aimed at achieving more universal benefits will prove to have been imaginary.

SUMMARY

The less developed countries have traveled a long road since the formation of GATT in 1948. Their early determination to keep their hands free to restrict their own import trade has not disappeared, but it is now overshadowed by the emphasis on their need to gain export markets. Original fears that they would be handicapped by lack of bargaining power have rarely been confirmed by actual experience.

The disappointment of less developed countries in the results that have been achieved is in part a reflection of their frustration over their own inability to develop the export capacity necessary to exploit those trade opportunities that have been opened up. And this frustration has found some release in an understandable but exaggerated impatience at the failure of developed countries to move more rapidly in removing the trade impediments that remain.

The public stance of the less developed countries toward GATT remains one of skepticism concerning its usefulness for their purposes. But the continuing accession of new less developed members and the restraint they have shown in the use of their overwhelming voting strength suggest that this stance may not reflect their true appraisal of GATT as an organization capable of helping them achieve their ends.

At the present stage of development of most of the less developed countries improved trade opportunities will be of little use unless a groundwork is laid by the creation of productive capacity, and this will require massive economic and technical aid. But increased export earnings not only will flow from the development of an adequate infrastructure; they can hasten its achievement. In order that artificial barriers to the development of those earnings be, as nearly as possible, abolished it is important that the less developed countries pursue that end in an international institution capable of obtaining favorable decisions from its members. In the trade field the developed countries have demonstrated that they are willing to undertake commitments in GATT, commitments which, being arrived at without the coercion of majority voting, they have generally carried out.

The United Nations Conference on Trade and Development

Richard N. Gardner

The United Nations Conference on Trade and Development (UNCTAD), held in Geneva from March 23 to June 16, 1964, was a diplomatic event of major importance—and a turning point in the evolution of international organization. It was the largest and most comprehensive intergovernmental conference ever held, involving 2,000 delegates from 119 countries. It was the first major conference in which the lines were drawn sharply on a North-South rather than on an East-West basis. And, what is of more lasting significance, it gave birth to continuing machinery that has already had a profound impact both on international institutions and national policies.

This continuing machinery, also called UNCTAD, is unprecedented in structure and far-reaching in scope. It includes a periodic Conference, supposed to meet at least once every three years; a 55-member Trade and Development Board, meeting twice a year; a 55-member Committee on Commodities and 45-member Committees on Manufactures, Shipping, and Invisibles and Financing Related to Trade; numerous subgroups and expert committees; and a large, independent secretariat in Geneva. Ranging broadly over the entire field of trade and development, UNCTAD has become a focal point for the discussion of economic problems of particular interest to the less developed countries.

Shortly after UNCTAD was born the UN's Undersecretary for Economic and Social Affairs, Philippe de Seynes, shrewdly observed:

> A new channel—or circuit—is being established through which gradually all problems are being routed, even those whose consideration was previously

Richard N. Gardner is Henry L. Moses Professor of Law and International Organization at Columbia University, New York. He served from 1961 to 1965 as United States Deputy Assistant Secretary of State for International Organization Affairs and was Vice Chairman of the United States delegation at the first UNCTAD Conference.

reserved for more antiseptic and reassuring forums; a channel characterized by a different combination of forces and a special ideology, one in which new criteria are applied to national policies and through which the world community is constantly confronted with proposals which the major centers of economic decision making cannot indefinitely overlook.[1]

UNCTAD has amply confirmed the justness of this description. It is appropriate, therefore, to seek detailed answers to some key questions: How did UNCTAD come about? What are its strengths and weaknesses as an international organization dedicated to helping the poor countries of the world?

THE ORIGINS OF UNCTAD

The decisions which led to the UNCTAD Conference of 1964 and to the continuing UNCTAD machinery were the result of important changes in world politics and economics which had their reflection in the United Nations.

Perhaps most fundamentally, the late 1950's and early 1960's were years of growing frustration for the less developed countries, years in which dreams of rapid economic development to follow in the wake of independence were rudely shattered. There was a marked decline in the prices of some key primary commodities on which developing countries rely for their export earnings. At the same time foreign aid failed to increase as rapidly as the less developed countries had hoped, and new aid was increasingly offset by repayment of principal and interest from past loans. Among the developing countries there was a growing conviction that nothing short of a fundamental reshaping of the world trading system could deal with their desperate and urgent problems.

The dissatisfaction of the less developed countries with their economic position was coupled with a growing disenchantment with the effectiveness of the UN's central economic forums. This disenchantment was understandable. With few exceptions the developed countries had failed to participate constructively or at a high level in the Economic and Social Council (ECOSOC) and the Second (Economic and Financial) Committee of the General Assembly. Too much of the time of these bodies was occupied in acrimonious and sterile cold-war debates which seemed irrelevant to the problems of the poor countries.

To be sure, the United States, joined by other developed Western countries, had used UN forums for the launching of constructive initiatives such as the Expanded Program of Technical Assistance (EPTA) and the UN Special Fund. But the really central questions of aid and

---

[1] Andrew W. Cordier and Wilder Foote (ed.), *The Quest for Peace* (New York: Columbia University Press, 1965), p. 189.

trade and finance were dealt with in other institutions—the International Bank for Reconstruction and Development (IBRD) and its soft-loan affiliate, the International Development Association (IDA); the International Monetary Fund (IMF); and the General Agreement on Tariffs and Trade (GATT). There was visible and progressive deterioration in the quality of representation, level of debate, and significance of work of ECOSOC, and an attempt to revive it by a ministerial meeting in 1960 proved a dismal failure.

The poor countries' disenchantment with ECOSOC was aggravated by what they regarded as its increasingly unrepresentative character. By the early 1960's the UN's original membership of 51 had more than doubled, and the less developed countries were close to a two-thirds majority. Yet ECOSOC was frozen at eighteen members, divided almost equally between developed and less developed countries. Efforts to enlarge the Council by Charter amendment were frustrated by Soviet insistence that the People's Republic of China (Communist China) would have to be seated first. It was only in December 1963 that the Soviet position changed and the Assembly voted to enlarge ECOSOC to its present membership of 27. By that time, however, the developing countries were committed to the displacement of the Council by machinery which would make full use of their numerical majority.

If the poor countries were disenchanted with the UN's central economic forums, they were no less disenchanted with the Headquarters Secretariat. There was a growing tendency to regard the Department of Economic and Social Affairs, staffed at upper levels mainly by citizens from developed Western countries, as unrepresentative and inadequately responsive to poor-country interests, a kind of "rich man's club." In actual fact, this Department, together with other parts of the UN Secretariat, had provided able and professional expression for the needs of the less developed countries, both in its periodic surveys of the world economy and in special reports highlighting the massive requirements for development assistance. Nevertheless, the poor countries were looking for a dynamic exponent of their interests—and they found one in the charismatic figure of Dr. Raúl Prebisch. To many less developed countries the Western-dominated Headquarters Secretariat looked alien and old-fashioned compared with the brilliant Argentine economist whose theoretical formulations and policy prescriptions fit perfectly their economic and political interests.

The various international economic agencies outside of New York shared some of the same disabilities in the eyes of the poor countries. The International Bank, the International Monetary Fund, and GATT, like the United Nations itself, were products of the wartime or early postwar period. The Western developed countries played the key roles in the drafting of their charters and in the management of their operations. Moreover, historic accident had left a major institutional gap which the developing countries were now determined to fill. For the Bretton Woods institutions had never been joined by the third great international economic agency envisaged in the planning for the postwar period—the International Trade Organization (ITO). Ironically, it was the lack of an international trade organization—due to the failure of the United States Congress to approve ITO or even the more modest Organization for Trade Cooperation's (OTC) presented to it in the mid-1950's—that provided the major excuse for the creation of UNCTAD—an agency in many respects less congenial from the point of view of the American Congress. One astute observer warned as early as 1956:

> I have no official documentation on the point that, unless we have the OTC, there will inevitably be other less suitable international agencies for the discussion of trade matters, but I strongly advise you to read the discussions on this matter which took place at the last session of the Economic and Social Council which recently closed here in Geneva. It is quite clear from these discussions that the tide is rising very strongly in the direction of trade questions being dealt with through the regional commissions of the United Nations and eventually through some new mechanism established within the United Nations, with the very strong political bias which inevitably prevails in United Nations debates.[2]

To some extent, of course, the institutional vacuum was merely symbolic. Although GATT in a formal sense was not an international organization, it began increasingly to behave like one. The United States, though not prepared to marry the lady it had been living with since 1947, settled down to a comfortable common law alliance, encouraging the formation of the GATT Council and the enlargement of the GATT Secretariat. These enabled GATT to do virtually everything OTC could have done. However, GATT did not contain the comprehensive provisions on commodity agreements, foreign investment, and restrictive business practices that had been contained in the ITO Charter, and the less developed countries became convinced that their interests required the creation of a forum for the comprehensive review of trade and development policy. Perhaps even more important was the fact that the developing countries considered the preoccupation of GATT with the reduction of trade barriers and the elimination of discrimination as largely irrelevant to—or even inconsistent with—their interests in development. While some of them pressed within GATT for greater emphasis on their spe-

---

[2] Eric Wyndham White, Executive Secretary of GATT, in a letter to the author dated August 16, 1956.

cial needs (producing such results as the GATT Action Program and the new Trade and Development Chapter), others pressed for a new forum which could absorb or at least compete with GATT. Indeed, some less developed countries pursued both strategies at the same time.

While the pressure from the less developed countries was the principal factor which led to UNCTAD, the Union of Soviet Socialist Republics and its allies played a significant supporting role. After the death of Joseph Stalin the Soviet Union began to take an active part in UN economic forums in an attempt to make common cause with the less developed countries and undermine Western controls on trade with the Communist world. The Soviet Union, which had boycotted the conferences called by the UN to establish ITO and which had roundly condemned the final product which emerged from them, astonished the summer 1955 session of ECOSOC by introducing a resolution urging ratification of the ITO Charter. This was the beginning of a series of resolutions proposing the establishment of a comprehensive world trade organization which were initiated or supported by the Soviet Union from 1955 to the UNCTAD Conference nine years later. In the light of the institutionalization of GATT without Soviet participation, of Soviet nonparticipation in the Bank and Fund, and of the negligible Soviet role in administration of UN economic programs, the launching of new trade machinery in partnership with the less developed countries seemed a way of breaking traditional Western hegemony in international economic institutions. It also seemed a way to expand Soviet trade and political influence with the uncommitted countries and bring pressure to bear on Western economic policies regarded as inimical to Soviet interests. By the late 1950's the European Economic Community (EEC) in particular emerged as a prime target of Soviet attack through the proposed UN trade conference.

Faced with this rising pressure from the less developed countries and the Soviet bloc, the developed Western countries were confused and divided. The Common Market had not merely created anxieties in Latin America, Africa, and Asia—it had created differences among the developed Western countries. United States and French strategy in economic as well as political forums seemed increasingly at cross purposes, and none of the rich countries—least of all the United States under the new Kennedy Administration—was anxious to accept responsibility for frustrating a trade conference and new trade machinery so ardently desired by the poor.

These developments in national policy, based in turn on fundamental changes in world politics and economics, all laid the basis for UNCTAD. But the decisive factor which brought it into being was the erosion of the voting position of the developed Western countries in the UN resulting from the admission of so many African and Asian countries (as well as East European Communist states). After the influx of seventeen new states in 1960, all of them from Africa with the exception of Cyprus, votes in the 1961 Assembly and the 1962 ECOSOC leading to the UNCTAD Conference were all but inevitable, as was the creation by the UNCTAD Conference of the continuing machinery with the same name.

In the fall of 1961 an event occurred in the Second Committee of the UN General Assembly whose significance was not fully appreciated at the time, even by specialists in UN affairs. This was the adoption of an amendment to what was to become Assembly Resolution 1707 (XVI) of December 19, 1961, entitled "International trade as the primary instrument for economic development." The amendment called upon the Secretary-General to survey the opinion of the UN Members on the desirability of calling an international trade conference under UN auspices. The vote was 45 in favor, 36 against, and 10 abstentions, with the Soviet bloc and most of the developing countries in the majority and with the developed Western countries and most of the Latin Americans in the minority. In the plenary session the countries which had declined to support the amendment voted for the resolution, several of them emphasizing that their affirmative votes represented no commitment as to the desirability of holding the conference.

When the Economic and Social Council met in the summer of 1962, the Secretary-General's survey showed a substantial majority of Members in favor of a trade conference. The United States delegation, which had led the opposition to the conference, changed its position, thus clearing the way for the adoption of ECOSOC Resolution 917 (XXXIV) of August 3, 1962, calling a UN Conference on Trade and Development and establishing a Preparatory Committee to consider the agenda and documentation for the conference.

Once a decision to hold a conference had been taken, it was clear that a primary objective of the less developed countries would be to create a permanent institution. Just what this institution was to be became a central issue at the Conference in Geneva in the spring of 1964. In his report to the Conference, *Towards a New Trade Policy for Development,* Dr. Prebisch endorsed the idea of "a new international trade organization" but significantly put the phrase in lower case.[3] He outlined a continuing

---

[3] *Towards a New Trade Policy for Development* (United Nations Publication Sales No: 64.II.-B.4 [UN Document E/CONF.46/3]) (United Nations, 1964), p. 100. This report is also contained in *Proceedings of the United Nations Conference on Trade and Development, Geneva, 23 March–16 June 1964* (United Nations Publication Sales Nos: 64.II.B.11–18 [UN Document E/CONF.46/141, Vols. I–VIII]) (United Nations, 1964) (hereinafter cited as *UNCTAD Proceedings*), Vol. II: *Policy Statements,* pp. 1–64.

organization based on periodic UNCTAD conferences, a standing committee, and

> an intellectually independent secretariat with the authority and ability to submit proposals to Governments within the framework of the United Nations.[4]

This formula, which developed through informal discussions with governments in the months before the Geneva Conference, represented an attempt to have the best of both worlds—to give the developing countries and the Soviet Union all the advantages of an ITO without the obvious disadvantage that a new juridical entity in the field of trade was even less likely than the old ITO to be approved by the United States Congress—or, for that matter, by other major Western countries.

The battleground for proponents of different concepts of what the continuing machinery should be was the Fourth Committee (Institutional Arrangements) of the Conference. The Soviet Union, together with Poland and Czechoslovakia, introduced a resolution calling for the immediate establishment of an International Trade Organization. The Latin American countries, which had mentioned ITO in their Alta Gracia declaration issued before the Conference, presented a somewhat ambiguous resolution calling for an ITO but endorsing an arrangement along the lines of the Prebisch formula. Countries from the Afro-Asian group presented a resolution proposing machinery of the sort recommended by Prebisch, with establishment of an ITO to be studied as part of the work of the continuing machinery. The United States, Canada, and other Western countries flatly opposed an ITO and sought a solution which would make maximum use of existing arrangements. Their formula, which eventually received the endorsement of France and most other Western countries, envisaged periodic UNCTAD Conferences called by the General Assembly and the transformation of the existing Commission on International Commodity Trade (CICT), which had been established as a commission of ECOSOC in 1954, into a Commission on International Trade with an expanded membership and a broad mandate to deal with all questions relating to the trade problems of the developing countries.

Given the voting power of the contending groups, an outcome along the lines of the Prebisch formula was inevitable. The Latin American and Afro-Asian draft resolutions were eventually merged in a joint resolution which paid lip service to the concept of an eventual ITO but provided for the establishment of the institutions specified in the Prebisch report. The Soviet bloc abandoned its ITO proposal in favor of this one,

[4] *Ibid.,* p. 100.

and the resolution was voted over the opposition of the Western group in a dramatic session on June 2, 1964. The last two weeks of the Conference were the occasion for hectic negotiations between the less developed countries and the Western group, resulting in the compromise embodied in the Final Act. This compromise was essentially the continuing machinery that Prebisch had advocated, with certain concessions to Western views on decisionmaking and coordination that will be subsequently discussed. ITO was effectively buried for the indefinite future by providing that the periodic Conference should review institutional arrangements in the light of experience, recommend any changes which might be necessary, and study all relevant matters, including "the establishment of a comprehensive organization."[5]

This institutional outcome was an unprecedented victory for the less developed countries. They had not only been able to call a conference which had been initially resisted by the developed countries; they had been able, for the first time in history, to create a major new international agency which the Western countries had not wanted at all. But the question remained: Just what could this new organization do to help the poor countries with their problems that was not already being done by existing organizations?

The answer to this question may be derived from looking more closely at UNCTAD as an international organization. Its special character lies in three main qualities. It is a new secretariat with a special ideology; a new center of decisionmaking to mobilize the demands of the poor against the rich; and a forum for the comprehensive examination of the whole package of trade, aid, and financial questions related to the economic development of the less developed countries.

Secretariat or "Sectariat"

All international secretariats in agencies concerned with the problems of the less developed countries are dedicated to promoting the interests of these countries. This is taken for granted by all the members. The UNCTAD Conference was remarkable, however, in that it saw the emergence of an international secretariat which actively espoused controversial points of view taken by the less developed countries and very largely opposed by the developed countries. The secretariat thus became a major

---

[5] *UNCTAD Proceedings*, Vol. I: *Final Act and Report*, Annex A.V.1 (Institutional Arrangements) (hereinafter cited as Institutional Arrangements), paragraphs 30 and 31. These paragraphs and the other paragraphs of the Institutional Arrangements contained in the Final Act of the UNCTAD Conference were subsequently embodied, with the same numbering, in General Assembly Resolution 1995 (XIX), December 30, 1964, which formally created the continuing UNCTAD machinery.

independent force exerting pressure for the reshaping of national policies.

One cannot think of any other international conference that was so profoundly influenced by the work of a secretariat as the first UNCTAD Conference at Geneva. To a very considerable extent Dr. Prebisch and his associates acted not merely as secretariat for the Conference but as secretariat for the 75 developing countries. Dr. Prebisch frequently met with the group of 75, and some of his principal associates actively assisted in the preparation of resolutions put forward by the group. Some of this could perhaps be explained in the light of the purposes of the Conference and the shortage of experienced advisers in the delegations of the poor countries. Nevertheless, some of the delegates of the industrialized West saw at Geneva an alarming departure from the secretariat impartiality to which they had become accustomed at the United Nations. As one of them put it, "This is not a secretariat—it's a sectariat!"

Even more significant than behavior at the Conference was the impact of Raúl Prebisch's brilliant report, *Towards a New Trade Policy for Development*. Both in its diagnosis and its prescriptions this document gave new impetus to the principal demands of the less developed countries. It focused attention on the concept of the "trade gap"—the gap between the foreign exchange that would be available to the developing countries through trade and the foreign exchange they would need to achieve the 5 percent annual growth rate in gross national product (GNP) laid down as the goal of the UN Development Decade. It made the very controversial estimate that this gap would amount to $20 billion a year by 1970 ($10 billion after allowing for foreign aid and foreign private investment). Moreover, although it did not quite say so in so many words, the basic assumption of the report was that the principal responsibility for filling this gap lay with the developed countries. When it came to recommendations for policy, the report focused mainly on what the rich could do for the poor by way of trade preferences, commodity agreements, compensatory finance, and increased aid on more favorable terms. It devoted a scant five pages to what the poor countries could do for themselves. And even this short section, while acknowledging the need for internal reform, warned that reforms must not be "a matter for international negotiation as a counterpart of financial cooperation."[6]

One of the central concepts in the Prebisch report was that steadily deteriorating terms of trade constitute one of the principal obstacles to the development of the less developed countries. According to this theory there is a persistent tendency for the prices of the primary commodity exports of the less developed countries to fall in relation to the prices of

[6] *Towards a New Trade Policy for Development*, p. 116.

their manufactured imports. The conclusion drawn from this was that the rich countries have an obligation to compensate the poor countries for losses due to these adverse changes in the terms of trade—compensation which could take place through direct action to maintain prices above market levels or by indirect action in the form of semiautomatic financial transfers.

The validity of this argument was questionable. The base year chosen by Dr. Prebisch to demonstrate an unfavorable trend in terms of trade— 1950—was a year in which commodity prices were unusually high due to the Korean War. For the decade of the 1950's as a whole the average terms of trade for the poor countries were better than in any previous decade in the preceding 100 years. Although the terms of trade did turn adversely for the poor countries in the early fifties and again in the late fifties and early sixties, they had begun to recover by the time of the UNCTAD Conference, and when the Committee on Commodities held its first meeting in 1965, the average terms of trade were about the same for the poor countries as they had been in 1958—a reasonably representative year unaffected by strong inflationary or deflationary factors—and substantially better than in the majority of years since the turn of the century. This was not to deny that serious price problems did exist for some commodities. But the overall picture was more one of price instability than of continuous decline. The picture did not seem quite as unfavorable as the Prebisch report suggested, nor did the pessimistic future predictions for commodity prices seem entirely convincing, taking into account the prospective growth of population and industrial production which, for a broad range of commodities, would assure a vigorous and growing level of demand.

It had to be emphasized, moreover, that terms of trade changes in and of themselves did not necessarily imply adverse consequences for economic development, still less any "exploitation." Rather they might reflect qualitative changes in the traded products or changes in factor costs. To put it very simply, the fact that a less developed country had to sell twice as many bushels of wheat as in a previous period to pay for a tractor was not necessarily harmful if the tractor could help to produce four times as many bushels of wheat.

Although subject to these criticisms, Dr. Prebisch's report and his tireless advocacy of its main themes both before and after the Geneva Conference had the salutary effect of sharpening awareness of the genuine commodity problems that do exist and stimulating the search for solutions. Since there are very few commodities for which new commodity agreements are practical, these solutions will have to take the form of financial aid. It is here that Dr. Prebisch's work has begun to bear fruit. While it is difficult to chart cause and effect relationships in such matters, it is likely that the preparations for UNCTAD by Dr. Prebisch and the Conference itself played some part in the decision of the International Monetary Fund to enlarge its compensatory finance arrangements giving more liberal access to Fund resources to less developed countries placed in payments difficulties because of a fall in export receipts from their primary commodities. Perhaps more important, the work of Dr. Prebisch helped stimulate the proposal on "supplementary finance" advanced at the Geneva Conference by the United Kingdom and Sweden. As subsequently developed by the staff of the International Bank in response to a resolution of the Conference, this proposal would go beyond the Fund's short-term lending and make an estimated $300–400 million a year of medium-term or long-term credit available to assure countries with sound development plans that these plans would not be disrupted as the result of unforeseen declines in export revenue that were beyond their control. In contrast to the Prebisch report the supplementary finance plan relates financial aid to declines in export proceeds rather than terms of trade and makes the payout not automatic but rather contingent on the satisfactory implementation of a "package" of development policies previously agreed upon with an international agency (presumably the International Bank).

There are, of course, technical questions about the practicability of projections of "foreseeable" export revenues. There are still more serious political questions about the willingness of developed countries to commit themselves to additional aid of this kind and about the willingness of developing countries to widen the area of international supervision over their domestic policies. But if these questions can be resolved and a "supplementary finance" plan put in operation, it will represent not only a triumph for UNCTAD but a new dimension in multilateral cooperation between developed and less developed countries.

The report of Dr. Prebisch to the Geneva Conference focused not only on the problem of commodity terms of trade but on the need to reduce the trade barriers of the rich countries that restrict the export opportunities of the poor. In this area it placed its primary emphasis on the proposal that developed countries depart from GATT's most-favored-nation standard and grant tariff preferences to less developed countries. The overwhelming majority of delegations at Geneva favored preferences, but they were divided on whether the preferences should be generalized, i.e., made available to all developing countries, or selective, i.e., limited to a few countries such as the overseas affiliates of the European Economic Community. The United States opposed preferences as a matter of principle on the grounds that they would establish permanent economic discrimination, foster uneconomic and noncompetitive production, and inhibit the reduction of tariff barriers between developed countries.

The idea of tariff preferences did not originate with UNCTAD, but there can be little doubt that UNCTAD gave it a political vitality it would otherwise have lacked. The Prebisch report, the debates and resolutions at Geneva, and the advocacy of Dr. Prebisch after the Geneva Conference, all mobilized overwhelming pressure on a reluctant United States. Moreover, in the years following the Geneva Conference Dr. Prebisch developed the preference plan in a way designed to encourage American support. He called for preferences in the form of advance installments of tariff cuts, emphasizing the temporary character of preferences and mitigating the main United States objections. In addition, he came down with increasing firmness on the side of generalized preferences as against the North-South kind of preferences which fragment the world into spheres of economic and political influence. Gradually, the United States began to see that generalized preferences might offer the best way to open up the exclusive arrangements between the Common Market and its African associates which work against the interests of both the United States and Latin America.

In the spring of 1967 Dr. Prebisch had the satisfaction of watching President Lyndon B. Johnson tell the inter-American heads of state conference at Punta del Este:

> We are ready to explore with other industrialized countries—and with our own people—the possibility of temporary preferential tariff advantages for all developing countries in the markets of all the industrialized countries.[7]

Whether the Common Market would accept this formula or whether some acceptable compromise could be worked out was a major question. But there was no doubt that, thanks in large part to the UNCTAD secretariat, a big step toward preferences for less developed countries had been taken.

If a preferential system is established, its benefits to the less developed countries are not likely to be as great as some have believed. Only a few of the more industrialized of these countries, e.g., India and Pakistan, Mexico and Brazil, are likely to enjoy the benefits. The disproportionate emphasis given the preference issue may have distracted attention from two things of much greater importance for the less developed countries—first, the reduction on a most-favored-nation basis of tariffs in industrialized countries which discourage the processing by the primary producers of their own raw materials, and second, the dismantling of nontariff barriers (quotas, consumption taxes) restricting the manufactured and

[7] Department of State *Bulletin,* May 8, 1967 (Vol. 56, No. 1454), p. 709.

primary product exports of the developing countries. Now that preferences are accepted in principle by virtually all countries, it remains to be seen whether the UNCTAD secretariat will be as effective in mobilizing political pressure for the amelioration and eventual elimination of such barriers as the long-term Cotton Textile Agreement, United States sugar quotas, and European consumption taxes on coffee and cocoa. The foreign exchange payoff from progress on these fronts would be many times greater than the payoff from a system of preferences. Admittedly, the political obstacles are also greater. But if UNCTAD could raise the banner of one-way free trade, to be put into effect by the developed countries for the developing countries in stages over the next generation, it might make a historic contribution to the problem of poverty in the world.

While the UNCTAD secretariat has had some success with supplementary finance and preferences, it has had little impact in stimulating the total amount of capital flowing from the rich countries to the poor. The Geneva Conference, like the UN General Assembly before it, called for an aid effort by the developed countries equal to one percent of their gross national products. Unfortunately, we are further from this target as of this writing than when the Geneva Conference was held, and the current figure is more like two-thirds of one percent. Moreover, despite the UNCTAD secretariat's emphasis on the problem, more and more aid is used up in the servicing of past loans. Although the UNCTAD secretariat began with its principal focus on trade, it has come, of necessity, to place increasing emphasis on the quantity and terms of aid. If, together with other international agencies, UNCTAD could get the developed countries to agree to staged increases in their aid efforts to reach the one percent target by 1975, this would mean a doubling of the present volume, taking into account the prospective increases in the developed countries' gross national products. This is surely a target worth shooting for.

Although the results have been uneven, the UNCTAD secretariat has proved a consistently vigorous advocate of the viewpoints of the less developed countries. How far the advocacy has gone beyond the traditional role of an international secretariat is illustrated by the statement made by Dr. Prebisch before the Second Committee of the General Assembly in December 1966 following unsuccessful negotiations for a cocoa agreement. Dr. Prebisch outspokenly characterized the "adamant position" of the United States in refusing to agree to a floor price higher than nineteen cents as "the main stumbling block" to agreement. With characteristic vigor he went on to say:

> I have taken risks which may seem greater than those which an international civil servant should have taken. I went to see the producers in

Cameroon and recommended compromises. I also saw the consumers. But there is something I cannot do, Mr. Chairman, and that is to recommend the producers to accept the floor price of 19 cents because, in all good conscience, I cannot. All the other compromises which I advocated, I advocated in good conscience, convinced as I was that a good settlement was possible. But I shall not do so in the case of prices, because I am sure that to accept the floor price of 19 cents would be to destroy the agreement. How can the floor price of 19 cents be accepted, seeing that, in the last twenty years, only once did prices fall below 20 cents? How can a sound agreement be built up on such a basis? How can the producers accept a price lower than the normal level of prices over the last twenty years?[8]

With such consistent advocacy of the viewpoint of the less developed countries, Dr. Prebisch and his associates have gained their confidence as few other international secretariats have done. One of the fascinating questions is the extent to which Dr. Prebisch and the UNCTAD secretariat will use their leverage to press for necessary changes in the policies of the less developed countries themselves. Among economists and practitioners of the art of economic development there is a growing consensus that a very large part of the responsibility for the failure of the less developed countries to make greater progress rests with those countries themselves. Many less developed countries have overvalued foreign exchange rates or severe inflation or inefficient state industries which make it impossible to export successfully, whatever trade policies are followed by the industrialized countries. Many are stifling their economic growth as well as their export capacity by excessive import restrictions which are driving up domestic production costs. Many are unduly dependent on large imports of food because of their failure to deal with the twin problems of food production and population growth. Many seem unwilling to tax their own wealthy classes or implement meaningful programs of land reform. And many are diverting to armaments scarce resources that are urgently needed for development.

Looking at the performance of many developing countries in recent years, one wonders whether the first UNCTAD Conference and the work of the secretariat which preceded it did not place too much emphasis on international arrangements for trade and too little on domestic policies for development. Since the Geneva Conference the exports of the less developed countries have grown beyond all secretariat estimates, but the rate of development in most countries has been disappointing. It is becoming more than ever apparent that what is required for development is not just dollars—whether earned through trade or received through aid—but the attitudes, practices, and institutions that make dol-

[8] UN Document A/C.2/L.937, December 9, 1966, p. 5.

lars productive. And this means the transformation of feudal political, economic, and social structures which serve to frustrate rapid and broadly shared economic growth regardless of what changes are made in international trading arrangements.

One of the significant developments in the continuing UNCTAD machinery has been the increasing willingness of Dr. Prebisch to discuss these fundamental truths. In his remarkable speech to the fourth session of the Trade and Development Board Dr. Prebisch emphasized that

> the tremendous effort which the developing countries must make to assimilate modern technology cannot be achieved effectively unless these countries, in turn, introduce basic reforms in their economic and social structure.[9]

He went so far as to say that, "Although I attach very great importance to international co-operation, the main point is the responsibility of the developing countries."[10] In that statement and more recently he has called for "simultaneous, convergent and properly concerted" measures[11] on the part of developed and less developed countries, in which increased measures of aid and trade by the rich would be met by increased efforts of self-help by the poor. And, in a significant reversal of the position taken in his report to the Geneva Conference,[12] he has declared that it is now "essential" to "link a policy of offering greater financial resources to the developing countries with undertakings on the part of those countries to follow certain lines of action. . . . "[13]

As of this writing, one of the great questions is the extent to which Dr. Prebisch's increasing concern with the internal responsibilities of the poor countries will be reflected in the work of UNCTAD. This subject was regarded as virtually forbidden territory at the first UNCTAD Conference. The addition to the agenda of the second UNCTAD in New Delhi of a new item entitled "improving the mobilization of internal resources" was a belated step toward recognizing what the less developed countries could and should do for themselves.

This, then, might be the UNCTAD secretariat's greatest challenge. Having established a new dimension for an international secretariat in speaking out on controversial issues, having won the confidence of the less developed countries, it is in a unique position to exert necessary influence on the poor as well as the rich. How successfully it does so will decisively influence the success of UNCTAD, the willingness of the rich

---

[9] UN Document TD/B/103/Rev.1, September 6, 1966, p. 14.
[10] *Ibid.*, p. 4.
[11] *Ibid.*, p. 15.
[12] See note 6 above.
[13] UN Document A/C.2/L.908, November 30, 1966, p. 9.

to make increased commitments, and the ability of the poor to realize their development goals.[14]

VOTING MACHINE OR CONSENSUS

UNCTAD provided the poor countries with new machinery to put pressure on the consciences of the rich. At the same time it has forced the international community to deal explicitly with a growing problem in international organization, the attempt of the majority of the poor to impose its views on the minority of the rich by the sheer weight of their votes. And it has given birth to new approaches to deal with this problem, approaches whose utility is now being tested in the UNCTAD machinery.

Putting greater pressure on the rich was a worthy purpose—and UNCTAD has fulfilled it well. The United States, the Soviet Union, France, the United Kingdom, and other developed countries have been engaged in a kind of "beauty contest" for the favor of the less developed; none of them has wished to bear the stigma of being indifferent or unsympathetic to the needs of the poor. The need to prepare for a new series of meetings devoted wholly to North-South economic questions has forced the rich countries to pay more attention to poor-country demands and, even when rejecting them, to come up with something constructive in the way of alternatives. Within some developed countries it has reinforced the position of those who want to do more for the less developed countries, providing new arguments to use in dealing with resistance to liberal trade and aid policies. In the United States, in particular, it has stimulated a search for new ways of helping the less developed countries not only within the government but in the business and academic worlds as well. Up to a point the possibility of majority voting may have strengthened this process; most developed countries will go some way to avoid being in a minority position in UN forums.

But the "pressure" theory of UNCTAD, particularly when exercised through majority voting, can be overdone. Indeed, experience has demonstrated that it can not only produce diminishing returns but even be counterproductive. Why this has proved to be so—and what has been done about it—is worth examining in some detail.

When the United Nations was founded, it had just 51 Members, mainly

[14] For further discussion of the policy issues examined in this section see the essay in this volume by Isaiah Frank, "The Role of Trade in Economic Development"; Harry G. Johnson, *Economic Policies Toward Less Developed Countries* (Washington: Brookings Institution, 1967); Richard N. Gardner, *In Pursuit of World Order* (rev. ed.; New York: Frederick A. Praeger, 1966), Chapters 5–7; and Association of the Bar of the City of New York, *Law and Policy-Making for Trade Among "Have" and "Have-Not" Nations* (Dobbs Ferry, N.Y.: Oceana Publications, 1968), which contains a discussion between Dr. Prebisch, Professor Stanley D. Metzger, and the author.

from Western Europe and Latin America, with approximate balance between developed and less developed countries. In the first fifteen years in the life of the Organization the periodic increases in membership tipped the balance more and more in favor of the less developed countries. But until the early 1960's, with the notable exception of symbolic resolutions calling for the creation of a Special UN Fund for Economic Development (SUNFED), important resolutions on economic issues were usually adopted on the basis of agreement between developed and less developed countries. Developed Western countries were usually able to negotiate acceptable resolutions with "moderate" less developed countries. Although there were clearly identifiable interest groups on economic issues, negotiations and voting did not usually take place on the basis of rich- and poor-country blocs.

With the advent of UNCTAD the pattern changed. By the spring of 1964, with the massive influx of new African states, the fraternity of the poor had grown to 75 countries. At the Cairo Conference of Nonaligned Nations in 1964 and in regional meetings the less developed countries developed a new sense of unity and discipline. They came to the Geneva Conference as a kind of "trade union" which caucused together, voted together, and negotiated through common spokesmen. From the point of view of the developed countries it seemed that unity among the 75 was often achieved by striking the highest common denominator of all their demands and that the new trade union was led by extremist rather than by moderate elements. What was perhaps most disturbing to the rich-country minority was the tendency of the poor to present demands on a "take-it-or-leave-it" basis and to use their two-thirds majority to vote resolutions over the opposition of the rich. One dramatic example of this tendency took place in the Fourth Committee of UNCTAD when the less developed countries and the Soviet bloc representing 30 percent of world trade voted proposals for new trade machinery over the opposition of twenty Western industrialized countries representing 70 percent of world trade. Since the new machinery was to be part of the UN rather than a new treaty instrument, the defeated minority was threatened with compulsory participation, at least to the extent of paying some 60 percent of the budget!

The Western countries did not come to UNCTAD with any proposals for special voting or other procedures to deal with the decisionmaking problem. To the extent the problem was recognized it was thought it could be dealt with by providing for equal representation on the continuing organ that would operate between the periodic Conferences and perhaps also by limiting in some manner the ability of the Conference to act independently of recommendations of the smaller organ. But it quickly became apparent that nothing like equal representation for the developed countries could be achieved. The institutional proposals voted over their opposition in the Fourth Committee gave the Western countries only fourteen seats out of 52 on the Trade and Development Board (it was only after strenuous negotiation that this was raised by the end of the Conference to eighteen out of 55). Moreover, the new behavior of the 75 at the Conference came as a shock to Western delegates accustomed to the more congenial traditions of the UN.

In mid-May, some two-thirds of the way through the Conference, the Western developed countries decided that new procedures to curb the "voting machine" of the 75 would have to be incorporated in any continuing UNCTAD machinery. The first proposal, embodied in the second Western draft resolution[15] introduced at the end of May, provided for a dual voting arrangement. A majority of the twelve principal trading states present and voting would have to be included in the normal majority requirement—two-thirds in the Conference, a majority in the Board. Subsequently this proposal was replaced in negotiation with a less restrictive one, namely, that a majority of the developed countries present and voting and of the less developed countries present and voting would have to be included in the usual majorities. The latter proposal was designed to be more attractive to the less developed countries since developed countries not among the twelve principal trading states had a somewhat better voting record from their point of view.

To justify these new voting requirements the developed countries argued that the increase in membership of the United Nations, coupled with the new tendency toward bloc negotiation and voting, made a change in procedures imperative. This was particularly necessary, they urged, in a new institution dealing with trade and finance, matters normally dealt with by negotiation rather than legislation. To be sure, the resolutions emanating from UNCTAD would be merely recommendations. But precisely because they were merely recommendations progress could only take place through a process of persuasion. Public opinion in the developed countries would react adversely to recommendations passed over the opposition of the developed countries but calling for action by them: Moreover, the currency of resolutions, as well as the prestige of the UN, would be debased by the passage of resolutions that were not followed by action. What was wanted, in the last analysis, was not voting but results.

Many of the delegates from the group of 75 acknowledged the force of some of these arguments. Some were even ready to accept the compromise dual voting formula which necessitated approval by a majority

[15] UN Document E/CONF.46/C.4/L.9/Rev.1, May 23, 1964.

of the developed countries as well as a majority of the less developed countries. But, in the final analysis, the 75 as a group rejected any dual voting plan. The necessary diplomatic groundwork for such a far-reaching proposal had not been laid; most of the 75 felt they had no authority from their governments to accept such a far-reaching change in UN procedures. To many of the poor-country delegates the proposal seemed to strike at the very source of the political strength they had been able to muster at Geneva. As one representative expressed it during negotiations on this subject:

> Those in possession must be relieved of their possessions. There are only two ways to do this—by force or by votes. We do not have the force, but we do have the votes. *And you are trying to take away our votes!*

To complicate matters further, France and some other Western countries began to have second thoughts about any special procedure which might appear to increase the legal or moral weight of decisions which satisfied the special requirements.

The UNCTAD Conference very nearly foundered on this fundamental question. The United States and other Western countries made it clear that they would not participate in any continuing UNCTAD machinery that did not contain some kind of special procedures. The less developed countries took a firm stand against any special voting procedures. In an attempt to break the deadlock Dr. Prebisch proposed that a conciliation procedure rather than special voting procedures be adopted. Unable to reach an agreement on a voting or conciliation formula, the Geneva Conference recommended the establishment of a Special Committee

> to prepare proposals for procedures within the continuing machinery designed to establish a process of conciliation to take place before voting and to provide an adequate basis for the adoption of recommendations with regard to proposals of a specific nature for action substantially affecting the economic or financial interests of particular countries.[16]

This ambiguous formula left in doubt whether conciliation would be in addition to or in place of special voting procedures and whether normal voting could take place once conciliation had failed. The less developed countries made their own views on this matter crystal clear on the last day of the Conference:

> There should be ample scope for reaching workable agreement on substantial issues. But . . . no arrangements designed for this purpose should derogate from the ultimate right of the proposed Board and the Conference to adopt recommendations on any point of substance by a simple majority

---

[16] Institutional Arrangements, paragraph 25(a). The Secretary-General appointed twelve persons to the Special Committee, which met at UN Headquarters during October 1964. The author served as the United States member.

vote in the case of the Board and two-thirds majority vote in the case of the Conference. The developing countries attach cardinal importance to democratic procedures which afford no position of privilege in the economic and financial, no less than in the political spheres.[17]

In view of the strong positions taken on both sides of this question the compromise eventually reached by the Special Committee in the fall of 1964 and incorporated by the nineteenth General Assembly as part of the basic resolution establishing the UNCTAD machinery was a remarkable achievement.[18] This solution takes the form not of special voting procedures but of conciliation which can be used to prevent voting for specified periods. Under the procedure conciliation can be initiated and voting suspended on any resolution, upon the motion of a comparatively small number of countries (ten in the Conference, five in the Board, and three in committees), or upon the motion of the President of the Conference or Chairman of the Board. The initiation of conciliation is automatic. However, guidelines are provided defining the kind of resolutions which are appropriate for the conciliation procedure.

Following a motion for conciliation, a conciliation group is appointed with adequate representation of countries interested in the subject matter. If the conciliation group reaches agreement at the same session of the Conference or Board, the agreed resolution can be voted. If it does not, the conciliation group continues its work and reports to the next session of the Conference or Board, whichever comes first. If, at the next session, the conciliation group has reached agreement, the agreed resolution can be voted. If it has not, a decision can be taken continuing conciliation for a further period or the original proposal or some variant thereof can be voted in the normal way. In the event that a vote is taken after unsuccessful conciliation, the resolution will cite the report of the conciliation group (which may contain minority as well as majority views), and the records of the United Nations will show how individual members voted on the resolution.

In effect the conciliation procedure provides a "cooling off" period, usually about six months, during which agreed solutions can be sought through quiet diplomacy. In the case of resolutions for which the developing countries wish UNCTAD Conference endorsement, the delay from one Conference to the next is three years during which time important changes may occur both in the cast of diplomatic characters and in government attitudes.

The conciliation procedure, of course, does not apply in the General

[17] "Joint Declaration of the Seventy-Seven Developing Countries made at the conclusion of the United Nations Conference on Trade and Development," *UNCTAD Proceedings*, Vol. I: *Final Act and Report*, p. 67.
[18] General Assembly Resolution 1995 (XIX), paragraph 25.

Assembly. The developing countries were not willing to provide that the Assembly should not adopt resolutions on economic matters while they are undergoing conciliation in UNCTAD. In establishing UNCTAD, however, the Assembly did promise to limit its competence in one respect so as not to modify the conciliation procedure or certain other carefully negotiated parts of the UNCTAD institutional arrangements (e.g., composition of the Board) to the disadvantage of the developed countries. It incorporated a provision drafted for this purpose by the Special Committee which states:

> The General Assembly expresses its intention to seek advice from the Conference before making changes in the fundamental provisions of the present resolution.[19]

And it adopted another provision drafted by the Special Committee which made clear that the conciliation procedure applies in UNCTAD organs to proposals to change these fundamental provisions.[20]

The existence of the conciliation procedure offers some interesting possibilities. The most obvious use of conciliation would be by a minority of developed countries in order to delay the voting of an unacceptable resolution presented by a majority of developing countries. However, conciliation could also be instituted by the minority of developed countries on a resolution on which they wished to engage the less developed countries in sustained dialogue but which in the absence of the conciliation procedure might be simply voted down and ignored. Conversely, the less developed countries might one day decide that their interests might be served by seeking to persuade the developed countries of the merits of a particular resolution through the conciliation procedure rather than by voting it immediately over the opposition of developed countries with no practical results.

But these speculations may be largely academic. The main value of the new procedure may come less in its actual use than in the subtle way its mere existence influences member governments toward compromise rather than voting on disagreed proposals. The strong stand of the developed countries on this issue served to drive home the lesson that they did not intend to be intimidated by majority voting. The conciliation procedure stands as a symbol of this determination and as a kind of deterrent. The *de jure* conciliation procedure has encouraged and institutionalized *de facto* conciliation. The Trade Board and its committees have followed the same pattern employed in the closing days of the UNCTAD Conference itself with small numbers of key representatives from the different groups of countries meeting under the auspices

[19] *Ibid.*, paragraph 32.
[20] *Ibid.*, paragraph 25(n).

of Dr. Prebisch or the chairman of the Board or committee, as the case may be.

Thanks to these developments, the formative years of the UNCTAD machinery have yielded a kind of solution to the "voting machine" problem. As of this writing, there has been no voting at all of disagreed resolutions. In the second meeting of the Trade Board *de facto* conciliation succeeded in changing a resolution of the poor countries on implementation of the UNCTAD Conference recommendations from an unacceptable inquisition into rich-country performance on each recommendation into a more generalized request for information. At the third meeting of the Trade Board the less developed countries drew back at the last moment from forcing a vote on a resolution opposed by the developed countries and calling for increased foreign aid appropriations by them.

It is difficult to predict how long this new and encouraging spirit will last. The composition of the Trade Board and its committees is more favorable than that of the periodic Conference to the search for agreed solutions. The developed countries have a greater proportion of seats in the Board than they do in the Conference. So do the more significant and more moderate of the developing countries. And the delegates in these organs tend to be trade experts rather than politicians. Moreover, UNCTAD has been on a kind of "trial period." If, after a longer period, results satisfactory to the developing countries are not being achieved on an agreed basis, *de facto* conciliation may break down and the formal conciliation machinery may get its first test.

COORDINATION OR FRAGMENTATION?

UNCTAD provided a new forum for the comprehensive review of trade, aid, and financial questions related to development. But it also raised new and difficult problems concerning the division of functions and the coordination of effort within the United Nations system. How these problems are dealt with will do much to determine UNCTAD's— and the UN's—effectiveness as instruments for economic cooperation in the years ahead.[21]

Much has been said in the United Nations about the need for a coordinated approach to economic development. Emphasis has been placed on country plans that look at the needs and resources of a country as a whole and call for mutually consistent programs in different sectors of the economy in pursuit of the overall plan. There has been general agreement on the need to relate action in all the different areas of policy, in-

[21] For another analysis of the coordination problem, based on 25 years of personal involvement, see the excellent essay in this volume by Walter M. Kotschnig, "The United Nations as an Instrument of Economic and Social Development."

cluding trade, aid, finance, and internal self-help, and on the need to avoid the waste of scarce resources.

For most Western Members of the United Nations, and for some other Members as well, these general principles have had specific institutional corollaries. These countries have sought to implement the Charter authority of the Economic and Social Council as the primary instrument for the coordination of UN economic and social activities, including those of the specialized agencies and regional economic commissions. They have tried to make ECOSOC, in practice as well as in theory, the central institution for the periodic review of economic problems, including those of trade and development, for the calling of conferences and the creation of new machinery, and for the systematic evaluation of the impact which UN programs have on economic development. They have endeavored to strengthen the authority and the quality of the central UN Secretariat, and in particular the Department of Economic and Social Affairs. And they have usually opposed the unnecessary proliferation of secretariats and conferences.

Quite understandably this concern with coordination has been overbalanced by other considerations in the minds of many developing countries. For them the primary concern has not been organizational neatness or financial responsibility, but immediate results. If traditional UN bodies were inadequate to their needs, new ones had to be created in which they would have greater control. Additional forums meant additional places to put pressure on the conscience of the rich. Additional budgets meant more money channeled to deal with their problems.

Well before UNCTAD the organizational considerations were losing out to the political. For all the talk about coordination the fourteen specialized and affiliated agencies pursued substantially independent roles (though some progress toward greater teamwork resulted from the creation of the UN Development Program [UNDP]).[22] Moreover, the less developed countries managed to get additional functions transferred from the Headquarters Secretariat to the regional commissions in which they had a greater measure of control.

UNCTAD represented a new stage in the process of fragmentation. The developing countries were largely successful in defeating efforts led by the United States to preserve, as far as possible, the powers of the central institutions. The developed countries, for the most part, wanted to confine the terms of reference of the new machinery to the trade problems of the developing countries; instead, its mandate runs broadly across the work of all UN agencies involved in trade and development.

[22] Money is usually the best coordinator. See the essay in this volume by Karl Mathiasen, "Multilateral Technical Assistance."

They wanted the new standing body dealing with trade to be a commission of ECOSOC; instead the Trade and Development Board wound up as a creature of the periodic Conference and virtually independent of ECOSOC. They sought to limit the size and number of the UNCTAD organs; instead they were obliged to accept the 55-member Trade and Development Board, the four large standing committees, and the cluster of subgroups and special panels. Perhaps most important of all, they sought to have the new machinery serviced by a small unit within the Department of Economic and Social Affairs; instead a large secretariat was established in Geneva independent of the Department of Economic and Social Affairs.

The decision to create UNCTAD as an autonomous set of institutions has caused some fundamental organizational problems. These were not unforeseen at the 1964 Conference. Indeed, as the author had occasion to state:

> If we agree that the trade problems of the developing countries should be considered as an integral part of the problems of development, then the establishment of a separate institution for [trade] with a separate secretariat and budget would result in an artificial division between trade and development frustrating that very integration of effort which we are all seeking. On the other hand, to place in such a new and separate institution the functions of development as well as trade would duplicate on a massive scale the ongoing work of the U.N. . . . . [23]

The issue of just what subject matter UNCTAD is to deal with is still not entirely clear. The first Conference was conceived mainly as a trade conference, but much of its fruitful work was done in its Third Committee, which ranged broadly over such matters as supplementary finance, quantities and terms of aid, debt servicing, private investment, and invisibles. Most of the less developed countries concluded that their interests would be served by giving the broadest possible competence to the new machinery since it gave them such a dominant role. And many of the developed countries, including the United States, were moved by developments during the first Conference to reconsider their original positions which sought to give UNCTAD narrowly trade-oriented terms of reference. As the 1964 Conference and subsequent developments have demonstrated, it is relatively harder for some developed countries to make concessions on trade issues than to make concessions on aid questions. Moreover, focusing UNCTAD on development as well as trade gives some opportunity for examining the internal policies of the less developed countries.

[23] Statement to the Fourth Committee of UNCTAD, United States Delegation Press Release, May 7, 1964.

For all of these reasons the Geneva Conference gave the continuing UNCTAD machinery broad authority to deal not only with trade but also with "related" problems of development. Since there is hardly any problem in development not related to trade, the subject matter of UNCTAD is virtually open-ended. But as a practical matter UNCTAD does not have the time and the resources to discuss everything. One of its central problems, therefore, is to focus its efforts on the top priority questions. The work of the Trade and Development Board in preparing for the second UNCTAD Conference in New Delhi showed how far UNCTAD still is from a satisfactory solution to this problem.

The resolution establishing UNCTAD reflects the rather unsatisfactory compromise between the idea that UNCTAD is to be the prime UN agency for the examination of trade and development issues and the idea that the responsibilities of the General Assembly and ECOSOC for co-ordination as laid down in the Charter are to be strictly preserved. One of the principal functions of the Conference is declared to be:

> Generally, to review and facilitate the co-ordination of activities of other institutions within the United Nations system in the field of international trade and related problems of economic development, and in this regard to co-operate with the General Assembly and the Economic and Social Council in respect to the performance of their Charter responsibilities for co-ordination; ... [24]

The Trade and Development Board is given broad powers to carry out functions in the field of trade and development while at the same time acting

> in conformity with the responsibilities of the Economic and Social Council under the United Nations Charter, particularly those of co-ordination, and with the relationship agreements with the agencies concerned.[25]

The terms of reference of its subsidiary organs dealing with manufactures, invisibles and financing, and shipping

> shall be adopted after consultation with the appropriate organs of the United Nations and shall take fully into account the desirability of avoiding duplication and overlapping of responsibilities.[26]

All of these provisions, written in at the Geneva Conference at the behest of the developed countries, have been largely dead letters. The UNCTAD organs have done just about what they have wanted to do and have occasionally ignored or even sought to displace the coordinating responsibilities of ECOSOC and the General Assembly. This confirms a truism about

[24] Institutional Arrangements, paragraph 3 (d).
[25] *Ibid.,* paragraph 20.
[26] *Ibid.,* paragraph 23.

the UN system which has been underlined in recent years—that constitutional provisions have about as much vitality as the majority's wish to abide by them.

The operation of the UNCTAD secretariat has accentuated this development. The references to the secretariat contained in the resolution establishing UNCTAD speak of a "full-time secretariat within the United Nations Secretariat"[27] and of "close co-operation and co-ordination between the secretariat of the Conference and the Department of Economic and Social Affairs."[28] These provisions were included at the behest of the developed countries which sought to avoid the creation of a substantially autonomous agency. Great emphasis was placed on the fact that the UNCTAD secretariat was spelled with a small "s." But the substantial autonomy of the new secretariat became assured when the third session of the Trade and Development Board decided to establish the secretariat in Geneva.[29] The work of the secretariat reflects the broad range of concern of the UNCTAD deliberative organs. With well over 400 employees, some 200 of them professional staff, it had a budget of $7.4 million in 1967.

Major policy changes are rarely carried out with organizational neatness. Confronted with charges about the proliferation of New Deal agencies, Franklin D. Roosevelt liked to say that he believed in creating four agencies to do a job because then one of them might actually do it. A certain amount of organizational upheaval is a reasonable price to pay for a major breakthrough toward improved forms of international cooperation. If UNCTAD has been "minding everyone else's business," perhaps this may stimulate everyone else to get on with their business more effectively. UNCTAD became a threat to established institutions as soon as the decision was taken in 1962 to hold the Geneva Conference. It can hardly be doubted that the threat of competition was a spur to activity in GATT, the International Monetary Fund, and the World Bank.

Moreover, the fact that UNCTAD has invaded some privileged preserves has not only stimulated activity; it may also have altered the approach to some key problems. Against the wish of most developed countries, for example, the Geneva Conference decided that the continuing machinery should take up the question of international monetary reform. Partly as a result of pressure in UNCTAD, discussions of this vital question, which had largely taken place in a developed country forum (the Group of Ten), were broadened to include developing countries (joint meetings of the Group of Ten and the Executive Board of the Interna-

[27] *Ibid.*, paragraph 26.
[28] *Ibid.*, paragraph 28.
[29] This decision did not only reflect the desires of developing countries. The Soviet Union and France, for political reasons, both wanted UNCTAD in Geneva.

tional Monetary Fund). Moreover, the idea of limiting the distribution of new liquidity to developed countries gave way to the idea that all countries should have a share in the new facilities. Finally, the report issued by the UNCTAD panel on liquidity gave additional circulation to the view that any new reserve units that might be created should be used for lending to the less developed countries. In all these ways UNCTAD has strengthened the position of developing countries in discussions of international liquidity. Whether this will prove helpful in putting pressure on the European creditor countries to agree to increases in world liquidity remains to be seen. In view of the sluggish growth of the world's monetary gold reserves and of the precarious reserve and payments positions of the United States and Britain the activation of new liquidity arrangements will be essential if the rich countries are to carry out really liberal aid and trade policies for the poor.

Nevertheless, problems of institutional fragmentation have been created, and they must be dealt with. They are particularly serious since UNCTAD has now been followed by another institution on the UNCTAD model, the United Nations Industrial Development Organization (UNIDO). Like UNCTAD, UNIDO has a large new secretariat, this one in Vienna, and it has a 45-nation Industrial Development Board. UNIDO is specifically charged with responsibility for "reviewing and promoting the co-ordination" of all UN activities in the field of industrial development.[30] Given this broad mandate and the past behavior of the poor-country majority which controls the Board, the various safeguards written into UNIDO's Charter about the coordinating role of ECOSOC may not be any more effective than similar provisions in the UNCTAD Charter.

"The UN," as someone put it recently, "is moving rapidly toward a state of affairs where everybody is going to coordinate everybody else." There is no central intergovernmental group or secretariat which can assign priorities and a rational division of labor for the UN system as a whole. Duplicating or overlapping functions are performed by several intergovernmental organs and secretariats. This is not merely wasteful of money and personnel. It makes it difficult to mount an effective interdisciplinary and integrated attack on trade and development problems. A number of different UN agencies are each dealing with a single piece of a large problem. The value of UN pronouncements tends to diminish when reports and resolutions, often repetitive and even contradictory, come from several different meetings and secretariats.

In his foreword to the UN budget estimates for 1967 Secretary-General U Thant issued a special word of warning about the implications of UNCTAD and UNIDO:

[30] General Assembly Resolution 2152 (XXI), November 17, 1966, paragraph 27.

The creation of autonomous units within the Secretariat, and therefore under my jurisdiction as Chief Administrative Officer, raises serious questions of organizational authority and responsibility. Moreover, such a trend is not altogether consistent with the concept of a unified secretariat working as a team towards the accomplishment of the main goals of the Organization. On the contrary, it may tend to have the adverse effect of pitting one segment of the Secretariat against another in competition for the necessary financial and political support for its own work programmes.[31]

UNCTAD's broad mandate and vigorous leadership have already raised a number of existing or potential jurisdictional issues. One of the most troublesome is in the important field of export promotion. For some time GATT's International Trade Center has circulated information on market opportunities for products of interest to the less developed countries. It has also arranged for the training of nationals of these countries in how to produce and sell more effectively in world markets. And GATT has advised individual countries on the trade aspects of their development plans in an effort to ensure that these plans take full account of the contribution that exports can make to economic development. The UNCTAD secretariat, eagerly seeking a more "operational" role, has cast a covetous look at such activities. So has UNIDO. And so have the regional economic commissions. Export promotion assistance of this kind is clearly one of the most practical and necessary contributions which international agencies can make to the development of the less developed countries. The question, however, is whether the various international agencies that feel they ought to be involved in this activity can cooperate effectively to do the job.

A second area of potential conflict is in the conduct of trade negotiations. Having taken over the functions of the UN Commission on International Commodity Trade and the Interim Coordinating Committee on International Commodity Agreements (ICCICA), UNCTAD clearly has jurisdiction as a forum for the negotiation of commodity agreements—and it has been exercising it vigorously for cocoa. But GATT also has jurisdiction in the commodity field, and the Kennedy Round negotiations inevitably required GATT to exercise that jurisdiction. Given the close relationship between trade negotiations on industrial and primary products and the close relationship between tariff and nontariff barriers, the commodity field seems destined to be a source of jurisdictional conflict between GATT and UNCTAD in the years ahead.

There are potential difficulties, too, in the area of industrial products. Most developed countries regard GATT as the only place to negotiate concessions on tariffs and other restrictions on industrial goods. Yet there

[31] General Assembly *Official Records* (21st session), Supplement No. 5, paragraph 20.

has been continuing pressure from some less developed countries to involve UNCTAD in "negotiations." While this may mean for the most
part the negotiation of resolutions rather than contractual commitments,
a difficult issue is presented by the drive for tariff preferences. If a system
of generalized preferences on behalf of all less developed countries is
worked out, where will the contractual commitments be made and which
institution will administer the various provisions that may have to be inserted to protect developed countries from market disruption and to assist
disadvantaged less developed countries that have lost their hitherto exclusive preferred status? GATT's claim to assume these responsibilities is very
strong, based on the provisions of the General Agreement and its historic
role in negotiations on industrial products. But, as the proponents of
UNCTAD have pointed out, GATT does not include many of the most
important less developed countries, nor does it include the Soviet Union
and other Eastern European countries whose participation in a preferential system may be desired.

In addition to jurisdictional problems there is the burden on Member
governments imposed by the proliferating conference schedule. There are
now three nearly year-round programs of meetings on trade and development: in GATT; in UNCTAD; and in the traditional UN forums—the
General Assembly, ECOSOC, and the regional economic commissions.
On top of these there are also the meetings of the UNIDO Board, the
Governing Council of UNDP, and the various specialized agencies. Ministers and senior officials of less developed countries are spending time
giving speeches or drafting resolutions in New York or Geneva which
might better be devoted to dealing with the problems of their countries
at home. Even the United States and other developed countries find it
difficult to release high-level manpower to attend all the meetings now
taking place in the UN system. Dr. Prebisch himself has sounded the
alarm in this connection. After noting that 60 percent of UNCTAD's
budget was spent on meetings, much of which might better be used for
studies in depth and small expert sessions and seminars, he has warned
that

> We are on a very dangerous slope. . . . We cannot ignore the fact that in
> UNCTAD—and I think this applies not only to UNCTAD but also to
> other United Nations activities—the proliferation of meetings has become
> so extreme that whenever I talk to representatives of the Governments
> concerned—and I am referring not only to the Governments of the big
> industrialized countries but also to the Governments of the developing coun-
> tries—I find the same concern. Why are there so many meetings? What did
> this meeting achieve? We cannot find qualified people to send to so many
> meetings! We cannot service them! There is a consensus that the number

of meetings must be reduced, a feeling which the Secretariat shares because
it knows that many meetings are unproductive and also because its analytical
and research work is seriously disrupted by the need to cater for a series of
such meetings. Yet despite this general conviction, and despite the fact that
all Governments—for I have never found any exceptions—are aware of the
situation, the number of meetings continues to increase. This involves a
great waste of money, in addition to the unfavourable effects on the Organization's efficiency and the attainment of its primary objectives. . . . [32]

The multiplication of meetings may not only be unduly burdensome
on Member governments; it may be counterproductive in terms of practical results. There is a point of diminishing returns in the theory that
the less developed countries should find every possible opportunity to put
pressure on the rich. At a certain point the multiplication of meetings simply means that the developed countries send lower-level representatives
and take decisions less seriously. Indeed, the repetition of the same demands in one meeting after another is less likely to result in a generous
response than in a hardening of the heart.

Recently there has been a growing awareness of these problems in the
international secretariats and in the national governments. The less developed countries themselves have begun to complain about the waste of
scarce human and financial resources resulting from inadequate coordination and the inflated conference schedule. There has been a slight but visible recovery of ECOSOC from its low estate at the time of the UNCTAD
Conference. With the support of the less developed countries ECOSOC
reorganized its Special Committee on Coordination as a Committee on
Program and Coordination. This new Committee has held joint meetings
with the Administrative Committee on Coordination (ACC) (which
brings together the heads of the specialized agencies) in an attempt to
evaluate the work of the UN family as a whole and make appropriate
recommendations to ECOSOC. In addition, special efforts are being made
to bring UNCTAD and UNIDO into an effective relationship with one
another and with other parts of the UN system. For example, UNCTAD,
UNIDO, and the regional economic commissions have agreed to send
joint teams of experts to selected less developed countries to consult on
problems of export promotion, and there is growing evidence of a willingness to envisage other joint projects. UNCTAD and GATT have
agreed to establish a joint International Trade Center, incorporating and
expanding the work hitherto done by the GATT Center in the export
promotion field.

It may be asked, however, whether all this will be enough. There is
little in UN experience or in the experience of national governments to

[32] UN Document A/C.2/L.908, November 30, 1966, pp. 14–15.

suggest that self-coordination can be fully effective. One day the United Nations may wish to consider a major consolidation and centralization of intergovernmental organs and secretariats in the economic field. Although powerful vested interests have now been created which will oppose such a development, the Member governments have the power to bring it about. Until now the less developed countries have considered that fragmentation might better serve their interests than coordination. The time may come, however, when this is no longer the case.

With this in mind we might well begin drafting a "grand design" for the consolidation of UN economic activities. The central element in such a design would be the establishment of a Director-General for Economic Affairs. Such an officer would be superior in rank to all but the Secretary-General himself. He would relieve the Secretary-General of responsibility for supervising economic functions, a responsibility which no Secretary-General has been able to perform successfully, given the pressure of his political duties. The Director-General, at the very least, would have administrative authority over the Headquarters Secretariat, UNCTAD, and UNIDO. Eventually, UN Members might agree on far-reaching constitutional changes which would give him real authority in relation to the specialized agencies.

There would be problems, of course, in such a centralization of authority. It may be difficult to find one man in whose hands the developed and less developed countries would be prepared to place such vast power. For the immediate future, we may have to move toward consolidation in small steps. The recent creation of the office of Undersecretary for Interagency Affairs may prove to be one such useful step, but it is too early to predict the results.

CONCLUSION

UNCTAD is still too new for us to see its full impact on international organization and national policy, but some things are already clear. UNCTAD has impressed the rich countries with the problems of the poor, has given impetus to new proposals, and has stimulated other international agencies to reexamine and intensify their efforts.

UNCTAD provided a new secretariat oriented to the viewpoint of the poor countries; it made new machinery available to put pressure on the rich; and it brought the trade, aid, and financial problems together in a new set of institutions. Each of these special qualities of UNCTAD has been useful; yet each has created problems. Fortunately, there is a growing emphasis by the secretariat on the responsibilities of the poor as well as the rich countries, a growing tradition of conciliation, and a growing concern with coordination.

UNCTAD will succeed in the measure that it turns from sterile debates over who bears responsibility for the poverty of the less developed countries to practical proposals for action by both rich and poor countries. It is safe to say that neither side is yet doing all that is necessary to deal with the problem of poverty. As Dr. Prebisch himself has said:

> There is no point in engaging in recrimination. I believe that we have already passed that stage and to continue in that vein will lead us nowhere. The responsibility lies on both sides. There is a complex of responsibilities which must be concorded and made to produce their effect by the formulation of a policy of development and international co-operation.[33]

---

[33] *Ibid.*, p. 5.

The International Monetary Fund

Edward M. Bernstein

Bretton Woods and Before

One would not ordinarily think of the International Monetary Fund (IMF) as of particular importance to the less developed countries. Nevertheless, in recent years the less developed countries have come to have a very high regard for the IMF; and the IMF, in turn, has become the great defender of the interests of the less developed countries. This entente has evolved out of the course of events. In the current discussions on international monetary reform the IMF has become the spokesman for universal participation in reserve creation. This suits the institutional interests of the IMF. At the same time it makes the IMF the advocate of the interests of the less developed countries.

This is not the role that had been intended for the International Monetary Fund. While the United States and the United Kingdom sponsored plans for a postwar international monetary organization open to all countries, there were people of influence who advocated less formal arrangements confined to a smaller group. Professor John H. Williams, then the economic adviser of the Federal Reserve Bank of New York, wanted to limit international monetary cooperation to the two key currencies (the dollar and sterling). When this view was criticized as too narrow, Professor Williams broadened his suggestion to include all of the key countries. At most these would have comprised the countries that subscribed to the Tripartite Declaration and the other countries now in the Group of Ten.[1] The argument for limiting the participants in interna-

Edward M. Bernstein was on the staff of the United States Treasury from 1940 to 1946 as principal economist and assistant to the Secretary of the Treasury. He was executive secretary and chief technical adviser of the United States delegation at the Bretton Woods Conference. From 1946 to 1958 Mr. Bernstein was director of research of the International Monetary Fund. He now heads a firm of research economists in Washington, D.C.

[1] The subscribers to the Tripartite Declaration of 1936 were the United States, the United Kingdom, and France, with the Netherlands, Belgium, and Switzerland subsequently adhering

tional monetary cooperation was that stability of the currencies of the less developed countries—and even of many of the developed countries—was not essential for orderly exchange arrangements and that such stability, in fact, could not be achieved outside the key countries.

Both the British and the American plans took account of the need for development finance; but this was to be provided through another institution. The British proposal for an International Clearing Union stated that one of the four main lines of approach in dealing with postwar economic problems would have to include "investment aid, both medium and long term, for countries whose economic development needs assistance from outside."[2] The United States proposed a Bank for Reconstruction and Development of the United and Associated Nations. This institution was established at Bretton Woods as the International Bank for Reconstruction and Development (IBRD) at the same time and with even larger resources than those of the IMF.

Actually, the reserve position of many of the less developed countries at the end of the war was quite strong. The wartime expenditures of the United Kingdom and the United States brought large foreign exchange receipts to the less developed countries which they were unable to use to purchase imports during the war. At the end of 1946, for example, India had reserves of $5.2 billion (nearly all in sterling), Argentina had reserves of over $1.6 billion, and Brazil had reserves of $760 million. For the less developed countries in the sterling area the reserve problem was the restraint that they were expected to exercise on their conversion of sterling into dollars. The initial draft of the United States proposal for an International Stabilization Fund had a provision which would have permitted a country holding excess sterling balances to sell them to the IMF. The provision, reminiscent of some current proposals for depositing excess balances of dollars and sterling with the IMF, was not adopted at Bretton Woods as it could have absorbed all of the convertible currency resources of the IMF.

MEMBERS AND QUOTAS

In its publication *International Financial Statistics* the International Monetary Fund classifies countries as either developed areas or less developed areas. The less developed areas include all countries except Europe, the United States, Canada, Japan, Australia, New Zealand, and South Africa. This is a convenient geographic division although it obviously has

to the Declaration. The Group of Ten, the ten industrial countries participating in the IMF's General Arrangements to Borrow, includes these countries (except Switzerland) and Canada, the Federal Republic of Germany (West Germany), Italy, Japan, and Sweden.

[2] *Proceedings and Documents of the United Nations Monetary and Financial Conference, Bretton Woods, New Hampshire, July 1–22, 1944* (Washington: United States Government Printing Office, 1948), Vol. II, p. 1549.

important exceptions if the test of a country's state of development is per capita income.

Of the 45 countries at the United Nations Monetary and Financial Conference at Bretton Woods 26 fall into the present designation of less developed areas. Of these, nineteen were from Latin America and seven were from Asia and Africa. The number of less developed countries holding membership in the IMF grew rapidly as more of the former colonial territories became independent. By the end of 1950 the number of less developed countries in the IMF had risen to 30 and by the end of 1958 to 43. At present the IMF has 106 members of which 81 are less developed countries and 25 are developed countries. Apart from Switzerland the members of the IMF include all countries not in the Communist bloc.

While the less developed countries comprise more than three-fourths of the members of the International Monetary Fund, they have about 27 percent of the total quotas, and only 25 percent excluding the Republic of China (Nationalist China). As the quotas represent in some sense a measure of a member's normal access to reserve credit from the IMF, the relatively low quotas of the less developed countries require some explanation. Of course, many of the less developed countries are very small and have a low level of output and trade. Actually, relative to their trade as measured by imports the less developed countries have larger quotas than the developed countries.

MEMBERS AND QUOTAS OF THE INTERNATIONAL MONETARY FUND

	End of 1947		End of 1957		July 31, 1967	
	Members	Quotas[a]	Members	Quotas[a]	Members	Quotas[a]
Developed countries	18	6,377	22	6,925	25	15,306
Less developed countries	27	1,545	42	2,091	81	5,675

[a] Quotas as allotted in million dollars. Payment has not yet been fully made on some quotas, including the Republic of China with a quota of $550 million.

Despite the fact that their quotas are a higher proportion of their trade the less developed countries are in relatively greater need of reserve credit than the developed countries. Many of the less developed countries have serious balance-of-payments difficulties because of a shortage of resources for development although this might not be regarded as a test of their need for reserve credit. Nearly all of the less developed countries have large year-to-year fluctuations in their balance of payments because of their dependence on exports of primary products for which prices change rapidly and considerably. The less developed countries hold a far smaller ratio of reserves relative to their imports than the industrial countries. The ratio would be even lower if it were not held up by the large reserves of a few less developed countries, mainly the oil-producing countries and one or two Far Eastern countries in the Vietnam war zone.

RESERVES AND IMPORTS, 1958 AND 1966

	1958			1966		
	Reserves end of year	Imports during year	Ratio of reserves to imports	Reserves end of year	Imports during year	Ratio of reserves to imports
	(million dollars)		(percent)	(million dollars)		(percent)
Less developed countries	9,225	26,600	34.7	11,255	39,800	28.3
Excluding Middle East, Libya, and Thailand	7,488	22,600	33.1	7,147	32,200	22.2
Developed countries	48,330	74,300	65.0	57,795	152,100	39.3

It is difficult to give the less developed countries quotas more nearly in accord with their relative needs because of the multiple functions of the quotas. The quotas represent some norm of drawing rights made available to members. To this extent there is a case for alloting quotas on the basis of the relative need of countries for reserve credit. At the same time the quotas are the source of the resources available to the International Monetary Fund for extending reserve credit. If the quotas of the less developed countries were increased relative to those of the industrial countries, the IMF would have a persistent problem of illiquidity. That is to say, the IMF would be short of the currencies of surplus countries so that it would have to limit the drawings of the deficit countries despite their larger quotas. As it is, the liquidity of the IMF is weak whenever the United States and the United Kingdom have payments deficits. That is why the IMF had to have access to supplementary resources from the surplus countries. This it now has through the General Arrangements to Borrow up to $6 billion from the Group of Ten.

There is still a third function that the quotas perform. They are the major factor determining the participation of a member in the management of the IMF, both in voting by the Governors and in voting by the Executive Directors. Actually, the voting arrangements are slightly more favorable to the less developed countries than they would be if they were based solely on quotas. Each member has a fixed number of votes (250) plus one additional vote for each $100,000 of its quota. Thus, while the less developed countries have less than 27 percent of the total quotas in the IMF, they cast more than 32 percent of the total votes. Of the twenty Executive Directors of the IMF nine represent less developed countries, including China. Of course, they cast only the votes of the countries they represent. But their presence on the Executive Board does give the less developed countries more voices to state their views.

In fact, the less developed countries have been treated very fairly in the two general and the various special adjustments of quotas. The standard increase in quotas in the two general adjustments were 50 percent of the original quota (effective in 1959) and 25 percent of the higher quota (effective in 1966). Thus, the standard increase would have been 87.5 percent of the original quota. Many of the large industrial countries (but not the United States or the United Kingdom) had a further special adjustment of their quotas. Even so, the less developed countries have had a much larger increase in their quotas than the large industrial countries. For example, the 25 less developed countries that have had continuous membership in the International Monetary Fund since 1946 had original quotas of $940 million. In the successive adjustments their aggregate quotas have been raised to $2,662 million—an increase of 183 percent. The Group of Ten had original quotas (prior to 1958) of $6,235 million. In the successive adjustments their aggregate quotas have been raised to $13,042 million—an increase of 109 percent. Whatever defects there are in the quota system, it is clear that the less developed countries have been allotted about as much in aggregate quotas as would be feasible under the present system of providing resources for the reserve credit operations of the IMF.

USE OF IMF RESOURCES

The International Monetary Fund holds about $21 billion of resources that can be drawn by members under stated conditions. The Articles of Agreement set formal conditions for drawing foreign exchange from the IMF. A member may draw up to 25 percent of its quota in a twelve-month period until its net indebtedness is equal to its quota, to make payments in accordance with the purposes of the IMF. Larger drawings in any one year or net drawings in excess of the quota can be made only under a waiver. The IMF can declare a member ineligible to use its resources on various grounds—mainly related to proper use of its resources to achieve the purposes of the IMF. This is a power that is hardly ever used.

The practical conditions governing drawings on the IMF are the policies established by its Executive Board. In the course of time some general rules on drawings have been developed. Countries have the overwhelming benefit of any doubt in drawing on the IMF to the full extent of their net creditor position (the gold tranche). Thus, a country has virtual assurance that it can draw on the IMF for the amount of the gold payment it has made on its quota and for the amount of its currency drawn by other members. For drawings beyond the gold tranche a member must give evidence that it is taking measures to restore its payments position. While the standards are not too stringent for drawings in the first credit tranche (a net debtor position of 25 percent of the quota), they become much more exacting with each successive credit tranche. Most drawings (or standby arrangements) are for amounts in excess of 25 percent of the quota and require a waiver. When granting a waiver the IMF can set specific terms and conditions for the use of its resources by the member.

All drawings must be repaid unless a member is a net creditor of the International Monetary Fund in excess of 25 percent of its quota. Thus, even drawings in the gold tranche must be repaid. The Articles of Agreement provide that a member should use its own reserves in equivalent amount with its drawings on the IMF unless its reserves are exceptionally small. Furthermore, a member must repay drawings whenever it has an increase in its reserves unless its reserves are exceptionally small. When a member has been indebted for a large amount and for an extended time, the IMF may require it to consult on measures to be taken to reduce its indebtedness. Under a policy adopted by the Executive Board members that draw on the IMF are required to give an undertaking that repayments will be made in three years with an outside limit of five. It should be noted that a member can repay the IMF in two ways: by giving the IMF acceptable convertible currencies (repurchases) or by drawings of its currency by other members.

The technical rules cannot convey the very great changes that have actually occurred in the attitude of the International Monetary Fund toward drawings during the twenty years of its operations. The IMF was relatively generous on drawings in 1947 and 1948, a period during which the uncertainties regarding the impending 1949 devaluations gradually began to hamper its operations with the European members. From 1949 to 1955 drawings were severely restricted, partly on the theory that use of IMF resources was not proper for members receiving Marshall Plan aid, partly because the United States was not satisfied with IMF policies on drawings and repayments. Since 1956 drawings on the IMF have been large although they have varied considerably from year to year, depending on the pattern of international payments. A great part of the drawings since 1961 has been to finance the payments deficits of the United Kingdom.

GROSS DRAWINGS ON THE INTERNATIONAL MONETARY FUND, 1947–1967
(million dollars; to July 31, 1967)

	1947–1948	1949–1955	1956–1960	1961–1963	1964–1967	Total
Total, all countries	675.7	540.7	2,467.2	3,395.5	6,310.2	13,389.3
Developed countries	574.1	222.5	1,399.9	2,157.5	4,921.3	9,275.3
Less developed countries	101.6	318.2	1,067.3	1,238.0	1,388.9	4,114.0

The less developed countries have been relatively large users of the resources of the International Monetary Fund. In the twenty years of its operations (to July 31, 1967) the drawings of the less developed countries have amounted to $4,114 million. Thus, the less developed countries account for 31 percent of the total drawings on the IMF. Relative to quotas, this is slightly more than the drawings of the developed countries. The relative share of the less developed countries in the drawings on the IMF is obscured by the very large transactions of the United Kingdom. The total drawings of the less developed countries have been only slightly less than the drawings of all the developed countries, excluding the United Kingdom.

As the data indicate, the IMF has been a very generous provider of reserve credit to the less developed countries. Drawings in larger or smaller amounts have been made by 43 of the less developed countries. Some of the less developed countries have only recently become members of the IMF and they will, no doubt, in good time make use of its resources. There are a few countries classified as less developed that have large reserves—particularly the oil-producing countries—and they may not find it necessary to make much use of the facilities of the IMF for a number of years.

The 81 less developed countries vary considerably in the size of their economies and in their quotas in the IMF. Fifty-eight of these countries have quotas of $50 million or less and 40 have quotas of $25 million or less. On the other hand, a number of the less developed countries have relatively large quotas, reflecting their considerable role in international trade and payments. These few members account for much the greater part of the drawings of the less developed countries. Ten of these countries have drawn $3,150 million, about 78 percent of the total drawings of the 81 less developed countries. Six have drawn $2,643 million, nearly two-thirds of the total drawings of all of the less developed countries.

QUOTAS, DRAWINGS, AND REPAYMENTS OF SELECTED
LESS DEVELOPED COUNTRIES
(million dollars; July 31, 1967)

	Quota	Drawings	Repayments	Net drawings outstanding
Argentina	350.0	425.0	333.5	91.5
Brazil	350.0	503.4	406.4	97.0
Ceylon	78.0	101.5	22.5	79.0
Chile	100.0	275.7	175.1	100.6
Colombia	125.0	247.6	140.0	107.6
India	750.0	1,000.0	582.4	417.6
Indonesia	207.0	172.5	115.4	57.1
Iran	125.0	121.0	107.0	14.0
Mexico	270.0	112.5	112.5	—
United Arab Republic	150.0	213.7	109.0	104.7
Total, ten countries	2,505.0	3,172.9	2,103.8	1,069.1

The record of the less developed countries in repaying their drawings is on the whole good. Of their total drawings $2,580 million (63 percent) had been repaid by the end of July 1967. The ratio of repayments is about the same as that of the developed countries. There have been instances in which a few less developed countries have delayed repayment beyond the usual time. And there have been instances in which arrangements had to be made for nominal repayment—that is, a repayment followed by an equivalent drawing. Nevertheless, the less developed countries have generally shown a high sense of financial responsibility in their operations with the International Monetary Fund. They recognize that use of the resources of the IMF involves the use of reserve credit; and nearly all of them recognize the necessity of restoring their position by repaying their drawings from the IMF.

Most drawings are now made under standby arrangements previously agreed upon with the International Monetary Fund. A member having a standby arrangement is assured of being able to draw up to a specified amount within a specified period, provided it pursues policies that have been agreed with the IMF. Such standby arrangements are usually made in conjunction with stabilization programs recommended by the IMF to restore the balance of payments, to undertake a change in parity, or to make an adjustment in the exchange system. At the end of July 1967 there were 24 standby arrangements in effect. Of these all but three were with less developed countries. They provided for agreed drawings up to a limit of $511 million of which $425 million remained unused at the end of July 1967.

By any reasonable test the International Monetary Fund has been generous on drawings by less developed countries. Of course, some countries have not been allowed to use their quotas to the full extent that they would have wished. Because of chronic balance-of-payments deficits a few of these countries had nearly exhausted their own reserves and if they had been allowed to draw further from the IMF, they would have exhausted their quotas as well. The limitations placed by the IMF on their drawings compelled corrective action that might otherwise have been delayed.

The discussions prior to Bretton Woods contemplated that the first credit tranche and half of the second credit tranche (37.5 percent of the quota after a member had used its own gold subscription) could be drawn with complete assurance. It would undoubtedly have been helpful to the less developed countries, with their greater scarcity of reserves, to have automatic access to this part of their quotas. In practice, however, it would not have been possible to provide greater automaticity in the use of IMF quotas, even in the first and second credit tranches, because the IMF does not hold sufficient resources in the form of currencies of the large surplus countries to permit such freedom in drawings. To finance greater automaticity the IMF would itself have needed absolute assurance from the Group or Ten countries that they would provide it with their currencies in any necessary amount. Clearly, the large industrial countries were not prepared to do this. Probably no member of the IMF, and certainly no less developed country, has been improperly deprived of the right to reserve credit. In any case, the argument for automaticity of any of the credit tranches of the IMF has become academic. The creation of a new reserve asset is now virtually assured. That will require the IMF to make a very sharp distinction between quotas, which represent reserve credit, and allocations of the new reserve asset which will represent a country's own reserves.

COMPENSATORY EXPORT FINANCING

Many of the less developed countries are dependent for a major part of their foreign exchange earnings on the export of one or a few primary products. Their export receipts fluctuate considerably, occasionally because of crop variations, but mainly because of changing conditions in world markets. The preface to Lord Keynes' Clearing Union proposal noted the need for measures

> to protect both producers and consumers from the loss and risk for which extravagant fluctuations of market conditions have been responsible in recent times.[3]

[3] *Ibid.*

At Bretton Woods some Latin American countries raised the question of their access to the resources of the International Monetary Fund in a period of falling prices and accumulating surpluses of primary products. They were assured, and correctly, that the resources of the IMF were intended to be used in such a situation. What the less developed countries wanted was some special privilege of drawing on the IMF in a period of adversity. What they got was Article V, section 4, of the IMF Agreement whereby the IMF, in granting a waiver to permit larger than normal quota drawings,

> shall take into consideration periodic or exceptional requirements of the member requesting the waiver. The Fund shall also take into consideration a member's willingness to pledge as collateral security gold, silver, securities, or other acceptable assets [commodities]. . . .

There has been no collapse of commodity prices comparable to that after World War I. Nevertheless, there have been large shifts in the export receipts of many of the less developed countries because of wide fluctuations in prices of basic commodities. There are some instances in which the export receipts of a country have fallen by 20 percent or more in the course of a few years. Very few of the less developed countries had sufficient reserves to maintain essential imports under such conditions. The inevitable response to a sharp drop in their export receipts was a corresponding reduction in their standard of living and in their development programs. To avoid this countries dependent on exports of primary products needed resources to pay for their imports until world markets recovered.

The problem of compensatory finance for exports received a great deal of attention from the United Nations and from the Organization of American States (OAS). In February 1963 the International Monetary Fund issued a report on *Compensatory Financing of Export Fluctuations.* The report included the decision of the Executive Board on two points. First, the IMF would be willing to adjust quotas of some members exporting primary products, particularly those with relatively small quotas, to make them more adequate in the light of fluctuations in their export receipts. Second, the IMF introduced a system of drawings designed to compensate for a temporary shortfall in export receipts, without regard to whether this was caused by a fall in prices or by other factors. Such compensatory drawings would normally not exceed 25 percent of the quota and they would be repayable in three to five years. A member had to satisfy the IMF that it was encountering payments difficulties attributable to conditions beyond its control and that it was ready to cooperate with the IMF in finding a solution to its payments difficulties. Even so, a member had greater assurance of being able to make a drawing under the compensatory credit policy than of making an ordinary drawing in the same credit tranche.

The policy on compensatory financing of export fluctuations applied to all members, whether developed or less developed countries and whether or not they were dependent on exports of primary products. In practice the adjustment of quotas under the compensatory financing decision was confined to the less developed countries. At various times in 1965 and 1966 the quotas of twelve less developed countries were increased for the particular purpose of taking account of their greater exposure to fluctuations in export receipts. The total quotas of these countries were increased from $382 million to $513 million—an average increase of 34 percent. In the general adjustment of quotas in 1966 many less developed countries were given a larger increase than the standard 25 percent. This larger increase was undoubtedly a reflection of the policy on compensatory export financing although it was not identified as such.

The 1963 policy was an important step in meeting one of the special problems of the less developed countries. Nevertheless, there was criticism that the new policy was too limited. The 1964 United Nations Conference on Trade and Development (UNCTAD) adopted a resolution recommending that the International Monetary Fund study various measures to liberalize the policy on compensatory financing of exports. In September 1966 the Executive Board amended its previous decision in response to this resolution.

The amount of drawings that could be outstanding under this policy was increased from 25 to 50 percent of a member's quota although the second 25 percent would be available only if the IMF was satisfied that the member was cooperating in an effort to find an appropriate solution for its payments difficulties. The IMF applies

> its tranche policies to drawing requests by a member as if the Fund's holdings of the member's currency were less than its actual holdings of that currency by the amount of any drawings [under the compensatory policy].[4]

In effect, this removes compensatory credits from the regular quotas of the IMF. In order to implement this policy the IMF will waive the provision limiting maximum outstanding net credit to a country to the amount of its quota. The new statement of policy clarifies the provisions for determining the shortfall in export receipts and for using increased export receipts to repay compensatory drawings. All in all, the new policy should provide the less developed countries with considerable assistance

[4] *Compensatory Financing of Export Fluctuations* (Washington: International Monetary Fund, September 23, 1966), p. 41.

in the form of additional reserve credit whenever the markets for primary products become seriously adverse.

There have been relatively few transactions under the compensatory export financing policy. The principal reason for this is that exports of primary products have held up very well since 1963. In the second report on *Compensatory Financing of Export Fluctuations* (September 1966) the International Monetary Fund stated that prices of primary products rose in 1963 and 1964 and fell by 9 percent in 1965 because of lower prices of agricultural products. The export receipts of 71 countries obtaining at least one-half of their export earnings from basic commodities other than petroleum rose by 11 percent in 1963, by 10 percent in 1964, and by 4 percent in 1965, despite the fall in agricultural prices. With lower export prices for primary products in 1966 and 1967 members have made more use of the new policy. In all, eight members (seven of them less developed countries) have qualified for compensatory drawings. The total amount drawn to July 31, 1967, was $178.7 million. In a few instances members drawing under the compensatory policy would probably not have been able to draw on the ordinary credit tranches of their quotas.

DRAWINGS AND REPAYMENTS UNDER COMPENSATORY EXPORT FINANCING

(to July 31, 1967)

Country	Year of drawing	Million dollars	
		Drawings	Repayments
Brazil	1963	60.00	37.50[a]
United Arab Republic	1963	16.00	
Sudan	1965	11.25	
Dominican Republic	1966	6.60	
Ghana	1966	17.25	
Ceylon	1967	19.50	
Colombia	1967	18.90	
New Zealand	1967	29.20	
		178.70	37.50

[a] Repayments consist of repurchases of $15 million in 1966 and $7.5 million so far in 1967 by Brazil; and sales of $15 million of cruzeiros to other countries in 1967 which have been applied by the IMF to repayment of Brazil's compensatory drawings.

EXCHANGE POLICIES OF LESS DEVELOPED COUNTRIES

As stated in its purposes the International Monetary Fund is intended to give confidence to members by making the Fund's resources available to them under adequate safeguards, thus providing them with opportunity to correct maladjustments in their balance of payments without resorting to measures destructive of national or international prosperity.

Essentially, what this means is that members are expected to keep their payments in balance, that when they have a deficit, they must restore their payments position without serious deflation and without relying on exchange restrictions and discriminations.

More positively, members are expected to abide by the fair exchange standards of the Articles of Agreement. These embrace a number of policies. First, a country must have a fixed exchange parity defined in terms of gold or the United States dollar and agreed with the IMF. Second, exchange rates must be maintained within one percent of this parity. Third, exchange must be available at a uniform rate for all current transactions. Fourth, no exchange restrictions may be placed on current transactions. This includes the obligation to maintain the convertibility of the currency for external transactions.

Obviously, a country cannot have exchange stability unless its international payments are reasonably well balanced over a moderate period of time. The obligation to maintain fair exchange standards, therefore, requires a country to follow policies designed to keep its balance of payments in order—above all, avoiding domestic inflation. If a member has a persistent payments deficit because of domestic policies, it is expected to stop the inflation although not to undertake deflation. If it has had a permanent change in its relative international economic position, it may propose a change in the par value of its currency.

These exchange standards have much more relevance to the large industrial countries than to the less developed countries. In fact, it is doubtful whether a system of fixed parities is best suited to a country dependent on exports of primary products if the prices of such export goods vary considerably from year to year. An attempt to maintain a fixed parity in a period of low and falling prices would result in sharp deflation and would almost certainly not be successful. Furthermore, with a fixed parity the export sector would bear the entire burden of falling prices and it would secure the entire benefit of rising prices. On the other hand, fluctuating exchange rates responsive to prices of export products would share the burdens and the benefits between the export and the import sector on the basis of the relative elasticity of supply for exports and of demand for imports. A country would still lose real income when export prices fall and gain real income when export prices rise. It would, however, be spared the secondary deflation and inflation that would result from a large fall or a large rise in export prices under a regime of fixed exchange parities.

The International Monetary Fund cannot relieve the less developed countries of their obligations on exchange rates and exchange practices. It can be very tolerant, and it is, in permitting them 1) to delay the setting of exchange parities, 2) to let exchange rates fluctuate, 3) to apply exchange restrictions, and 4) to continue inconvertibility of their currencies. Actually, and quite properly, the IMF places more stress on the domestic financial policies of the less developed countries. This is on the reasonable assumption that unless a country has a fairly strong payments position, based on appropriate domestic policies, there is very little it can do to abide by the exchange standards of the IMF.

On the whole, the less developed countries have not done badly in maintaining fixed par values for their currencies. Thirty-five of these countries have had no change in the par values they originally agreed with the IMF. Of these, 21 were established within the past five years during a rather favorable period for the payments position of the less developed countries. Fourteen countries (six of them in Latin America) have kept their original par values unchanged over a period of ten to twenty years. Thirteen countries have had one or more changes in par value but are maintaining the new parities reasonably well. Ten countries (nine of them in Latin America) have par values which are not used in actual exchange transactions. They may have free rates, multiple exchange rates, or *de facto* fixed rates different from the agreed par values. Twenty-three countries have never agreed with the IMF on par values. With few exceptions these countries have become members within the past five years.

Apparently, many less developed countries want to maintain a system of fixed parities and some of them have succeeded in doing so. Nevertheless, most of the less developed countries depend on exchange controls to a greater or less extent to support their exchange rates. Very few of them have accepted the obligation of maintaining external convertibility of their currencies. Only fifteen of the 81 less developed countries had made their currencies convertible by the end of July 1967. Twelve of these countries are in the western hemisphere and two are oil-producing countries. Of the 25 developed countries that are members of the International Monetary Fund fourteen have made their currencies convertible. It is this great dependence on exchange controls, even more than the difficulty of maintaining parities, that distinguishes the exchange practices of the less developed countries from those of the industrial countries.

IMF ATTITUDE TOWARD INFLATION

No question has caused more difficulty in the relations of the less developed countries with the International Monetary Fund than the question of inflation. The less developed countries have come to regard the IMF as the embodiment of orthodoxy on the inflation question. The large industrial countries, on the other hand, regard the IMF as much too tolerant toward the inflationist policies of the less developed countries. The IMF itself has tried, not without some success, to adopt a pragmatic attitude toward the fiscal and credit policies of the less developed countries. Obviously, the IMF would be very happy to see its members follow policies that would maintain a high degree of price stability and avoid large balance-of-payments deficits. As this is impractical for most of the less developed countries, the IMF has become tolerant of expansionist financial policies provided they are not disruptive—that is, they do not involve a degree of price inflation that impairs domestic production and inhibits exports.

There is an exaggerated view of the extent to which the less developed countries are in a state of inflationism—that is, large-scale and persistent inflation. Data on money and prices are published for most of the less developed countries in *International Financial Statistics*. The money supply statistics are much more dependable than the price statistics although their interpretation is more complex. Of the 40 less developed countries for which data are available seventeen had a twofold increase, or less, in their money supply between 1958 and 1966 and may be classified as not having a disturbing inflation problem. Five of the 40 countries had a five- to 25-fold increase in their money supply and may be classified as having a very serious inflation problem. The other eighteen countries increased their money supply twofold to fivefold and may be classified as having a moderate to bad inflation problem. In 26 of the 40 less developed countries the cost of living index rose by 50 percent or less between 1958 and 1966. In the other fourteen countries the cost of living index rose from 50 to 3,000 percent. The inflation experience was probably much the same in the other 40 less developed countries for which money and price data are not available.

There are half a dozen countries, four in Latin America and two in the Far East, in which the rate of inflation is completely disruptive to the economy. There are perhaps another dozen countries in which the rate of inflation causes some difficulty for the economy, particularly in the balance of payments. In most of these countries the inflation is caused by a development program requiring more resources than can be secured from domestic savings and capital inflow and aid. In a very few countries the inflation has acquired a self-generating character in which different sectors of the economy struggle for an excessive share of the national product. The attempt of each sector to defend its share of the national product from erosion through inflation results in a spiral of rising prices and wages. In such countries the greatest difficulty in restoring stability is the well-established expectation of continuing inflation.

The staff of the International Monetary Fund is far less dogmatic on the inflation problem than is generally assumed. They have always recognized that development will involve a rise in prices, at least in some sectors, and they have not regarded such a rise in prices, incidental to development, as evidence of inflation. The report of the IMF to the government of India in 1953 made these observations on *Economic Development with Stability:*

> Economic stability is consistent not only with a high degree of price flexibility, but even with some movement in the general level of prices. In every country, a rise in the proportion of the national income going into investment sets up forces that induce an upward adjustment of prices in the sectors in which expansion is relatively large. Such a rise in prices need have little effect on prices in other sectors. This functional rise in prices should not be confused with an inflationary rise in prices. Even if the Government of India had all the resources needed for development, so that there could be no problem of inadequacy of resources, some readjustment of prices would and should occur in conjunction with the implementation of the Five Year Plan.[5]

The staff of the International Monetary Fund has recognized that because of their great dependence on exports of primary products the less developed countries have much less control over the behavior of domestic prices than the large industrial countries. A rise in the prices of export goods will raise incomes and expenditures and bring about a higher level of domestic prices to match the rise in export prices. On the other hand, a fall in the prices of export goods will lower incomes and expenditures. If the monetary authorities are unwilling to see the domestic economy deflated to match the decline in export prices, they will have to undertake offsetting fiscal and credit policies to prevent a serious decline in the domestic sector of the economy. Most underdeveloped countries are not prepared to accept alternate periods of inflation and deflation in response to the rise and fall of prices of their basic export commodities. They prefer to permit a rise in domestic prices when export markets are good and to prevent a fall in domestic prices when export markets are bad. One may regret a policy that results in this ratchet type of inflation. In most countries it cannot be avoided so long as there are large fluctuations in the prices of basic commodities.

Less developed countries have much greater difficulty than the high-income countries in maintaining monetary stability. It is much more difficult for them to reduce consumption and investment in response to a

[5] P. 5.

decline in their real output (including lower terms of trade for their exports) or to transfer real resources from consumption to investment to permit an accelerated rate of development. To recognize these difficulties, however, is not the same as to condone a persistent inflation. Too often, the monetary authorities in less developed countries justify a rampant inflation as if it were a necessary condition for development when, in fact, it is only the result of an unwillingness to follow unpopular fiscal and credit policies. It is a mistake to identify accelerated development with rapid inflation. It should be possible for the less developed countries to use fiscal and credit policies in a constructive way, to encourage an expansion of output and an increase in investment without generating such a degree of inflation as to undermine the efficient functioning of the economy.

The staff of the International Monetary Fund does a great deal of useful work on inflation. It provides technical assistance of a very high quality in the fiscal field and in central banking. There may be a tendency for the staff of the IMF to depend too much on formula in prescribing remedies for inflation for the less developed countries. This is inevitable when an international organization undertakes to advise 81 less developed countries with widely different institutional arrangements. In any case very little can be done to terminate inflation until governments are willing to take strong and unpopular measures to restore monetary stability. The IMF has always been ready to help its members by cooperating with them on a stabilization program that combines domestic policies, exchange reform, and financial assistance. Although these programs have not always been successful, they have in a number of instances been the decisive factor in encouraging governments to deal boldly with the inflation problem.

THE RESERVE PROBLEM

The present interest in the reserve problem dates from 1958 when the International Monetary Fund published its report on the adequacy of reserves.[6] While the report provided a useful collection of statistics, it made no constructive contribution to an understanding of the reserve problem. This was not due to any lack of technical ability on the part of the staff of the IMF. The negative character of the report reflected the quaint idea of the Managing Director (who undertook personal supervision of the report) that under the gold standard the world economy could get along with any amount of reserves, provided countries would adapt their money, income, and price policies to the availability of reserves.

[6] *International Reserves and Liquidity* (Washington: International Monetary Fund, 1958).

The one positive recommendation of the 1958 report was to increase the quotas of members by 50 percent. Even this recommendation was made under pressure from the United Kingdom and the United States. The report failed to note that the liquidity of the IMF, its ability to finance the drawings of its members, would be seriously impaired if the United States and the United Kingdom were to have balance-of-payments deficits. It took the IMF three years to admit that it would need supplementary resources from the surplus countries to finance the drawings of the deficit countries. It was the United States, while C. Douglas Dillon was Secretary of the Treasury, rather than the IMF that took the initiative in the General Arrangements to Borrow under which the Group of Ten agreed to lend up to $6 billion to the IMF when additional resources are needed to avoid a crisis in the world monetary system.

The International Monetary Fund was late in recognizing that there is a long-run problem of assuring an adequate but not excessive growth of monetary reserves. During the past ten years there has been only a very small increase in the gold reserves of the countries outside the Communist bloc. Most of the increase in monetary reserves in this period has been in the form of official holdings of dollars and has been the consequence of the United States balance-of-payments deficit. More recently, all of the newly mined gold has been absorbed by industrial uses and private hoards so that except when the Union of Soviet Socialist Republics sold gold to finance imports of wheat there has been no increase at all in the gold reserves of the Western countries. The surplus countries of Europe are much less willing now than they were a few years ago to increase their reserves in the form of dollars. In any case, it is not in the long-run interest of the United States to have a large and steady increase in foreign official holdings of dollars, particularly when its own reserves are not increasing. It has been apparent for some time that if monetary reserves are to grow at a rate suited to an expanding world economy, it will be necessary to have a new reserve asset to supplement gold and foreign exchange.

Professor Robert Triffin proposed the conversion of the International Monetary Fund into a world central bank empowered to create reserves through loans and investments. Such a world central bank would try to regulate the growth of reserves from year to year to achieve international monetary stability. Another proposal was to create a new reserve asset composed of all the leading currencies (reserve unit) and to have these reserves grow at a regular rate, without regard to the balance of payments of individual countries or their need for reserve credit. If such a reserve asset were created, it was proposed to back it with the currencies of the Group of Ten, to allot the new issues to the participating countries, and to grant the IMF an amount of resources equivalent to the equitable share of other members (mainly, but not exclusively, the less developed countries) to be used for their special benefit.

This proposal for a reserve unit was not acceptable to most of the less developed countries. An expert committee appointed by UNCTAD recommended that the less developed countries should participate directly in the creation of reserve units and should be allotted an equitable share of any new issues. Furthermore, the UNCTAD committee recommended that most of the backing of the new reserve asset should be used to finance development—say, by investing the strong currencies in World Bank bonds. Such a system would have imposed on the prospective surplus countries the risk of acquiring and holding a reserve asset ultimately backed by claim on the less developed countries. None of the Group of Ten would have agreed to accept and to hold a new reserve asset of this sort.

The International Monetary Fund did, after a time, assert its jurisdictional claim that "reserves are the business of the Fund" and that all of its members must participate in the creation of reserve assets. The United States and several other countries in the Group of Ten gave strong support to a universal system under the IMF or a subsidiary of that organization. In its annual report for 1966 the IMF discussed two alternative forms of reserve creation—the reserve unit and automatic drawing rights.

> In the longer run . . . [a] scheme, operating through Fund units [i.e, reserve units], might prove somewhat more flexible and for that reason more suited to meet the need for a reserve asset in which countries might ultimately be holding a substantial part of their total reserves.[7]

In July 1965 Secretary of the Treasury Henry H. Fowler announced that the United States was prepared to enter into negotiations on a contingency plan for creating reserves to supplement gold and foreign exchange. The deputies of the Group of Ten and their technical assistants have been studying the problem of reserve creation constantly in recent years. In 1966 the Group of Ten invited the Executive Directors of the International Monetary Fund to hold joint meetings with them on a contingency plan. As a result of these meetings the ministers of finance and the governors of the central banks of the Group of Ten reached an agreement in London on August 26, 1967, for the establishment of a new reserve facility in the IMF. This agreement has been approved by the Executive Directors and the Board of Governors of the IMF. The contingency plan will require an amendment to the Articles of Agreement of the IMF, the ratification of which is expected in late 1968 or early 1969.

---

[7] International Monetary Fund, *Annual Report of the Executive Directors for the Fiscal Year Ended April 30, 1966* (Washington, n.d.), p. 19.

The plan calls for the establishment of a special drawing account in the International Monetary Fund in which all members of that institution will be able to participate. The resources, obligations, and operations of the special drawing account will be completely separated from the ordinary quota subscriptions and quota drawings of the IMF. On the proposal of the Managing Director, with the concurrence of the Executive Directors, and after the approval of the Board of Governors the IMF will allocate special drawing rights (SDR's) to all members of the IMF in proportion to their quotas. As the special drawing rights are intended to meet the need for a regular growth of reserves, decisions to allocate special drawing rights will be taken for a basic period, ordinarily about five years, during which allocations will be made at specified intervals. Before the expiration of a basic period the Managing Director will recommend allocations of special drawing rights at an appropriate rate for a new basic period. It is expected that in the initial basic period allocations will be between $1 billion and $2 billion a year.

The special drawing rights will be transferable from one country to another, either directly or through the intermediation of the International Monetary Fund, for currencies that are convertible in fact. Countries will be able to use these special drawing rights to meet balance-of-payments deficits but not to change the composition of their reserves. Countries that use special drawing rights will have an obligation to restore their position so that their holdings will average 30 percent of their cumulative allocations over the preceding five years. The purpose of the reconstitution provision is to make sure that countries use other reserves in addition to special drawing rights to meet their payments deficits. Countries will be obligated to accept special drawing rights until their holdings are equal to three times their cumulative allocations. Where necessary the IMF will direct transfers of special drawing rights to countries with a balance-of-payments surplus or with large reserves.

Despite the name the special drawing rights are true reserve assets and not a form of reserve credit. They can be transferred directly from one country to another in the accounts of the International Monetary Fund in much the same way as other reserve assets are transferred. The accounting unit for special drawing rights is one dollar in gold. Their value will be guaranteed in terms of gold although it may be decided to alter this if there is a uniform change in the price of gold. Interest will be paid at a moderate rate on balances of special drawing rights, the cost being borne by countries in proportion to their cumulative allocations. Operations can begin, however, only with the approval of an 85 percent vote of the participating countries. While this will give the European Economic Community (EEC) countries a veto, they are not expected to prevent the implementation of the plan. The London agreement to create a new reserve asset is thus a landmark in the evolution of the international monetary system.

Concluding Observations

There is a common interest that will bring the less developed countries and the International Monetary Fund even closer together in the future. In any international organization of universal membership the less developed countries inevitably comprise the vast majority of all members. Merely because of their numbers the less developed countries must absorb much of the attention of the management and staff of the IMF. At the same time the growing need for reserves and reserve credit will require greater dependence of the less developed countries on the financial and other help of the IMF.

The International Monetary Fund has learned much about the less developed countries. There is little that is doctrinaire in the attitude of the IMF toward the exchange and payments problems of the less developed countries. Quite properly, the IMF seems to be more concerned with the inflation problems of these members. Fortunately, the less developed countries seem to have come to the conclusion that inflation is not of itself helpful to economic development. Many of them are eager to follow policies designed to maintain stability. The IMF is the best source of technical assistance on fiscal and credit policy for the less developed countries. With mutual respect and understanding the IMF and its members can cooperate in dealing with the inflation problem.

The less developed countries, with few exceptions, have a far greater deficiency of reserves than the developed countries. This is understandable. Reserves represent real resources and the less developed countries are under constant pressure to use all available resources to finance their development. The plan for special drawing rights will make it possible for reserves to grow at a rate suited to the needs of the world economy. This is important for the less developed countries not only because they will share in the allocations of special drawing rights but because the growth of reserves will permit world trade and payments to continue to expand. As exporters of basic commodities, as countries dependent on foreign capital and foreign aid, the less developed countries have a great interest in an expanding world economy. The International Monetary Fund, which will administer the new reserve plan, is fully aware of the importance to the less developed countries, as well as the large industrial countries, of an adequate growth of reserves.

The World Bank Group

Roy Blough

Introduction

THE World Bank Group consists of three closely affiliated intergovernmental institutions: the International Bank for Reconstruction and Development (hereinafter referred to as the Bank, IBRD, or the World Bank), the International Finance Corporation (IFC), and the International Development Association (IDA). These institutions are the chosen multilateral instruments of governments for providing external capital on a global basis to help finance the development of the world's low-income countries.

The purpose of the present essay is to examine the policies followed by the World Bank Group in carrying out its functions, with special reference to the influence of these policies on the volume of the flow of external capital to low-income countries and on the economic development achieved by the use of such capital.

The Bank, together with the closely related International Monetary Fund (IMF), was planned at the Bretton Woods Conference of 1944 and opened its doors for business on June 25, 1946. Established by a multilateral treaty, the "Articles of Agreement" or charter, IBRD had as its central objectives assistance in the postwar "restoration of economies destroyed or disrupted by war" and the "development of productive facilities and resources in less developed countries." The methods contemplated were, among others, "to promote private foreign investment by means of guarantees or participations" and to "supplement private investment by providing . . . finance . . . out of its own capital, funds raised by it and its other resources."[1] The Bank's loans were to be a supple-

Roy Blough, a member of the Board of Editors of *International Organization,* is S. Sloan Colt Professor of Banking and International Finance, Graduate School of Business, Columbia University, New York.

[1] Article I of the Articles of Agreement of the International Bank for Reconstruction and Development. The statistical information regarding the operations of the World Bank Group was

ment to those that could be secured through commercial and other channels, not a substitute for them. It was anticipated that in the main the loans would go to meet the foreign exchange requirements of specific projects.

The Articles of Agreement give the Bank authority to set interest rates and other terms of loans. However, there can be no doubt that the Bank was intended to be run on "sound" banking principles and not to be used as an instrument for making open or hidden grants. All loans made by the Bank were to be guaranteed by the governments of the benefiting countries with repayment in the currencies borrowed. The Bank was to charge a commission from which a reserve fund would be established. Moreover, to raise funds by borrowing in the world's capital markets the terms of the loans made by the Bank would necessarily be "hard," that is, their rates and maturities would have to approximate those prevailing in the private capital markets. The Bank would, however, be able to loan when private investors and financial institutions were unwilling to do so and on somewhat more favorable than prevailing terms. The Bank is not obliged to earn a return on its capital, and it can borrow at more favorable rates than can private borrowers and most governments, for several reasons. The loans made by the Bank represent a broad spread of risks, default on them would be a serious matter for the guaranteeing governments, and while the Bank's bonds and other debts are not the obligations of any one government, they are in effect insured by the unpaid and callable capital subscriptions of all the member governments.

The other two institutions of the World Bank Group were established to fill gaps in the supply of external capital that could not be filled by the Bank without major changes in its philosophy and methods of operation. Although very constructive in promoting economic development the Bank's "hard" loans left unfilled a considerable need in countries

derived primarily from International Bank for Reconstruction and Development and International Development Association, *1965–1966 Annual Report* (Washington, 1966); International Finance Corporation, *Annual Report 1965–1966* (Washington, 1966); and from prior annual reports. The literature concerning the Bank Group is voluminous. The materials issued by the Bank that were consulted include the summary proceedings of the annual meetings of the Boards of Governors, especially International Bank for Reconstruction and Development, International Finance Corporation, International Development Association, *Summary Proceedings, 1966 Annual Meetings of the Boards of Governors* (Washington, 1966); also International Bank for Reconstruction and Development, *The World Bank—Policies and Operations* (Washington, 1956) and International Bank for Reconstruction and Development, *The World Bank, IFC and IDA: Policies and Operations* (Washington, 1962); issues of *Finance and Development,* a review published quarterly by the IMF and IBRD; a series of pamphlets on operations in various geographical areas, for example, International Bank for Reconstruction and Development, *The World Bank Group in Malaysia* (Washington, 1967); and the press releases of the three institutions. In preparing this essay the writer also had the benefit of interviews with a number of officials of the Bank and of other organizations having relations with the Bank.

presenting good development projects but not having sufficient prospective financial ability to service loans offered on conventional terms. This need could be met only through grants or "soft" loans, that is, loans for long terms at low rates of interest. However, it was believed undesirable to involve the Bank itself in making both hard and soft loans. After considerable delay the institutional gap was filled by the establishment in 1960 of the International Development Association to provide "development credits," that is, 50-year loans bearing no interest, except a small annual "service" charge, and requiring no governmental guarantee. The funds for IDA development credits have come with minor exceptions from governments. Administratively, the Bank and IDA have the same Executive Directors, officers, and staff; thus the two are, for operational purposes, one organization.

The Bank also lacked the flexibility to give specific promotion to private entrepreneurship in economic development. In 1956, after several years of consideration, the International Finance Corporation was established with a view to fill this gap. The funds for IFC have come from member governments, supplemented recently by loans from the Bank. Although IFC has some of the same officials as the Bank, it is, in contrast to IDA, run as a separate organization. However, it is an integral part of the World Bank Group, performing services for the Bank, receiving loans from the Bank, and joining with the Bank in some financing operations.

While the Bretton Woods negotiators contemplated universal membership in the Bank, the Eastern bloc countries, with the exception of Yugoslavia, did not become members. As new nations have joined the United Nations, most of them have also joined the Bank. As of June 30, 1966, IBRD had 103 members, IDA 96 members, and IFC 81 members.[2] Only three IFC member countries were not in IDA, while eighteen IDA countries, mostly in Africa, were not in IFC; all IDA and IFC countries must of course be members of IBRD. All members of IBRD must also be members of the IMF.

The structure, control, and basic policies of the Bank, IDA, and IFC are set by the articles of agreement establishing each of these institutions. The pattern of the Bank is typical. Within the framework of its Articles of Agreement ultimate control is in the Board of Governors on which each member country has a Governor; the Board normally meets once a year. Responsibility for the general operation of the Bank, under powers delegated by the Board of Governors, is in the Executive Directors, of whom there are twenty, five appointed by the five countries

---

[2] On July 8, 1966, Portugal became a member of IFC, bringing the total to 82.

having the largest number of votes and fifteen elected by groups of countries.[3]

Control in the Board of Governors and the Executive Directors is highly concentrated in a few countries as the voting power of member governments is closely proportional to their subscriptions to the resources of the institution. According to Article V, section 3, of the Bank's Articles of Agreement each member of IBRD is to have 250 votes plus one additional vote for each share of stock held; except where otherwise specifically provided all matters before the Bank are to be decided by a majority of the votes cast. Furthermore, under Article VIII amendments have to be accepted by three-fourths of the members having four-fifths of the total voting power in order to become effective. As of June 30, 1966, the voting power of individual member countries ranged from 25.5 percent for the United States and 10.5 percent for the United Kingdom down to only 0.13 percent for each of three other countries. Sixteen countries had more than one percent each of the voting power. Therefore, in the Executive Directors, for example, a majority of all votes for a measure can be cast by the joint action of the representatives of four countries, the United States, the United Kingdom, the Federal Republic of Germany (West Germany), and France, together with India and the Republic of China (Nationalist China), or by the action of those four representatives together with the representatives of various combinations of two groups of states casting votes for as few as seven additional countries.

The operating staff of the Bank is headed by the President, who in practice has held a strong position with respect both to operations and to the interpretation of Bank policy and leadership in determining it.

As of June 30, 1966, the Bank had over twenty years made net loan commitments of nearly $9.6 billion, IDA since 1960 had made net commitments of about $1.4 billion, and IFC had made total net commitments of almost $0.2 billion, or a total for the World Bank Group's lifetime commitments of approximately $11.2 billion.

New commitments of loans, credits, and investments of the Group in the fiscal year 1965–1966 totaled $1,158.9 million, including IBRD loans of $839.2 million, IDA credits of $284.1 million, and IFC equity and loan commitments of $35.6 million. Total commitments were about $200 million less than in the previous fiscal year, while disbursements increased from $844 million in 1964–1965 to $957 million in 1965–1966. Thus, the order of magnitude of development financing by World Bank Group funds was an annual rate of roughly $1 billion.

[3] One appointed member is selected by each of the following: the United States, the United Kingdom, the Federal Republic of Germany (West Germany), France, and India. Of the elected representatives only one is responsible to a single member, the Republic of China (Nationalist China).

Using a slightly different basis, the Organization for Economic Co-operation and Development (OECD) estimated that in 1965 the World Bank Group committed 55.2 percent of the total commitments of $1,904 million of multilateral agencies to less developed countries. United Nations agencies committed 13.6 percent, and the remaining 31.2 percent was committed by regional intergovernmental agencies in Europe and Latin America.[4] According to another OECD computation the loans and credits supplied by the World Bank Group have been constituting about one-tenth of the total flow of official and private funds to the less developed countries and about one-sixth of official funds, both multilateral and bilateral.

The orders of magnitude to have in mind concerning the financing of economic development by the World Bank Group are thus in the range of $1 billion annually or about one-tenth of total public and private capital flows to developing countries. Some comments on the significance of these figures will be made later in this essay.

While the supply of external capital is by no means the only important factor limiting the rate of economic development, virtually all participants and observers are agreed that it is a crucial one today, that the total flow of funds to less developed countries is grossly inadequate, and that the terms on which much of the capital is available are too rigorous for many of the countries to meet at this time. It should not be assumed, however, that the deficit must be made up by the Bank. Some types of capital needs, for example, may not be appropriate for the Bank Group to meet. But Bank officials have estimated that $3 or $4 billion more could be invested annually over the period 1967–1970 in projects meeting the Bank's standards if lack of ability to repay were not the obstacle. In this situation the policies followed should both promote efficiency in the use of available funds and increase the available funds.

POLICY QUESTIONS FOR THE WORLD BANK GROUP

The World Bank and its associated institutions are dedicated to the promotion of economic development in the less developed countries and areas. The policies followed by the Bank and by the member countries with respect to the Group can have a critical bearing on the effectiveness with which economic development is promoted. The following questions indicate some major objectives for policy.

1) What policies has the Bank Group followed to maximize the effectiveness of its funds in promoting economic development? How, if at all, could the effectiveness be increased?

[4] Calculated from *Development Assistance Efforts and Policies: 1966 Review* (Paris: Organization for Economic Cooperation and Development, September 1966), p. 36.

2) What policies has the Bank Group followed to maximize the amounts of funds available to it? How, if at all, could these amounts be increased?

3) What policies has the Bank Group followed to increase the amounts of funds flowing to less developed countries through other channels and to improve the effectiveness of the use of those funds? How, if at all, could the success of the Bank Group in these efforts be increased?

The first and second questions above relate to the Bank Group as financing institutions. The third question relates to the Group as a force for leadership in the world community of nations and business enterprises.

As a few examples will indicate, the questions are all interrelated. The lending policies of the Bank determine the terms on which it must secure funds, thereby also determining or at least setting limits to the sources from which the funds can be secured. Conversely, the success of the Bank in securing funds on various terms will set limits on the lending policies that it can follow. Again, the Bank might succeed in diverting to itself funds from other channels but at the cost of reducing the total flow of funds.

The approach to these questions should be evolutionary. The situation has changed over two decades, as has knowledge. Professional and, to a lesser extent, public understanding of how best to use external financing to promote economic development has evolved substantially over the postwar period, thanks both to experience and to major study and research. This evolution should be reflected in changes in the Bank's policies, and it has been at least to a degree.

In considering the policies of an institution like the Bank the central fact to note is that in general the institution can do only what its governing members are willing to have it do. Praise or blame for policy ordinarily must rest with the governments themselves. The Executive Directors, the President, and the staff, however, do have an area of discretion in interpreting and applying policy and the opportunity and responsibility to exercise leadership in seeking to change it.

The work of the Bank over the years has not lacked for praise, including a measure of self-praise, or for criticism, including criticism by possibly envious competitors. Not surprisingly the Bank has been criticized by those member countries that have not received as much as they would have liked on more favorable terms and subject to fewer conditions. Some of this criticism has been made by the Governors in their statements at the annual meetings. Beginning with the 1965 meeting, the gist of these statements has been made readily available in the published reports of the meetings. Some critics of Bank policies may not be fully aware of how far changes have taken place in recent years.

LENDING POLICIES OF THE WORLD BANK GROUP

Purposes of the Loans

With the postwar economic reconstruction far in the past the Bank loans and IDA development credits are made to assist in economic development. In general, they finance only the foreign exchange requirements of projects. However, the Bank's charter does state that local currency loans may be made when local currency cannot be raised by the borrower on reasonable terms or when the project gives rise indirectly to an increased need for foreign exchange. Prior to 1964 these provisions were interpreted rather narrowly, which gave rise to criticism that the distinctions between the requirements for foreign exchange and for local currency were sometimes unreal.

Over most of its history the Bank has made loans almost exclusively for specific development projects rather than for support of development programs in which the particular application of funds was determined by local authorities. Project loans have many advantages. Projects can be carefully planned and a cost-benefit analysis applied. The expenditure of funds according to the plan can be readily checked. Especially when resources are scarce, these are important merits. For the most part, moreover, development programs must in any event be broken down into projects in order to be implemented. Whether this can be done more effectively by an outside agency or by the recipient country depends largely on the training, experience, and integrity of the officials making the decision.

The heavy emphasis on project loans has come under increasing criticism. For one thing, the larger projects tend to be the ones financed by the Bank. Not only are they more visible, impressive, and challenging, but they also involve a lower percentage of overhead costs since the costs of planning, investigation, and supervision do not increase proportionately with the size of the project. However, financing large projects is not necessarily the most constructive use of external funds or of the local resources that usually make up the bulk of the cost. In some countries there are few if any large projects that would be practical to undertake. More important, the much greater need may be for numerous smaller projects that would not be practical for the Bank to administer on a project basis and for funds to support the maintenance and efficient utilization of existing facilities.

The Bank has in fact been moving toward the greater use of program financing. One Bank official recently estimated that about 20 percent of the loans currently being made would qualify as program loans. These include, among others, the so-called "impact" loans under which the

Bank provides foreign exchange needed by a donor country as a result of shifting internal resources to a development aid program. There have also been a few "maintenance" loans in which foreign exchange is made available to purchase materials and replacement parts needed to make use of existing capacity in the less developed country. Loans to local development banks also usually qualify as program loans.

It should also be remembered that the Bank has been a leader in encouraging the formulation of development programs by the less developed countries and accordingly is not oblivious to the need for program financing to be supplied from some source, if not by the Bank.

If a proposed plan for long-term supplementary financing to meet unforeseeable shortfalls in the export proceeds of the developing countries should be adopted with IBRD as administering agency, the Bank would become much more deeply involved in program financing. A 1964 recommendation of the United Nations Conference on Trade and Development (UNCTAD) requested IBRD to study the feasibility of such a new "scheme" which

> should aim to deal with problems arising from adverse movement in export proceeds which prove to be of a nature or duration which cannot adequately be dealt with by short-term balance of payments support.[5]

The scheme thus would be added to and would go beyond the IMF's short-term supplementary financing. IBRD made the study,[6] which presented a plan under the terms of which a developing country and an administering agency would reach an agreement on the country's export expectations, its development program and policies, and the amount of unexpected shortfall in export earnings to which it could feasibly adjust without disrupting the agreed development program. The forecast would normally cover a period of four to six years and would become part of the development program. If a disruptive shortfall in export earnings then occurred, the agency would help the country find funds from any available sources and would itself make up the remaining deficit which would be transferred into long-term indebtedness to the agency. The funds needed to carry out the scheme were estimated in the study at $1.5 billion to $2.0 billion for an experimental period of five years or about $300 million to $400 million a year. The Bank's staff report was favorable to the plan; no action has been taken by the Bank management.

[5] Article I of Recommendation A.IV.18 (supplementary financial measures) of *Proceedings of the United Nations Conference on Trade and Development, Geneva, 23 March–16 July 1964*, Vol. I: *Final Act and Report* (United Nations Publication Sales No: 64.II.B.11 [UN Document E/CONF.46/141, Vol. I]) (United Nations, 1964), p. 52.

[6] *Supplementary Financial Measures: A Study Requested by the United Nations Conference on Trade and Development, 1964* (Washington: International Bank for Reconstruction and Development, December 1965). Figures on estimated funds needed are on p. 13.

It is expected that the subject will be further studied by the continuing machinery of UNCTAD, as requested in the 1964 Conference's recommendation.

The economic sectors in which the Bank Group finances development also have undergone substantial evolution although the loans of the Bank continue to be devoted primarily to the installation of economic infrastructure. The largest category has been transportation, which accounted for 34.5 percent of the cumulative total loans and credits through June 30, 1966, and 43.1 percent of those made in the fiscal year 1965-1966.[7] Transportation projects have been supported in fifteen different countries and territories and have been of all sizes and types, including roads, canals, railways, ports, and inland waterways.

Electric power projects have been a close second to transportation projects, accounting for 30.8 percent of the cumulative total and 28.6 percent of the 1965-1966 loans and credits. Water supply, sewerage, telecommunications, and other public service projects also have received support in relatively minor amounts.

The loans and credits to industry, including manufacturing and mining, constituted 15.8 percent of the cumulative total loans and credits and 20.7 percent of those made in 1965-1966. Nearly half of the latter total took the form of commitments to increase the resources of ten development finance companies in six countries. By the end of June 1966 the Bank Group as a whole had supported 25 such companies in 21 countries with nearly $500 million of loans, credits, and investments.[8]

Agricultural development projects received 9.2 percent of the cumulative total loans and credits and 13.6 percent of those in 1965-1966. About one-third of the latter amount was to supply funds for investment on farms through credit institutions in a half dozen countries. Because of the difficulties of administering small loans and extending necessary technical services the Bank has made use of central banks and private banks in the recipient countries as media for relending funds to farmers and cooperatives. Of course, many of the electric power and transportation projects also have been highly important in promoting agricultural development.

The Bank Group first started financing education in 1962 and through June 30, 1966, had made loans and credits for education equal to 0.9 percent of total cumulative loans and credits and 3.0 percent of those for 1965-1966. Virtually all of the funds have been spent on the construction of buildings and the supply of equipment, with about one-half

[7] Except as otherwise indicated statistics in this section are from the IBRD-IDA *1965-1966 Annual Report*.

[8] IFC, *Annual Report 1965-1966*, p. 11.

going to secondary education, one-fourth to university education, and the remaining one-fourth to vocational training and postsecondary school training projects. Almost all of the funds supplied for education purposes have been made in the form of IDA credits.

Postwar reconstruction accounted for 4.5 percent of cumulative loans, all in the first few years of the Bank's operation. The small remainder of loans not included in the categories thus far mentioned went for general development and project preparation.

Terms of Loans and Credits

IBRD determines the rate of interest, including commission and administrative charges, maturity and grace periods, and other terms of loans. The underlying principle on which the interest rate to borrowers is set is that it be sufficient to pay the cost of borrowing, cover administrative costs, and leave something to put into reserve against possible future losses. Historically, the total annual charge by the Bank on outstanding loans was made up of a rate roughly equal to the Bank's borrowing costs at the time the loan was made, plus a one percent "commission charge," plus a fraction of about one-fourth of one percent per annum to meet administrative costs. The commission charge was set by the charter at from one to $1\frac{1}{2}$ percent for the first ten years and was to be segregated in a special reserve to meet the Bank's obligations in case of need. After the first decade the Bank was no longer restricted as to the commission rate, and its reserves rose to a level which, while not necessarily excessive, was embarrassingly high and became the source of criticism by Bank Governors who objected to the high interest rates being charged. The policy accordingly was modified as of June 30, 1964, to lower the commission rate and cease building up the reserve.

The interest rate charged on the Bank's long-term (greater than ten years) loans has ranged from 4 percent to $6\frac{1}{2}$ percent. In practice the Bank has been slow to raise its interest rates to meet the rising cost of capital. At present the interest rate formally charged is 6 percent while the cost of borrowing is around 5.3 percent, the commission and administrative cost markups thus being substantially less than one percent.

The Bank also makes a charge against undisbursed portions of its loans. At first this charge was $1\frac{1}{2}$ percent; in 1950 it was reduced to three-fourths of one percent, and since July 1964 it has been three-eighths of one percent.

Prior to 1965 the Bank followed a policy of extending credit to all borrowers at rates based on the above formula regardless of the applicants' apparent credit qualifications. Any differences in rates between borrowers could be attributed to different loan maturities or to changes in the Bank's borrowing costs. However, loans made to Japan and Italy during the fiscal year 1964–1965 were at rates of 6½ and 6¼ percent, respectively, when the standard rate was 5½ percent. A higher rate was charged to these countries in part because the Bank did not wish to compete with the market where the countries obtained most of the funds for the projects. Apparently the loans were made by the Bank because of earlier commitments when these countries were in a more difficult credit position and are not likely to set a precedent.

Insofar as possible loans are made in the foreign currency that is needed for the project, thus minimizing balance-of-payments problems for the country supplying the funds. However, purchases with the funds are not tied in any way to buying from any particular country; indeed, the Bank insists on the money being spent where it will buy the most. The loan repayments are guaranteed against devaluation and are to be repaid in the currency loaned or an acceptable substitute.

Prior to the fiscal year 1963–1964 the Bank's policies with regard to the maturity and the grace period (the period between the time the loan is made and the time when repayment begins) were "that the [maturity] term should bear some relationship to the useful life of the equipment or plant being financed" and that the grace period should be "determined by the time estimated to be necessary to bring the project into operation." Most maturities were in a ten- to 25-year range with a grace period of from two to five years. In recent years IBRD has paid more attention than previously to the debt situation of the borrower, as is indicated by loans with maturities as long as 35 years and grace periods as long as ten years. During 1960 the weighted average maturity of IBRD loans was 22.9 years, while in 1964 the figure was 24.9 years. All education loans have been for a term of 30 years.

IDA development credits are made on a no-interest basis but have an annual "service charge" of three-fourths of one percent of the outstanding balance. The maturity of the credits is 50 years and the grace period is ten years. The principal is to be repaid at the rate of one percent of the original credit per year during the eleventh through the twentieth years and 3 percent during the 21st through the 50th years.

When a loan agreement includes both a Bank loan and an IDA development credit, the composite terms of the whole financial package can vary from one extreme to the other, depending on the relative importance of the two.

Procedural Requirements

The procedures which are required by the Bank before a loan is granted are mainly designed to assure that the project has a high priority for economic development. However, the ability to repay the loan also needs to be determined, and the rigors of the procedure undoubtedly impress the prospective purchasers of Bank bonds and thereby encourage investment in them. The Bank looks upon its relationship with the borrowing country as a long-term one. Before considering any loan applications by a country it insists on making an economic survey to determine the country's stage of development, its needs, its potentialities, and its resources. On the basis of this survey projects are identified that merit further careful study. Preinvestment field study, frequently undertaken in cooperation with the Special Fund component of the United Nations Development Program (UNDP), then is carried on to analyze the technical and economic feasibility of the project. The contribution of the project to the income of the country, the period of time required, and other factors are examined. In the case of manufacturing and mining projects these analyses are made for the Bank by the staff of IFC. The Bank staff is directly responsible for the analyses in other sectors but may secure assistance from the United Nations Educational, Scientific and Cultural Organization (UNESCO) for educational projects and the Food and Agriculture Organization (FAO) for agricultural projects. Some preinvestment studies are paid for by the UN Development Program; others in general are charged to the borrowing country.

Although the general result of the analysis by the World Bank staff is very constructive in distinguishing high-priority from low-priority projects, the question has been raised whether too much weight may not sometimes be given to the project evaluations in determining whether the loan or credit is to be made. Superficially these evaluations appear to have a high degree of quantitative certainty, but this very fact suggests that they also have an element of arrogance or presumption since cost-benefit calculations can rarely be made except within a substantial range of error. Also, it is not easy for the outside observers to accept the statement that it makes no difference in the appraisal of the project as to whether funds will come on hard terms or on soft terms. Certainly it should make a difference. The high rate of discount that must be applied to future benefits for hard-loan financing may understate important benefits that would be recognized if the discount was applied at a lower rate.

If on the basis of the studies and other considerations the decision is to grant the loan, the country is assisted in preparing its application for funds from the Bank. Alternative sources of financing are considered as well as the possibility of using joint sources. If some part of the loan needs to be made on soft terms, this is decided upon. If the policies of the country are considered not favorable for development, progress in changing these policies may be required as a condition for making the loan.

The making of a Bank loan or IDA credit does not mean that the funds are immediately turned over to the borrower. The funds are made available for disbursement only as they are actually needed so that there may be a long period between making the loan and paying it out.

When the loan is negotiated, a statement indicating the allocation of the proceeds is made, subject to revision, and disbursement is checked against this list. Actual payment may be made directly by the Bank to the supplier, or the Bank may agree to reimburse a commercial bank for payments made by it under an approved letter of credit, or the borrower may be reimbursed for actual expenditures. Where practicable, documentation is required attesting to the transaction, shipment of goods, and payment, if this has been made.

These disbursement procedures give a high degree of assurance that loan proceeds are used for the purpose for which the loan was granted. The procedures obviously are facilitated by the policy of loaning for specific projects. The Bank claims that, on the one hand, the procedures have not been objected to by borrowers and, on the other hand, that they are an important reason why the Bank is considered to be a "sound institution."[9]

The Bank continues to take an interest in the country receiving the loan or credit after the disbursement has been made, sending missions to restudy its economic situation, inspecting the projects which have been financed, helping the country to develop new projects, and providing technical assistance.

Conditions Imposed

In addition to the terms and procedures thus far mentioned the Bank in practice has made loans conditional on two types of actions by the recipient country. One type is the introduction of appropriate accounting, disbursing, and other business practices. In some cases personnel changes may be called for. It might seem that there would be no objection to this type of condition since the recipient country has more trouble repaying funds if some are wasted and since wastage clearly is not fair to capital-supplying countries whose resources and often tax revenues are being used. Nevertheless, not infrequently there is objection that these conditions constitute a national humiliation indicating that the country is not to be trusted. A hidden motive in some cases may be resentment at being unable to "ride the gravy train" or to use the funds for political purposes.

The other type of condition relates to changes called for in the eco-

9 Norman G. Jones, "Disbursing World Bank Loans," *Finance and Development*, March 1967 (Vol. 4, No. 1), pp. 51–55.

nomic policies of the country. These might involve, for example, new taxes, reform of tax administration, stronger monetary policy, changes in foreign exchange rates, or even a far-reaching stabilization program. In at least one case the charging of certain electric power rates was required.[10] From the viewpoint of promoting economic development economic policy changes may be crucial in improving the chances that the development project or program will succeed. Undoubtedly the setting of such conditions also helps to increase the confidence of prospective buyers of Bank bonds and the willingness of the taxpayers of developed countries to contribute funds to IDA.

The imposition of economic policy conditions has, however, been a source of frequent criticism of the Bank, and in the cases of Turkey and Brazil this practice led to temporary ruptures between the country and the Bank.[11] The conditions are looked on not as an element of support for politically difficult reforms but too often as a "price" for getting the loan, a price to be escaped if possible. In many cases, however, the reasons for resenting the conditions may be justified. The conditions are characterized as: humiliating denials of independence and sovereignty; patronizing evidences of the smug assumption that "Papa knows best"; frequently mistaken requirements because of failure to understand special conditions and needs; and sometimes premature demands because of insufficient recognition of the inevitable delays in achieving reforms.

Objection to conditions placed on international loans is, of course, made even more strongly when the loan comes from a single country. Indeed, one of the arguments for using multilateral institutions for providing aid is that recipient countries are more willing to accept conditions and make policy changes at the instance of a multilateral organization than of any one country since there is less of an appearance of "economic colonialism" and surrender of sovereignty. But the multinational character of the Bank has not circumvented the problem of resistance to conditions, mainly because no one likes to do unpleasant things, especially when required by someone outside the country, but undoubtedly also in part because the Bank is dominated by a few industrial countries, particularly the United States. The pressures which were exerted for the creation of the United Nations Capital Development Fund as an additional mechanism of international lending stemmed partly from a desire for more money but partly also from the desire of the recipient countries to have a greater role in determining the conditions under which funds were to be distributed. It would be interesting to know what part of the pressure came from the desire to have a greater

[10] Wolfgang G. Friedmann, George Kalmanoff, and Robert F. Meagher, *International Financial Aid* (New York: Columbia University Press, 1966), p. 411.

[11] *Ibid.*, p. 412.

role and what part from the belief that the conditions would be less onerous. To the extent that the latter was the case the question must be asked whether the conditions the Bank imposes are really excessively onerous.

There are, of course, limits to the effective pressure that can be brought to bear to secure acceptance of conditions. The size of the loan may be too small, the political leadership of the country may be unwilling or unable to secure policy changes, and other lending agencies may be willing to supply the funds with less onerous conditions. National governments of developed countries have not hesitated to supply funds for political reasons, and private capital especially is alert to improvements in local conditions and moves in rapidly when the situation becomes favorable.

State-Owned Industries and Development Banks

The Bank has a history of refusal to lend to state-owned manufacturing and mining (including petroleum) industries while making many loans for government infrastructure projects and state-owned transportation, communication, and electric power industries. The distinction can be justified on the practical grounds that infrastructure projects rarely attract private investors and that even in the United States public utility industries are inevitably either owned or are closely controlled by some level of government.

The unwillingness to help finance state-owned industrial projects has been extended also to state-owned development banks, even though many of these are engaged chiefly in lending to private industry. The Bank Group has accepted the development financing company as a valuable intermediary, especially in financing projects that are too small for the Bank to wish to administer. IFC has helped organize such companies and has become a shareholder in seventeen of them in fifteen countries.[12] But none of this support has gone to state-owned institutions.

It is difficult to escape the conclusion that the basic reason for this type of discrimination has been ideological with respect both to the countries holding the major voting power and to some Bank officials, at least in earlier years. In addition to this, Bank officials have seen some rather horrible examples of state-owned industries that were badly mismanaged and run on a political basis where nothing could be done to change the situation. Certainly in many countries state-owned industries have been less efficient and more political than those that are privately owned. By applying a general rule Bank officials are able to avoid the

---

[12] David Grenier, "IFC: An Expanded Role for Venture Capital," *Finance and Development*, June 1967 (Vol. 4, No. 2), p. 139.

administrative problems of making case-by-case judgments, as well as the unpleasant repercussions from informing government officials that their industries or development banks were too inefficient or political to merit financial support.

The Bank's policy has long been under attack from countries that either had no private enterprise base or for other reasons preferred state ownership of certain industries, as well as from many students of the subject. In 1965 George D. Woods, President of the Bank, in speaking to the Economic and Social Council (ECOSOC) of the United Nations, recognized that the Bank had been

> reluctant to finance State-owned industrial enterprises primarily because of the great difficulty of assuring that they would be managed on a business-like basis, free of political pressures

but expressed awareness that in some countries "a shortage of private savings and of industrial entrepreneurship harshly limits what purely private capital can accomplish" and stated that the Bank was

> therefore embarking upon a re-examination of our policies as applied to such cases to see whether there are ways, other than through completely private ownership, in which effective management of industrial ventures can be assured.[13]

If the reexamination has led to any change in policy in the two years since this speech was made, it has not come to the present writer's attention.

Geographical Distribution of Loans

The combined total of $1,123 million in Bank loans and IDA credits made in 1965–1966 went to 32 countries including a regional project in three East African countries. Making up the total were Bank loans of $839 million made to 29 countries of which only five received IDA credits. IDA credits of $284 million were made to eight countries, including three that received no Bank loans, indicating their fiscal weakness.[14]

The 32 countries receiving loans and credits in 1965–1966 included twelve in Africa, one (New Zealand) in Australasia, three (Finland, Portugal, and Spain) in Europe, eight in Asia and the Middle East, and eight in Latin America.

With respect to the distribution of the amounts of loans and credits by regions of the cumulative total to June 30, 1966, and of the latest year, 1965–1966, Asia and the Middle East ranked first in size in both the cumulative and the latest annual totals, and the western hemisphere

---

[13] Address by George D. Woods to the Economic and Social Council of the United Nations, March 26, 1965. (Reprint issued by IBRD.)

[14] Statistics in this section are taken from the IBRD-IDA *1965–1966 Annual Report*.

(Latin America) was next in both. Europe was third in the cumulative total but lower in the latest annual total. Less than one-fourth of the European cumulative total was for postwar reconstruction. Africa ranked fourth in the cumulative total but third in the annual total; a delayed beginner, this continent presumably will receive increasing proportions in the future.

There was no quickly apparent correlation of loans and credits either positively or negatively according to per capita income. For example, in 1965-1966 India received the largest total ($191 million) and Mexico the second largest ($154 million). However, the Indian figure was altogether IDA credits, while the Mexican figure was altogether Bank loans. The fact that Europe, which has low-income countries but not so low as elsewhere, has received as much as it has for economic development indicates that the Bank has been concerned with finding projects that could pay the cost as well as with putting funds where the need was greatest. Bank Governors for several countries not receiving IDA credits were critical of this fact and of the heavy concentration of the credits in India in their statements at the 1966 meeting of the Board of Governors.

Investment Policies of IFC

IFC is the investment banking arm of the World Bank Group. By means of the terms of its financing IFC seeks to promote economic development through the catalytic stimulation of private investment in industry in developing countries.[15] Its investment policies in its early years were constrained by a prohibition against investing in equity securities— a prohibition insisted on by the United States—which was subsequently removed by an amendment to the IFC Articles of Agreement in 1961. Another handicap, which limited the number and size of operations it could undertake, was the small amount of capital—about $100 million— at its disposal. This is in the process of being overcome by the amendments in 1965 to the charters of IFC and IBRD permitting IFC to borrow from IBRD up to $400 million.

Thus far IFC has invested or otherwise pledged about $150 million and has sold off to private investors approximately $57 million of securities held. The total capital involved was $895 million so that private investment averaged $5 for every $1 of IFC capital. Recently IFC has shown substantial growth, the $35.6 million commitments in 1966 being over 40 percent greater than in any previous year. Until borrowing from the Bank was authorized, the largest commitment made by IFC from

---

[15] This section is based primarily on Grenier, pp. 133-142, and IFC, *Annual Report 1965-1966*.

its own resources to any single enterprise was $6 million. This limit has now been raised to $20 million.

IFC is now engaged in practically every form of investment banking operations, almost exclusively in manufacturing although with a few investments in other fields. It has made major commitments in iron and steel, pulp and paper, textiles, cement, and fertilizers. Its primary investment criteria are economic priority for the country; potential profitability; need for new money not available on reasonable terms from private sources; private equity sponsorship; opportunity for local investors to participate; and the unlikelihood that the project would go ahead in the absence of IFC participation. Given these criteria, IFC may invest in equity shares, combine a loan and equity investment, underwrite issues to the public, bring together foreign and domestic partners, provide financial entrepreneurship, or put up the "first money" to get a project started or the "last money" to fill a remaining gap. IFC expects to make a profit, and on the 23 commitments which it has closed out it made a profit on 21, with an average annual return on the 23 commitments of 12.15 percent.

As previously noted, IFC also has helped establish or reorganize private development financing companies.

Methods of Increasing Available Funds

Since the supply of external funds to promote economic development is inadequate, a crucial question is in what ways, if at all, the supply can be increased. And, since this essay deals with the World Bank Group, it must be asked how the funds that it provides can be increased. To introduce the topic it is necessary to describe the methods by which the Group now secures its funds.

The two major sources of new funds of IBRD are capital subscriptions and borrowing in the capital markets; a minor source is income from operations. There has also been a substantial turnover of loans through repayment by borrowers and by the sale of early maturities in the capital markets.

The authorized capital of the Bank started at $10 billion and has since been twice raised. Capital subscriptions have reached $22.4 billion, of which, pursuant to the Bank's charter, 10 percent, or $2.2 billion constitutes the paid-in portion while the remainder can be called if necessary to meet the Bank's obligations on borrowings or on loans guaranteed by it. This callable portion is in effect a guarantee fund which provides a solid basis for the excellent credit rating of Bank bonds. The United States' callable share of the obligation was $5.7 billion as of June 30,

1966. It is significant that the debt of the Bank has never exceeded the United States' obligation and that when this amount was approached the capital of the Bank was increased.

The protection afforded creditors by the unpaid capital subscriptions, together with the governmental guarantees required on loans made by the Bank, would in some circumstances be sufficient to assure the market for World Bank bonds. However, in the early years of the Bank this was not the case. Credit standing is a matter of psychology and law as well as of assets. The history of international loans had been a dismal one when the Bank started business, and the Bank was a new and untried institution. Moreover, the legal situation presented obstacles. In the United States the Securities and Exchange Act, the National Banking Act, and other laws needed to be changed at the federal level, while restrictions on investments by trusts, pension funds, insurance companies, and other financial institutions had to be removed at the state level. A long campaign to educate investors and legislators was necessary. In other countries there were comparable legal or administrative obstacles. On balance, the Bank's conservative policies of "sound" banking were fully justified during the early years when it was establishing its credit.

Through June 30, 1966, the Bank borrowed a total equivalent to $5.2 billion, of which $2.8 billion was outstanding on that date. Meanwhile, the Bank had sold to investors $2.0 billion of its holdings and had received repayments from borrowers of $1.1 billion. Of the $2.8 billion of funded debt outstanding $2.1 billion was in United States dollar obligations, the balance being in Canadian dollars and six European currencies. The largest European currency obligations were in deutsche marks equivalent to $338.6 million and Swiss francs equivalent to $174.8 million. Many of the American dollar obligations have been sold outside the United States; it has been estimated that about half of the total Bank obligations are held abroad. About $200 million of dollar loans have been purchased by central banks using accumulated dollars which the banks wished to invest. The most recent of these loans have been in the form of two-year paper at $5\frac{3}{8}$ percent interest.

The net income of the Bank for the fiscal year 1966 was $143.7 million. Prior to 1964 all income was placed in a special reserve account but was available for lending by the Bank. Since that time part of the income has been transferred to IDA for its lending as development credits.

Although the IDA Articles of Agreement authorize it to borrow in financial markets, the interest-free terms of its development credits give it no basis for borrowing at this time. All of its funds have come from governments ($1,552 million through June 1966), transfers of income from the World Bank ($125 million), and net income ($10 million).

The member countries consist of eighteen Part I high-income countries which subscribed $751 million of the $1,000 million authorized capital and 78 Part II low-income countries which subscribed $248 million. Part I countries paid in 100 percent of their subscriptions in gold and convertible currencies while Part II countries paid in 10 percent in this form and 90 percent in their local currencies. Additional funds have been received in the form of supplementary contributions from Part I countries and by the release in convertible form of parts of the local currency contributions of the Part II countries.

While the World Bank may transfer additional amounts of its profits to IDA, this source cannot be relied on for major increases. With its uncommitted funds virtually exhausted IDA must return to the Part I countries for further subscriptions if it is to continue to provide substantial amounts of development credits. IDA began this process in the spring of 1967.

The funds available to IFC for investment have come from three sources: capital subscriptions, a turnover of funds by sales of portfolio holdings, and loans from IBRD. The capital subscribed as of June 30, 1966, was $99.4 million of an authorized $100 million. IBRD and IFC amended their charters in 1965 to permit lending by IBRD to IFC in effect up to $400 million, which would make it possible for IFC to invest up to the limit of five times the capital and surplus that its charter provided. Thus far, a line of credit of $100 million has been extended to IFC, none of which has yet been drawn down.

A fairly widespread criticism of the Bank over the years has been that its insistence on being a "sound" bank combined with hostility toward possible competition has kept the flow of funds to less developed countries lower than was both needed and feasible. In the early 1950's during the efforts in the United Nations to create a Special United Nations Fund for Economic Development (SUNFED) the Bank privately took a strong stand against such a fund being authorized to make soft loans. Toward the end of the decade, however, the Bank enthusiastically supported the founding of IDA as its own "soft-loan window." Bank officials also opposed the establishment of the Inter-American Development Bank (IDB) and the Asian Development Bank. However, it should be noted that the Bank changed its position regarding the Asian Development Bank and assisted in its design and that present relationships between the Bank and the Inter-American Development Bank are very cordial and cooperative.

Some observers have interpreted the attitude toward SUNFED and toward the regional banks as reflecting the view of a monopolist fighting the emergence of competitors who would offer better terms to borrowers.

While belief in the desirability of a single source of multilateral loans may not have been absent from the minds of some bank officials, other considerations undoubtedly were much more important. It was feared that the Bank's principles of making loans on sound projects to responsible borrowers would be undermined if these loans had to compete with soft loans or with loans made for political reasons. To avoid such undermining of borrower discipline soft loans should be administered nonpolitically by the Bank in conjunction with and supplementary to its hard loans.

Criticisms are currently heard that the Bank by adhering to its basic style of operations has failed to do what it might have done to increase the flow of funds to less developed countries through its own channels. In particular, criticisms are heard that the Bank has not made substantial use of its authority to guarantee private loans to developing countries and that it has reacted negatively to proposals to subsidize rates of interest for economic development borrowing. The Bank in fact has made no use of its authority to guarantee loans made directly by other investors. It has, however, sold to such investors, especially to banks, parts of its loans, either as participations at the time the loan was negotiated or later out of its portfolio. In recent years such sales have been without its guarantee, the last guarantee apparently having been made in 1955. Usually it is the early maturities that are sold, and this fact, together with the high regard in which the Bank's judgment on loans is held, has made the issues salable without its guarantee. Of course, every loan is guaranteed by the government of the recipient country, and formerly some loans to the newer countries were guaranteed also by one of the metropolitan powers.

Banks buy loans from IBRD not only for interest yield but in some cases with a view to developing profitable relations with the borrowers, as well as to maintaining close relations with the Bank, which has large amounts of money to place in time deposits.

The amounts of sales of loans from portfolio have fallen off in recent years because with rising market interest rates such sales could be made only below par. The sale of participations in current loans has been affected to some extent by the United States' investment guidelines that apply to foreign loans although not to the Bank's bond issues. However, the effect has probably been minor since the guidelines do not apply to the issues of the less developed countries.

The question of subsidizing interest arose in connection with the plan proposed at the 1964 UNCTAD by Governor D. Horowitz of the Bank of Israel. The Horowitz Plan called for IBRD, IDA, or some other intergovernmental institution to borrow in the market at the interest rate necessary and loan the funds to IDA to be reloaned to developing countries on soft terms. The loans would be guaranteed by the industrial countries members of IDA. The interest differential would be made up by an "interest equalization fund" created and maintained by annual appropriations of the industrialized countries, each assuming its proportionate share.

IBRD agreed at UNCTAD to make a staff study of this plan.[16] The language of the staff report can only by interpreted as a negative view although no policy position has been taken on the matter by the Executive Directors. One objection raised to the Horowitz Plan is that the Bank's market for bonds might be confused if IBRD sold two kinds, one carrying the usual guarantees and the other with a national subsidization of interest and guarantee of final payment. Aside from this possibility of confusion the principal risk for the Bank would be in realizing over a long term of years the promises of governments to provide interest subsidies. The Bank would have no recourse if a government changed its mind, for example, when a successor government took over.

The argument made in favor of the Horowitz Plan is that it could greatly increase the flow of "soft-loan" funds because governments would be more willing to guarantee the principal and subsidize the interest rate over the life of the loan than to provide the same amount of money in a capital sum. Governor Horowitz originally thought that an additional $3 to $4 billion could be raised over ten years in this way but later reduced the figure to $500 to $600 million over a five-year period.

In seeking to assess whether the Horowitz Plan would substantially increase the flow of funds from the market to the developing countries two principal questions are involved. One, a question of judgment regarding financial markets, concerns the capacity and willingness of the financial markets to absorb additional securities of international organizations. The Bank appears to hold the view that there is at any time a fairly fixed total amount that portfolio managers would wish to invest in such securities in view of the maturities, interest rates, and risks involved and that this amount is not enough greater than the present flow to justify introducing a new method of tapping it. The other question of judgment is a political one: Would governments over the years be willing to enter into long-term commitments to guarantee the loans and to appropriate annually the interest subsidy. Governments might be reluctant to commit themselves in this manner and, moreover, might fear that the precedent would encourage private interests that are pressing hard for interest subsidies for other projects.

[16] *The Horowitz Proposal: A Staff Report* (Washington: International Bank for Reconstruction and Development, February 1965).

The budgetary cost to the taxpayers would be less through interest subsidization than by capital contribution, but the cost would not be negligible. In an example given in the World Bank staff report on the Horowitz Plan the deficit in interest was $1,386 million to finance principal sums of $3,000 million. The economic cost to the contributing countries in real resources would not be substantially affected by the financing plan.

Proposals such as the Horowitz Plan imply that multilateral programs are superior to bilateral programs since governments can now apply a comparable subsidization plan in their bilateral programs, along with investment guarantees and other incentives to foreign investment. If only one kind of financing were appropriate for economic development, perhaps it should be the kind done by the World Bank and IDA. But there are many kinds of requirements and many sources of funds. It may well be that the Bank's contribution to subsidized loans can be more practically made through consultative groups and economic analysis than through plans of the Horowitz type.

One of the ways in which at least temporary expansion of loans to developing countries has taken place is through supplier credits subsidized by the government of the exporting country through guarantees and loans below market rates. Bank officials have been critical of supplier credits, attributing to their excessive use much of the debt service difficulty met by various countries, at least in South America. Critics of the Bank note that the use of supplier credits avoids the supervision that the Bank likes to exercise over borrowing countries. Supplier credits also have a real defect, however, in that salesmanship is brought to bear in promoting projects that may be of low priority in order to place an order which the seller's government will underwrite by guarantees and subsidies. Overselling and overborrowing are encouraged. The result as seen by the Bank is that the fiscal ability of low-income countries to pay for carefully planned projects of high priority is impaired and resources accordingly are wasted. The less developed countries, however, often defend supplier credits as their only available source of funds in the face of the conservatism of the Bank. Movements toward supplier credits have brought IBRD into a degree of conflict with the Export-Import Bank of Washington and comparable agencies in other countries which are vigorously competing for export markets.

In general, the methods that have been proposed to expand funds for lending by IBRD and IDA do not overcome the impediments that limit the flow of official funds to the less developed countries. In some cases, no doubt, the inability of a recipient country to absorb and make good use of funds continues to be a limit. For the most part, however, the factors that limit the flow of official funds to less developed countries are the amounts and costs of funds available in the financial market, the inability of the recipient less developed countries to repay the principal and interest on borrowed funds either because of low income or lack of foreign exchange, the willingness of taxpayers of donor countries to pay higher taxes in order to finance aid, and the balance-of-payments deficits of some major donor countries.

The factors that affect market absorption of Bank bonds include the general supply of and demand for long-term funds, the interest rates necessary to attract these funds from alternative investments, and public confidence in the quality of the loans. The amounts of bonds that could be sold by the Bank at some interest rate undoubtedly exceed the amounts that the Bank would and could loan to the less developed countries at the interest rates necessary to service the bonds.

The debt position of many countries is not encouraging. According to a World Bank study of 99 countries[17] the service on external public debt rose from an average of 8 percent of merchandise exports in 1960 to 9 percent in 1965, and in some countries the burden was much heavier. Unless the less developed countries can solve the problem of meeting debt service by earning larger amounts of foreign exchange through expanded exports, the flow of official funds to less developed countries will be increasingly dependent on government contributions, both bilateral and multilateral. The economic capacity of the industrial countries to support a much larger flow of aid cannot be questioned. The constraints are mainly political, contributions of governments depending on how important the governments believe the economic development of less developed countries to be and on the willingness of their taxpayers to bear the cost.

The taxpayers in the various donor countries are not unaware of the cost of foreign aid. For example, the competition between expenditure priorities in the United States Congress finds foreign aid, whether bilateral or multilateral, with practically no constituency to support it. In West Germany the significance of aid contributions in the national budget has been a political factor. The press of the United Kingdom has referred to the burden on taxpayers in discussing the position to be taken toward new contributions to IDA.

The major complicating problem of an economic character has been deficits in the balance of payments, particularly of the United States and the United Kingdom. There is of course no adverse balance-of-payments effect when real resources (goods and services) are transferred from the donor country to the recipient country. The problem arises when funds

[17] IBRD-IDA, *1965–1966 Annual Report*, p. 33.

from a donor country that is in a deficit position are spent by the recipient country for goods and services in countries with a surplus balance of payments and with a redundancy of the deficit country's currency. The same problem applies to private investment, purchase of World Bank bonds, and government contributions to IDA, although not necessarily to the same degree.

In the United Kingdom financing IBRD and IDA has not been a matter of much concern on balance-of-payments grounds, despite the deficit, since the amounts of funds supplied by the United Kingdom to these organizations have been substantially exceeded by the purchases of British goods paid for from the loans made by the organizations, especially to India and Pakistan. In the United States, however, the balance-of-payments dilemma obviously is very much on the minds of the fiscal and monetary authorities. Their concern may be excessive since there is considerable delay between the making of a World Bank loan or credit and the disbursement of the funds, which in the interim are deposited within the country from which they were borrowed. The United States balance-of-payments deficit has resulted in pressures to delay giving approval for the floating of certain World Bank bond issues in the United States. Undoubtedly it was also the reason for a delay of several months in the response to proposals for the replenishment of IDA funds; the favorable terms of the response when it came were somewhat obscured by provisions designed to afford protection against possible adverse consequences of contributions on balance-of-payments deficits.[18]

TECHNICAL ASSISTANCE

The function of providing technical assistance is carried on by many multilateral and bilateral agencies, and there are many kinds of technical assistance services designed to fulfill many purposes. While the technical assistance services rendered by the World Bank Group sometimes are directed to other goals, they are focused primarily on what the recipient countries need in order to apply for and effectively use loans and credits

[18] At the Rio de Janeiro annual meeting of the IMF, September 26, 1967, United States Secretary of the Treasury Henry H. Fowler said,

As of last March, I was authorized by President Johnson to support the IDA replenishment at a substantially increased level, provided that account should be taken of the balance of payments problems of deficit donor countries in deciding how IDA's new resources would be made available.

While this can be interpreted to imply relating expenditures in some way to contributions, or vice versa, it should be noted that the Secretary went on to say,

Nothing in the United States plan would require IDA to make any changes in its present policies with respect to the allocation of its resources to countries and projects, or with respect to international competition in procurement, and no such changes are contemplated in this proposal.

from the Bank and what the Bank needs in order to make its loans and credits intelligently. As previously indicated, the Bank from the beginning has followed the policy of not making loans in a country until it has completed a comprehensive economic survey of the country, sending for that purpose an economic mission in which other agencies sometimes participate. The reports of these surveys have been published in a series of very useful books. Missions also study particular problems in a variety of fields, as discussed earlier. In addition, the Bank endeavors to keep abreast of economic developments within the borrowing countries.

The emphasis on economic and engineering studies has put the Bank in a position to advise other prospective donors and lenders, as well as to discern the possibilities of additional loans or emerging problems with respect to loans already made.

While the Bank's various economic studies are not a part of its formal technical assistance program, they are in fact an important form of technical assistance. These studies may cover any or all of a whole range of economic policy issues, including such diverse subjects as the methods of formulating development policies and the appropriate rates of foreign exchange. The Bank's advisers in the member countries commonly discuss many matters of current and long-term interest with the country's officials concerned with them.

As part of its program to help improve the administration of economic affairs in the member countries the Bank established the Economic Development Institute (EDI) in 1956. Over the following decade 600 officials from more than 90 countries participated in the courses of the Institute. Until 1962 the offering was limited to an annual six-month general course on development, conducted in English. Since that date several new courses have been added to meet such needs as improving the techniques of project identification, evaluation, and execution. Some courses are now conducted in Spanish and some in French.[19]

COORDINATING ACTIVITIES

While an administrative case might be made for concentrating international assistance for economic development in the hands of one agency, such as the Bank, in actual fact the sources of capital funds and technical assistance are numerous, including global multilateral organizations, regional development banks, bilateral governmental programs, and programs of private foundations and other nonprofit organizations. Private business investments made with the expectation of profit can hardly be

[19] IBRD-IDA, *1965-1966 Annual Report*, p. 19.

classified as aid, regardless of their value for economic development, but businesses often are the source of aid in addition to their investments.

The value of having aid come from numerous sources of funds is that more in total is likely to be transferred since the special concerns and interests of different donors can be promoted, particularly when aid is given on a bilateral basis. However, in the absence of coordination funds are likely to be used wastefully while the countries receiving assistance may not be receiving what is appropriate to their development requirements; the tendency is for recipients to play donors off against each other with the results that neither the amounts nor the uses of the funds give a well-balanced development and important needs are not met.

Because of its broad membership, the substantial funds available to it, and its emphasis on economic and project studies the Bank has emerged as a natural leader for improved coordination of assistance. It has taken important initiatives to improve coordination through closer consultation between the providers of assistance and through better planning and execution by the recipients of assistance.

The experience of the Bank in coordinating aid from a variety of sources began with its chairmanship of a consortium of interested governments and institutions established in 1958 to meet a foreign exchange crisis in India. The Bank organized a second consortium in 1960 to coordinate assistance to Pakistan. These consortia involved not only consultation and study of the situation but also the pledging of funds by the members of each consortium.

The Bank has continued to promote the coordination of assistance for other countries through "consultative groups" which are similar to consortia except that there is no pledging of funds. The consultative group exchanges information with the recipient country and between its members with a view to determining what the needs are and how they might best be met. Consultative groups have been established under the Bank's leadership in nine countries: Colombia, the Republic of Korea (South Korea), Malaysia, Nigeria, Peru, the Sudan, Thailand, Tunisia, and Morocco. The group for Nigeria is at present inactive. This particular Bank policy has received virtually unanimous commendation. For example, of the Governors attending the 1966 Bank meeting a large number commented quite favorably on this operation, with very few reservations.

And, indeed, these activities of the Bank in promoting the coordination of aid provided by various national governments and international organizations would seem to be a major contribution. IBRD is in an excellent position to take leadership in consultative groups because it has money to put into projects if it decides to do so, it has made the greatest efforts to secure comprehensive and adequate information, and it has perhaps the best-trained and most experienced staff in the economic development field. Thus the Bank is able to provide help and exert influence in many directions, including the Inter-American Committee on the Alliance for Progress (CIAP).

The opportunity of a recipient country to present its needs in an organized fashion before a committee of possible contributors is valuable in that one first-rate presentation may take less time and effort and be more effective than many partial presentations. Moreover, with possibly interested donors present there is a considerable likelihood that more money will be secured and that it will be allocated in ways that will permit the recipient country to do many things it wants to do while satisfying each of the donor countries that it is putting its money into what it considers most important and best suited to its aid.

On the other hand, appearing before a committee of possible donors is not without its humiliating aspects since the recipient country is in effect throwing itself on the mercy of others. Moreover, the possibilities of bargaining between different prospective donors is minimized. On balance, however, the merits of coordination outweigh the demerits. The recipient country would be in a far more difficult position if all of the funds available to it came from one source, which would accordingly have enormous economic power.

Accomplishments and Problems

The foregoing discussion suggests how the policies of the Bank have evolved in various directions, mostly away from some of the rigorous banking standards of the formative period. It also suggests how the Bank continues to be under criticism regarding both matters under its control and matters not under its control. In these concluding paragraphs it is time to return to the consideration of certain policy questions that were raised earlier.

One question concerned the effectiveness with which Bank funds have been used in promoting economic development. Speaking generally, there can be no doubt that the methods developed by the Bank to assure the proper and efficient use of funds provided by it have constituted a major contribution. Historically, intergovernmental loans to less developed countries were commonly motivated by political considerations, and little if any check was made on whose pockets they went into and to what uses they were put. Private loans were motivated by expectations of profit; any development achieved was incidental except as it contributed to profit. The United States bankers who seduced Latin American governments to borrow during the 1920's did not set a good example.

Through its emphasis on sound projects and its careful procedures the Bank brought a new dimension of effectiveness to international lending and set the example for other organizations and governments.

On lesser points the case is not so clear. The Bank may be adjudged slow in recognizing the importance of program lending, the value of financing more than the foreign exchange component, and the desirability of soft loans. But it has done so and is adapting its lending policies to new situations. The general policy of not lending for state-owned manufacturing and mining enterprises and development banks is widely interpreted as being narrowly ideological and not worthy of an international organization; it is to be hoped that the reexamination of policy promised by the Bank's President will lead to a case-by-case rather than a general policy approach to this matter. The conditions imposed on the governments of borrowing countries at times appear to be for the purpose of assuring the profitable operation of the borrowing company, which stretches beyond reasonable limits the concept of sound economic policy. The reliance on apparently precise cost-benefit analyses in deciding on loans can result in neglecting more fundamental economic considerations; such analyses are scarcely applicable to program lending.

The problem of grants and soft loans remains a central and very puzzling one for development finance. The situation is very awkward. On the one hand, there is not enough debt-servicing capacity in many less developed countries to support their borrowing the needed amounts of official capital on a hard-loan basis. On the other hand, there is probably not enough transferable capital in the world to meet the demands of developing countries on a grant basis or even on a very soft-loan basis. Such capital must be rationed, and the institution doing the rationing cannot avoid the charge of discrimination and arbitrariness nor the fact of it. No satisfactory formula for allocating grants or soft loans has come to light. Because of this problem the narrow membership base of Bank control may be expected to be increasingly attacked.

Disappointing to everyone are the amounts of money raised and lent by the Bank Group today. The amounts of hard loans are limited by both demand and supply factors. High interest rates discourage potential customers while the reluctance of some governments to have large amounts of Bank bonds sold in their currencies and countries limits supply. The amounts of IDA soft loans are limited to some extent by the Bank procedures for determining the quality of the project or program, but the real limit is the willingness of governments and taxpayers in industrial countries to draw on their large and rising national incomes for purposes of making the funds available through IDA.

The complaint that the Bank has not done what it could in raising money is subject to heavy discount. Undoubtedly there are methods by which more funds could be gotten for immediate crash programs. But the international financing of development is nothing less than a very long-term proposition. For the longer pull there seems nothing substantial to recommend beyond the Bank's practice of drawing on financial markets for hard-loan funds and on the contributions of governments for soft-loan funds. This is essentially a problem for the governments. The Swiss government has set a good example in its recent proposal to loan the equivalent of $12.1 million to IDA on the same terms as the IDA credits and with no tieing or other strings attached.[20]

Many people would like to see a larger proportion of official funds channeled through the World Bank Group. If there is anything about Bank policy that has kept the proportion down, it is not apparent in public discussion. Probably what has kept it down is the short-run appeal of putting the funds bilaterally where the donor particularly wants them to go for purposes of special interest to him. Also, the appeal of using regional organizations that bring the countries of a region into closer relationship cannot be overlooked.

In this situation the leadership of the Bank in coordinating the contributions to development finance from various governments and organizations may over the future come to be its greatest contribution to economic development. But it is important to recognize the crucial requirement of the Bank in carrying out its coordinating activities that it be very well supplied with cash. Only with money, particularly money available on soft terms, can the Bank achieve and assure well-balanced economic development financing "packages" without which the rightly praised consultative groups may end in frustration.

The Bank's greatest contribution probably has been to make economic development lending respectable. Given the financial support it deserves, the Bank Group may be expected through its lending, its technical assistance, its special expertise, and its coordinating and promotional activities to make a continuing and even greater contribution. Its future depends heavily on whether it receives that financial support.

---

[20] IDA Press Release No. 67/10, July 4, 1967.

Regional Development Financing

HENRY SIMON BLOCH

OBJECTIVES OF REGIONAL DEVELOPMENT BANKS

REGIONAL development banks can serve as focal points for regional and subregional cooperation, thus promoting economic integration. They are institutions whose objectives are neither national nor global and whose leadership and staffs have a regional outlook.

The first and immediate challenge confronting these regional development banks is the financing of regional projects which are beyond the reach of national development banks. The International Bank for Reconstruction and Development (IBRD) has devoted only limited resources to such projects, with a few spectacular exceptions, especially the Indus River project. A purely national approach to planning and financing development does not make sense in most of Latin America and Africa because many nations on these continents are "minicountries," too small to form economic units of development. Many national borders have been determined by political and diplomatic history rather than by economic factors; frequently, they cut across natural development units such as river basins or mineral deposits. Moreover, except in Europe, the very dearth of strong national institutions makes regional development banks important; they provide additional financial intermediaries to be interposed between the developing regions and the world financial centers, as well as between various national financial institutions of the member countries of the regions concerned.

A second challenge facing regional development banks is to provide support to the poorer nations in their regions, which by and large have

HENRY SIMON BLOCH is Adjunct Professor of Public Law and International Relations at Columbia University and a Director of E. M. Warburg & Co., Inc. Thanks go to his colleague and collaborator, Professor W. B. Bassett of the Graduate School of Business, and to Dr. K. E. Lachmann, Chief of the Fiscal and Financial Branch of the United Nations who cooperated on a United Nations report on regional development financing prepared by the author in 1966. This essay is part of a research project on regional banks of the School of International Affairs, Columbia University, New York.

not received as much aid per capita as the richer ones. The third challenge is industrialization, which involves diversification of production and economies of scale. The long-range goal—closer to realization, perhaps, in Latin America than elsewhere—is that of financing economic integration. The underlying philosophy here is that even national projects must be viewed in their subregional or regional context.

Although they do have basic objectives in common, the differences between the regional development banks themselves are quite strong.

The European Investment Bank, a consortium of donors, must not be considered as a proper instrument for financial integration of the European Economic Community (EEC). Financial integration of the Common Market countries would require a joint monetary system and possibly a joint central bank. It would further require harmonization of financial policies, strong regional financial legislation, and institutions applicable to and operating in all six countries. The arguments which are used to demonstrate the weakness of the European Investment Bank cannot be applied to regional development banks in developing nations. The Inter-American Development Bank (IDB) is already seasoned, and, as the financial arm of the Alliance for Progress, it operates within a framework of regional institutions. Its President has for some time referred to it as the "Bank for Economic Integration." The Asian Development Bank is a partnership of developing and developed nations, with the United States and Japan playing major roles in its financing and organization. As the development of Southeast Asia may eventually become one of its goals, this study includes a discussion of the so-called Lower Mekong development scheme. The African Development Bank (ADB) is a consortium of recipient countries, *sui generis* because of its rigid exclusion of nonregional partnerships.

Any examination of regional development banks must, however, be more speculative than historical and more analytical than descriptive because the emergence of these public international banks with development activities devoted to specific regions is so recent (see Table I) that their true impact has not yet been felt.

Before sketching profiles of the regional development banks let us first briefly comment on the World Bank's role.

THE WORLD BANK AND THE REGIONAL DEVELOPMENT BANKS

The International Bank for Reconstruction and Development served as the organizational model for the regional banks; yet, the establishment of these banks was the result of a feeling that the World Bank was overcentralized, that it did not give sufficient voice to the developing coun-

TABLE I: THE REGIONAL BANKS[a]

Bank	Headquarters	Organized[b]	Authorized Capital (in Millions of United States Dollar Equivalents)	Membership				
				Total	Developed Countries	Less Developed Countries	Regional Countries	Nonregional Countries
European Investment Bank	Luxembourg[c]	1958	1,000	6	6	0	6	0
Inter-American Development Bank	Washington	1960	3,150	21	1	20	20	1
African Development Bank	Abidjan	1965	250	29	0	29	29	0
Asian Development Bank	Manila	1967	1,100	32[d]	16	16[d]	19[d]	13

a Based upon available data as of June 30, 1967.

b The year of organization is not synonymous with the year the institution was legally created; rather, it is an approximation as to when the bank began to internally function as a going concern.

c The headquarters of the European Investment Bank was in Brussels until the merger of the European Coal and Steel Community and the European Economic Community executive bodies into a single Commission located in Brussels. To compensate Luxembourg for the loss of the High Authority of the Coal and Steel Community the European Investment Bank's seat of operations was shifted.

d Includes Western Samoa.

tries in its decisionmaking, and above all that its focuses were global and national but not regional. However, in order to be effective the regional banks must have the cooperation of the World Bank; each of them encounters different needs, many of which can only be satisfied through such cooperation.

Indeed, the regional banks have adopted the World Bank's *procedures* and *terms of lending*. Both the World Bank Group and the regional banks adhere to the principle of separation of bankable from nonbankable activities and use separate windows for soft lending. Still, there are striking differences in certain *loan policies,* demonstrating a variation in political coloration, among which the following are most noteworthy: 1) The Inter-American and African Development Banks support publicly owned development banks. (The policy of the Asian Development Bank is still to evolve.) The practice of the World Bank and of the International Finance Corporation (IFC) is to finance only private development banks. This alternative to the policy of the World Bank Group may become particularly significant in those cases where established government development banks could be used as effective channels for development financing. 2) The Inter-American Development Bank does not insist on strict profit standards in its electricity loans, as does the World Bank. (The policies of the African and Asian Banks are still to evolve.) 3) The charters of the regional banks allow direct lending to private enterprises and subordinate government units without requiring government guarantees, as is the case with the World Bank.

There are a number of smaller projects which the Inter-American Development Bank finances, and the African Development Bank will certainly deal with smaller projects than does IBRD. It seems to the author, however, that in the long run the emphasis of the regional development banks will not necessarily be on such projects. Once regional projects really get going, the proportion of smaller projects may have to be reduced.

The World Bank has repeatedly announced that it will broaden its policy, and several of its recent activities have given proof of a change in attitude. This is an evolution, not a revolution. It can only be accomplished because the Bank's creditworthiness is thoroughly established and because a staff of competent economists has been developed to undertake macroeconomic analyses. In a recent speech its President, George D. Woods, declared that the World Bank Group now feels that "the country is the project."[1] This is perhaps the clearest endorsement of the "program" approach as against the mere "project" approach although the

[1] The tenth Gabriel Silver Lecture at Columbia University, under the auspices of the School of International Affairs, on April 13, 1967.

latter still has validity in many cases, both for the World Bank and, especially, for the smaller loans of regional banks.[2]

The World Bank Group cannot work on the regional principle because its decisionmaking structure is not designed for decentralization. Sitting in Washington, the board of twenty Executive Directors representing over 100 countries makes decisions on proposals submitted by the President. Thus highly centralized, the World Bank has no experienced, well-established, powerful regional field offices and during its over twenty years of existence has set up no network of decentralized regional institutions. This task fell rather to the regional development banks. As shown in Table II, the developing countries have a relatively greater voice in the regional development banks than is allowed by the voting pattern of IBRD. The voting is weighted more in favor of the poorer countries in the African than in the Asian Development Bank and in the Asian than in the Inter-American Development Bank.

THE EUROPEAN INVESTMENT BANK[3]

In Europe the concept of the Six was a post-Marshall Plan development, and the European Investment Bank was created with the specific objective of becoming *the* Bank of the Common Market. It has financed ventures in the less developed areas of the Six, helping them to overcome the temporary disadvantages occasioned by the tariff reductions of the Common Market. It has been entrusted with the management of monies for the European Development Fund, which is providing Common Market financial support to associated members in Africa and territories overseas. The Bank also has become a potent lender to associated members in accordance with special provisions in the Convention of Association. In Africa it has a large potential, especially if, as is hoped, a close working relationship with the African Development Bank can be achieved. However, its resources are too small in relative terms, and the national financial institutions of Europe are so powerful that the Bank's position as *the* Bank of the Common Market does not, in reality, have the importance which its image would suggest. Furthermore, as stated above, conditions for financial integration of the Six do not presently exist.

THE INTER-AMERICAN DEVELOPMENT BANK

The idea of an inter-American banking operation is not new; it initially appeared at the First International Conference of American States in

[2] A very significant analysis of the Bank's new policy was presented to the Canadian Political Science Association by Irving S. Friedman, the Economic Adviser to the President, on June 7, 1967. In December 1967, at the annual review of development financing activities by OECD, the Common Market countries criticized IDA for directing insufficient funds toward Africa.

[3] A full treatment of the European Investment Bank and the European Coal and Steel Community (ECSC) will be available in a forthcoming book by Henry Simon Bloch and William Bruce Bassett as part of the above-mentioned project.

TABLE II: VOTING POWERS[a]

[Figures Represent Percent of Total Voting Power]

Bank	Developed Members	Less Developed Members	Nonregional Members	Regional Members	Voting Power[b] of Regional Members in the World Bank
European Investment Bank	100	0	0	100	16.7
Inter-American Development Bank	42.5	57.5	42.5	57.5	7.8
African Development Bank	0	100	0	100	6.8
Asian Development Bank	65.3	34.7	37.3	62.7	17.6[c]

[a] Based upon available data as of June 30, 1967.

[b] These figures represent Board of Governors meetings, where each World Bank member may cast its vote. However, in Executive Director meetings the less developed countries have even less voice because an Executive Director cannot split his votes if the countries he represents disagree. In Executive Director meetings the developed countries have 73.6 percent of the vote, whereas in Board of Governor meetings they have 66 percent. Only in ADB, among the regional banks, can an Executive Director split his vote.

[c] Cambodia and Western Samoa are not members of the World Bank.

1889-1890 in Washington. Similar proposals came up regularly thereafter but were rebuffed by the United States which objected to competition with private banking. In May 1940 the United States joined other nations in signing a convention for the establishment of an inter-American bank. In spite of strong support by President Franklin D. Roosevelt and Adolf Berle, Assistant Secretary of State for Latin America, the Senate, still opposed to competition with private banking, refused to ratify the convention. The idea was revived at the International Conference of American States at Bogotá (1948) and at inter-American conferences in Washington (1950), Caracas (1954), Petrópolis, Brazil (1954), and Buenos Aires (1957). In every instance the United States took the position that existing lending institutions—IBRD and the Export-Import Bank—were sufficient and that no additional agency would be needed. Finally, in 1959 the United States took the leadership in establishing the Inter-American Development Bank, which began functioning in 1960. Incidentally, United States policy during the organizing phase of IFC and the Asian Development Bank was characterized by similar policy reversals.

Among Latin American nations there was a persistent feeling that IBRD was too rigid in its requirements, that its lending policy was too conservative, that it did not furnish sufficient economic and financial assistance in the preparation and execution of national development programs, and that· it did not give them enough voice in policymaking for their region. Moreover, there was a great deal of dissatisfaction with the amount of aid given to Latin America by the United States, as well as with lack of cooperation among Latin American nations themselves.

It was pointed out that between 1945 and 1957 only 2½ percent of all United States aid went to Latin America, and of this one-fourth was military assistance. Between 1945 and 1960 Yugoslavia, for example, received more funds from the United States than did all Latin American countries combined. From 1945 to 1957 less than 20 percent of World Bank loans were committed in Latin America. This period covered European postwar reconstruction, and it was only after this goal had been accomplished that the World Bank and the United States turned their major efforts toward the developing nations. Since that time IBRD has generated the International Development Association (IDA) which gives soft loans to the poorer countries; it has begun to encourage educational and other social financing activities; it has established the Development Advisory Service and initiated consultative groups which provide borrower participation in the planning and review of projects.

Creation of the Inter-American Development Bank, by itself, brought about more unity among Latin American countries than had any other institution, political or economic, in the hemisphere. Symbolic of this, as well as of the incumbent's prestige, was the reelection by acclamation in 1964 of the Bank's President although during the first election in 1960 there had been a near deadlock. Since the first election the runner-up has worked closely with the President as one of the Bank's senior officials. Even more illustrative is the fact that at a time when Bolivia had no diplomatic relations with Chile it was a Bolivian governor of the Bank who proposed the reelection of the Chilean President.

Some of the early IDB activities were a continuation of World Bank studies. For instance, the World Bank had already planned for regional projects in telecommunications for Central America and for a Pan-American Highway before IDB began its operations. In these and many other activities the Inter-American Development Bank has coordinated its own activities with those of the World Bank. In addition, the two banks have participated together in consultative groups for Ecuador and Colombia, the former headed by IDB and the latter by the World Bank.

IDB's loan activities demonstrate that the choice of objectives by the regional development banks has been determined to some extent by the process of elimination. The World Bank's position as the most massive lender in the public power field has led the Inter-American Bank to concentrate on agriculture, industry, mining, water supply, education, and housing. IDB's financing of transportation and electric power was less than 10 percent, for each of these sectors, of its total bank authorizations up to the beginning of 1967.[4] Of striking interest are the Bank's newer activities which are only minimally reflected in the historical distribution of its total loan activities. These include preinvestment studies, credit lines for export financing of capital goods by Latin American countries to other Latin American countries, and also considerable support for the Central American Bank for Economic Integration (CABEI).

In 1967 the Inter-American Development Bank was charged by the Meeting of American Chiefs of State at Punta del Este with specific activities in the field of economic integration. It will take a long time before the specific procedures and methods for creation of a common market in Latin America are agreed upon and longer still before actual economic integration can take place.

It is quite possible that Latin America's experience may be the opposite of Europe's. In Europe the Common Market was the first stage in the process of integration, but progress in subsequent stages has suddenly come to a halt. There is still no integrated European capital market[5] and no strong regional financial organization; however, the Six have strong

[4] Transportation, 8.6 percent; electric power, 8.2 percent. (Inter-American Development Bank, *Seventh Annual Report: 1966* [Washington, 1967], p. 5.)

[5] The Columbia University School of International Affairs is sponsoring a study on European financial integration by E. S. Kirschen, edited by Henry S. Bloch and William Bruce Bassett.

national economies and strong national financial systems, while most nations of Latin America (Mexico is a notable exception) lack strong national financial foundations. In Latin America the need is greater than in Europe for strong regional institutions to underpin the weaker national institutions. The Inter-American Development Bank could well be much more instrumental in promoting integration than the European Investment Bank has been.

A regional perspective is kept in sight through the Inter-American Committee on the Alliance for Progress (CIAP).[6] CIAP sets up goals on a continental basis but with country-by-country objectives. Once the financing of intraregional exports of capital goods by the Inter-American Development Bank is sufficiently expanded, it can become an important support action for the development of a capital goods industry on a continental scale. In Europe, where national capital goods industries existed, the problem was one of tariffs and duties; in Latin America the industry itself has to be financed. As of now, the capital export financing program is far too small. However, in the Central American Common Market (CACM) Latin America has an experiment in economic integration which has already progressed in a manner unique to the developing world.

THE ASIAN DEVELOPMENT BANK

The Asian Development Bank is an association of developed and developing nations. Equity shareholders include the United States, the United Kingdom, the Federal Republic of Germany (West Germany), Belgium, the Netherlands, and Italy, but not France. In addition, Switzerland, normally coy when it comes to joining international organizations, has become a full-fledged member.

The United States–Japanese partnership in the Asian Development Bank, solidly backed by a $200 million participation by each of the two countries, had two effects. One was a strong financial base and the other the Western image, which was strengthened when European countries, especially West Germany, became partners. The Union of Soviet Socialist Republics (Soviet Union) did not join the Asian Development Bank although it was formally invited, nor did any of the Eastern European countries. Indonesia entered only after a change of government. Burma and Outer Mongolia have been formally invited but have not accepted membership.

The charter is by no means a United States–Japanese dictated instrument and includes many clauses to which these countries objected. The groundwork was laid by purely Asian committees, advised by an Inter-

[6] On CIAP see Raúl Sáez, "The Nine Wise Men and the Alliance for Progress," elsewhere in this volume.

American Development Bank expert, UN staff and consultants, and a representative of the President of the United States.

The voting pattern was the subject of serious negotiations. The United States and Japan made major concessions to allow the poorer countries a much greater relative voting power than they possess in the Inter-American Development Bank.

The very choice of the Bank's site involved political adjustments: The Philippines granted diplomatic recognition to Malaysia and Singapore when Manila was chosen as the site of the Bank's headquarters. So important was the prestige of location that Iran made a very attractive offer of participation, subject to location in Teheran, and refused to join the Bank when Manila was chosen as its headquarters.

The first elected President is a Japanese, but his election is due at least as much to his personal qualities and international financial standing as to his nationality. It was he who was primarily responsible for Japan's success on the world capital market. The first Vice-President, who is an Indian, is also one of the prominent international financial experts of Asia with World Bank experience.

In its first operations the Bank, like the Inter-American Development Bank, may continue projects already conceived, such as the Pan-Asian Highway. The Indus River project has been pioneered by the World Bank, which has devoted the bulk of its financing in Asia and the Far East to India and Pakistan. Despite this fact both countries acquired major shareholdings in the Asian Development Bank and so, of course, expect the institution to be very active on their subcontinent. A major future challenge to the Asian Development Bank lies in Southeast Asia, which is today one of the world's great danger zones. For this reason and because it illustrates the potential benefits of subregional cooperation and economic integration the Lower Mekong Basin development scheme will be discussed in some detail.

The Lower Mekong Development Scheme

Development of the Lower Mekong Basin could have a considerable multiplier effect on the development of the entire subregion, specifically the riparian nations of Thailand, Vietnam, Laos, and Cambodia.[7]

The riparian countries at present cannot utilize the energy which hydroelectric projects on the Mekong River could produce. This creates a need for phasing of the Mekong's development so as to keep it in step with the economic development of the riparian countries. If development

[7] See the various studies by the Committee for Coordination of Investigations of the Lower Mekong Basin, the so-called Mekong Committee. See also C. Hart Schaaf and Russell H. Fifield, *The Lower Mekong: Challenge to Cooperation in Southeast Asia* (Princeton, N.J.: D. Van Nostrand Company, Inc., 1963).

of the Mekong is to proceed by stages, each stage would still require an investment which would not be bankable in conventional terms. As new hydroelectric resources are made available, the problem arises as to how long it will take the four riparian countries to be able to utilize them.

Two strategies for the development of the Mekong have been envisaged: 1) The first approach would time the development of the Mekong's hydroelectric resources with the development of the riparian countries induced by this process. It would be necessary to assure at each stage a demand large enough to absorb the energy produced over the amortization period applied to the invested capital. 2) The second approach would be to use the resources of the Mekong as a triggering device for the acceleration of the economic growth of the four countries, with a first investment "package" enabling them to utilize the resources put at their disposal by the development of the river and to create financing of future mainstream developments. The first investment "package" would be amortized and reimbursed only toward the completion of the successive stages of river development.

In this perspective investments during the early stages of river development are always maintained one step ahead of the absorption of the newly created resources by the four riparian countries. This presupposes a strategy which implies two prerequisites.

The first is external financial support for the "first investment package," either in the form of grants or in the form of soft loans. There will be need also of local cost financing. Money, however, could only be put to proper use if a long-term economic development plan was devised for the entire subregion.

The second prerequisite would, therefore, be a four-nation economic development plan as a framework for national development plans. This, in turn, would require the pooling of resources as well as of markets. Such pooling of markets would require as a minimum a common market for domestically produced commodities but should lead eventually to effective use of the enormous water resources made available.

The Mekong Committee has mobilized multilateral and bilateral contributions without prejudging future financial policies. These policies will probably involve the Asian Development Bank, possible regional special funds consigned to it, or subregional financing institutions.

While the project is multinational, one of the lessons to be drawn from it is that in the preinvestment phase local contributions to the United Nations Special Fund studies could only be obtained because of *localization* in *one* given country of each aspect of the preinvestment studies. Furthermore, countries which made bilateral contributions were approached with a list of preinvestment projects and were offered a choice of financing either one complete project, several complete projects, or only a part of selected preinvestment projects. This meant the setting up of a donor consortium but it did not mean—as is frequently believed—a true multilateral recipient organization.

In a politically sensitive area where multinational approaches are extremely difficult, maximum reliance was placed on parallel and externally coordinated national activities without multinational cooperation among the recipient nations.

If it is to be executed effectively, the Mekong development requires, however, multinational investment and managerial institutions.

The following have been proposed: 1) a common authority for coordination and planning of regional development, with budgetary powers for the programming of investments; and 2) a water resources agency.

Here, the first and minimal alternative is to organize enterprises for the sale of energy and water to national institutions of the four riparian countries. The second and much more ambitious alternative is to create the key instrument for implementation of a regional development plan. There may have to be subsidiaries for the production and distribution of energy which would function on the multinational level more or less as Electricité de France functions on the national level. There would also have to be a subregional enterprise for the agricultural development of the newly irrigated areas. Finally, there would have to be a subregional transport enterprise. In all of these alternatives the participation of all four riparian states is assumed.

Additional requirements will include: 1) complementary infrastructure investments, such as roads, canals, and bridges; 2) four-nation universities, training centers, and applied research centers to be financed bilaterally or multilaterally or by foundations for which this might be a particularly interesting activity; and 3) multinational industrial enterprises. Without basic industries the take-off stage will be very hard to attain by the riparian countries. Their limited resources are insufficient for effective industrialization. Here is where the Asian Development Bank could play a major role. Naturally, the exact formula which would be acceptable to the riparian governments and to the Asian Development Bank cannot now be envisioned. Private enterprise might have an important role in this investment program for industrialization.

THE AFRICAN DEVELOPMENT BANK

In Africa the situation is very different from that which prevails in Asia and Latin America. Many of the African nations have only very recently emerged from colonial status. Many of them have had access to the Bank only because up to independence the colonial powers served as guarantors and negotiators of loans. Furthermore, the United States did not have as large and well-established an aid-providing activity in Africa as it had in Asia and Latin America.

The African Development Bank was created under the sponsorship of the United Nations after more than two years of negotiations. An African delegation representing most of the continent traveled to the major capitals to elicit foreign interest. Finally, it was decided that in a continent where regional economic activities meant action across currency zones, across linguistic barriers, and across established trade and financial patterns the difficult task of self-help could be better accomplished by an African institution completely free of foreign equity participation.

Twenty-nine independent African countries have, so far, joined the African Development Bank; South Africa is not eligible for membership, and Libya, Madagascar, Chad, Gabon, the Central African Republic, and Burundi have not joined.[8] Of this latter group it is significant that five are associated with the EEC, and, consequently, have access to alternative financial support. Nevertheless, most of the African associate members of the Common Market (thirteen) have subscribed to membership in the African Development Bank.

The African states had to assume a relatively heavy financial burden to establish the Bank as a viable institution. Although the authorized capital was set at $250 million, well below the capitalization of the other regional banks, this figure in fact represents a greater contribution than that which the *developing* countries of Asia made to the Asian Development Bank and is almost equivalent to the Latin countries' contribution to the Inter-American Development Bank. While in the Inter-American and Asian Development Banks half of the paid-in capital is in local currency, the one-half of African Development Bank capital that is paid in by members must all be in gold or convertible currencies. On the basis of full subscription and payment of original authorized capital (about $220 million has been subscribed) and with account taken of the fact that a few African countries, most notably the United Arab Republic, are in arrears the African Development Bank is to receive $125 million in gold or foreign exchange. The original paid-in capital of the Inter-American Development Bank was $125 million in United States dollars; and the Asian Development Bank is to receive $75 million in gold or convertible currencies from developing countries in the region.

Moreover, the African Development Bank has been given the exceptional power to require members to lend local currencies to the Bank; only the European Investment Bank has similar power.

---

[8] Botswana and Lesotho at the time of writing have not yet decided for or against membership.

In view of the enormous problems of development in Africa and the Bank's relative lack of capital the African Development Bank must obtain cooperation by non-African governments and institutions. The government of the United Kingdom has announced that it will set up a "special fund" in the Bank, and expressions of active interest in participating in worthwhile projects have been received from other governments. Noteworthy is the expected participation, through a trust fund, of the United States.

The World Bank Group has opened an office close to the African Development Bank's headquarters in Abidjan, and it is hoped that active collaboration between the two will ensue. The United Nations Development Program (UNDP) is giving the African Development Bank support in its preinvestment and investment promotion activities, but it will be some time before the Bank can borrow large amounts in foreign capital markets on the strength of its own creditworthiness. If the Bank develops its reputation as an organizer of feasibility studies and as a solid financial institution, it will be able to attract additional capital to the region through parallel financing, trust funds, and participation in loans.

The scope and manner of the Bank's operations have been set out by its charter in the broadest and most flexible terms in order to enable the Bank to secure the greatest leverage from its resources, whatever the economic and political conditions it may encounter in years to come. Yet, given the limitations of the small equity capital available, the management is subject to specific rules as to its disposal,[9] such as maximum lending limits for national and multinational projects. Paid-in capital can be lent only for bankable projects and on commercial terms. The Bank does not make loans from its equity capital for social projects such as housing construction, rural water supply, and hospitals. It cannot lend for general budget support, for balance-of-payments support, or for refinancing of existing debts.

The governments of Tanzania and Zambia have requested the African Development Bank to assist in a project to which the Bank could only make a relatively small contribution: It concerns the financing of a railway from the Zambian copper mines to the port of Dar-es-Salaam in Tanzania. Total cost is estimated at $300 million. The World Bank previously refused to finance this project, and it is most uncertain whether funds will ever be found for such a heavy investment, as outside help would have to be as politically motivated as the request.

In late April 1967 the African Development Bank announced its first

[9] Many of which are embodied in the *Text Concerning the Loan and Investment Policy of the African Development Bank and Its Procedures*, approved by the Executive Directors in December 1965 laying the foundation for the Bank's operations.

loans. A $3 million loan was granted for the improvement of two trunk roads in Kenya which link up with existing roads in Uganda and Tanzania. Parallel financing for the project was attracted, with the United States Agency for International Development (AID) contributing an additional $3 million. Total cost may amount to $10 million.

This loan, although a national one, was significant for the two neighboring states and provides an example of how the regional development banks can promote subregional cooperation. In mid-1966 ministerial talks which had been taking place between the three nations on a subregional common market broke down over disagreement regarding the formula by which a proposed East African development bank would disburse its pool of funds. After the African Development Bank loan Kenya indicated its willingness to reopen negotiations on the formula under conditions more favorable to Uganda and Tanzania. Thereafter, events moved swiftly, and on June 6, 1967, the heads of state of the three countries signed a treaty establishing an East African Economic Community and Common Market, which includes, among other institutions, an East African Development Bank.

At the time the loan to Kenya was announced the African Development Bank approved a small equity investment in a proposed national development bank in Sierra Leone in which the government holds an equity interest, thus demonstrating that restrictions applicable to IFC investments are not followed by the African Development Bank.

FINANCING

Attracting additional foreign capital into its region is one of the most important functions of a regional development bank. Acting alone, developing countries generally do not have the creditworthiness to obtain sufficient long-term development finance on reasonable terms. Acting jointly through a regional development bank, they may increase their borrowing power.

The regional development banks are structured for three types of financial resources: 1) paid-in capital; 2) funds raised in capital markets by borrowing on the security of reserves and callable capital; and 3) special funds. In general, the last two types are resources which a bank attracts from outside the region for use in developing member countries. A bank's success in acquiring such resources reflects its ability to provide additional capital to the region and determines the extent to which it can wield politico-economic leverage in promoting regional cooperation and economic integration.

Mobilization of finance by the regional development banks has brought about joint cooperative action by member countries. The subscribed capital, through its paid-in portion, makes possible the joint use of capital subscribed by individual members. The callable portion of members' subscriptions is payable to the bank in gold or convertible currency if needed to meet bank liabilities on borrowings or guarantees for ordinary operations. The pooling of callable capital enables the banks to offer greater security than that which can generally be offered by any individual developing country. This greater security through joint action attracts more lenders, both from within and outside the region.

The regional development banks are limited in their borrowings by that portion of their callable capital which is fully available and acceptable to potential lenders. The Inter-American Development Bank has made a commitment to lenders not to let its total funded debt rise above the uncalled portion of the United States subscription. In April 1967, when the Board of Governors held its annual meeting in Washington, the Governors voted to increase authorized capital by $1 billion without requiring additional paid-in capital from subscribing members.[10] Subscription to this increase by the United States would increase the Inter-American Development Bank's United States callable capital to over $1 billion out of a total authorized capital of $3,150 million.

On January 17, 1967, the Inter-American Development Bank floated a public offering in the United States of $50 million, 25-year bonds, paying 5.2 percent interest. No Latin country—not even Mexico—could command such favorable conditions or interest. This bond issue was the fourth sold by the Bank in the United States capital market and brought the Bank's total bond sales in that market to $275 million. The Bank has also borrowed or arranged to borrow a total of over $200 million in capital markets outside the United States.

The World Bank and the Asian Development Bank have the advantage of counting among their members all the major countries where sizable borrowing operations are feasible. Callable capital subscriptions (as distinct from subscribed capital) providing adequate security for the Asian Development Bank include $100 million by the United States and $100 million by Japan, $75 million by other developed countries outside the region, and over $53 million by Australia and New Zealand.[11]

The African Development Bank will have to establish its credit standing through its record of operations over a period of years because its

[10] All members must pay in a portion of their capital subscriptions. In 1967 the first member of the British Commonwealth, Trinidad and Tobago, met the prerequisite of becoming a member of the Organization of American States (OAS) and joined IDB. This comes as a result of a major OAS concession: permission for members to receive trade preferences from outside the region.

[11] Total capital subscriptions were double the callable amount for the United States and Japan.

callable capital is wholly African-subscribed. The European Investment Bank borrows on the guarantee of $750 million callable capital from its six members, and its charter allows borrowing up to 250 percent of this amount.

The Inter-American, the African, and the Asian Development Banks must negotiate step-by-step to overcome a number of handicaps, including imposition of taxes on the issuance of securities by European national and local governments. The bonds of the Inter-American Development Bank have been made eligible for trust investments in the United Kingdom. In the United States federal legislation has been passed in order to make Inter-American Development Bank securities eligible for investment by national commercial banks. The Treasury has ruled the bonds eligible to serve as guarantee for United States government deposits with commercial banks. Legislation has also been enacted in a number of major states making the bonds eligible for purchase by financial institutions which are subject to state regulations. Thus, in the United States, a member country, the Inter-American Development Bank had to obtain, first, federal legislation, then, an executive ruling by the Secretary of the Treasury, and, finally, special legislation by a number of important states in order to be successful on the American capital market.

The World Bank and others have found that the world capital market cannot under its present structure absorb massive additional issues for development purposes, even with government guarantees. It may, therefore, be asked whether there is too much reliance upon flotation in the public markets; perhaps more issues could be better sold through direct placements. In some cases the placements would provide a major saving by reducing registration, underwriting, and management costs.

Whenever capital market conditions ease up, there is a backlog of so-called high-quality issues to be taken up, e.g., top United States corporate obligations (which sometimes include the advantage of a convertible feature, thus adding a speculative promise to financial security) or bonds of developed countries. As the market becomes easier for such issues, it does not necessarily become easier for issues of a less attractive financial character.

In his United Nations report[12] the writer made a case for the use of financing by central banks and public or semipublic agencies as lenders to regional development banks for ordinary resources. Reference was made to the World Bank which for a number of years has been placing

---

[12] See "Regional Development Financing," by Henry S. Bloch, in cooperation with the Fiscal and Financial Branch of the Department of Economic and Social Affairs, United Nations Conference on Trade and Development, February 9, 1966 (UN Document TD/B/AC.4/R.3); and Henry S. Bloch, *Le Financement Régional et le Développement de l'Amérique Latine* (No. 315) (Brussels: Société Royale d'Economie Politique de Belgique, March 1966).

short-term and longer-term notes with central banks. Since publication of that report the Inter-American Development Bank has demonstrated that it is able to obtain such financing, and there is no reason why the Asian and African Development Banks should not also be able to use this method.

The World Bank has regularly placed two-year, and sometimes longer, notes and bonds with central banks. These funds have regularly been rolled over as the notes and bonds matured by replacing them wherever central banks have a surplus of dollars. The Bundesbank of West Germany has been a major purchaser. These placements furnish IBRD with financial resources which, when combined with long-term borrowings, do not present too great a reliance on short-term funds for long-term investments. The potential of this technique is illustrated by the March 1967 placement of $100 million, two-year notes, with 43 countries and the United Nations. The 43 countries included a wide variety of developed and developing nations, among them the Republic of Vietnam (South Vietnam), Ghana, Libya, Morocco, and France.[13]

The Inter-American Development Bank has begun to use the same method. On April 15, 1966, it sold an issue of $65 million in short-term bonds. Of these $25 million were 5 percent, one-year bonds; $29 million were $5\frac{1}{8}$ percent, two-year bonds; and $11 million were $5\frac{1}{4}$ percent, five-year bonds. A total of $57 million of the issue was sold to central banks or other governmental financial agencies in fifteen of the Bank's Latin American member countries. The remaining $8 million was sold to governmental entities in Spain and Israel. Again, on April 18, 1967, the Inter-American Development Bank directly placed $30 million more short-term bonds with central banks and government financial agencies in fourteen of its Latin member countries. This second direct placement with governments consisted of $16 million in one-year bonds, yielding 5 percent, and $14 million in two-year bonds, paying $5\frac{1}{8}$ percent.

Let us look briefly at a third type of financial resources for regional banks, namely, special funds. These special funds are comparable to IDA funds: Because they are used for loans on soft terms the regional development banks must depend upon government contributions to obtain them. However, unlike IDA, the regional banks may accept special funds which are tied to purchases in the contributing country. In addition, these special funds may be administered in a manner quite different from IDA which grants interest-free loans (with a service charge) only to those countries which meet "national need tests."

The Inter-American Development Bank's Fund for Special Operations

[13] For details see Press Release 67/10, March 6, 1967, of the International Bank for Reconstruction and Development.

and the Social Progress Trust Fund[14] are administered separately from ordinary resources (capital contributions and borrowings). Both funds are principally financed by the United States and are distributed on a soft-loan basis. In the case of the soft loans granted by the Inter-American Development Bank's special funds interest rates vary depending upon whether the funds are used to serve economic or social development. A national need test is not applied. Similar so-called "special funds" are planned for the Asian and the African Development Banks.[15]

PROSPECTS AND PROPOSALS

If the political and economic prerequisites are fulfilled, the regional development banks can play a major role in the financing of economic integration. Development financing institutions have evolutionary capacity; they can spawn subsidiaries, create affiliates, and amend their charters. For financial institutions generally the administrative structure is of lesser significance in the decisionmaking process than for central government authorities. There is an "open form" approach to the administration of such institutions rather than a rigidly predetermined pattern.

Most important, however, financial institutions, national as well as international, are endowed with a high degree of self-determination. Just as central banks, the International Monetary Fund (IMF), and the Bank for International Settlements (BIS) have lives of their own, so the international development financing institutions possess technical independence—though not political independence—from government machineries. Like the voting blocs in the International Monetary Fund they are relatively stable and often continue to function quite satisfactorily while political tension exists between members. Development financing organizations have in many ways proved themselves factors of unity not only in declarations but also in political actions. Governments which have no diplomatic relations with each other may, for example, cooperate in a regional development bank.

The executive directors of these development banking institutions are in practice the final authorities on the interpretation of the charters or articles of agreement. They can, therefore, allow these institutions to reinterpret their terms of reference as conditions change.

If the regional development banks can fulfill their task as banks for integration, they will acquire an importance far beyond that which their

[14] The Social Progress Trust Fund is almost totally depleted, and in large part its activities are being assumed by the Fund for Special Operations.

[15] Creation of a multimillion-dollar agricultural fund under the management of the Asian Development Bank was approved by the second ministerial conference on Asian economic development, held in Manila on April 27–29, 1967.

founders had imputed to them. If they prove too weak financially (which is not likely to be the case with the Inter-American and the Asian Development Banks but is a certain danger with the African Development Bank), other institutions will have to bridge the gaps. In any case, the regional development banks, to function as true banks, must rely to a considerable extent on use of finance beyond their own capital and earnings.

Regional economic integration may proceed by development of subregional economic communities. The classic example is the Central American Common Market which is served by CABEI. If this Central American Common Market is to continue on its path toward stronger economic integration of its member states, the evolution must be facilitated by continued close cooperation with the Inter-American Development Bank. In Africa subregional associations have shown a tendency to rise and fall because they are not strong enough to survive political crises on their own. The success of subregional groups depends upon the availability of a reservoir of crisis support from larger regional institutions. The reemergence of the East African Common Market is a case in point. The new impetus for subregional economic development in East Africa, though it may be short-lived, is due to a farsighted gesture of the African Development Bank, responding to an initiative by the government of Kenya. If Southeast Asia is to have the benefits of economic integration, it will be through massive injections of capital and, most likely, with the strong support of the Asian Development Bank, either as a supplier of finance or as a magnet for and manager of external contributions.

The regional development banks will be ineffective if they are not able to tap considerable funds in North America and Europe. The Inter-American Development Bank has shown the way in the use of supplier relationships to obtain external financing, to achieve direct placements, and even to enter capital markets. However, regional development banks must not be dependent on underwriting syndicates and the use of private capital markets because their demands are too great and the motive for their financing activities is frequently too political for the strictly commercial type of national or international underwriting. This, of course, is true only within limits; certainly, callable capital can serve as a guarantee and provide leverage for some publicly underwritten private loans. Nevertheless, the relending of these resources only on commercial terms cannot meet the requirements of the regions. As this limitation is slowly being recognized, some of the ideas on interest subsidization, so brilliantly advocated by the Governor of the Bank of Israel, David Horowitz, have elicited a great deal of attention. The basic concept of interest subsidization, already effective in various national schemes, may eventually become applicable in some form on regional scales.[16]

Recent years have shown a very interesting trend toward use by the World Bank and the Inter-American Development Bank of short-term placements with central banks, which help improve maturity schedules and provide a bridge for short-term needs. There are other governmental and semigovernmental financial institutions holding substantial resources which could release limited assets for purposes justifiable in politico- and socioeconomic terms, below market terms, though not as contributions *à fonds perdu.*

As the capital market is presently organized, there are severe limitations to the methods of bond sales, and only very limited sources of finance are being tapped even by governments of developed countries. The underwriting syndicates have been widened in recent years, and there has been a resurgence of large transatlantic selling syndicates. Unfortunately, these impressive groups have taken up only miniature amounts compared to the needs of the developing countries. At the beginning of 1967 the World Bank had a funded debt of only $3 billion and callable capital of over $20 billion, $5.7 billion of which was callable from the United States. Thus, the security ceiling of callable capital is somewhat academic as market conditions do not allow massive use of even the highest quality borrowing power.

Two methods to improve the situation are suggested: one relatively modest and one requiring a more innovative approach. The modest proposal envisions better access to capital markets by agreements negotiated between the regional development banks and nonmember capital-exporting countries; by obtaining special tax and regulatory exemptions; by qualifying as legal investments in fiduciary situations, and by a more flexible approach to distribution techniques, including direct placements with governmental financial institutions of supplier countries. In this connection it might be useful to recall the earlier efforts of the "blue-chip" World Bank. In Switzerland, a nonmember country, the World Bank had to conclude a special agreement to obtain a legal status facilitating the issuance of securities. In many ways this agreement with Switzerland can be considered a model of the arrangement which the regional development banks should negotiate with nonmember capital exporters.

A more ambitious method is a coordinated institutionalized approach by the developed countries toward direct lending to the regional development banks, as well as toward assistance in the placement of the banks' bonds. Coordination of lending could be accomplished through the cen-

---

[16] On the Horowitz Plan see the essay by Roy Blough in this volume. See also UNCTAD and IBRD documentation on the subject.

tral banks of developed countries. Regional development banks could issue bonds to governmental financial institutions.[17] These might be special, nonmarketable issues which could only be negotiated between governments. Such bonds would be held to redemption, removed from the fluctuations of the capital markets. The feature permitting transfer between governments would give them a reserve attribute which would increase their appeal, allow developed countries to adjust to reserve fluctuations, and provide a consistent source of finance for the development banks at a low rate of interest. In addition central banks could improve and coordinate public flotations. To assist in sales of marketable securities the central banks of developed countries should be given explicit power to conduct open-market operations with the public securities of the regional development banks. This would support the market and increase their attractiveness to investors; the regional development banks would obtain greater amounts at less cost.

Major developed countries are already members of the Asian Development Bank, the United States is a member of the Inter-American Development Bank, a number of other developed countries are participants in specific financing of Inter-American Development Bank projects, and developed countries may be expected to provide resources also to the African Development Bank. Therefore, future borrowing by these institutions should be coordinated. Such coordination is vital for the regional development banks if they are to have sufficient and dependable financial resources to promote regional cooperation and economic integration.

The purchase of nonmarketable securities and open-market operations in public issues can maintain a steady flow of additional resources to the regional development banks without subjecting them to dependency upon periodic authorizations and appropriations by legislative bodies. At present the central banks of most capital-exporting countries control or influence the amount and number of foreign flotations on their capital markets. It would be highly beneficial to the regional development banks if these controls were coordinated through institutionalized cooperation between central banks.

The regional development banks have the arduous task of establishing themselves as financial institutions in order to tackle the complex duties imposed upon them by their member countries. There is great danger in competition for funds by the regional institutions. Eventually, this competition will make itself felt, and there is realization that regional financing without global coordination and global approaches could become self-defeating. Indeed, regional development banks have the possibility of changing the financial map of the developing world.

[17] See Bloch, *Regional Development Financing,* and Bloch, *Le Financement Régional et le Développement de l'Amérique Latine.*

Multilateral Technical Assistance

TECHNICAL assistance remains a poorly under-
stood tool for promoting development. Programs continue to grow, but
persistent questions are raised about their effectiveness by practitioners
and academic observers. Today's uncertainty contrasts dramatically with
the exuberance which attended the launching of two landmark technical
assistance programs, the Point Four Program of the United States and the
Expanded Program of Technical Assistance (EPTA) of the United
Nations.

Disillusionment may be the beginning of wisdom, however. An increased awareness of the obscurities of technical assistance and a growing
sense that knowledge and ideas cannot be quickly—or usefully—transferred across cultural and societal boundaries can bring a more realistic
understanding of the art. Those concerned with technical assistance will
need to be patient as well as persevering. More thought must be given
to purposes. Experimentation, evaluation, and research must be strengthened. Only gradually will we be able to improve our grasp of the diverse
ways whereby intangibles can be adopted by one society from another.

This brief study on multilateral assistance is set in such an experimental
context. No definitive course for multilateral technical assistance will be
charted in the next few pages. The essay will suggest first how vast
and vague the concept of technical assistance is. It will then review the
history of the major UN programs, the Expanded Program of Technical
Assistance and the Special Fund, which have now been merged into the
UN Development Program (UNDP). These quite different endeavors
illustrate how diverse technical assistance programs can be. After this
beginning an effort will then be made to select trends for multilateral
technical assistance, with particular attention being paid to the predilec-
tions of bilateral donors which dominate technical assistance work.

KARL MATHIASEN III, formerly a senior staff member at The Brookings Institution, is Executive
Director of the University of North Africa Association in Washington, D.C.

Finally, a plea for continuing open-mindedness, for diversity of means, and for further experimentation—a persistent theme throughout these pages—will be discussed more directly.

Other programs might have served as examples of multilateral technical assistance. The International Bank for Reconstruction and Development (IBRD) recently has stimulated new technical assistance activities in agriculture and education. With the help of the United Nations Educational, Scientific and Cultural Organization (UNESCO) and the Food and Agriculture Organization (FAO) the Bank hopes to increase the number of project opportunities and to improve the execution of major investment projects. Regional programs of technical assistance, like those supported by the Organization of American States (OAS), have achieved notable successes, even while depending primarily on one source of funds.

But UNDP, comprised of two important and long-standing program elements, is devoted exclusively to technical assistance and preinvestment. While the United States supplies nearly 40 percent of the resources for the program, other donors and recipients as well exercise influence on its policies. UNDP now finances 80 percent of the technical assistance which the UN and the specialized agencies undertake, and it continues to grow both in scope and in size. UNDP epitomizes both the problems which beset multilateral institutions charged with program administration and the unique opportunities open to them.

THE SCOPE OF TECHNICAL ASSISTANCE

What is meant by technical assistance, what common assumptions underlie its purposes and programs? A useful description was approved by the Twelfth International Congress of the International Institute of Administrative Sciences in Vienna in July of 1962:

> Technical assistance consists in the transmission of learning, knowledge, and techniques or material and human resources in order to help those who receive it to solve specific problems in a more suitable manner in keeping with their needs. It is an external contribution which assumes a very wide variety of forms: visits of experts and technicians, receiving fellowship holders, organizing courses and seminars, exchanging or disseminating information or documents, and supplying material and equipment, and occasionally financial means.[1]

As Sidney C. Sufrin points out in citing this definition in *Technical Assistance—Theory and Guide Lines,* the stress is "on knowledge and

[1] *Technical Assistance in Public Administration: Lessons of Experience and Possible Improvements* (Vienna: International Institute of Administrative Sciences [Twelfth International Congress], July 1962), p. 12, quoted in Sidney C. Sufrin, *Technical Assistance—Theory and Guide Lines* (Syracuse, N.Y: Syracuse University Press, December 1966), p. 44.

information, with material and financing being of secondary importance."[2] John H. Ohly of the United States Agency for International
Development (AID) emphasized this point even more strongly in an
internal paper used by AID for orientation purposes. He stressed that the
results of technical assistance

> are always in the first instance intangible, rather than tangible, changes
> in the character of the receiving society and its people—new methods of
> thinking, altered work habits, a higher level of popular knowledge, im-
> proved skills, the availability of more information, the acquisition of dif-
> ferent values, new or improved governmental and non-governmental
> organizations, and other transitions in the society's general process of
> operation . . . the transfer of intangibles from a person in one society to a
> person in another society, and the effective use thereof by the transferee,
> are the core of the process.[3]

Little wonder, then, that so few attempts are made to state theories of
technical assistance and that these often imprecise, preliminary statements
offer little guidance to technical assistance operators.

The results of technical assistance are often as unanticipated as they
are intangible. The criteria for measuring success or failure still elude
us. When closely examined, many apparent successes or failures yield
contradictory evidence. A strong case might be made that all projects
succeed in some ways and fail in others. After analyzing a large number
of technical assistance projects of different agencies qualified observers
have not been able to identify individual elements or clusters of factors
which were present in all of the more successful cases and absent in the
less successful ones.

An analogy can perhaps be drawn to the field of education where arguments still rage about the best and most useful techniques of teaching or,
to be more accurate, for helping others to learn. In technical assistance
and in education we are in the early stages of experimentation and understanding. In both we now appreciate that no single technique will suffice
to transmit ideas to highly varied populations. Technical assistance agencies, like schools, must employ a variety of approaches to succeed in their
multifaceted ventures.

The lack of a scientific approach to technical assistance not only makes
measurement and evaluation distressingly difficult but also challenges
the skill and the patience of the most astute administrators. Regrettably,
the ambiguity of technical assistance tempts practitioners to devise highly
personalized approaches and prompts the development of hasty program

[2] Sufrin, p. 45.
[3] John H. Ohly, "Human Resources, Institutions and Technical Assistance," in *Orientation
Handbook* (Agency for International Development) (Washington: United States Government
Printing Office, 1964 [revised 1965, 1966]), Unit II, p. 22.

philosophies. Clearly, agencies must do a better job of evaluating their actions and admitting their inadequacies. Equally as clearly, agencies' enthusiasms for their particular approaches must be restrained. It is only logical to assume that in different countries, with widely diverse values and perceptions of need, responses to recipients' requests for aid also must vary.

With the passage of time two persistent themes have tended to dominate technical assistance: institution building and human resource development. Donors have learned the hard way that the cultural and value changes technical assistance seeks may prove evanescent unless they are institutionalized in the local setting. If no local institutions exist to which new concepts of change can be grafted, donors have sought to stimulate the growth of innovative institutions capable of keeping the change process reinvigorated. Donors also attach increasing importance to human resource development and emphasize education and training to create a fertile ground for sowing the seeds of change. All countries from the least to the most advanced require more, and more specialized, people to undertake the new tasks which accompany growth and change.

Institution building and human resource development offer no magic nor great promise of success, however, for technical assistance ventures. They do serve to emphasize the long-range nature of technical assistance by stressing the importance of institutionalizing change and developing people who can stimulate change in receiving societies.

Those who suggest that carefully designed institution-building and human resource development programs satisfy the wide variety of requirements for technical assistance are oversimplifying in their haste to lend certainty to the practice of technical assistance. Massive training efforts are needed in many fields and at a variety of levels. These diverse educational activities may be quite scattered and may not contribute to the growth of institutions over the short term. Technical assistance advisers and operators are needed by recipient countries to perform a range of experimental and communication activities which may never have institutional dimensions.

It is not surprising, then, that the means chosen by technical assistance agencies are now almost as varied and numerous as the goals sought. Technical assistance activities encompass multimillion dollar ventures like the United States project designed to produce a land-grant college in an African country. As many as 30 American technicians will be needed each year for fifteen to twenty years, and the recipient must supply personnel and extensive monetary support. Technical assistance also encompasses a $20,000 UN project which simply provides one International Labor Organization (ILO) adviser to a Central American country for twelve months. Another sends students from a Central African country abroad for general training at a cost of $40,000 over several years. Projects also finance the purchase of trucks and cars to transport advisers, training aids to assist them in their demonstrations, and agricultural tools to provide initial supplies for innovators and entrepreneurs. Technical assistance includes, as well, the seconding of French and United Kingdom citizens to teach in local schools or to perform tasks for struggling new government bureaucracies. If the United States Peace Corps and other volunteer programs are included, the range of means and activities becomes even more extensive.

The apparent proliferation of technical assistance efforts and people is particularly bothersome, however, to major donors like the United States. The policies of UN agencies, their small and scattered projects, are singled out again and again for criticism. Unhappily, the roots of the United States' concern appear to be the growth of UN budgets and the UN's increased multilateralism rather than any sense that UN projects do not serve the purposes of UN technical assistance.

Multilateral Technical Assistance

What might be appropriate tasks for multilateral technical assistance agencies? Multilateral technical assistance is increasing in size and its future seems assured, but it probably will not dominate the technical assistance field. While popular with recipients, donors evince more enthusiasm for bilateral programs, and these conflicting desires and pressures will keep both channels in use.

Each of the technical assistance agencies—bilateral or multilateral—has the competence to conduct a limited range of activities, and the selection of activities should reflect its purposes and attributes. Unfortunately, this has not always been the case. Few suggestions, for example, have been advanced for increasing the complementarity of bilateral and multilateral programs, yet such proposals are badly needed. Some clues to the strengths and weaknesses of multilateral technical assistance can be found by a brief look at the history of EPTA and the Special Fund.

The Expanded Program of Technical Assistance

A review of EPTA, prepared for the fifteenth anniversary of the Program, characterized it as follows:

> For the Expanded Programme is the sum of a very large number of individual endeavours, most typically personified by the Asian or African trainee setting out alone for a fellowship course in Europe or America; the irrigation engineer from Australia surveying a river basin in Latin America

with a handful of local assistants; the accounting officer from India training a group of accountants in an African ministry. Even where the expert works as a member of a team representing different disciplines required for the same project, the characteristics of individual endeavour and person-to-person assistance or exchange of knowledge prevail.[4]

This paragraph conveys the essence of the Expanded Program of Technical Assistance. It also sets the scene for much of the discussion about the quality of UN technical assistance. The individual nature of EPTA's enterprises, the extensiveness and thinness of 1,500 projects in more than 130 countries and territories, raises eyebrows. In addition, the lack of agreed emphasis on selected fields, sectors, or types of programs opens the Program to criticism. While to its proponents the virtue of EPTA-type assistance lies in its responsiveness to the varied desires of recipients, to its critics it seems scattered, unprogrammed, uncoordinated, and thus limited in both impact and value.

The History and Growth of EPTA

The Expanded Program of Technical Assistance, established by the UN General Assembly in 1949, recognized that some specialized agencies already were conducting technical assistance programs. Their executive heads were appointed to a Technical Assistance Board (TAB) to manage EPTA, and the Secretary-General subsequently was empowered to select an Executive Chairman for TAB.

A Technical Assistance Committee (TAC) comprised of country members approved, with limited review, TAB's recommendations and, subject to the approval of the Economic and Social Council (ECOSOC) and the General Assembly, authorized the allocation of funds to the "participating organizations," i.e., the specialized agencies and the UN itself, which carry out technical assistance in public administration, economics, etc. Although this system of allocating EPTA resources was changed later so that funds were distributed on a country-by-country rather than on an agency-by-agency basis, the specialized agencies wielded considerable authority over the design of the EPTA program until it was merged with the Special Fund in 1966, as described below.

ECOSOC did lay certain restrictions upon the agencies which restrained them from economic and political interference in the internal affairs of the recipient countries. UN technical assistance was to be given only to, or through, governments and in the form desired by each country, and the participating organizations were to "avoid distinctions arising from the political structure of the country requesting assistance, or from the race or religion of its population."[5]

[4] UN Document E/TAC/153, pp. 72–73.
[5] ECOSOC Resolution 222 A (IX), August 15, 1949, Annex I.

As for the recipients, each country decided for itself if it was eligible for assistance. Neither EPTA management nor UN governing bodies attempted to define a "developing country" as opposed to a "developed" one, and some observers have questioned this restraint. Aside from the difficulty of agreeing on criteria, however, the Expanded Program was conceived as a pooling and sharing of resources. No country, even the most developed, was to be excluded. Countries such as Greece, Israel, Lebanon, Portugal, the Republic of China (Nationalist China), Saudi Arabia, and Venezuela were still net recipients of EPTA aid when the Program was merged with the Special Fund. That is, their contributions to EPTA did not match the aid they received. Only Japan has changed its status from net recipient to net donor, though it still receives EPTA aid. Finland, Italy, and Luxembourg are apparently the only three countries which ever relied on EPTA, later terminated their requests for aid, then continued solely as donors.

The picture which emerges is a perplexing one, particularly for Americans. We consider aid appropriate only for poor countries and, conversely, urge developed nations to share the aid burden. Continuing increases in the biennial program figures for such countries as Yugoslavia and Venezuela, for example, and the substantial programs still being undertaken in Israel and Lebanon inevitably raise questions about the UN's criteria for distributing the extremely limited resources available to it.

Program Emphases

As pointed out above, it is difficult to delineate clear program emphases which have characterized EPTA at various stages in its history. During the first years of EPTA survey and advisory missions tended to predominate, providing appraisals of the extent and nature of recipients' problems and resources. Some countries still request EPTA survey missions to reassess their progress, but the proportion of funds for surveys has declined in part because of the increased survey activities of other programs like the Special Fund.

There were equal numbers of fellows and experts during the first fifteen years of EPTA, approximately 30,000 in each category, but more than three-quarters of total EPTA expenditures were for experts' services and for equipment they needed. The substantial proportion of EPTA resources devoted to the provision of experts reflected the nature of countries' requests, their ideas of the function and purpose of EPTA, and the substantial number of training opportunities offered by the other aid programs. Moreover, the UN, like most donors, preferred and prefers to train nationals in their own countries. Local training programs have been emphasized both by the Expanded Program and, as will be seen later, by the UN Special Fund.

Personal observation, as well as the limited size and duration of EPTA projects, leads one to conclude that EPTA has not emphasized "institution building" as much as technical assistance agencies like AID and the Special Fund have. Since the Fund's creation EPTA projects have investigated, laid the groundwork for, or strengthened institutions. Some of these EPTA efforts resulted in Special Fund institution-building projects.

The EPTA element of UNDP continues to be typified by relatively small, short-term, practical projects directed at targets of opportunity, often without any apparent or consistent thread running through them. In this respect, although the term "gap filling" has become one of opprobrium in the lexicon of technical assistance agencies, EPTA personnel often describe their task as filling the gaps left by other donors or carrying out the technical assistance tasks others do not wish to undertake.

EPTA has always demonstrated a heavy if disconcerting reliance on the capacity of each receiving country to define its priorities and to request the kinds of assistance it needs. In the least developed countries, where UNDP activities are concentrated, government machinery is weak and often unequal to the tasks of formulating priorities and coordinating aid. As a consequence, TAB and now UNDP assign Resident Representatives to those countries receiving significant amounts of UN assistance. Their purpose is to provide stronger UN leadership and more continuous central guidance in the field.

In ideal circumstances an increasingly sensible and meaningful dialogue should occur between the Resident Representative speaking for the United Nations agencies and the host country development coordinator expressing the priority needs of his ministries. Where host country coordination is weak, however, the Resident Representative has little authority to exert effective control or to restrain members of the UN family. In these cases he must plead both with the host country government to develop and maintain its priorities and with his own family of agencies not to "sell" projects but to respond to the country's expressed needs.

Staff review of country EPTA programs both in the field and at headquarters has been little more than cursory. Technical problems are reviewed as well as problems of feasibility, cost, and adequacy of project description. But there is still no rigorous testing of EPTA-type projects against any previously agreed set of national priorities or program criteria.

Perhaps EPTA evidenced a tendency to make a virtue of necessity, for the specialized agencies were unwilling to accept preordained programming priorities. But the EPTA staff exhibited as well as important sense of restraint and an unwillingness to push preconceived notions of development priorities. Assuming that responsibility for preparing EPTA

project proposals must rest with the country, the Resident Representatives tried to respond wherever possible to country requests.

EPTA-type resources are still more "scattered" than in cases where aid
resources are "programmed" by the donor. Bilateral donors usually make
clear their preferences for particular substantive fields or specific kinds
of projects. They may even recommend or suggest projects if requests
are not forthcoming or if requests are not for the "right kinds" of activity.
This more assertive approach does not characterize EPTA operations.

EPTA resources are distributed among countries in accordance with
country targets, not in response to specific requests. The method by which
country targets are established has a rather mystical quality about it.
According to the fifteenth anniversary report on EPTA the country
target is

> the notional total of EPTA funds which, on best existing estimates, are
> likely to be available to help meet the country's basic assistance requirements
> in the two-year programme period. . . . [The target is] fixed partly on the
> basis of assistance projects already under way; . . . partly in the light . . .
> of the country's general needs and capacity and its particular requirements
> for new kinds of assistance; and partly according to the concern of the
> Executive Chairman for considerations of equity, as well as efficiency, in
> the proposed allocation of funds.[6]

Both the militancy of the specialized agencies and the political influence of the recipients have helped maintain the country target pattern.
The agencies feel that they have a major stake in maintaining their portion of EPTA resources, particularly as they have increased their staffs
substantially to assist in the implementation of EPTA activities. The
recipients have wanted to be assured of a share of these resources since
they could program their use with a minimum of donor interference.
They have resisted any marked increases for particular countries or regions.

The rather permissive relationships between the specialized agencies,
the recipient, and the Resident Representative elicited some frank comments in the EPTA report:

> In the worst of circumstances—now rarely encountered as the priority-
> making machinery of Governments has improved—visitors from the agen-
> cies will have operated with insufficient knowledge of or regard for the
> country's over-all priorities and for the accepted co-ordinating function of
> the Resident Representative. Thus they may have stimulated ministries to
> ask for the continuation or institution of projects whose importance or
> urgency would seem doubtful in any systematic assessment of the country's
> real needs. This kind of thing happens without ulterior motives: technical

<hr>

[6] UN Document E/TAC/153/Rev.1, p. 73.

assistance is so largely an enterprise of as well as for human beings that if it continues to sustain some doubtful undertakings and even some "pet projects" this seems more often than not the result of well-meant enthusiasm and idealism.[7]

In this circumstance meaningful initiative for coordinated programming of EPTA-type resources must come from the host government. Unless these governments have the capacity to formulate and adhere to their own priorities, the specialized agencies—and other donors as well—will largely determine the pattern of external resource allocations. The UNDP Resident Representative is not likely to be provided with the specific guidance, the authority, or the staff to force a program mold either on the specialized agencies or on the recipient country.

THE SPECIAL FUND

The United Nations Special Fund departed significantly from the philosophy of EPTA. The Special Fund was established to accomplish a number of priority tasks. It distinctly was not to respond to any and all requests from the recipient governments. Yet, in a more general sense, the Fund has been both responsive and extremely creative.

From the beginning the Special Fund stressed projects which would lead to early results, seeking to hasten capital investment by carrying technical assistance into the preinvestment sphere. Large projects, averaging $1.5 million in cost, were emphasized, apparently on the assumption that other organizations would pick up small projects. Interest in projects lasting less than four or five years was limited. The Special Fund laid particular emphasis on procedures designed to assure that projects were well planned, adequately and technically organized, and sufficiently financed. Similarly, projects had to be integrated into national development programs if such existed. Special Fund assistance might have been marginal, but the staff hoped it could be decisive in stimulating investment.

The requirements for substantial host government participation and financial contributions, while flexible, were never waived, as they occasionally were in the history of EPTA. Provisions for host country follow-up had to be clearly stated, and the relationship of this activity to the activities of other donors had to be clearly specified. To quote a Special Fund guideline, projects

> should respond to certain basic criteria such as the early applicability of
> projected results, a substantive advance in relation to prior knowledge, the
> building up of a satisfactory institutional framework for the continuation

[7] UN Document E/TAC/153, pp. 77–78.

by the government of the work undertaken during the "partnership period," and should also have a positive impact on the government's investment policy.[8]

From the beginning of the Program surveys, training, and research were the three areas selected for emphasis. Briefly, activities were required to meet one of the following three sets of criteria:

1) Surveys were to aim at prompt investment or increased productivity, and general reconnaissance surveys were not usually supported. To assure adequate technical services for a survey project the Special Fund occasionally entertained a request for technician training or, alternatively, used the program for the provision of Operational, Executive, and Administrative Personnel (OPEX) to provide required personnel.

2) Training projects were to be of a technical nature with an identifiable relationship to economic development. The training of instructors, foremen, and other supervisory personnel, as well as engineers and others directly involved in production, received emphasis. The Special Fund, like most donors, averred that "the training of trainers" was likely to have optimum impact in assisting developing countries. While the Special Fund preferred to help establish institutions designed to meet long-range basic needs, it accepted requests for emergency programs even if standards had to be relaxed and training courses accelerated to provide urgently required personnel. In general, the Special Fund sought training programs which could be incorporated into larger institutions.

3) Research projects were to be of an applied research nature though basic research projects were open for consideration if it was clear that they led to applied research activities and early application. Research activities were required to provide adequate opportunities for demonstration and dissemination of the findings of the research undertaken. Training of national personnel was to be included in these projects, and projects were to be selected only if there was a clear prospect of technical breakthrough in a chosen field.

In 1965, for instance, there were 522 Special Fund projects as compared with 2,000 EPTA projects in 130 low-income countries and territories. The total cost of the projects was $1,151 million, of which the recipient governments paid $673 million and the Special Fund contributed $478 million. The Special Fund component was financed through contributions pledged by 115 countries. Of the total number of projects 223 were resource surveys and feasibility studies, 195 were devoted primarily to training in specialized fields, and 104 emphasized applied research.

Through 1965 nearly 43 percent of the Fund's resources had been expended to supply international experts, and almost 14 percent had been

[8] UN Document SF/PGL/S, p. 4.

used to obtain contractual services. Imported equipment utilized another 28 percent of the Special Fund's availabilities while fellowships accounted for less than 3 percent. The remaining 12 percent of the funds expended by 1966 was used to cover both direct costs to the Special Fund and agency overhead costs. The funds provided by recipient governments were utilized to cover the cost of local project personnel, buildings, and facilities, and local equipment, supplies, and services.

By the end of 1965 it was claimed that follow-up investments in Special Fund projects amounted to $1,068 million, of which $751 million was foreign investment. The cost to the Special Fund of the 25 projects which "produced" these investments was estimated at $19.2 million. Obviously, it is a moot question whether investment interest preceded or followed the surveys.

Ambitious for an even greater investment response to Special Fund activities, the staff recommended new ventures to the Governing Council of UNDP in January 1966 to stimulate new investment activity. Pilot or demonstration plants were recommended for financing, on a reimbursable basis where necessary. A pyrethrum plant was proposed for Rwanda, with earnings from the plant to be used in that country to develop other industrial operations. A potassium salt project was recommended for Poland under similar arrangements. A third project proposed funding of the final engineering designs for a railroad in Gabon. In this case, if investment did occur, the Special Fund was to be repaid. In addition to these new ventures the Special Fund staff proposed new projects in work-oriented adult literacy projects, a research and training program in community development, and the expansion of the Latin American Demographic Center.

The relationship between EPTA and the Special Fund activities in those 130 countries where both operate is growing stronger. Not only have EPTA experts assisted host country governments in preparing requests for the Special Fund, but they have also helped in some cases after the Special Fund has ended its support, providing advice and guidance for an additional period of time. Both areas of relationship, preproject and postproject, can be expected to receive more attention in the merged UNDP.

Unlike the Expanded Program of Technical Assistance the number of Special Fund projects in any one country is limited due to the size of the projects and the limited resources available. While the Special Fund estimates that the projects run a total of four or five years in length, they often continue for a total of six or seven years, much longer than the eighteen- to 24-month average life of EPTA projects. The emphasis of the Special Fund on institution building is plain and pronounced.

While agriculture is emphasized by the Special Fund, as well as by EPTA, agricultural projects commanded 40 percent of Special Fund resources as compared with 25 percent of EPTA resources. Education projects were also more important in the Special Fund than in EPTA.

The philosophy of the Special Fund and the management principles that characterized its operation provided some sharp contrasts with those which typified the activities of EPTA. The Managing Director of the Special Fund administered it in a more direct and centralized fashion. While the Council of the Fund established broad policies, he was responsible for their interpretation, for recommending approval of projects, and for selecting the implementing organization. The specialized agencies had less power and influence in the Special Fund than in the Expanded Program of Technical Assistance. The Resident Representative was the "Director" of Special Fund projects in the country and played a key role in the development, negotiation, and administration of Special Fund projects. This was clearly not always the role of the Resident Representative with regard to EPTA projects.

The selection of surveys, training institutions, and research facilities as priority areas was but one reflection of a very clear "donor" philosophy which typified Special Fund operations. As pointed out previously, this tendency was rather assiduously avoided in the Expanded Program.

UNITED NATIONS DEVELOPMENT PROGRAM

In the fall of 1965 the long-discussed merger of EPTA and the Special Fund into the UN Development Program took place. The General Assembly approved the merger with only nine abstentions and without an opposing vote. The merger was termed "a truly significant step" by Secretary-General U Thant, which

reaffirmed one of the basic purposes of the United Nations, and put our world organization in the very front-line of the global war on want—a struggle that is perhaps the most critical of these times, and certainly the most critical in which men ever have engaged themselves.[9]

The terms of the merger call for the continuation of EPTA and Special Fund activities along present lines for at least two years. The programming approaches described above have been retained although a single Governing Council has been created to guide both program elements. The Governing Council is rather large, primarily because the recipient nations were determined to be well represented, and the very size of the Council places much of the leadership and policy responsibility on the Administrator and the Coadministrator, Paul Hoffman and

[9] UN Document ST/SG/SM/396.

David Owen, respectively. The specialized agencies may well have been stripped of some of the influence they managed to retain in EPTA. They are represented on a new Interagency Consultative Board, an advisory body which appears to have less policy influence than TAB had on the Expanded Program.

The imaginative and sensible leadership of Paul Hoffman and David Owen will provide impetus for new departures and for continued experimentation. As indicated above, the Special Fund has already initiated new activities which extend the concept of preinvestment to the very threshold of investment. The Coadministrators will also need to react to pressure for increased amalgamation of the two program elements.

The United States, for example, was an early proponent of the merger as a means of making UN technical assistance more efficient. In 1963 this position was endorsed by an impressive advisory committee convened by the Department of State at the instigation of the Bureau of the Budget. The Advisory Committee on International Organizations, chaired by Sol Linowitz, declared it

> essential . . . that the international agencies themselves simplify and improve the machinery and coordinate more closely their own planning, programming and operations at Headquarters and in the field in order to assure a common approach to the recipient countries and their needs.[10]

Obviously, UNDP offers attractive opportunities for increased efficiency and economy. The headquarters staffs of the two programs have been substantially merged. Over time the terms and conditions for both parts of the program will become more similar. Moreover, an increasingly strong relationship can be expected between the type of experiments and investigations typical of EPTA programs and the preinvestment programs of the Special Fund. There are dangers, however, in extending the merger concept too far. Further experimentation is needed with both EPTA and Special Fund kinds of technical assistance. Efforts to develop criteria common to both could be untimely and harmful. Yet, under continuing pressure from the major donors this may happen all too quickly.

FUNCTIONS OF MULTILATERAL TECHNICAL ASSISTANCE

Given the absence of hard-and-fast criteria for allocating and employing technical assistance resources, how might one conceive of the UNDP role? The selectivity of bilateral donors is a principal factor which must

---

[10] *The Technical Cooperation Programs of the United Nations Assistance* (Department of State Publication, The Report of the Advisory Committee on International Organizations) (Washington: United States Government Printing Office, 1963), p. 9.

be considered. In the first place, bilateral donors allocate resources for political, economic, and development reasons and limit their aid to a selected group of countries. None of the major donors pretends to extend aid evenhandedly to all countries. Each tends to concentrate on countries where it traditionally has played a major role or where it wishes to extend its political or economic influence. The United States, in particular, concentrates aid where it considers its own security to be at stake. While these tendencies are more apparent in the allocation of capital than technical resources, the concentration of French personnel in North and West Africa, British technical aid to Commonwealth and associated countries, and the increasing inclination of the United States to limit technical assistance to Latin America and to countries of South and Southeast Asia are cases in point.

In the second place, bilateral donors quite logically concentrate their limited resources in countries which have the most apparent growth potential. Within the countries selected for attention they usually aid larger, more populous countries which dominate the region, appear to be most stable, and give most promise of rapid economic progress.

Finally, within these selected countries the donors express interest only in particular fields of activity or in certain types of projects. France's interest in education, particularly at the higher levels, and the emphasis of the Federal Republic of Germany (West Germany) on vocational training centers and technical on-the-job training in industry are but two examples. The United States, in addition to its preference for large institution-building projects, makes every effort to program all of its aid in closely relating fields so that its efforts are mutually reinforcing.

In the context of this selectivity the emphases of the Special Fund and EPTA make considerable sense. Impatient with technical assistance surveys which do not really stimulate capital investment, the Fund has moved into the grey area between technical assistance and capital investment to create more opportunities and to force the pace of investment. By maintaining its traditional, responsive stance EPTA also has helped balance the more selective and assertive approach of the bilateral donors. EPTA has continued to finance small, investigatory, and pilot activities.

One hopes that the same imagination applied to the Fund will lead EPTA to experiment more consciously with—and to evaluate more carefully—these experimental, seed efforts which can help develop better project opportunities for all donors, for this experimental role is tremendously important. The new United Nations Institute for Training and Research (UNITAR) might serve as a repository of technical assistance information, analyzing, as well, the value of specific types of experiments in technical assistance to avoid repeating unnecessary mistakes. UNITAR could make the results of these analyses readily and centrally available. Unless other donors—and recipients—are aware of the results of UNDP experiments and investigations, much field work will be repeated unnecessarily.

Multilateral programming and evaluation devices must help keep a reasonable balance in the aid equation by reducing the invidious aspects of the giving and taking of aid. The mutual evaluation activities in the Alliance for Progress show how multilateral institutions can ease the strain inherent in aid relationships by involving both recipients and donors in reviews of development planning and performance. The review of country planning efforts by the "Nine Wise Men" and the subsequent evaluation activities of the Inter-American Committee on the Alliance for Progress (CIAP) are striking innovations. The Committee, comprised of acknowledged development experts from several countries, annually reviews the development performance of Latin American nations. These intensive examinations, often lasting five or six days, help coax countries on to increased effort. The donor avoids being both prosecutor and judge and obtains, as well, useful guidance for increases or decreases in aid. Recipients also become more anxious to improve the quality of their efforts but without the usual feeling of being prodded by an interfering and overbearing donor.

The regional commissions of the United Nations might provide a forum for similar mutual endeavors. Despite past resistance within UN Headquarters to the delegation of programming responsibility to the regional commissions UNDP should seek to strengthen their capacity to review the regional implications of individual projects and to prepare regional or subregional programs. The Governing Council and the Coadministrators may reserve to themselves the final responsibility for project approval, but regional advice on major institution-building, pre-investment, and pilot investment programs can have both short- and long-term benefits. Over the short term UNDP might find it easier to avoid marginal technical assistance investments in response to strong national pressures. Over the long term consultation with the regional commissions can increase their professional standing and their capacity to program development resources directly. Increased emphasis on the Latin American common market and the Economic Commission for Africa's (ECA) efforts to encourage an African free trade union and a common market lend added purpose to a regional approach.

The use of country targets by EPTA for the allocation of resources is another case in point. While "notional" targets arrived at in some mystical way are difficult to accept, UNDP should continue to experiment with the concept of providing resources to recipient countries to be used for development activities of *their* choosing. The psychological importance of such "free" resources should not be underestimated. Even in countries which have achieved acceptable rates of growth it is a delicate and difficult task for recipient and donor to agree on technical assistance priorities. It requires of both a remarkable breadth and capability to exchange views, to communicate needs and concerns, and from these exchanges to develop projects which are feasible, for which the donor has the skills, and which are addressed to needs considered fundamental by the recipient.

For those countries which are farthest removed from the conventional wisdom and standards of the developed countries the capacity to discuss and consider needs with donor agencies is extremely limited. The channels of communication are hazardous, and heavy-handed donor programming can be injurious and become a source of suspicion and resentment. These are the very countries which need technical assistance of all kinds.

Concern about infringements on national sovereignty can be reduced if one agency responds to the recipients' requests without prejudice, assuring them adequate resources to program the priority technical assistance activities they select. Although donors are prone to consider this approach wasteful, there is no proof that donors' criteria are less risky. In any case, no shortcut to learning by trial and error has been devised, and recipients must experience failure if they are ever to succeed in designing viable development projects.

The Coadministrators may develop over time better criteria for allocation of EPTA resources among countries. Perhaps more resources should be allocated to those recipients which receive aid from only one principal donor. In these countries EPTA resources could help alleviate a feeling of complete dependence on one donor's sense of priorities. A good case also can be made for allocating a greater proportion of EPTA resources to the poorest countries and those farthest down on the development potential scale. These countries have extremely limited resources to conduct developmental activities of their own choosing. They are dependent principally on technical assistance for growth and development. Until technical assistance endeavors have helped them formulate new project opportunities and broadened their base for preinvestment and investment activity, they have little opportunity to attract aid from others. Multilateral institutions may have to shoulder heavy burdens in countries where other donors fear to tread.

Other criteria might be used to alter the pattern of EPTA allocations. The continued acceptance of the country target concept, however, is contingent upon Governing Council agreement that the resources thus provided serve a useful purpose. The allocations must be justifiable in development as well as psychological terms.

Individual projects proposed by the recipient, of course, must fall within agreed and reasonable bounds. Clearly, the project must be feasible, i.e., UNDP staff must feel that the proposed project is sensibly planned and can be accomplished. UNDP must also assure itself that the participating agencies or other contractors have the skills and other resources needed to implement the project. The Resident Representative should also ask the receiving country to demonstrate the importance of the request in terms of the recipient's *own* priorities. If the recipient cannot do so or demonstrates a tendency to request unproductive projects year after year, the threat of reduced allocations should be employed. Prior to such actions, however, the Resident Representative should seek every means of strengthening the government's own capacity to single out its needs and to put them in some rank order.

The mutuality of UNDP may give the UNDP Resident Representative a unique opportunity to help in this manner. Country planning, the development of priorities, and the coordination of development efforts are important for the least developed countries where technical assistance plays a central role, yet the capacity to perform these functions is exceedingly weak. While the Resident Representative is usually described as a coordinator of UN activities, he has a significant opportunity to strengthen the hand of the government, not, as is the tendency of some bilateral donors, to try to do the country's job from the outside.

In allocating limited staff resources to support the work of the UN Resident Representative the UNDP Coadministrators should attach increased importance to the opportunity which the Resident Representative will have to aid and assist the recipient in the accomplishment of development tasks. Bilateral donors cannot expect to become directly involved in internal planning, but the UN Resident Representative may well have substantial access to internal government planning. Where this is not possible, the UN activities are designed to support country goals, with account being taken of the fact that such coordination has marginal value, particularly where the UN effort is only a small part of total aid.

In selecting tasks appropriate to UNDP it is important to remember that UN personnel engaged in technical assistance enjoy a certain halo effect. As a recent study pointed out, UN people:

> are representing the recipient country's own club; they are rendering a service to which the recipient is entitled and for which he need not beg; their presence has been approved in advance. . . . The United Nations is relatively impoverished; it is not threatening anyone—only trying to help; its technicians are not as well paid or supported as those in the bilateral programs; the operation is relatively small-scaled, and proceeds at a slower pace with a minimum of equipment and fanfare. The recipient

neither demands nor expects as much from United Nations technical assistance, and is not as indignant about its shortcomings as it is about those of the bilateral programs. The whole work atmosphere is decidedly different from that of most other programs, and the United Nations technician can use this to his advantage.[11]

This essay has suggested that it may be useful to have UNDP carry out assistance activities in a manner that differs substantially from the approaches of the major bilateral donors, particularly the United States' Agency for International Development. Clearly, it would be foolish to try to compartmentalize EPTA, AID, and the Special Fund and to claim that each is a distinctly different technical assistance instrument. Nevertheless, EPTA might be said to lay the groundwork, through limited investigations and pilot activities, for the more substantial institution-building and human resource development programs increasingly preferred by AID and by other donors. The Special Fund, with its historic emphasis on preinvestment and its new interest in pilot plant and reimbursable projects, devotes more attention to the other end of the technical assistance spectrum, spurring hard to prepare projects and attract support for capital investment.

As UNDP increases in size, it probably will undertake a broader range of activities than other programs. After all, UN people can play varied and quite sensitive roles which other technical assistance personnel are denied. The future of UNDP activities seems bright, but unless the UN and the agencies accept technical assistance as a long-range undertaking and develop career systems to support their programs, results will continue to be disappointing. Technical assistance is an important part of the development profession and agencies must take more seriously the selection, training, and assignment of people. Fortunately, the source of supply for career technical assistance personnel needed by the UN has been broadened by the United States' Peace Corps, other volunteer programs, and the UN associate expert scheme.

Whatever the course of UNDP, planners and practitioners must be prepared to accept continuing ambiguity. If one reviews all of the informal ways in which knowledge has been communicated in the past and the ways in which values are more widely shared, it becomes apparent that the paths for extending and transferring ideas have not been fully explored. It is too early, then, to halt or to limit creative experimentation with varied techniques and approaches, though it is surely time to insist upon more careful evaluation of all of our endeavors.

[11] Robert W. Iversen, "Personnel for Technical Assistance," *Technical Assistance Research Project Staff Report* (Syracuse, N.Y: Syracuse University Press, March 1966), p. 21. (Mimeographed.)

The Consortia Technique

INTRODUCTION

INTERNATIONAL organization of aid presents two basic difficulties: 1) Major economic development aid should best be conceived as a supplement to total national development effort, not to single parts of it. This means that a program approach rather than a project approach should be applied in financing. Only a program can show whether projects are additional and optimal. While every program must be spelled out in projects, the sum total of individually worked out projects will not add up to a program.

2) Each country's development program should be helped by a truly international, i.e., multilateral, effort of an integrated sort. In view of the multitude of presently existing national and international agencies and consortia offering economic assistance this is an urgent and by no means accomplished task. To attempt the solution of this problem not only as a theoretical ideal but also as an operational proposal which should have good chances of being implemented in the not too distant future is indeed so difficult that one has to beware of perfectionism which makes the better the enemy of the good. The "better," i.e., the ideal case, will therefore be only mentioned briefly, listing reasons why this does not seem to represent a realistically practical solution. How to arrive at the second-best rather than the third-best solution, however, deserves a closer examination. Consortia are frequently mentioned as a decisive progress; it will be argued, however, that their performance up-to-date has weaknesses which make them only a second- or third-best solution.

I

The ideal solution for efficient multilateral financing of economic development would seem to be one all-embracing international agency

PAUL N. ROSENSTEIN-RODAN is Professor of Economics at the Center for International Studies, Massachusetts Institute of Technology, Cambridge, Massachusetts.

which would integrate and fuse all the present sources of aid. This solution seems to be best on balance of all considerations but even that is by no means certain. It is true that suspicions of political strings might be removed if international rather than national agencies administered aid but even an international organization is not necessarily above this suspicion of political influences working within it. The difficulties of the International Bank of Reconstruction and Development (IBRD) to establish itself as the highest authority in economic development of underdeveloped countries—although it has made great progress in recent years— is a good example. A competition between an illogical multitude of different agencies may sometimes improve their efficiency. It does not make sense, however, to pursue further this excursion into non-Euclidean bottlenecks. If we treat an unrealistic ideal solution, we might as well assume unrealistically that the international institutions would function with an ideal efficiency and conscience. The solution of one all-embracing international agency is unrealistic for the following reasons:

1) In the present political climate governments and congresses of the developed countries are not prepared to channel all their foreign aid into an international organization. Even under the present largely bilateral arrangement (more than four-fifths of international aid is provided that way) there is great difficulty in raising the volume of aid adequately. If all aid were to be channeled internationally, it seems that only a fraction of the present volume of aid (say one-half or up to optimistically two-thirds) might be obtained. If that is so, then the sacrifice of that amount of aid is not worth it, especially since the drawbacks and failings of bilaterally administered international aid can be effectively reduced by an agreement to apply the same criteria which would make it a second-best solution.

2) Practical difficulties of creating additional agencies are overwhelming; even expanding existing agencies is by no means easy. The problem of mobilizing sufficient staff and experts for an all-embracing international aid agency would be very great even if the personnel of existing international agencies were to be absorbed by it.

Since the ideal solution is unrealistic anyway, it does not seem worthwhile to list other reasons.

II

The second-best solution is *bilateral aid within a multilateral framework*. Because of the serious difficulties of administering aid through one central international organization, a second-best solution seems to represent a more realistic achievable target. This solution might combine the advantages of an international spirit (notably, sufficient volume and flexibility of aid) and avoid the serious disadvantages of straight bilateral aid (lack of coherent and uniform criteria for aid). Such a system of "bilateral aid within a multilateral framework" would ideally involve three features:

1) An agreement by each nation contributing aid bilaterally to try to apply internationally agreed-upon criteria for aid and to notify an international (or regional) coordinating committee of every conventional or unconventional loan or grant contemplated or given to underdeveloped countries.

Today most aid negotiations are conducted bilaterally. They give rise to justified or unjustified suspicions of political strings. Internationally agreed-upon common criteria tested and applied by an international committee independent of both creditors and debtors (see the third point below) would remove frictions which result from such suspicions. Such a committee should therefore be able to insist more emphatically on some efficiency conditions and could thereby achieve better results.

2) An international or regional organization for consultation and coordination of aid to underdeveloped countries.

The Development Assistance Committee (DAC) of the Organization for Economic Cooperation and Development (OECD) is a feeble, unsatisfactory, insufficient beginning of such an organization on the international scale.[1] It must be hoped that such activity will improve in the near future, leading to an international agreement on the principle of how the burden of aid—suitably measured, i.e., distinguishing between trade (including private investment) and aid, and taking account of the real burden involved in long-term and low-interest rate loans with or without long grace periods and grants—should be shared among contributing countries.

Longer-term commitments of aid would be more easily obtained within an international framework of burden sharing. Long-term pledges are essential for efficient planning. Continuity of aid is often even more important than the amount. It is more difficult to realize it if the danger exists that some countries may discontinue or reduce aid and may receive debt repayment from other countries' aid resources.

3) An international staff of technicians ("Committees of Wise Men") with prestige and capability to work out the evaluation of the development programs and recommendations of aid to be received by underdeveloped countries.

Such recommendations should serve as a basis for the disbursement of both bilaterally and multilaterally administered aid and effectively realize

---

[1] The fault is not in the organization itself but in the member governments' reluctance to commit themselves to a delegation of aid decisions.

a separation between programming and financing; that would remove any suspicion of political strings and make aid truly a mutual partnership.

An international committee of recognized prestige and expertise—like an International Court of Economic Justice—applying purely functional criteria can evaluate to what extent national effort is sufficient or insufficient and can recommend varying amounts and terms of aid tied to quantitatively and chronologically fixed targets of national fulfillment without being automatically accused of interfering in matters of national sovereignty. It can do that only if it is reasonably certain that its recommendations will be followed not only by aid-receiving but also by aid-providing countries.

III

On an international scale some lip service is paid to this philosophy, but it is not in fact applied. For Latin America the Alliance for Progress tried to apply that solution. The Committee of Nine represented an institution such as the international committees of wise men mentioned above. CIAP (Inter-American Committee on the Alliance for Progress) represents one such consultative and coordinating agency which was to try to follow up the recommendations of the Committee of Nine both with the underdeveloped and the contributing countries. In its relations with the contributing countries it has to deal not only with the partners in the Alliance for Progress but also with other countries and therefore with DAC.

The fact that the Committee of Nine was disassociated from administration of aid could in fact increase its effectiveness in this respect since it has and should exercise freedom to criticize the aid programs of contributing countries as well as the development programs of the recipient countries.

IV

An independent multinational committee would symbolize the separation of financing and programming and the complete multilateralization of aid decisions, although not of aid administration. Some *de facto* delegation of aid decisions has been realized under the Marshall Plan when recommendations of the Organization for European Economic Cooperation (OEEC) were applied by the United States. OEEC was a political organization following some functional criteria. The Committee of Nine as an independent nonpolitical organization represented one step further in an effective delegation of decisions not subject to political negotiations. It was perhaps too ambitious a design when neither the creditor nor the debtor governments were as yet willing to limit their sovereign rights by effectively and formally delegating aid policy decisions so formally and so completely. How to arrive at a suitable solution in this field presents enormous difficulties so that an ideal solution can only be gradually approached while in the interim period a second-best solution might prevent the better from being the enemy of the good.

The best solution would be reached on the basis of an international agreement on sharing the burden of aid and on multilaterally supervised criteria on how to distribute that aid. The total aid of each contributing country should amount to an agreed quota. How the quota is distributed for each country between various contributing agencies, however, need not be determined by this committee. It may be left to a political committee. In other words, the contributor to any single country's development program might represent a different pattern and different proportion from those which obtain for aid to underdeveloped countries as a whole.

Such an agreement is not yet arrived at although public opinion and conscience in the West seem to recognize its desirability and seem to be groping gradually toward its realization.

V

In practice today multilateral contributions are being negotiated and obtained through the technique of consortia. Their advantage is not only that of mobilizing resources from different countries or agencies but also that of assessing the country's development effort and its strategy as a whole and not limiting its attention to single project analysis. The economic report can thus better evaluate the country's development prospects, its absorptive capacity, and its capacity to repay.

If a country's program is well worked out, a high proportion of aid can consist in "program loans." When a program is not so well worked out, a higher proportion of aid consists in "project loans." In all cases, however, the study of the country as a whole avoids the danger of not seeing the wood for the trees.

In spite of this advantage the consortia technique if not coordinated and integrated by an additional international agreement may be far from the best solution. Its main drawback for the recipient countries seems to be that it becomes somewhat haphazard and accidental whether each country will in fact receive the suitable amount and composition of aid. This would only be possible if one, some, or all countries were willing to "underwrite" the residual amount of aid (i.e., the amount required to make up the total lending appropriate for this country) and also to underwrite the supply of the necessary proportion of unconventional loans. Otherwise, consortia established for different underdeveloped countries may represent in international financing the equivalent of single project loans as contrasted with more desirable program loans. In the same sense in which single projects do not add up to a program individual consortia decisions need not result in an appropriate proportion of external aid required for different countries. In other words, the relative amounts of aid alloted to each country would not be based on one coherent criterion.

Besides mobilizing aid funds from many quarters the consortium technique has the great advantage of being suitable for lending on the basis of a program which shows whether the projects composing it constitute *additional* investment and whether they follow criteria of priority (optimality). The program approach can therefore mobilize external resources for projects which are too small to be separately financed, for some "local currency expenditures," and notably also for two types (measures) of restructuring the economy which normally do not constitute "bankable" projects.

The first refers to "developmental outlays" which do not fit the orthodox definition of "capital" or "investment" but represent a necessary national effort which requires additional external resources. When more teachers are engaged for improving education, that is classified as current account expenditure, while construction of school buildings is considered as investment. In the same way the expansion of extension services in agriculture is considered to be current account expenditure, while the use of tractors is an investment. From the economic point of view there is no difference between the two: The distinction between capital and income cannot bear the burden which is frequently put on it.

The second type of "nonbankable" project consists of expenditures necessary for restructuring the economy which should also be considered as part of necessary national investment. When economies rely to an excessive extent on exports of tropical food products (coffee, cocoa, bananas, sugar, etc.), they have to diversify their exports. This is more easily said than done. The effort to realize diversification must necessarily take several years. During the first, second, and third years of such an effort, no visible improvement of exports appears on the surface. The restructuring of exports is a project which has a gestation period of, say, five years when no increase in yield materializes during the first four years. Yet unless this effort is undertaken now, the diversification will not take place five years later. The investment necessary in such a long gestation project necessarily requires external assistance.

To be able to finance such restructuring measures constitutes a typical advantage of the program approach. Such an approach could theoretically be applied by every single aid agency coordinated according to the principle of "bilateral aid within a multilateral framework" without necessarily using the consortium technique. In practice, however, the program approach was mainly used by the consortia—where IBRD, for instance, used teams of technicians to evaluate country programs—while the so-called program loans of the United States' Agency for International Development (AID) other than those through consortia were confined to programs of monetary stabilization (disinflation).

VI

In August 1958 the International Bank for Reconstruction and Development established a consortium for aid to India. The original meetings to cover the last two and a half years of the Second Plan period only indicated broad magnitudes of aid which participating countries intended to make available. Authorizations of aid subscribed by eleven participants between 1961–1962 and 1965–1966 amounted to $4,698.7 million. The second consortium organized by IBRD was for Pakistan in 1960. The consortium aid pledges between 1961–1962 and 1965–1966 amounted to $2,050 million. Other consortia were established by OECD for Greece in 1960 and Turkey in 1965. Consulting groups were established by IBRD for Colombia (1963), the Republic of Korea (South Korea) (1966), Malaysia (1966), the Sudan (1964), Thailand (1965), Tunisia (1962), as well as for Morocco, Nigeria, and Peru. The Inter-American Development Bank (IDB) established a consortium for Ecuador in 1965.

VII

Originally the consortium was created as an emergency measure for loans to India. As such it has brilliantly fulfilled its purpose. India, however, presented some special features which may not be apparent in the case of other countries. It represented a very high proportion of aid needed for all underdeveloped countries. The contribution to the India consortium might therefore more closely correspond to the "desirable" contributions to aid as a whole.[2] This naturally does not apply to smaller countries. In the case of other consortia, although they are not yet numerous, slightly different procedures have already been introduced. In some cases, for instance, the United States declares that it will match the contributions both of all other countries *and* of international agencies; in other cases the United States only offers to match the contributions of other countries but not those of international agencies. In the longer run,

[2] In fact it does not come up to it either: Two dollars of aid per head of population is markedly less than aid to some other smaller countries with lower national development effort.

moreover, the "matching" should be applied not only to the amount of aid (loans above ten years maturity) but also to the measure of aid, based on the present-day value of discounted future repayments, including the proportion of unconventional loans. The technique of consortia alone, that is, not supplemented by a "loan fund of last resort," does not seem to be able to solve such problems.

VIII

A coordinating committee must see to it that the amount and composition of aid available to an underdeveloped country should not depend on the haphazard willingness of countries other than the United States to subscribe the necessary quota of both conventional and unconventional loans. This might lead to the undesirable result that country A might receive all that is recommended while country B may receive less. Some countries or agencies might be willing to finance some more attractive-looking projects and leave the rest to other sources of financing.

This is a matter of urgent concern to securing the targets of the modern development creed. Promotion of consortia may be a good instrument for a partial and intermediate solution of the overall financing problem; but it cannot solve the whole problem. One form or another of underwriting a "loan fund of last resort" must logically complement the consortia technique.

The Organization for Economic Cooperation and Development

Goran Ohlin

The problems of development assistance have loomed large on the OECD agenda ever since its establishment, first as the Organization for European Economic Cooperation (OEEC) and then as the Organization for Economic Cooperation and Development (OECD). Briefly recapitulated, OEEC was created in 1948 to provide for the joint European execution of the Marshall Plan and for the close economic cooperation that the United States' aid offer had launched. Whatever the actual contribution of OEEC, the postwar European economic recovery was remarkably quick. Few international organizations have been thus blessed with the satisfaction of seeing their objectives so amply fulfilled.

While the end of the dollar shortage and the restoration of convertibility did not render European economic cooperation unnecessary, Europe had been divided into six and seven and the world into North and South. Although OEEC's original raison d'être had been realized, the machinery which had been established still functioned—procedures for intergovernmental consultation and cooperation and a secretariat of high caliber. The plan to convert this machinery to new tasks, first of all by including the United States and Canada, seems in retrospect both natural and warranted.

On the official level a communiqué issued in December 1959 by the chiefs of state of the United States, the United Kingdom, the Federal Republic of Germany (West Germany), and France stated that the economic progress of Western Europe had made it possible for the industrial countries in the West to cooperate in 1) policies to promote the develop-

Goran Ohlin is presently associated with the Federation of Swedish Industries, Stockholm, Sweden. He was previously a Fellow of the Development Center of the Organization for Economic Cooperation and Development.

ment of less developed countries; and 2) the coordination of their own policies for trade, growth, and stability.

As matters advanced, the United States put forward another proposal for directing special attention to the task of enlarging capital flows to the underdeveloped countries and to the coordination of development assistance. Consequently, in January 1960 a number of governments announced their intention of forming a group for this purpose, and the Development Assistance Group (DAG) was created.[1]

In May of the same year it was formally decided in the course of the remodeling of OEEC that DAG was to be constituted as a committee of the new OECD. However, the work on the new convention and the subsequent ratifications dragged on into the fall of 1961 when the Organization finally changed its name. The Development Assistance Committee (DAC) then officially took up its place as part of the Organization for Economic Cooperation and Development.

As a result of its prehistory DAC is in some respects different from other OECD committees. One peculiarity is that DAC members are not necessarily members of OECD, and conversely far from all members of OECD are in DAC. Japan was a member of the original DAG and stayed on in DAC although it did not become a member of OECD until 1964. Australia, a nonmember of OECD, was admitted to DAC early in 1966. The Commission of the European Economic Community (EEC) is a member on a separate basis as the operator of an independent assistance program. On the other hand, only donor countries are members and even among them some were slow to join. Norway and Denmark did so in 1962 and 1963, respectively, Austria in 1964, and Sweden in 1965.

Another survival, perhaps more important, from DAC's earlier prototype is the rule that the Committee has a permanent Chairman, supplied by the United States, who is not a regular delegate to OECD. The two Chairmen DAC has so far known—Ambassador James Riddleberger and Ambassador Willard L. Thorp—have done much in virtue both of their personalities and their wide experience of economic diplomacy to mold the style of the Committee and, for that matter, the style of the post itself. In the elusive manner that characterizes the work and influence of the Committee as well the Chairman has become a "semi-independent official, in but not quite of the OECD, capable of leadership in the procedures of the DAC and the policies of its members."[2]

---

[1] The original members were Belgium, Canada, France, Italy, Portugal, the United Kingdom, the United States, and West Germany; Japan was included at the very first session.

[2] Seymour J. Rubin, *The Conscience of the Rich Nations: The Development Assistance Committee and the Common Aid Effort* (New York: Harper & Row [for the Council on Foreign Relations], 1966), p. 80.

In the Secretariat the Committee has been served by the Development Department, and the role of the Secretariat has been extremely important. Along with DAC's Chairman it has consistently been the spokesman for more aid and better aid. It has also made a major contribution to the intellectual definition of aid policies by establishing joint categories for the measurement and appraisal of the aid effort and by creating a common language for the discussion of the many disparate measures falling under "development assistance."

Actually, no branch of OECD remained entirely outside the development nexus. Especially in the work relating to trade policy, but in other areas as well, the problems of developing countries increasingly impinged on tasks originating in the cooperation among member countries.

Some mention should also be made of the Development Center although by its very design it stands somewhat to the side of the main organs of OECD. The notion that OECD should set up some sort of center for applied research and teaching in the development field cropped up early. It was not until late 1962, however, that the role of such a center had been tentatively defined, and only in the course of 1963 did the Center begin to take shape as a "semi-autonomous" branch of the Organization charged with a broad mandate to

> bring together the knowledge and experience available in participating countries of both economic development and of the formulation and execution of general economic policies; to adapt such knowledge and experience to the actual needs of countries or regions in the process of economic development and to put the results at the disposal of the countries concerned by appropriate means.[3]

Thus, the Center was not primarily meant to serve DAC. Its President was responsible directly to the Secretary-General, and his task was to be guided by the needs of the developing countries. The first President of the Center was a prominent French politician, Robert Buron, with long experience of French decolonization. Assisted by an academic economist as Vice-President he was to operate the Center in consultation with five high-level economists. In spite of this collegiate touch academic research did not become a major activity of the Center. Its work program has included the creation of a documentation service for the benefit of economic policymakers in developing countries, the arrangement of a number of seminars for higher civil servants held in the capitals of some of these countries, and a program to improve cooperation between training institutes and research institutes in the field of economic development.

However, the relationship—or lack of relationship—between DAC and the Development Center has been a source of much confusion even in the

[3] "The OECD Development Centre," *The OECD Observer*, October 1963 (No. 6), p. 12.

OECD Council which took the decision to create the Center. As a result the activities of the Center have been subject to frequent and frankly skeptical reviews by the Council. Especially the experiment with itinerant seminars has been under fire from critics disputing the possibility of such a program having much intellectual impact in the course of a few weeks on government servants who still attend to their regular duties on a half-time basis. They have been defended as a way of establishing significant contacts in smaller countries, as occasions for frank discussion of concepts of development, and as opportunities for the Center to study varieties of development experience. Of the seminars held by 1966 (in Cameroun, Ivory Coast, Guinea, Iran, Peru, Ecuador, Cambodia, and Ceylon) the best were marked by enthusiastic high-level participation, the worst by sullen attendance of a motley crew.

In 1967, as Buron was succeeded by the French economist André Philip, yet another reappraisal of the Center's work began. There are strong pressures to bring the Center closer to DAC, and its research department has begun to assist the DAC Secretariat in various matters. But so far it seems that if the Chairman of DAC may be described as "in, but not quite of the OECD," the opposite may be said of the Center which has tended to be of, but not quite in, the Organization.

From an early date OECD also rendered technical assistance to its own less developed members. The only development assistance provided by OECD itself, it has been administered by the Secretariat and has taken the form of aid in economic policymaking and in various areas of planning. A major project in a slightly different category has been the Mediterranean Regional Project which represents a considerable effort to design the development of educational facilities in consonance with the manpower requirements of general development plans.[4] Extensive surveys were undertaken in the participating countries, serious research on the economics of education was brought to bear on the problem, and new institutions were sponsored and supported. It seems too early to appraise the effects of this singularly long-term project, but it has attracted much interest in other parts of the world, especially among educational planners in Latin America, and it has drawn the Secretariat into various forms of collaboration with developing countries outside OECD. Contacts between OECD and the third world have thus increased along somewhat unanticipated channels. However, any attempt to throw some light on the work of OECD in relation to economic development must first of all focus on the most important expression of OECD's concern with economic development on a world scale, namely, DAC.

---

[4] This project covered Greece, Italy, Portugal, Spain, Turkey, and Yugoslavia.

The Development Assistance Committee

DAC has no funds of its own, but out of the total flow of public and private capital going to underdeveloped countries at least nine-tenths originates in DAC member countries, and most of it flows in bilateral channels. The potential importance of DAC and OECD activity in the field of aid policy might therefore seem very large. But it must be remembered that bilateral aid to developing countries is usually bilateral for some good reason. To a large extent it springs from historical circumstance or some particular interest. This is why the work of DAC must to a large extent be an exploration of the margins within which a joint or common policy exists or can be created.

At a London meeting in March 1961 DAC adopted a resolution on the common aid effort which expresses the central premise on which the work of DAC has been based. The notion of a common effort implied, in the words of a perceptive observer of DAC, that the broad motives and aims of the donors in the group were "if not identical, at least compatible."[5] It was recommended that members should strive to "secure an expansion of aggregate volume of resources made available to less developed countries and to improve their effectiveness. . . . "[6]

One objective of United States policy at the time was to urge Europeans to increase their share of development aid which was usually thought to be low until DAC statistics showed otherwise. "Burden sharing" required the assumption of a joint effort and also of rules for the sharing. The London resolution recommended a study of the principles for an equitable determination of member contributions. Such studies have been made, exploring the possibilities of an allocation or appraisal of the burden on the basis of a proportional or a progressive levy on incomes but also revealing the great difficulties involved. The definition of the "burden" is not self-evident—according to some suggestions aid should be seen as part of an overall Western security policy and lumped with military expenditures, but even on a more limited view of development assistance it was clear that hard-term loans of a commercial nature are less of a burden than soft aid. As for ability to pay, it was recognized that balance-of-payments problems might make aid a greater sacrifice. Above all, however, such studies and considerations ran up against the basic problem that development assistance is a name that covers a multitude of things and that quite often donor countries are not themselves clear as to whether they engage in it as a promotion of their own interest or as an act of splendid generosity. When the first is the case, any talk of a burden would be sheer hypocrisy.

[5] Rubin, p. 5.
[6] Text of resolution on common aid effort in "Development Assistance Group Concludes Fourth Meeting," Department of State *Bulletin,* April 17, 1961 (Vol. 44, No. 1138), p. 554.

It is not surprising that in the end no members have been anxious to introduce rigid formulas and explicit criteria into this delicate matter. The Secretariat has nevertheless continued to calculate aid flows as percentages of national income, and comparisons on this basis are common in the Committee's discussions. However, it is more accurate to say that DAC itself, with its continuous surveillance of members' aid policies, is an instrument for, among other things, a kind of burden sharing. Where a formula would fail to meet the complexity of the problem, reliance is placed on what OECD terms "confrontation."

Actually, in DAC work mutual exhortation has probably been more important than the notion of sharing a given burden. The expansion of flow of resources to the underdeveloped countries and the improvement of the quality of development assistance have been the main subjects of the Committee's attention.

Has it been effective? Itemizing a number of the subjects which have had a prominent place on the Committee's agenda, one might well get the impression that much of its work must have been in vain. The overall volume of the flow of capital to developing countries has almost stagnated since DAC was established. The terms of aid—rates of interest and repayment conditions—have been discussed for years, as it has long been clear that debt service is becoming a major problem to many developing countries. Some limited progress has been made but hardly enough to make a dent in the debt problem. Even less progress has been made in attempts to discourage aid tying. The tying of aid to procurement from the donor is a source of irritation both to recipients and other donors. It has been repeatedly discussed, deplored, and regretted in DAC, but the practice has become more prevalent rather than less so.

Sobering as this record is, it would be rash to pass a negative verdict on DAC's performance. In a number of ways the work of DAC has undoubtedly affected both the theory and the practice of development aid.

At the heart of this work is the Annual Aid Review. In reply to a Secretariat questionnaire each member government submits a memorandum on the state of its aid program. It is then examined at a Committee meeting, with three other countries acting as the principal examiners. As in the similar reviews of members' general economic policy in OECD's Economic Policy Committee the country under review is represented by a delegation of officials from its capital. Some queries are prepared in advance by the Secretariat and a good many more are usually asked by members in the course of the meeting which may last a full day or more. At the completion of the country examinations the Chairman prepares his report on the year's review.

The Annual Aid Review has been termed an exercise in shame tactics.

Aid officials showing up for the grilling seem, at least the first few times, to take criticisms to heart more than do seasoned diplomats. Inadequate performance has often been blamed on an indifferent public opinion or even government, and the mood at the review may at times be that of a camaraderie of men with a shared cause. This may indeed bolster their resolve, and the thought of next year's accounting before professional colleagues in Paris may spur them on. It should be remembered, however, that aid officials do not by themselves make aid policy, and it would be difficult to identify individual improvements of aid policies clearly attributable to the Aid Review. The slight softening of aid terms in the early 1960's was perhaps in part attributable to the manifestation of international opinion at these and other DAC meetings. But it has probably been more important that the 1960's have been a period of groping consolidation of aid administration in many donor countries. The sharing of experience through the Aid Review was at the very least a substitute for the extensive mutual study of conditions in other donor countries that would otherwise have been called for.

The Aid Review is basic and recurring, and although the Chairman and the Secretariat have managed to create a certain amount of variety by appending different themes each year to the stock questions about the "aid effort," it is becoming something of a routine. But DAC has also roamed a wide field of other tasks in an experimental exploration of its possibilities. It has, for example, held a number of meetings with a geographic focus, discussing aid problems in large regions or individual countries in the developing world—Latin America, the Far East, East Africa, Thailand, Indonesia, Pakistan, and others. In Thailand a scheme for on-the-spot cooperation among donors was the result, but for the most part hopes of actual coordination have been dashed, and even the best-prepared meetings have remained exchanges of views of uncertain usefulness.

In a different category DAC has put in a good deal of work in the study and discussion of specific technical aspects of aid policy—the debt problem and the terms of aid, ways of estimating aid requirements, the possibility of establishing criteria of performance for aid recipients, etc. Some of this work has resulted in the adoption of recommendations to member governments. The more solemn ones have been adopted at the so-called "high-level meeting" which is held in the summer before DAC, like the rest of Paris, closes shop during the month of August. In 1965, for instance, the meeting recommended to members, among other things, to meet the one percent target (i.e., the minimum percentage of national income which the 1964 UN Conference on Trade and Development [UNCTAD] requested economically advanced countries to supply as financial resources for the less developed countries), to soften terms in specified ways, and to mitigate the evils of aid tying. In 1966 they were asked to give more emphasis and attention to agricultural assistance and food aid.

In an appraisal of all this work one must distinguish between at least three different types of activity—fact finding, education, and exhortation. Of these the last would on the face of it seem to have been the least successful. In spite of all efforts to raise the dignity of the "high-level meeting" it has not become an occasion at which member governments exchange binding pledges. Even if the DAC resolutions are not ignored by member governments, it would be difficult to show that they are taken very seriously. Their most important function may well be to articulate the doctrine of DAC and the spirit in which its deliberations are held.

In contrast, there is no disputing the great contribution that DAC has made to the analysis and understanding of the problems of development aid. The whole statistical picture of international development finance has been largely the product of the OECD Secretariat, responding to DAC needs. The reports on *The Flow of Financial Resources to Less-Developed Countries* have become indispensable sources, and the Chairman's reports, under the title *Development Assistance Efforts and Policies,* have been remarkable and authoritative documents which have probably contributed more than any other literature to the public understanding of aid issues.

The only flaw in this achievement occurs as an inevitable consequence of the Committee's terms of reference which tend to mask the heterogeneity of bilateral aid under the bland cover of "development assistance." The notion that development assistance flows out of the bounty of rich countries toward the "third world" as a whole and that it should be a natural task to take from some according to their abilities and give to others according to their needs has at times seemed to be the working doctrine of the Secretariat. In DAC it has furnished a sort of lowest common denominator on the basis of which all assistance could be discussed. The evident weakness of this procedure is that the deep complexities of aid policy, no matter how apparent they have increasingly become to members of the Secretariat and how familiar they are to delegates, have rarely been touched upon in Committee meetings—though they obviously have in corridors—and never alluded to in its publications.

But the fact-finding effort of DAC does not stop with what is made public. DAC has requested and received valuable studies of a great number of subjects. As one result of this research, as well as of the dialogue between donors which is its business, DAC has served an educational function. The whole concept of bilateral development assistance was so new in the late 1950's that there was hardly even a common language in which to discuss it. DAC has not been the only international forum for the discussion of aid problems, but it has been the only one where bilateral aid programs have been scrutinized in detail. Although it would be difficult to prove, it is hard to escape the impression, as already mentioned, that this has had some impact on the ways of planning and administering aid in many member countries. It is probably on the technical level and among aid administrators that DAC's influence has been greatest.

Beyond that level DAC does not easily reach. But the basic decisions about aid policy, decisions about its volume and direction, are made elsewhere—in high echelons of ministries of finance and foreign affairs or in cabinets. Some proposals to enhance the effectiveness of DAC have focused on this problem and would, for instance, have the Chairman pursue more direct contacts with member governments or publicize the Committee's strictures of governments which perform poorly as donors.

Clearly DAC can never be more than its members permit it to be, but its task is to be slightly more than the sum of its members. When member countries seem to agree that the Committee serves a purpose, it may well be because DAC helps to structure a relatively uncharted field of activity. In most member countries there is a gap between the theory and the practice of aid which cannot be closed merely by improvement in the practice for it is equally important to understand the issues better. In this zone between diffuse images and confused realities DAC has had a margin for maneuvers which has been skillfully used by its Chairmen. As time passes, the usefulness of DAC might decline if aid policy settled into fixed patterns. But this is unlikely to happen. It is virtually certain that the international aid system will have to change character. The present reliance on large-scale lending inevitably produces a debt problem of absurd dimensions. There would seem to be only three basic alternatives: 1) Aid could be put on a grant basis; 2) present loan aid could be supplemented by systematic measures to reschedule and consolidate debt and defer repayment; or 3) aid must be sharply reduced. The issue obviously presents itself in a different light in different recipients, but the shadow of the debt problem looms large over international aid. DAC is already deeply involved in this problem and will not run out of tasks.

UNCTAD AND OECD

In the spring of 1964 the first UNCTAD convened in Geneva, and over a thousand delegates met for what were probably the stormiest sessions so far of an international body devoted to development problems.

The Conference had an immediate impact on the work of OECD. The impression that the industrial countries had been put on trial and subjected to unreasonable and peremptory demands gave rise to a defensive mood which, when OECD resumed work in the fall of 1964, threatened for a while to obscure the fact that most of the issues raised at Geneva had been on the agenda of OECD for a long time.

In part, of course, this was precisely why UNCTAD hurt. On the part of the developing countries there had been no conspicuous expression of approval of the efforts of donor countries, individually or collectively, but, on the contrary, a fair degree of belligerence. At any rate the personal reaction of many Western delegates was one of indignation and irritation. And it was certainly true, as the Chairman of DAC pointed out in his report of 1965, that most of the conceivable suggestions to stimulate development assistance and increase its effectiveness already received regular attention.

But the Geneva Conference also touched some truly sore spots. In the area of trade policy controversy was genuine and deep. Nor was it just a matter of extravagant demands from the less developed countries. As Ambassador Thorp diplomatically put it in his 1965 report, trade policy "must take into account not only highly respected economic theories but also various long-established national and international policies. . . . "[7] What the UNCTAD confrontation on these issues—preferences, access to markets, international price manipulation for primary products—had brought out was a sharp rift among OECD members themselves. This lack of agreement was acutely distressing during the Conference where it was regretted also by many delegates from the large group of developing countries who wanted to negotiate in a serious spirit with the Western group.

After the 1964 Conference a special Working Party on UNCTAD Issues was immediately set up in OECD, and Australia, New Zealand, and Finland were invited to participate in it. In this group the recommendations passed at Geneva were systematically examined. OECD also began to play a certain part in other efforts to harmonize the positions of the countries in the Western group.

Within OECD matters affecting trade policy fell under the competence of the Trade Committee which became more involved with the problems of the developing world than before. There was also a certain amount of blurring of the lines between the Trade Committee and DAC —joint meetings, shared documents, etc. The new tendency after the first

[7] *Development Assistance Efforts and Policies of the Members of the Development Assistance Committee: 1965 Review* (Report by Willard L. Thorp, Chairman of the Development Assistance Committee) (Paris: Organization for Economic Cooperation and Development, September 1965), p. 12.

UNCTAD to see the problems of trade and aid in a joint perspective imposed a certain strain on the established division of labor in OECD where tariff matters had been rather studiously kept out of the work of DAC and its Secretariat and aid problems had not been touched upon in the Trade Committee. Probably this institutional separation accounts for part of the lack of adequate preparation for the Geneva Conference.

In DAC one response to Geneva was the creation of special groups to study two issues of central importance in any appraisal of the overall aid performance of the donors. One such issue was whether and how one could estimate the aid needs of the developing countries. At Geneva Raúl Prebisch had cited a UN estimate of a trade gap of twenty billion dollars for 1970, but much lower estimates had been prepared by others, and many donor countries were citing the lack of suitable projects as one reason for their unimpressive rate of aid expenditure. A Working Party on Aid Requirements, aided by a special Expert Group on Analytical Techniques, examined this problem very thoroughly. In this analysis a sharp distinction was drawn between the need for external capital and the need for foreign exchange, as in some underdeveloped countries the so-called savings gap and in others the currency gap seemed to be the major bottleneck for growth. Especially in the least developed countries the most serious shortage is usually in technical and administrative skills, and analytic and econometric estimates of such requirements seemed impossible. In all cases the notion of absolute and indispensable aid requirements is inadequate unless the growth target on which they are postulated is realistic, which cannot be determined without thorough study of the recipient's capacity for the making and implementation of development policy. Although analytic techniques were shown to have valuable applications, most DAC members seemed to find specific estimates of aid requirements too rigid and arbitrary to be of much use in practical economic diplomacy.

Although DAC was not seeking any reasons to abandon its traditional doctrine that an increase in the volume of assistance was highly desirable, there was, both in the Committee's work and in individual donor country's aid policy, a new emphasis on the importance of the performance of recipients, of self-help. To be sure, there had always been concern about inefficient use of aid, but it was also inevitable that one reply to UNCTAD would be to insist on the underdeveloped countries' own share of responsibility.

A Working Party on the Financial Aspects of Development Assistance was similarly set up to study in depth a second issue, the problem of external indebtedness of the developing countries. This task has come increasingly to involve the Working Party with those particularly serious

cases where debt consolidation is imminent or has already become necessary. This group also sought to arrive at a common position on various
UNCTAD recommendations, such as that on "supplementary financial
measures" which had been developed in some detail by the staff of the
International Bank for Reconstruction and Development (IBRD).

One should not imagine that the intensified effort of joint study and
consultation could remove all the conflicts within the Western group
generated by the 1964 UNCTAD. Especially when seen from the OECD
point of view it is an absurd exaggeration to think of its member countries as a solid bloc, particularly as regards the great and unresolved issues of international trade policy. What is clear, however, is that whatever
discord remains will at least not be the result of inadequate preparation
and lack of mutual consultation. Future confrontations in the continuing
UNCTAD machinery will reveal how much the change amounts to.

CONCLUSION

What has it all amounted to so far? How should one rate the contribution of OECD to economic development? Such questions may be foolish
but they are not quite meaningless. Like any other organization OECD
is under constant appraisal by members and nonmembers alike. But it is
peculiarly difficult to evaluate a contribution which falls largely in the
intangible realms of diplomacy.

Unlike most international organizations in the economic field OECD
is not an operational agency charged with a specific task which it accomplishes with greater or lesser efficiency. It is primarily a forum, a tool to
stimulate and structure communication between its members and to enhance their comprehension of the issues they face, at best leading them
into greater agreement.

Proposals to change OECD in the direction of a more executive agency
fail to take into account the important fact that its members strenuously
oppose such tendencies. The Organization's consultative character is very
firmly insisted upon, and suggestions for "operational" projects are firmly
dismissed. Although it seems clear that its members differ considerably
in their appreciation of OECD, there is much implicit approval in their
position, and in the wide spectrum of cooperation that it sponsors it undoubtedly meets a great number of genuine needs.

The specific contribution to bilateral development policies may have
been greater in the early days of DAC than it is now. Aid policies in
member countries have stabilized, and the mixture of persuasion and
intimidation in DAC work has less of a bite than when policy was still
fluid. On the other hand, UNCTAD has provided a new and tangible

task in which coordination seems both more urgent and more attainable than in bilateral aid administration in the field, where DAC has signally failed to achieve it.

Among nonmembers and especially in the underdeveloped countries opinions about OECD range from ignorance and indifference to wariness. OECD is a discreet organization, barely known to the public even in its member countries. When it is known at all to the third world, it is often misunderstood. As a "rich man's club" it attracts suspicions of a power which it does not possess. On the other hand, administrators in numerous underdeveloped countries have come to appreciate the spirit and proficiency of the OECD Secretariat, and in UNCTAD matters OECD steps naturally into the role of opposite party in a dialogue which both sides wish to become constructive.

The absence of any representation of the underdeveloped countries in DAC and OECD work might be expected to give this work a different character from that of larger international organizations. It undoubtedly makes possible a greater frankness, and the relatively modest size of the operation is probably conducive to efficiency. But in the context of development assistance there is little to distinguish the doctrine prevailing at OECD from that at the UN or its affiliated agencies. OECD members certainly pursue many aid operations in which considerations of their own specific interests are dominant, but the heterogeneity of such pursuits rules out any rallying of OECD around any heavily self-interested Western objectives. Theories of the conspiratorial neocolonialist character of Western aid are certainly not confirmed in the deliberations at Château de la Muette.

The Nine Wise Men and the Alliance for Progress

RAÚL SÁEZ S.

BACKGROUND OF ECONOMIC RELATIONS WITHIN THE INTER-AMERICAN SYSTEM

THE inter-American system represents the first attempt to implement the idea of regional cooperation. Regardless of general world opinion about the system's success, since its inception at the beginning of the nineteenth century the nations of the Americas have tried to establish a juridical order capable of solving their mutual problems, to jointly face the defense of the hemisphere, and to preserve peace in the region. In fact, however, these policies, initially expressed by the Monroe Doctrine of 1823, were first pursued unilaterally and later, after the First International Conference of American States in 1889–1890, through an ineffective collective body. They did not achieve the desired objectives and in fact only led to such violent forms of imperialism as the "big stick policy" and interventionism.

This century-long experiment did not come close to achieving the ideal of political equality nor a modicum of respect for the interests of the various countries involved, but it was at least the framework of a system capable of solving the conflicts of the nations of the region. There was, on the other hand, no proviso whatsoever for joint action toward a solution for Latin American social and economic problems. Yet, as time passed, the subdivision of Latin America into many states, the chaotic political evolution of many of them, and their disadvantageous geographic location regarding the developed nations, which were the sole sources of capital and technology, progressively magnified those problems.

RAÚL SÁEZ S. is Executive Vice-President of the Chilean Development Corporation. Formerly, he was the Chairman of the Panel of Experts of the Alliance for Progress, the Nine Wise Men.

Prior to 1914 Latin America turned to the European capital market for resources to solve its problems through long-term loans used to finance public works or fiscal and balance-of-payments deficits. According to Brazilian economist Rómulo Almeida those sources of external financing were then, relatively speaking, much more abundant than they are at present. At the same time he acknowledges the fact that the extra cost of those European resources in commissions and associated expenses, as well as their utilization without definite goals in mind, such as specific projects or programs, meant sizable wastage out of proportion to the results obtained through the investment of those funds.

The post-First World War depression was followed by a boom in the 1920's which improved the export situation and led to Latin America's first important technological advance; unorganized and haphazard, this advance was financed in a manner similar to that of the prewar period. All of this activity took place without any participation by the inter-American system and without any conception of the objectives of the social and economic development of the Latin American area as a whole.

The depression of the 1930's and the Second World War once again created special conditions for Latin American development, the foremost being an incentive toward achieving self-sufficiency.[1] This effort was undirected, however, nor did it result in coordinated action on the part of the Latin American countries. Nonetheless, all of this made clear to the Latin American leaders that their countries could not go on depending on the export of basic products and that it was necessary to both increase agricultural productivity and make a corresponding effort in industry to create jobs for the men displaced from the farms.

However, the thirties witnessed a political change of far-reaching consequences for inter-American relations. United States President Franklin D. Roosevelt initiated a vast internal program for economic recovery and social progress known as the New Deal, whose philosophical backbone was the contention that government should intervene to a much greater extent in influencing the course of the economy. In inter-American affairs the "big stick" and interventionist policies were replaced by the "good-neighbor" policy.

> By treaties, interventionism was discarded. Accepted was the policy of mutual respect, juridical equality of States, and settlement of disputes by negotiation. Offensive economic protectionism was replaced by a program of mutually beneficial tariff adjustment.[2]

[1] This incentive was provided by a change in the terms of trade favorable to industry, but at the same time it is necessary to recognize that this phenomenon was not a transitory one developed by the particular conditions created during those two periods but was rather a manifestation of the beginning of a long-term trend.

[2] Milton Eisenhower, "The Alliance for Progress: Historic Roots," in John C. Dreier (ed.), *The Alliance for Progress: Problems and Perspectives* (Baltimore, Md: Johns Hopkins Press, 1962), pp. 6–7.

For the first time in the history of inter-American relations economic problems were brought to the fore although the principal instruments originating from this change were essentially oriented toward accepting the juridical equality of sovereign states, regulating peaceful coexistence among the nations, and guaranteeing hemispheric security. The most important documents embodying these new conditions were those acknowledging the principle of nonintervention, which appears in the Charter of the Organization of American States (OAS) of 1948, and the principle of collective security which as contained in the 1947 Inter-American Treaty of Reciprocal Assistance (Rio Treaty) stated that an armed attack upon one American state should be considered an attack upon all signatories of the Treaty.

The OAS Charter did, in Articles 26 and 27, acknowledge explicitly the importance of economic matters in hemispheric affairs and the need for cooperation within the spirit of good neighborhood, as well as the desirability of consultation to provide help in the case of difficult conditions in a given country. In fact, however, these avowals proved to be no more than expressions of good intentions. After World War II, notably after 1952, Latin America witnessed a deterioration of its relative position at the same time that its economic needs grew more pressing and social pressure became more acute. At first the United States through the Export-Import Bank provided financing for American exports; this financing, although growing, was totally insufficient to meet the demand. In the 1950's this help was supplemented with ample programs of technical assistance on the pattern of the Point Four Program which were not always well coordinated with the more evident needs of the various countries. Substantial quantities of food were also sent out on very liberal terms to alleviate emergency situations. At the same time more flexible financing regulations were set up, and some conditions of trade with the United States became more favorable. But neither at the Ninth International Conference of American States, held in Bogotá in 1948, nor at the 1954 Meeting of Ministers of Finance and Economy of the American Republics at Quitandinha, Brazil, nor at the Buenos Aires Inter-American Economic Conference of 1957 was it possible to convince the United States of the urgent need for a program to help Latin America. It was incontestable, according to Hernando Agudelo, that the United States' lack of interest in the postwar economic and social problems of Latin America hurt the nationalist feelings of those Latin Americans who looked to international cooperative efforts for assistance in modernizing their societies.[3]

[3] Hernando Agudelo Villa, *La revolución del Desarrollo* (Mexico City: Editorial Roble, 1966), pp. 53-54.

The Economic Commission for Latin America (ECLA), created in 1948, has played a leading role in calling attention to the seriousness of the socioeconomic problems of Latin America. It produced the concept of the need for planning development "from within" and pointed out the advantages of expanding both the markets and the availability of natural resources by means of a regional integration scheme. Partly due to the action of ECLA and partly due to the policies of the interested governments various instruments of economic coordination came into being, the most significant of which were the General Treaty for Central American Economic Integration signed at Managua, Nicaragua, in 1960 and the 1960 Montevideo Treaty establishing a Free-Trade Area and Instituting the Latin American Free Trade Association (LAFTA). It is necessary to underline these initiatives, as in each process of integration, even in its most elementary stages, there is a recognition of the need for simultaneous cooperation between those that integrate as well as for multilateral decision and concerted action. In the late 1950's such conditions began to characterize the Latin American movement.

The creation of the Inter-American Development Bank (IDB) followed much the same pattern although with a most important difference. This new organization is made up of all members of the inter-American system, including the United States which had opposed the creation of this bank for many years. It is interesting to remark on the reasons Milton Eisenhower advances to justify this bank, particularly in view of the ever critical nature of the relationships between the United States and its neighbors south of the Rio Grande. Those reasons are a very basic part of the advantages of a multilateral organization. According to Dr. Eisenhower:

> First, decisions on loan applications *would be made co-operatively;* thus there would be no justification for identifying the United States with project developments that might, while improving the economies, continue to strengthen the prevailing order. Second, if conditions were attached to loans, in the hope of spreading more widely the benefits of economic growth, the intervention involved or implied *would have been collectively determined.* In other words, an agency of the Americas might help to solve the dilemma: desirable social changes might be fostered through credit, while avoiding the malodorous charges that had arisen as the United States sought *sincerely but unilaterally* to promote economic development in Latin America.[4]

I want to stress these advantages derived from the multilateral characteristics of IDB as they are an answer to the needs of Latin American development and are an implicit condition for the Alliance for Progress.

[4] Eisenhower, in Dreier, p. 12. Emphasis added.

THE ALLIANCE FOR PROGRESS: THE IMMEDIATE ANTECEDENTS
AND ITS CREATION

This then was the background of the situation existing in Latin America at the beginning of the 1960's, as well as the main features of the contribution of the inter-American system to the solution of the pressing socioeconomic problems of the area. Dr. Eisenhower, main adviser to the United States administration in the 1950's, remarked that Latin Americans watched

> with amazement our spending of billions of dollars in Europe, the Middle East, and the Far East under the European Recovery and Mutual Security Programs. Deeply disturbed by our failure to give them a significant role in these programs and to meet fully their demands for public loans, they contend that here is proof that we consider other areas more important to our welfare.[5]

It is difficult to express this situation in terms of figures. Dr. Agudelo estimates that from the close of World War II to the end of the 1950's Western Europe had received $37 billion; the Near East and Africa, $7 billion; Asia and the Pacific, $13.6 billion; and the American republics, only $1.7 billion.[6] But it is not necessary to have accurate figures to back the statements of the Panel of Experts of the Alliance for Progress, official designation of the so-called Nine Wise Men, in its second report to the Inter-American Economic and Social Council (IA-ECOSOC) at São Paulo, Brazil, in November 1963. Concerning the situation before the creation of the Alliance for Progress the Panel said:

> The inter-American conferences and specialized meetings on economic and social subjects made no progress except in the field of recommendations and theoretical studies. It is true that the Charter of the Organization of American States contains provisions designed to facilitate the solution of these problems, such as those relating to the settlement of political disputes by peaceful means and to the preservation of the peace. But while these provisions and the instruments that support them have been applied with some effectiveness, the standards for the establishment of vigorous and stimulating cooperation in the economic field have been consistently neglected and undervalued. For this reason it was being asserted, with varying reasons, that the inter-American system was in a state of crisis, that its institutions were ineffective and that its operational mechanisms lacked the dynamism needed to cope successfully with present-day problems.[7]

[5] Milton Eisenhower, *The Wine is Bitter: The United States and Latin America* (New York: Doubleday and Company, Inc., 1963), p. 72.

[6] Agudelo, p. 52.

[7] "Second Report of the Panel of Experts: October 1, 1962, to September 30, 1963" (OAS Document OEA/Series H/X.4), p. 1.

It was within this framework that a definite concept took shape which was the concrete antecedent allowing the formulation of that audacious program called the Alliance for Progress. This concept developed not only from the Economic Agreement of Bogotá signed in 1948[8] and the unsuccessful attempt to work out a program of action at the Economic Conference of Buenos Aires in 1957. There are other efforts more immediately responsible for the inspiration of the philosophy of the Charter of Punta del Este.

Perhaps the first proposition that should be remarked on is the report prepared by a group of experts for consideration at the Meeting of Ministers of Finance and Economy of the American Republics, called by ECLA, in 1954 at Quitandinha, Brazil. In this document[9] it was recommended that Latin America, in a way paralleling the experience carried out in Europe in the Organization for European Economic Cooperation (OEEC), benefit from the creation of a group of experts on economic development. The reasons that were given to justify the application of this idea to Latin America and that imparted a sense of joint and soundly responsible effort to the problem of Latin American development were the following:

> *That* in preparing internal measures aimed at facilitating the full utilization of international co-operation it might, in certain cases, benefit the Latin American countries to receive the prior opinion of an independent group of experts;
>
> *That* owing to the confidence this group might inspire in the interested governments and international credit institutions, the advice of such experts could also contribute to harmonizing different points of view and facilitating negotiations;
>
> *That,* in order to discharge their duties to the best of their ability, the experts should act in a personal capacity and as entirely independent of the institutions appointing them. . . .

The Quitandinha report thus enunciated with precision all the features of the Panel of Nine Wise Men that would later be acknowledged in the Charter of Punta del Este with less clarity. It can also be asserted that the spirit of the first provision involves, no doubt, the need for planning development on a national scale in order to make optimal use of international economic cooperation. The Quitandinha proposal remained only an antecedent for a possible solution to be implemented when conditions for an integral program were definitely present in the hemisphere.

[8] "Economic Agreement of Bogotá" (OAS Document OEA/Series A/4 [SEPF]). This treaty was signed with so many reservations that it was totally ineffective.

[9] "International Co-operation in a Latin American Development Policy" (UN Document E/CN.-12/359, September 1954), Recommendation No. 8, p. 136.

In August and September 1958 the Brazilian government presented for consideration by the governments of the other American states two aides-mémoire defining what was designated as Operation Pan America. These aides-mémoire defined the purpose of the operation in five points easily recognized in the later Charter of Punta del Este. They can be summarized as follows:[10]

1) The first and second points define "development" as the attaining of a minimum rate of per capita growth which would allow a cumulative and self-sustained process of expansion and at the same time the achievement of a rate of growth for the gross production of the area considered as a whole big enough to initiate a self-perpetuating process of development at a satisfactory speed. 2) The third point stresses the need to determine the magnitude of the resources required to complement the national economies in order to achieve the desired objectives. 3) The fourth point refers to the need to identify the bottlenecks affecting the Latin American economies which should be eliminated by means of *individual or collective action*. Among the more salient bottlenecks were limits on international trade and the lack of a regional market. 4) Lastly, the fifth point is a generalized expression of the alternatives for action open to Latin America to achieve the proposed objectives.

But perhaps the most fundamental trait of Operation Pan America is its *multilateral character*. The first aide-mémoire states specifically:

> Operation Pan America *is conceived as involving the joint action* of the twenty-one republics of the Western Hemisphere, the preservation of its *strictly multilateral nature* being indispensable. Bilateral matters will continue to be handled through the channels normally followed in such cases without becoming part of the aforesaid Operation.[11]

This imaginative project, containing many of the elements needed to convert it into a practical and constructive plan, went through the long bureaucratic process of the Special Committee of the Organization of American States to Study the Formulation of New Measures for Economic Cooperation, the Committee of Twenty-One, which approved a large number of resolutions that led nowhere. After twenty months of delays and negotiations President Juscelino Kubitschek of Brazil presented a new aide-mémoire[12] directly to the President of the United States which in addition to reiteration of the ideas of Operation Pan America contained a precise plan of action. Among the stated aims it is well to

---

[10] *Documents on International Affairs: 1958* (London: Oxford University Press [for the Royal Institute of International Affairs], 1962), pp. 429–433.

[11] *Ibid.*, p. 430. Emphasis added.

[12] "La 'Operación Panamericana' y los Trabajos de la 'Comisión de los 21'" (OAS Document OEA/Series H/X.3.1.1), pp. 54–55.

single out one that is again taken up in a special manner in the Charter of Punta del Este; this goal is, namely,

> to insure satisfactory prices and terms for the raw materials and basic commodities fundamental to the economic and social stability of Latin America.

Lastly, a third antecedent defining fundamental aspects of the Alliance for Progress is the 1960 Act of Bogotá. Following a long period of stagnation of the Operation Pan America proposals President Dwight D. Eisenhower expressed the willingness of the United States government to earmark resources for social development on the condition that this assistance be tied to the carrying out of certain administrative and organizational reforms by the recipient countries. This decision led to passage of a bill in the United States Congress authorizing an important sum for social development purposes. The American states, convened in Bogotá shortly thereafter for a new session of the Committee of Twenty-One, finally approved a document that partially embodied President Kubitschek's proposals and explicitly incorporated initiatives of a social nature. From an operative viewpoint the Act of Bogotá only presented a solution for the social problems; these would be dealt with through the IDB Social Progress Trust Fund and would be financed largely by the funds authorized by the United States Congress. Nonetheless, conceptually, the Act represented a big advance in inter-American cooperation and reinforced the tendencies that cropped up during the whole process I have described.

Thus, we can distinguish four well-defined features of this document. In the first place the acknowledgment of the necessary simultaneity of economic development and social progress is expressed in the statement that the purpose of the Special Fund is

> to support the efforts of the Latin American countries that are prepared to initiate or expand effective institutional improvements and to adopt measures to employ efficiently their own resources with a view to achieving greater social progress and more balanced economic growth.

In the second place, the just-mentioned quotation and Title I of the Act acknowledge the need for and describe the nature of the proposed institutional changes, a definition that never before had been so explicitly stated in an inter-American system document, in particular as regards the "measures for the mobilization of domestic resources" (Title I, Part E). Also, there is an acknowledgment, although not imperative, of the convenience of preparing national development plans and of the need for additional mobilization of internal capital. Finally, the last chapter of the Act carries as its title "Multilateral Cooperation for Social and Economic Progress" which eloquently expresses the clear *multilateral orientation* of all efforts to organize Latin American development.

It is easy to understand, then, that when United States President John F. Kennedy made his historic call for the creation of an Alliance for Progress in March 1961 he invoked precisely the ideal of collective effort that apparently had made much progress in the minds of Latin Americans. "Therefore," he said,

> I have called on all the people of the hemisphere to join in a new Alliance for Progress—*Alianza para Progreso*—a vast co-operative effort, unparalleled in magnitude and nobility of purpose, to satisfy the basic needs of the American peoples for homes, work and land, health and schools—*Techo, trabajo y tierra, salud y escuela.*[13]

The emphasis of President Kennedy on cooperative effort should be noted, an emphasis he repeatedly used in this and many other of his speeches with singular insistence. Further, whoever wishes to review the ten concrete points of this speech will find there all those ideas which were the aspirations of Latin American leaders: a decade of sustained maximum effort to which the United States would contribute resources sufficient in quantity and nature to achieve successful development; long-term national plans to mobilize widely the resources of every country; support for economic integration; case-by-case examination of commodity market problems; adequate use of American agricultural surpluses in emergencies and special programs; help to advance science and technology in the area, specifically, the expansion of technical training programs, as well as a more intense cultural interchange; and a reaffirmation of the collective security system. This long enumeration of objectives concluded with a clear call for reforms. "This political freedom," said the President,

> must be accompanied by social change. For unless necessary social reforms, including land and tax reform, are freely made; unless we broaden the opportunity of all of our people; unless the great mass of Americans share in increasing prosperity, then our alliance, . . . our freedom will fail. But we call for social change by free men, change in the spirit of Washington and Jefferson, of Bolívar and San Martín and Martí, not change which seeks to impose on men tyrannies which we cast out a century and a half ago. Our motto is what it has always been: "Progress yes, tyranny no— *Progreso sí, tiranía no!*"[14]

It is in this spirit that the Charter of Punta del Este was signed on August 17, 1961. That spirit is clearly expressed in a declaration adopted by IA-ECOSOC at Punta del Este which states that

[13] John W. Gardner (ed.), *To Turn the Tide* (a selection of public statements by John F. Kennedy) (New York: Harper & Brothers, 1962), p. 163.

[14] *Ibid.*, pp. 167–168.

> Assembled in Punta del Este, inspired by the principles consecrated in the Charter of the Organization of American States, in Operation Pan America and in the Act of Bogotá, the representatives of the American Republics hereby agree to establish an Alliance for Progress: a vast effort to bring a better life to all the peoples of the Continent.[15]

The Charter of Punta del Este is, by itself, an original and ambitious document. The fact that to a large degree criticism of it is oriented to weighing the amounts of financial assistance that are promised and those that are actually given hides the deep meaning of this document. Perhaps the Charter ought to be likened to a new type of *contrat social* that acknowledges the need for and tries to establish a new mode of international coexistence. It is a contract that defines the legal relationships between the nation-members of a society, that is, in Rousseau's terms:

> a form of association which will defend and protect with the whole common force the person and goods of each associate, and in which each, while uniting himself with all, may still obey himself alone, and remain as free as before.[16]

The signatories of the Charter have accepted, within this *contrat social*, a new concept:

> the responsibility of all for individual and collective development; the urgent need for supplementing the political forms of democracy with an economic democracy which would give all a share in an increasing prosperity more and more justly distributed among peoples and individuals.[17]

This is the true importance of this document, still today not well understood by those who should be the first to fight for its integral application.

At the beginning of the Alliance for Progress it might rightly have been said that it was a program unknown to everybody.

> I have the impression that the U.S. entered upon this program without being prepared to carry it out, convinced that Latin Americans were, since it was a program that they themselves had proposed. The surprising discovery was that the Latin Americans were not ready either, and the idea that was adopted, and which to my mind is reasonable to promoting the development of Latin America, has been accepted only at the level of the technical experts and the economists, but does not form a basic part of the criterion of the governments, of the political leaders, of the industrial leaders and producers in general, and of the people themselves.[18]

---

[15] "Alliance for Progress" (OAS Document OEA/Series H/XII. 1), p. 3.

[16] Jean Jacques Rousseau, *The Social Contract and Discourses,* trans. G. D. H. Cole (New York: E. P. Dutton and Company, Inc., 1950), pp. 13–14.

[17] See the address by Raúl Sáez at the tenth meeting of ECLA, Mar del Plata, Argentina, May 1963, contained in UN Document E/CN.12/SR.88(X).

[18] Raúl Sáez, "The Alliance for Progress" (address delivered at the gathering of members of the Institute of Engineers of Chile in Santiago, July 26, 1962). Author's translation.

That is why the Nine Wise Men in their first report to IA-ECOSOC were able rightly to ask themselves whether or not after such a short time—from the signing of the Charter of Punta del Este in August 1961 to October 1962—it could be said that the Alliance was in crisis, a crisis whose causes might be rooted in these five facts: 1) lack of knowledge on the part of the members about the Latin American origins of the Alliance; 2) lack of practical application of its intended character as a cooperative, multilateral effort; 3) lack of understanding of its revolutionary content and consequent absence of popular support; 4) lack of Latin American leaders at the international and national levels; and 5) inadequacy of the inter-American system mechanisms to achieve the purpose and mobilize the means of action for the Alliance.[19]

In 1964, three years after the signature of the Charter, the first United States coordinator for the Alliance for Progress tried to draw attention to the Alliance's intended nature in view of the lack of understanding of the program. Speaking at a commencement at Lewis and Clark College in June 1964, Teodoro Moscoso stressed that the Alliance was not and could never be a success as a United States program. It had been conceived as a vast *cooperative* program, and as such it demanded much more from Latin America than it did from the United States. If there was little or no will to this end in Latin America, he warned, if there was a lack of political leadership to fight for and support the goals and methods of the Alliance for Progress, then the assistance of the United States would bring only isolated improvements. The United States could not by itself achieve the fulfillment of the grand design.

However, as Paul Rosenstein-Rodan underlines,

> most Latin American countries forgot the multilateral principle agreed upon in an atmosphere of euphoria at Punta del Este and the United States all too willingly complied with their wishes. This principle, which consisted in submitting aid decisions to an independent and functional organ, which is the backbone of the Alliance for Progress and of any enlightened international aid policy, received . . . less and less lipservice until it was practically dropped at the Buenos Aires CIES [IA-ECOSOC] Conference in March 1966.[20]

At that point the Inter-American Committee on the Alliance for Progress (CIAP), established at the suggestion of the Nine Wise Men, had been operating for two years.

---

[19] "Report of the Panel of Experts to the Inter-American Economic and Social Council" (OAS Document OEA/Series H/X.3 [Document 17]), pp. 38–48.

[20] Paul Rosenstein-Rodan, "La marcha de la Alianza para el Progreso," *Progress 1966/67* (New York: Vision, December 1966), p. 172. Author's translation.

THE ALLIANCE FOR PROGRESS AND THE ROLE OF THE NINE WISE MEN

It might seem strange that six years after the signature of the Charter of Punta del Este it is necessary to begin by giving an interpretation of its meaning. But this need becomes evident when the examples given above are reviewed and when the many occasions are recalled in which authorized voices have pointed to deviations or important disagreements with respect to what in this study we consider has been the consistent interpretation of the Charter's meaning by the Nine Wise Men. "The idea is spreading," said the Committee of Nine,

> that the Alliance is a contingent program, at the mercy of every event in the cold war and of every difficulty of the countries committed to the effort.[21] The great concepts of permanence, of continuity, of long-term tasks, of self-help, are apparently being subordinated to the immediate difficulties of balance-of-payments disequilibria [,] to budget deficits, to the tendency to develop certain isolated projects that have a social impact and to the ups and downs of world tension, i.e., to circumstantial conditions that can obscure the real philosophy of the Alliance.[22]

The interpretation given here is the result of a careful analysis by the Nine Wise Men of the text of the Charter and its antecedents as well as of the problems entailed in the development of Latin America.[23]
The fundamental objective of the Alliance for Progress is

> to enlist the full energies of the peoples and governments of the American republics in a great cooperative effort to accelerate the economic and social development of the participating countries of Latin America, so that they may achieve maximum levels of well-being, with equal opportunities for all, in democratic societies adapted to their own needs and desires.[24]

The Charter points out that to attain this objective it will be necessary to undertake action in three principal fields: 1) national plans for economic and social development; 2) economic integration of Latin America; and 3) the defense of basic export commodities. It is easy to understand the close interrelations between these three different fields of action. For instance, it is impossible to expect success by development programs that do not take into account the critical common problems of the defense of basic products and the regional economic integration plans, whose aims include, among others, the expansion of markets. The Charter sets very definite goals in the economic and social aspects of development.

---

[21] Currently, the Vietnam war, for instance.

[22] "Second Report of the Panel of Experts," p. 2.

[23] The points of view of the Nine Wise Men are developed in the reports to IA-ECOSOC, in particular, in the two reports already cited, and in the IA-ECOSOC meeting in Lima (1964).

[24] "Title I: Objectives of the Alliance for Progress" of the Charter of Punta del Este, contained in OAS Document OEA/Series H/XII.1.

Probably the only important field where not enough has been said is the one referring to international commerce in general, beyond the export of basic commodities.

This is, no doubt, the most effective program ever formulated for the integral development of a region; in order to carry out this vast task the countries of the inter-American system signed a formal agreement:

> This declaration expresses the conviction of the nations of Latin America that these profound economic, social, and cultural changes can come about only through the self-help efforts of each country. . . .
>
> The United States, for its part, pledges its efforts to supply financial and technical cooperation in order to achieve the aims of the Alliance for Progress.
>
> . . . .
>
> The United States intends to furnish development loans on a long-term basis, where appropriate running up to fifty years and in general at very low or zero rates of interest.[25]

These explanations and quotations basically define the Alliance and its aims. The Alliance *is an association of peoples and governments created to make a great cooperative effort.* To what end? *To accelerate economic and social development,* to better distribute welfare, to offer to each person equal opportunities. What is the basic condition? To make a great national effort within a *democratic society.*

However, association and cooperation imply responsibility of all associated members in decisions and execution; in other words, *multilateral responsibility* is an unavoidable consequence of the nature of the program. Rightly, the Committee of Nine insisted in its first report:

> It is essential to emphasize *that the concept of multilateral effort is perhaps the part of the machinery whose improvement should interest the Latin American countries most.* More important than the multilateral organization itself is the multilateral attitude or spirit that the Charter proposes.[26]

But what has been the result of this experiment? Have the Nine Wise Men played a significant role as a multilateral body with an effective capacity to make decisions and to check their execution? In the first place, it is necessary to describe very briefly the origin of the Committee, "a panel of nine high-level experts" as the Charter calls it.

At the 1961 Punta del Este meeting Jorge Sol, then Executive Secretary of IA-ECOSOC, explaining the preliminary work, pointed out that in the case of Latin America

> the idea was from the beginning to look for and study formulas capable

---

[25] "Declaration to the Peoples of America," contained in OAS Document OEA/Series H/XII.1, p. 4.

[26] "Report of the Panel of Experts," p. 36. Emphasis added.

of placing the efforts of the Alliance for Progress on a *multilateral co-operation base*.[27]

At the same meeting United States Secretary of the Treasury C. Douglas Dillon stated:

> If a group of highly capable and impartial experts was established, my government would expect their recommendations to be very important when deciding *how to spend our resources for the development of Latin America*. We would expect other friendly governments, potential suppliers of capital, . . . would also accept these recommendations from the experts *as a major factor in their decisions about help for Latin America*.[28]

There is here an explicit acknowledgment of acceptance of the principle of multilateral decision. But it is surprising to see in the statements of all the other delegations that save for some passing remarks about this concept none accepted this idea with intensity and emphasis. It is not only a doctrinary aim of Latin America, but it is also an essential part of any collective program in which there is a vital necessity to solve problems of common interest with resources that may be ample but will always be limited and therefore have to be shared by all, a program, finally, in which failure of some countries to live up to their commitments inevitably affects all the others.

The main topic of discussion at the Punta del Este meeting was the document providing for a coordinating committee presented by the United States. This document contained the necessary basis for the beginning of a system of multilateral decision. But it was rejected. Why? Historian Arnold Toynbee, underlining Mr. Dillon's proposal to establish an inter-American committee on development, says:

> The experience of the implementation of the Marshall Plan for Europe tells powerfully in favour of setting up a strong steering committee of this kind. At least, this seems to have been one of the principal causes of the Marshall Plan's success. It was therefore natural and proper that the structure and power of the proposed Committee should have been the main focus of the discussion at the Punta del Este Conference. It is perhaps also ominous that this was the point on which the U.S. delegation met with opposition.

He goes on to add that

> the larger Latin American countries wished to water this proposal down; and the terms of the declaration of 17 August 1961 seem to indicate that, in this conflict of wills, the larger Latin American countries' wishes prevailed. In this document the word "committees" does not appear.[29]

[27] "Reunión Extraordinaria del Consejo Interamericano Económico y Social al nivel ministerial" (OAS Document OEA/Series H/XI.1), pp. 101–102. Author's translation.

[28] *Ibid.*, p. 139. Author's translation.

[29] Arnold Toynbee, *America and the World Revolution and Other Lectures* (London: Oxford University Press, 1962), p. 229.

The panel of experts, once nominated according to the procedures established in the Charter, realized the impossibility of making a useful contribution to such a fundamental program within its terms of reference. The Alliance, like any other development effort embracing several countries, must look for the solutions of problems which are common to all of those countries but at the same time should try to help integrate their economies; by its very nature it becomes a program that must be carried out simultaneously on two different but intimately connected levels—internal national development and collective development of the region as a whole. It is the simultaneity of these two actions that unavoidably confers on the Alliance the character of cooperative, multilateral effort.

What was the panel's responsibility? As expressed in the Charter's own terms

> each government, if it so wishes, may present its program for economic and social development for consideration by an ad hoc committee, composed of no more than three members drawn from the panel of experts referred to in the preceding paragraph together with an equal number of experts not on the panel.[30]

That is to say, in effect the panel is nothing but a list of names from which to draw to make up one-half of an *ad hoc* committee for the evaluation of a national program. But evaluation by an *ad hoc* committee *is not even compulsory*. Further, the *ad hoc* committee turns out a report, and if *the interested country consents,* it can be presented to IDB or other institutions or countries which might participate in the plan's financing. In addition to these two limitations the action of the *ad hoc* committees is also restricted because according to the Charter

> the ad hoc Committee shall not interfere with the right of each government to formulate its own goals, priorities, and reforms in its national development programs.[31]

It is true that the Charter acknowledges the fact that

> the recommendations of the ad hoc committee will be of great importance in determining the distribution of funds under the Alliance for Progress which contribute to the external financing of such programs.[32]

In the words of an eminent statesman Latin American governments "with complete determination and forethought made the group of experts practically powerless, and in fact created only a list of names."[33]

[30] Charter of Punta del Este, contained in OAS Document OEA/Series H/XII.1, pp. 15–16.
[31] *Ibid.*, p. 16.
[32] *Ibid.*
[33] Alberto Lleras Camargo, "Un informe sobre la Alianza para el Progreso" (OAS Document OEA/Series G/V [c-d-1103], June 15, 1963), p. 13. Author's translation.

Right from the beginning the Panel sat down to tackle the task of performing useful work in the most important program ever proposed to solve the problems of Latin America. It decided, *de facto,* to become the Committee or Panel of Nine and began to work out, as such, a set of regulations for its own work.[34] Those regulations established, among other things, the obligations of defining some norms for the presentation of plans and common evaluation criteria, of making specific studies of general interest, of helping spread knowledge of the Alliance, of preparing an annual report on the progress of its activities, of cooperating with the various financial organizations that must collaborate with the Alliance, etc. At the same time a Coordinator, an Undercoordinator, and a Technical Director of the Committee were designated, and the appointment of a small staff was obtained under the direct control of the Committee to support the work of its members.

Naturally, these arrangements, although they made it possible for the Nine Wise Men to work much more effectively in their only area of responsibility, that is, as members of an *"ad hoc* committee" to evaluate a national development program, did not allow the Committee to participate officially in other fundamental tasks of the Alliance which derive from its multinational and cooperative character. The Alliance's success is a matter of importance not to one or several countries in the region but to all of them. The nature and amount of external aid, the cooperation in the Alliance for Progress program by the countries that do not belong to the inter-American system, the problem of trade in basic products, and the question of regional integration are some of the many multilateral aspects of the Alliance. In the absence of a representative body that might take action the Nine Wise Men began to act in these areas, discreetly but firmly, in the conviction that the worst mistake that could be made would be to have the program show as its only outward face the image of the United States Coordinator.

Convinced that planning constitutes a prime requisite for the Alliance, the Nine Wise Men insisted in every instance on the need to look on external financial help as financing for a planned, overall program, since outside assistance for development has no meaning if external credit continues to be granted on the basis of individual projects sometimes unrelated to the highest priorities in the plan. It is obvious, also, that planning and its successful implementation are the only measuring rod for gauging, multilaterally, the efforts and achievements of the various countries in a collective program for development such as the Alliance.

[34] This decision was recognized officially some ten months later by OAS Resolution A-6/M 62 approved at the first annual meeting of IA-ECOSOC at the ministerial level, October 27, 1962, in Mexico. See OAS Document OEA/Series H/XII.4.

Planning also constitutes the most adequate means for making the goals of the various nations of the region compatible with one another, rendering it impossible for the production objectives of one severely to damage economic conditions existing in another. Lastly, from the beginning the Nine Wise Men underscored the importance that should be attributed to planning and to the evaluation of plans by a single group that might judge which elements in each country might facilitate or hinder the longer-term and more fundamental objectives of integration.

In spite of these efforts and the good will shown by Agency for International Development (AID) employees managing the resources assigned to the program by the United States, as well as by some international credit institutions, outside help continued to be granted fundamentally on the basis of bilateral negotiations. Even in those cases where the recommendations of the *ad hoc* committee's reports were taken into consideration, this procedure cannot be said to have had the definite multilateral character that had been rejected at Punta del Este. In vain the Committee of Nine's Coordinator requested that the recommendations of the *ad hoc* committees for Chile and Colombia be put into effect as tangible evidence of the validity of the spirit of the Alliance. "This would also be," he said,

> the most effective means of convincing the peoples of Latin America that the conditions governing assistance are limited to those contained in the reports, which are the result of technical and impartial studies, and are not the result of other requirements that would deprive the Alliance of its character as a cooperative and multilateral effort.[35]

Convinced that the results of a program as ambitious as the Alliance could not be obtained by utilizing the procedures contained in the Charter, the Nine Wise Men proposed the outright revision of all the inter-American system mechanisms to adapt them to the newly created conditions, a proposal that was duly accepted by the OAS.[36]

THE INTER-AMERICAN COMMITTEE ON THE ALLIANCE FOR PROGRESS (CIAP) AND THE MULTILATERALIZATION OF THE ALLIANCE FOR PROGRESS

It is possible that the problem of the nature of a multilateral operation is a question of semantics. Consequently, it seems essential to agree on the meaning given to this expression in this study.

[35] "Exposición del señor Raúl Sáez en nombre de la Nómina de los Nueve," plenary session of IA-ECOSOC at the ministerial level, October 23, 1962 (OAS Document OEA/Series H/X.3), p. 6. Author's translation.

[36] OAS Resolution A-8/M 62, October 27, 1962, contained in OAS Document OEA/Series H/XII.4, p. 25.

When speaking about the hemisphere's collective security nobody doubts the multilateral character of the juridical instrument being applied and who applies it: the Rio Treaty of Reciprocal Assistance and the OAS. But when speaking about economic and social development, what is or are the proper mechanisms? What is or are the instruments? In fact, among the organizations that deal with the economic and social aspects of the inter-American system there are several which have a certain multilateral character. IA-ECOSOC defines the hemisphere's economic policy and in virtue of that capacity approved the Charter of Punta del Este and the creation of CIAP. IDB's own activity, in which there is a power of decision by the member countries, limited and balanced but shared by all, has a certain multilateral character.

Many examples may be given outside the inter-American system. Within the socioeconomic field we can mention the large international credit institutions such as the International Bank for Reconstruction and Development (IBRD), in which all member countries may vote in the deliberations but in which the vote is proportional to the share of the total capital. This means, in fact, there is a certain amount of fiction regarding its multilateral character as decisions are made by the lending countries.

The technique known as the financial consortium, in which several countries and/or international credit institutions jointly participate in financing a national program, also exhibits the features of a multilateral system. Its direct, simultaneous application to a group of underdeveloped countries does not seem to be possible without an intermediate mechanism, independent of the countries supplying financial and technical resources and of the borrowing countries; this mechanism should be authorized to make the decisions. Otherwise, the consortium technique simply becomes financing of loans by an international credit institution; thus, using present criteria, program financing disappears and becomes the usual project financing system. Consequently, the main advantage that it might be possible to attribute to the few consortium experiences carried out is lost.

In some cases the Alliance has tried to apply the system of advisory groups. As its name implies such a system has no multilateral character since its purpose is merely to inform and not to participate in making decisions or in following up the execution of plans, two characteristic features of all the other multilateral instruments referred to.

Throughout this study we have tried to identify multilateral action within the Alliance for Progress with the possibility of evaluating national development programs by an impartial mechanism utilized by all member countries requesting aid. This mechanism should apply common criteria, and all the countries involved should accept the obligation to use this evaluation to decide the allocation of resources. In practice, it is conceivable that the responsibility for the evaluation and the supervision might fall on a group of experts of great reputation chosen on a personal basis. As Professor Rosenstein-Rodan has sometimes called it, it would be a kind of "court of international justice, or economic arbitration." The allocation of resources, which may come from various sources and be of different natures, which may be open to negotiations, part bilateral, part multilateral, or which may or may not be granted to a certain extent because of emergencies or other contingent reasons, may perfectly well be the responsibility of another organization, one with a political nature but also with a capacity for multilateral decisionmaking regarding those financial resources with no definite ties. It must, of course, be acknowledged that because of its nature this latter, more "pragmatic" mechanism cannot have the freedom of judgment of the former, and, consequently, the best alternative seems to be a combination of both types of organization.

Possibly these conceptions may be considered too theoretical. However, it is well to recall that at the 1963 United Nations Conference on the Application of Science and Technology (UNCSAT) its President, M. S. Thacker, suggested

> that a *world brain trust* or committee of wise men be formed to examine the development plans of the various countries and to receive their progress. The committee would be composed of "great scientists and technologists" and the heads of the specialized agencies, and would be designed to overcome the presently uncoordinated planning among numerous agencies.[37]

In the same manner a draft report of the UN Committee for Development Planning suggests consideration in the future of

> suitable international institutions to survey progress annually, and where appropriate, to organize agreements for specific actions by developed and developing countries. Nations would pledge themselves to take part in the review and other exercises arranged by these institutions.[38]

However, there is a much more fundamental fact than those we have mentioned and that is the undisputed success of the Marshall Plan. When the countries of Europe signed the convention for the creation of OEEC on April 16, 1948, the signatory countries formally recognized the fact that their economies were interdependent and that the prosperity of each

---

[37] *Report of the United States Delegation to the United Nations Conference on the Application of Science and Technology for the Benefit of the Less Developed Areas,* Geneva, Switzerland, February 4–20, 1963 (prepared by the Agency for International Development for the Department of State) (Washington: United States Government Printing Office, 1963), p. 259. Italics in original.

[38] Unpublished draft, Santiago, Chile, April 1967.

of them depended on the prosperity of all. They promised to cooperate closely and

> to agree on the full utilization of their own capacities and possibilities, to increase their production, to modernize their industrial and agricultural equipment, to increase their interchange and to progressively reduce the obstacles to their mutual commerce, to favor full employment, to review and to maintain the stability of their economies as well as the confidence in their national currencies.[39]

This is not the place to analyze the vast number of multilateral studies made by OEEC nor by its successor, the Organization for Economic Cooperation and Development (OECD). The interesting thing is to observe how a multilateral mechanism acted in the application of the Marshall Plan, because although it was a reconstruction program for a group of European countries without technical or administrative limitations, it may be that many of the problems encountered are fundamentally similar to those present in a regional development effort. A technical committee made up of government representatives proposed the economic programs to the OEEC Council which decided *de facto,* not *de jure,* how to allocate the help furnished by the United States; the Council's recommendations were in fact accepted by the United States. These decisions reflected the principles of cooperation and the compromises made by the member countries of OEEC.

This is the concrete example which, in the opinion of the Nine Wise Men, might be the basis of a similar structure designed to direct the Alliance for Progress. The proposal diverges substantially from the idea, often defended by high-echelon political representatives of the United States, of channeling the resources for the Alliance for Progress through international mechanisms like IBRD. In such bodies decisions are made by countries not directly interested, without consideration for the needs of the area as a whole and, above all, without enlistment of the necessary solidarity of the participating countries. It might be easier to have IDB play the just-described role, but that would entail a substantial modification of its operating system which might possibly make the Bank lose its capabilities as a banking instrument, equally necessary for the purposes of the Alliance.

The position of the Nine Wise Men was clear. After obtaining in Mexico in 1962 the designation of two Latin American personalities to propose a new mechanism—former Presidents Juscelino Kubitschek and Alberto Lleras Camargo—and after examining the reports of both, they presented for the consideration of IA-ECOSOC in São Paulo, Brazil, in

---

[39] *Au service de l'Europe* (3rd ed.; Paris: Organization for European Economic Cooperation, 1956), p. 11. Author's translation.

1963 a concrete proposal for the creation of a committee for inter-American development which embodied and reinforced the ideas of both Presidents.

The proposal of the Committee of Nine contained in its second report was singularly concrete.[40] Fundamentally it established that CIAP should have the authority to *execute, coordinate, and represent multilaterally the program* of the Alliance for Progress according to the Act of Bogotá, the Charter of Punta del Este, and the mandates of the competent inter-American bodies. Among the executive functions was included one which was much debated at the São Paulo meeting:

> *to decide* about the allocation of the Alliance funds according to the recommendations of the ad hoc Committees responsible for the evaluation of the programs.

The Wise Men were, of course, conscious of the fact that this unrestricted proposal went beyond any delegation of sovereignty, *de facto* or *de jure,* that might be acceptable to the largest contributing country, the United States. But they also realized that to make out of this effort an alliance of the peoples of America it was necessary to create a strong mechanism, capable of fulfilling the transcendental tasks required. The Coordinator, speaking for all of them, put it in these words:

> It would be damaging to organize today one more instrument, which through lack of effectiveness might only be an additional instance in the already complex process of the implementation of Latin American development. The multilateral responsibility demanded by the Alliance would be reinforced if it established a more positive means of intervention of this Committee in the allocation of the external resources required for the program. However, it [the Committee] only wishes to remark at this juncture that in view of existing legal difficulties to make more explicit the power of globally defining the resources, more important than the written text of the agreement, is the intention that the countries express regarding the fulfillment of the recommendations CIAP might make, as happened, for instance in the case of the Marshall Plan.[41]

The intention of the Committee of Nine was perfectly clear and well defined: to separate the technical functions, which were carried out fully independently by the Committee and involved the evaluation of programs and the review of how the countries were putting the policies to work and carrying out the reforms they accepted in their own plans, from the more general implementation activities, regarding foreign aid,

---

[40] "Second Report of the Panel of Experts," pp. 87–121.

[41] "Exposición General hecha por el Señor Raúl Sáez de la Nómina de los Nueve," second annual meeting of IA-ECOSOC, São Paulo, Brazil, November 12, 1963 (OAS Document OEA/Series H/X.4 [CIES/534]), pp. 16–17. Author's translation.

for instance, a political responsibility that the Committee believed should belong to CIAP. If due to the scarcity of the total available resources or due to considerations of another kind it was not possible to follow the recommendations of the Committee of Nine, CIAP should not modify those recommendations by its own initiative since they stem from a functional appreciation of a set of data. Consequently, it should consult with the Committee to jointly agree on the modifications that might or should be suggested to the countries. Economic considerations are not the sole element that should be taken into account within the Alliance for Progress since the decisions are essentially of a political nature, but economic recommendations cannot and should not be altered by political considerations: in other words, political considerations leading to a final decision must not be made first, with economic recommendations modified to make these fit into political decisions but, on the contrary, economic decisions which certainly are the most important should be made on the basis of a functional economic judgment. The Ministerial Council of OEEC discussed its political problems in economic terms. The Council of Economic Advisers to the United States government is an independent corps whose prestige is based on the high technical quality of its economists. Its proposals may be changed by the Executive or by Congress but the mere fact of its existence causes functional economic considerations to have a greater influence on political matters. It is important to consider that when an independent technical judgment has been made, it is necessary to produce good reasons if one wishes to back a political decision different from the technical recommendation. In other words, technical judgment forces political decisions to become rational; this is a condition that seems to be a necessary requisite for good management on a national or supranational scale. For this reason the Nine Wise Men insist throughout their report on keeping the two bodies—the Committee of Nine and CIAP—independent but in close working contact.

Governor W. Averell Harriman, head of the United States delegation, gave his support to the creation of a strong multilateral organization.

> A strong permanent committee of the IA-ECOSOC, working under the leadership of a distinguished Latin American chairman, can and should give a vigorous new impetus to our common efforts.

And he further added:

> However, we should not fail at this meeting to come to an agreement on the establishment of *this new permanent multilateral organ* of the Alliance for Progress. For our part my government is ready to participate in the CIAP in a truly meaningful manner *and is prepared to give great weight to its recommendations.*[42]

[42] "Address by the Honorable W. Averell Harriman," second annual meeting of IA-ECOSOC, São Paulo, Brazil, November 13, 1963 (OAS Document OEA/Series H/X.4 [CIES/537]), p. 3. Emphasis added.

Considering these and other phrases of the text as well as the references made in the address and during the meetings to the OEEC and Marshall Plan experiences it could be inferred that a strong CIAP might be the beginning of an instrument of *de facto* decisions provided the Latin American governments so proposed.

In fact, the situation, as in Punta del Este, was not yet sufficiently ripe. There was resistance on the part of the existing organs of the inter-American system which felt menaced by the appearance of a mechanism with great powers of decision. The authority of such a mechanism to decide how to allocate resources was not accepted even in its most limited manifestations and remained only an expression of good will. According to a resolution adopted at the second annual meeting of IA-ECOSOC at the ministerial level CIAP was given limited power "for determining the distribution among the several countries of public funds under the Alliance for Progress. . . . " The member states agreed that when providing financial and technical assistance through their own agencies and when instructing their representatives in the various international organizations that provide such assistance, they would give special consideration to the recommendations of the Inter-American Committee on the Alliance for Progress.[43]

CIAP's creation was, despite criticism, an important step toward multilateralism. It was possible to preserve the main functions of representation, coordination, and multilateral fulfillment of the Alliance proposed by the Committee of Nine, but again no use could be made of this opportunity to obtain two fundamental results outlined in the Committee's first report, one beneficial to the good relations of the United States with its southern neighbors and another regarding the process of integration.

First, CIAP would, by making external financial aid a cooperative and multilateral effort, eliminate or considerably reduce the difficulties that accompany such aid where it is treated as a bilateral arrangement between the country aided and the United States or between the country and certain financial groups.

Secondly, in examining each national program within the broader framework of the needs and possibilities of the region as a whole the Committee would achieve one more step toward the essential objective of working together for the development of a Latin American common market.[44]

In his interesting and well-documented book Dr. Agudelo quotes a commentary in *Comercio Exterior de México* regarding the creation of CIAP:

[43] Resolution 1–M/63, January 7, 1964, contained in OAS Document OEA/Series H/XII.6.
[44] "Report of the Panel of Experts," p. 36.

The multilateral character of decisions about the management and allocation of resources and the supervisory faculties of CIAP were defeated in
the debate at São Paulo. The United States was not willing to try in Latin
America what so successfully had been tried with the Marshall Plan: "To
grant the countries receiving American help power to distribute it."[45]

A few days before he died President Kennedy reasserted his decision
to give CIAP full responsibility:

> We have labored to build a structure of cooperation and common efforts
> for years to come. No nation in the Americas can deny that much more
> must be done to strengthen and speed our efforts, that there have been
> setbacks and disappointments.
>
> That is why we intend to support strongly the leadership of the new
> *Inter-American Committee for the Alliance for Progress.* . . . [46]

Now What?

The creation of CIAP was a step in the right direction. Potentially,
even with the limited powers granted to it at São Paulo its field of action
is very wide. On the other hand, at the IA-ECOSOC meeting held in
Buenos Aires in March 1966 it was agreed to eliminate the Panel of
Experts provided for in the Charter.[47]

Such a decision, to those who constituted the Committee of Nine and
who in that capacity fought for the creation of a strong CIAP, seems to
be a serious mistake. To transfer the function of passing technical, impartial judgment on plans, along with the other responsibilities of the
Nine Wise Men, to a group which must give weight to political considerations is to join two elements that should have been kept apart at least
until the appearance of a multilateral mechanism vested with all necessary powers of decision and other functions such as have been mentioned
here as desirable.

Time will tell if that measure was or was not adequate. In the meantime it can be said that CIAP has received clear manifestations of support
from United States President Lyndon B. Johnson but has not expanded
its multilateral action in the specific fields of decision and fulfillment
within the Alliance for Progress. That is, CIAP might use more of its
potential power to influence decision.

This action may be urgent if it is recalled that President Johnson stated
on its fifth anniversary that the Alliance for Progress would not come

[45] Agudelo, p. 197. Author's translation.
[46] Allan Nevins (ed.), *The Burden and the Glory* (New York: Harper & Row, 1964), p. 161.
Emphasis added.
[47] Resolution 27–M/66, April 1, 1966, contained in OAS Document OEA/Series H/XII.11,
p. 55.

to an end after the ten-year period announced in the Charter but would
be extended for another ten years with new and more ambitious goals
than those originally established. Moreover, the document signed on
April 14, 1967, at Punta del Este is a solemn reassertion by the presidents
who declared themselves

> pledged to give vigorous impetus to the Alliance for Progress and to em-
> phasize its multilateral character, with a view to encouraging balanced
> development of the region at a pace substantially faster than attained thus
> far. . . . [48]

Besides, it is necessary to keep in mind that the main program established at the April 1967 meeting of American chiefs of state in Punta del
Este was the pledge to create a Latin American common market. Such
a fact by its very nature requires the presence of an organization capable
of multilateral action. Consequently, as a function of its development
and of the probable creation of subregional markets the concept of multilateralism will become a familiar idea to the rulers and peoples of America. Therefore, what is bound to happen in the near future forces us to
think again more definitely about the need to give to CIAP or to any
other mechanism of the system features which might perhaps be similar
to those of OEEC at the earliest possible date. Probably, when the time
comes, the absence of a highly technical, impartial mechanism will be
noted.

The question then arises as to whether it will be difficult for the United
States to accept the fact that the inter-American system is evolving toward
a multilateral organization. I think that history, even the most recent,
shows that this is not so and that it is rather momentary situations, local
resistances, the defense of minor interests, the fears, and painful experiences of past occasions which have hindered a more rapid evolution of
this process. If the ideas of the League of Nations and of the United
Nations are concepts born in the United States, if the most successful of
multilateral efforts—the Marshall Plan—had its direct inspiration in that
country, if even originally the proposal of the Alliance involved the concept of multilateral action, why should there be unsurmountable difficulties if the Latin Americans are not opposed to it? It is well remembered that already in 1963 the House committee reporting on the Foreign
Assistance Act of 1963 expressed the view that the success of OEEC in
Europe supported the hope that similar organizations operating in the
western hemisphere would help attain the objectives of the Alliance
for Progress.

[48] "Declaration of the Presidents of America," contained in "Meeting of American Chiefs of
State, Punta del Este, Uruguay, April 12–14, 1967" (OAS Document OEA/Series C/IX.1), p. 57.

Even the amendment introduced in 1966 to the Foreign Assistance Act recognizes at least the need for approval by CIAP. It provided that loans should be made only for those Latin American social and economic development projects and programs *which were consistent with the finding of and recommendations of the Inter-American Committee* on the Alliance for Progress in its annual review of national development activities.

That is, conditions seem ripe for the multilateral mechanism sponsored by the Nine Wise Men. The fact that it has not become a reality does not mean that the Alliance for Progress has not had significant impact on Latin America. Given the many factors independent of the program which have affected the Latin American area it is difficult to identify the beneficial effects it has produced. Progress in the coordination of development, improved planning systems, improvements in taxation and fiscal revenue, significant advances in realizing the social problems, progress in education and health, some administrative reforms, and the acceleration in some countries of agrarian reform are many points in favor of the Alliance. Important but insufficient.

The Alliance for Progress has lacked a vital impulse that can come only from the realization that this is Latin America's own program. Tasks are done with inspiration only when one becomes aware of one's own responsibility. Let us give Latin America that responsibility.

Multilateral Assistance:

Possibilities and Prospects

FRANK M. COFFIN

THIS essay aims to assess the prospects of a larger role for multilateral assistance in world development. It does not attempt to review the familiar, often extreme, arguments made in favor of either bilateral or multilateral aid.[1] It rejects the notion that the realizable possibilities of the many multilateral institutions and programs treated in detail in the other essays in this volume can be assessed as a unitary whole. The effort here will be to identify the specific kinds of multilateral aid which have especial potential of political support from aid-giving countries in the near future. As for the more distant future the reader is forewarned that the domestic politics of assistance, at least in this decade of stagnating support of aid of all kinds, recognizes no significant distinction between multilateral and bilateral aid. The web of will to help others develop is finely and infrangibly woven.

THE MULTILATERAL SPECTRUM

In appraising the current total aid effort the author has accepted the definition and statistics of "official aid" of the Development Assistance Committee (DAC) of the Organization for Economic Cooperation and Development (OECD) which excludes private investment, other non-governmental activities, and export credits. It includes only 1) actual contributions (as distinguished from commitments) 2) made by govern-

FRANK M. COFFIN is a United States Circuit Judge on the Court of Appeals for the First Circuit, with chambers in Portland, Maine. The author was formerly Deputy Administrator of the United States Agency for International Development and has served as the United States representative to the Development Assistance Committee of the Organization for Economic Cooperation and Development. He served earlier in the Congress as a Representative from Maine and was a member of the Committee on Foreign Affairs and the Joint Economic Committee.

[1] A perceptive general discussion of pros and cons is that of Robert E. Asher, "Multilateral Versus Bilateral Aid: An Old Controversy Revisited," *International Organization*, Autumn 1962 (Vol. 16, No. 4), pp. 697–719.

ments 3) for capital loans of one year or more, capital grants, technical assistance, the provision of agricultural commodities, and contributions to international organizations. "Multilateral assistance" in the strictest sense —the projects and programs administered by international or regional organizations—is financed largely from the national contributions just mentioned in the form of annual appropriations, capital subscriptions and purchases of bonds, and loans and participation in portfolios and from investment income, interest, and repayments of loans. So viewed, the flow of multilateral assistance, net of amortization, amounts to only about $1 billion a year, or one-sixth of the official aid of non-Communist countries.[2] The addition of the aid from the Communist countries, perhaps $500 million a year, would not perceptibly change this fraction.

The prospect of increasing this amount because of an ideological preference for multilateral aid lies with the strong "internationalists"—Denmark, Norway, Sweden, and the Netherlands. While the average multilateral contribution of Development Assistance Committee members in 1966 was only 10 percent of their total capital aid and multilateral contributions, these four countries averaged a 63 percent allocation to international agencies.[3] Their enthusiasm for international aid stems from their size, a lack of postcolonial responsibilities (except the Dutch), the difficulty of mounting and staffing a sizable bilateral program, and their genuine interest in international cooperation. In all of their cases, however, this "good" record of supporting international organizations masks a lagging overall aid effort, all of these countries being far below the DAC average percentage of total official aid flow to national income. As far as these countries are concerned, one would hope that they would even more vigorously fulfill their internationalist tradition and exercise initiative in making increased contributions to the International Development Association (IDA), to regional and national development banks, and to consortia. Since, however, their total capital and multilateral aid is only about 2 percent ($105 million) of the fifteen-country total, even a dramatic effort on their part would not in itself have a marked effect. Nevertheless, the catalytic effect of such an effort on others should not be underestimated.

[2] International Bank for Reconstruction and Development and International Development Association, *1965-1966 Annual Report* (Washington, 1966), p. 39. In 1965 the total official bilateral aid and contributions to multilateral agencies to these countries was $6,212.2 million; in 1966 it was $6,431.7 million. (*Development Assistance Efforts and Policies of the Development Assistance Committee: 1967 Review*, A Report by Willard L. Thorp, Chairman of the Development Assistance Committee [Paris: Organization for Economic Cooperation and Development, 1967], Table 4, p. 189, Table 5, p. 191.)

[3] From an analysis of *Development Assistance Efforts and Policies: 1967 Review*, Table 5, pp. 190–191. The Development Assistance Committee is composed of fifteen OECD member countries (Australia, Austria, Belgium, Canada, Denmark, the Federal Republic of Germany [West Germany], France, Italy, Japan, the Netherlands, Norway, Portugal, Sweden, the United Kingdom, and the United States) and the Commission of the European Economic Community (EEC).

The great bulk of multilateral contributions—50 percent—comes from five countries whose multilateral contributions range only from 3 to 18 percent of their total bilateral capital aid and multilateral contributions. They are France, West Germany, the United Kingdom, Japan, and the United States. Their contributions to international agencies amounted in 1966 to only $255 million.[4]

To discuss multilateral assistance in such a restricted sense, however, is to underestimate both the present scope and the future prospects of effective multilateral efforts. For the term "multilateral" is invoked in aid discussions to signify the benefits of harmonized or coordinated policies, programs, and projects. These benefits are not confined to the operations of an international agency. If one looks at the essence of multilateralism rather than at any specific institutional form, one sees a broad spectrum.

Most thoroughly multilateral are the operations of the global agencies: the International Bank for Reconstruction and Development (IBRD), its International Development Association (IDA), and the International Finance Corporation (IFC) in the field of capital assistance; and the United Nations Development Program (UNDP), as well as the UN specialized agencies, in the field of technical assistance. The family of major regional development agencies is now seemingly complete with the European Development Fund (EDF) and the European Investment Bank (EIB) of the European Economic Community (EEC), the Inter-American Development Bank (IDB), the Central American Bank for Economic Integration (CABEI), and, most recently, the Asian Development Bank and the African Development Bank (ADB). This by no means forecloses other institutions with a regional reach, such as the newly proposed Caribbean development bank.

Often overlooked in discussions about multilateral assistance are the consortia and consultative groups which combine national contributions and administration with the leadership of an international agency or a country. Such groups either exist or are in prospect for no fewer than twenty countries, accounting for roughly 80 percent of total official aid.[5]

A form of limited multilateralism is the joint participation of two or more nations in a regional project, such as the development of both the Lower Mekong and the Indus Basins. Finally, multilateral coordination of

---

[4] *Ibid*.

[5] For World Bank-led efforts see Roy Blough's "The World Bank Group" elsewhere in this volume. The Inter-American Development Bank has assumed leadership of such an effort in Ecuador. The Organization for Economic Cooperation and Development leads consortia for Greece and Turkey. Most recently, the Netherlands has assumed leadership of a concerted approach to Indonesian development.

national aid policies is the objective of the Development Assistance Committee of OECD.[6]

Viewed in this perspective, multilateral assistance already dominates the world scene. This fact only underscores the need for discriminating analysis in discussing why and where multilateral effort should be increased.

THE SPECIFIC OPPORTUNITIES FOR INCREASED MULTILATERALISM

Taking first the existing global and regional institutions, one observes that the unique advantage of internationally administered aid lies in the assumption that an international agency, being presumptively devoid of political taint, can enter into a better partnership with a developing country and can exercise more acceptable influence on its economic and social policies. This concept lies at the root of the belief in the superiority of the multilateral dollar. The recipients get more dignity with their dollar and the contributors get more development for theirs.

The Global Institutions

While this tenet is hopefully true, it has not yet been clearly proven in practice. The two prime examples of international leadership are those of IBRD-IDA and the United Nations Development Program. The World Bank, commencing cautiously from a rather neutral stance in its consortia and consultative groups, has, under the prodding of its contributing members, assumed a perceptibly stronger role. But while its rich members complain of too permissive a posture, its development clients complain of excessive interventionism. Its vocation, which it has begun to pursue seriously, is to tread this tortuous path.

The United Nations Development Program is the result of a recent effort to merge the preinvestment and technical assistance activities of the Special Fund and the Expanded Program of Technical Assistance (EPTA) into a coordinated and priority-minded force. The task is monumentally difficult—to produce a centripetal thrust out of the centrifugal tendencies of the various assistance programs of such well-entrenched, specialized institutions in the UN family as the World Health Organization (WHO), the UN Educational, Scientific and Cultural Organization (UNESCO), and the Food and Agriculture Organization (FAO). But again, a beginning has been made.

No sophisticated observer would argue that IBRD-IDA should be *the* monopoly source of capital assistance and thus find itself thrust into the

[6] The essay entitled "The Organization for Economic Cooperation and Development" by Goran Ohlin, which appears elsewhere in this volume, contains a detailed historical account of DAC's efforts to achieve policy consensus on several key issues.

very eye of the global political storms which would rage about its decisions. Nor would one urge that *all* bilateral technical assistance experts (including, for example, over 90,000 from DAC member countries and probably over 10,000 from Communist countries) be assigned to the UN (whose experts presently number about 9,000) or that the UN attempt to master the myriad of intranational contracting arrangements with business firms, governmental entities, labor unions, nonprofit groups, and educational institutions that increasingly constitute the heart of bilateral technical assistance.

The realizable opportunities are more modest. In the case of the World Bank Group the major immediate need is not only to "replenish" IDA but to gain acceptance of the notion that this very liberal instrument of development under seasoned and committed international management deserves sustained support at remorselessly escalating levels from the rich countries. That donor countries may feel that IDA makes too little impact on policies of receiving countries or that receiving countries may chafe under what they consider to be too tight a rein proves only that this institution is close to the vital center of an effective partnership in development.

But for countries burdened with current serious balance-of-payments deficits or for countries which may fear such imbalances in the future and wish to "play it safe" IDA and its international bidding procedures create problems both economic and political in nature.[7] Even if a government and its citizenry become economically sophisticated enough to overcome the argument that giving away goods and services makes them poorer, the more formidable balance-of-payments argument tilts the domestic political scales in favor of stringently tied bilateral aid. There are palliating devices such as allocating a project in a consortium to the lowest bidder, provided that the country is willing to furnish the financing; compensating for the higher cost of tied aid by additional grants or interest subsidies; or allowing aid recipients to make purchases from other developing countries. But the result of all such devices is still an undesirable mercantilistic patchwork system with irritants for donors, competitors, and users. Not the least of the irritants is the fact that tied aid adds about 15 percent a year in increased prices to the official aid bill[8]—or an amount, $1 billion, about equal to the total net flow of multi-

[7] The distribution of IDA credits in the short run may favor some countries. For example, there is some indication that the United Kingdom's share of IDA-financed procurement has exceeded its share in contributions to IDA. However, projections of past experience are probably not a reliable basis for predicting the longer-range future.

[8] Address by Irving S. Friedman, Economic Adviser to the President of the World Bank, to the Conference for Corporation Executives, School of Advanced International Studies, The Johns Hopkins University, Washington, April 28, 1967.

lateral assistance from international agencies. More radical surgery is needed.

The full potential of internationally financed and administered assistance will not be realized until international cooperation in the monetary field has brought about new arrangements increasing world liquidity and consequently diminishing the disruptive effects of minor fluctuations in flows of trade on the reserve position of the major trading countries.

As for the United Nations Development Program it is clear that it should play an increasingly significant role. That role, however, seems most likely to emerge as 1) more effective recruiting, programming, and coordination characterize Headquarters administration and 2) the United Nations Development Program Resident Representatives in the field are allowed by donor and recipient governments to perform a strong leadership coordination role. To the extent that this role is fulfilled the benefits of multilateral technical assistance can be realized within the traditional bilateral framework.

The Regional Institutions

The unique opportunity of the regional institutions is to concentrate upon the financing of adjustment problems involved in movements toward continentwide or regional economic integration. Also deserving of support from donors are a growing number of significant regional projects. The Lower Mekong Basin, the Indus Basin, malaria eradication, and power, communications, road, and railroad networks are examples. Other candidates for capital grants or long-term loans are a growing number of competently managed development banks serving a country or a subregion. These offer smaller donors a productive use of funds with no administrative obligations. Finally, among existing institutions there are the consortia and consultative groups offering scope for different degrees of donor interest and kinds of participation under centralized leadership. Increased and sustained support of these ongoing enterprises, together with more positive policy direction, is essential.

New Initiatives

In addition to existing institutions and programs there are promising new initiatives and ideas. Indeed, the significant policy thinking on assistance problems has recently, largely because of the first United Nations Conference on Trade and Development (UNCTAD), been directed to multilateral programs. The most ripe for action is the World Bank study of supplementary financing. This study proposes that developing nations submit their plans and policies of development to an international agency. The agency and a developing country would agree on a "policy package" calculated to realize development targets. Should such a nation suffer losses in export earnings because of events beyond its control, it would receive assistance to compensate for these losses. Burdens are placed on both donors and recipients. The financial obligation of the donors might run to $300–$400 million a year.[9] And the obligation of the recipients would be to submit their country plans and policies for scrutiny by the responsible international agency and to adhere to agreed-upon programs. This imaginative proposal deserves an equally imaginative and bold response as well as serious consideration in forums like UNCTAD. While no panacea, its concept of reciprocal obligation gives it political feasibility even in a period of parsimony.

A second proposal stemming from the first UNCTAD—the Horowitz proposal, named after its creator, the head of Israel's delegation and Governor of the Bank of Israel—contemplates the raising of development funds by borrowing on the private capital market. The investor would have a security guaranteed by governments. The funds would be loaned on concessional terms, and the difference in interest rates paid to the investor and paid by the loan recipient would be met by government appropriations contributed to an "interest equalization" fund.[10] In a period when governments are not willing to increase their aid budgets significantly the device of triggering sizable funds for development through relatively low (but long-enduring) annual contributions for interest subsidies may be the kind of crazy quilt addition to the fabric of assistance which the times allow. Despite uncertainty about the capacity of the market to absorb such bonds this concept may yet produce feasible national or multilateral offspring.

Still in the field of aid there is the new concept of world, regional, national, and provincial centers of research and training devoted to the accelerated production of key foods. With the present crisis in agriculture there is a recognized need to marshal energies toward the improvement in quantity and quality of basic crops. A proposal for a pilot project has been made to OECD involving the creation of multinational institutions for training and research. If launched, this project would deserve the support of all nations able to help in solving the problem of survival for many of the world's peoples. There is reason to believe that the multiplying effect of such institutions—not necessarily confined to agriculture— would be impressive beyond that of most traditional infrastructure proj-

[9] John Pincus, *Trade, Aid and Development* (New York: McGraw-Hill [for the Council on Foreign Relations], 1967), pp. 330–331.

[10] See the discussion in Pincus, pp. 333–334; and Jacob Kaplan, *The Challenge of Foreign Aid* (New York: Frederick A. Praeger, 1967), pp. 369–370. Despite an unenthusiastic report by the World Bank on this proposal both authors see merit in further consideration of its possible adaptations.

ects. For example, a Rockefeller Foundation investment of some $10–$15 million in developing Mexican semidwarf wheats has already yielded hundreds of millions of dollars in increased production and the newly discovered "Philippine miracle rice" promises yields of seven tons of grain on plots now producing two tons.

Apart from aid, but having the potential equivalent of increased assistance, are the opportunities to expand commodity agreements; to engage in a multinational effort to give some time-limited tariff preferences and easier market access to developing countries; and to move toward a better system of international liquidity—essential, as has been pointed out above, to reaching a long-range solution to the problems of tied aid—with the by-product of putting more purchasing power into the hands of the developing countries. Exploration of all these avenues of growth stimulation has at least passed beyond the point of initial generalizations. While the task of the scholar and expert is far from complete, there is some reason to hope that officials and parliamentarians are beginning to give serious consideration to steps that might be taken.

This brief sketch of present and impending opportunities for increased multilateral assistance does not ignore very real areas for new efforts which can best be made by bilateral programs. The recruitment, training, and retention of a high-quality cadre of technical advisers in government, in universities, and in business is a continuing challenge of high priority. More particularly, there is a need to experiment with ways of encouraging the effective transfer of entrepreneurial skills to developing countries. In the past this kind of effort has all too often been cloaked in self-defeating dogma by both proponents and opponents. It is now becoming more and more clear that whatever the mix of public and private enterprise may be in a given country or whatever its articulated ideology the contributions to development of a dynamic private sector can be of incalculable value. While guaranty programs, not only bilateral but also multilateral, need to be more fully exploited, there is need for increased resort to joint government and private business operations. West Germany has taken an initiative in allowing some governmental subsidizing of the training activities of private firms. To go several steps farther, industrial facilities could be financed by aid with the successful bidder required not only to construct a plant but to manage, train, staff, and build up sales, eventually turning the facility back to local ownership. Finally, there is a need for a rising, rather than a diminishing, grant component in bilateral aid not only to offset the ominous rising tide of debt servicing but also to undertake certain activities (such as agricultural investment) where profit or repayment ought not to be expected.[11]

[11] For a persuasive plea for the return of a significantly larger component of grant aid see Kaplan, pp. 310–319.

Nevertheless, even with a more adequate treatment of the opportunities for increased bilateral assistance it is probable that at least in the immediate future the major interesting and useful opportunities for increased assistance are multilateral. But to say these opportunities ought to be seized is not to say that they will be.

POLITICAL REALITIES

When we confront political reality, we see three areas of restraint on increasing multilateral assistance: the present levels and trends of global aid, the attitudes and policies of key governments, and the pervasive problem of public support of aid in any shape or form.

The stark fact underlying any consideration of the feasibility of increased multilateral assistance is that global economic official aid has remained at roughly a static absolute—and declining proportional—level since 1961. It consists of three significant components: the aid given by the members of the Development Assistance Committee; the aid administered by the various international and regional organizations and largely derived from these nations; and aid from Communist countries. The DAC nations' aid flow has remained at about $6 billion for five years. Perhaps a sixth of this amount has been in the form of food, reported at a higher value than world prices. Grant aid has diminished and average loan terms, after some slight progress in 1963 and 1964, are not much softer than they were in 1962.[12] The flow of net disbursements from international institutions is about $1 billion. Even a generous estimate of the flow of official aid resources from the DAC nations is no larger than one-half of one percent of their gross national products.[13] The Union of Soviet Socialist Republics, Eastern Europe, and the People's Republic of China (Communist China) contribute even less, about one-tenth of a percent of their combined gross national product.[14]

The five key countries, accounting for 89 percent of non-Communist aid, are the same countries which give the bulk of the contributions re-

[12] *Development Assistance Efforts and Policies: 1967 Review,* Table V.3, p. 76, and Table V.4, p. 77. The figures for 1966 show some slight improvement as to average maturity period and interest rate over those for 1965 but no improvement over 1964. And the United States Congress in 1967 took one more step toward hardening the terms of aid loans by doubling the interest rate from one to 2 percent during the ten-year "grace" period.

[13] This figure is arrived at by dividing the World Bank's figure of $1,250 billion representing the gross national product of the economies represented by the DAC nations (IBRD-IDA, *1965-1966 Annual Report,* p. 38) into the DAC figure of $6,431.7 million representing the flow of official aid in 1966. A lower figure, three-tenths of one percent, is derived if we take the estimate of official and private resource flows, net of repayments of profits and other income, of $4.5 billion and an estimate of $1,500 billion as the combined gross product of the developed countries. These are the estimates used by Friedman.

[14] This is the figure if we estimate their combined gross product at $500 billion; their aid flow in 1965 was estimated at $500 million. (IBRD-IDA, *1965-1966 Annual Report,* p. 39.)

ceived by the international institutions—West Germany, France, Japan, the United Kingdom, and the United States. While a political analysis of each of the critical five countries is beyond the scope of this study, the point to be made is that pragmatism rather than ideology may well bring about, in the short run, some increased emphasis on multilateral aid.

Perhaps the only country of the five to have an ideological preference for such an emphasis is the United Kingdom—but that preference is traced chiefly to pronouncements of British officials and has little scope for realization after provision for dependent territories and members of the British Commonwealth of Nations, particularly in the context of the United Kingdom's continuing balance-of-payments crisis. Recently, however, despite a decline in Britain's official aid disbursements its contributions to multilateral agencies have been expanding together with bilateral expenditures for technical assistance. Since the United Kingdom, with Sweden, sponsored the proposal at the first UNCTAD for supplementary financing to compensate developing countries for temporary shortfalls in export earnings, it is not too much to expect that it would be responsive to a request by an international agency for funds for such a program. Admittedly, it is likely that such funds would be produced by a transfer from other programs rather than as a result of an increased aid commitment.

The United States, while not so ideologically favorable to multilateral assistance as Britain, is more multilateral in deeds than its administration often cares to acknowledge to the Congress. In 1967, for example, the Johnson Administration, while presenting to the Congress another "bare bones" aid request at a disappointingly low level, also requested $960 million over the next three years to replenish the coffers of IDA, $200 million for the Asian Development Bank, and "consideration" of a possible contribution to the African Development Bank. The 1967 meeting of chiefs of state of the Organization of American States (OAS) at Punta del Este, Uruguay, stimulated increased emphasis on Latin American regional development with the possibility of increased funds for the Inter-American Development Bank.

These observations might ordinarily be a basis for moderate optimism about an increased emphasis in the United States on multilateral aid. Support not only of the United Nations agencies but of the various regional institutions as well seems to be a cardinal element in United States aid policy. Multilateralism seems to be favored in principle both by key leaders in the United States Senate and by many influential groups and individuals. But all of this is quite irrelevant in a period when support for economic assistance programs in the United States Congress has reached an all-time low. Preoccupation with the war in Vietnam, with its traumatic impact on urgent domestic programs, has riddled the ranks of aid supporters on Capitol Hill, who at best were never a confident majority. The disastrous fate of the Administration's severely pared aid request in 1967 in terms both of monetary slashes and of qualitative restrictions gives little hope that the United States will in the near future resume an aid program consonant with its resources and past tradition. The impact of this retreat by the United States in the war against global poverty must by the very size of its program cancel out any immediate hopes for overall improvement in the total flow of resources to the developing nations.

Even without Vietnam the prospects of substantially increased multilateral aid from the United States would be dim so long as it feels itself forced by its continuing balance-of-payments deficits to tie 90 percent of its aid-financed purchases. The tying policy, begun as a necessary but unpleasant expedient in 1960, threatens with time to harden into cherished doctrine. For example, the most recent United States official aid request to Congress pointed with pride to a reduction of non-United States aid purchases from $934 million in 1961 to an estimated $107 million in fiscal year 1968.[15] And United States officials, despite an overall positive contribution to the United States balance of payments by the World Bank Group, have felt compelled to couple a generous offer to replenish IDA funds with conditions amounting to tied aid. True, they have plumbed the depths of their ingenuity to minimize the impact, but as long as international liquidity rests on the conventional system of national currency balances, multilateral aid seems bound to be plagued with tortured improvisations.

If the United Kingdom and the United States find themselves well disposed in policy but indisposed in capacity toward greater multilateral assistance at the moment, the situation is reversed in West Germany and France. Each country is less hampered by political and financial restraints, but neither is warm to the concept of greater multilateralism: West Germany, because of its traditional requirement that aid be used to dissuade countries from recognizing the Democratic Republic of Germany (East Germany) and its insistence that aid be used to promote German exports; France, because of its preoccupation, for cultural, political, and economic reasons, with its former territories in Africa and its present coolness toward any enterprise which in any way might limit or influence its freedom of maneuver in international affairs. But West Germany, for all its timorousness toward consortia (based largely on its past predicaments in being singled out as the residual donor to meet a consortium pledge

---

[15] Agency for International Development, *Proposed Foreign Aid Program FY 1968* (Washington: United States Government Printing Office, 1967), p. 75.

target), is a major supporter of the European Development Fund and also participates in the Asian Development Bank half a globe away.

Until recently one would have placed Japan in the same ardently pro-bilateral category as France and West Germany. But 1965 saw the establishment of the Asian Development Bank in which Japan is a major participant and Japan's sponsoring of a Southeast Asian Development Conference. The pull of regional events, opportunities, and pressures has advanced Japan on a multilateral path, even though confined to its adjacent area, where any number of academic arguments would have been unavailing.

In sum, despite the general pall cast by the struggle in Vietnam, the balance-of-payments difficulties of the United Kingdom and the United States, and the coolness toward multilateralism in the other major aid-giving countries, the very proliferation of multilateral institutions and programs is creating some pressure for response at a time when there seems to be no other appealing reason for increasing aid.[16] But there are implicit hazards. For the regional institutions to flourish and serve their purpose they must have adequate and continuing support on the most liberal terms. If donors have not made this kind of commitment, the seeds of frustration will have been sown. Additionally, if the lure of the new institutions dilutes support of the global World Bank agency, IDA, world development will not have been advanced. At some point diminishing returns will set in.

This leads inevitably to the basic question: What is the political feasibility of substantially increased aid of any kind? For without a quantum increase the prospects of healthily increasing multilateralism are dim.

This is a fallow time for development assistance. Apart from the adventitious creation of new institutions in Asia and in Africa and the discussion of novel proposals nothing else is moving aid to a higher priority in the major chancelleries of the world. Although the United States, leader in this domain since the Marshall Plan, beleaguered by a war, a continuing deficit in its balance of payments, and fears of inflation, has—at best—held the line against massive retrenchment, it has also hardened

---

[16] The way in which proposals to create institutions have generated their own pressure is similar to that described by Isaiah Frank in writing about the first UNCTAD:

> When a responsible Western government is faced with a series of international meetings on an issue such as tariff preferences for less developed countries, it cannot simply send someone to sit on his hands. As part of its preparation, the government will reëxamine its policies; it will react to proposals put forward by an international secretariat; it will often suggest alternatives; it may draw upon the resources of the academic community for analysis and ideas; it may sound out various domestic interest groups; and, increasingly, it will consult with other advanced countries in seeking a concerted position.

("New Perspectives on Trade and Development," *Foreign Affairs*, April 1967 [Vol. 45, No. 3], p. 521.)

the terms of its loans and diminished the proportion of its grant aid. And few voices sound in protest.

France, in the forefront in terms of proportion of aid to its wealth, has seen its aid decline both absolutely and proportionately. Though its spokesmen have on occasion blandly offered to join others in striving for a goal of 1.5 or even 2 percent of net national income, there is no sign that it would lead such a movement.

West Germany takes refuge in its constitutional requirement to balance its budget and its difficulties in raising funds on the capital market and hopes to maintain its present aid level another year. After that there are no predictions.

Japan's official aid flow has recently doubled, but as a percentage of national income it is still not much over half the DAC average. Japan speaks more positively of taking seriously the United Nations' goal of one percent of national income but cautions that achieving this is some years off. In the meantime it persists in requiring fairly hard terms.

The United Kingdom, despite the stirring aid initiatives of its Labor Government in 1964, not only reduced its overseas program by 10 percent in 1966 but revoked the Cabinet status of its new Ministry of Overseas Development in 1967.

The only progress in recent years in increasing aid levels (apart from Japan) has come from smaller countries starting from a generally low base: Austria, Canada, Denmark, the Netherlands, and Sweden. But their total official aid amounts to only 6 percent of that for all the DAC countries.

Historians may some day note the irony of rich nations growing richer at an incredible pace yet not finding the will to give the help which their wealth and technology allow at a time when it would make a significant difference in world development.

Problem: How to Generate Will

The political feasibility of a dramatic impetus in multilateral development assistance is at bottom simply a question of will and motivation. But to pose the question thus starkly is to expose the immensity of the problem. History reveals many instances where the will of the people of a nation has been aroused for the purpose of protecting or propagating a religious faith, defending or taking territory, guarding or aggrandizing a dynasty, or sustaining or cutting down a tyrant. But there has never been a time when the common people of many diverse nations have felt it part of their life and work to help the common people of a far greater number of nations.

Can anything be done? In the face of such a challenge the political feasibility of increased levels of aid is not a matter of waiting for better public opinion polls but of striving to produce a climate of opinion where the unthinkable becomes the possible. If a "warm front" is to be generated, the first requirement is a widely shared sense of purpose. Attempts to spell out particular "national interests" of donor nations sound less and less convincing as the colonial era recedes, as military bases become obsolete, and as alternative sources of aid multiply. A new interest in redefining purpose in less national terms is beginning to appear in many countries. While various United Nations spokesmen and agencies have long preached the objective of development for the sake of humanity, the most dramatic and significant recent statement is the fifth encyclical of Pope Paul VI, "On the Development of Peoples."[17] Saying that "the new name for peace is development," the Pontiff elaborated in impressive detail and eloquence the ethical and spiritual bases for giving first priority to global development. The Protestant and Orthodox World Council of Churches, meeting at Geneva in 1966, sounded a similar concern. Humanists, religionists, and academics are coming to acknowledge the ethical root of development assistance and are less ashamed of admitting it.

But the more serious involvement of the world of the rich in the business of development has another side to it—that of quickening the pulsebeat of its own societies which are in danger of losing themselves in self-contained affluence. The papal encyclical touches on this in these words:

> If today's flourishing civilizations remain selfishly wrapped up in themselves, they could easily place their highest values in jeopardy, sacrificing their will to be great to the desire to possess more.[18]

To these grander concepts can be added the interest of all nations in maximizing trade, financial solvency, cultural interaction, political responsibility, and stable population levels and in minimizing military adventurism. All of these and more are part of a yet-to-be articulated common doctrine of purpose.

While the search for such a common doctrine goes on, and as an essential part of the search, two strategic forces ought to be marshaled on both the national and international level: 1) the executives of the aid-giving countries, their parliamentarians, their publics, churches, and other voluntary organizations; and 2) the officials, parliamentarians, and citizens of the aid-receiving countries.

As to the first, there is a proposal on the table. Addressing the Economic and Social Council (ECOSOC) of the United Nations on December 20, 1966, George D. Woods, President of the World Bank Group,

[17] *The New York Times*, March 29, 1967, pp. 23–25.
[18] *Ibid.*, p. 24.

called for "a joint and thorough examination" by the industrialized countries "of what they are trying to achieve in their relationships with the developing world." This, he said, deserved a priority comparable to that given matters of defense, monetary, and trade policy. He urged that such an effort should engage foreign ministers and finance ministers as well as development ministers. The objective would be "to lay down new goals and new approaches and to give a new emphasis to the development assistance effort of the industrialized nations." It would be consistent with, and a way of reaching, the goal of "an international policy for economic development" as suggested by Secretary-General Raúl Prebisch of UNCTAD.[19]

Such a suggestion should be acted upon for the simple reason that it has never been tried on such a basis. The annual "high-level" meeting of the Development Assistance Committee may boast a foreign minister or two but their appearance is often perfunctory. The work is left to the second-echelon development ministers. Aid, for some foreign ministers, is only of peripheral interest. For most finance ministers it is an unpleasant subject, challenging their normal instincts to safeguard their treasuries. Governments do have a "first team." If development assistance is to be played well, that team must involve itself.

The parliamentarians of the industrialized countries, on the other hand, do meet together in various forums, such as the broadly based but casual Inter-Parliamentary Union, the Atlantic-oriented North Atlantic Treaty Organization (NATO) Parliamentary Assembly, and the European-based Council of Europe. But there is no forum for the parliamentarians of the aid-giving countries where economic questions of trade, monetary policy, or aid are systematically discussed with preparation and in depth. Yet this is a world in which parliamentary action on such questions is of vital importance. Such a forum should be devised, and parliamentarians of developing countries should be invited to participate. The benefits would be twofold: There would be a recognition that countries other than one's own were deeply involved in the assistance effort; and the exchange between the lawmakers of the rich and the poor ought to be healthy and humbling for both sides. There is, of course, the risk that the net result might be to provoke a destructive confrontation and to reenforce preexisting prejudices. That risk is well worth taking, for it is inconceivable that the task to be done in the decades ahead can be accomplished without more influential, knowledgeable, and committed parliamentarians.

The citizenry, however, is the most important component of an effort to create a more hospitable climate of opinion. While former colonial powers have been accustomed to make sustained sacrifices for distant

[19] IBRD Press Release, December 20, 1966, pp. 5, 6.

lands, the challenges of development in today's world are quite different. And countries without a colonial tradition face these challenges with no precedent. Although every other function of government has built-in advocates, development assistance is a function without a significant or influential domestic constituency. In every industrialized country there are groups of intellectuals and idealists at one extreme and self-interested contractors at the other who support that country's aid program. But the great mass of the population is untouched and unconcerned.

Just as there should be an effort to convene foreign ministers, finance ministers, and development ministers and just as there should be an effort to convene parliamentarians, so should there be an effort to assemble in a permanent organizational framework citizens and citizen organizations that should be concerned with development assistance. In each industrialized country there ought to be a major organization, linking the individuals and groups possessing the ability to channel information and insights to the ranks of churchgoers, businessmen, laborers, farmers, housewives, and students. The entire cross-section of a nation should be represented.

In the United Kingdom there is the valuable Overseas Development Institute supported by internationally minded British firms. Citizens' groups are associated with aid efforts in Canada, West Germany, the Netherlands, and Scandinavian countries. Other countries have a variety of groups interested in one or another aspect of development activities. In the United States the Society for International Development, with worldwide membership, has long been a focus for discussion of problems of development, while the Council on Foreign Relations and the Foreign Policy Association have included assistance problems in their programs and publications. The very complexity of a largely urban society, however, suggests the need for a separate organizational vehicle serving as analyst, clearinghouse, broker, and catalyst, embracing existing groups, and having as its sole objective the creation of a more knowledgeable and sympathetic public opinion concerning the problems and needs of development. A foundation-sponsored effort is now under way in the United States to explore the feasibility of such an organization, at once comprehensive in membership and single-minded in purpose.

Such national organizations should be linked together internationally. When two or more national groups have been organized, an *internationale* should be formed. Thus established, it should proselytize and expand with the objective of forming an international movement for the advancement of development assistance in all industrialized countries.

It would not only develop materials, such as films, books, leaflets, and newsletters, as well as programs for their use but would also arrange for the sending of representatives of the rich countries to the poor and the bringing of representatives of developing countries to address the complacent audiences of the rich countries. Being privately financed, it could and should conduct searching examinations of the aid programs of the industrialized countries. It and its national affiliates could become a respected and influential voice in advancing an international policy of economic development.

As to the second of the strategic groups mentioned above, the developing countries themselves can play a much greater role in creating the collective will that is a prerequisite to a larger flow of aid. At present there is only a trickle of communication—and that through official channels. The officials, parliamentarians, and citizens of developing countries constitute the best interpreters of development assistance anywhere. They live with the problem. They know it better than anyone else. They fully realize its imperative and purpose in their lives. Thus, when representatives of developing countries visit the industrialized countries, whether they be students, technicians, businessmen, academicians, or tourists, they should capitalize on the goodwill and interest with which they are received—to the benefit of both their hosts and themselves. Much like the position of an important client discussing a business proposition with a great bank, so too there is no want of dignity on either side of the development transaction even though one is borrowing and the other is investing. The result is an undertaking which serves both parties well.

With this in mind developing countries should realize that the industrialized countries have a major problem in the public acceptance of really significant levels of aid. They should further realize that they can help resolve this problem. Few governments could, however much they might wish to, subsidize the importation of foreigners to propagandize aid. But developing countries themselves can train and send speakers for the omnivorous service club appetite, for community forums and university seminars, and for the programs of the many aid-interested organizations in every industrialized country. They can prepare and circulate films, TV strips, articles, and books. They can even arrange to become acquainted with hostile parliamentarians. To the extent that comprehensive citizen aid-supporting activities develop in the industrialized countries these efforts can be an important resource. That such activities cannot be most effectively undertaken by individual developing countries is apparent. There would thus seem to be much sense in the developing countries organizing a joint effort, perhaps in collaboration with donor country citizen organizations, for the promotion of development assistance.

Does UNCTAD have a role to play in marshaling these important forces in both the developed and developing countries? No easy answer can be made to this. UNCTAD seems to have enough to do in managing its confrontations of officials on substantive questions. No constructive purpose would seem to be served at the moment in bringing together the large numbers of ministers, parliamentarians, or citizen group representatives of UNCTAD's member countries. One boggles at the prospect of the fixed positions and set speeches that would bid fair to break all records of hortatorial exhaustion.

Nevertheless, still to be solved in the development sphere is the structural problem of providing flexible international institutional devices for useful communication between the officials, individuals, and groups who collectively determine the quantity, quality, and uses of development assistance. If UNCTAD could recognize that many of its goals lie beyond the power of executive branch officials seated at its table, that "saying so does not make it so," and that it has a responsibility to help create a climate of understanding on the part of both aid givers and aid users, it might then play a uniquely useful role as moderator of limited, informal, and useful discussions.

UNCTAD could arrange a series—perhaps as part of a systematic program—of meetings on development problems for selected parliamentarians from both developed and developing countries. It could provide leadership for launching similar sessions for assistance-oriented citizens' groups of donor countries with participation by influential spokesmen from receiving countries. And it could take the initiative, long overdue, of developing information, materials, and speakers whose audiences would be the very countries to which UNCTAD properly addresses its challenges.

There remains one other note to sound. If adequate response is to be made by the relatively rich to the demands and needs of the absolutely poor, then all reservoirs of skills and matériel should be tapped. The time may thus hopefully not be far distant when greater cooperation between East and West is possible, at least in the area of development assistance, and when the Soviet Union and the Eastern European countries will participate fully in this enterprise of the century.

The next few years will probably not be years of historic achievement. But if people of goodwill in countries North and South, East and West, bend their every effort, these can be years of historic decision and preparation. Let not the weasel words "political feasibility" cloak something quite a matter of the spirit—on the part of both the haves and want-to-haves.

Private Foreign Investment and International Organizations

Stanley D. Metzger

More rapid industrial and agricultural development of the economically underdeveloped three-quarters of the globe is the most important long-run task in international relations, with the sole exception of avoiding major warfare. While economic development depends primarily upon domestic efforts to marshal and direct resources, both human and material, the marshaling and direction of supplementary external resources can assist materially in attempting to achieve that objective. While the major external resources necessary to supplement domestic efforts will continue to be governmental and intergovernmental assistance, there has been for some time now, and will doubtless continue to be, a substantial insufficiency of such resources.

Private external resources which assist economic development are thus at the least a desirable addition to the external governmental resources which are required to supplement domestic measures.

Moreover, even apart from the capital resources transferred to less developed countries through private investment, it can serve as a potent instrument for economic advancement. Given the shortages of skilled managerial and technical personnel in underdeveloped countries now existing and continuing to portend for a long time to come, the extended use of private instrumentalities for transferring external resources, which is especially noteworthy for its infusion of such skilled personnel into the less developed economy, may well be the most efficient way of promoting development in certain important areas of industry and commerce.

These assertions would probably be subscribed to, with varying degrees of enthusiasm, by considerable numbers in all countries.

Stanley D. Metzger is Professor of Law, Georgetown University Law Center, Washington, D.C.

Yet, unlike agriculture, labor, health, education, public lending for economic development, monetary affairs, and other major elements in international economic and social life, private foreign investment has no public international "home agency" whose job it is to nurture and foster it and to promote its welfare.

For private investment has been accorded grudging recognition and inspired ambivalent feelings. The history of private investment had not led by the close of World War II to a generally favorable attitude to its propagation. It had been associated with economic development of less developed countries to be sure, but it was widely believed that such development had been subordinated to its desire for high private earnings for the purpose of repatriation and distribution as dividends to those already well off. In addition, foreign investment had often been associated with and was closely integrated in the political tutelage of metropole powers over colonial territories. In the postwar age of burgeoning nationalism, private foreign investment was, therefore, looked at with very skeptical eyes—it might be desirable but only if carefully hedged about with restraints to guard against a recurrence of the past.

This skepticism on the part of putative capital-importing countries was matched by the concern of capital-exporting countries, as spokesmen for their businessmen, regarding the security of investments in the face of "political" risks of expropriation and of inability to repatriate earnings or capital because of "balance-of-payments" exchange restrictions.

The preoccupation of both the capital-exporting and capital-importing countries with their respective fears had two major consequences. It ensured that there would not be created a chosen public instrumentality to foster private investment since there was such disharmony concerning its role in economic development. And it dominated the terms of what became an ideological international discourse concerning private foreign investment during the 1945–1965 period.

In counterpoise, there evolved throughout the same period a practical approach to the relationship between private foreign investment and economic development which sought to accommodate the needs of the capital-exporting and capital-importing countries while inventing new nonideological techniques for handling the "fear" problems.

Various international organizations were the scene of the ideological confrontation which dominated the private foreign investment-underdeveloped country running dispute during most of the period. Recently, international organizations have begun to play a substantial role in the practical approaches which had their origin in national legislation, especially as the ideological disputation has receded from international forums.

This essay, concerned as it is with the actual, not the potential, relationship between private foreign investment and international organizations, will attempt to outline the main currents in this development and to indicate those which augur better for the general welfare.

THE IDEOLOGICAL DEBATE

Prior to World War II, the main elements of the debate about "protection" of private foreign investment had been made clear. It hinged about the capital-exporting countries' demand that host governments pay just compensation—payment that is "prompt, adequate, and effective"—when they "take" property of foreign nationals. The capital-exporting countries stated that this demand was a requirement of customary international law.[1]

Capital-importing countries resisted the demand, as well as its asserted basis. While the resistance comprised countries as disparate in their ideological orientation as Latin American countries and the Union of Soviet Socialist Republics, the Latin countries had entered the opposing lists far earlier. Adhering to the "Calvo Doctrine" (Carlos Calvo had been Argentine Foreign Minister in the 1870's), they took the position that as a matter of principle they were only obliged to accord foreign nationals whose property is taken equal treatment with their own citizens.[2] This means that if they choose to pay no compensation to their own citizens whose property is taken, they are under no obligation to compensate foreign nationals similarly situated.

The classic formulations were those of the United States and Mexico in their exchanges of notes of 1938 concerning the Mexican expropriations which began in 1915 and continued into the 1930's when oil properties were taken. Are there

> universally recognized principles of the law of nations [which] require, in the exercise of the admitted right of all sovereign nations to expropriate private property, that such expropriation be accompanied by provision on the part of such government for adequate, effective, and prompt payment for the properties seized

regardless whether "its financial or economic situation makes compliance therewith difficult," as the United States claimed?

[1] See Green Haywood Hackworth, *Digest of International Law* (Washington: United States Government Printing Office, 1942), Vol. III, pp. 658–660, for the United States formulation in its 1938 note to Mexico. See also Arghyrias A. Fatouros, *Government Guarantees to Foreign Investors* (New York: Columbia University Press, 1962), pp. 303–338; and Stanley D. Metzger, "Property in International Law," *Virginia Law Review*, May 1964 (Vol. 50, No. 4), pp. 594, 598–607.

[2] Hackworth, *Digest of International Law* (Washington: United States Government Printing Office, 1943), Vol. V, pp. 635–636; and American Law Institute, *Restatement of the Law, Foreign Relations Law of the United States* (Philadelphia, 1965), Section 185, Reporters' Notes Section 2.

Or, as Mexico asserted, is there

> in international law no rule universally accepted in theory nor carried out in practice, which makes obligatory the payment of immediate compensation nor even of deferred compensation, for expropriations of a general and impersonal character like those which Mexico has carried out for the purpose of redistribution of the land[?]

For if there were, Mexico averred, a

> transformation of the country, that is to say, the future of the nation, could . . . be halted by the impossibility of paying immediately the value of the properties belonging to a small number of foreigners who seek only a lucrative end.[3]

The debate, though framed in terms of property protection, perhaps had deeper connotations. It reflected, on one hand, the suspicion on the part of the underdeveloped country that the capital-exporting country, in the guise of protecting its foreign investors, was seeking to restrain economic and social development along nonprivate enterprise lines in the face of the poorer country's efforts to establish or maintain maximum freedom of action to do so. On the other hand, it signified the concern of the capital-exporting country to maintain the "whole structure of . . . international trade and commerce" by opposing other than "orderly change" in property rights of foreigners—which meant opposition to all disorderly change if foreign interests were dominant. It also included a dollars-and-cents dispute about whether, how much, when, and in what form payments must be made if property is taken. These aspects were rarely separated in the postwar debate.

The postwar debate took place at the Geneva and Havana conferences on the Charter for an International Trade Organization (ITO) in 1947-1948, at the Ninth International Conference of American States at Bogotá in 1948, in the General Assembly of the United Nations from 1951 sporadically until 1966, in the Organization for Economic Cooperation and Development (OECD) from 1958 until 1962 and sporadically since, and at the Buenos Aires Economic Conference of the Organization of American States (OAS) in 1957. It is noteworthy that each was a forum for debate on policy and principles—none were "operating agencies," a subject to which we will advert later. In addition, there has been a procedural convention sponsored by the International Bank for Reconstruction and Development (IBRD) which qualifies as part of the ideological approach to the problem. Each exhibited, with relatively minor differences, the point and counterpoint, thrust and counterthrust, of the competing positions. As might be expected, no agreement has been ar-

[3] Hackworth, Vol. III, pp. 658–659, 657–658.

rived at though the consequence of the debate has been a weakening of the principles supported by the capital-exporting countries, largely the result of the growth of numbers of independent, underdeveloped countries, and the growing realization by some of the major capital-exporting countries, especially the United States, of the greatly lessened importance and the growing sterility of the disputation. A brief résumé of this experience may be demonstrative of these assertions.

A word of caution is in order. It would be a mistake to think that the lengthy debate on property protection matters had crucial practical significance. Private foreign investment continued to be desired, and it went to many countries where good commercial reasons—markets for sales, sources of supplies—existed, despite this debate. One can say that there were two levels of discourse being carried on—the ideological and the practical—and while they did touch from time to time, their interference with each other was much less than it might have been.

THE ITO CHARTER

The ITO Charter of 1948 represented the "chief official attempt at a general multilateral treaty embodying some sort of code for foreign investment. . . ."[4] As it emerged in 1948, it contained generalized provisions recognizing the value of private foreign investment; avoiding "unreasonable or unjustifiable" actions injurious to the foreign investors' interests; for "reasonable security for existing and future investments"; and for giving "due regard to the desirability of avoiding discrimination as between foreign investments. . . . " It also recognized the right of capital-importing countries to interfere with foreign investments through screening, restrictions on ownership, and other "reasonable" requirements.[5]

Nothing in the 1948 Charter dealt with compensation for expropriated foreign property. The earlier Geneva draft of the Charter,[6] however, had contained an Article 12 (2) (b) which had stated:

> Members shall make just compensation if the property, in which a national of another Member has an interest, is taken into public ownership or placed under public management or occupation.

[4] A. A. Fatouros, "An International Code to Protect Private Investment—Proposals and Perspectives," *University of Toronto Law Journal*, 1961 (Vol. 14, No. 1), p. 79.

[5] *Ibid.*, p. 80; and Articles 11 and 12 of the Havana Charter in *Havana Charter for an International Trade Organization, March 24, 1948* (Department of State Publication 3046) (Washington: United States Government Printing Office, 1948).

[6] *Draft Charter for the International Trade Organization of the United Nations, Embodied in the Report of the Second Session of the Preparatory Committee of the United Nations Conference on Trade and Employment at Geneva, Switzerland, April–August 1947* (Department of State Publication 2927) (Washington: United States Government Printing Office, 1947).

But a note to Article 12, referring to the form of compensation deemed to satisfy the obligation of "justness," read:

> A Member's obligation to ensure the payment of just consideration or just compensation to a foreign national (insofar as it is an obligation to make payment in currency) is essentially an obligation to make payment in the local currency of that Member.[7]

The note was significant in several respects. Nineteen leading countries (including major Western, capital-exporting countries such as the United Kingdom, Canada, France, and the Netherlands, then suffering from balance-of-payments deficits) had sponsored it, indicating that in 1947, far from there being a rule of international law requiring remittance in foreign exchange of currency paid in compensation for takings, there was in fact only an obligation to make payment in the local currency of the taking state. Secondly, the statement of the nature of the obligation ("essentially in local currency") paralleled the right acknowledged in both the Articles of Agreement of the International Monetary Fund (IMF)[8] and the typical United States bilateral treaty of friendship, commerce, and navigation[9] to control remittances, even of just compensation payments, when necessary for exchange reasons. Third, such a note tended to allay the concern of underdeveloped countries that a lack of exchange would inhibit their ability to "take" foreign property since they could always pay enough local currency if there were no exchange repercussions from such payment. Finally, in consequence of the foregoing, the United States, which had been the progenitor of Article 12, actively sought, and succeeded in achieving, its excision from the 1948 Charter.

The ITO Charter provisions on foreign investment—what they contained and what they omitted in view of the negotiating history—proved to be one of the reasons for the failure of the Charter to receive support in the United States and hence, eventually, to fail.[10]

[7] *Ibid.*, pp. 14, 13.

[8] In *United States Statutes at Large*, Vol. 60 (79th Congress, 2nd Session, 1946), Part 2 (Washington: United States Government Printing Office, 1947), and *Treaties and Other International Acts Series* (hereinafter cited as *TIAS*) 1501 (Department of State Publication 2512) (Washington: United States Government Printing Office, 1946), Article VI, section 3, states: "Members may exercise such controls as are necessary to regulate international capital movements. . . . "

[9] See for example, Article XII of the Treaty of Friendship, Commerce and Navigation Between the United States of America and Japan in *TIAS* 2863 (Department of State Publication 5312) (Washington: United States Government Printing Office, 1954); see also Metzger, *Virginia Law Review*, Vol. 50, No. 4, pp. 606–607; and Herman Walker, Jr., "Modern Treaties of Friendship, Commerce and Navigation," *Minnesota Law Review*, April 1958 (Vol. 42, No. 5), pp. 805–824, reprinted in Stanley D. Metzger, *Law of International Trade: Documents and Readings* (Washington: Lerner Law Book Company, 1966), Vol. I, pp. 24–29.

[10] William Diebold, Jr., *The End of I.T.O.* (Essays in International Finance No. 16) (Princeton, N.J.: International Finance Section, Department of Economics and Social Institutions, Princeton

THE BOGOTÁ AGREEMENT

The Economic Agreement of Bogotá,[11] signed May 2, 1948, at the Ninth International Conference of the American States, was another multilateral agreement which attempted to deal with protection of foreign private investment. Like the ITO Charter, it foundered in substantial part on this issue. A provision recognizing the importance of private foreign investment was, as usual, no problem, nor were those promising "equitable treatment" and forbidding "unjustifiable restrictions" on earnings-transfers. But Article 25, specifically requiring that any expropriation "shall be accompanied by payment of fair compensation in a prompt, adequate and effective manner," drew eight reservations in the form of restatements of the Calvo Doctrine—that the question of compensation would be finally determined by whatever local law might provide.

Efforts in 1949 and 1950 to supplant these reservations by an agreed revised article or by a single reservation acceptable both to the United States and the many reserving Latin American states proved unavailing. Nor was this a consequence of lack of diligence. As the American negotiator the writer can testify to the innumerable cups of coffee at the Pan American Union building at countless weekly sessions, as well as perhaps 30 drafts of suggested new language, which went into the salvage effort. It was as clear at the end as it had been apparent at the outset that the difference could not be bridged by language.

This was really the last multilateral negotiation effort in the direction of protection. The 1957 Buenos Aires Economic Conference witnessed a halfhearted and foredoomed effort to update and hence revive the draft Bogotá Agreement (which had never entered into force). By that time, all knew that the lines were so clearly drawn that no one had a hope of agreement. The American spokesman and the Mexican spokesman for the Latin American countries arranged privately that there would be a simple 30-minute speech by each containing their respective age-old positions, with no rebuttals, in order to minimize tensions and hence disappoint those who doted on circuses and conflicts. That was the end of the matter at Buenos Aires. Succeeding Inter-American Conferences have not witnessed any revival of the property protection issue,[12] both the

University, October 1952), pp. 11–24; and National Foreign Trade Council, *Position of the National Trade Council With Respect to the Havana Charter for an International Trade Organization* (New York, 1950), pp. 5–6, 53–60.

[11] Economic Agreement of Bogotá in *Treaties and Conventions Signed at the Ninth International Conference of American States* (Pan American Union, Law and Treaty Series No. 25) (Washington: Pan American Union, 1948).

[12] Fatouros, *University of Toronto Law Journal*, Vol. 14, No. 1, p. 73.

United States and the Latin Americans having concluded that it is an arid and sterile discourse.

OECD

Beginning in 1958, and culminating in 1962, when the Organization for Economic Cooperation and Development circulated without endorsement, or indeed any "decision on the principle and content," a draft convention on the protection of foreign property, it had been considering drafts, sponsored by the German and Swiss governments, designed to protect private foreign investment by commitments from capital-importing countries. The 1962 draft convention required that foreign investment should not "in any way" be impaired by "unreasonable or discriminatory measures"; that the host country "shall at all times ensure the observance of undertakings given by it in relation to" such property, with any breach of contract to be treated as an international law violation (a proposition not widely accepted as a statement of international law); that compensation, according to the 1938 United States formula, be paid if property is expropriated; that the "freedom of transfer of current income from and proceeds upon liquidation of such property" is recognized by host countries (compare the ITO Charter note to Article 12); and that disputes on the interpretation or application of the convention will be settled by arbitration (compare the Latin American Calvo Doctrine viewpoint).

The American view of this exercise, on the part of some European capital-exporting countries with little postwar negotiating experience in this area, was unsympathetic. Commenting on the drafts which, with little change, became the 1962 draft convention put forward solely by capital-exporting countries and passed on to governments by OECD, the United States Department of State stated:[13]

> The experience of the Department of State over many years has convinced us that the bilateral treaty of friendship, commerce, and navigation offers the most practical means of affording treaty protection to American investors abroad. Multilateral negotiations have been found to produce unsatisfactory results, and the reasons are not difficult to perceive. There are great variances among nations as to the degree to which they are prepared to bind themselves legally to accord fair treatment, even among those which in fact accord fair treatment in practice. Some countries with federal constitutions, including Australia, Canada, and the

13 U.S. Congress, House, Committee on Foreign Relations, *Ad Hoc* Subcommittee, *Hearings, on H. J. Res. 160, to create a commission to study and make recommendations for the security of American foreign investments and the prevention of claims against the United States*, 85th Congress, 1st Session, 1957, p. 14. See also Stanley D. Metzger, *International Law, Trade and Finance* (Dobbs Ferry, N.Y: Oceana Publications, 1962), pp. 164–165; and Metzger, *Virginia Law Review*, Vol. 50, No. 4, pp. 612–613.

United States, have special problems which limit the commitment they can undertake. Efforts at general uniform arrangements tend to break down over the differences among individual countries and their varying legal systems and economies. Consequently, bilateral negotiations during which adjustments can be made to take care of individual differences, may be expected to produce the best results as far as United States interests are concerned.

We have come to these conclusions after three major multilateral attempts to provide a uniform system of protection for international investment. Each resulted in failure. In 1929, an international conference met at Geneva under League of Nations auspices, to consider a carefully prepared draft convention on the treatment of foreigners and foreign enterprises. Because of the reservations each country felt obliged to attach, the effectiveness of the proposed convention was so reduced that the project was abandoned. A second attempt was the section on economic development in the abortive ITO Charter, which, in order to accommodate the varying views of participating countries, equivocated on certain fundamental principles, including the standard of compensation in case of the expropriation of property.

Differences between legal systems, between national policies, and differences as to economic interests created in each case insuperable obstacles to the establishment of uniform principles applicable to each of the many countries concerned. Experience over the past few years in the U.N. with resolutions designed to encourage private investment, which have stimulated strong reactions against any forthright declaration of principle, further indicate the futility of multilateral efforts under present conditions.

While the OECD convention is not yet dead, it is fair to say that it is moribund, especially in view of developments at the UN to which we now turn.

UN Resolutions

The United Nations became seized of the private foreign investment problem as early as an ECOSOC resolution of 1947,[14] prior to the ITO Charter episode. The 1952 and 1954 resolutions recognizing the useful role of such investment but at the same time stressing the right of people freely to use and exploit their natural wealth and resources indicated the continuing tension between the need for additional resources and the suspicion of the putative provider which has characterized attitudes toward private investment in recent years. Perhaps the most important resolution in this area was adopted by the 1962 General Assembly. After a struggle the underdeveloped countries succeeded in watering

[14] UN Document E/255, February 5, 1947, pp. 12–13.

down the traditional formulation of "just" or "full" compensation in respect of takings to "appropriate compensation." While the United States made statements for the record that "appropriate" compensation meant the same thing as "prompt, adequate and effective compensation," this could hardly be convincing in view of the negotiating and voting history of the resolution. Any efforts to secure commitments against discriminatory takings or obligatory arbitration were doomed from the outset.[15]

The 1966 General Assembly made further substantial steps in the same direction in actions taken on the International Covenant on Economic, Social, and Cultural Rights and the International Covenant on Civil and Political Rights and in a new resolution on "permanent sovereignty over natural resources." Article 1, paragraph 2, of both Covenants had provided for the exercise of the right of permanent sovereignty over natural resources in accordance with the "principle of mutual benefit, and international law"—a provision which reflected the uneasy balance of forces through language which avoided rather than solved the key issues. In 1966 a majority of countries at the General Assembly voted for the addition of an independent article in each Covenant stating that,

> Nothing in the present Covenant shall be interpreted as impairing the inherent right of all peoples to enjoy and utilize fully and freely their natural wealth and resources.

The intention was to remove any obstacles to expropriation of private foreign property or to the cancellation of contracts or concessions which might be thought to reside in the reference, in Article 1, paragraph 2, to the "principle . . . of international law."

Another provision of one of the Covenants adopted in 1966, Article 2, paragraph 3, of the Covenant on Economic, Social, and Cultural Rights, is relevant to private foreign investment. That controversial paragraph (adopted by a vote of 41 in favor, 38 against, with 21 abstentions, in committee) reads,

> Developing countries, with due regard to human rights and their national economy, may determine to what extent they would guarantee the economic rights recognized in the present Covenant to non-nationals.

This limitation of the right to discriminate on the basis of nationality to "developing countries" tends to negate the inference that the "normal" disabilities on aliens (i.e., to engage in shipbuilding, radio station broadcasting, aviation on the same terms as nationals) found in the laws of almost all countries, developed as well as developing, were uppermost

[15] General Assembly Resolution 1803 (XVIII), December 14, 1962; see Stephen M. Schwebel, "The Story of the U.N.'s Declaration on Permanent Sovereignty over Natural Resources," *American Bar Association Journal*, May 1963 (Vol. 47, No. 5), pp. 463–469.

in the minds of the proponents of the paragraph. Rather, as the American representative in the committee stated, "authoriz[ing] in virtually unqualified terms discriminatory treatment of nonnationals by a certain group of states...,"[16] it appears to enable developing states to engage in measures affecting private foreign investment, such as discriminatory takings and payment therefor, believed by many developed countries to be inconsistent with international legal principles.

Finally, the General Assembly in 1966 adopted the latest in the series of resolutions relating to "permanent sovereignty over natural resources." The apparent aim of this resolution insofar as it concerned private foreign investment was to increase receptivity in world public opinion of measures of less developed countries whose object will be in the direction of greater "government supervision over the activity of foreign capital to ensure that it is used in the interests of national development" (preamble). Thus, operative paragraph 3 stressed the importance of "strengthening" the ability of developing countries to undertake the maximum possible development of their natural resources "themselves."

Operative paragraph 5 affirmed the right of developing countries

> to secure and increase their share in the administration of enterprises which are fully or partly operated by foreign capital and to have a greater share in the advantages and profits derived therefrom on an equitable basis, with due regard to the development needs and objectives of the peoples concerned and to mutually acceptable contractual practices, and calls upon the countries from which such capital originates to refrain from any action which would hinder the exercise of that right.[17]

The references to "equitable basis" and "mutually acceptable contractual practices" of course give some aid and comfort to private foreign investment in its effort to stave off the erosion of the older international legal principles which had been long espoused by capital-exporting countries. But in consequence of the weight of numbers of the developing countries, their increasing political importance, and the growing weakness of the legal principles urged by the capital-exporting countries in the face of the obvious want of any sort of "consensus" that they persist—which is the essence of any assertion that they are existing "international law"— the capital-exporting countries must expect to continue to have to wage a gradually losing, rearguard action in international organization debates as long as the debate is carried on in ideological terms.

[16] Department of State *Bulletin,* January 16, 1967 (Vol. 56, No. 1438), p. 105. The texts of the two Covenants are reprinted in that issue of the *Bulletin* on pp. 107–121. The "new" article is Article 25 of the Economic Covenant and Article 47 of the Civil and Political Rights Covenant.

[17] UN Document A/6518, November 21, 1966, the report of the Second (Economic and Financial) Committee, reprints the text of the resolution, which was adoped by the Assembly on November 25, 1966, 104 for, none against, with 6 abstentions (including the United States), as General Assembly Resolution 2158 (XXI).

The IBRD Arbitration Convention

The latest in the international efforts by capital-exporting countries to legislate conduct by host countries toward private foreign investment is the IBRD Convention on the Settlement of Investment Disputes Between States and Nationals of Other States.[18] The purpose of the Convention is to encourage the submission of legal disputes concerning private foreign investments between the investor and the host government to international arbitration rather than the usual local remedies in agencies and courts and to establish any breach of a contractual obligation so to arbitrate as an international law violation; it makes any arbitral award pursuant to the Convention enforceable within a state on the same basis as an award of its own court. The idea behind the Convention is that the assurance that government private investor contracts which contain commitments to arbitrate investment disputes will be internationally enforceable and will encourage otherwise hesitant investors to invest in economically helpful development enterprises.

Any country can become a party to the Convention while specifying that resort must first be had to its local remedies, though this would so elongate the proceedings as to work at cross-purposes with the central purpose of the Convention, which is obviously to create a relatively quick procedure so as to restrain action deemed harmful to the investment. Additionally, a country can become a party to the Convention and never insert an arbitral clause in any contract between it and an investor; this, too, would render negatory any effect the Convention might have.

The Convention is obviously applicable only where an investment in a host country is made pursuant to a contract with a government, and such a contract contains an agreement to submit to arbitration. This, in effect, rules out the United States and practically all other developed countries, where investments are made without contractual arrangements with host governments.[19] In fact, it is difficult to see how the Convention can apply to situations other than concession contracts.

Some 25 capital-importing countries signed the Convention, mostly African countries. Of non-African countries, only Malaysia, Pakistan, and the Republic of China represent underdeveloped countries. No Latin American countries signed, they having jointly so declined during negotiations, for obvious reasons earlier discussed. None of the other major underdeveloped countries signed.

[18] A convenient place to find the IBRD Convention and the report of its Executive Directors on it is *International Legal Materials,* 1965 (Vol. 4), pp. 532–544 and 524–531.

[19] *International Legal Materials,* 1966 (Vol. 5), pp. 649, 662, 664, and particularly 666–667 and 667–670 where the State Department's Legal Adviser made it clear, under close questioning by Senator Frank Church, that the Convention had no practical relevance so far as the United States' being required to arbitrate is concerned and Undersecretary of the Treasury Joseph W. Barr emphasized the "small step" forward which it represented.

It seems clear that the IBRD Convention will have extremely limited utility or effect; perhaps, however, it saves a certain amount of face for some capital-exporting countries which had been strong supporters of the "codes." The United States, which had opposed the substantive codes after a futile effort to achieve them twenty years ago, supported the IBRD Arbitration Convention at no real cost and with no substantial expectations concerning its utility.[20] At the end of the tiresome four-year journey toward its completion, there were probably no more than a handful of people in the sponsoring institution who believed that it represented a major step and many more who were simply glad that it was over so that serious matters of economic development could be attacked with more single-minded attention. A membership of less than half the 120-odd UN Members—and many of those of lesser importance—with no indication of significant use even by them, was most unimpressive.

A more important difficulty with the Convention than its ineffectuality, however, is the attitude toward economic development which it bespeaks.

Most students of economic development have long since come to the view that it requires nothing less than the transformation of "traditional" societies predominantly based on

> subsistence or near-subsistence agriculture and/or the bulk export of a few primary commodities, in which per capita income grows slowly or may even be declining as a result of population pressure,

into a modern society in which

> growth of per capita income is internalized in the social and economic system through automatic mechanisms promoting accumulation of capital, improvement of technology and growth of skill of the labor force.[21]

To create a modern society out of an underdeveloped "traditional" one obviously requires deep-seated changes at every turn.

Liberation from "colonialism," redistribution of property and income, and economic planning toward material capital accumulation are insufficient prescriptions even in those cases where they are appropriate. Political stability and a "reasonable impartiality of governmental administration to provide an institutional framework for planning innovations," a legal institutional framework to lessen noneconomic risks, a social system "permitting mobility of all kinds" and "characterized by the depersonalization of economic and social relationships" in order to provide "maximum opportunities and incentives for individual advancement on the basis of productive economic contribution" are some of the additional requirements for modernization.

[20] See above, note 19. See also Metzger, *Virginia Law Review*, Vol. 50, No. 4, pp. 615–617.

[21] Harry G. Johnson, *Economic Policies Toward Less Developed Countries* (Washington: Brookings Institution, 1967), pp. 44–46.

It seems clear, then, that legal development, along with economic, social, and political development, must be a part of a truly modernizing society. For principled determination of conflicts in economic and social relations is the very meaning of that "depersonalization" which is necessary for the widest individual advancement in a system where careers are open to talent, not rigidified into those caste or class patterns which are the hallmark of the traditional societies sought to be modernized.

How does one foster or hinder legal development? One would think that a major way to foster development is through developing local legal institutions, training of teachers and students, and providing these institutions with socially necessary taks befitting their purposes. An institution, like an individual, becomes more proficient through progressive application to more difficult tasks which challenge its abilities and build upon the deposited experience of successfully handled jobs. On the other hand, one way to hinder development is to denigrate the function and betray lack of confidence in the ability of a person or institution to master it. Avoidance of local legal remedies accomplishes the latter, not the former, purpose. Fostering international arbitration instead of the progressive building up of local legal institutions is the reverse of that legal development which is part and parcel of economic development. It is a throwback to the old attitude that less developed countries are perpetual children, incapable of dispensing justice in their courts and unable to learn—that they are somehow inferior to more developed countries and likely to remain so for a long time to come.

This attitude, so reminiscent of similar views so common to the internal lives of too many countries, cannot commend itself to the underdeveloped world and should not be part of the armory of others truly interested in the modernizing of the less developed countries, in the interest of the well-being of all.

What has been said should not be taken to imply that local litigation, as distinguished from "international" litigation, is a good thing; far from it. Litigation in any form is combat, bloodless though it be; combat indicates a failure of cooperative enterprise, as strikes indicate a failure of collective bargaining. Businessmen know better than others that litigation between entities that depend upon each other for the continuous successful functioning of their enterprises is a last resort, resembling the divorce court. It does mean, however, that if international arbitration, rather than local litigation, is insisted upon in these extremities, the chances of reconciliation—of resuming once again the path of cooperative endeavor—are rendered even more remote by reason of the attitude, above described, implicit in the insistence.

THE PRACTICAL APPROACH

Following the debacle on private foreign investment at the 1947–1948 Geneva and Havana conferences on the ITO Charter the United States took stock of the state of customary international law as it related to property protection and the chances of achieving a multilateral agreement improving upon it and decided, *sub silentio,* that neither adequately removed the "fear" obstacle, whatever real role it played, to increased private foreign investment which could be useful in economic development.

The then existing (and presently existing) state of customary international law on protection if property is taken may usefully be summarized at this point.

When a private foreigner's property is taken, he must exhaust his local legal remedies, up through the highest court or administrative tribunal in the taking state—which can take years, as may indeed be the case if his property is subjected to condemnation proceedings in his own country. At the end of this local remedial process he may or may not receive the full value of his property as of the time of taking, but if he does not, the host country cannot, in view of the continued unsettlement of this phase of the law, be said to have violated international law. And there will be no forum to which his own country can hail the host country to litigate the matter in the absence of the latter's consent.

If he does in fact receive the value of his property, he may or may not be permitted to remit it in his own currency, depending upon whether the host country in its lawful discretion decides to permit remittance. If it is an underdeveloped country, there is strong likelihood that it maintains exchange restrictions and cannot spare the exchange.

Beginning in 1948, the United States embarked upon an investment guaranty program designed to overcome the deficiencies of customary international law and to offer the kind of protection which was not negotiable with foreign countries on a multilateral, or indeed a bilateral,[22] basis. During the past nineteen years more than two billion dollars worth of investment guaranty contracts have been written, insuring American private foreign investments for small premiums against the risks of expropriation and inconvertibility of earnings or principal. The investor, following an expropriation, if one occurs, need only pursue his local remedies for one year; he would then turn over his claim to the United States government and receive dollars to the face amount of the investment upon which he had paid premiums.[23]

[22] Metzger, *Virginia Law Review,* Vol. 50, No. 4, pp. 614, 622–625.
[23] For a description of the United States program see Walter S. Surrey and Crawford Shaw (ed.), *A Lawyer's Guide to International Business Transactions* (Philadelphia: American Law

The United States writes such insurance for American investments in over 60 underdeveloped countries.[24] The only obligations of the host country, until 1961, were to agree to recognize the subrogation of the United States, upon payment on a contract, to the claim of the investor, if his investment had been approved by the host country, and to settle such claim by arbitration failing a settlement by negotiation between the two governments.[25] In the 1961 foreign aid legislation the Administration sought and secured authority to loosen even these mild requirements, acquiring authority for the President to make "suitable arrangements" for protecting the interest of the United States government. Since then several agreements loosening the earlier arbitration requirements have been negotiated, as well as one with Argentina which avoids any implication that it may be departing from Calvo principles by signing the agreement.[26]

It is most instructive that during the nineteen years of the program there has not been any significant loss to the United States government on account of expropriation guaranty contracts. This indicates that the deliberate omission of any requirements that the host country assume increased "legal" commitments to the investor has not proved to be less protective of the approved investment. It tends to indicate that an attitude which is more trustful and confident accomplishes more than suspicion in creating climates of goodwill and fair dealing.

It is also noteworthy that the investment guaranty program satisfies the fears of the investor through a subsidy of his risk by the capital-exporting country while at the same time not trammeling the freedom of action of the capital-importing country. Hence, it finesses the earlier

Institute-American Bar Association, 1963), pp. 336–346, and references therein, particularly note 121; and Arnold Rivkin, "Investment Guaranties and Private Investment," *Federal Bar Journal,* October 1959 (Vol. 19, No. 4), pp. 357–366. Lawrence A. Collins and Aaron Etra, "Policy, Politics, International Law and the United States Investment Guaranty Program," *Columbia Journal of Transnational Law,* 1966 (Vol. 4, No. 2), pp. 240–296, represents the most comprehensive recent treatment.

[24] Surrey and Shaw, pp. 341–342; and Collins and Etra, *Columbia Journal of Transnational Law,* Vol. 4, No. 2, pp. 295–296.

[25] See, e.g., the Agreement Between the United States of America and Afghanistan, June 5 and 9, 1957, in *TIAS* 2972 (Washington: United States Government Printing Office, 1958); and the Agreement Between the United States of America and Ecuador, March 28 and 29, 1955, in *TIAS* 3230 (Department of State Publication 5955) (Washington: United States Government Printing Office, 1956).

[26] Protocol to the Agreement Between the United States of America and the Republic of Argentina, signed December 22, 1959, June 5, 1963, printed in *International Legal Materials,* 1963 (Vol. 2), pp. 776–782. Article 3 (B) of the Agreement states:

> [N]either questions under the Constitution and the laws of the Argentine Republic as to the motive, occasion for or legitimacy of an expropriation nor the final decision reached in the Argentine judicial process on *any question* of the Argentine Constitution and laws may be reviewed by the Arbitral Tribunal, since these are matters, within the internal jurisdiction of the Argentine Republic.

(Emphasis added.)

conflict of "principle" between the two countries, deideologizing the disputation.

It also removes the "fear of expropriation" and the "fear of inability to remit" preoccupations which might have restrained greater private investment in underdeveloped countries.

Since the launching of the American investment guaranty program, the Federal Republic of Germany (West Germany) and Japan have instituted similar programs of smaller size and scope for their investors, and several other countries, including Denmark, Norway, and Switzerland, are in various stages of establishing their own national programs. In addition, there has been substantial sentiment among smaller developed countries, underdeveloped countries, business groups, and publicists for the adoption of a multilateral intergovernmental investment guaranty system to supplement national schemes for those that have or will have them and to provide a guaranty system for the investors of those countries which choose not to adopt national schemes.

In 1962, at the request of the Development Assistance Committee (DAC) of OECD, IBRD undertook a study of the problems involved in establishing a multilateral institution for making investment guaranties. Its analytical report without recommendation tended to magnify the problems involved, perhaps because of reluctance on the part of the Bank at that time to undertake the administration of the program. The fact that the Bank had taken on the task of promoting the Arbitration Convention may have been a contributing factor even as it was an error in judgment.

However, in 1963, not satisfied by the report, OECD held a number of meetings of experts from capital-exporting countries to examine the feasibility of establishing a multilateral system supplementary to the national schemes.[27] Incidentally, the fact that this initiative was taken by OECD so soon after its circulation of the draft convention on protection of foreign property indicates its own lack of confidence that underdeveloped countries would accept the obligations sought to be imposed upon them by that document.

In 1964 the OECD Secretariat prepared a report for DAC, based upon the experts' meetings, which outlined a multilateral investment guaranty scheme which it considered to be both feasible and desirable. DAC asked the Secretary-General of OECD to consult with interested member governments and to prepare draft articles of agreement for a multilateral

[27] The text reflects the report of IBRD to the Secretary-General of the United Nations of September 20, 1965, on the status of the International Bank studies on multilateral investment guarantees, reprinted in *International Legal Materials*, 1966 (Vol. 5), pp. 92–95, and material from Metzger, *Virginia Law Review*, Vol. 50, No. 4, pp. 625–627.

program, reflecting governmental views and the conclusions of the secretariat report.

These consultations were still under way when, in the spring of 1964, the United Nations Conference on Trade and Development (UNCTAD), whose actions reflected the desires of its substantial majority of underdeveloped countries, requested IBRD to "expedite its studies on investment insurance," in consultation with governments in both developing and developed countries. This positive interest in progress toward a multilateral investment guaranty scheme on the part of the UNCTAD-underdeveloped countries must be compared with their hostility toward "codes" which would obligate them beyond present requirements and the subsequent nonparticipation of the most important developing countries in the later IBRD Arbitration Convention.

IBRD had informed UNCTAD, during its discussions leading to its request that IBRD expedite its studies, that OECD was discussing the matter and that it (IBRD) would wait conclusion of these deliberations before acting.

On June 18, 1965, OECD transmitted to IBRD a "Report on the Establishment of a Multilateral Investment Guarantees Corporation," setting forth the principal features of a multilateral scheme[28] and indicating that it was one which would be "likely to receive the widest support among the organization's members," which were developed countries in overwhelming part.

IBRD made the OECD report available to its members, conducted preliminary consultations among its member states through their Executive Directors, and has prepared draft articles not yet made public, which at the time of writing were being discussed by the Executive Directors of the Bank. It seems clear from general expressions of countries to the Bank, as well as from the Bank's having moved positively as far as it has toward the effectuation of a multilateral investment guaranty scheme after its own very lukewarm attitude in 1962, that the dominant responses thus far, from developed and developing countries alike, are favorable.

The OECD report, and, it is understood, the Bank's draft articles which are based upon the report, outlines an approach to a multilateral guaranty scheme which is closely related to the actual private investment of a particular capital-exporting country in a host underdeveloped country.[29] The scheme would offer guaranties against noncommercial (i.e., political) risks for new private investments, provided that the investment originated

[28] *International Legal Materials,* Vol. 5, pp. 93–94.

[29] The major European countries indicated, at the OECD experts' meetings and continuously thereafter, an unwillingness to subscribe to a paid-in fund which would back investment guaranty contracts without regard to the particular nationality of the investor so long as he was a national of a subscribing state.

in a capital-exporting country which was a member of the scheme and was to be made in a developing country which was also a member. It would be administered by a new entity affiliated with the Bank, with its own Council operating on a one-country, one-vote basis. The President of the Bank would serve as Chairman of the new entity's Board of Directors, on which capital-exporting and -importing members would be represented, the former in the majority.

Losses would be shared among the capital-exporting countries only, under a formula which would reflect both the extent to which each country's nationals had made use of the program on a global basis and the extent to which its nationals had purchased guaranties for investments to be made in the particular country in which a loss had occurred. Approval by both the country of origin and the host country would be a prerequisite to issuance of a guarantee, thereby enabling a capital-exporting country to control its maximum potential liability for losses, and the capital-importing country the nature and extent of the investment. No special "code" of treatment would be associated with this multilateral scheme; and neither IBRD's Arbitration Convention nor any other devices which might be considered inconsistent with their interests by the underdeveloped countries would be tied to the new scheme.

It is still too early to say with assurance that a multilateral investment guaranty scheme, to supplement national schemes where they exist and to provide protection where they do not, will be established in the next few years. The prognosis, however, is favorable. It reflects the growing realization on the part of developed and developing countries alike, that the investment guaranty device, whether national or multilateral or both, offers the most substantial prospect—the most practical approach—to increase security for private investment without breeding suspicion and the traumatic recollection of the past which attends the other solutions which have engaged so much attention in the past.

CONCLUSION

It would be pleasant to be able to conclude on the note that the practical approach had prevailed over the arid ideological discourse, after a difficult twenty-year struggle, as the story thus far related would appear to indicate. While this continues to be the likely outcome, recent United States unilateral actions attempting to force underdeveloped countries to apply standards of protection going well beyond international law requirements indicate that we will continue to witness for some time two inconsistent approaches to the relationship between private investment and developing countries. At the very time when wiser heads in both developed and developing countries were eschewing divisive and futile ideological debate which took little account of their mutual needs and aspirations, the Congress, over the opposition of the United States Administration, enacted amendments to the foreign aid legislation and to the act authorizing augmentation of the "soft-loan" component of the Inter-American Development Bank (IDB).[30]

Briefly, these amendments to United States foreign aid legislation in 1962, 1963, and 1965 called for suspension of American assistance to any foreign government which after January 1, 1962, 1) nationalizes American-owned property, or 2) repudiates or nullifies a contract with an American, or 3) imposes "discriminatory taxes" or "restrictive maintenance or operational provisions" or takes other actions having "the effect" of nationalization; and fails within six months

> to take appropriate steps, which may include arbitration, to discharge its obligations under international law toward such citizen . . . including speedy compensation for such property in convertible foreign exchange, equivalent to the full value thereof, as required by international law, or fails to take steps designed to provide relief from such taxes, exactions, or conditions, as the case may be. . . .

This legislation was adopted in the face of the strongest advice against it. Ambassador W. Averell Harriman was so aroused by it that he expressed himself in very blunt language:

> *You can't dictate to people. If the United States threatens to take away aid under these conditions there is not a country in the world that would not tell us to go to hell.*[31]

The Department of State advanced six reasons against it.[32] 1) Such

---

[30] *United States Statutes at Large,* Vol. 76 (87th Congress, 2nd Session, 1962) (Washington: United States Government Printing Office, 1963), pp. 260–261; *United States Code Annotated,* Title 22: *Foreign Relations and Intercourse* (St. Paul, Minn: West Publishing Co., 1964), 2370 (e), pp. 227–228; Foreign Assistance Act of 1963, Section 301 (e), *United States Code: Congressional and Administrative News, 88th Congress-First Session, 1963* (St. Paul, Minn: West Publishing Co., 1963), pp. 425–427; and Public Law 89–6, 89th Congress, 1st Session, March 24, 1965, reprinted in *International Legal Materials,* 1965 (Vol. 4), p. 458. The last-named enactment requires that the "voting power of the United States" in the Fund for Special Operations of IDB "shall be exercised for the purpose of disapproving any loan from" that Fund for "any project, enterprise, or activity in any country" where the President has suspended United States assistance because of the Hickenlooper Amendment.

[31] Richard B. Lillich, "The Protection of Foreign Investment and the Hickenlooper Amendment," *University of Pennsylvania Law Review,* June 1964 (Vol. 112, No. 8), p. 1116, quoting the New York *Herald Tribune,* January 7, 1964, p. 10 (international edition).

[32] Lillich, *University of Pennsylvania Law Review,* Vol. 112, No. 8, p. 1127; and Metzger, *Virginia Law Review,* Vol. 50, No. 4, pp. 619–620. As Lillich points out, however, in 1963, when the amendment was further tightened, while Agency for International Development (AID) Director David E. Bell was not enthusiastic in indicating no objection, the Secretary of State, though unhappy about congressional attempts to "legislate foreign policy," reversed the State Department's very marked antagonism of just a year earlier, stating that the amendment was "a good thing." (Lillich, *University of Pennsylvania Law Review,* Vol. 112, No. 8, p. 1126.)

legislation would make it appear that our aid programs "are substantially motivated by a desire to protect U.S. private investment and that they are, in effect, tools of U.S. capital." 2) A vital element of United States foreign policy is placed at the mercy of one unreasonable action by a foreign official, who might be goaded by groups desirous of just such a denouement. 3) The legislation could retard "some of the economic and social reforms we seek in connection with our aid program, particularly in Latin America"—land reform "may well require expropriation of existing estates, some of which may be owned by U.S. nationals," which we expect would be compensated, but the fear that the United States would consider the compensation inadequate or the procedures unfair and hence cut off all aid might well inhibit the land reform action. 4) The requirement that aid be cut off could "commit our whole policy" into the hands of an intransigent American citizen whose acts could provoke expropriation and prevent reasonable settlement yet whose claims might be difficult for the United States to assess. 5) A decision as to the reasonableness of compensation often being difficult, an *ex parte* judgment by the United States that it disagrees with a court in a host country "is hardly calculated to win respect." 6) Finally, "flexibility, rather than a rigid rule, is required." The "interests of the United States as a nation require the balancing of many factors, and the availability of our foreign assistance must depend on the same factors." The

> injection of the U.S. foreign assistance programs into condemnation proceedings would at best advance the interests of the American citizen whose property is expropriated only marginally, and, on the other hand, it can seriously injure the vital U.S. national interests which the foreign assistance program is assigned to further.

This ill-advised effort to enunciate new principles of property protection under the guise of restating existing international law came at the very time when the Supreme Court of the United States had stated that

> there are few if any issues in international law today on which opinion seems to be so divided as the limitations on a State's power to expropriate the property of aliens . . . [this] disagreement as to relevant international law standards reflects an even more basic divergence between the national interests of capital importing and capital exporting nations and between the social ideologies of those countries that favor state control of a considerable portion of the means of production and those that adhere to a free enterprise system.[33]

Lillich further questions, quite cogently, whether this change of view had any substantial factual basis (*ibid.*, pp. 1127–1128). At the April 1967 annual meeting of the American Society of International Law Andreas Lowenfeld, former Deputy Legal Adviser of the Department of State, indicated a substantial number of additional complications in connection with the administration of the Hickenlooper Amendment.

[33] *Banco Nacional de Cuba* v. *Sabbatino, United States Reports,* Vol. 376: *Cases Adjudged in*

It also came at a time when efforts to accommodate interests on a practical basis were bearing fruit, as can be seen from the wide support of both developed and developing countries for the investment guaranty device, bilateral and multilateral, which did not attempt to lay down new rules of conduct. Indeed, the really noteworthy development in the past few years has been the growth of the practical approach on the part of farsighted businessmen, of new countries seeking more rapid economic development, and of knowledgeable diplomats.

Despite aberrations such as these foreign aid conditions, which are really a throwback to an earlier era of combat from which almost all had hoped that we had emerged at long last, the practical approach to economic development, enlisting the active participation of private foreign investment in a cooperative, not antagonistic, spirit, appears to be the sensible way in which countries will find that they can accomplish their tasks. At all events, it is the only feasible approach for nations and for international organizations.

For the practical, cooperative approach to the involvement of private foreign investment in the essential task of economic development of less developed countries serves the true interests of developed and developing countries alike, and that of the participating individuals as well. Less developed countries more and more are coming to see that ideological proscriptions are a poor substitute for, and may even impede, the successful input of resources (capital, technical, expertise) which is so necessary to rapid development.

Private foreign investment more and more is coming to see that there is no single foreordained way to invest successfully in an underdeveloped country—that joint ventures with local capital, with local government, with investment guarantees, and in varieties not even yet dreamed of, may be necessary and even desirable if the twin objectives of development and earnings are to be achieved. The investors are not only themselves becoming deideologized, as are the great majority of countries; they are finding that this process may even be bringing about a sense of adventurousness and innovation (could we say sense of commitment?) which resembles frontier days in our own country. This, it is suggested, is what really suits our nature. To the extent that the future relationship between private foreign investment and international organizations can encompass an intensification of this positive, practical approach to economic development—and avoid the tired and useless ideological squabbles of the past twenty years—it will serve us all well—the developed and the developing countries.

the Supreme Court at October Term, 1963 (Washington: United States Government Printing Office, 1964), pp. 428–430.

Education for Development

ROBERT W. COX

THE relationship between international organization and developing countries is one of interdependence: developing countries place hope in disinterested help through international agencies; and the needs of the developing world provide stimulus to the expansion of international organization. Yet these two contemporaneous processes of political development—the growth of international organization and nation building in developing areas—may not always be in step. Education is a convenient viewpoint from which to examine this relationship, with its element of discord and of convergence of interest. Education is a prominent aspiration of governments and people in developing countries and is widely considered to be a most efficacious instrument for modernization. This subject-matter limitation also makes it possible to focus on two international organizations: the United Nations Educational, Scientific and Cultural Organization (UNESCO) as the agency primarily responsible for educational systems; and the International Labor Organization (ILO) because of its recent emphasis both on training in occupational skills and on the relevancy of the manpower factor for educational policy.

Executive heads of international organizations are concerned with the institutional continuity of their organizations, often with expanding the tasks and strengthening the authority of these organizations and sometimes with playing a role toward international integration. Their choices of activities and programs tend to be made in relation to these primary political goals.

Governments of aid-receiving countries have a different perspective. They regard international organizations instrumentally in relation to their own primary goals, which vary with regimes, i.e., the preservation of the

ROBERT W. COX is the Director of the International Institute for Labor Studies. This Institute was created by the International Labor Organization (ILO) in 1960 as a center for education and research. This essay expresses the thinking of the author and in no way commits ILO.

existing order of society or its transformation toward a vision of a future society. Economic development is also viewed instrumentally toward these ultimate ends. If one shifts from governments to population groups, a greater number of goals come to light for which economic development is instrumental.

Aid-giving governments view the economic development of less developed countries and the activities of international organizations in this regard from yet different perspectives: as means toward creating a friendly disposition on the part of developing countries and toward avoiding dangerous disturbances in the international system for the security and stability of which they have both a special interest and a special responsibility.

Thus, in considering the role of international organizations in the education and manpower field with reference to economic development it is necessary to weave in and out of a complex web of goals. The choice of international organization programs and the way they are carried out are the products of a mixing and meshing of these differing goals.

The complexity is not reduced when the subject is approached from the standpoint not of goals but of the way in which the relevant variables interact in the process of modernization, as seen from the national perspective. To consider human resources development (education and manpower) as the independent variable and economic growth as the dependent variable would present an incomplete and possibly false view of the process. Both need to be shown in a dependent relationship to politics and power.[1]

The set of domestic variables referred to below in considering the process of modernization thus comprises four elements: 1) social stratification and its implications for power relations among social groups; 2) political leadership; 3) educational policy; and 4) economic growth.

Among them a fifth is introduced, namely, the influence of international organizations, in the effects of which we are particularly interested.

It is not possible to do more here than suggest an approach which would take sufficient account of some of the complexities mentioned. As a first step, human resources development is considered from the perspective of international organization. As a second, the policies advocated by international organizations are viewed within the process of moderniza-

[1] David E. Apter, in *The Politics of Modernization* (Chicago: University of Chicago Press, 1965), p. 223, has distinguished between "modernization" as an early phase and "industrialization" as a later phase:

> It is important to consider the political rather than the economic variable as independent in modernizing societies because the ensemble of modernization roles is not integrated by a dynamic subsystem based on rational allocation, as is the case in industrial societies. Instead the subsystem is usually the . . . political group such as the army or bureaucracy (or in some instances, a religious body).

tion (with the aid of some loosely sketched models). Finally, some questions are put concerning the role of international organization in relation to developing polities.

THE INTERNATIONAL ORGANIZATION PERSPECTIVE

The programs of international organizations have grown in response to changes in the world environment both through demands made by their memberships and initiatives and opportunities seized by international civil servants.

One such initiative was an "operational" manpower program launched by the newly appointed Director-General of ILO in 1948 and 1949. From one perspective this may be seen as an institutional adaptation by ILO to the post-World War II environment.

The first target of the program was European manpower: The program could thus appear as an auxiliary to the Marshall Plan. (The Union of Soviet Socialist Republics at that time was in a position of aloofness and sometimes hostility toward ILO.) Subsequently, at the time United States President Harry S. Truman initiated his Point Four Program ILO's attention shifted from Europe to the developing areas. The early manpower program expanded into other fields of technical cooperation, but manpower activities continued to dominate, today accounting for about 40 percent of ILO's expenditures.

Trade unions became highly politicized in the Cold War, their international policies polarized on the issue of anti-Communism. The emphasis by the ILO Director-General on manpower put to the fore a technical matter which, though it did not arouse the same emotional involvement as cold-war issues, was able to maintain trade-union support as being useful and noncontroversial. The program also found favor with ILO Employer delegates and some governments not only for its own merits but because it represented a shift away from ILO's traditional work of drawing up international legal standards of labor legislation. Western trade unions supported warmly the standards approach as a means of legitimizing their bargaining demands; employers opposed it (presumably for the reason unions supported it); and many governments, especially the growing number from the developing areas, considered that practical aid rather than more model laws was what they wanted. Manpower activities thus, for ILO, represented an important area of consensus in an environment bedeviled with ideological and political conflict and a significant expansion of ILO's tasks. This development has been so important that it would be difficult to imagine ILO today sustaining sufficient support for the residue of its programs (none of which have such a broad appeal as the manpower program) and maintaining its place in the world if its manpower activities were to cease.[2]

UNESCO's concentration upon educational development was a means to strengthen its authority and expand its task. The earlier period of scattered activities sustained politically on a basis of "you support my project and I'll support yours" was succeeded by a definition of clearer organizational goals in the shape of a few major programs. More forceful initiative by the UNESCO Director-General found ready allies in the national ministries of education in the developing areas who could make use of this external pressure in addition to that of domestic groups toward a policy of educational expansion.

UNESCO introduced a new method, inspired perhaps by the methods used earlier by the North Atlantic Treaty Organization (NATO) and the Organization for European Economic Cooperation (OEEC): the fixing of goals for expansion by representative regional conferences followed by periodic assessment of how far these goals are attained. Conferences of ministries of education were held in Karachi (for Asia) in January 1960; Addis Ababa (for Africa) in May 1961; and Santiago (for Latin America) in March 1962.[3] These conferences not only set targets— seven-year universal compulsory education for Asia by 1980, six years of education for Africa by 1980, and six years for Latin America by 1970— they were also occasions for education ministers and their officials to confront ministers of economics or finance with their claims for a larger allocation of resources and to do so with the support of international organization specialists, professors of economics, and other "independent" experts. UNESCO also associated other international and regional organizations with these conferences, rallying support for the policy thrust.[4]

The International Bank for Reconstruction and Development (IBRD), the UN Children's Fund (UNICEF), and the UN Special Fund all came around to the view that education is a vital priority component in eco-

[2] The vigor of ILO's defense of its acquired position as the international agency responsible for vocational training, management development, productivity improvement, etc., in the industrial field when the United Nations Industrial Development Organization (UNIDO) was being created by the UN General Assembly is a token of this perception of a vital organizational interest. In the outcome ILO's competency was preserved. See General Assembly Resolution 2152 (XXI), November 17, 1966; the negotiations are reported in ILO Document G.B. 167/18/25 of November 11, 1966.

[3] Separate from this series but contributing to the same current of thought was the conference convened by the Organization for Economic Cooperation and Development (OECD) for countries of Western Europe and North America in October 1961 which consecrated as part of the now conventional wisdom the proposition that educational investment is good for economic growth.

[4] ILO has more recently adopted the same method for setting regional goals for training and employment creation, beginning with the American region. See the "Ottawa Plan of Human Resources Development" approved by a regional conference held in that city in September 1966. Similar "plans" for Asia and Africa are in preparation.

nomic development plans qualifying for their financial assistance;[5] and
this gave the UNESCO leadership the further argument that its promotion of planned educational expansion would help governments of developing countries get their share of the available finance since education
was "in" with the financial agencies.

Together with the systematic use of internationally organized pressures
on national action through the institutional device of regional targets
followed by evaluation an educational development ideology was elaborated, giving preeminence to the role of education as a motor of economic progress.[6] Many sources contributed to the elaboration of this
ideology: A group of American scholars provided the reasoned basis for
it;[7] United States foundations threw their support behind efforts to work
it out; the International Economic Association focused professional interest upon the economics of education;[8] and OECD, the United Nations,
ILO, and UNESCO officials put together from this emerging body of
thought the rationale of their advocacy of education and training as the
highway to development. UNESCO stood at the center of this, using its
social science arm to promote the elaboration of a development doctrine
and methodology which was applied through an expansion of the tasks
of its educational arm and encouraging the endorsement of the doctrine
by other international agencies whose concurrent activities could sustain
the UNESCO drive.

The main tenets of this ideology are that investment in human resources is very likely to produce a higher return in terms of economic
growth than investment in physical capital and that such investment is

[5] The views of Paul G. Hoffman as Managing Director of the Special Fund are in the pam-
phlet by him, *One Hundred Countries: One and One Quarter Billion People* (Washington: Albert
D. and Mary Lasker Foundation, 1960), especially pp. 11, 31, 35; and in his *World Without
Want* (New York: Harper & Row, 1962), pp. 53–54. The World Bank approach is described in
an article by its President, George D. Woods, "Sow Education Aid, Reap Economic Growth,"
Columbia Journal of World Business, Summer 1966 (Vol. 1, No. 3), pp. 37–42. The Inter-
American Development Bank (IDB) also stresses loans for higher education, linking this with its
aim to promote Latin American integration by advocating a "common market of knowledge and
talent." See a speech by Felipe Herrera, President of IDB, at Bank headquarters, Washington,
D.C., September 12, 1966.

[6] The term ideology is used to mean doctrine designed to produce action, an interpretation of
realities intended as a guide for acting upon it. Ideologies may be limited in scope, e.g., to education and economic development or the role of international organization in world politics, as well
as comprehensive interpretations of historical change.

[7] Especially Frederick Harbison and Charles Myers (following earlier work by Theodore Schultz)
through the work of the Inter-University Project on Labor in Economic Development, the studies
of which were backed by the Ford Foundation and the Carnegie Corporation, New York. See
Frederick Harbison and Charles A. Myers, *Education, Manpower, and Economic Growth: Strategies of Human Resource Development* (New York: McGraw-Hill, 1964). The most comprehensive interpretation by the Inter-University Project is in Clark Kerr and others, *Industrialism and
Industrial Man: The Problems of Labor and Management in Economic Growth* (Cambridge, Mass:
Harvard University Press, 1960).

[8] E. A. G. Robinson and J. E. Vaizey (ed.), *The Economics of Education* (London: Macmillan,
1966).

also socially more beneficial because it improves individual welfare and earning capacity.[9] A subsidiary proposition is that the content of education should be more scientific and technical so as to relate more to the needs for modernizing the economy. Some readjustment of wage and salary differentials between different types of occupations is also recommended to give incentive for the acquisition of technical skills over literary and legal education. The prevalent opinion among the professors, the international officials, and the foreign aid program officials (though not among the political leaders of many recipient countries) gives preference to the expansion of secondary and higher education in those countries in the early stages of growth before an attempt to bring about universal primary education, the reason being that shortage of subprofessionals, supervisors, technicians, and managers creates bottlenecks for development and thereby also prevents expansion of employment opportunities for the less educated. And ILO has added as a qualification to unmitigated enthusiasm for the development potency of education that employment-creating targets should be kept in line with school-filling targets: More jobs should be created as more people are educated and trained. Finally, economic development planning should be comprehensive so as to relate the planning of investment in education and training with manpower planning and the planning of investment in physical capital.

Without at this point considering the merits and criticisms of this ideology with reference to economic development it is necessary to point out its attractiveness to the international organizations. Organization leaders perceived in the 1950's that economic development was a challenge to their ability to bring about peaceful change in the international system. But it became clear once again—as it had been made clear in the aftermath of Bretton Woods—that the big powers were not prepared to place the very large sums required for any international programs of economic development under the administration of international officials in structures that would be, much more than the Bretton Woods institutions, responsive to the wills of the less developed countries.[10] By the end of 1957 the Special United Nations Fund for Economic Development (SUNFED) project for a capital development fund, which had been the subject of pressures and negotiations during the mid-1950's, was shelved, and the substitute adopted by the General Assembly was the Special Fund, an

[9] Those who pursue the goal of educational expansion dispose also of a second line of attack. If it is objected that in some circumstances the economic growth argument does not justify greater investment in education, then education can be advocated as a "human right." This second line is, however, strictly speaking, distinct from the educational development ideology.

[10] The other issue area in which international organization might have been expected to play a role with potential to change the international system was disarmament or arms control. But the prospects were even more bleak. The big Western financial contributors took the position that progress toward disarmament was a precondition for more economic development aid.

agency with a lesser order of funds to deal in "preinvestment," to foster projects which would enhance the capacity of underdeveloped countries to absorb more capital (which might come through other channels).[11] In the "preinvestment" concept education and training had an honored place. The educational development ideology gave greater qualitative importance to the kinds of things that the international organizations had left to do and enhanced their prestige vis-à-vis bilateral programs which had much larger funds at their disposal.

Furthermore, the simple relationship posited between education and economic development avoided many awkward questions concerning the will of governments to undertake population control measures or fiscal, land, or other institutional reform and to deal with the economic consequences of attitudes bred of social tradition or of poverty. Such questions which lead straight to matters of social stratification and political leadership are embarrassing for international agencies which have to give the appearance, in technical assistance, of being servants to established regimes.

From a UNESCO organizational standpoint there can be little doubt of the success with which the educational development ideology was applied. It lent support to and provided a rationale for a constellation of pressures toward the expansion of investment in education. The sum spent on education and training by international organizations has been rising through the 1960's. The same is true of bilateral aid programs.[12] The proportion of national budgets in the developing countries devoted to education has been rising markedly more rapidly than their national incomes.[13] Education has been claiming successfully an increasing share of all resources available for development, national, bilateral, and multilateral. It is a tribute to the leadership of UNESCO particularly that such an impressive impact could be made upon economic development policies throughout the world. From the standpoint of strengthening the effectiveness and authority of international organization this must be accounted a marked success. Whether it advances the cause of economic development is a separate question.

THE DOMESTIC PERSPECTIVE OF MODERNIZATION

To this latter question we must now turn in order to provide a framework for assessing the interaction of international organization activity

[11] John G. Hadwen and Johan Kaufmann, *How United Nations Decisions are Made* (Leyden: A. W. Seythoff, 1960), pp. 85–111; and James Patrick Sewell, *Functionalism and World Politics: A Study Based on United Nations Programs Financing Economic Development* (Princeton, N.J: Princeton University Press, 1966), pp. 97–122.

[12] E.g., the United States' International Education Act, 1966, and the high proportion of French bilateral aid going into the export of teachers.

[13] "Education, science and communication in the UN Development Decade," *UNESCO Chronicle,* June 1966 (Vol. 12, No. 6), p. 229.

with national situations. The framework should be broad enough to comprehend the role and effect of educational and training systems in the context of modernization. The simplest way to approach this schematically is to sketch out several models which state presumed relationships between the variables referred to at the beginning of this discussion.[14]

Model X: The Perpetuation of Existing Social Stratification

In this model the educational system reflects and perpetuates the existing structure of power relations between social strata. Neither the social stratification nor the educational system is conducive to economic growth; but this has not prevented economic development occurring in some sectors.[15] The social strata may be described as follows: 1) a small group traditionally deriving its power in the main from land and buttressed by close association (through family connections) with religious and military institutions; 2) an urban "middle" stratum; 3) skilled manual workers, committed and adapted to the modern sector; 4) an urban "marginal" stratum not fully adapted to "modern" culture, subsisting in unskilled trades or unemployed; and 5) the traditional rural stratum.

During this century the power of the urban middle stratum has grown at the expense of the traditional power-holding upper strata. This shift has been accompanied by adaptations rather than by revolutionary upheavals. The urban middle stratum, while deriving power from industry and commerce, has not challenged the cultural values of the old aristocracy, which remain dominant. Its acceptance of these values, including a disdain for manual work, distinguishes this social group from the ascetic entrepreneurs of the "Protestant ethic." The old landowning family adapts too: It delivers its clients' votes to the political party run by urban "middle" elements in return for a free hand in local affairs. The church and the military broaden the recruitment of their elites to reflect the urban middle stratum's position of social and political power.[16]

---

[14] This is all very tentative and subject to verification. The models which follow are drawn from some recent studies which include a broader set of variables than measures of manpower, education, and economic growth. I am particularly indebted to James S. Coleman (ed.), *Education and Political Development* (Princeton, N.J: Princeton University Press, 1965).

[15] Although the elements of this model are drawn in the main from studies about Latin American countries, the model is not meant to be a series of generalizations about Latin America. Its purpose is to suggest some relationships in terms of which particular situations can be analyzed. In some respects model X seems to fit other countries with long-established educational traditions and an absence of recent revolutionary upheaval in social structure, such as India, while at the same time certain developments in Latin America may have broken out of this framework. The volume published by the UNESCO International Institute for Educational Planning, *Problems and Strategies of Educational Planning: Lessons from Latin America*, ed. Raymond F. Lyons (Paris: UNESCO, 1965), contains some articles which have been helpful in delineating the characteristics of this model.

[16] See John J. Johnson (ed.), *The Role of the Military in Underdeveloped Countries* (Princeton, N.J: Princeton University Press, 1962), especially pp. 109–129.

In this social structure education is the avenue of mobility; but the educational system operates to preserve rather than to change the structure. It is education in the old Western European tradition with a high valuation on training for the "liberal" professions. The system functions primarily as a means of selection to entry into these professions and analogous occupations, i.e., preeminently government employment. Educational expansion increases opportunities for upward mobility of urban middle and working class people.

Secondary school pupils come in their large majority from the upper and urban middle strata. For the most part they study academic subjects, only a minority going to the commercial or industrial secondary schools which are regarded as "second-class." The qualifications of secondary school teachers are also poor on the average, as many are part-time teachers. The defects of the secondary school are carried over into the university: inadequate standards of scholarship, compounded by an absence of research, and the lack of a self-sustaining and mutually stimulating intellectual community. These are the consequences of a system in which teaching is a part-time occupation and where both the professor's chair and the student's diploma are valued more for the social status they confer than for the content of the educational process they symbolize.

Despite the fact that there has been a marked expansion of primary education in rural areas this education is ill adapted to rural needs. Its content is not patently relevant; it is not organized to take account of the exigencies of agricultural work; teachers are ill qualified, their appointment often enough being a form of political patronage at the disposal of local magnates. The expansion of rural primary education may reflect an awakening demand on the part of rural populations or a quickened sense of duty on the part of governments; but its inadequacies, the low average years of schooling, and the high dropout rate render it of little positive effect toward the improvement of agriculture. And in the case of those relative few who stick with it primary education tends to be regarded instrumentally as a means of escape from rural work. Primary education is also not well adapted to the urban "marginal" group.[17] Expansion of existing educational systems does little to integrate these groups or make them economically more productive.

The output of the educational system is as ill adapted to industrial development as to rural needs. Some countries close to this type have, it is true, experienced high rates of economic expansion in recent decades; but it would be difficult to attribute this to educational causes. In fact, the reverse may well be the case because those countries in which the urban

---

[17] Marshall Wolfe, "Social and Political Problems of Educational Planning in Latin America," in *Problems and Strategies of Educational Planning*, pp. 26–27.

middle stratum has been growing most rapidly (as a consequence of the expansion of education) have been least dynamic economically.[18] Calculations of the supply of "high-level manpower" for economic development which are based upon the output of the secondary schools and universities are thus unconvincing evidence of productive skills and aptitudes. Expansion of this type of education may be counterproductive. It might be more useful to find out more about the background of those whose aptitude and skill for industrial expansion have been demonstrated.

If, by and large, the educational system in this model functions so as to maintain prevailing value-patterns and the existing social structure, educational expansion creates dysfunctions. The urban stratum demands an increase in secondary education, supported by other aspirants to "middle" status among the better-off urban workers.[19] This in turn creates a demand for more government jobs which may prove to be a drag on economic expansion and a stimulus to further misallocation of human resources (e.g., more teachers to train more students who in turn will demand more government jobs).

The personal conflict inherent for the secondary school and university student between defense of his acquired social status and lack of constructive outlets engenders unrest among students, politicizing the universities. Student discontent is directed overtly toward demands for participation in the government of universities and includes implicitly an element of informal apprenticeship for selection to membership in the political elite. It tends to be anomic, radical in its attack on authority, but not to represent any consistent or fundamental challenge to the social power structure which, archaic as it seems, has proven able to sustain extraordinary inequalities and tensions. If, however, the educational system were to produce a large and growing number of alienated "educated unemployed," there would be a possibility of this type of discontent crystallizing into forceful social movements, i.e., providing leadership to awaken rural society and the "marginal" population in the towns.

Model Y: Populist Political Leadership

This is a more volatile model, more characteristic of a newly independent country.[20] Social stratification is much more fluid than in model X. The educational system functions less as a preservative of previously existing social relations; on the contrary, high expectations are placed in it as an instrument for fashioning a new future society. However, education

[18] *Ibid.*, p. 21.

[19] *Ibid.*

[20] This model is drawn mainly from literature about some African countries; but the same comment has to be made as about model X, i.e., it is not intended as a generalized description but as an analytical construct.

and educational expansion can for a developing economy lead to a mis-allocation of resources and may also produce some seriously destabilizing effects in the political system, at least in the short term.

The traditional structures of social authority vary considerably but in virtually all cases are subnational, that is, they refer to tribal or communal units smaller than the contemporary nation-state. The nation-state exists juridically, but the great task now is to give the people a sense of national identity. This task is being undertaken by a political elite composed of individuals of different backgrounds, often of humble origins with reference to the traditional social authorities but sometimes combining the aura of high status in the old authority system with a new revolutionary role. This political elite has a strongly populist orientation uniting it and legitimating its power; and populist ideology determines its policy choices in nation building.

Education is regarded by this elite as a major instrument of nation building; and this valuation appears to be widely shared, creating a popular demand for expansion of education, especially primary education.[21] The goal of universal primary education is seen as necessary to create the communications system of a modern society, enabling closer contact between the political elite and the population. It is also a requisite for the introduction of modern production processes. And it is an aspect of the "human rights" aspirations of populist nationalism toward overcoming inequalities.

Secondary and higher education are also regarded by the political and economic elite and those aspiring to join them as the channel of upward mobility. It was through the educational system that the present political leadership was recruited.[22] Civil service and public sector employers, as well as employers in some of the larger foreign-owned undertakings, make educational level the criterion of access to higher-level jobs. The absence of a thriving private sector in which entrepreneurial initiative determines success, irrespective of the level of formal education, closes out alternative channels of upward mobility. (A resulting aberration is an excessive emphasis on diplomas.) Thus, along with the populist demand for universal primary education there is a demand from aspirants to elite status for the expansion of secondary and higher education.

[21] Hadley Cantril, in *The Pattern of Human Concerns* (New Brunswick, N.J.: Rutgers University Press, 1965), presents results of attitude surveys in some developing countries. One is struck by the cross-national differences in the extent to which education features in people's hopes for their country, e.g., for 47 percent of the Nigerian sample compared with 11 percent of the Indian and 6 percent of the Brazilian. Cantril finds a more general contrast between the Nigerians, enthusiastic about the potentialities of their newly achieved independence and especially high in their hopes both for themselves and for their country, and the more "lethargic" Brazilians and Indians (pp. 70, 77–85, 156).

[22] Michael Debeauvais, "Education in Former French Africa," in Coleman (ed.), *Education and Political Development*, p. 85.

Is the populist-led expansion of education changing the social power structure?[23] What happens typically is a growth of tensions between the political elite which takes power at the time of independence and the elite of technicians and civil servants and between these newly established elites and the generation of students behind them.[24] The political elite's rapid rise to power has the effect of inflating expectations in the efficacy of education as a means of access to elite status. This inflation of expectations leads in turn to frustrations as secondary school and university graduates realize the positions of power are already preempted. The newer elite of technicians and administrators, especially those in the key economic sectors, are better educated than the political leaders but subordinated and suspect. The politicians react in defense of their acquired positions by resorting to the anti-intellectualist strain in populism. This further alienates the students in secondary and higher education. The economic technicians' problem may be at least temporarily resolved by a military take-over in which they come to share power with that other set of technicians—the army officers.

The commitment to rapid expansion of primary education, noble in moral intent, has some serious negative consequences. One, as in model X, is to drain off the potentially more able from rural communities, general education being regarded as incompatible with manual and especially agricultural work. This is one important source of a more general problem: the "unemployed school leaver," i.e., those with a few years of primary education who aspire to clerical jobs which do not exist. For the economic system the investment in production of these "school leavers" is a misallocation of development resources. For the political system they are a destabilizing factor, prone to anomic outbursts, readily recruited to demagogic messianist agitation. For the educational system itself the effects are declining quality (due to larger and larger classes and shortage of qualified teachers) and rising costs (exacerbated by the large proportion of repeaters in primary grades who in turn act as a block to learning by new pupils).[25] The cost factor alone puts governments in the painful alternative of either abandoning the goal of universal primary education or of eliminating those pupils who prove unable to learn—either of which is offensive to populist aspirations.

Similarly, the expansion of secondary and higher education, in addition

[23] Aye Ogunskeye thinks, as regards Nigeria, that education may have some influence but is probably not decisive in supplanting the traditional tribal authorities. See Aye Ogunskeye, "Nigeria," in *ibid.,* p. 140.

[24] James S. Coleman, "Introduction: Education and Political Development," in *ibid.,* p. 27 ff.; Seymour M. Lipset, *The First New Nation: The United States in Historical and Comparative Perspective* (New York: Basic Books, 1963), pp. 72–73; and Apter, pp. 71 ff., 133 ff.

[25] See a series of articles in *Le Monde* by B. Girod de l'Ain, "L'école dans le tiers monde," especially November 28, 1966.

to the politically significant frustrations already mentioned, is also leading to the production of more graduates than can be absorbed by the economy.[26] One explanation long popular is that education is of the wrong kinds, having a literary and legal bias when technical graduates are needed. But this is no longer a sufficient reason because more emphasis has been given to the technical content of education and now there appears the phenomenon of unemployed technical graduates, plus a "brain drain" of scientific specialists and technicians from underdeveloped to industrialized countries. Another explanation lies in the inflated earning expectations of graduates. They demand salaries comparable to those offered to attract their predecessors, the colonial administrators; but new jobs at this cost cannot be created in sufficient numbers by poor countries.[27]

Model Y poses a number of critical questions: Does an attempt to provide universal primary education conflict seriously in the competition for scarce resources with the initiation of rapid economic development? Have the economic benefits of educating high-level manpower been overstressed in recent development ideologies? Does heavy emphasis on education at the early stages of modernization involve serious threats to political stability? The negative appraisal of educational expansion is probably most apparent in the short term. Long-term perspectives may argue that economic disequilibriums and political disorder are to some extent inevitable in the process of modernization but that the goals of modernization will never be attained unless an informed and competent population is created through education. However, we all live in the short term—politicians especially.

Abandonment of educational expansion goals would be politically unrealistic for populist political leadership. Thus, one should look for adaptations rather than reversals in policy. The political system adapts typically to the dangers of the "school-leaver" problem by introducing schemes of

[26] Educational output in developing countries has since the 1950's tended to increase substantially faster than gross national product which in turn has risen faster than wage-paid employment. See a forthcoming publication of the International Institute for Educational Planning, *Manpower Aspects of Educational Planning: Problems for the Future.*

[27] Countries which want rapid economic development through planning need more administrators than were required to run a colonial territory in which governmental functions were much more limited. Education does not offer salaries or status sufficient to attract graduates, and so their surplus does little to diminish the shortage of qualified teachers. W. Arthur Lewis thinks the oversupply of educated people is a temporary thing.

> In the long run the situation adjusts itself because the premium on education diminishes as the number of the educated increases.
>
> .   .   .   .
>
> As the premium on education falls, the market for the educated may widen enormously. Jobs which were previously done by people with less education are now done by people with more education. The educated lower their sights, and employers raise their requirements.

(W. Arthur Lewis, "Education and Economic Development," *International Social Science Journal,* 1962 [Vol. 14, No. 4], p. 687.)

compulsory civic service, "youth brigades," and so forth. While this is offensive to the liberal conception of individual human rights, it is quite consistent with populist conceptions of human rights through collective action for national emancipation. The school system, too, adapts to the condition of society. Too great a load is placed upon it as an instrument of nation building.[28] The culture of the school, derived from Western models and often taught by metropolitan teachers in the metropolitan language, is far removed from the culture of the family environment. There is nothing in daily experience outside the school to sustain the ideas taught in school. As a result these ideas are not easily understood; they are mimicked.[29] And as schooling expands, pressures for "localization" are greater, and the school system conforms increasingly to the cultural fragmentation of the nation. Only the secondary and higher schools—especially the boarding schools—can sustain modern cultural attitudes for the minority which passes through them. The gap between national elite and "localized" popular culture remains great. Since the school system is unable to provide the institutional framework for nation building, this framework must be sought elsewhere, to wit, in the institutions run by the modernized elite. Hence the recent prominence of the military backed by bureaucratic technicians who may appear as the combined institutional force strong enough to resist the disintegrating effects of traditional tribalism or communalism and newly induced anomic disorder and messianism.

Some of the problems raised by this model may be seen as questions of phasing in the transformation and modernization of societies.[30] It may be that the most propitious moment for expanding primary education is after urbanization and industrialization have proceeded some distance.[31] Then populations exist which can use general education more effectively to adapt to economic opportunities. By the same token possibly more re-

[28] Coleman, in Coleman (ed.), *Education and Political Development*, p. 22.

[29] Francis X. Sutton, "Education and the Making of Modern Nations," in *ibid.*, p. 67.

[30] See Burt F. Hoselitz, "Investment in Education and Its Political Impact," in *ibid.*, p. 543:

> At certain periods investment in a given set of non-human resources and at other periods investment in human resources brings about a higher sustained growth of average income.

Thomas Balogh is angrier:

> It is quite illegitimate to claim that an educational system which in the framework of the United States has been accompanied by a certain rate of growth would, in a different framework, be accompanied by a similar growth rate or a growth rate which can be calculated on the basis of the educational status (assessed qualitatively) alone. Such a quantity of education in the feudal-aristocratic countries of South America, the colonial-aristocratic areas of British Africa, and the litterateur-colonial areas of French Africa would produce not merely no growth but possible refusal to work on farms, an increase in urban unemployment, subversion, and collapse.

(*The Economics of Poverty* [New York: Macmillan, 1966], p. 91.)

[31] Daniel Lerner, *The Passing of Traditional Society: Modernizing the Middle East* (Glencoe, Ill: The Free Press, 1958), p. 60.

sources should be devoted to employment creation in the modern sector before there is a large-scale expansion in the output of secondary and higher education. An important intervening variable between education and economic growth is attitudes—toward work, toward what constitutes fair rewards, and toward the future of the nation and the individual's identification with it. Education without any change of the economic environment does not change attitudes but builds frustrations. Conversely, a change in the economic environment may create the conditions in which a change of attitudes can be constructively influenced by an expansion of educational opportunity. In this interim phase particularly, some forms of education may be both relatively cheap and especially propitious in helping to improve the economic environment, namely: apprenticeship; short subprofessional training for secondary school leavers; industrial training for adults on the job; and some forms of practical training designed to turn peasants into farmers in combination with investment in agriculture.[32] These do not create frustrations if they are geared, as they should be, to economic opportunities. The opportunities, however, may be limited to relatively small groups of workers who have become partially acculturated to the modern economic sector. The problem of effective penetration of rural populations remains paramount and unresolved.

Model Z: Modernization with Alternative Channels of Upward Mobility

A third development model is suggested by James Coleman on the basis of an analysis of Soviet, Japanese, and Philippine cases.[33] It is interesting mainly for comparison. In these cases a modernizing elite (the Communist Party elite in the Soviet Union in the early 1920's, the Samurai governing class in Japan in the early 1870's, and the United States' colonial officialdom in the Philippines at the turn of the century) adopted mass education as an instrument for political unification and for the creation of a technically competent population. They were successful in improving political communication between elite and population (though not uniformly in inducing conformity), and they avoided the problem of the "educated unemployed." They were able to do this because: 1) In none of these cases was education thought of as conferring a right to political elite status; 2) higher education was flexible and practical in orientation, making for a close adaptation to economic opportunities; and 3) there were auxiliary channels of upward mobility. In these

---

[32] See Lewis, *International Social Science Journal*, Vol. 14, No. 4, pp. 692–693; and Hoselitz in Coleman (ed.), *Education and Political Development*, p. 564.

[33] Coleman, "Introduction to Part II," in Coleman (ed.), *Education and Political Development*, pp. 225–232.

respects, it may be added, the model presents analogies to the United States, just as it contrasts with Europe.

It is the third characteristic which is most remarkable in its contrast with the situations portrayed in models X and Y, where aspirations for upward mobility focus on the educational system. Coleman suggests that

comparisons of historical development of educational systems in modern societies strongly support the proposition that where alternative channels of mobility exist, a politically dysfunctional intellectual proletariat is less likely to appear.[34]

Yet we may well ask whether the notion of alternative channels of mobility is not now becoming illusory even in industrialized capitalist countries. Is not the increasing technical specialization of all productive activity making educational qualifications a condition for upward mobility, not perhaps a substitute for but a necessary complement to entrepreneurial initiative? Does this not therefore mean that for lack of alternative channels of upward mobility developing countries will have to solve through educational policy the problems of recruitment to the political and economic elites and the related problems of limiting the creation of an educated unemployed? Model Z shows that a determined modernizing elite can effectively use educational expansion as an instrument of mobilization, but it offers little hope that the political and economic dysfunctions of rapid expansion can be ignored.

FUNCTIONALISM, PLURALISM, AND FUTURE OPPORTUNITIES

From the foregoing it may be inferred that the official educational development ideology has been efficacious for strengthening UNESCO and ILO; but an analysis of education in the process of modernization suggests some politically destabilizing and economically constricting consequences of a simple, uniform policy of expanding education and training. In the light of this can we envisage some better adjustment of the action of international organizations and of their institutional growth to the dynamics of national political and economic modernization?

More comprehensive planning could be the answer. Those scholars who have best contributed to the elaboration of the educational development ideology always maintained that action should be adapted to the

---

[34] *Ibid.*, p. 231. Though no private sector offers alternative channels of mobility in the Soviet Union, the continual adjustment of the educational system to the needs of the economy and the planned management of labor supply avoided the creation of disaffected "intellectual unemployed." Coleman concludes that the real dilemma for the developing countries' leaders is that

they possess neither the disposition to emulate the Japanese or Philippine pluralistic example, nor the organizational and administrative capacity to pursue effectively the totalitarian alternative.

(*Ibid.*, p. 232.)

specific situation of each country. The technical international officials concerned are nearly all advocates of a comprehensive planned approach. "Comprehensive planning" is the key phrase in the revision of official ideology now going on within the technical departments of international agencies where there is awareness of the dysfunctional effect of earlier simplistic enthusiasm.[35]

This is not, however, a matter amenable to bureaucratic problem solving. There are structural difficulties in getting a proper fit between fragmented responsibility for international action and coherent domestic development policy. A coherent policy may be defined as the coordinated use of appropriate instruments at the national level to achieve feasible goals. The structure of international organization is such that separate agencies are each responsible for different instruments: UNESCO for the school system; ILO for labor market machinery and on-the-job training; and the Food and Agriculture Organization (FAO) for rural extension services, for example. The political relationships inherent in international organization activity are such that the separate aims of government ministries and different local groups combine with particular international agencies to create pressures for the expanded use of certain instruments. Thus, despite an intellectual acknowledgment on the part of international officials of the need for comprehensive planning the political structure of international organization-national government relations is such that priority tends to be given to the chosen instruments rather than the coherent plan.[36] UNESCO in the nature of things is inclined to support expansion of existing educational systems and so may sometimes lend its influence to domestic pressures for maintaining through these systems values inimical to economic development. Similarly, the structure of ILO political relationships inclines that organization to support programs which benefit the relatively small but committed industrial worker group in developing countries.

To the extent that officials of the functional international organizations themselves prefer comprehensive planning (and deference to priorities other than those of their own wares) they risk losing support of their particular clients. International bureaucracies, however, are so responsive

---

[35] Evidence of this "revisionism" is apparent in a new report, prepared through collaboration among technical secretariats, "Development and Utilization of Human Resources in Developing Countries: Report of the Secretary-General" (UN Document E/4353/Add.1), Part II, paragraph 107, p. 18. The International Institute for Educational Planning, founded by UNESCO in 1963, has produced studies and sponsored discussions making for a critical reappraisal of the educational development doctrine.

[36] The "coordinated programs" prepared in concert by the international agencies through the Administrative Committee on Coordination (ACC) are carefully negotiated between the central bureaucracies of the agencies. Their function is to provide a guide for orderly relations between the agencies and an assurance to the Economic and Social Council (ECOSOC) that such relations are satisfactory and fruitful.

to client interests that this is not likely to go very far. Comprehensive planning at the local level where local administrative structures are weak relative to the administrative structures of international organizations may become complicated by the need for negotiation among organizational interests at the international level.[37]

The problem is not only one of structure; it links with the general ideology of international organization. The best-formulated theoretical justification of the system of segmented responsibilities among international organizations is the theory of what can be called functionalist pluralism.[38] International organizations with functionally specific goals bring into their orbit functionally specialized technicians or interest groups at the national level. By promoting aims and projects in which these subnational groups are interested international organizations at the same time encourage pluralism within the nation and international integration. Internationalism is obstructed primarily by integral nationalism; the structure of world government will be created piecemeal by transnational alliances of groups which are competing within each nation, which alliances in turn help to break down the unity of the nation-state. Extrapolated, the future political process of world government is envisaged as pluralistic, characterized by competition between constellations of functionally defined interests rather than competition between nations.

This is an ideology of international organization which accorded well with the reaction against Fascist totalitarianism in the 1930's and 1940's among a set of nations in which the elements for pluralistic competitive internal politics were already present. It accords less well with a world environment in which many newly independent states are engaged in

[37] The report of the Secretary-General on human resources in the developing countries contains this plea:

> It is important that the international organizations avoid giving inconsistent and conflicting advice on the selection of priorities. There is a danger, if agencies do not co-operate closely, that an individual agency, on the basis of its specialized knowledge of the urgency of needs in its own field, might give advice which would deviate from, or be inconsistent with, that which would be appropriate if the total needs and resources of the country were taken into account.

(*Ibid.*, Part II, paragraph 107, p. 18.) The only structural proposal adapted to this problem is the reference in a footnote to the suggestion by the Administrator of the UN Development Program (UNDP) that there should be in each country a "cabinet" of agency field representatives under the chairmanship of the Resident Representative. What, one may well ask, is the cumulative bias which the "unplanned" influences of international organizations give to national development policies? Possibly to give more weight to social, humanitarian, and welfare measures than would otherwise be the case. It should not, however, be inferred that more comprehensive planning of international action at the national level would reverse this bias to neglect humanitarian considerations.

[38] This theory has been formulated by various authors. A notable contributor is David Mitrany, *A Working Peace System: An Argument for the Functional Development of International Organization* (London: Oxford University Press [for The Royal Institute of International Affairs], 1943). Functionalist theory has been critically reassessed by Ernst B. Haas, *Beyond the Nation-State: Functionalism and International Organization* (Stanford, Calif: Stanford University Press, 1964); and Sewell, *Functionalism and World Politics*.

the task of nation building. These states exist juridically prior to the people over whom they rule having found a sense of identity as a nation. It is the task of the political elites of these countries to provide the symbols and the experience of collective action which will foster a national identity. They thus often try to suppress internal factionalism and the competition of political and economic interests. These are pre-nation-states seeking to become nation-states, whose elites are promoting forms of integral nationalism and of socialism as a means to that primary goal. And it is this nationalism which is providing a stimulus and driving force to the task expansion of international organization at the present time.

This radically changed environment calls for a reformulation of general international organization ideology. It is not necessary to abandon the goal of a pluralist competitive polity—this is a value choice which no set of circumstances can oblige anyone to abandon. But it is necessary, if one wishes one's ideology to be effective as a guide for action (which is the purpose of an ideology), to conceive this goal as attainable through strategies adjusted to a typology of different situations.

It is now becoming possible to define such typologies and their associated strategies as a result of recent studies in comparative politics of developing areas which have helped to delineate the groups among which political competition occurs in countries at various stages of modernization and industrialization. One line of competition (noted above) in new nations is between the first-generation political leaders and the technicians of the civil service. Within the civil service concentrations of technical competency can also be descried: Economic management and planning attracts many of the best talents, while other ministries get the less able or less qualified. The question posed for international organizations—in the perspective of a pluralist ideology—is whether it is not better at this stage of development to build on poles of strength in the national bureaucracies and encourage a sense of community among civil servants as a group under the leadership of their most able elements rather than to act on assumptions concerning the desirability of promoting intra-bureaucratic competition between ministries for resources such as might be more appropriate to a later and more complex stage of industrial and administrative development. David Apter has argued that technicians, planners, and scientists, even though in developing countries they are not typically advocates of liberal democracy, by their very functions demand and create supplies of information and encourage fuller communication between population and elite. They also demand freedom of scientific research and free debate on ideas in the scientific field.[39] These are first

---

[39] Apter, pp. 175–176. It can also be argued that their professional solidarity with others in their field—not only at home but chiefly in the outside centers of learning from which they draw their models—moderates (in the sense of Mitrany's functionalism) the integral nationalism inherent in nation building.

steps toward the conditions in which liberal democracy might be possible. Much could be achieved toward this rethinking of the ideology of international organization by a closer intermixing of the two channels of political science that have analyzed, on the one hand, the politics of development, on the other, international organization.

At present the governments of developing countries are supporting the creation of new international organizations which cover the same fields as older organizations or combinations of older organizations but whose purposes are defined in terms of development problems, such as the UN Conference on Trade and Development (UNCTAD) and the United Nations Industrial Development Organization (UNIDO). (A separate organization for science and technology was proposed but not created.) There is a combination of motives: the belief that more organizations mean more funds for development; the belief that the new organizations created by the votes of the developing country majority will be more responsive to that majority's will whereas the older organizations, by habit of mind and by structure of decisionmaking, are more responsive to the industrialized countries which were *their* creators; the opportunity to create within the international civil service as a whole centers of bureaucratic influence which will fabricate ideologies designed to upgrade the interests of developing countries and press these interests with vigor vis-à-vis the international financial agencies.

The older organizations, including ILO and UNESCO, have responded to these structural initiatives from the developing countries by defending their competencies, expanding (or offering to expand) those of their activities that interest developing countries, and expressing confidence in the efficacy of interorganizational arrangements for coordination and planning (e.g., ACC).

The present state of the structural dialectic of international organization in relation to the function of economic development is one of tension between the older functionalism of ILO, UNESCO, and FAO and the newer functionalism of UNCTAD and UNIDO. No clean-cut synthesis is in prospect; but accommodations are made by negotiation between these differing conceptions. The direction of these accommodations will be determined in large measure by the constellations of environmental forces which lie behind each form of organization; and the most important question about a prospective shift in this respect which could have impact upon the structure of international organization concerns the possibility of closer understanding between industrialized countries of East and West as to policy for accelerating economic development of the poor countries.[40]

---

[40] The "older" functionalist organizations might play the role of broker in probing the possibilities of East-West consensus on development policy.

Finally, a remark about the programmatic counterpart to these structural questions in the specific area of education and manpower is in order. The defects in the official educational development ideology derived from the insufficient account it took of the ways in which social stratification and political power shape education and limit economic development potential. Two questions which could be put as a preliminary to fixing the educational aspects of development policy are: 1) What is the emerging pattern of roles critical for modernization? 2) How can the politically inarticulate groups be brought into participation in modernization? These questions are both pluralist in their implications.

No attempt can be made here to suggest answers to these questions, answers which would in any case have to be grouped in relation to typologies of modernization. Some recent work in political science has focused on the formation of career and entrepreneurial roles.[41] The pattern of roles and role formation determines the potential form of political competition or pluralism. Changes in the pattern of roles are very closely linked with changes in attitudes. Very little is known about this which is operationally useful, yet changes in attitudes and role formation are critical determinants of change in social stratification and political leadership which in turn condition prospects for economic and political development.

Lucian Pye's study of Burma stressed how personality factors act as a block to development.[42] The deficiency of "associational sentiments" resulting from traditional upbringing precludes individuals from according each other the confidence necessary for innovative organization building. E. C. Banfield's study in Southern Italy made analogous observations.[43] Oscar Lewis' studies in the "culture of poverty" suggest there may be common traits of personality which would obstruct the effective organization of poor people for common goals.[44] These studies all point up the importance of organization-building skills and begin to throw some light on the problem of arousing participation by the rural and the urban "marginal" populations. But very little is yet known about how this can be done. Very little attention has been given to the development of organization-building skills, compared with the efforts expended in training administrators and technicians. Concern for pluralism, however, would argue for some balance in this respect, especially at a time when civil servants are in many places allying with military administrators to oust the

---

[41] Particularly in Apter.

[42] Lucian W. Pye, *Politics, Personality, and Nation-Building: Burma's Search for Identity* (New Haven, Conn: Yale University Press, 1962), pp. 38–41, 52–55.

[43] E. C. Banfield, *The Moral Basis of a Backward Society* (Glencoe, Ill: The Free Press, 1958).

[44] Oscar Lewis, "The Culture of Poverty," *Scientific American,* October 1966 (Vol. 215, No. 4), pp. 19 ff.

political entrepreneurs. Training for trade-union leadership is one offering in this direction.[45] The problems of leadership in rural communities are more difficult for an international organization to come to grips with.[46] If, as suggested earlier, it is good policy to strengthen bureaucracies, it would also seem good policy to balance this with programs to strengthen nonbureaucratic entrepreneurs (including political entrepreneurs). International organizations might devise programs to reach these role players.[47]

Such a program implies the adoption by the international organization of an activist role which is certainly likely to encounter local obstacles. The extent to which an international organization can persist in its course despite such obstacles depends upon the strength of the alliance supporting its policies. This brings us back to the crucial question of East-West understanding on development policy. To be able to base an activist role upon such a consensus would enable international organization to sharpen the definition of its distinctive personality in world affairs. And it could be a step toward linking in an interacting and mutually sustaining way the processes of political development at national and international levels.

[45] Harold K. Jacobson, "Ventures in Polity Shaping: External Assistance to Labor Movements in Developing Countries" (unpublished paper presented to a round table convened by the International Political Science Association, Grenoble, September 1965).

[46] Wolfe, in *Problems and Strategies of Educational Planning*, p. 24, suggests the development of peasant organizations is a precondition for effective rural education in Latin America:

As peasant unions and other mass organizations penetrate the countryside and as agrarian reform looms larger on the horizon, the educational planner is beginning to encounter more insistent and specific rural demands for education. . . .

And in another article in the same volume, "Some Notes on Rural Educational Policies," he states on p. 74:

In most parts of Latin America this goal [effective rural primary education] seems to be within reach if there is a sufficiently strong and coherent demand for such type of education. This would imply the emergence of political leadership responsive to rural wants and anxious to secure rural support, on the one hand, and a certain degree of political and economic organization of the rural people themselves, on the other.

[47] The International Institute for Labor Studies, Geneva, offers education for potential leaders in the social policy field. The Institute is in fact searching for better answers to the two questions: Who are the potential leaders? What kind of education is good for them? See my article, "Four Keys to the Purpose of Institute Educational Action," in the International Institute for Labor Studies *Bulletin*, October 1966 (No. 1), pp. 8–21.

Toward a World Population Program

RICHARD N. GARDNER

THE world is witnessing not only a population explosion but a family planning revolution. For the first time in history there is concrete evidence that people throughout most of the world accept the need for family planning and desire that family planning services be made available to them. And for the first time in history we have the technical means to implement family planning programs—the pill, the intrauterine contraceptive device (IUCD), and other methods. Moreover, research now under way suggests that reliance on a contraceptive pill that must be taken daily or an IUCD that is presently unsatisfactory to 25 percent of those using it will some day be of only historical interest—mere shadows reflecting the dim dark ages in the history of family planning. Already researchers have had success with an injectable contraceptive that provides long-standing immunity from pregnancy.

It is clear that the problems facing most less developed countries in the field of family planning are neither popular resistance to contraception nor lack of imagination on the part of family planning experts. The major problems are inadequate funds, weak administration, insufficient personnel, and, in some cases, lack of will on the part of government to get on with the job. The question is: What can be done to overcome these problems through bilateral and multilateral assistance? Specifically, what can be done through the United Nations and its family of agencies?

POPULATION GROWTH AND ECONOMIC DEVELOPMENT

The facts about the world population explosion are now well-known. It took hundreds of thousands of years, from the beginning of life on

RICHARD N. GARDNER, Henry L. Moses Professor of Law and International Organization at Columbia University, New York, served as Deputy Assistant Secretary of State for International Organization Affairs from 1961 to 1965. In a speech to the United Nations General Assembly in December 1962 he made the first United States offer to help other countries control population growth.

earth to the beginning of this century, for the population of the world to reach 1.5 billion. In the first two-thirds of this century this number doubled to the present total of something over 3 billion. In the last one-third of this century, if present trends continue, this figure will more than double to over 7 billion.

This unparalleled increase in man's numbers is causing problems even for highly developed countries. The United States, with a population growth rate of about $1\frac{1}{2}$ percent a year, is likely to see its present population of 200 million reach more than 300 million by the year 2000. Uncontrolled fertility is adversely affecting the health of mothers and children, family life, and opportunities for decent housing, education, employment, and a better standard of living. The relatively high birth rate in poverty-stricken families is an important contributing cause of their poverty; it condemns a significant portion of the American people to living in conditions of economic and cultural deprivation. Rapid population growth is adding other strains to American society in the form of air and water pollution, the breakdown of mass transportation, overcrowding in urban areas, the depletion of precious natural resources, and the destruction of needed recreation areas and open spaces.

The results of present population trends are even more ominous in the less developed areas of the world. The average annual increase of population in these countries is approximately 2.5 percent—sufficient to double the population every 28 years. In many countries the annual growth rate has reached 3 percent or more. In Latin America, the region of the world where population growth is highest, total population will rise from something over 200 million today to approximately 600 million at the end of the century if present trends continue. Comparable figures for population growth in key countries in other parts of the world, if present trends continue, are no less frightening: India, from 500 million to one billion; Indonesia, 100 million to 200 million; the United Arab Republic, 30 million to 70 million. And then there is the People's Republic of China (Communist China), about whose population so little is known, which at present growth rates is likely to increase from 800 million to at least 1.2 billion.

Public discussion of the population problem has focused attention on the relation between the number of people and the supply of food. In the less developed countries as a whole food production in recent years has failed to keep pace with population growth. In the 1965–1966 crop year food production per capita in Asia, Africa, and Latin America actually declined by 4 to 5 percent. The Food and Agriculture Organization (FAO) has estimated that world food production will have to increase at least threefold by the end of the century to provide an adequate diet for the world's increased numbers. Such an increase seems impossible without a thoroughgoing transformation in existing agricultural institutions and techniques in the less developed areas. As a consequence of present trends in food production and population the developing countries are becoming increasingly dependent on the United States to meet their growing food deficits. But massive food tranfers of ever-growing magnitude cannot go on indefinitely. Quite apart from the economic and political problems involved, the day may come when even the United States will no longer be able to fill the developing countries' food deficits. The specter of world famine in the 1970's or 1980's is all too real unless drastic changes are made in food and population policies.

Yet the reason for reducing present rates of population growth in the less developed countries is not exclusively—nor even primarily—that of avoiding starvation. These countries, whose citizens have an average income of little more than $100 a year, are seeking rapid increases in their living standards. To achieve these increases they must achieve a substantial rate of investment as well as meet their current consumption needs. Yet it is all many of these countries can do to enlarge total economic product as fast as the additional mouths to feed—so that little or nothing is left over for additions to capital stock. Recent economic studies have indicated that the costs in both domestic investment and foreign aid of preventing one birth are of the order of one percent of the costs of supplying an additional person with the present low standards of living over his lifetime. Thus, effective family planning can enormously increase the potential of the limited capital resources of the less developed countries for expanding per capita levels of living.

The United Nations set as the goal of its Development Decade the achievement by 1970 of an annual growth rate of 5 percent a year in the national income of less developed countries. At the present time the rate of investment required to reach this objective is not being achieved in many of these countries because resources which might otherwise be available for investment must be used to provide necessities for a rapidly growing population. Moreover, even if the United Nations 5 percent target should be achieved, present rates of population growth would greatly dilute its impact on individual levels of welfare. For the many developing countries with population growth in the region of 3 percent a year achievement of the United Nations target figure would mean increases in individual living standards of only 2 percent a year—in other words, average annual increases per capita of about $2.

Nor can the menace of population growth be calculated in economic terms alone. In many countries population growth—even when accompanied by modest increases in per capita income—may threaten the basis of the good life and perhaps the very foundations of civilized society. The population increase and migration from the countryside have outstripped the capacity of many of the world's great cities to supply minimum levels of housing, sanitation, education, and transportation. Uncontrolled fertility has been accompanied by increasing resort to abortion —both legal and illegal. Moreover, increasing numbers of illegitimate children are growing up without the benefits of family life. These conditions multiply individual frustrations and take their toll on society in the form of delinquency, crime, revolution, and even war.

Unfortunately, there are no quick and simple solutions to the many problems associated with rapid population growth. It will take time before appropriate measures for the limitation of births can be made available to all who would make use of them. And even if birth rates decline, future increases in population will result from the population growth of the past as more people pass through the childbearing years. Moreover, the application of modern science and medicine in less developed countries will further reduce the death rate and spur population growth.

Thus, development policy for the less developed countries will have to reckon with large and continuous increases in population. Family planning will not quickly or easily alter the demographic facts of life. Nor can it be a substitute for other measures to help the less developed countries. Nevertheless, the success with which the world applies a policy of voluntary family planning in the next few years can spell the difference between rates of population growth that are compatible with human dignity and those that spell certain misery for a growing majority of people in the world.

The Family Planning Gap

We hear a great deal these days about the "aid gap" and the "trade gap" and the "food gap." But none of these gaps can be closed unless we reduce the "family planning gap"—the gap between the number of married women who now have access to modern birth control techniques and the number who would make use of them if given the opportunity.

A rough approximation of the world's "family planning gap" and the cost of closing it can be made using demographic statistics from 1965, the most recent year for which the necessary figures are available.[1] World population in 1965 was 3.3 billion. Of this total about 43 percent, or 1.4 billion, were in the main childbearing years 15–44. Half of these, or 700 million, were women. It is estimated that about 80 percent of these women, or 560 million, were married. About 430 million of this 560 mil-

[1] Grateful acknowledgment is hereby made to the staff of the Population Council for help in preparing the following estimates.

lion were in the less developed countries of Latin America, Africa, and Asia.

Studies carried out in the less developed countries indicate that, on the average, about 20 percent of married women are sterile or subfecund, are currently using contraceptives, or have an absent husband, and that another 30 percent are pregnant, lactating, or want a child. In other words, a total of 50 percent are not exposed to the risk of unwanted pregnancy, leaving 50 percent who are exposed to this risk. This means there are some 215 million women in the less developed countries exposed to the risk of unwanted pregnancy. Of this 215 million, 169 million are in Asia, 27 million in Africa, nineteen million in Latin America. If Communist China is excluded, the total figure for the less developed countries would be 140 million. It is estimated that the number of women exposed to unwanted pregnancy in developed countries is about ten million so that the global family planning gap involves about 225 million women, or 150 million if Communist China is excluded.

Most of these women are older married women since allowance has already been made for those wanting another child. Based on studies in the less developed countries, it would appear that about one in four of these women gives birth to a child each year. This means that the 150 million women exposed to unwanted pregnancy outside of Communist China give birth to about 37.5 million children per year. Since the total number of births outside of Communist China is 95 million a year, we reach the astonishing conclusion that about 40 percent of the children born in the world as a whole outside of Communist China are unwanted in the sense that they would not have been born had their mothers had access to modern methods of family planning! These figures suggest the staggering toll in terms of individual suffering and social cost resulting from the absence of family planning services.

What would be the cost of closing this family planning gap? In the Republic of Korea (South Korea), where one of the most successful national family planning programs has been established, the average cost per man or woman given family planning advice and materials has been $5.14 per year. Most of this sum represents the cost of clinics, vehicles, communications equipment, and—most important of all—the training of doctors and health workers. The cost of contraceptives is a minor factor. In less developed countries an IUCD can be supplied for about $2\frac{1}{2}$ cents, other simple devices for a similarly low cost. Even a year's supply of pills costs only about $1.50 to $2.00, and this figure is rapidly going down.

The Korean figure of $5.14 must be doubled to about $10 to be applicable to the less developed countries as a whole since most of them are much less advanced than Korea in transportation, communication, education, and health services. Moreover, experience shows that a further increase of 40 percent has to be made in the estimate to allow for normal attrition, for the fact that many men or women discontinue use of a particular device, necessitating a duplication of the initial expenditure. Thus, it would cost about $14 on the average to provide an average woman in the less developed world with one year's protection against pregnancy.

The approximate cost of filling the family planning gap, therefore, is as follows: for the less developed world as a whole (215 million women exposed to unwanted pregnancy) about $3 billion; for the less developed world outside of Communist China (140 million women exposed to unwanted pregnancy) about $2 billion. These figures, it should be noted, give the cost of building up presently nonexistent or inadequate family planning services to provide one year's protection against unwanted pregnancy. The annual cost after the initial buildup would be somewhat less. And the health network created to provide family planning assistance could provide other services as well.[2]

What would happen to the world's vital statistics if the family planning gap were closed? The present figures per thousand are: birth rate, 36; death rate, 15; net increase, 21. Without unwanted births outside Communist China the new figures per thousand would be: birth rate, 25; death rate, 15; net increase, 10. In other words, the elimination of the 37.5 million unwanted births per year outside Communist China would reduce the world's annual population growth from the present level of 2.1 percent to one percent.

This one percent figure applies to the world as a whole and still assumes high birth rates in China. The elimination of the 37.5 million unwanted births per year outside Communist China would reduce the annual increase in population in the world outside Communist China to one-half of one percent. Assuming the continuation of present death rates, population growth in the world outside Communist China can be reduced to one percent at one-half the $2 billion annual cost estimated above—or about $1 billion a year.

So far we have made no distinction between countries with official policies favoring or permitting family planning programs and countries without such policies. Obviously, nothing can be spent in countries that

<hr/>

[2] It is difficult to get an average cost estimate that will apply to the ten million women in the developed countries exposed to unwanted pregnancy. The greater average level of health standards, communications, transportation, and education is a factor reducing the cost of providing family planning services in developed countries below what it is in less developed countries. On the other hand, the general cost structure and the standard of health service considered acceptable is higher; and more sophisticated contraceptives (the pill) are more likely to be used. Assuming that the $14 per person employed for less developed countries is a reasonable point of reference for developed countries, we would have to add something like $100–$200 million to the figures given above to get global cost estimates for closing the family planning gap including developed as well as less developed countries.

do not permit family planning programs to be established. In the less developed countries outside Communist China there are about 75 million women exposed to unwanted pregnancy in countries that favor or permit family planning. The cost of closing the family planning gap in these countries is therefore about $1 billion. This breaks down into $921 million for Asia, $76 million for Africa, and $53 million for Latin America. For the three largest Asian countries outside Communist China the annual cost of closing the family planning gap comes to $616 million for India, $126 million for Pakistan, and $140 million for Indonesia.

Obviously, the obstacle to closing the family planning gap is not just money. In addition to lack of funds family planning programs are hampered by the absence of administrative capacity, the absence of trained personnel, the absence of education, the absence of effective communications, and, perhaps most fundamentally, the absence of the will to get on with the job. We could not spend $1 billion per year in UN Member States permitting family planning even if this sum of money were available. But this rough estimate does have usefulness as a target figure against which to measure the adequacy of the sums now being spent for the purpose.

When the day comes when we can use as much as $1 billion for family planning in UN Member States permitting such programs, we will not only alleviate suffering for millions of people; we will save their governments billions in education, housing, health, and other costs. Most important of all, we will eliminate something more dangerous in its long-term consequences for civilization than even the hydrogen bomb—the production of millions of unwanted children destined to grow up in the world without adequate parental care or adequate opportunities for a decent life. It is difficult to imagine another use for $1 billion that would do more to relieve human suffering and bring greater benefits to the human race as a whole.

GUIDELINES FOR ACTION

In view of the grave threat which present rates of population growth pose for economic development and of the vast dimensions of the family planning gap it is obvious that a greater investment must be made in programs of family planning. More will be said of this later. But money alone will not do the job unless it is related to sound policy. The following are some guidelines for national and international action that may facilitate progress in this difficult and still controversial area. While there is nothing like unanimity on all these points, there is evidence of growing support for all of them, support from both experts and laymen, developed and less developed countries, and members of all religious groups.

First: We should be concerned with the quality of life.

The central objective of development policy is to promote the welfare and dignity of the individual human being. We must be concerned not only with economic needs but also with those political, cultural, and psychological needs that are fundamental to all men. Aggregate statistics like gross national product and industrial and agricultural production, while necessary tools of analysis, may be quite misleading as indicators of progress in this broader sense when they are accompanied by rapid population growth. Even per capita income figures by themselves cannot be considered a sufficient standard by which to measure successful development.

As noted earlier, present rates of population growth can not only retard increases in per capita income—they can bring famine, cause critical conditions in health, education, and housing, aggravate overcrowding in the cities, and breed social tensions, frustration, and violence. If we are concerned with successful development in the broader sense, we must focus on individual welfare as well as gross statistics and on noneconomic as well as economic indicators. And if we are concerned with the quality of life, we have no choice but to be concerned with the quantity of life.

Second: We should seek the maximum dissemination of knowledge and the maximum freedom of choice.

At least two out of every three persons in the world as a whole and about nine out of ten in the less developed countries are without modern family planning information and services. We should seek to make information and services available to all these persons who wish to have them. If we do this, we will eliminate a particularly objectionable form of discrimination existing in the world today—discrimination against persons who are denied family planning information and services by virtue of poverty or ignorance or other factors beyond their control.

Freedom to limit family size to the number of children wanted is a basic human right. Our aim should be to enable every couple to determine the family size it wants by means of its own choosing. This aim cannot be achieved when modern family planning services are not available. When they are made available, however, there should be no coercion. Individuals should be free to determine family size and methods of regulating pregnancy in the light of their personal needs and religious and cultural values.

If we wish to make a success of a program of voluntary family planning, time is of the essence. The rate of world population growth is so great—and its consequences so grave—that this may be the last generation that has the opportunity to limit population growth on the basis of free choice. If we do not make voluntary family planning possible in this generation, we may make compulsory family planning inevitable in future generations.

Third: Family planning begins at home.

Family planning policy should be applied consistently at home and abroad. Developed countries should not ask less developed countries to do things they are not prepared to do themselves. They should not give the impression that they favor limiting the population growth of other peoples but not that of their own people.

Rich countries like the United States must practice what they preach if their words are to carry weight and their efforts overseas are not to be misunderstood. Of course, the principal reason for accelerating family planning programs in developed countries is that such programs are beneficial for those countries. If it is good for Asian and African and Latin American women to be free from unwanted pregnancy, it is also good for American women.

Fourth: Assistance to a country in family planning should be solely at the request of that country.

In family planning assistance, as in other types of assistance, a donor country or international agency can only act with the consent and cooperation of the recipient country. If international cooperation in family planning is to become a reality, it must respond to the needs and demands of the countries concerned.

Fifth: The principal responsibility for implementing programs of family planning in a particular country must be taken by the people of that country themselves.

In this area of foreign assistance, as in every other, we can only help people to help themselves. Aid and advice in family planning can be an important supplement to domestic efforts, but it is bound to fail if those efforts are inadequate. The basic commitment in terms of policy and leadership and trained people must come from within the country concerned.

Modern forms of family planning are not going to be brought to Indian peasants by social workers from New York. People will only accept new and strange methods of family planning if they are strongly endorsed by their own government and presented by individuals they trust and understand.

Sixth: Family planning programs should be part of expanded programs of health and social services.

Some people think of family planning as essentially a mechanical problem to be solved by means of some technological miracle. But as Dr. Frank W. Notestein, President of the Population Council, has said:

> If, by a miracle, we learned to make prayer an effective means of contraception, we would not have the organizational and educational machinery to make very efficient use of the discovery.[3]

To bring modern methods of family planning to vast rural populations requires a network of health and social services that does not exist in most of the countries concerned. It requires administrators, doctors and auxiliary personnel, vehicles, dispensaries, medical implements, communications equipment—as well as pills, IUCD's, and other contraceptive devices. To reduce the birth rate in India, for example, to a point where economic growth becomes meaningful, the government of India in the next decade must encourage over 50 million couples to practice family planning. Considering that India has more than 375 million people who cannot read, 550,000 separate villages, and only 3.5 million couples now practicing family planning, it is obvious that the job cannot be done without strengthening presently inadequate rural services.

Moreover, the acceptance of family planning will be facilitated if it is not a separate program but rather one element in a total package of services for maternal and child care. A woman is likely to be interested in the pill or the IUCD when it is explained to her by the same health worker who has delivered her child. As M. G. Candau, Director-General of the World Health Organization (WHO) has summarized:

> The integration of family planning services with other health activities uses existing health facilities and personnel, prevents the fragmentation of health services, utilizes personnel that has traditional contact with patients and avoids weakening what is often a limited basic health program.[4]

Seventh: Family planning is not a substitute for foreign aid—what is needed·is more of both.

Nothing could be more certain to frustrate the objectives of both family planning and foreign aid than to consider the former a substitute for the latter. For the foreseeable future we will require more of both.

We have already noted that family programs cannot succeed without a

---

[3] "A Critical Evaluation of National Family Planning Programs," Statement to the 8th International Conference of the International Planned Parenthood Federation, Santiago, Chile, April 1967, p. 11.

[4] Statement to the 43rd session of the Economic and Social Council (ECOSOC), WHO Press Release WHO/24, July 14, 1967.

massive investment in health and other basic services. This will require additional external financing. To be sure, family planning can reduce the amount of international assistance needed to produce a given increase in per capita income and may hasten the day when some countries can become substantially self-supporting. But, in the foreseeable future, even with the most vigorous action in family planning, it will take a substantial increase in international aid to reach living standards in the less developed countries compatible with minimum human dignity. At the very least, the developed countries should be thinking of a steady escalation of their aid efforts to reach by 1975 the target of one percent of their gross national products recommended by United Nations bodies. Given their present rates of economic growth, this would mean a doubling of the foreign aid effort of the developed countries.[5]

From a psychological point of view, moreover, family planning programs are likely to meet resistance at the governmental and popular level if they are presented as a means of cutting back investment in a country's war on poverty. Statements that "one dollar invested in birth control is worth 200 dollars in aid" only arouse suspicions that the rich countries are offering IUCD's with one hand and taking back aid funds with the other. The Black Power extremists in the United States who have urged American Negroes to resist family planning programs have their counterparts in other countries who will exploit any evidence that family planning is being used by the rich to avoid their responsibilities to the poor.

Eighth: Assistance in dealing with the population problem should be related to the maximum possible extent to the work of international agencies, particularly the relevant agencies of the United Nations.

The reasons why multilateral aid may in some situations prove more effective than bilateral aid are well-known, and evidence to support them is provided elsewhere in this volume. In a sensitive area like family planning the case for multilateral aid is particularly compelling. International agencies can help promote a broad consensus on the nature of the population problem and on what ought to be done about it. They can help countries share responsibility for taking controversial steps that may be opposed by particular domestic interests. They can help prevent family planning from becoming a cold-war issue involving political ideologies or a subject of disagreement between national or racial groups. In the nuclear age, no race or nation achieves wealth or power through unregulated fertility. International agencies are in an excellent position to transmit this vital message.

[5] For a proposal to this effect see the author's "Time for a New Marshall Plan," *The New York Times*, June 3, 1967, p. 30, and his statement included in Association of the Bar of the City of New York, *Law and Policy-Making for Trade Among "Have" and "Have-Not" Nations* (Dobbs Ferry, N.Y: Oceana Publications, 1968).

The United Nations and its family of agencies are thus the logical place for cooperative action to deal with the population problem. But how much has the UN system been able to do in the past? How much can it do in the future?

The UN's Slow Beginning

The United Nations was excruciatingly slow in coming to grips with the population problem. For the first decade and a half of its existence virtually nothing was done by the UN or its agencies in the field of family planning.

Historians may judge this omission to be one of the most serious failures of the world organization. Action in these crucial years could have reduced the population problem to more manageable proportions. The opportunity was lost—and now the world must make up for lost time in an atmosphere of population crisis.

The inactivity of the UN in these years, however, was but the reflection of the attitudes of its Members. The predominantly Catholic countries of Latin America and Western Europe, together with the Communist bloc, opposed any UN action in support of family planning. The United States and other Members with significant Catholic minorities supported the "hands-off" policy not merely for fear of domestic political repercussions but out of a reluctance to provoke a confrontation on this issue that might weaken the UN. A few less developed Members and the Scandinavian countries pressed for action, but they did not have the votes. There was simply no shared sense that a population problem existed—and even less was there a consensus on what to do about it.

Accordingly, in the UN's first fifteen years, although population problems were occasionally referred to by delegates, there was not a single debate in the General Assembly or the Economic and Social Council (ECOSOC) devoted to the population problem. The Secretary-General and other UN officials had little to say about it—and avoided any proposals for action. In Dag Hammarskjöld's 1955 reorganization the demographic section of the UN Secretariat was even downgraded from a Division to a Branch and its staff substantially reduced. By the late 1950's and early 1960's B. R. Sen, Director-General of the Food and Agriculture Organization, and Eugene Black, President of the International Bank for Reconstruction and Development (IBRD), were warning about the consequences of existing rates of population growth, but doing something about the problem was outside the scope of their agencies.

In the World Health Organization, the UN agency which would have to bear a major share of the responsibility for implementing a family planning program, the situation was particularly unfavorable. According to Article 1 of its Constitution WHO was created to further "the attainment by all peoples of the highest possible level of health." This objective was vigorously implemented through programs of disease eradication—progress in control of malaria, smallpox, cholera, yaws, and trachoma was spectacular—and through work in environmental sanitation, nutrition, and maternal and child care. Unquestionably, these activities made a major contribution to economic development. Sickness is a major cause of low productivity in the less developed countries not only because it reduces the efficiency of workers on the job but because it also removes experienced workers from the labor force by premature death or incapacity.

Nevertheless, WHO's rather one-sided approach to its mandate to raise health standards was, paradoxically, creating new problems. Advances in death control, unaccompanied by any action on birth control, further aggravated the demographic imbalance. In the 1950's population in the less developed countries not only grew at an unprecedented rate, but that rate itself grew at an unprecedented rate. The principal responsibility, of course, was by no means that of WHO. The aid programs of the United States, the United Kingdom, France, and other developed countries were no less unbalanced in emphasizing death control unaccompanied by birth control, and so were the development plans of the less developed countries themselves. But as the principal international agency concerned with health WHO certainly helped to reinforce this dangerously unbalanced approach. The resulting trends worked against economic development and the achievement of acceptable health standards as well.

Some members of WHO sought to change the Organization's costly abstention from action in family planning—but without success. At the second World Health Assembly in 1949 Ceylon asked WHO to consider a family planning program on a world scale. The British delegate replied that family planning was not a proper concern of WHO, and the matter was dropped. In 1950 Ceylon proposed that WHO create an expert committee on the health aspects of population. This seemingly benign proposal was defeated without discussion by a vote of 30 to 1, with 5 abstentions. In 1952 Norway revived the committee idea, provoking a heated debate in which Ireland threatened to withdraw from the Organization if the proposal was adopted. The United States and other important contributors took the position that the proposal was premature and politically dangerous to WHO. It was dropped without a vote. As late as 1961 Ceylon and Norway could not even gain acceptance of the modest proposal that the Director-General collect information on what countries were doing with regard to family planning.

But it would be wrong to pass a wholly negative judgment on the UN's record on population during these first fifteen years. While nothing was done to support family planning efforts, the groundwork for later action was being laid. WHO's increasing emphasis on the training of doctors and on the strengthening of national health services helped to create an infrastructure essential to the implementation of family planning programs. Increasing funds for this infrastructure were made available not only from WHO's regular budget but from UN Headquarters institutions—the Expanded Program of Technical Assistance (EPTA) and the UN Special Fund.

There was perhaps an even greater contribution made by the UN in the field of population during these early years. One has to understand a problem before one can act effectively to deal with it. The UN did much to make this understanding possible: through the population unit in the UN Secretariat; through the Population Commission (a group of experts meeting every two years); through the World Population Conference held in 1954 under UN auspices; through the demographic work of the regional economic commissions; and through the regional demographic research and training centers established in Latin America, Africa, and Asia.

The significance of these UN activities should not be underestimated. When the Population Commission met for the first time in 1947, demographic statistics, including census and vital statistics, were so incomplete that it was hardly possible to speak of world population trends or of world population problems. Without the devoted labors of the population and statistical sections of the UN Secretariat, operating under the Population and Statistical Commissions, one might not be able to discern even now the outlines of the world population problem or the problems of the major regions. Moreover, the UN played a major role in encouraging and assisting Member governments to obtain factual information on the size, composition, and trends of their populations and on the interrelation between population growth and economic development. It helped train nationals of less developed countries in census taking and demography. Slowly but surely it helped alert the new leaders of the developing nations to the dangers of too rapid population growth. The UN system was not yet ready to face the issue of family planning; but the basis for a breakthrough was being laid.

1962–1967: The Years of the Breakthrough

The breakthrough to UN action on family planning began in December 1962. In that month the General Assembly finally reached the agenda item "Population growth and economic development" which the Swedish government had first introduced a year earlier. It not only held the first debate in its history on the population problem, but it adopted by a vote of 69 in favor, none against, and 27 abstentions, a historic resolution calling for a program of international cooperation.[6] Beginning with this resolution, the UN family began to lay the legislative and institutional foundation for direct support of national family planning programs.

What was responsible for the breakthrough? As already suggested, the years of slow and careful accumulation of basic factual information by UN bodies helped awaken the concern of the membership. So did the pioneering work of private agencies. The International Planned Parenthood Federation, with affiliated organizations in many UN Member States, and particularly the Planned Parenthood Federation of America, influenced public opinion and official attitudes around the world. The Population Council and the Ford and Rockefeller Foundations supported research leading to cheaper and better contraceptive techniques and demonstrated their effectiveness in less developed countries. Other private agencies too numerous to mention also played a part. In the December 1962 debate on population the red cover of an eloquent pamphlet entitled "Does Overpopulation Mean Poverty?," financed by the Albert and Mary Lasker Foundation, could be seen at the places of many UN delegates.

A decisive role in the breakthrough was also played by the less developed countries themselves. India, Pakistan, Tunisia, and Egypt were stimulated by their own experiences with exploding population growth to press more vigorously for UN action. And by 1962 the less developed countries had the votes they previously lacked to override the Catholic countries of Latin America and Western Europe.

Another element was the changing attitude of the United States. The UN debate of December 1962 triggered a dramatic change in American policy which in turn provided new impetus for further UN movement. This electric interplay of United Nations and United States action on population provides an excellent illustration of how international organizations can be instruments of progress on sensitive issues. It is worth describing in some detail.

Until December 1962 the United States government had no policy on population—or perhaps it might be more accurate to say it had a policy against United States government involvement in family planning programs at home or abroad. Agency for International Development (AID) missions were under instructions which prevented them from providing aid or advice of any kind in this field, in line with President Dwight D. Eisenhower's statement that "I cannot imagine anything more emphatically a subject that is not a proper political or governmental activity or

[6] General Assembly Resolution 1838 (XVII), December 18, 1962.

function or responsibility."[7] It was with that statement, indeed, that President Eisenhower had repudiated the historic recommendations of his foreign aid panel headed by General William H. Draper, Jr., urging United States aid for family planning programs in developing countries.

The election in 1960 of John F. Kennedy, the first Catholic ever to be President of the United States, was interpreted by some as an insuperable barrier to any progress in United States population policy. Indeed, an attempt by the author to include a reference to population in the report submitted to the President-elect by his Task Force on Foreign Aid in January 1961 was rejected on this ground. But President Kennedy took a pragmatic, farsighted view of the population problem uninfluenced by religious doctrine. And as a Catholic he was better equipped than his predecessor to assess the domestic political reaction and deal effectively with it.

During 1961 and 1962 the population problem received increasing attention within the Department of State and AID, but there was reluctance in many quarters to urge a new policy upon the White House. Some specific catalyst was needed to bring the issue into the open. It came in December 1962 when the General Assembly finally reached the Swedish item. Suddenly, the United States had to "stand up and be counted." The author obtained authority to serve as the United States representative in the debate, and, in a speech approved by President Kennedy himself, told the General Assembly that the United States not only favored a more active UN role on population but that it was itself now willing to

> help other countries, upon request, to find potential sources of information and assistance on ways and means of dealing with population problems.[8]

Shortly thereafter new instructions were issued to AID missions around the world citing this statement as the new basis for policy. President Kennedy in April 1963 confirmed the new policy in response to a press conference question, declaring that we need to "know more about the whole reproductive cycle" and that this knowledge should then "be made more available to the world."

President Lyndon B. Johnson picked up strongly where President Kennedy left off. In his State of the Union Message of 1965 he declared:

> I will seek new ways to use our knowledge to help deal with the explosion in world population and the growing scarcity in world resources.[9]

In the period 1965–1967 he made more than 30 statements reiterating his

---

[7] *The New York Times,* December 3, 1959, p. 18.

[8] Richard N. Gardner, "Population Growth, Economic Development, and the United Nations," Department of State *Bulletin,* January 7, 1963 (Vol. 48, No. 1228), p. 18.

[9] Department of State *Bulletin,* January 25, 1965 (Vol. 52, No. 1335), p. 96.

concern with domestic and foreign population problems. At home the Johnson Administration began making family planning services available in programs of the Office of Economic Opportunity and the Department of Health, Education, and Welfare. Overseas it clarified and strengthened the deliberately ambiguous offer of assistance contained in the 1962 General Assembly speech. In March of 1965 AID gave its overseas missions a mandate to respond to requests for technical, financial, and commodity assistance in support of family planning programs. The only limitation on this mandate was that AID would not consider requests for contraceptive devices or equipment for their manufacture. In April 1967 even this qualification was removed, and in September 1967 AID announced a grant to India for the purchase of contraceptives. None of these actions produced any significant adverse domestic reaction. Indeed the United States Congress wrote confirming authorizations of Administration policy into the foreign aid and Food for Peace legislation as well as various domestic health and antipoverty bills.

These, then, were some of the factors making possible the 1962 resolution of the General Assembly and the more ambitious UN actions that were to follow. In retrospect the 1962 resolution looks comparatively mild. But in the circumstances of the time its cautiously worded provisions represented a big step forward.

First, the Secretary-General was requested to conduct an "inquiry" among Member States "concerning the particular problems confronting them as a result of the reciprocal action of economic development and population changes." This inquiry, which took the form of a questionnaire sent to each Member of the UN and its specialized agencies, helped focus the attention of responsible officials in all countries on the implications of population trends for economic and social planning, to open up channels of communication between policymakers and local demographic experts, and to encourage governments without competent experts of their own to seek outside assistance. When the answers to the inquiry were compiled, analyzed, and laid before the membership two years later, the UN had before it the most complete information ever assembled on the attitudes and policies of governments on the population problem. It left no doubt of the need and desire of less developed countries for international assistance in initiating and carrying on family planning programs.

Second, the Economic and Social Council was asked, in cooperation with the specialized agencies, regional economic commissions, and the Population Commission, to

> intensify its studies and research on the interrelationship of population growth and economic and social development, with particular reference

to the needs of the developing countries for investment in health and educational facilities. . . .

This directive stimulated a substantial increase in the work program of the population section at UN Headquarters, the regional economic commissions, and the regional demographic research and training centers, and encouraged correlative studies of problems in public health and education by WHO and the United Nations Educational, Scientific and Cultural Organization (UNESCO).

Third, the Economic and Social Council was directed to report its findings with respect to all of the foregoing to the General Assembly. This laid the basis for the Assembly's next leap forward in 1966.

Fourth, UN agencies were asked to encourage and assist governments, especially of the less developed countries,

> in obtaining basic data and in carrying out essential studies of the demographic aspects, as well as other aspects, of their economic and social development problems.

Fifth, the World Population Conference scheduled for 1965 was requested to

> pay special attention to the interrelationship of population growth with economic and social development, particularly in the less developed countries. . . .

It was of enormous importance that this resolution was carried without any negative votes. But this meant the loss of a key section that had been included in the original resolution urging

> that the United Nations give technical assistance, as requested by Governments, for national projects and programmes dealing with the problems of population.[10]

This section was widely interpreted as calling for UN technical assistance in the implementation of family planning programs. There was uncertainty about whether it would involve the UN in training persons in the use of contraceptive devices and whether the UN would actually distribute those devices. The paragraph was approved by a narrow margin in the Second (Economic and Financial) Committee, but in the plenary, where a two-thirds majority is required on important questions, it failed of adoption by a vote of 34 in favor, 34 against, and 32 abstentions. A number of countries that voted in Committee for the resolution as a whole with the technical assistance section included abstained in the separate vote on the section. The United States was one of these, but it took pains to emphasize that the elimination of the paragraph would in

[10] UN Document A/C.2/L.657.

no way detract from the existing authority of the UN to grant technical assistance upon request to Member governments.[11] Abstention on the controversial section—and its consequent defeat—was the price that had to be paid for achieving a broad consensus among the membership. It was also the price the United States and some other Members had to pay for this first big step forward on population, given the uncertain state of domestic opinion.

In retrospect, it seems clear that the price was both necessary and worth paying. The General Assembly debate showed that, for all the movement that had occurred in national attitudes on the population problem, there were still significant differences among the membership. At least four different viewpoints could be identified.

The first viewpoint was represented by the government of Sweden and the other sponsors of the resolution—Ceylon, Denmark, Ghana, Greece, Nepal, Norway, Pakistan, Tunisia, Turkey, Uganda, and the United Arab Republic. These twelve nations argued that population growth posed grave problems for economic and social development and that urgent action was required to deal with it. They advocated a major increase in United Nations activity in the population field, including technical assistance in family planning. Support for this viewpoint was expressed by most Moslem countries (e.g., the United Arab Republic, Tunisia, Turkey, and Pakistan), some countries of Asia (e.g., India, Nepal, Thailand, Malaya, and Japan) and some countries of Africa (e.g., Ghana, Guinea, and Uganda). This viewpoint found little support in Latin America.

A second viewpoint—expressed by a substantial number of Member States including France and other countries of continental Europe, some French African countries, and some Latin American countries—conceded the existence of population problems in some areas but argued that action by the UN should be deferred pending further study. They opposed the controversial technical assistance section and took the initiative in introducing the proposal for an inquiry on Member countries' population problems.

A third viewpoint was advanced by Argentina and Ireland, with support from a few other countries, principally in Latin America. These countries questioned the existence of a population problem, challenged the right of the UN to discuss it, and were particularly outspoken in opposing a UN program in family planning financed from technical assistance funds to which they were contributing.

A fourth viewpoint was expressed by the members of the Soviet bloc. During the General Assembly debate the Union of Soviet Socialist Re-

[11] Department of State *Bulletin*, January 7, 1963 (Vol. 48, No. 1228), p. 19.

publics and some of the Eastern European countries expounded the traditional Communist position that Western discussions of the population problem were based on "neo-Malthusian fallacies" and that population problems would cease to exist under Communism. This position was poorly received by the less developed countries. One representative of a less developed country even chided the Soviet Union for favoring planning in all sectors of economic life except the human sector—the one most important in its implications for economic and social growth.

When the statements and voting records of these four groups are analyzed, it becomes clear that the elimination of the technical assistance paragraph made possible affirmative votes on the resolution by many countries in the second group and abstentions instead of negative votes by many countries in groups three or four.

Moreover, subsequent UN actions triggered by the 1962 Assembly resolution soon confirmed that no practical significance attached to the removal of the technical assistance section. The countries of the Economic Commission for Asia and the Far East (ECAFE), much more united on this issue than the General Assembly, took up the demand for technical assistance at the Asian Population Conference of 1963 and at the annual ECAFE meeting in 1964. In 1967 ECAFE went as far as to establish a center in Bangkok to assist its members in the implementation of their family planning programs. Building on the 1963 and 1964 ECAFE actions, the Economic and Social Council at its summer 1965 session requested the Secretary-General

> to provide . . . advisory services and training on action programmes in the field of population at the request of Governments desiring assistance in this field.[12]

And in December 1966 the cycle was completed when the General Assembly unanimously approved a resolution calling on UN agencies

> to assist, when requested, in further developing and strengthening national and regional facilities for training, research, information and advisory services in the field of population. . . .[13]

Equally important, the UN Secretariat, encouraged by the 1962 resolution, dropped its previous reticence on family planning. The Population Branch at UN Headquarters was strengthened and raised to the status of Division. Milos Macura, an able Yugoslav demographer, was made its Director, an appointment that helped keep population out of ideological controversy. Even without the technical assistance section, the UN Secretariat in 1965 responded to a request from India and sent an expert mission to advise that government on its family planning program. Popula-

---

[12] ECOSOC Resolution 1084 (XXXIX), July 30, 1965.
[13] General Assembly Resolution 2211 (XXI), December 17, 1966.

tion was increasingly featured in statements of Secretary-General U Thant and Philippe de Seynes, the Undersecretary for Economic and Social Affairs. On the occasion of Human Rights Day, December 10, 1966, the Secretary-General issued the following response to an appeal by twelve heads of state of less developed countries for action to deal with the population problem:

> In my view, we must accord the right of parents to determine the numbers of their children a place of importance at this moment in man's history. For, as one of the consequences of backwardness, rates of population growth are very much higher in the poor two-thirds of the world than they are among the more privileged countries and it is being increasingly realized that, over the two or three decades immediately ahead, when present world-wide efforts to raise food production will not have yielded the fullest results, the problem of growing food shortage cannot be solved without in many cases a simultaneous effort to moderate population growth.[14]

In the summer of 1967 the Secretary-General used the occasion of his annual statement to ECOSOC to call for "a bolder and more effective program of action" to deal with the population problem.[15]

The growing support for family planning in the central UN institutions was reflected in the work of key UN agencies. Perhaps the most important step forward was taken by Henry R. Labouisse, Executive Director of the United Nations Children's Fund (UNICEF). In a report issued in March 1966 he urged that UNICEF enter the field of family planning as a logical extension of its existing work in maternal and child care. He pointed out that UNICEF's maternal and child care centers were among the best places to conduct family planning programs. He proposed that UNICEF resources be used, among other things, not only for the education and training of nationals of developing countries in family planning techniques but also for the distribution of contraceptive supplies. This report was the subject of heated discussion in the summer 1966 session of the UNICEF Executive Board, particularly when it was proposed that UNICEF meet requests for family planning assistance from India and Pakistan which had already been rejected by WHO. Action on the Executive Director's report was deferred, but in a mail poll taken after the Executive Board meeting the aid to India and Pakistan was approved. The projects have a total cost of $800,000 and include contraceptive materials to be used in maternal and child health programs. In its summer 1967 session, the UNICEF Executive Board adopted a policy permitting assistance to family planning activities as part of national health services.

---

[14] UN Press Release SG/SM/620, December 9, 1966, pp. 1–2.
[15] UN Press Release ECOSOC/198, SG/SM/51, July 11, 1967, p. 3.

UN agencies concerned with education and communication have also begun to prepare for a role in the family planning effort. The UNESCO General Conference of November 1966 called on the Director-General to appoint a special committee

> [to] defin[e] Unesco's responsibilities in the population field, and to consider, in particular, the following fields for possible Unesco action: (i) to carry out sociological studies on social, cultural, and other factors influencing attitudes for family planning . . . ; (ii) to function as a clearing house for exchange of sociological research and knowledge in the field of family planning.[16]

The 1967-1968 UNESCO program, moreover, provided for research by UNESCO at the request of member states into the effectiveness of various information and education techniques related to family planning. And the Science and Technology Branch at UN Headquarters accepted a grant from the Ford Foundation for a study of the motivational and communications aspects of family planning. With the help of this grant a computerized system for the exchange of family planning information is being established.

The World Health Organization, always the most sensitive point in the UN system for discussion of family planning in view of its special responsibilities in medical assistance, has also begun to move—though not without difficulty. Assisted by a grant of $500,000 from the United States in 1963 for research on "problems of human reproduction" (the neutral phrase was carefully chosen at the time to include problems of sterility as well as of fecundity), a WHO scientific group issued reports concerning the safety and effectiveness from a medical point of view of the pill and the IUCD. M. G. Candau, the Brazilian Director-General who had followed a somewhat hesitant policy on family planning in the past, presented proposals for an expanded WHO role in family planning to the 1965 World Health Assembly. In approving the Director-General's proposals, the Assembly requested him to develop further his proposed program both in the field of reference services (studies on medical aspects of sterility and fertility control methods and health aspects of population dynamics) and

> in the field of advisory services . . . on the understanding that such services are related, within the responsibilities of WHO, to technical advice on the health aspects of human reproduction and should not involve operational activities; . . . [17]

At the 1966 World Health Assembly, however, an attempt to strengthen

16 United Nations Educational, Scientific and Cultural Organization, *Approved Programme and Budget for 1967–1968* (Paris, January 1967), p. 328.

17 World Health Assembly Resolution WHA 18.49 of May 21, 1965.

this mandate ran into difficulty. A coalition of Western European, Communist, Latin American, and French-speaking African countries defeated a resolution that would have authorized the Director-General to extend WHO's advisory services in family planning "through such means as expert advice in programme planning and execution, training personnel and program evaluation" and that would have asked him also to study

> how family planning services could be integrated in the overall health planning—particularly in the maternal and child health services—of those countries, which feel the need thereof; . . . [18]

The opponents of this resolution urged that WHO should proceed slowly with family planning activity and not promote any particular population policy. Several countries expressed concern lest WHO's limited resources be diverted from traditional health work to family planning activities. The Director-General himself spoke against the resolution, warning that in some less developed countries malaria and tuberculosis services had already suffered from the diversion of funds to family planning. "To promote family planning at the expense of the health services," he declared, "was not a decision for an international organization working in the health field."[19] In the end the 1966 World Health Assembly approved the Director-General's proposed program in family planning based on the previous year's resolution and confirmed that

> the role of WHO is to give Members technical advice, upon request, in the development of activities in family planning, as part of an organized health service, without impairing its normal preventive and curative functions; . . . [20]

In the light of the controversy at the 1966 World Health Assembly, of WHO's refusal to take on the India and Pakistan projects subsequently undertaken by UNICEF, and of the caution frequently displayed by WHO representatives in interagency meetings on population, it is uncertain how far WHO is now prepared to go. The Director-General's strong emphasis on population in his report to the 1967 summer session of ECOSOC, however, provided some grounds for optimism:

> The World Health Organization has continued to provide information on biological, clinical and public health aspects of fertility, sterility, family planning and fertility regulation. Several Governments have requested different forms of advice such as those related to setting up or strengthening family planning in association with maternal and child health services, or integrating family planning programmes within such services. Requests for advice on the side effects of modern contraceptives, on the

[18] World Health Organization *Official Records* (19th Assembly), No. 152, p. 368.
[19] *Ibid.*, p. 384.
[20] World Health Assembly Resolution WHA 19.43 of May 20, 1966.

development of a bio-medical research unit in reproductive physiology, and on a review of research are being implemented with a view to making recommendations for further development and priorities upon request from Member States . . . WHO is prepared to assist, upon request, in the evaluation of family planning services in Member States.[21]

With so many agencies finally moving in response to the challenge of population growth the UN family seems on the way to implementing a "co-ordinated inter-agency programme" of expanded research and advisory services of the kind urged by the Population Commission at its thirteenth session in 1965.[22] An important instrument for achieving that coordination is the subgroup of the Administrative Committee on Coordination (ACC) established in 1966 and including representatives of UN agencies now involved in the population field. Indeed, as the Secretary-General told the 1967 summer session of ECOSOC,

> The United Nations now has at its disposal the institutional infrastructure which, given some additional means, could be put to more effective use in support of large scale programmes.[23]

WANTED: A WORLD POPULATION PROGRAM

Thanks to the breakthrough of 1962–1967 there is no longer any question of the willingness of the United States and the United Nations to grant assistance to less developed countries in the field of family planning. But policy has not yet been fully translated into program. To put it bluntly, the ratio of talk to action is still distressingly high.

The United States aid program has still barely touched this vital aspect of economic and human development. In the fiscal year 1967 AID provided less than $9 million for activities related to population, a sum which was less than four-tenths of one percent of total United States foreign aid spending. Much of that $9 million was used for academic studies, statistical studies, and attitude studies—studies which were extremely useful but which did not in themselves increase the availability of family planning information and techniques to those who wished to have them. Only in one country, Turkey, did AID provide a significant amount of aid going beyond studies and this was in the form of jeeps for family planning workers and support for an educational effort. That single program in Turkey costing $3.5 million accounted for more than one-third of AID's fiscal year 1967 population budget. For fiscal year 1968 AID

---

[21] WHO Press Release WHO/24, July 14, 1967, p. 5.
[22] For the Commission's report see Economic and Social Council *Official Records* (39th session), Supplement No. 9.
[23] UN Press Release ECOSOC/198, SG/SM/51, July 11, 1967, p. 3.

planned to spend about $20 million for assistance to family planning programs.

The situation is scarcely better in the United Nations. Of the $130 million UN regular budget for 1967 only $1.7 million is devoted to population work. This sum, which had to support the work of the Population Commission and the Population Division at UN Headquarters as well as that of the regional economic commissions, was almost entirely devoted to research and training in statistics, demography, and the economic aspects of population growth. Various UN agencies are spending small additional amounts for population work, but except for the two UNICEF projects totaling $800,000 there is little by way of direct support for family planning programs. Only a minuscule portion of WHO's $70 million annual budget is employed for this purpose.

Unless there is a vast increase in this very small amount of international assistance available for family planning, adequate programs to reduce birth rates in the less developed countries will never materialize. In India the current five-year plan allots $306 million over five years for population, or an average of $61 million per year. A dozen other countries have adopted national family planning programs with services included as a basic element of national health activities and with budgets ranging from a few thousand dollars to many millions. In more than 50 countries private voluntary groups, affiliated with the International Planned Parenthood Federation, are pressing locally for more vigorous action. In almost every case, public or private, lack of funds is a major obstacle to expanding programs—programs which are popular, beneficial from a health point of view, and extremely important to overall economic objectives. Although some of the needed funds can be raised within the less developed countries, there is a great and growing need for technical assistance to train administrators, doctors, and health workers and for other assistance to pay for vehicles and communications equipment not locally available. Without assistance of this kind the new scientific developments which have simplified and will further simplify contraception will be largely meaningless for the less developed countries.

With these facts in mind an increasing number of individuals and private organizations have begun to call for a vast expansion of international assistance for family planning programs. In December 1965 a Committee on Population[24] formed as part of President Johnson's National Citizens' Commission to offer recommendations to the United

[24] The author served as Chairman of this committee. Its other members were Eugene R. Black, Cass Canfield, Dr. Leslie Corsa, Jr., Gardner Cowles, A. W. Dent, General William H. Draper, Jr., Mrs. Albert D. Lasker, David E. Lilienthal, John D. Rockefeller, 3rd, Mrs. Edith S. Sampson, George N. Shuster, and Dr. Aaron Stern. For the text of the report see Richard N. Gardner (ed.), *Blueprint for Peace* (New York: McGraw-Hill, 1966), Chapter 6.

States government during International Cooperation Year made the following key recommendations:

> That the U.S. Government be prepared to make available upon request up to $100 million a year over the next three years to help other countries implement programs of family planning and strengthen national health and social services necessary for the support of family planning programs.

> That U.S. assistance to other countries in all of these areas be related to the maximum possible extent to the work of multilateral agencies, particularly the relevant agencies of the United Nations, including the World Health Organization, the United Nations Children's Fund, and the United Nations Development Program.[25]

In the spring of 1967 Senator J. William Fulbright, together with eighteen cosponsors, introduced S. 1264, a bill to amend the Foreign Assistance Act. Both Senator Fulbright and Senator Charles Percy, in presenting the bill, cited the key recommendations of the Committee on Population and declared that their bill would substantially implement them. It authorized the appropriation of $50 million per year for three years, plus available United States-owned foreign currencies, for use in support of voluntary family planning programs in friendly foreign nations. It stipulated that this support should be made available, under procedures to insure that no coercion is involved, to foreign governments, UN specialized agencies, United States and foreign nonprofit organizations, universities, hospitals, accredited health institutions, and voluntary health or other qualified organizations. It authorized a wide variety of action including demographic studies, medical and psychological research, personnel training, instruction and staffing of clinics and rural health centers, training for doctors, manufacture of medical supplies, dissemination of family planning information, and the provision of medical assistance and supplies to individuals who desire such assistance.

In November 1967 the Fulbright bill was enacted into law as a new Title X of the Foreign Assistance Act of 1961 entitled "Programs Relating to Population Growth." Its provisions were essentially the same in substance as when originally introduced, except for the fact that the $50 million for three years was reduced to $35 million for the fiscal year 1968 and the final language specified that this sum was available only to support family planning programs. The reference to multilateral assistance was altered to authorize contributions to "the United Nations, its specialized agencies, and other international organizations and programs."

During the 1967 foreign aid hearings the author submitted an illustrative budget to show how as much as $100 million a year in dollars and

[25] *Ibid.*, p. 140.

local currencies might be effectively spent on family planning programs.[26] This budget, shown in the table below, includes $20 million for training, $6 million for additional AID staff, $10 million for demonstration projects, $10 million for information programs, $15 million for commodities (including equipment, transportation, and supplies), $11 million for research and evaluation, $8 million for private nonprofit organizations, and $20 million for UN and international organization programs. Broken down geographically it shows $42 million for Asia, $26 million for Africa, $19 million for Latin America, and $13 million for training and supporting assistance in the United States, including UN Headquarters.

Three of the categories of assistance noted in this table require special explanation. The first is the $15 million category for commodities. This category would include the purchase of contraceptive devices themselves where United States financing is regarded as necessary for the achievement of effective programs. The Fulbright bill explicitly authorizes the use of aid funds for the purchase or manufacture of such supplies, a use that AID now regards as appropriate. This type of expenditure may be increasingly necessary as foreign countries move out of the planning stage into large-scale implementation of programs. It is likely to be required now that experience has demonstrated that the pill will play a major part in family planning programs along with the IUCD. Since the pill is more expensive, there may be occasions when the United States government will need to provide financial assistance to help make it available.

The second category is financial support for private agencies. The Ford and Rockefeller Foundations, the Population Council, the Planned Parenthood Federation of America, and the International Planned Parenthood Federation, not to mention other organizations, can often carry on informational activities, research, and pilot projects better than government agencies. At the time the Fulbright bill was introduced AID had made grants of only $400,000 to private agencies. The proposed figure of $8 million a year would be commensurate with the enlarged scope that should be afforded to private institutions in this field.

The third category of assistance is to UN agencies. Without a major new initiative by the United States and other aid donors a significant UN program of aid to family planning will never get off the ground. What is needed, indeed, is a World Population Program directed by the UN and financed by a special fund of voluntary contributions. The United States should offer up to $20 million a year for this program, not subject to the usual matching requirements, and encourage contribu-

---

[26] For congressional reaction to the illustrative budget and to the author's proposal for a World Population Program under UN auspices see U.S. Congress, House, Committee on Foreign Affairs, *Hearings, Foreign Assistance Act of 1967*, 90th Congress, 1st Session, 1967, Part V, pp. 971–1011, and Part VI, pp. 1127–1157; and U.S. Congress, Senate, Committee on Foreign Relations, *Hearings, Foreign Assistance Act of 1967*, 90th Congress, 1st Session, 1967, pp. 47–74.

PROPOSED $100 MILLION UNITED STATES AID BUDGET FOR FAMILY PLANNING

(Including Counterpart Funds Where Available)

Areas	Training (Including Facilities)	AID Staff	Demonstration Projects	Information	Commodities, Equipment, Transportation Supplies	Research and Evaluation	Private Groups	UN and International Agencies	Totals
Asia	9	3	3	4	8	4	4	7	42
Africa	3	1	4	4	4	3	2	5	26
Latin America	2	1	3	2	3	2	2	4	19
United States	6	1	—	—	—	2	—	4	13
	20	6	10	10	15	11	8	20	100

tions from as many other countries as possible, toward a total program goal of $50 million annually. If this modest beginning is successful, a substantially greater level of effort will then be in order.

Some part of the funds from the World Population Program could be used to expand the UN's existing work in providing demographic information and training demographic specialists. But the bulk of the funds should be used for operational activities in direct support of family planning programs. In specific terms the World Population Program should finance:

1) *Increased staff* at UN Headquarters and in the regional economic commissions *to help countries prepare projects in family planning* that could be supported by the UN.

2) *Training centers* for personnel needed in family planning programs —doctors, health workers, administrators, communications specialists.

3) *Pilot or demonstration projects* to get national or regional programs under way. Interdisciplinary teams drawn from different UN agencies— doctors, administrators, demographers, economists, communications experts—could work in model areas with host government personnel. Aided by advice and training from the UN on the organization, administration, execution, and evaluation of programs, the host countries could gradually learn to carry forward nationwide programs through their own efforts.

The World Population Program should be directed by the Secretary-General of the UN through the Administrator of the UN Development Program (UNDP). The various UN agencies like UNICEF, WHO, and the regional centers should be given funds to execute projects, but a centralized budget and administration at UN Headquarters would encourage more effective teamwork in regional and country programs.

Many UN Members, including the United States, have a general policy against establishing new voluntary programs in the UN system. As a general rule this is sound, but exceptions are justified when there is no other way to do a particular job that needs doing. The United States made an exception to this rule when it launched a separate voluntary program in WHO for malaria eradication and when it made its voluntary contribution of $500,000 for the WHO research program in human reproduction.

A new voluntary program is now a necessity if the UN system is to give effective assistance to family planning. As a practical matter it will not be possible to get sufficient funds in the UN regular budget or in the UN agency budgets for family planning in competition with other activities. As noted earlier, the Director-General of WHO has already warned against diverting funds from WHO's customary activities to family planning efforts. Other UN officials may take a similar view. Moreover, since certain countries still have reservations about the use of their money for family planning, it is best to have a separate fund for this purpose for those that are prepared to contribute. A separate voluntary fund in which UN Members that wish to give family planning aid provide it to those that wish to receive it effectively bypasses the political problem.

To help get the program started and to stimulate lagging bilateral aid efforts in population more could be done through another international organization, the Organization for Economic Cooperation and Development (OECD). The International Bank's consortia for India and Pakistan and OECD's consortium for Turkey could also be involved. Each of these countries has initiated nationwide family planning programs, but there are great shortages of personnel to train doctors and health workers in family planning techniques. The consortia members should consider the feasibility of creating a "doctor pool" which India, Pakistan, and Turkey could draw upon for family planning assistance. The trainers of medical personnel could be made available directly to these countries or indirectly under UN or WHO auspices. In general, there should be a greater effort to stimulate additional aid in family planning from the Scandinavian countries, Japan, and the United Kingdom, all of which are in a position to do more in this field.

The prospect—encouraged by hearings on the Fulbright bill—that additional United States aid might be made available for a United Nations program in family planning produced a swift response at UN Headquarters. The Secretary-General told the summer 1967 session of ECOSOC that the Secretariat had prepared a minimum five-year plan for the expansion of the UN's population work and that he would ask the General Assembly for gradually increased budgetary appropriations. Then he added:

> I have decided to establish a trust fund to which I hope governments and institutions will pledge voluntary contributions. This would help us to lay the ground for training centers as well as for pilot experiments which will assist the less developed countries in establishing and expanding their own administration and programmes.[27]

The United States and other countries immediately indicated their willingness to contribute.

The trust fund opened in the summer of 1967 could be the first step toward a World Population Program and toward a really effective response by the UN to the challenge of population growth. At least, one earnestly hopes so. In the long run this might prove to be the Organization's most vital contribution to human welfare second only to keeping the peace. In a matter of such transcendent importance to humanity as a whole the United Nations belongs at the very center of the picture.

[27] UN Press Release ECOSOC 198, SG/SM/51, July 11, 1967, p. 3. See also "Additional Financing of the Expanded United Nations Population Programme," aide-mémoire circulated by the UN Secretariat to governments and private agencies in July 1967.

International Cooperation in Food and Population

INTRODUCTION

It is characteristic of our time that its most pro-
found problems are global, involving all men, yet the nations into which
men have divided themselves have never been as numerous nor as sharply
diverse. A hundred years ago poverty was the common lot of most human
beings; today we find two sets of nations staring at each other across the
oceans, one rich and one poor, with a growing gap between them. The
technological revolution has continuously improved the levels of living
in the rich countries; in the poor ones its principal effect has been to
multiply human misery by causing a rise in human numbers at rates
higher than ever before experienced.

The growth of populations and the lag in development are interrelated
—each worsens the other. Together, they have created a specter that
haunts the poor countries—whether there will be enough food in the
future to feed their peoples.

This specter will be exorcised for coming generations only if population growth can be drastically slowed. But in the next twenty years it is
equally necessary to bring about an unprecedented increase in world
food supplies. No likely reduction in rates of population growth in the
poor countries will lower by more than 10 or 15 percent the amount of
food they will need in 1985. Moreover, a marked improvement in human
diets over the next two decades may be essential to lower birth rates.
The problems of food and population can be solved only by the joint
efforts of the rich and the poor countries on a scale never before

ROGER REVELLE is Director of the Center for Population Studies, Harvard University, Cambridge,
Massachusetts. The author wishes to express his appreciation of the extensive help given by
Carl Nathan in many aspects of the preparation of this essay.

attempted. The question then arises: How shall their efforts be organized? How can international bodies and the nations themselves best work together to accomplish these enormous tasks?

Probable Relation Between Nutrition and Family Planning

In developed countries infant mortalities are nearly always less than 50 per thousand live births. But in the less developed countries, with very few exceptions, 50 to more than 150 children out of every 1,000 die before the age of one year. In a family of four or five children the probability that all will grow up is often less than 50 percent.

When average infant and child mortality is high, the variance is also high; the chances in an individual family that several children will die are frighteningly large. In all these countries parents desire a high degree of assurance that one of their sons will grow up to be a man, and they are willing to assume the burden of having too many children in order to gain this assurance. Availability of contraceptive devices may thus be relatively unimportant until the desired number of living children is secured. Low infant and child mortality, and public awareness that mortality is low, may be one of the necessary preconditions for reducing fertility.

The population problem of our time has been created by lowering death rates, yet we are faced with the paradox that an essential element in curing it may be to lower infant and child death rates further still, perhaps down to the levels existing in the Western world. If this is so, then the quickest possible increase of food supplies, both in quantity and quality, is of utmost urgency for the long term as well as the short because poor nutrition in the poor countries strikes fiercely at the children. The principal killers are the diseases of childhood that result from a combination of infection and malnutrition.

A relatively small crop failure in the United States has little effect, but in India it means that millions of children may die before the next eight months have passed. Even with a normal harvest a fifth of all Indians probably live on less than 1,600 calories a day, in contrast to our 3,000. Consequently, a partial crop failure reduces the diet of many poor persons to disastrously low levels.

The Dimensions of the World Food Problem

To meet human nutritional needs for calories, food supplies in the developing countries will have to be approximately doubled by 1985. In terms of cereal grains alone this means an increase of 300 million tons.[1]

---

[1] President's Science Advisory Committee, Panel on the World Food Supply, *The World Food Problem* (3 vols.; Washington: The White House, May and November 1967), Vol. 2, pp. 655–657.

The total quantity of protein must also be doubled, and the proportion of high-quality protein (containing a balance of amino acids similar to that in eggs and milk) must be increased. Part of these requirements could be furnished from the abundant harvests of the United States, Canada, Australia, and a few other developed countries provided these countries expand their cultivated areas and continue to raise yields per acre. But most of the increase must come from the developing countries themselves.

In Latin America and Africa large areas of arable land are not now cultivated, and these could be put under the plow, though at considerable expense. In Asia, which contains most of the world's hungry people, almost all the arable land is already cultivated.[2] In this continent an increase in food supplies could be obtained in part by reducing losses to pests but mostly by raising production through higher yields per acre, either by increasing the number of crops per year, or the weight of the harvest from each crop, or both.

In order to increase the number of crops per year irrigation developments will be required and often farm machinery to enable the farmers to prepare the land for seeding in the short time available between crop seasons. To increase yields per crop a combination of inputs is needed: adequate and timely irrigation water; large amounts of chemical fertilizers; high-yielding crop varieties, that is, varieties which will respond to fertilizer by producing more humanly edible material; pest control; improved farm tools and, in many cases, farm machinery; and better farming practices.

These inputs will need to be purchased by the farmers, using the proceeds from the sale of at least part of their crops. Thus, the necessary increase in food supplies cannot be obtained with traditional subsistence agriculture. It will be necessary for the farmers to make the transformation to market agriculture. The corollary is clear. The farmers will need customers who can afford to buy a large fraction of what they produce, and these customers will exist only if there is general economic growth. If there is to be "effective demand" for food, the means of buying the food—the purchasing power—must be available. National income must grow at a rate which permits consumers to purchase their food requirements. Hence, agriculture cannot be developed in isolation but only as part of the overall economy.

On the supply side agricultural production likewise depends on overall national production. Manufactured inputs—fertilizers, pesticides, and machinery—must be imported or produced domestically. If they are to be imported, the economy must generate sufficient exports or must be

[2] *Ibid.*, pp. 429–434.

able to rely on a net inflow of foreign assistance or investment. If they are to be produced domestically, the nonagricultural sectors must expand to meet the needs of the agricultural sector.

Conversely, overall economic growth in most developing countries largely depends on agricultural growth. Many nonagricultural industries are based on agricultural raw materials, including food products. Most of the resources used for agriculture are not transferable to other types of production.

Agricultural development as an essential basis for economic growth is in most developing countries a more meaningful and realistic goal than total self-sufficiency in food production. No developed countries have such self-sufficiency; in fact, one of the results of development is an improvement and diversification in human diets which involves greatly expanded international trade in livestock and poultry feeds, beverages, tropical fruits, animal fats, and vegetable oils.

The necessity for overall economic growth and rising consumer incomes, combined with present widespread malnutrition and undernutrition, means that future demands for food will increase more rapidly than population size. Up to 90 percent of the incomes of the poorest people in the less developed countries now go for food. As their incomes rise, they will want more and better things to eat. It is especially important that the diets of children be improved to create one of the necessary preconditions for family planning—lower child mortalities. From these considerations the annual compound growth rate of food demand can be estimated at 4 percent or more from 1965 to 1985 or at least 120 percent over the twenty-year period.

A primary characteristic of modern agriculture is that it is a highly technical business based on scientific knowledge. This has come about very recently even in the developed countries. Only within the last 25 years, anywhere in the world, have yields increased rapidly. The agricultural revolution in the United States since 1940 is one of the great events of history in terms of sheer scientific and technical accomplishment.

A destructive fallacy of the postwar era has been the notion that the agricultural technology of the developed countries in the temperate zones could be easily adapted for use in the poor countries of the tropics and subtropics. The standard approach of technical assistance has been, "We know how and we can show how." The fact is that we do not know how.[3]

The technology for raising yields in each locality must be created through applied local research and this research must be continuous.

3 *Ibid.*, pp. 614–639.

Consider, for example, the Japanese variety of rice which gives an increased yield of about ten pounds for every pound of nitrogen applied as fertilizer. It would seem to be a simple matter to introduce this variety in India where the local rice variety shows a poor response to more than a few pounds of nitrogen. But the Japanese variety cannot be grown successfully in India because the hours of sunlight during the growing season are not as long as in Japan. A new variety adapted to the Indian diurnal rhythms and resistant to Indian plant diseases is required. But pathogenic viruses and fungi mutate to produce new strains which virulently infect previously resistant crops. The plant geneticist is hard pressed to modify his plant varieties to keep ahead of their microbial enemies. In the long run there may even be a question of whether he or the fungi will be the smarter. Similar problems demanding new technical knowledge and new development arise in every aspect of tropical and subtropical agriculture. To make the quantum jump to market agriculture many cultural and social problems must be solved, as well as technical ones.

We are faced with two central facts: If the people of the poor countries are going to get enough to eat, they must practice market-oriented agriculture; and there must be overall economic development. They cannot concentrate, as they have always done in the past, on the relatively simple problem of improving subsistence agriculture. They must urbanize, industrialize, develop their entire economies. At the same time they must create the research and teaching institutions, the transportation and communications systems, the incentives for farmers, and the social conditions required for modern, scientifically based agriculture.

These are not problems that can be solved in a year or ten years. The solution will take at least two generations. They must be approached not as in the past, with short-term, quick payout programs or with gimmicks of various kinds but with realistic, long-continued, large-scale action. Any review of these problems shows that they cannot be solved without very great contributions from the developed countries.

THE ROLE OF THE DEVELOPED COUNTRIES

Capital Assistance

The solution will require heavy capital investment—of the order of 100 billion dollars during the next twenty years for agriculture alone in the less developed world (outside of the People's Republic of China [Communist China]). About one-fourth of this amount will be needed for purchases of equipment and material from the United States, Europe, and Japan which are not produced in the less developed countries.

To double agricultural production by 1985 needed investments in fertilizer plants and distribution systems have been estimated at $30.5 billion; investments in facilities for manufacture, formulation, and distribution of pesticides at close to $2 billion; and about the same amount to manufacture and distribute farm tools and machinery. The costs of the last to the farmers would be more than $30 billion.[4] Capital costs of irrigation works could be roughly $100 billion by the year 2000 or $35 billion by 1985 if 35 percent of the potential irrigation developments are completed by that date.[5]

Capital investments required for agriculture for India alone (containing slightly less than a third of the population of the underdeveloped world outside of mainland China) from 1964 to 1986 have been independently estimated[6] at $30.5 billion. Neither of these estimates allows for investments in facilities and people for research, education, and extension or for costs of fertilizers, pesticides, and seeds to the farmers.

Far larger capital investments will be required for the overall economic growth that is necessary to transform subsistence farming into modern agriculture in the poor countries. To achieve the needed 4 percent annual growth rate in food demand and supply, national incomes must rise by about 5.5 percent per annum, and this means that the level of capital investments must be raised by an average of roughly $20 billion a year over the next two decades to at least 15 to 20 percent of the gross national products of the developing countries. Capital and technical involvement of developed and developing nations alike will be required on an unprecedented scale.

The direct costs of family planning programs are relatively small. Probably about $350-450 million per year, mostly in rupees, would be all that could be effectively spent in India, even if social and economic conditions were such that most couples could be induced to practice strict family planning. This would include $100-150 million in foreign exchange for contraceptive materials (because of the difficulties of building a steroid manufacturing capability, oral contraceptives should probably be imported, at least at first) and the remainder for distribution facilities, paramedical personnel, educational materials, advertising, administration, and subsidies to midwives and parents. Adequate nutrition and economic change are probably preconditions for population control, and hence the indirect costs are very much greater, but they are included in the above estimates for agricultural and economic development.

---

[4] *Ibid.*, pp. 375–403.
[5] *Ibid.*, pp. 449–450.
[6] *Ibid.*, p. 676.

Food Aid

From 1954, when Public Law 480, the Agricultural Trade Development and Assistance Act, was enacted, through 1966 the United States sold on concessional terms or donated to the less developed countries 147 million tons of agricultural commodities valued at $13.5 billion.

It is likely that the needs of the poor countries for food aid will continue to increase for some time to come. If both food demand and food production in the developing countries grow at the required rate of 4 percent per year, net imports will need to be 50 to 60 million tons in 1985 as compared to 23 million tons in 1965.

While the needs of the poor countries for food aid are growing, so is grain production in the developed countries. The record world crop of 274 million metric tons of wheat in 1966 resulted both from increases in acreage and from higher yields. Wheat acreage in the United States was increased by over 15 percent in 1967, and a record production of 41 million metric tons was forecast. In the future the productive capacities of Canada, Australia, Argentina, and the Union of Soviet Socialist Republics will probably continue to expand, with resulting strong competition for markets.

The combination of growing needs for food aid, stiffening competition in commercial markets for grains, and United States dependence on dollar earnings from agricultural exports makes it highly important that in the future food aid should be the joint responsibility of the developed nations. Most actual aid will be bilateral, but the organization and financing of concessional sales should take place in a multilateral framework. The agreement reached in the Kennedy Round of tariff negotiations that other developed nations would contribute up to 4.5 million tons in a multilateral food donation program is a step forward.

Since needs for food aid can be expected to fluctuate widely from year to year, depending on weather conditions in the less developed world, and cannot be predicted until it is too late to change agricultural production programs in the developed countries, relatively large stocks will need to be built up and held for concessional sales. This should be in part a joint responsibility of the developed countries, but some stocks should also be built up in the poor countries wherever storage facilities exist or can be erected at reasonable cost.

In these countries food aid should be used to stabilize prices for the benefit of both farmers and consumers. This will require accumulation of reserve food stocks.

Food aid other than disaster relief should be considered as an interim program to buy the time needed for agricultural development. It cannot be looked upon as a long-range, permanently subsidized program which couples our excess production capacity with the food needs of the developing countries. There are many reasons for this, but the simplest is that in the long run our capacity will be insufficient.[7]

Trade Cooperation

Agricultural exports are the principal source of foreign exchange for many developing countries, and their economic plans have usually stressed expansion of these exports to help pay for needed imports. However, simultaneous attempts by several countries to increase the value of their agricultural exports have tended to oversupply the international market and have succeeded mainly in reducing the prices of farm products relative to industrial goods. For this and other reasons the "terms of trade" for the poor countries have shown a downward trend ever since the early 1950's. World prices of industrial products, compared with those of farm products, were 20 percent higher in 1964 than they had been a decade earlier. A 10 percent decline in their terms of trade costs the poor countries in a year about as much in foreign exchange as the annual total of United States economic aid. The 20 percent drop over the last fifteen years has largely negated the helpful effects of capital assistance on their balance of payments.

The United Nations Conference on Trade and Development (UNCTAD) has been the principal forum for the poor countries to express their dismay at this turn of events. But it has not produced any fundamental improvement. This will come only if the United States and other developed nations modify their import policies to encourage increased consumption of export commodities from the developing nations. Nearly all developed countries protect their own high-cost beet sugar production, thereby reducing the market for one of the products in which the tropical countries have a clear comparative advantage. Moreover, they usually allow sugar to be imported only in raw form, thus impeding development of refining industries in the poor countries. Similar policies can be cited in the protection of rice, oilseeds, cotton, and fruits.

Liberalization of trade relations between the developing nations themselves may be fully as important as between the developed and developing nations. In particular, the developing countries should be encouraged to expand their food trade with one another as well as with the developed world.

Improved international intelligence concerning crop conditions and plans to buy and sell is needed to rationalize complex international mar-

[7] Roger Revelle, "Population and Food Supplies: The Edge of the Knife," *Proceedings of the National Academy of Sciences of the United States of America,* August 1966 (Vol. 58, No. 2), pp. 340–341.

keting. International commodity study groups embracing the leading producing and importing countries meet regularly, chiefly under the leadership of the Food and Agriculture Organization (FAO), to exchange intelligence on rice, oilseeds, oils and fats, bananas, citrus fruit, tea, various fibers, and rubber.

None of the international commodity agreements has been notably successful in keeping prices up or in helping to shift production to items which may be in short supply in the future. In the latter sphere perhaps the most hopeful device is the International Coffee Agreement's Diversification Fund.

"Classical" Technical Assistance

In some problems of development Western scientific and technical knowledge can be applied directly or can be easily adapted to conditions in the poor countries. In agriculture and population control, for example, Western technicians can help with design of irrigation works, fertilizer plants, and contraceptive factories; surveys of soil and water resources; identification and analysis of country problems; methods of collecting vital statistics and other demographic data; and establishment and evaluation of administrative procedures. Among the most fundamental uses of existing technology are in systems analyses of the cost effectiveness, needed level of expenditures, and the optimum sequence of steps for alternative ways of increasing agricultural production. These alternatives, which can be employed singly or in combination, may include: use of fertilizers and other inputs to raise yields on presently cultivated land where there is already an assured water supply; development of irrigation on land now under cultivation to provide more adequate, timely, and assured water; irrigation development, plus use of other inputs, to allow double or triple cropping on presently cultivated land; or extension of the cultivated area by putting potentially arable but presently uncultivated land under cultivation.[8]

Technical Assistance of the Second Kind—Research and Education

In many questions of tropical and subtropical agriculture and human fertility control the Western world has little technology to transfer. But its scientists and technicians possess the ability to produce new technology through experimental research. A fundamental conclusion is that there must be a new concept of technical assistance. Instead of "know-how, show-how" the new concept must be one of cooperation between specialists in the developing and the developed countries learning together how to solve the wide range of problems for which at present there are

[8] *The World Food Problem*, Vol. 1, pp. 29–30.

no answers. The key is the doctrine of the Rockefeller Foundation, which emphasizes that its staff members work with, rather than direct, the scientists and technicians of the developing countries.

As Mosher has pointed out, research in development assistance has two roles. The first is to discover the knowledge needed to carry on assistance more effectively. Here, the *results* of research are important. Second, research is a teaching tool, understandable across cultural differences and neutral with respect to previous beliefs and experience. Here, it is the *method* of research that is important.[9]

Technical assistance of the second kind is well illustrated by the major contributions to agricultural research in the poor countries that have been made by the Rockefeller and Ford Foundations since World War II. The Rockefeller Foundation's efforts began with a program in cooperation with the government of Mexico that resulted after twenty years in a substantial breakthrough in wheat production.

In the early 1940's average wheat yields in Mexico were eleven bushels per acre, and the country was importing half of all the wheat it consumed. Most wheat was grown during the dry season to reduce losses from stem rust. The government created a new agency in its Ministry of Agriculture, the Office of Special Studies, with a Rockefeller man in charge. He assembled a staff of young American agricultural scientists and Mexican "counterparts." By application of modern techniques of research in plant breeding they developed new rust-resistant varieties with short, stiff straws to avoid "lodging" of heavy-headed plants, thereby permitting profitable use of high levels of nitrogen fertilizers. These varieties were insensitive to differences in diurnal rhythms of sunlight and darkness, thus adding considerably to their geographical adaptability. By 1964 yields had climbed to 37 bushels per acre, a three-and-one-half-fold increase, and 95 percent of the wheat harvest was grown from improved seeds developed in the Foundation project. Mexico now has a surplus of wheat and is beginning to assist other nations by providing its high-yielding wheat seeds, training young scientists, and lending its own wheat specialists.

In 1965 an accelerated wheat improvement program patterned after Mexico's was initiated in West Pakistan in a cooperative project with the Ford Foundation. On the basis of results to date Pakistan may well achieve self-sufficiency in wheat production by 1968 or 1969 and could have an exportable surplus after that time. India bought 18,000 tons of Mexican wheat seeds in 1966, at the time the largest importation of seed

[9] Arthur T. Mosher, "Research on Rural Problems," in *Development of the Emerging Countries: An Agenda for Research,* ed. Robert E. Asher and others (Washington: Brookings Institution, 1962), pp. 78–79.

stock in history; under good circumstances up to 40 percent by weight of the Indian wheat harvest in 1967–1968 could come from the Mexican varieties.

An equally dramatic transformation could occur during the next few years in the production of rice, the staple food of most of the world's people, through use of new varieties developed by the International Rice Research Institute. This is a truly cooperative enterprise, located on land donated by the Philippine government, supported financially by the Ford Foundation, directed technically by the Rockefeller Foundation, governed by a Board of Trustees from six countries, and staffed by personnel drawn from the rice-producing nations of South and Southeast Asia and from the United States. With sufficient fertilizers and pest control and timely water supplies the best new varieties created by the Institute have yields per crop up to five times those of the native varieties now used. Both India and Pakistan, working respectively with the Rockefeller and Ford Foundations, have initiated cooperative programs with the Institute and will soon be planting the new rice seeds over wide areas.

The new wheat and rice varieties could become major change agents in international agriculture to match the role of hybrid corn in the United States 30 years ago. They have captured the imagination of political leaders in India, Pakistan, and other developing nations.[10]

Technical assistance of this second kind is probably essential to accomplish the needed reduction in rates of population growth in the poor countries. Rapid declines in fertility levels have occurred during the last twenty years in Japan and several European countries, but the conditions in these nations differed markedly from those in the poor nations: literacy rates were high; many couples already were deliberately controlling their fertility; and there were strong motivations to limit family size. We need to find, to learn how to bring about, and to discover how to help people recognize the changes in living conditions in the less developed countries that will lower the benefits to individual families of having more than two or three children and increase their costs. At the same time basic and applied research is needed to develop methods of fertility control that are easier to introduce and to use than the present oral contraceptives and mechanical devices.

The Rockefeller Foundation has distilled the following set of guidelines for technical assistance of the second kind: Such aid takes time and the Foundation is ready to persist in each project for as long as need be.[11]

[10] Albert H. Moseman, "The Social and Economic Consequences of World Hunger" (unpublished manuscript).

[11] J. G. Harrar, *The Agricultural Program of the Rockefeller Foundation* (New York: The Rockefeller Foundation, 1956).

It is worth offering only if there is a real local desire to accept and utilize it. It should support projects within the capacity of the nation in order to avoid frustration and capitalize on success. The people, the government, and the trained personnel must be involved in the project so closely that it will be ongoing when the Foundation pulls out. Quality should always be emphasized. Success is most likely where there is progress on a broad front, not in narrow "bottleneck" sectors.

The Foundation's programs are integral parts of the appropriate agencies of the host government. Rockefeller personnel are selected for quality, personal as well as scientific, and for willingness to serve on a career basis. Emphasis is on research, but research results are put into action as quickly as possible.

Education for Agriculture

Such education involves both kinds of technical assistance. The developing countries lack the research and educational institutions and the educated manpower that are necessary for the sustained creation and application of agricultural technology. It has been estimated that by 1980 in India alone the number of college graduates with B.S., M.S., or Ph.D. degrees in agriculture should be increased from the present 10,000 to 130,000. In addition, 50,000 engineers, nutritionists, food technologists, and economists will be needed by that date, as well as 75,000 in other professions. From 300,000 to 600,000 subprofessionals will be required. For the less developed world as a whole these numbers should probably be multiplied by two to three.[12]

There are not enough trained persons in the less developed countries to teach the numbers of scientists, extension workers, and other specialists who will be needed. It will be mandatory to add to their human resources the very large resources of the United States land-grant colleges, private foundations, and industry, and the expertise of the Europeans and the Japanese. Some education, particularly of new faculty members, can be given in the advanced countries, but most should be in the less developed countries with their unique conditions and special problems. This will require institution building on a very large scale.

FUNCTIONS OF INTERNATIONAL AND NATIONAL AGENCIES

The United Nations and its specialized agencies, the international regional organizations, and the various international trade bodies have played important and often unique roles in attacking the problem of food supply in the world's poor countries. So far they have been of little importance in attempts to control population growth.

[12] *The World Food Problem*, Vol. 2, pp. 611–614.

Some of the unique functions exercised by multilateral agencies have been:

1) Compilation and dissemination of worldwide or regional economic surveys, technical studies, commodity reports, and statistics on production, prices, demographic variables, etc. Up to the present these have been very uneven in quality because the compiling agencies have felt obliged to accept the figures produced by each member country regardless of its level of statistical competence or objectivity, and, in general, because of a desire not to hurt any member's feelings. For example, it took the Economic Commission on Asia and the Far East (ECAFE) ten years to win the right to print an objective survey of progress in the region without censorship by the member governments. Yet when the draft of its 1966 annual survey contained the statement that at the present rate of progress India would take over 100 years to achieve Japan's 1966 per capita income levels, New Delhi objected, and the statement was expunged by ECAFE's Director. The staff were said to be demoralized and incensed at their Director for giving in once again.[13]

2) Organization of international forums, technical and economic conferences, and consultations in which governments can exchange views on their policies for food and agriculture and arrange coordinated actions and their representatives can share new information and ideas concerning common problems.

3) Global dissemination of public information on world agricultural needs and difficulties. Much of this information has been propagandistic and self-serving, for example, the widely quoted statement that 60 percent of the people in the poor countries are malnourished is little more than a rather bad guess, and yet it has been repeatedly used in public statements by FAO.

4) Management or assistance of commodity marketing and information arrangements for agricultural products in international trade.

5) Sponsoring negotiation on international agreements on resource utilization and help in their financing. The Indus Waters Treaty between India and Pakistan, which was negotiated under the auspices of the International Bank for Reconstruction and Development (IBRD), is the best example. The Bank has taken the lead in raising funds for the dams, canals, and other development works that were required to implement the treaty.

6) Coordination by the Bank, especially during the last few years,

[13] L. F. Goodstadt, "What's Wrong With ECAFE?," *Far Eastern Economic Review*, December 22, 1966 (Vol. 54, No. 12), p. 597.

of bilateral capital assistance furnished by the developed countries to the poor ones, including support for agricultural development. IBRD has chaired joint meetings of bilateral donors and has organized consortia of developed countries willing to supply aid to a particular country.

7) Raising of private capital in the international money market for loans to the poor countries.

8) Management of food aid contributed by several agricultural surplus nations. So far this has been done on a rather small scale and for special purposes by FAO, the UN Children's Fund (UNICEF), and the United Nations Relief and Works Agency for Palestine Refugees in the Near East (UNRWA). The chief difficulty has been that of matching contributions of food with donations of cash or facilities needed for storage, transportation, and distribution.

9) Arrangement of international cooperative activities against animal and plant diseases and pests, for example, FAO's campaign for controlling the desert locusts of North Africa and the Middle East.

Some of the most important functions have been carried out both by multilateral and bilateral agencies, though the latter have usually operated on a much larger scale. These include:

1) Provision of capital assistance from public funds for loans, credits, and grants to the poor countries.

2) Provision of "classical" technical assistance, such as surveys of soil and water resources, assignment of experts to advise or teach farmers and fishermen, help with analyses of country problems, and training programs.

In three areas bilateral assistance has been predominant, though multilateral agencies have not been excluded. These are:

1) Provision of food aid. In the past this has come almost exclusively from the United States and has consisted largely of surplus commodities which needed to be disposed of for domestic political reasons. As a consequence it met only in part the needs of the recipient countries.

2) Underwriting or guaranteeing private sector investments.

3) Provision of technical assistance "of the second kind." Bilateral government agencies have been able to involve universities and departments of their own governments in research and teaching. The most successful international creation and application of new technology has been done by the foundations, especially the

Ford and Rockefeller Foundations. Some regional multilateral
agencies have helped to organize and manage research and training institutions like the Inter-American Institute of Agricultural
Sciences at Turrialba, Costa Rica.

As the urgency and complexity of agricultural development become
more apparent, aid agencies of all types are beginning to collaborate.
A single project may be aided by a foundation, the United States government, the World Bank, the International Development Association
(IDA), a regional development bank, FAO, the World Health Organization (WHO), and a regional United Nations commission, as well as
by private businesses. At a higher level consortia of bilateral donors have
been created, as well as long-term arrangements for cooperation among
multilateral agencies—for example, FAO, the World Bank, and the
Inter-American Development Bank (IDB). One can now speak of poly-
multilateral aid.

Multilateral Capital Assistance Agencies

The World Bank and the International Development Association

The organization, policies, and functioning of these agencies are described elsewhere in this volume. Here we are concerned with their role
in the development of agriculture.

The World Bank's doctrine used to be that loans are most effective for
development if they clear urgent and basic bottlenecks, such as the lack of
power or water, through the support of clearly defined projects, each of
which will be directly productive. It made some so-called program loans
—infusions of funds for a variety of projects in a number of economic
sectors, the allocation to be decided to some extent by the recipient. But
until 1964 almost all Bank loans for agriculture in the developing countries were of the project type. Critics charged that such narrowly defined
loans were unsuitable for broad development programs and allowed the
Bank too much control over the course of development. The Bank replied
that it did not consider projects in isolation but in the context of priorities
within a development plan (much of the Bank's technical aid consisted
in developing such priorities). Moreover, the narrowly defined project
requirement was interpreted much more loosely than the charter or reports of the Bank suggested. Sometimes one loan was made for several
different purposes. A 1960 loan to the Belgian Congo aimed to make a
soil survey, settle and train farmers, plant perennial cash crops such as
tea, build compost, slaughtering, and meat processing plants, establish
cattle breeding stations, and promote cattle disease control.

Recently, there have been several important modifications of the directly productive project approach. In 1960 the soft-loan International Development Association was established and placed under the administration of the Bank. By 1964 the Bank had resolved to expand its agricultural operations considerably, especially to emphasize the use of intermediate credit institutions, and in 1965 it declared its intention to support "projects which involve a comprehensive approach to agricultural development."[14]

The Inter-American Development Bank, the United States Agency for International Development (AID), and the Ford Foundation all currently speak of "integrated area" projects in which resource effectiveness is to be maximized by providing all the necessary inputs simultaneously in one geographical area. The World Bank supports nothing so broad or so difficult to administer.

But it does make loans to national financial institutions which relend the money locally. One of the trends in multilateral lending for agriculture is just this—to funnel funds through agricultural development or credit banks which can then support a large number of small projects of many kinds, providing financial and technical advice to the borrowers, in many cases, along with the loan. The trend is marked in the Inter-American Development Bank; it appeared in the World Bank around 1960 and especially after 1964.

In 1965–1966 about a third of the agricultural lending of the Bank, together with that of IDA, went through these credit institutions. The Bank notes, with a nostalgic backward glance at its former concentration on such simple projects as dam building, that

> such lending is probably the most difficult in the whole field of development finance . . . it is difficult and costly to administer the many small loans required and at the same time to extend technical services to ensure the productive use of credit.[15]

Throughout its existence the Bank has complained of the inability of developing nations to absorb capital in the sense that there is a "lack of well-prepared and well-planned projects ready for immediate execution,"[16] especially in agriculture. In an attempt to drum up business that could meet its own standards the Bank began to offer technical aid oriented toward identifying, evaluating, and preparing projects within the context of priorities in each nation. Recently, the Bank has intensi-

---

[14] International Bank for Reconstruction and Development, International Development Association, *Annual Report 1964–65* (Washington, 1965), p. 7.

[15] International Bank for Reconstruction and Development, International Development Association, *1965–1966 Annual Report* (Washington, 1966), p. 12.

[16] International Bank for Reconstruction and Development, *Fourth Annual Report to the Board of Governors: 1948–1949* (Washington, 1949), p. 9.

fied its search-and-prepare operations. The UN Special Fund (now part of the UN Development Program [UNDP]) provided impetus in this direction, paying for preinvestment studies by the Bank. In 1965–1966 the Bank sent 115 missions to prepare, appraise, and supervise agricultural projects; FAO, under an agreement with the Bank, participated in 34 of these missions and sent out 40 of its own to identify projects and draw them up. Specific projects are studied intensively. In Chile, for example, a proposed groundwater irrigation scheme was preceded by a water re-source survey which indicated that the groundwater reserves were insufficient.

Frequently, in making project evaluations the Bank has found that it must begin with the fundamentals and put together a general picture of the recipient nation's needs and resources. Until recently these reports have been chiefly descriptive compilations, rather than analyses. In the last few years, however, the Bank has pioneered in making more search-ing studies, for example, of problems of water and power development and agricultural productivity in West Pakistan. These are based on exten-sive collection of new data by consultant firms and include detailed, comprehensive, and highly sophisticated economic and technical analyses.

From a financial point of view the Bank's operations in agriculture are difficult to measure. As of June 1966 it had lent $744.9 million for agriculture, forestry, and fishing, representing 7.8 percent of its total lending over twenty years (including postwar reconstruction). The Bank points out that

> the total . . . lent directly for agriculture and forestry . . . does not ade-quately measure the extent to which Bank financing has stimulated farm output[17]

in the sense that its massive investments in power, transport, and indus-trial development all contribute to agriculture. For example, a number of the transportation loans have been expressly to connect remote agricul-tural areas to a nation's road system.

Sixty percent of the Bank's agricultural lending, in 36 separate project loans, has been for irrigation and flood control, often combined with hydropower development; another 17.9 percent has been for farm mech-anization; and livestock improvement has received 10.4 percent.

The International Development Association, described in Roy Blough's essay in this volume, has also devoted an increasing fraction of its re-sources to agriculture. As of June 1966 IDA had allocated 250 million dollars, or 19 percent of its credits, to projects in agriculture, compared with 7.8 percent for the Bank (though the value of the Bank loans was

[17] International Bank for Reconstruction and Development, *Eleventh Annual Report: 1955–56* (Washington, 1956), p. 10.

about three times that of the IDA credits).[18] Seventy-four percent of the IDA agricultural credits were for irrigation alone, compared with 60 percent for the Bank.

The Chandpur Irrigation Project in East Pakistan which received a $9 million credit in July 1963 illustrates the increasing emphasis of the World Bank and its affiliates on broad projects. A part of the second five-year plan for East Pakistan, the project was designed to provide drainage and flood protection to 135,320 acres, with about 109,000 acres to receive pump irrigation. Technical aid and extension services were planned to help the farmers use the water effectively, adopt "improved cultural practices," establish cropping and rotation patterns, and use fertilizers and improved seeds; credit facilities were to be provided these farmers as well.[19] This is a far cry from the earlier irrigation projects of the World Bank which usually stopped at the sluice gate.

The Inter-American Development Bank

This institution, whose origins and functioning are discussed in Henry Bloch's essay in this volume, has played an important role in agricultural development in the hemisphere. Some of its projects are classic examples of the type favored by the United States Export-Import Bank, such as the modernization of a meat-packing plant, but others have a broad scope. An example is a land resettlement project in Mexico which received a $ 25.5 million hard loan in 1963, over a fourth in Mexican currency. The loan will be used in a 130,000-acre area, which will be prepared for intensive cultivation of cash and food crops. Five million dollars were earmarked for

> such auxiliary services as research, technical assistance, experimental farms, demonstration fields and the organization of cooperatives for rural credit, cattle raising, agricultural machinery and marketing.[20]

The Fund for Special Operations of IDB is financed from contributions by member governments. In this sense it is the twin of IDA. Both make soft loans, though the Fund's loans can be repaid in local currency. By 1964 42 percent of the Fund's loans had been funneled through smaller development lending institutions.

A typical loan in agriculture was the $1.1 million extended to Bolivia in 1963 for agricultural credit in support of Bolivia's broad program for agrarian reform. The program, which was also supported by AID, envisioned the creation of 50 rural development centers in ten years to

[18] IBRD-IDA, *1965–1966 Annual Report,* pp. 76–77.
[19] *Development Credit Agreement* (Credit No. 40 Pak), International Development Association, July 26, 1963. Since 1963 this project has apparently run into several difficulties.
[20] Inter-American Development Bank, *Fourth Annual Report: 1963* (Washington, 1964), p. 28.

provide health, education, and extension services to surrounding farmers. IDB's funds were to provide credit through several of these centers for short-term loans.

The Fund for Special Operations supports a new type of loan: one made solely for technical assistance. An example is the 1963 loan of $3.8 million to a Mexican planning commission to make preinvestment studies in the Lerma-Chapala-Santiago Basin, an area of 49,000 square miles in ten states of the central highlands. All but $600,000 of the loan was in Mexican currency.

The Social Progress Trust Fund of IDB was established in 1961 by an appropriation of funds from the United States Congress. Though the Bank is the administrator, the United States, as the sole contributor, has set criteria for the selection of projects, and the Fund is a major mechanism for United States participation in the Alliance for Progress. The result is a new kind of bilateral aid with a multilateral stamp. Of IDB's three sections it is the most liberal and the most devoted to "social overhead" projects.

One of the Fund's requirements is that recipient governments reform their system of landholding where it hinders improved land use.[21] Specific injunctions direct that "projects must benefit directly the cultivating farmers, such as landless laborers, small tenants and sharecroppers . . . " with priority for "an 'area approach' in which a whole zone is taken for integrated development. . . ."[22]

From the time of its first loan in 1961 until the end of 1963 IDB had invested $243 million in agriculture, or 28 percent of its funds. Of this total $126.5 million came from the section of Ordinary Capital Resources, $50 million from the Fund for Special Operations, and $66.3 million from the Social Progress Trust Fund. In less than three years IDB had loaned one-third as much for agriculture as the World Bank throughout its twenty years of operation.

"Equilateral" Technical Assistance Agencies

The system of budgeting and control of the quasi-independent "specialized agencies" like WHO and FAO has two effects: Each of the poor members logrolls for a share so that resources are spread too thin and there is little chance to establish or stick to a set of priorities; and the major contributors fight hard to keep the budget as small as possible. Consequently, the specialized agencies seek a large part of their operating funds outside the regular budget.

[21] Social Progress Trust Fund, *Fifth Annual Report: 1965* (Washington: Inter-American Development Bank, 1966), pp. 606–609.

[22] *Ibid.*, pp. 607–608.

In general, policies and programs are undertaken only if they meet with the concurrence of a great majority of the members and the indifference of the rest. This usually rules out subjects that are controversial, unconventional, or even experimental. As a result the organizations in their work for the developing countries have been confined largely to classical technical assistance.

The World Health Organization and the Population Problem

Because of the controversial nature of the population problem WHO has been able to play only a minor role in attacking it and that only very recently.

WHO was established in 1948; shortly thereafter, the delegate from Ceylon requested consideration of the problems of birth control. He was squashed by the United Kingdom's delegate. Two years later Ceylon proposed that an expert committee on the health aspects of the population problem be established; the resolution was defeated without discussion by a vote of 30 to 1. It was reintroduced by Norway in 1952, whereupon the delegates of Ireland, Italy, and Belgium threatened to withdraw from the Organization if it were passed. The United States took the position that discussion was premature, and the resolution was dropped without a vote. After a lapse of eight years in 1960 India and Sweden were able to bring up the matter again, but the Western countries managed to defer more than a cursory discussion. In 1961 Ceylon and Norway moved that the Director-General be requested to collect information on family planning activities in the member countries. They were defeated by a vote of 31 to 13, with 25 abstentions.

The debate was transferred to the UN General Assembly in 1962, when Sweden introduced a resolution on "population growth in economic development" calling for a program of international cooperation in population problems. The General Assembly adopted the resolution with no negative votes but with 27 abstentions, including the Soviet bloc which claimed that there was no problem, only neo-Malthusian fallacies. The resolution had been emasculated by the removal of a clause recommending that the UN give technical assistance, when requested by governments, for national programs dealing with population problems. But it did call for a world population conference in 1965 and endorsed the view that the UN should assist the less developed countries in studies of the demographic aspects of economic and social development.

Finally, in 1965 a resolution authorizing WHO to do something about the "health aspects of world population" was passed by the World Health Assembly. The Director-General was requested to develop a program in the fields of reference services, studies on medical aspects of methods of sterility and fertility control, and health aspects of population dynamics. He was also authorized to give technical advice to member governments at their request on the health aspects of human reproduction, provided no actual operations were involved. During the following year WHO used a grant of $500,000 from the United States to convene a scientific study group on the safety and effectiveness of intrauterine devices and oral contraceptives. The group concluded that they were safe and effective.

In 1966 the United States joined with other countries in urging that WHO be authorized to provide on request expert advice on program planning and execution, training of personnel, and evaluation of family planning programs. The Director-General was to be requested to study how family planning services could be integrated into overall health planning. The resolution was opposed by many of the African nations, the Latin American countries, France, Belgium, and the Soviet Union. Among the most articulate opponents was the Director-General himself. He deplored the fact that some less developed countries were diverting as much as 22 percent of their funds from public health services to family planning programs. "To promote family planning at the expense of the health services was not a decision for an international organization working in the health field."[23] A substitute resolution was finally passed stating that WHO could give members technical advice upon request in the development of activities in family planning as part of an organized health service, provided its normal preventive and curative functions were not impaired. WHO's 1967 regular budget contained an allocation of $40,000 for birth control research, out of a total of $59 million. It is hard to take this very seriously.

WHO's dismal record in population problems is all the more deplorable because in this field above all others assistance by a multilateral agency could be expected to be more effective, since it should meet with less suspicion and more acceptance, than assistance from a single country, particularly if that country is rich, thinly populated, and predominantly white.

The Food and Agriculture Organization

The regular budget of FAO is now about $25 million per year, of the same order as the amount spent on agriculture by the Ford and Rockefeller Foundations. But it is responsible for expenditures of several times this amount from the Expanded Program of Technical Assistance (EPTA) and the Special Fund of the United Nations (now combined as

[23] World Health Organization, *Plenary Meetings*, Part II: *Nineteenth World Health Assembly* (Geneva, 1966), p. 384.

the United Nations Development Program), other UN agencies such as UNICEF and the World Bank, the developing countries that participate in its projects, and special grants and trust funds given by member governments and private donors.

The Organization directs its concern to farm, forest, and sea, in subjects ranging from pest control to international trade in agricultural commodities, land tenure, marketing processes, credit, nutrition, and agricultural education. Besides a prodigious amount of publishing designed to inform and persuade FAO gives technical assistance, mostly of the "classical" kind. Although some of its assistance is furnished at the level of governmental planning and economic policymaking and thus resembles that of the World Bank and the other multilateral lending agencies, most consists of technical advice and training for farmers, housewives, and specialists and is aimed at general development rather than specific investment projects. It also helps to promote and carry out regional cooperative programs among the developing countries, assists the World Bank and other lending agencies in developing and appraising investment projects, and makes analyses of national and international problems related to agriculture. The following examples illustrate some of its activities.

A Netherlands expert sent to Uttar Pradesh, India, in 1951 found that 50,000 flayers and tanners produced goods worth 60 million rupees annually, yet worked under severe social-religious disabilities. The leather workers were Chamars, an untouchable caste, who had to flay animals which had died naturally, wherever they were found. The expert organized them into a pilot center where he trained them in efficient, hygienic methods of flaying, curing, and tanning. He set up marketing cooperatives and built corrals for moribund cattle so that they could be flayed promptly upon expiring. The project was so successful that the Chamars were soon joined by educated agricultural students who later became supervisors of the 24 rural flaying, curing, and carcass utilization centers and 32 tanning centers that were in operation by 1956. The leather products earned high prices and brought the village flayers up to twice the average per capita income in the area. The workers were especially proud of smelling better.[24]

Under plague conditions in North Africa and the Middle East a swarm of desert locusts may cover 50 square miles, fly thousands of miles, and settle many tons to the acre to strip off all vegetation. FAO began in 1951 to coordinate national programs of locust control, providing a modicum of funds and equipment. In 1960 a $2.5 million UN Special Fund project was inaugurated to expand the effort, especially in research.

[24] *Millions Still Go Hungry* (Rome: Food and Agriculture Organization, 1957), pp. 13–15.

When this was used up in 1966, some of the member nations began to set up their own trust fund, administered by FAO's new "Commission for Controlling the Desert Locust in the Near East." The member nations of the Commission have agreed to maintain permanent national locust control services, hold reserves of the appropriate supplies, encourage research and training, help implement common policies, and cooperate in storing supplies belonging to the Commission itself. The Commission in turn will plan joint programs, maintain strategic caches of supplies, keep all members informed about infestations and current technology, and promote informational exchanges among members. A similar commission is being set up for East Africa.

During the last few years FAO has begun preparation of an Indicative World Plan for Agricultural Development, with the objective of analyzing

> the problem as a whole in an integrated way and in sufficient detail to serve as a basis for policy guidance to the developing countries and for developed countries as well as for ourselves. . . . The main purpose is not to produce a series of documents or reports. It is to create a new technique of working with developing countries in their agricultural planning and programming.[25]

The plan has two time horizons, 1975 and 1985, and will appear in a preliminary version in 1968. Its aim will be to set goals, indicate alternative policies, describe the inputs, economic incentives, and institutional changes they would require, and state the implications for investment and manpower needs. It remains to be seen how far the results will go toward the country-by-country, multisectional, and interdisciplinary analyses that are needed as a basis for action.

FAO collaborates with UNICEF and WHO in "applied nutrition" programs. These have usually been planned for rural areas and combine encouragement of home food production, including poultry raising and vegetable gardening, with school lunches, feeding of preschool children, training of housewives in practical nutrition and food preservation, and other activities designed to make maximum use of existing food supplies and resources. UNICEF has been spending only about $2.5 million a year on these programs, and the contributions from FAO and WHO are even smaller, but the principal shortage is probably the inability of the international organizations to enlist trained personnel who can organize and carry out the projects. An objective appraisal might show that the United States' Peace Corps and its counterparts in other developed countries could do as good a job.

[25] "Indicative World Plan for Agricultural Development" (Food and Agriculture Organization Document WS/45027/2, April 15, 1966), p. 8.

The Agency for International Development and Public Law 480

In the attack on problems of agriculture and population there are both interactions and separation of roles between the international agencies and bilateral programs. Judgment of the significance and potential of the international agencies therefore requires some discussion of bilateral aid. The largest program is that of the United States, and here it is appropriate (though not customary) to begin with a success story.

During the 1950's agricultural production in the Indus Plain of West Pakistan, containing the largest single irrigated area on earth, was not keeping up with the rate of population growth. Yields per acre were among the lowest in the world and in many places were diminishing year by year.[26]

A sharp reversal began in 1960 and is still continuing; the harvest of major crops increased by nearly 5 percent per year or 27 percent over the second plan period from 1960–1961 to 1964–1965. The principal component in this remarkable upturn was a great expansion in the use of the sweet groundwater that underlies the northern Indus Plain, through both public and private "tubewells"—large deep wells with motor-driven pumps.

Over the five-year period individual farmers installed some 30,000 relatively small private tubewells which increased total irrigation water by 9 percent.[27] Several thousand large public wells were also drilled, and these, together with a number of surface water projects, increased the irrigation supply by an additional 10 percent. The public and private groundwater development also permitted more timely and flexible use of water by the farmers.

The United States Agency for International Development played an essential role in this dramatic change. It supported the engineering for the public tubewell program, helped make surveys of groundwater quality and quantity, and arranged for the hydrologic and economic analyses that proved the feasibility of both public and private wells. It loaned the funds for construction of the public wells. Other loans provided foreign exchange for the electrical power system to operate public wells and some of the private ones and allowed a liberalization of import policy which freed such basic commodities as pig iron for the small machine shops that manufactured well pumps and casings and diesel

[26] The White House-Department of Interior Panel on Waterlogging and Salinity in West Pakistan, *Report on Land and Water Development in the Indus Plain* (Washington: The White House, 1964), p. 1.

[27] Walter P. Falcon and Carl H. Gotsch, "Agricultural Development in Pakistan: Lessons from the Second-Plan Period," in *Development Policy I,* Winter 1967–1968, published by the Development Advisory Service of the Center for International Affairs, Harvard University, Cambridge, Massachusetts.

engines. Whole streets in many Punjabi cities are now devoted to such manufacturing; 120 diesel engine shops sprang up in one town between 1961 and 1965, and about 250 engines a month were produced.[28]

More than 15 percent of West Pakistan's wheat requirements, worth close to 50 million dollars, were supplied under United States Public Law 480. These and other food aid commodities were almost undistinguishable from dollar assistance in relieving the foreign exchange situation, for without them food imports would have had to be purchased with scarce hard currency.

By establishing buffer stocks of PL 480 wheat the Pakistani government was able to decontrol and stabilize wheat prices. In the past the farmers of West Pakistan had protected themselves against price and yield uncertainties by growing foods for home consumption, rather than concentrating on cash crops and depending on the market (or the government) for food grains. Now the farmers rapidly learned that they could purchase wheat at reasonable prices in the market. The PL 480 program thus gave them an impetus to move into higher-valued cash crops.[29]

In East Pakistan PL 480 wheat was used to support an extensive program of rural public works which reduced the severe seasonal underemployment that existed in the rural areas.[30] Each year several thousand miles of drainage ditches were dug, and thousands of miles of secondary roads were constructed. The roads gave access to many heretofore isolated villages, and this helped to lower the costs of fertilizer and other goods to the farmers and to raise the prices they received. The laborers were paid in cash rather than in wheat. Many experts feared this would prove inflationary: everyone "knew" that the rice eaters of East Bengal would never eat wheat and hence the rupees put into circulation would produce excess demand for rice and other commodities not supplied under Public Law 480. It turned out, however, that rice eaters will eat wheat if the price is right. With an internal subsidy of approximately one-third considerable wheat was sold in the open market for more than enough rupees to finance the works program.

Support of university-to-university programs has been among AID's most successful ventures in technical assistance, at least when these have been continued over a sufficiently long time. For twelve years, for example, under contract with AID or its predecessor agencies North Carolina State University has been cooperating in research and teaching with the Agrarian University of Peru and the Peruvian Ministry of Agricul-

---

[28] *Ibid.*, p. 12.

[29] *Ibid.*, p. 61.

[30] Richard V. Gilbert, "The Works Programme in East Pakistan," *International Labour Review*, March 1964 (Vol. 89, No. 3), pp. 213–226.

ture. Since 1961 Agrarian University's enrollment and budget have doubled, and more than 150 Peruvians have earned M.S. or Ph.D. degrees.

AID is currently supporting some geographically integrated or "package" programs much like Ford's Intensive District program in India in order to demonstrate the superiority of provision of all inputs in combination rather than singly. In West Pakistan, for example, it has made loans for tubewell installations in two million-acre tracts and centered the bulk of its agricultural effort in these areas, including provision of fertilizer, high-yielding seeds, credit, farmer training, and education of specialists, to achieve a multiplier effect.

Like the World Bank AID has found that national agricultural credit institutions in the recipient countries are often effective in lending to medium-sized holders and in following up the loan with technical advice. By June 1966 AID had loaned more than $150 million to be relent in this way. United States-owned local currencies worth nearly $40 million have been loaned for agribusiness development within host countries as "Cooley Loans." These have supported private enterprises from popcorn products to livestock vitamins, from cheese factories to bakeries.

In fiscal 1967 AID proposed to increase its overall agricultural expenditures by a third to about 512 million dollars (two-thirds of the World Bank's lending for agriculture since 1948), of which 30 percent would be for imports of fertilizers.

AID loans are made under the Alliance for Progress and under World Bank consortia, as well as in a strictly bilateral framework. In his 1967 message on foreign aid President Lyndon B. Johnson proposed the "objective that 85% of our development loans be undertaken in a regional or multilateral framework"; he mentioned support of the African, Asian, and Inter-American Development Banks and stated that the United States would exert its influence to ensure that the World Bank consortium for India became the primary vehicle for all aspects of development aid, including food aid, "from grants of funds to evaluation of performance."

By far the most serious weaknesses of United States bilateral aid have been its kaleidoscopic shifts of policy and its inability to make or keep long-term commitments. These reflect a more fundamental failure—the lack of a clear-cut, disinterested strategy that could be understood and supported by the people of the United States. In the absence of strategy its tactics have necessarily been *ad hoc*—aimed at symptoms instead of causes. Between 1948 and 1967 eleven different directors administered our foreign aid programs (not counting the separate management of food aid); each apparently had different ideas and was subject to different pressures.

John Montgomery has eloquently summarized the history of these two decades:

> Most foreign aid doctrines in the past have been the result of waves of sentiment, fads in economics and social science, and accidents of leadership. Point Four programs reflected as much the personality of Henry Garland Bennett as they did post-war economics or the needs of the less-developed countries. Later phases have concentrated on bankers' approaches, or led to domination of programs by auditors and accountants, or turned to multilateralism as an escape from politics, or invented institution-building as an approach to technical assistance, or discovered macro-economics as a means of justifying resource allocations. Some of these phases represent flashy new ideas, official discoveries of appealing old ones, or Congressional pressures for reforms. One of the great tragedies . . . has been the lack of continuity in programs and theories, coupled with a failure to place foremost a thoughtful examination of the processes and the results of foreign aid activities.[31]

It was only to be expected that our twists of policy would eventually come full circle.

In 1950 the administrator of the Technical Cooperation Administration defined Point Four as

> simple, down-to-earth, self-help to assist other peoples to increase their food production, better their health conditions, and improve their educational system; . . . [32]

President Johnson, in his State of the Union Message of January 12, 1966, said,

> This year I propose major new directions in our program of foreign assistance to help those countries who will help themselves.
>
> We will conduct a world-wide attack on the problems of hunger and disease and ignorance.

But recently something new has been added—assistance in family planning. In January 1967 AID declared that it "has a strong policy regarding family planning activities, and has given them highest priority."[33]

This is a marked change from the attitude that prevailed even a few years earlier and reflects a wider change in United States public opinion and government policy. AID is approaching its newly assumed responsibilities with commendable restraint and sophistication. Of all the possible areas of assistance from the rich countries to the poor ones this is the most emotionally charged and could easily boomerang. At the same time what should be done is by no means clear.

[31] John D. Montgomery, "The Challenge of Change," *International Development Review,* March 1967 (Vol. 9, No. 1), p. 8.

[32] Henry Garland Bennett, quoted in President's Science Advisory Committee, Panel on World Food Supply, *The World Food Problem,* Vol. I, p. 119.

[33] Agency for International Development, "Recommendations for A.I.D. Action in Support of Population Control Programs" (mimeographed), January 5, 1967, p. 21.

Although there have been high hopes for family planning programs using intrauterine devices, and birth rates appear to have gone down in some countries, notably in the Republic of Korea (South Korea) and the Republic of China (Nationalist China), the part played by the birth control programs is not clear. Many of the devices seem to have been used by older women who were already controlling their fertility in other ways. The officers in charge of AID's family planning program have recognized the importance of postponing the age at which women have their first child and of longer spacing between pregnancies, even though they also recognize that fertility control usually begins with married couples who already have their desired number of living children.

Perhaps the most important decision they have made is that AID will supply contraceptive materials, such as the "pills," to countries that request this assistance. The hormone-like substances in the oral contraceptives are expensive and difficult to make without a highly sophisticated pharmaceutical industry. AID also plans to help in the production of educational materials, training of medical and paramedical personnel, collection of vital statistics, demographic analyses, evaluation of programs, transportation in rural areas, and applied research.

MULTILATERAL VS. BILATERAL AID

Many earnest men have urged that the United States and other developed countries channel most, or all, of their assistance to the poor countries through multilateral agencies. In this way economic aid would be transformed, according to Senator J. William Fulbright, "from a national charity, and an instrument of cold-war competition, to an international responsibility," and an end would be put to "the peculiar and corrosive tyranny which donor and recipient seem to exercise over each other in bilateral relationships."[34]

Senator Fulbright has further stated that:

> The aid-providing countries of the world should terminate bilateral programs and channel their development lending through the World Bank and its affiliated agencies, especially the International Development Association . . . the Bank and its affiliates should be authorized to dispense the increased development funds . . . as they now dispense limited amounts, that is, according to social needs and strict economic principles.[35]

This is, no doubt, an idealistic position, but it rests on a grave misunderstanding of the needs of the less developed countries and the nature of the assistance they require.

[34] J. William Fulbright, *The Arrogance of Power* (New York: Vintage Books, 1966), p. 240.
[35] *Ibid.*, p. 238.

We have seen that the amount of capital investment in foreign currency required for agriculture alone is about twice what is now being provided. The total needed for the overall economic progress that must take place if the problems of population and food supply are to be solved is likewise about double the present flow of capital to the poor countries, especially if their adverse terms of trade, loan repayments, and "brain drain" (which can be thought of as a kind of reverse flow of investments) are taken into account. Yet we have also seen the evidence from the World Bank's difficulties in finding "bankable" projects that the developing nations, at their present levels of education, technology, and social structure, may be unable to absorb capital at a much higher rate than at present. And we have found that these weaknesses cannot be overcome simply by transferring existing technology or giving advice based on our Western experience. New technologies must be discovered and new experience gained through research, experimentation, and education in cooperation with the peoples of the poor countries themselves.

This can be accomplished only if research and teaching institutions in the advanced countries become deeply and fully involved over periods on the order of decades and generations, rather than years. It is not enough simply to engage individual specialists; groups of wise and willing men are needed who are used to working together, who can call on a wide range of resources, and who can enlist large and growing numbers of colleagues both in their own country and in the country where they are working. These are the characteristics of universities and government departments and of the great United States foundations. Members of these organizations have demonstrated repeatedly that they can work effectively and happily with their counterparts in the poor countries without much trace of a "peculiar and corrosive tyranny."

It is difficult to see how any of the existing international agencies could establish the necessary supporting relationship with these institutions or what purpose would be served if they did.

The right kind of relationship does not now exist between AID and American universities, but experience of other government agencies shows that it could be created. In the past AID has operated under the fallacy that the task of technical assistance was simply to transfer knowledge and that this job demanded mainly programs of advice and training. It was assumed that universities had staff members who knew what to do and could do it directly during relatively short assignments in the developing nations or indirectly by teaching students from those nations. If not, they could hire experts on short appointments.

We now know that the universities need to build up their faculties and the government agencies their research staffs for continuing involvements between the campus or the experiment station and the field. For example, our land-grant colleges need additional faculty members with a primary long-term commitment to research and teaching for international agricultural development. The practical problems of development must be made academically respectable—an accepted basis for promotion and status in the academic community. The faculty members involved must have a chance to work with their own graduate students in the developing countries, and the students must be able to participate in research programs. One of the fundamental requirements is assured funds on a large scale and for a long term. Most of these funds will have to be provided by the federal government. To this extent at least bilateral aid must continue for many years to come.

If the international organizations did not exist, they would have to be invented. But both multinational and binational modes of action are needed. The issue is not to choose between them; rather it is to find ways in which they can be related to each other and can effectively interact. The international agencies can play a central role in the formulation and analysis of the problems of the poor countries. These activities are aided by international comparisons, and the governments of the poor countries should have a major voice in conducting them. Planning, coordination, and assignment of responsibility for both capital and technical assistance can be most effectively conducted internationally, and much "classical" technical assistance can be provided by international organizations. But most technical assistance "of the second kind" can be undertaken only by educational or other institutions of the developed countries and these institutions can be most easily supported by their own governments.

The Application of Science and Technology to Development

SHERMAN E. KATZ

THE United Nations Advisory Committee on the Application of Science and Technology to Development has said:

> The considered view of the Committee is that, in present circumstances, the wider and more intensive application of existing knowledge, suitably adapted to local conditions, provides the best prospect of securing rapid advancement in the developing countries.[1]

In agriculture, industry, the development of natural resources, housing, transportation and communications, public health, and education such application is not only possible but urgently needed. This essay attempts to evaluate the role of the United Nations, the United Nations Educational, Scientific and Cultural Organization (UNESCO), and the International Atomic Energy Agency (IAEA) in the transfer of science and technology to the less developed countries. The deficiencies disclosed by this evaluation indicate the desirability of a new program, a United Nations science corps.

The construction of a dam for irrigation and power purposes, a typical development project, illustrates the integral part science and technology play in the development process: Hydrologists study the movement of water in the river bed to select the proper site for the dam; geologists

---

SHERMAN E. KATZ is a student at Columbia University Law School and Columbia University School of International Affairs, New York.

This essay was originally prepared for a seminar in international organization and administration given by Richard N. Gardner at Columbia Law School in the spring of 1967. The exclusive consideration of the programs of the United Nations Educational, Scientific and Cultural Organization (UNESCO) and the International Atomic Energy Agency (IAEA) as part of the UN effort to apply science and technology to development should not be interpreted to imply that other programs have not been significant. Rather, it is the result of the organization of the seminar for which the essay was written.

[1] Economic and Social Council *Official Records* (39th session), Supplement No. 14 (UN Document E/4026), p. 7.

determine whether the selected site can support the dam; architects and civil engineers design and construct the dam itself; hundreds of skilled workmen participate in this construction; mechanical engineers design turbines to generate power; electrical engineers design transformers to transmit the power generated; irrigation engineers select an irrigation system to carry water into the fields; and agronomists study the soil and select the proper crop. If the irrigation project is part of a larger program of rural resettlement, public health specialists are consulted concerning proper sanitation measures. Finally, educators come into the villages to teach the basic sciences.

In addition to these applications of existing knowledge new developments in the nuclear sciences and space exploration can accelerate economic development. Not only can nuclear energy serve as a power substitute for the fossil fuels, but the heat generated in a nuclear reactor can also be used to desalinize water. It is conceivable that such dual-purpose nuclear power plants, if built on a sufficiently large scale, can produce water cheaply enough for agricultural use. Satellites transmitting photographs of 400-by-800-mile sections of earth can provide information for crop development and natural resource surveys. Weather photographs from satellites have obvious agricultural utility provided there are trained meteorologists to analyze the data received.

The utilization of science and technology, new or old, is implicit in any development program. The phrase "science and technology" may, however, be misleading and thus requires the following caveat. "Science and technology" refers not to any single field of knowledge or skill but to a broad spectrum of knowledge and myriad skills. Therefore, the fact that several UN agencies "carry on work in the field of 'science' does not automatically entail duplication of effort."[2] For example, the study of nuclear desalinization of water by IAEA can hardly be considered a duplication of UNESCO's program to train hydrologists. This point should be kept in mind when evaluating the "science programs" of such agencies.

This essay asks three questions about UN participation in the adaptation and application of science and technology to development: 1) How has the UN formulated its role; 2) how well has it performed that role; 3) how could it improve its performance? The first question is considered with reference to the UN Conference on the Application of Science and Technology for the Benefit of the Less Developed Areas (UNCSAT) held in Geneva in 1963 and to the work of the Advisory Committee created to follow up the accomplishments of that conference. The second

[2] Letter to the author from George M. Fennemore, Division of International Scientific Organizations, United States Department of State, Washington.

question is directed to the performance of two agencies, UNESCO and IAEA, which from their titles seem to have a special responsibility for the application of science and technology to development. The third question raises a proposal for a new UN program.

A CONFERENCE AND A COMMITTEE: A CHALLENGE TO THE UNITED NATIONS

The idea for a UN conference on science and technology originated in the UN Scientific Advisory Committee in 1961. The purpose of the conference was to consider the problem of how science and technology could best be harnessed to help accelerate the process of economic and social development. It was hoped that participants from the less developed countries would obtain information about possible applications of late advances in science and technology to the solution of their development problems while the more advanced countries would enlarge their understanding of the needs of the developing areas of the world. The scope of the conference is indicated by the twelve principal subjects considered: 1) natural resources; 2) human resources; 3) agriculture; 4) industrial development; 5) transport; 6) health and nutrition; 7) social problems of development and urbanization; 8) organization, planning, and programming for economic development; 9) organization and planning of scientific and technological policies; 10) international cooperation and problems of transfer and adaptation; 11) training of scientific and technical personnel; and 12) communications. A total of 1,910 papers on these topics was submitted to the conference with subjects ranging from "the improvement of tropical beef cattle" to "the progressive development of a national telecommunications network and its integration into a global system."[3] From February 4 to February 20, 1963, 1,665 delegates from 96 countries and 108 specialized and related agencies conferred at the Palais des Nations in Geneva.

What did the conference accomplish? According to one delegate the most successful meetings at the conference were the small, informal sessions designed to allow a free exchange of ideas. The chairman of one such session asked each of the delegates from the less developed countries to prepare a list of the problems he had encountered in mineral exploration—not geological problems but problems of organization. After the delegates had read their lists, the representatives from the developed

---

[3] *Science and Technology for Development: Report on the United Nations Conference on the Application of Science and Technology for the Benefit of the Less Developed Areas* (hereinafter cited as *Report on UNCSAT*), Vol. VIII: *Plenary Proceedings, List of Papers and Index* (United Nations Publication Sales No: 63.I.28 [UN Document E/CONF.39/1, Vol. VIII]) (New York, 1963).

countries were asked to suggest solutions to the problems raised. This kind of communication, partially in sessions but mainly in the conference papers, now collected in an eight-volume summary,[4] was a major achievement: the review of existing knowledge for the application of science and technology to development. P. M. S. Blackett of the United Kingdom described this stocktaking aspect of the conference as "a supermarket where delegates from the less developed countries can window-shop to help them decide on priorities."[5]

The conference provided a forum where new research could be discussed, research with high potential value to the less developed countries in fields such as desalinization and solar and nuclear energy.

The attention of the scientists of the world was drawn to the immense problem of science and development. It was submitted that scientists had been burying themselves with narrow specialities and neglecting the wider implications of their work. Abba Eban of Israel called this a "galvanizing of the scientific conscience."[6] Never before had so many scientists thought about economic development.

The conference showed the leaders of the new countries that the intelligent use of science and technology is a prerequisite to economic progress.

But what concrete results has the conference produced? Many of the delegates from the less developed countries wanted a new agency set up specifically to deal with applications of science to development. M. S. Thacker of India, President of the conference, conveyed this proposal to Secretary-General U Thant. The Secretary-General and the directors-general of all the specialized agencies who had accepted responsibility for "follow-through" decided at a postconference meeting of the Administrative Committee on Coordination (ACC), May 2–3, 1963, that rather than create a new agency the possibilities and resources of the existing agencies should be further developed and coordinating arrangements between them should be strengthened. For this purpose ACC established a Subcommittee on Science and Technology to meet periodically to review the interagency working relations.

The Secretary-General in his report on the conference to the Economic and Social Council (ECOSOC) suggested the establishment of an advisory committee on science and technology "to keep all aspects of the subject under review." It would be composed of

> scientists, economists and administrators of the highest calibre with an intimate knowledge of the activities of the United Nations agencies concerned. . . . [7]

[4] *Ibid.*, Vols. I–VIII.
[5] Conveyed to the author by a source wishing to remain unidentified.
[6] *Idem.*
[7] UN Document E/3772, p. 78.

The suggestion was adopted by the Economic and Social Council in Resolution 980A (XXXVI) of August 1, 1963, wherein the Council

> *Decides* to establish an advisory committee on the application of science and technology to development, consisting of fifteen members appointed by the Council, on the nomination of the Secretary-General after consultation with Governments, on the basis of their personal qualifications, knowledge or experience in this field, with due regard to equitable geographical representation, the committee to have the following functions:
>
> (*a*) To keep under review progress in the application of science and technology and propose to the Council practical measures for such application for the benefit of the less developed areas;
>
> (*b*) To review, in close co-operation with the Administrative Committee on Co-ordination, the scientific and technological programmes and activities of the United Nations and related agencies and propose to the Council measures for their improvement, including the establishment of priorities and elimination of duplication;
>
> (*c*) To consider specific questions referred to it by the Council, or by the Secretary-General, or by the executive heads of the specialized agencies and the International Atomic Energy Agency;
>
> (*d*) To study and advise the Council as to the need for making changes of organization or other arrangements which would advance the application of science and technology for the benefit of developing countries; . . . [8]

The General Assembly asked the Committee

> to examine, in keeping with its terms of reference, the possibility of establishing a programme of international co-operation in science and technology for economic and social development, in which scientists and technicians of the highly developed countries would, as a matter of priority, help to study the problems of the developing countries and explore suitable solutions, having regard to limitations upon the material resources and trained personnel currently available to the developing countries; . . . [9]

In short, the United Nations has given this Committee the task of finding an effective follow-up to the 1963 conference.

As its terms of reference indicate, the Advisory Committee is an advisory body without any executive power of its own. It makes recommendations to the Economic and Social Council. Its members serve not as representatives of their countries but as individuals personally qualified to carry on the work of the Committee. Among the members of the Committee serving their second three-year terms are: Pierre Auger of

---

[8] The Committee membership was increased from fifteen to eighteen by ECOSOC Resolution 997 (XXXVI), December 18, 1963.

[9] General Assembly Resolution 1944 (XVIII), December 11, 1963.

France, former Director-General of UNESCO; M. S. Thacker of India, President of the Geneva conference; Sir Norman Wright of the United Kingdom, former Deputy Director-General of the Food and Agriculture Organization (FAO); Abdus Salam of Pakistan, well-known physicist; and Sir Ronald Walker of Australia, former President of the Economic and Social Council. Representatives of several UN organs, including FAO, IAEA, the International Labor Organization (ILO), UNESCO, the UN Industrial Development Organization (UNIDO), the World Health Organization (WHO), and the World Meteorological Organization (WMO), as well as the International Bank for Reconstruction and Development (IBRD) and the regional economic commissions, have attended most of the meetings of the Committee. Since its first session, February 25–March 6, 1964, the Committee has met seven times and issued four reports on its work.

The work of the Committee thus far can be divided into two phases: 1) identifying problems that merit concerted attack by means of special research; and 2) proposing a world plan of action.

The Committee established two criteria for research problems worthy of concerted attack: whether a solution would offer unusually great benefits by application in developing countries; and whether the state of science and technology in a particular field was such that a breakthrough might be realized if a massive, coordinated attack on the problem was made. It was hoped that by establishing a limited list of particularly important problems it would be possible to draw the support of foundations and similar private institutions in addition to bilateral governmental and United Nations resources in solving the problems. While recognizing that specific problems should be defined in the light of the particular needs of the developing countries the Committee identified eight objectives of outstanding importance to development in general as a first step in composing its list of problems for concerted attack: 1) the provision of adequate food supplies; 2) the improvement of health; 3) more complete understanding of population problems; 4) the most effective exploration and utilization of the natural resources of developing countries; 5) industrialization; 6) better housing and urban planning; 7) improvements in transportation; and 8) raising levels of education, including new educational techniques.[10]

The Committee then described three or four specific research problems in each area ranging from the control of the tsetse fly, under the objective of adequate food supplies, to the study of the relative effectiveness of different stabilizing agents with varieties of soil for road-building purposes, under the objective of improvements in transportation. Even this

[10] Economic and Social Council *Official Records* (39th session), Supplement No. 14, pp. iii–v.

limited list encompassed too much to focus sharply the attention of the scientific community on a few top priority problems.

It should be noted that the Committee excluded from this list those problems on which there is already sufficient existing knowledge and where the main objective is therefore to secure the application of such knowledge on a far more comprehensive scale in the developing countries.

The second phase of the work of the Committee, now in progress, is the world plan of action for the application of science and technology to development. The purpose of the proposed plan was suggested in paragraph 13 of the Committee's third report:

> For its part, the Committee feels very strongly that the time has now come for the United Nations and related organizations to take firm decisions leading to effective action to implement such of its proposals as are found acceptable. It is with a view to facilitating such decisions and to promoting such action that the Committee now proposes to the Council the very important step of launching the international co-operation programme envisaged by the General Assembly and elaborated in this report.[11]

The Committee added that it was not advocating amalgamation of existing programs into a single, centrally directed operation or a new fund and organization similar to the United Nations Development Program (UNDP) or the World Food Program (WFP). Rather, "what is proposed is a world campaign which comprises a Plan of Action."[12]

The Committee suggested these four objectives for the plan:

(*a*) To assist the developing countries to build the necessary structure of institutions (national and, when appropriate, regional) and to train the necessary skilled personnel on which their capacity to apply science and technology to their development will depend;

(*b*) To promote the more effective application of existing scientific knowledge and technology in the development of the less developed countries and, with that in view, to improve the arrangements for the transfer and adaptation of knowledge and technology already available in more developed countries, and at the same time, to develop a more favourable climate in developing countries for the adoption of innovations in the techniques of production;

(*c*) To focus increasingly the attention and mobilize the efforts of scientists and research organizations in highly developed countries as well as in the developing countries on problems whose solution will be of special benefit to the developing countries, and to encourage co-operation of developed and developing countries to this end;

---

[11] Economic and Social Council *Official Records* (41st session), Supplement No. 12 (UN Document E/4178), p. 5.

[12] *Ibid.*

(*d*) To promote a greater knowledge among Governments, the scientific community, the general public and especially young people, in developed as well as developing countries, of the needs of the developing countries for science and technology; . . .[13]

The Committee proposed general plans for the accomplishment of these objectives. In regard to the first objective the Committee proposed a "Five Year Plan on Basic Structures" costing $190 million, to be financed by the specialized agencies, UNDP, and the World Bank.[14] The plan envisages the establishment of national policymaking bodies for science and technology, the strengthening of existing research institutes, and the establishment of special purpose regional institutes to study problems selected by countries of the region according to their own needs. The plan also contains several goals for the developing countries in regard to education and training, such as doubling the number of people who receive secondary education, establishing national universities with faculties of science, technology, medicine, and agriculture, providing for the training of science teachers, and building an adequately manned mobile agriculture extension system. The "Five Year Plan" appears to be less a plan and more a suggestion of priorities for building the necessary structure for science and technology. The Committee gave no indication as to which UN agency should execute the five-year plan.

For the transfer of technology, the second objective of the world plan of action, the Committee proposed: 1) several steps to be taken by UNESCO and UNIDO (then the Center for Industrial Development [CID]) to reduce the cost of technical journals and other books; and 2) the establishment by UNIDO of several experimental pilot technology transfer centers staffed by "engineers with a dynamic orientation towards assessing and meeting the needs of the developing industry in their area" and capable in their extension work of providing advice as to the most appropriate technology or equipment to be chosen.[15] One of many examples of problems to which technology must be applied was that of weed control, which, according to the Committee, could have a significant impact on total agricultural output. The Committee concluded from its examples that the major obstacles to the transfer of existing technology are: 1) insufficient knowledge in some developing countries of the benefits that may be derived from the many applications of existing knowledge; 2) the lack of essential capital resources (especially foreign currency); and 3) the lack of adequately trained local manpower.[16] Its

[13] *Ibid.*, p. 84.
[14] *Ibid.*, pp. 19–20.
[15] *Ibid.*, p. 27.
[16] *Ibid.*, p. 67.

recommendation indicated that the Committee itself had no ideas on how these obstacles could be overcome:

> The Committee would favour an inquiry by the United Nations family into the many factors involved in meeting these requirements [the obstacles] in the best way, and recommends that all possible steps should be taken to increase the resources available . . . to encourage and assist in the application and adaptation of existing knowledge in the developing countries; . . . [17]

To facilitate accomplishment of the third objective of the world plan of action, focusing scientific attention on problems worthy of concerted attack, the Committee reduced its list of problems slightly and added more detail concerning the particular aspects of the problems it thought should be investigated. For example, the Committee made specific recommendations for basic and applied research in the area of drought and salt-resistant plants and suggested application of the results on a pilot scale in developing countries situated in arid and semiarid zones. Cooperation in this effort, the Committee felt, could take the form of assistance by developed countries working with existing arid-zone or desert institutes or relevant university departments. The plan of attack, as well as the follow-up, would require the efforts of an international team of scientists representing a variety of specializations.[18]

The fourth objective of the world plan of action is the promotion of greater knowledge in developed and developing countries of the needs of the developing countries for science and technology. The Committee recommended

> The undertaking of a detailed study of the ways and means by which an appropriate milieu can be built up to create the requisite interest and appreciation in science and technology on the part of leaders of opinion, and the development of effective methods to this end, especially through the analysis of examples of cases in which this has been achieved; . . . [19]

The publication of a popular book on the application of science and technology to development with special emphasis on UN programs and the preparation by the specialized agencies of a series of popular paperbacks for widespread distribution were also suggested.

The difficulty of obtaining, in the words of the Committee, "firm decisions leading to effective action" is clearly demonstrated by the difference in wording of the draft resolution prepared by the Advisory Committee for the enactment of the world plan of action by the Economic and Social Council and the resolution actually adopted by ECOSOC.

[17] *Ibid.*, p. 68.
[18] *Ibid.*, p. 49.
[19] *Ibid.*, p. 82.

The first three operative paragraphs in the Committee's draft resolution read,

> *The Economic and Social Council,*
>
> . . . .
>
> 1. *Decides* to conduct a World Plan of Action for the Application of Science and Technology to Development;
>
> 2. *Adopts,* as objectives of the Plan:
>
> . . . .
>
> 3. *Approves* as guidelines for the Plan of Action and the roles of the United Nations organizations, Governments and the scientific community, the recommendations contained in the third report of the Advisory Committee; . . . [20]

The resolution adopted by the Council reads,

> *The Economic and Social Council,*
>
> . . . .
>
> 1. *Welcomes* the proposal of the Advisory Committee designed to establish a World Plan of Action . . .
>
> 2. *Endorses* the objectives for the proposed plan set forth by the Advisory Committee:
>
> . . . .
>
> 3. *Urges* United Nations organizations . . . to give priority attention to the third report of the Advisory Committee. . . . [21]

The original draft resolution asked the agencies to prepare "detailed operational targets with financial estimates based on the Plan of Action." The adopted resolution asks the agencies for

> detailed statements indicating the extent to which their current or planned programs and activities are designed to intensify and accelerate the accomplishment of the objectives set forth in the Plan together with such pertinent financial data as may be available . . . by January 1, 1968.[22]

In short, no "firm decisions leading to effective action" have yet been made. Rather, ECOSOC has "endorsed" four objectives in terms of which the agencies will analyze their present and planned operations.

But the idea of a world plan of action has not been forgotten. The Council resolution also asks the Committee to examine the statements of the agencies with the purpose of

> (*a*) Ascertaining the range and extent of that which is being done, or which is planned, to achieve the [plan's] objectives . . . ;

[20] *Ibid.,* p. 84.
[21] ECOSOC Resolution 1155 (XLI), August 5, 1966.
[22] *Ibid.*

(*b*) Identifying and drawing attention to those areas in which present or planned activities leave gaps or apparent imbalances;

(*c*) Defining and elaborating in greater detail the content of the proposed World Plan of Action; . . . [23]

The Advisory Committee has suggested a three-stage approach to the agencies for the preparation of their statements:

Stage I: Current and future programs of the United Nations family.

The agencies should state what they are now doing and planning in terms of the eight priority areas (adequate food supplies, etc.) defined by the Committee. A suggested further analytic procedure here is to point out the elements in the programs dealing with: (a) national policies for science and technology and the general development of appropriate infrastructures; (b) human resources (education, training, etc.); and (c) dissemination and transfer of information.

Stage II: Definition of activities in the application of science and technology needed to attain optimum levels of development.

Here the agencies are asked to describe "in systematic and quantitative form" their views on the level of the application of science and technology they believe should be reached within five years in terms of the objectives of the world plan. The same eight elements considered in Stage I would be considered here. The Committee has suggested that this stage be prepared in terms of two or three representative types of "theoretical developing countries" covering "existing conditions in terms of population, income, etc.," in order to overcome the problems of the quantity of work involved in a country-by-country analysis and the "implication that such activity would be an interference with national planning."

Stage III: Defining the extent to which the programs of the UN family meet the objectives of the proposed world plan of action.

The Economic and Social Council has asked the agencies to indicate the

> extent to which their current or planned programmes and activities are designed to intensify and accelerate the accomplishment of the objectives for the proposed World Plan of Action.

This in effect means comparing what is being done (Stage I) with what needs to be done (Stage II). This comparison would point out the present gaps or inadequacies in meeting the objectives of the world plan and

[23] *Ibid.*

should allow identification of those areas where new or reinforced activities are needed by the agencies.[24]

The agencies and the Committee have agreed that development consultants should be sent to the agencies to aid in the preparation of Stage II. It seems ironic that agencies presumably in the business of development must turn to consultants to get a picture of optimum development. At the seventh session of the Committee, May 1–5, 1967, it was mentioned that the consultants would be coming to the agencies in the fall. It is questionable whether the agencies will be able to meet the deadline of January 1, 1968.

The preparation of these statements is a useful exercise not only for the formulation of the world plan but also because it forces the agencies to take a hard look at what they are now doing for the application of science and technology to development and to compare that with what they should be doing. In terms of the first question this essay asks about the United Nations, how the UN has formulated its role in the transfer of science and technology to the developing countries, the agency statements are perhaps the first conscious effort at definition of that role by the UN.

The Advisory Committee on the Application of Science and Technology to Development has placed the challenge of the Geneva conference before the members of the UN family of organizations. The UN agencies must now ask themselves what they have done in the past to face that challenge and what they can do to meet it in the future.

What Has Been Done: UNESCO and IAEA

The science programs of the United Nations Educational, Scientific and Cultural Organization and the International Atomic Energy Agency should give at least the beginning of an answer to the question, "How has the UN helped apply science and technology to development?"

Although many agencies are concerned with the various sciences related to their functional areas (FAO with the agricultural sciences, for example) only UNESCO is concerned with science per se as part of the world's knowledge to be shared and utilized by all. Only UNESCO is engaged extensively in activities such as improving the teaching of the basic sciences, the establishment of national science policies, and the organization of the international scientific community. It is UNESCO, then, which lays the groundwork for the adaptation and application of existing knowledge. Therefore, its program must be examined carefully to understand what the UN has done.

[24] See the draft working paper prepared by the secretariat of the Advisory Committee on the Application of Science and Technology to Development, December 19, 1966, paragraph 6.

The approved UNESCO budget for 1967–1968 allocates $36,441,674 to "Natural Sciences and their Application to Development," slightly less than one-third of the agency budget.[25] This allocation includes $9,051,281 from the UNESCO Regular Program Budget total of $61 million; and $4,727,003 from the technical assistance side and $22,661,390 from the Special Fund component of the United Nations Development Program.[26] Figures from the approved 1967–1968 budget are given wherever possible in the following discussion of the science activities of UNESCO.

The science program of UNESCO is divided on the agency's organizational chart into two categories: "Advancement of Science" and the "Application of Science to Development."[27] The artificiality of this division is illustrated by two advancement of science programs. The international Indian Ocean expedition, cosponsored by UNESCO and the International Council of Scientific Unions (ICSU), was a six-year (1959–1965) investigation of the relatively unknown, 28-million-square-mile Indian Ocean. Forty research vessels from 24 countries examined the ocean's topography, circulation, and the distribution of plant and animal life. Part of the new knowledge about the ocean obtained by the expedition is the presence of an untapped food supply of fish off the Arabian coast, a highly practical discovery immediately applicable to the development of the region. The International Hydrological Decade (IHD), 1965–1975, is a concerted drive to get the data needed to ensure the rational use of water. UNESCO, the chief sponsor, hopes to raise the level of hydrological research in countries which are already engaged in it and to introduce and develop hydrology in regions for which data is nonexistent. Accordingly, the $1.5 million allocated to IHD by UNESCO for 1967–1968 includes "the training of hydrologists."[28] A prerequisite of dam construction or any other water development program is a trained hydrologist able to measure water currents and to discover underground sources of water. Therefore, IHD will equip developing countries with the skills required to harness natural resources while it advances hydrological science.

The underlying philosophy of UNESCO's "Application of Science to Development" program, the second category, is that assistance is given to help developing countries become scientifically independent. UNESCO believes that without scientific autonomy the state is obliged to have recourse to foreign experts and scientists and technical equipment in-

[25] *Approved Programme and Budget for 1967–1968* (UNESCO Document 14C/5 Approved) (Paris, January 1967), p. 5.

[26] *Ibid.*

[27] *The Activities of UNESCO in Science and Technology* (UNESCO Publication No. MC/-NS.64/XIII.5a/A) (Paris, 1964), p. 20.

[28] *Approved Programme and Budget for 1967–1968*, pp. 228–229.

definitely. The transfer of knowledge and know-how plus adequate equipment has a justifiable place in the program of UN agencies because of its "immediate practical applicability and the way in which it lends itself to international co-operation" according to this philosophy.[29] Nevertheless,

> each country must strive to build up its own scientific and technical potential, that is, the sum of the national skills and resources which it must have at its disposal for defining and solving all the problems that it has to face in the sphere of science and its practical applications.[30]

To help the developing countries achieve scientific autonomy UNESCO programs assist them in 1) science planning and 2) the execution of science policy in three phases: (a) the formation and maintenance of a sufficiently large and qualified body of scientific and technical workers; (b) the organization of a substructure of national scientific institutions; and (c) the implementation of priority research programs in the fields of natural resources and industry.

Science planning means the establishment of a science policy and a national agency to execute that policy. UNESCO aid in formulating policy and an executive authority comes in two stages:

> First of all, at the request of the government concerned and under the Regular Programme [$300,000], the Organization sends an expert, who, in the course of a short-term mission (lasting only a few weeks), assesses the situation and the problems connected with the organization of research in accordance with the government's objectives. He then lays before the government various suggestions regarding structure and, where appropriate, submits preliminary draft schemes. . . .
>
> In the second phase, a longer-term mission of experts, made available under the United Nations Expanded Programme of Technical Assistance [$399,900], can prepare final draft schemes and help to establish the executive machinery and carry out the work plan. This assistance also contributes, mainly through fellowship and training courses, to the training of national scientific personnel (in research, teaching or administration) who will later keep the machinery in operation.[31]

UNESCO sent out twenty planning missions, either Stage I or II, in 1965-1966 and foresaw that twenty more would go out during 1967-1968. The funds appropriated to these missions seem inadequate in view of the fact that a science policy is central to scientific autonomy, the goal of UNESCO assistance.

The greatest portion of the UNESCO science budget is spent on the "execution of science policy" and specifically on the "formation and main-

[29] *The Activities of UNESCO in Science and Technology*, p. 12.
[30] *Ibid.*
[31] *Ibid.*, p. 13.

tenance of a sufficiently large and qualified body of scientific and technical workers."

UNESCO's approach in regard to "scientific workers" has been to attempt to improve the teaching of the basic sciences at the university and higher technical level, including postgraduate training. UNESCO allocated $1,715,000 to be spent in this area during 1967–1968.[32] UNESCO "expert missions" had helped modernize the science faculties of universities in 32 countries by the end of 1966. For courses in special branches of study (soil science, hydraulic engineering, petroleum geology, etc.) UNESCO has established a network of seventeen international postgraduate courses in European universities.[33] UNESCO has taken a particular interest in the teaching of agricultural science ($2,314,500 for 1966–1968).[34] In cooperation with FAO, UNESCO gives training courses for university teachers of agricultural sciences and sends out advisory missions to aid in the planning of rural polytechnical institutes.

UNESCO aid to the formation of a qualified body of "technical workers" includes $17 million for the establishment and operation of technical and vocational educational institutions. Of this sum $15.5 million comes from the Special Fund component of UNDP for the execution of 50 projects for the education and training of civil, electrical, mechanical, petroleum, biomedical, and other types of engineers. These projects range from one to five or six years in length and often entail substantial financial investment by the recipient state. Typical of the training offered in the less developed countries is the Uganda Technical College project:

> An institution providing training in the fields of mechanical, electrical and civil engineering, also telecommunications, applied chemistry and ceramics. Total costs for the entire 6-year duration (1962–1968) are estimated at $5,145,805 which includes the Special Fund allocation of $1,171,100 and a government contribution of $3,974,705.[35]

At the end of 1965, 200 UNESCO experts from 36 countries were teaching in 32 countries in training institutions with a total student enrollment of 18,000.[36] UNESCO programs are clearly making a substantial numerical contribution to the pool of trained technical workers in the less developed countries.

[32] *Approved Programme and Budget for 1967–1968,* pp. 189–198.

[33] See Daniel Behrman, *Web of Progress* (Paris: United Nations Educational, Scientific and Cultural Organization, 1964), pp. 29–50, for personal observation by the author of four international courses: mathematics in Budapest, soil sciences at Ghent University in Belgium, hydraulic engineering in the Netherlands, and physics in Sweden.

[34] *Approved Programme and Budget for 1967–1968,* pp. 266–273.

[35] *Ibid.,* p. 256.

[36] *UNESCO: Twenty Years of Service to Peace* (UNESCO Publication No. MC.66/D.63/A) (Paris, 1966), p. 50.

UNESCO assistance in the organization of national scientific institutions, the second phase of "the execution of science policy," has been limited but indicative of the kind of institutions needed. In India a Power Engineering Organization and a Central Mechanical Engineering Research Institution have been established. A National Institute of Petroleum is now in operation in Argentina. An international institution of seismology and earthquake engineering in Japan is under consideration. A common system of measurement is essential to the successful operation of a national research network; UNESCO is executing a Special Fund project in the United Arab Republic for the establishment of a national metrology laboratory.

The "implementation of priority research programs in the fields of natural resources and industry" is the third phase of UNESCO's aid to "the execution of science policy." UNESCO comments that while it is "neither competent nor equipped to deal with the planning and launching of industrial production proper,"[37] its terms of reference and experience qualify it for the work of scientific inventories and research in relation to natural resources. Therefore, UNESCO projects have concerned the development of modern prospection methods (geological and geochemical prospection), applied research in the soil sciences, research for the utilization of raw materials in Latin America, hydrological research as part of the International Hydrological Decade, and methodological research and studies on the ecological possibilities of the arid and humid tropical zones.

Although UNESCO has considered itself hampered in the area of technological research by the lack of the articulation of objectives of national development plans, it is presently the executing agency of nine UNDP projects with specific development-objective orientations. One is a four-year project in Cambodia (1967–1970) for training personnel in the hydraulics of rivers and river control structures. UNDP is contributing $900,000 and the Cambodian government will add $400,000. A six-year project in India is described as

> a project to develop plans and prototypes for new equipment, give consultative aid to industry, train a cadre of high level scientists and engineers, and act as clearing house for information on design production and heavy engineering technology.[38]

UNDP will pay $785,553 of the total cost of $3,864,074.

The UNESCO philosophy of "scientific autonomy" rests on the proposition that the developing countries must acquire the capability of solving their own scientific and technological development problems and thereby

[37] *The Activities of UNESCO in Science and Technology*, pp. 15–16.
[38] *Approved Programme and Budget for 1967–1968*, p. 262.

decrease reliance on outside assistance. This philosophy, however, should not block from view the more immediate goal of making full use of science and technology to accelerate economic and social progress. The goals are by no means incompatible. Perhaps because the former goal, scientific autonomy, has monopolized its attention UNESCO has been blind to methods by which both goals can be achieved simultaneously. One such method appears below in the proposal of a UN science corps.

The International Atomic Energy Agency is an autonomous member of the United Nations family, retaining independence in policy, programming, and budgetary matters. It received nine of its eleven million dollar 1966 budget from assessments on its 94 members and from voluntary contributions.[39] In addition it makes charges for some of the services it provides and it receives some funds from UNDP.

In the words of its Statute the objectives of IAEA are to

> seek to accelerate and enlarge the contribution of atomic energy to peace, health and prosperity throughout the world . . . [while ensuring] that assistance provided by it or at its request or under its supervision or control is not used in such a way as to further any military purpose.

The Agency divides its program into five groups: 1) nuclear power and reactors; 2) life sciences (agriculture, biology, medicine); 3) physical sciences (physics, chemistry, hydrology); 4) regulatory activities; and 5) technical assistance.

For electric power alone nuclear reactors remain economically infeasible for most developing countries. At best they may be practical in a partially industrialized or urbanized society. Although generating costs are declining, in order to justify the high fixed costs of nuclear power there must be "large concentrated loads" such as industrial or urban centers can provide.[40]

More promising for the less developed countries are the "dual purpose" nuclear power-desalinization plants now under careful study. The heat generated in the production of nuclear power can also be used to boil sea water into steam, the first step in desalinization. Feasibility studies have shown that with very large nuclear power plants, 25 times bigger than any now built, the cost of producing electric power could be cut to about one-tenth of a penny (United States cent) per kilowatt hour, while at the same time fresh water for human consumption could be produced from sea water at about ten cents per 1,000 gallons of water. The large plant now contemplated in the United States for the Los Angeles area

[39] G. Robert Keepin, "Inside IAEA Today," *Nuclear News,* 1966 (Volume 9, No. 1), pp. 13–14.
[40] Sir John Cockcroft, "The Impact of Atomic Energy on Society," *Atomic Energy Review,* December 1966 (Vol. 4, Commemorative Issue), p. 8.

will not be able to reduce the cost of water below 22 cents per 1,000 gallons. Agricultural use, however, cannot support desalinized water costing more than one-tenth of that amount.

The UN Advisory Committee on the Application of Science and Technology to Development is only one of many voices which have called for the intensive study of the desalinization process in the hope of a breakthrough which would reduce the cost to a level suitable for agricultural use. Dual-purpose plants for water for human and industrial use are now under consideration for Israel, Mexico and southwestern United States, the United Arab Republic, Greece, and Tunisia. Their combined capacity would be about 550 million gallons per day; the entire capacity of the desalinization plants built in the last decade using conventional fossil fuels is about 50 million gallons per day.[41]

In the area of the life sciences IAEA and FAO established a Joint Division of Atomic Energy in Agriculture in October 1964. Out of this division have come two important "finds." First, in the area of soil fertility it has been possible through intensive fertilizer uptake studies of rice and maize using radioactive tracers to determine the optimum methods of fertilizer use in maize and rice production. Second, the Joint Division has developed the "sterile male" technique for the eradication of the Mediterranean fruit fly and the tsetse fly. This technique involves the development by radiation-induced mutation of a hardy, sexually aggressive species, sterilization of the males of this species, and subsequent dispersal of the insects in the infected area.[42] An FAO-IAEA-UN Special Fund three-year project was begun in 1965 to demonstrate the scientific and economic feasibility of this method in seven Central American countries. "Sterile males" bred in Israel have recently been sent to Capri for a similar demonstration. Elimination of the tsetse fly, it will be recalled, is one of the research problems worthy of concerted attack according to the Advisory Committee.

In the physical sciences the use of radioisotope tracers in hydrology is the outstanding contribution of nuclear science to development. The rate of water flow and the direction of underground water, sand movement and siltation in harbors, rivers, and estuaries, and water pollution can all be more accurately measured with tracers than with ordinary hydrological techniques. Tritium tracers were used in Lake Chala on the border between Kenya and Tanzania to follow the movement of underground water into and out of the lake in order to solve a question of water rights between the two riparian states. As this technique would

41 Ibid., pp. 9–10.
42 Atoms for Peace, Health and Prosperity (Vienna: International Atomic Energy Agency, December 31, 1965), p. 12.

indicate, IAEA is an active participant in UNESCO's International Hydrological Decade.

The Agency's regulatory activities concern the safe transport of radioactive materials and the establishment of safeguards to ensure that nuclear materials are not diverted into any military use.

Technical assistance from IAEA takes the form of experts, equipment, and fellowships. Much of this assistance goes to those member states which have at earlier times received Agency assistance in the planning, installation, and "start-up" of research reactors. Among the principal fields of the experts' work are radioisotope applications in agriculture and medicine, prospecting for nuclear raw materials, production of nuclear fuel, and nuclear engineering. Three million dollars, nearly one-third of the 1966 budget, was devoted to technical assistance.[43]

The International Center for Theoretical Physics in Trieste is an unusual and noteworthy aspect of the Agency's technical assistance program. Established in 1964 by IAEA and UNESCO, the Center is designed to foster through training and research the advancement of theoretical physics with special regard to the needs of the developing countries. The "associateship" plan of the Center has been favorably noted by the Advisory Committee on the Application of Science and Technology to Development and commended to other agencies.[44] Associateships are conferred on selected leaders of research in the developing countries which give them the privilege of being able to come to the Center every year at any time of their own choosing for one to four months with travel and subsistence paid by IAEA and with no other formalities except a letter to the Center. This privilege is conferred upon the associates for three years by an international committee. About 50 associateships are given, approximately the total number of active theoretical physicists in the developing countries.

The Advisory Committee felt that if this program was well publicized, it could help considerably in halting the brain drain. Active scientists could be persuaded not to exile themselves permanently abroad since they would be offered through an associateship an opportunity of working in a stimulating research atmosphere for up to one-third of their working year while spending the bulk of the year in their own countries. The Committee noted that the World Health Organization operates a similar program.

Another international institution established by IAEA and commended to the other agencies by the Advisory Committee is the Middle Eastern

[43] *The Agency's Programme for 1967–68* (IAEA Document GC[X]/332) (Vienna, July 1966), p. 6.

[44] Economic and Social Council *Official Records* (41st session), Supplement No. 12, pp. 19, 79–80.

Regional Radioisotope Center for the Arab Countries. In 1963 the Agency, the United Arab Republic, and other Arab states established this center in Cairo to train specialists in isotope applications and radiation protection and to conduct radioisotope research in subjects of interest to the participating countries. The center is financed by technical assistance funds administered by IAEA and by the participating countries. The United Arab Republic, as host state, converted its national radioisotope center into a regional one and pledged an annual contribution to the operating costs of the center.

Some of the research carried on with the assistance of IAEA can lead to highly practical results for the less developed countries in areas such as desalinization, pest control, and the varied uses of isotope tracers. Much of this research, however, must be done in and by the developed countries as the result of present economic realities. IAEA performs an important service for the developing countries by directing the attention of the nuclear community to those problems worthy of concerted attack because of their potential benefit to development in the event of a breakthrough. The occurrence of such breakthroughs cannot be relied upon by the less developed countries in view of their uncertainty. Developing countries with immediate, pressing, economic and social problems cannot and should not expend their own resources on entrance into fields of unforeseeable return value. The prestige of having one's own nuclear reactor may lead to shortsighted decisions in this area. At present atomic energy unfortunately has only limited application to the basic problems of adequate food supplies, utilization of natural resources, better housing, etc. It is to these problems that the following proposal is directed.

What Can Be Done: A United Nations Science Corps

The basic problem with the UNESCO philosophy of scientific autonomy is that it passes the buck of initiating programs for the wider and more intensive adaptation and application of existing knowledge back to the developing countries without providing the means. It does not overstate the case to say that less developed countries have neither plans nor knowledge: neither plans for the business of improving food supplies and health, utilizing natural resources, and whatever other development objectives are appropriate to their condition and environment; nor the knowledge of the technology needed to carry out such plans. Most requests for aid to the specialized UN agencies from the less developed countries come on an *ad hoc* basis, often reflecting which minister in the country has prevailed in the fight for priority, rather than on the basis of any carefully considered development plan.

The amount of UN-sponsored training in practical management and development skills specially related to the needs of the developing countries is inadequate. Programs of agricultural and industrial extension work to promote the practical application of known technology are insufficient in size and number. Such programs go to the heart of the problem: transfer and adaptation of existing knowledge. Much of the training now given is too specialized to be of present use in the ordinary processes of development. Those who have useful training may become a part of the educated unemployed because of the dearth of development programs.

What then is the *need?* The need is for the mobilization of men of knowledge and men of experience: men of knowledge in all fields, not only in the sciences of development such as agronomy, hydrology, etc., but also science administrators, economists, sociologists, political scientists; men of practical and technical experience of all kinds such as management specialists, business executives, lawyers, community developers and town planners, public utilities and road-building experts, designers of vehicles, and communications experts. These men are needed to help the developing countries apply science and technology to their own development problems through the formulation of development plans and the training of men in the basic skills necessary to carry out those plans.

How can this mobilization be accomplished? To be sure, the lack of financial resources has been a real obstacle in the path of UN organizations interested in accelerating development through science and technology. But men can be mobilized by intangible as well as tangible rewards. The UN agencies have failed to capitalize on the intangible asset they possess in greatest abundance: prestige. They can capitalize on that asset through the creation of a United Nations science corps.

The members of the UN science corps would be drawn from universities, scientific institutions, industry, foundations, and professional groups in all of the developed countries. Each person selected by the administering agency, perhaps UNESCO, would be given one to three years leave with full pay in order to work in a less developed area in one of two capacities: 1) as a member of a full-time team of experts sent to a national government for the formulation of development plans and/or science policy specially adapted to the national development objectives; or 2) as a member of a regional training center teaching practical scientific, management, and industrial skills in accordance with a curriculum designed by the countries of the region and doing extension work in the methods and adaptation of technology, particularly in agriculture and industry.

The consulting teams on planning would be joined by the UN Resident Representative or other person familiar with the various types of

UN assistance available. The teams would spend at least their first six months familiarizing themselves with the "problem," i.e., the present condition and aspirations of the country, in collaboration with the department ministers and the head of state. The eight basic problem areas identified by the Advisory Committee in its second report might be used as a point of departure. The plans which are ultimately produced should be realistic, quantitative wherever possible, and specific as to the economic and social benefits expected to be produced. The importance of such plans cannot be overemphasized because it is only with specific development objectives and closely integrated science policies that the logjam of *ad hoc* requests and programs can be shaken up and reorganized and the institutions of better-equipped countries enabled to participate actively in the adaptation and application of existing knowledge to development.

The regional training center is recommended rather than training programs in each country because development problems generally are regional rather than national. Many countries in the geographic regions of Latin America, the Arab states, Africa, Asia, and Southeast Asia have primitive agricultures and industries which they wish to develop along modern lines and similar resources with which to attack these problems. Water supply, power supply, transportation, communications, and public health can all be dealt with most effectively on a regional level. In the United States New York and the surrounding New Jersey and Connecticut areas illustrate the artificiality of "state" borders in regard to economic and social development problems. Although all the countries in these regions are in the process of development, some are more advanced than others and therefore have useful experience, both successes and failures, to share. Most of the small emerging countries cannot be independent of their neighbors in matters such as roads, transport, telecommunications, river basins, fisheries, etc.

To complete the case for regionalism, a neophyte regional institutional framework recently established by UNESCO could be used as the basis for the regional training centers. The Latin American Center for the Application of Science and Technology to Development was established in São Paulo, Brazil, by agreement of the Latin American states at a conference in Santiago, in 1965. UNESCO has converted its Science Cooperation Offices for Arab States (Cairo), for Asia (New Delhi), and for Southeast Asia (Djakarta) into "Regional Centers for Science and Technology." It has such a regional center in Nairobi for Africa, and another center is now contemplated for West Africa.

The same case for regionalism can be made for the "planning" work as well. Indeed, the science corps planning teams should encourage individual countries to envision their development in the larger context of the complementary roles they can play in the region. Unfortunately, many of the less developed countries, newly independent, are unwilling to take such an international outlook at this time.

The regional training centers would be designed to provide the skilled manpower necessary to make the application of existing knowledge possible. A massive attack on the basic problem of human resources is what is contemplated. The particular areas of study would be selected by the countries of the region themselves on the basis of their development plans. The center would have close contact with the national universities and previously established institutions so as to coordinate the total training effort of the region. In the case of development problems unique to one country or best handled by on-the-spot examination and training, extension programs would be established by the regional center.

Imagination must be the keynote to fieldwork on the solution of problems and to planning as well. The Advisory Committee provides several examples: Where solar energy is available, it can be used in rural areas for small-scale power units for pumping water and other purposes; two-thirds of the world's total livestock are in developing countries and the value of the skins and hides for leather export can be increased as much as 75 to 100 percent by the improvement of local preprocessing; non-moving, nonexposed parts of machinery (baseplates, pedestals, holders, tables, etc.), which constitute the largest proportion of weight and are usually cast iron, can be replaced by cheaper local materials, notably by high-grade cement concrete, thereby saving iron or iron imports in developing countries hampered by iron shortages.[45] The eight-volume summary of the Geneva conference[46] is divided according to the major subject areas considered: natural resources, agriculture, etc. Each volume is filled with ideas for the application of existing knowledge in the various fields and therefore might become the handbook of the corpsmen working at the training centers and in the field.

It may be asked why public and private institutions can be expected to send personnel to the science corps. Scientific institutions and private foundations already have small international programs which send professors to teach at universities abroad and, more recently, send lawyers to advise newly independent governments. For them the science corps would not be a new concept but would mean coordination of their efforts and direction to places in the world where those efforts could best be used. The universities could extend the sabbaticals which they already grant to allow participation in the science corps. Their motivation need not be altruistic in view of the unique experience which the science corps

[45] Economic and Social Council *Official Records* (41st session), Supplement No. 12, pp. 34–42.
[46] *Report on UNCSAT*, Vols. I-VIII.

professor could share with the university community upon his return. The sense of mission created by the proper public announcement of the formation of the science corps might help persuade the universities and other groups to participate. The motivation for industry would be two-fold: one, the goodwill that follows from service in behalf of the public welfare; and two, the education of its own executives to the needs and therefore the market potential of the less developed countries. Governments might enhance this motivation by giving tax credits to business corporations for the amount of salaries paid to personnel while serving in the science corps.

Underlying all of these factors are the glamor and the prestige that go with working "for the United Nations." There are thousands of highly qualified, experienced, top-level executives and professionals in the 40–50 and 50–60 age groups who would like nothing better than the opportunity to serve as "consultants" to less developed countries and win the public recognition that would follow. The UN might even enhance this motivation by creating a system of awards for "distinguished service in the cause of world peace." The creation and successful operation of the "International Executive Service Corps" by the private business community of the United States in order to provide management and technical assistance to business enterprises in developing countries indicates the presence of an untapped source of interest in the economic development work of the UN.[47] In short, obtaining the necessary manpower is not an obstacle to the creation of a science corps.

UNESCO may be best equipped to administer the science corps by virtue of its long-standing close relationship with the international scientific and university communities. It has worked with scientific institutions and universities in research projects (the Indian Ocean expedition, etc.), in its international scientific and technological services (abstracting scientific journals, etc.), and in its "international courses" program and its teaching of the basic sciences. UNESCO has also been the principal architect of a growing network of "bilateral links" connecting universities and scientific institutions in the developed countries with their counterparts in the developing areas. UNDP, now the principal source of international developmental aid, may be in a better position to absorb the administrative costs of organizing the science corps. UNDP also has experience in all phases of development from the preinvestment survey to the establishment of an institute for the training of industrial mana-

---

[47] In this program top management level business executive volunteers are assigned to companies of all sizes in developing countries. They serve as consultants in the solution of the entire gambit of business problems for periods of three to four months. In two and a half years 273 projects have been completed in 35 countries and 300 more projects have been undertaken.

gers and supervisors and therefore has a working knowledge of the administrative manpower needs of the developing countries.

Finally, it may be asked why not create a new "science" agency to administer the science corps as well as all other aspects of "science" which are now scattered throughout the UN agencies. The answer lies in the caveat offered at the outset of this essay. "Science" is useless as a functional classification because it encompasses limitless territory. Few aspects of the development work of the United Nations are not concerned with one science or another. Any effort to lump all "science" together under one roof will result in a hopeless morass.

As noted at the outset, in present circumstances, the wider and more intensive application of existing knowledge, suitably adapted to local conditions, provides the best prospect of securing rapid advancement in the developing countries. As long as the United Nations lacks the resources to bring about this application itself, it should do all it can to stimulate action by others. A United Nations science corps could be an effective method of promoting such action.

Wanted: A World Development Plan

JAN TINBERGEN

THE CASE FOR A WORLD INDICATIVE DEVELOPMENT PLAN

DEVELOPMENT planning has become a routine activity for large numbers of corporations as well as for public authorities at various levels, particularly national governments. The time has come to make an attempt to create a framework for all these activities at the highest, that is, the world, level. Several of the most important arguments in favor of the construction of such a world "indicative" development plan[1] will thus be discussed in this introductory section.

To Avoid Duplication in National Planning

The national plan of any country, irrespective of its precise character, always needs as part of its data a set of figures about the world markets for its imports and exports. In quite a few national planning agencies extensive analyses of the probable expansion of world supply and demand and of prices are made. Such analyses require projections of the probable development of a group of autonomous factors, say, public expenditure and private investment, for a number of foreign countries. They also need estimates of the crops of some major agricultural products. Finally, they require knowledge of a number of coefficients or standard ratios of various kinds for the countries and commodities analyzed. Clearly, there is a considerable degree of duplication in much of this work which could be avoided if an international system of information and coordination was in existence which would in fact be a type of planning operation on a world scale.

JAN TINBERGEN is Professor of Development Planning, Netherlands School of Economics, Rotterdam. He was formerly Director of the Dutch Government Central Planning Bureau from 1945 to 1955.

[1] By an indicative plan we mean one that is not imposed on any institution but only serves as a guideline for the activities of the institutions concerned (governments, enterprises, families, and so on).

To Supply Market Analysis Materials for Business

In addition to national planning agencies numerous large enterprises are also making studies of the type just discussed, usually concentrating in their later stages on some commodity groups. A number of the more general indicators of probable developments of incomes, prices, and costs which would be the by-products of an international planning operation would therefore facilitate their work. There is also the possibility, which will be discussed later, that the specific studies characteristic of market analysis work as done by business for individual, narrowly defined commodities could be useful to both national and international public planning work.

To Contribute to the Establishment of an International Order

Today's world urgently requires a reinforcement of all orderly procedures of peacekeeping and the relevant forms and types of cooperation between nations. In other words, there is a pressing need for an international order instead of the junglelike behavior of national governments. This is an old topic with a variety of aspects, above all, political and military. In the present situation it is difficult to see what can be accomplished in the political and military fields and it is, moreover, outside the scope of this essay to discuss them. Yet the socioeconomic background is also important. Since economic and social problems are among the most urgent considerations for the larger part of the world—the low-income countries—an international order must have important tasks in this field, too, as has been recognized from the start by the builders of the United Nations Organization. This is clear from Article 1 (3) and from Articles 55–72 of the Charter of the United Nations. For present-day circumstances these articles are, however, far too general and too vague to be of any help in really establishing an international order. Consequently the General Assembly at its 1498th plenary meeting on December 19, 1966, adopted Resolution 2218 (XXI), which in Part A requests the Secretary-General

> to prepare a concise and systematic survey of the various principles, directives and guidelines for action in the field of development, as contained in the resolutions, declarations and similar texts of the United Nations and related agencies and in other relevant sources;

and in Part B

> to elaborate . . . a preliminary framework of international development strategy for the 1970's within which initial efforts could be concentrated on the elaboration of specific goals and targets for individual sectors and components.

A world indicative plan is an indispensable ingredient for a proper answer to both requests; quite apart from that we think it an essential element as well for any international order in the economic and social fields. Generally speaking, the United Nations family of institutions is much too weak to represent a real international order in the field of economic policies. In order to be stronger these institutions should be endowed with more economic power. Such power can be used satisfactorily only if there is an international economic policy and this again requires a plan.

In the next paragraph and in the next section of this essay we will elaborate on this.

To Specify the Aims of International Economic Policies

Although most political decisions are still taken at the national level, the nature of the problems to be solved has already imposed on national governments various forms of international cooperation in economic policies. The technical elements involved simply compel even the most nationalistic government to admit the necessity of such cooperation. In the end it will become clear that the division of the world into autonomous nations is outmoded and further technological and other extranational development will at some point break up this outmoded structure. Already the existing weak forms of cooperation, in order to be carried out as efficiently as possible, need the background of a set of aims to be pursued. Efficiency requires that no inconsistent policies be pursued. It is inconsistent, for example, to strive for the economic development of low-income countries without adapting to that aim the commercial policies of the developed countries. Finally, any inconsistency will also hurt the interests of the developed countries, not to speak of the damage already done to the interests of developing countries. Even though we will never be able to avoid all inconsistencies which may arise in 100-odd country plans, some of the most serious may at least be reduced.

Again, the only way to formulate a consistent set of policies in the international economic sphere is to construct an indicative world plan. In it a number of aims will have to be formulated with regard to the growth·in incomes and in production in the various parts of the world and in the sectors of which the plan is composed. The consequences for investments, consumption, and trade will be estimated. Some of the most important means to be applied to influence the economies in the direction desired can be derived. These then can be the "directives and guidelines for action" which together are identical to the "framework of international development strategy" asked for in the General Assembly resolution quoted above.

To Exert Pressure on the Developed Countries

It is now generally known that the results of the Development Decade are disappointing. The Secretary-General of the United Nations has elaborated on this painful subject on various occasions.[2] In his inaugural address to the Institute of Social Studies at The Hague Hans Linnemann spoke of the Development Decade as the "plan that failed." The reasons are several, of course. A very serious aspect of the lag of development behind the modest goals so far set is that one of the principal bottlenecks is lack of foreign exchange, or in other words, financial assistance by the developed countries. It is embarrassing, to say the least, that it is a failure on the side of these countries which increasingly has become a dominating feature of the situation. While in the early phases of the United Nations' development efforts the absorptive capacity of developing countries could be said to be the main reason for the widening gap in welfare between the richer and the poorer countries, this argument no longer applies. For the past several years the President of the International Bank for Reconstruction and Development (IBRD), George D. Woods, has declared that the World Bank family of institutions—especially the International Development Association (IDA)—could channel some $3 or $4 billion more per annum to the developing countries. The representatives of the governments of the prosperous countries by their vote endorsed the General Assembly resolution quoted before which

> *calls upon* all concerned to make the utmost effort possible towards the realization of the modest targets of the present United Nations Development Decade.

Yet, the United States Congress has repeatedly reduced the President's proposed amounts of aid, and similar trends prevail in some European countries. These tendencies display a dangerous lack of comprehension of those countries' longer-range interests. One widespread example of such misunderstanding is that an adverse balance-of-payments situation often is considered by a prosperous country as an excuse for not stepping up its assistance. The other more serious misunderstanding at play is that public opinion in these countries does not see the dangers to its own populations springing from a situation of despair in some of the largest developing countries. Other aspects of the future economic situation giving rise to particular concern are the employment situation (and the ensuing tensions) to be expected in several developing countries and, of course, the food situation.

The lack of activity in the international development field is also partly

---

[2] See *The United Nations Development Decade at Mid-Point: An Appraisal by the Secretary-General* (United Nations Publication Sales No: 65.I.26 [UN Document E/4071/Rev.1]) (New York, 1965) and subsequent reports.

due to the absence of institutions responsible for world welfare as distinct from the welfare of individual nations and endowed at the same time with more economic power. If, say, the UN Secretariat were given a much larger budget, it could exert pressure, by the way it spent the money, on Member governments just as a federal government can influence state governments by changing the means of subsidizing some state activities or the orders placed in a certain state. Once some eminent statesmen were charged with such a worldwide responsibility, they would probably follow a policy different from the present, simply because they now only have national responsibilities.

A world indicative plan may also help to exert pressure on the governments and the publics in the prosperous countries since it can show by alternative sets of figures what a desperate situation is bound to develop if "the utmost effort possible" is not made by "all concerned," especially those which can relatively easily afford to make the efforts expected from them.

The above arguments are not new and have not been ignored by the few who, notwithstanding the insufficient support they get from public opinion, have nevertheless tried to create the beginnings of world indicative planning. In a number of international institutions within and outside the United Nations family of agencies activities have been started which are a sound basis for future work.[3] Meanwhile, the United Nations Committee for Development Planning had its first meeting and made its first report to the Economic and Social Council (ECOSOC)[4] outlining a program of future work, especially of the Center for Development Planning, Projections, and Policies at United Nations Headquarters.

The present essay will elaborate on a number of the technical problems of planning at a world level, some of which have been set out in another article by the author.[5] Following a distinction we proposed elsewhere[6] between the tasks, the methods, and the procedures of planning we will deal with these in succession in the remaining sections of this essay.

TASKS OF AN INDICATIVE WORLD PLAN

The tasks of an indicative world plan may be summarized as the specification of a world development policy or strategy and will be dis-

[3] For a brief survey of these activities see Jan Tinbergen, "International Economic Planning," *Daedalus,* Spring 1966 (Vol. 95, No. 2), pp. 537–544.

[4] "Economic Planning and Projections, Report of the Committee for Development Planning on its first session" (UN Document E/4207 and Add.1–2, May 12, 1966).

[5] Tinbergen, *Daedalus,* Vol. 95, No. 2, pp. 544–557.

[6] J. Tinbergen, *Central Planning* (Studies in Comparative Economics No. 4) (New Haven, Conn: Yale University Press, 1964), pp. 8, 14, and 22.

cussed more systematically in the present section. It is useful to distinguish between the qualitative and the quantitative aspects of the specification.

Qualitatively the specification of any policy and hence also of an international development policy consists of listing the aims of such a policy and the means to be used. Both will be discussed here only in their main elements.

For practical purposes we think the main aims are the growth of production and hence incomes and the distribution of the growth among the countries of the world and among the social groups involved. As a consequence of a specification of these growth and distribution figures the distribution of the growth envisaged over the various industries and other economic activities will also be determined.

The means needed to attain the main aims are manifold and have to be applied at many different levels: at the national level; at lower levels, down to local authorities and private firms and individuals; and also at supranational levels. For an international development policy the latter are the most important ones. Among the means, investments in capital goods as well as in human beings, through education and training stand out. Such investments can be public or private. Public investments can be undertaken by the authorities themselves; private investments can be encouraged and stimulated by a system of insurance against noneconomic risks, by tax facilities and subsidies, and by various types of technical assistance, both from public and from private organizations, including private business. The appropriate choice of the sectors to be developed, for instance, agriculture or various types of manufacturing industries, must also be given attention. With regard to education the methods to be used are no less important than the extent of the educational facilities offered.

Large financial resources will be needed in order to effectuate an investment program. A considerable part of such resources must be provided by the developing countries' own governments. This implies that the collection of taxes as well as saving on current expenditure will be an important factor.

Another set of means must be applied in order to safeguard the flow of necessary imports into developing countries. This can be done, first of all, by the expansion of export earnings by those countries. Since a large portion of the developing countries' exports consists of primary commodities, market regulations for some of these commodities will be necessary in order to create some stability in export proceeds. It is an open question which markets actually need regulation. In any case those characterized by a long production period, such as a long growth period for trees producing a product (coffee, rubber), are in need of controls. Other markets need regulation if they are in fundamental disequilibrium as a consequence of past policies; sugar is one of these. Even if some long-term stability has been organized or can be expected a priori, the well-known irregular short-term fluctuations due to crop variations require a system of supplementary finance. Under such a system a country whose export proceeds were below the most reasonable forecasts would receive supplementary revenues from a fund created for this purpose. An outline of such a system was made at the instigation of the first UN Conference on Trade and Development (UNCTAD).[7]

For some primary and some other export products the developing countries experience difficulties as a consequence of restrictive trade policies of the developed countries. This is true, *inter alia,* for sugar, for some ores, and for textile products. These restrictions must be reduced. In addition, most developed countries' tariffs show an "antiprocessing structure": Raw materials are imported freely or at low import duties whereas these duties are higher for processed articles. So far little has been done to change this structure, which constitutes a brake on the industrialization of developing countries.

While as high a rate of expansion of exports as possible remains desirable, it will not be sufficient to enable the developing countries to import all the capital goods and raw materials they need for their development. Direct financial transfers therefore remain necessary and at higher levels than at present.

Many other elements of a well-designed development policy could be added to the list given already. For the present purpose we only mention a policy of family planning. As long as the expansion of the developing countries' population is not slowed down, several of the other measures proposed are of small importance. Thus, an increase in general efficiency which is basic in later stages of development does not work out favorably in many respects if there is still a surplus of unemployed.

While a general recognition—perhaps in the text of some development charter—of the need for using the means summarized here is desirable, it is much more important that a development strategy be expressed quantitatively. In all practical walks of life tasks can only be set—and efficiency checked—if they are given numerical expression. If we really are in earnest about development policies, we must commit ourselves to hard figures even if some danger of arbitrariness is involved. As long as no figures are mentioned, even the smallest contribution made in any

---

[7] See *Supplementary Financial Measures: A Study Requested by the United Nations Conference on Trade and Development* (Washington: International Bank for Reconstruction and Development, December 1965).

direction may serve as an excuse for postponing larger efforts. Most of the programs set out above are being pursued already, but the crucial point is that they are not being carried out on a sufficiently large scale. Figures are therefore needed. But such figures must be mutually consistent and that is exactly what a plan tries to bring: a coordinated set of targets and means. To a large extent the targets determine what the magnitude of the means must be. Let us therefore first discuss the targets. Among these the average growth targets for the developed and the developing countries stand out.

The targets must satisfy the fundamental condition that the gap in well-being between developing and developed countries must eventually be narrowed. Since it would be difficult to reduce the rates of growth of the developed countries and perhaps would not even be desirable for the developing countries themselves, we think that an overall annual rate of increase in their real national product per capita of some 3 percent—being the average performance over the last fifteen years or so— remains desirable. If one starts from this premise, there is practically no escape from an average annual target rate of growth for the total national incomes of the developing countries of 7 percent. The only counterargument so far produced is that this goal is difficult to attain. It would be more difficult to deal with the consequences ten years from now of a rate of growth less than 7 percent. Most of us still do not seem to understand how serious the challenge is that we are up against.[8]

Granted the need for an average rate of growth of 7 percent for the developing world as a whole, one of the tasks of the planners is to differentiate this target between countries with a lower and a higher rate of population growth, a lower and a higher initial level of income, and lower and higher potentialities. The one published exercise in this problem by Paul N. Rosenstein-Rodan[9] was made as early as 1960 and in my opinion needs revision. I cannot help feeling it was too modest.

From the rates of growth for single countries we can derive the rates of growth needed in various industries as well as the distribution of these sectors over countries. I consider this the main planning problem involved and I will make a few suggestions for its solution in the next section of this essay.

We also need a specification of the extent to which the various means

[8] Max F. Millikan regards the criterion chosen here as an undesirable way to argue that a much higher rate of growth than the prevailing one is needed for the developing countries. His main argument to arrive at the same conclusion is that only with the rates of growth mentioned is there a real prospect that a shortening of the period of dependence on large-scale aid can be attained. However one looks at the matter the common conclusion is that the growth rates just quoted are what we need.

[9] P. N. Rosenstein-Rodan, "International Aid for Underdeveloped Countries," *Review of Economics and Statistics*, May 1961 (Vol. 43, No. 2), pp. 107–138.

must be applied. Here we have to be aware of the margins of error existing in our best estimates. Among these means financial transfers and training rank high. They have to be derived from the total investments needed and from the needs for trained manpower by deducting what the developing countries can do by themselves. Thus, the level of financial transfers from developed to developing countries, which still constitutes the most important single figure among the means, cannot be estimated with precision and may contain an error of more than one billion dollars per annum. Yet all practical evidence suggests that the figure—now estimated at some $10 billion by the Organization for Economic Cooperation and Development (OECD)[10]—must at least be raised by the amount of $3 to $4 billion mentioned on various occasions by the President of the World Bank. It is my contention that we must also set tasks for the individual prosperous countries, that is, define and accept some criterion of distribution. In principle, that proposed by Rosenstein-Rodan is the best before us.

Such a specification of the financial assistance to be produced by the developed countries should be matched by targets to be set for the resources to be made available for development purposes by the individual developing countries. One can even think of a sliding scale of foreign contributions depending on the efforts made by each developing country itself.

Quantitative targets in the fields of market regulations and of trade policy generally may be expressed in terms of prices of single commodities or levels of single import duties, but they may perhaps more comfortably be expressed in terms of macrotargets for total imports from developing countries by individual developed countries or for the percentage of total imports into the latter that has to originate from developing countries.

There are two other important targets. Developing countries should set themselves export targets to be attained through a more systematic export promotion policy. Several developing countries suffering from inflation should also establish targets in the field of tax collection in order to curb inflation.

Summarizing, we feel that for an effective international development policy numerical tasks have to be formulated for individual countries—both developed and developing—with regard to the main aims and means of such a policy. Since an effective policy is in the broader interest of all countries, we must overcome the difficulties, however large they

[10] *Development Assistance Efforts and Policies of the Members of the Development Assistance Committee: 1966 Review* (Report by Willard L. Thorp, Chairman of the Development Assistance Committee) (Paris: Organization for Economic Cooperation and Development, September 1966), p. 27.

seem, if we want to be serious at all about the subject. The figures most needed are those concerning the envisaged growth of income and production by countries and sectors, the financial transfers and the internal public finance by countries of origin and destination, and trade figures by countries. The smaller developing countries may be grouped in order to reduce the amount of detail. The estimation of the figures mentioned typically represents the task of an indicative world plan.

METHODS TO BE USED

By the phrase "methods" we indicate the scientific process of establishing a first draft of the consistent set of figures which any plan aspires to be. It is far beyond the scope of an essay of this kind to give adequate treatment to the question of what methods are available; in fact, one could fill a library with what has been written about the subject. We want only to stress some aspects which still seem in need of more attention than has been given to them so far.

For a problem of the complexity shown such methods have to be mathematical. But there are mathematical methods of very different degrees of sophistication. All procedures able to make a useful contribution must be tried out and their results checked against each other. There can be no doubt that approximative methods or models only are possible; one limit is set by the computer capacity but much narrower limits are set by the needs of communicating about the subject with those responsible for the final decisions. While others are much more qualified than I am to devise detailed and complicated models of the mathematical programming type, I will make an attempt at sketching a model which may be helpful as a check and for communications purposes.

In a planning exercise of the type described the element of distance and mobility of products cannot be neglected. Since it is virtually impossible to introduce transportation and similar costs to overcome distances for each commodity individually, a classification of commodities according to their degree of mobility seems to be attractive. One such category would be domestic products or nontradables,[11] that is, products which cannot be imported or exported for technical or cultural reasons (buildings, many services, very perishable goods, goods only in demand by local consumers, and often electricity; also, as a first approximation, very heavy goods). Together their production amounts to one-half of national income in most countries. Another category, covering primarily most agricultural, mining, and manufacturing products, will be called international goods or tradables. It is characteristic for the former cate-

[11] This expression is Ian M. D. Little's.

gory that their production must be equal to the demand exerted by the nation in which they are produced, and it may be assumed that once the income targets for the country have been fixed, their demand and hence their production can be derived directly.

The planning problem of estimating the production increases by country and commodity groups then reduces to the category of international commodities. What we are after here may also be called the "best division of labor" between the countries of the world. More precisely formulated it is the problem of minimizing costs of the production of all these goods under a number of restrictions. Costs must be seen as opportunity costs neglecting the "costs" of abundant resources, even if they are paid, in other words, using shadow prices wherever necessary. Costs must also be seen as long-run costs, taking into account gains from learning. Then, costs must be interpreted to imply costs of complementary production processes. In our context this means that the expansion of any international industry in any country requires the expansion of a number of national industries, including needed infrastructural provisions, and of some international industries producing heavy goods (if we have not classified them as national already for that very reason). I have devised a method known as the semi-input-output method in order to estimate these complementary costs.

The main restrictions are of two types. First, total demand for each commodity group will be determined by the increase in incomes. Second, the production increases planned for any single country must be sufficient to attain the income targets set for that country. Both types of restrictions depend therefore on the income targets chosen. This underlines the importance of the choice of these targets, the principles of which were discussed in the previous section.

One implication of the restrictions should be clearly understood. Any single group of commodities should not necessarily be produced where it is cheapest. This might well lead to too small an income increase in the less developed countries. The plan should not try to find the absolute minimum of the joint production costs of all goods, but a relative minimum: The developing countries may have to produce a number of goods in which they are not yet competitive but in which they are "as competitive as possible."

In a previous article I briefly sketched the main factors to be taken into account in finding this relative minimum of costs.[12] We will now elaborate somewhat on possible methods to find the optimum as defined. Suppose that the endowment of natural resources were the same everywhere and our approach to the problem of transportation obstacles were

[12] Tinbergen, *Daedalus*, Vol. 95, No. 2., p. 551.

accepted as sufficient. Later we will remove these oversimplifications. Proceeding from these assumptions, however, the main problem remaining is the distribution of the industries and the countries of the world by their degree of capital intensity. By the capital intensity of an industry I mean the ratio of capital (including educational capital) to (unskilled) labor used in the industry. For some industries this is not a fixed ratio but a range of ratios.[13] By the capital intensity of a country is meant the ratio of capital to labor (defined in the same way) the country is endowed with after deduction of the quantities of both factors needed for the domestic industries. Both the countries and the industries (in the widest sense) can be arranged in the order of their capital intensity. The best division of labor in these simple circumstances would then be a specialization in each country—as far as its international industries are concerned—such that the order in which the countries are arranged coincides with the order in which the industries are arranged. Of course, no more should be produced of each international commodity than its world demand which can be estimated from the income targets set. Having arranged the commodities in order of their capital intensity and knowing the demand for them and having also arranged the countries according to their capital endowment per capita, we would then suggest that the least capital-intensive products be produced by the countries having the smallest amount of capital per head; the next least capital-intensive products by the country endowed with the second smallest amount of capital per head, and so on. Even so it will happen that the poorest countries will then have too little capital. This should be provided to them by capital transfers or so-called aid.

So far the exercise is simple. We must now introduce the element of national resources. This can be seen as a correction on the distribution thus far obtained, tending to replace some of the industries provisionally allocated to each country by others more in accordance with the countries' endowments and the industries' needs for some natural resources. It will be necessary to recognize a large number of natural resources, each to be represented by some primary commodity. The problem to be solved is what influence should be given in any country's industrial structure to the presence or absence of a number of specified natural resources. I think a similar method can be followed as was sketched for the capital factor, now using several factors and consequently applying more complicated methods, known to the mathematician as "multidimensional," for both the ordering of the products and of the countries.

---

[13] See Gerard Karel Boon, *Economic Choice of Human and Physical Factors in Production: An attempt to measure the micro-economic and macro-economic possibilities of variation in factor-proportions of productions* (Contributions to Economic Analysis, 35) (Amsterdam: North Holland, 1964).

It stands to reason that for the final decision about the extension of any industry in any country the usual project appraisal must be undertaken. But a first crude sketch may well be obtained with the aid of the method just suggested or of similar methods.

Finally, the element of transportation costs may also be brought in in a more refined way. For some categories of heavy goods these costs may be introduced explicitly. Here we are only in the first stages of systematic research, especially when economies as a whole are considered, but some methods have been suggested.[14] It is also possible to study this factor for each industry separately as a further correction of the initial approximations.

The methods discussed so far are meant to be directed at finding a first approximation for a consistent set of figures for production increases. A confrontation of these figures with the increases in consumption to be expected will yield indications about the changes in exports and imports implied.

The first approximation discussed should be seen as the set of figures which the central planning agency submits to the "lower-level" agencies involved. These will have to carry the main burden of the planning work, but they need some frame of reference comparable to what is known in the Union of Soviet Socialist Republics as the "control figures," in India as the "plan outline," and what without a special name was also practiced by the Organization for European Economic Cooperation (OEEC) during the Marshall Plan period. This brings us to the last subject to be discussed, the procedure for world planning.

PROCEDURE FOR INTERNATIONAL PLANNING: CONCLUDING REMARKS

We use the word procedure here to indicate the succession and nature of contacts with the outside world needed by a central agency for constructing its plan. It is now generally understood that the first act in a planning process is the submission by the central planning agency to the responsible policymakers of a first set of tentative targets and means. The policymakers are then supposed to approve them, possibly after amendments have been indicated. This first set of broadly consistent figures is then sent to various lower levels with a request to submit more detailed partial plans. These "lower levels" may be and should be geographical as well as sectoral levels or national governments as well as branch representatives if they exist. These partial plans must again be coordinated, that is, made consistent, by the central planning agency.

---

[14] See a forthcoming publication by the Netherlands Economic Institute, *The Element of Space in Development Planning.*

More than one round of consultation with the lower levels may be necessary. Finally the integrated plan is submitted again to the policymakers for their final approval.

At the world level this procedure is a much more difficult issue than at the national level. For one thing there is no world government. There is only a very weak analogue, the General Assembly of the United Nations, with the Economic and Social Council as its organ in socioeconomic matters. Elsewhere I defended a procedure in which the Council might play the role of the central policymaker.[15] I suggested that another character be given to the annual meetings of ECOSOC and that indeed world targets be discussed there as well as—following the example of OEEC—policies of individual countries in the light of these targets. I submitted that a subtle mixture of tact and courage would be needed and that a scientific approach to the problems must be attempted.

The other enormous difficulty for any world planning, even if indicative only, is the size of the area covered: in fact, the world at large. This means that more than 100 governments are involved. There is also the problem that many industries are not sufficiently well organized at the world level to be partners in the process.

The number of 100 or more necessitates an intermediary level for which the UN regional economic commissions are the only bodies available in most of the world—but not even this mechanism exists in the Western Asian region and the Asian Communist area. The latter area probably does not want any cooperation of this kind, and hypothetical figures for it may have to be estimated by, say, the Economic Commission for Asia and the Far East (ECAFE). Anyway these complications imply a planning procedure taking more time, with the likelihood that figures may have to be inserted into the plan which have not actually been estimated in each case by the governments of all the countries involved.

In some industries, such as agriculture, an old well-established agency like the Food and Agriculture Organization (FAO) exists, fully able to play the part supposed to be fulfilled by sector representatives. For manufacturing some worldwide private organizations exist although it is not certain that they are sufficiently equipped to cooperate. Such cooperation should be encouraged nevertheless. Also, the UN Industrial Development Organization (UNIDO) may be able to make useful contributions. In some service industries, especially in the field of transportation, capable organizations exist. Their cooperation must be sought. In the education sector the UN Educational, Scientific and Cultural Organization (UNESCO) and in the health sector the World Health Organization (WHO) are the natural partners.

[15] Tinbergen, *Daedalus*, Vol. 95, No. 2.

Business as well as trade unions should be asked for their advice and suggestions. Here some organizations are available. Moreover, the International Labor Organization (ILO) will be available. Generally, the cooperation of all of the United Nations specialized organizations should be sought as a matter of course. This is true in particular also for UNCTAD.

The procedure in outline then looks as follows: The United Nations Center for Development Planning, Projections, and Policies starts out by constructing a first set of broadly consistent targets and means figures. This is submitted to ECOSOC and through it to the General Assembly. After possible amendment this "plan outline" is then submitted to the UN regional economic commissions which would consult the governments of their region. Simultaneously the plan outline is submitted to the specialized agencies and to some interested private organizations.

It will be a great experiment for the Center for Development Planning, Projections, and Policies to receive the reactions of a number of these "lower levels" and to see whether some common denominator can be found for their coordination. One is inclined to "wait and see" what the first exercise will bring. Like every other new human activity world planning is a process of experimenting in which trial and error as well as a learning process will play their part. It will require a sense of proportion and much wisdom and courage to cut off unimportant issues in order that the relevant ones get the attention they need.

The right timing for initiating the procedure will be the most difficult problem. The subject of the exercise probably should be the period 1971-1980; it is hardly conceivable to consider an earlier period, however desirable it may be. Even then the timing will allow little leeway.

In conclusion we want to emphasize that this essay has been only a very crude sketch of how a world indicative plan might be constructed. A large number of details have been left untouched. Partly this has been done because they are well-known to every planner and to most policymakers. Partly it has been done because so many decisions on details can only be taken after the experiment has been started and difficulties have been experienced which could not have been foreseen. Even so, there are compelling reasons to implement the operation, first and foremost because it is so necessary and, also, because our experience with planning at lower levels gives us confidence that the difficulties are not unsurmountable.

International Agencies and Economic Development:

An Overview

ROBERT E. ASHER

I

UNCTAD I, the United Nations Conference on Trade and Development held in Geneva in the spring of 1964, marked a major milestone in international concern with and approaches to the problems of less developed countries. The principal achievements of this mammoth, contentious, allegedly economic gathering, however, were in the political realm. Economic issues of great importance were raised but not resolved. Instead they were consigned for study and consideration to the elaborate continuing machinery born at Geneva, as well as to various previously established agencies, and eventually to the agenda for UNCTAD II, convened in New Delhi in early 1968.

Will UNCTAD I and II prove to be milestones on the road to a global partnership of rich and poor countries, to a revolution of rising frustrations, or to an uneasy federation of regional and ideological blocs? The evidence is mixed. In 1945, according to the Preamble of the United Nations Charter, "the peoples of the United Nations" proclaimed their determination "to promote social progress and better standards of life in larger freedom" and "to employ international machinery for the pro-

ROBERT E. ASHER is a member of the Senior Staff of The Brookings Institution, Washington, D.C., and Vice-President of the Society for International Development. The author notes his considerable indebtedness to the other contributors to this volume and would gladly acknowledge each borrowing but for the very nature of an overview and the exigencies of space. The interpretations and conclusions contained in this essay are the author's and do not necessarily represent those of collaborators in the present undertaking, of fellow members of the Brookings staff, or of administrative officers of The Brookings Institution.

motion of the economic and social advancement of all peoples." Whatever its feasibility at the time—when more than half of the people presently alive and more than half the nations now in the UN had not yet been born—the problems facing mankind today, the political will and economic capacity to deal with them, and the institutional framework for doing so have changed drastically since the closing days of the Second World War.

The ground rules for international economic cooperation that were drawn up in the 1940's under the leadership of the United States were aimed primarily at preventing actions found harmful by the major powers during the 1930's, not at promoting practices helpful to the emerging nations. Since about 1950, however, the international community has devoted an enormous amount of attention to the manifold problems of the low-income countries, gradually modifying the original ground rules and introducing many innovations, including various forms of development assistance. The spokesmen for the less developed countries nevertheless continue to think they are condemned to live in a world they never made under arrangements designed to perpetuate their underdog status.

In their view, the time for a "new international division of labor" is overdue. In economic terms, they mean by this more domestic processing of the primary products they have to date been exporting; more rapid industrialization, with opportunities for specialization in certain types of manufacturing; and greater assurance of the wherewithal to help them meet their development goals. Their aspirations, however, are not confined to the economic sphere; they are also profoundly political.

No government, least of all that of the United States, thinks of itself as insensitive to the needs of others or wedded to the status quo. The United States has been instrumental in launching a bewildering array of intergovernmental agencies, institutions, commissions, programs, and campaigns. These have been endowed with sufficient resources to do some good (by stealth, it has been said), to get in each other's way, and to make it difficult for all but the most persevering of analysts to discover what is really happening. Some of this machinery fits neatly into the UN system, some fits loosely, and some is totally outside.

The less developed countries—"the fraternity of the impatient," they have been called by Harlan Cleveland—appear, however, to regard the United States as a principal defender of the status quo.[1] They consider

[1] See "The Fraternity of the Impatient," U.S. Department of State Press Release 335, July 22, 1964, subsequently published in the Department of State *Bulletin*, August 17, 1964 (Vol. 51, No. 1312), pp. 241–248. Assistant Secretary Cleveland included the United States in the fraternity. Noting that the post-UNCTAD joint declaration of the 77 developing countries expressed great impatience, he said to the UN Economic and Social Council (ECOSOC): "For our part, we not only honor and applaud their impatience—we share it. Welcome to the 'fraternity of the impatient,' we say." (*Ibid.*, p. 246.)

the major innovation of the postwar era—the extension of grants, loans, and technical assistance on a modest scale from more developed to less developed countries—as little more than a "token effort." They are much more aware of what remains to be done than of the steps already taken.

The situation is strikingly similar to the civil rights struggle in the United States, but with two significant differences. The challengers in the development arena, though they inhabit the same rapidly shrinking planet as the challenged, are not subjects of one specific government and cannot be accommodated through established political processes. Secondly, and more important, they are not a minority group. On the contrary, they constitute the overwhelming majority of mankind. They seek an end to second-class citizenship, a better chance to acquire dignity and status, to earn a livelihood and educate their children, to speak up and be heard as persons and nations rather than as petitioners. This means not only heroic efforts at self-help but also cooperation with others in obtaining real integration instead of token integration in a wider, more humane, more forward-moving community of nations.

A "new international division of labor" can benefit the more developed as well as the less developed countries. Mutual education is needed; instant development is impossible, but a century of imperceptible gradualism will be unacceptable. Time is a critical factor. As Americans should have learned from the civil rights struggle in their own country, measures that would be hailed with joy at one moment in history will be attacked as inadequate, ineffective, and insulting a few years later—if the psychological moment for adopting them has passed. Feelings of frustration can cause the frustrated to abandon integration as a goal and nonviolence as a technique.

Attitudes are more important than machinery. The problem at the international level is surely not the lack of machinery but of sufficient fuel, committed engineers, and an agreed itinerary. More specifically, multilateral efforts to promote development are predicated upon the notion that the national interests of the participating governments, though not identical, overlap sufficiently to permit each nation to benefit in its own peculiar way from cooperation with others. It is thus conflicting conceptions of these national interests that prevent the machinery from more quickly fulfilling its high-sounding purposes.

Despite the solidarity of the less developed countries at UNCTAD I and other evidences of international cooperation, the sense of international community is not particularly potent as of this writing. Nationalism continues strong, and on every continent country after country has grown more inward looking, more nationalistic, more assertive about its rights, and more reticent about its responsibilities. The communications gap between rich and poor, notwithstanding all the talk, is as wide as the income gap. The Cold War is no longer an automatic stimulus to action by the more affluent nations on behalf of the less affluent. The intransigence of the development process itself, which makes a mockery of "development decades" and early "take-offs" into self-sustaining growth, is discouraging. The evidence that development does not necessarily lead to peace, stability, and goodwill toward men is plentiful.

While circumstances have thus conspired to complicate incredibly the tasks of the organizations whose activities have been reviewed in this volume, their achievements are far from negligible. The object of their solicitude—the less developed world—has not been standing still. Its record is in many respects remarkable. An adequate foundation for further progress has been built.

How, in brief, has this come about? What machinery is in place? What problems have been tackled? What successes and failures should be noted?

II

Today, no development problem can be permitted to surface without an accompanying demand that an agency be established to "solve it" or, as a minimum, "to give the problem the importance it deserves." No previously established international agency can afford to admit that it is not primarily a development agency. The Universal Postal Union (UPU) and the Intergovernmental Maritime Consultative Organization (IMCO) will doubtless consider complaining to our editors about the insufficient attention given to them in this study of international organization and economic development.

In 1958, in a review of international economic cooperation since the close of the Second World War, I urged that the main (though not the sole) goal of the UN system be a much more vigorous pursuit of the

> vitally necessary job of concentrating additional resources from both developed and underdeveloped countries on raising levels of living among peoples no longer resigned to poverty, hunger, disease, and subordinate status.[2]

I was aware of certain lacunae in the panoply of international machinery—most notably, an agency of the stature and breadth of the International Trade Organization (ITO) called for by the Havana Charter of 1948 and a financial agency able to provide grant aid to less developed countries and truly long-term loans at nominal rates of interest. However, I sounded no clarion call for the creation of a series of new agencies.

[2] Robert E. Asher, "Economic Co-operation Under UN Auspices," *International Organization*, Summer 1958 (Vol. 12, No. 3), p. 300.

Reporting to the Economic and Social Council (ECOSOC) were four regional economic commissions and a number of functional commissions dealing with transportation and communication, social problems, human rights, statistics, narcotic drugs, and other matters. There were specialized agencies in the fields of manpower, health, education, food and agriculture, civil aviation, telecommunications, postal services, meteorology, international investment, and monetary policy. An International Atomic Energy Agency (IAEA) and the already-mentioned Intergovernmental Maritime Consultative Organization had just come into being.

The General Agreement on Tariffs and Trade (GATT) was operating as a partial substitute for the stillborn ITO and making encouraging progress in reducing tariffs and liberalizing trade. The International Bank for Reconstruction and Development (IBRD) had made lending to low-income countries, especially for electric power, transportation, and economic overhead projects, respectable. The United Nations itself was firmly engaged in operational activities through its Expanded Program of Technical Assistance (EPTA). The vigorous campaign of the less developed countries for a capital assistance fund under the aegis of the United Nations had not been successful but had already led to such important by-products as the creation of the International Finance Corporation (IFC) as an affiliate of the World Bank which would invest in private industrial enterprises in the less developed countries, and the UN Special Fund to finance "preinvestment" undertakings in those countries.

Some notable multilateral initiatives had been taken outside of the UN framework. The Organization for European Economic Cooperation (OEEC) had greatly liberalized trade and payments within Western Europe. Three European "communities"—the European Economic Community (EEC) or Common Market, the European Coal and Steel Community (ECSC), and the European Atomic Energy Community (Euratom)—had been created. The Colombo Plan, however, remained one of the few such initiatives that involved developing as well as developed countries. To summarize, there appeared in 1958 to be no dearth of intergovernmental machinery.

Since then, as even the most casual reader of this symposium will have noted, the creation of international machinery has continued unabated. In global terms UNCTAD is politically the most important addition, for reasons well set forth in the essay by Richard N. Gardner. At the regional level the Alliance for Progress which is a multilateral undertaking but not an agency (though it embraces certain agencies described elsewhere in this study) is politically and economically highly significant. So, too, are the establishment of the International Development Association (IDA) as a second affiliate of the World Bank, the creation of the European Development Fund (EDF) and the Inter-American Development Bank (IDB), and the opening of regional development banks in both Asia and Africa. In promoting development, financial institutions have an asset—money—which enables them to launch productive projects as well as to recommend policies, make studies, run seminars, negotiate agreements, and engage in the more costless international activities to which other agencies are perforce limited.

Other new machinery worthy of mention in this incomplete catalog includes:

The extensive substructure of UNCTAD, comprising, *inter alia,* a 55-member Trade and Development Board which meets twice a year, a 55-member Committee on Commodities, 45-member Committees on Manufactures, on Shipping, and on Invisibles and Financing Related to Trade, and a secretariat of several hundred people in Geneva under Dr. Raúl Prebisch of Argentina;

The United Nations Industrial Development Organization (UNIDO), like UNCTAD an organ of the General Assembly, which has a 45-member Industrial Development Board, an "action-oriented" mandate that stresses operational activities rather than research, and a relatively autonomous secretariat in Vienna under Dr. I. H. Abdel-Rahman of the United Arab Republic;

A World Food Program (WFP) in Rome set up in 1963 under the joint sponsorship of the United Nations and the Food and Agriculture Organization (FAO) to use food surpluses, cash contributions, and services such as shipping for both emergency relief and economic and social development;

"Centers" within UN Headquarters such as the Center for Development Planning, Projections, and Policies and the Center for Housing, Building, and Planning and centers elsewhere such as the joint International Trade Center being established by GATT and UNCTAD;

Institutes galore, among them the UN Research Institute for Social Development in Geneva; the UN Institute for Training and Research (UNITAR) in New York; Institutes for Economic Development and Planning in Latin America, Africa, and Asia set up with the help of the Special Fund in cooperation with the regional economic commissions of the UN; an International Institute for Labor Studies established by the International Labor Organization (ILO); and an International Institute for Educational Planning spun off by the UN Educational, Scientific and Cultural Organization (UNESCO);

The Advisory Committee on the Application of Science and Technology to Development;

Last and as yet least, the capitalless UN Capital Development Fund.

The sole notable move toward consolidation has been the merger, effective January 1, 1966, of the Expanded Program of Technical Assistance and the Special Fund into the United Nations Development Program (UNDP).

Although the creation of new development agencies dominated by the less developed countries has been a major pastime of the international community during the 1960's, the bulk of the real work, insofar as the international promotion of economic growth and social change is concerned, continues to be done by the previously established agencies. Those agencies, moreover, have undergone profound changes in response to the pressures and needs of the low-income countries and new attitudes on the part of the high-income countries. Though the old stereotypes live on in the debates, the machinery established in the 1940's and the 1950's is focused as never before on current problems of the low-income countries.

The World Bank Group (the International Bank for Reconstruction and Development, the International Finance Corporation, and the International Development Association) has increased the annual level of its commitments to less developed countries from under $300 million in 1956 to about $1.2 billion in 1966. Formerly concentrating its resources heavily in electric power and transportation and inclined to remain aloof from other international agencies, the World Bank Group has stepped up its financing of agricultural and industrial development and exhibited a new and timely willingness to lend for educational development. It has worked out cooperative and fruitful relationships with FAO and UNESCO, overcome the misgivings it once had about technical assistance and soft lending, and, through the consortia and consultative groups it has convened and serviced, raised a multilateral umbrella over a sizable volume of bilateral assistance.

The International Monetary Fund (IMF), long regarded by many of the less developed countries as a citadel of economic orthodoxy rather than a source of short-term assistance, has become a much more flexible instrument. Gross drawings by less developed countries, which amounted to only $420 million during the years 1947–1955, exceeded $1 billion in 1956–1960 and more than $2.5 billion during the years 1961–1967.[3] Of special interest to less developed countries is the provision made by the

---

[3] For details see Edward M. Bernstein's lucid essay elsewhere in this volume.

IMF in 1963 and substantially liberalized in 1966 for the compensatory financing of foreign exchange deficits due to shortfalls in export proceeds below the level of the medium-term trend and beyond the control of the exporting country.

GATT, particularly since its innovative report, *Trends in International Trade,* published in 1958, has become acutely conscious of the need to maintain and expand the export earnings of the less developed countries through measures other than the reciprocal reduction of tariff barriers. A new Part IV of the General Agreement, entitled "Trade and Development," entered into force in 1966 and, as John W. Evans reports, brought to an end the period during which the GATT contained neither

> textual recognition of the role of exports in economic development nor a constitutional framework for many of the activities in which the Contracting Parties had been engaged

since 1958.

The contributions of the International Labor Organization and the United Nations Educational, Scientific and Cultural Organization to the conventional wisdom of the mid-1960's about the supreme importance of investment in human resources are delightfully described by Robert W. Cox. The Food and Agriculture Organization, a club in which the less developed countries have long felt more at home than in most of the pre-1960 intergovernmental agencies, has been serving them more relevantly and diligently since launching its Mediterranean Development Project in 1958. It has been moving away from the provision of technical assistance on an uncoordinated, retail basis and become deeply concerned with the strategy of agricultural development.

The heavy emphasis in multilateral agencies, old as well as new, on problems of the less developed countries might appear to provide a basis for the charge that the international economic machinery has somehow been stood on its head and is now neglecting the problems of the industrialized nations in order to concentrate exclusively on those of the low-income countries. Closer scrutiny, however, would show that the charge is false.

The principal protagonists and beneficiaries of the recently completed Kennedy Round of tariff negotiations which preoccupied GATT for four exhausting years (1963–1967) are the major trading areas of the non-Communist world, especially the United States and the European Economic Community. Real benefits will accrue to the less developed countries, benefits more substantial than many of us expected, but the deepest cuts were made in tariffs on items of most interest to the principal negotiating partners.[4]

---

[4] "Although such concessions were, of course, extended by the MFN [most-favored-nation] rule to developing countries as well, they were in general irrelevant to the latter." "Tariff Averages for

Similarly, the equally protracted negotiations on international monetary reform involving the creation of a new reserve asset, the SDR or special drawing right, have been of paramount interest to the major industrial countries, in this case the so-called Group of Ten in the IMF. The gross drawings of the more developed countries on the Fund during the years 1947–1967 exceed $9 billion, of which nearly $7 billion has been drawn during the 1960's. However, all IMF members, including the 81 less developed countries, can benefit from the new arrangement.

The World Bank continued until quite recently to be used by Australia, Finland, Japan, and other developed countries as a source of long-term credit. It has promoted and protected the interests of private international investors, most of whom are in high-income nations. The intergovernmental machinery in the fields of civil aviation, telecommunications, meteorology, and shipping is obviously not neglectful of the interests of developed countries.

The Organization for European Economic Cooperation, launched during the Marshall Plan period, has been transformed into the Organization for Economic Cooperation and Development (OECD) in which the United States, Canada, and Japan have joined the former OEEC states as full members. Only a small part of the far-flung program of this organization—primarily work of the Development Assistance Committee (DAC), the Trade Committee, and the semiautonomous OECD Development Center—is devoted directly to expediting growth in the less developed world.

The more developed countries, it seems to this observer, have all the machinery they want, plus the ability to create more when they feel so inclined. They suffer primarily from division in their ranks, an ailment from which no group of nations is immune.

III

Reverting to our main theme, multilateral efforts to promote growth and change in the low-income world, and reviewing the present array of machinery, it is reasonable to ask: What has it accomplished? What accounts for the proliferation? What trends are discernible? Who, if anyone, is minding the store—in other words, exercising some overall control? Let us postpone for the moment consideration of the first and most fundamental of these questions and address ourselves briefly to the others.

Insofar as the proliferation of machinery is concerned one must bear

Products of Interest to Developing Countries as Compared with Other Products" (United Nations Conference on Trade and Development Research Memorandum No. 13/2, August 4, 1967 [provisional draft, mimeographed], p. 8.)

in mind the low base from which it all started. Development was hardly recognized as an international problem two decades ago although it was deemed worthy of the attention of the newly established International Bank for Reconstruction and Development—*after* the necessary priority had been given to reconstruction. Almost every national government now has a much more complicated, disorderly panoply of agencies for dealing with economic and social problems than it had ten years ago. No one is happy about this, least of all congresses, parliaments, and treasuries, but expansion at the national level tends to be accepted with greater equanimity than expansion at the international level.

Most of the growth at the international level is a perfectly normal response to increased need. As one after another of the "keys" to development fails to open the door, as the infinite complexity of the unlocking process is revealed, as the interrelationships between economic, social, attitudinal, and institutional changes become better understood, and as new stages of development are attained, revised strategies and different pinpointings of effort are required. The desired objectives can sometimes be achieved by modifying the terms of reference or work programs of agencies already in being. At other times new machinery will be needed.

The balance in favor of new machinery has been massively tipped by the great increase in the number of sovereign states, their voting strength in intergovernmental forums, their self-evident qualification for the label "less developed," and their discontent with the agencies they have inherited. As Professor Gardner has reminded us, the less developed countries are not concerned about organizational neatness but about immediate results. When existing machinery appears to them to be inadequate, their response tends to be a vote for new machinery in which they will have greater control.

The establishment of an organization, moreover, creates the illusion of an attack on a problem and thus tends to satisfy demands for action without really answering the question of what should be done to solve the problem. Unfortunately, illusions too must now be bigger and better than they used to be; demands that could once have been satisfied by setting up a small committee today require as a minimum response the establishment of a sizable agency.

Does it do any good to set up machinery by a majority vote that does not include the votes of the nations expected to provide, in the form of money and expertise, most of the muscle and at least part of the brain? Not much good, but some. Governments that stand aloof grow uncomfortable when they could be sitting in chairs awaiting them at conference tables. The prospect that the machinery will be run entirely by others—without their own steadying hand at the helm—is too dreadful to contemplate. Once their participation is obtained, funds and good works may follow.

Furthermore, the more developed countries, which frequently oppose the initiatives of the less developed countries for new machinery and a voice more nearly commensurate with the share of the low-income countries in world population, have themselves exhibited ingenuity in adding workrooms and dormer windows to the organizational structure. They cannot blithely blame the less developed countries for all of the proliferation.

The prospect of rival machinery is often the best way to jog existing agencies out of well-worn ruts. The trouble is that by the time the substantive objective has been achieved and the proposed new functions have been more or less subsumed by existing agencies the propagandists for a new agency have become convinced by their own propaganda and insist on carrying through their threat. Given the good performance of the International Development Association, it is almost shocking that the less developed countries have continued to devote so much energy to establishing a UN Capital Development Fund and so little to keeping IDA alive and growing. The recalcitrance of the developed countries whenever the resources of IDA require replenishing highlights even more revealingly the present state of international economic cooperation.

Multilateral machinery grows and evolves not only in response to genuinely pressing needs, to needs that once were pressing but have already been substantially met, to the desires of vocal delegates, to the ambitions of secretariats and prospective members of secretariats, and to the hope that more machinery for development will result in more resources being devoted to development; it proliferates also because machinery begets machinery. The establishment of an Economic Commission for Europe (ECE) leads almost inevitably to economic commissions for every other major region. The existence of a worldwide organization to promote agricultural development requires in fairness to industry the establishment of a worldwide organization to promote industrial development. The justification that originally helped to support the creation of a Food and Agriculture Organization—that three-fourths of the people in the world derive their livelihoods from agriculture—can later be turned around to support the establishment of an Industrial Development Organization on the ground that there are too many people in agriculture and not enough in industry.

The success of a global preinvestment fund managed by Paul Hoffman has helped bring into being a Preinvestment Fund for Latin American Integration under the aegis of the Inter-American Development Bank. A regional development bank for Latin America, coming to fruition after a 70-year history, promptly gives rise to agitation for regional development banks in Asia and Africa.

The converse of the foregoing is also true: Established bureaucracies fight to preserve their empires and their policy standards and to protect them from invasion or subversion. The World Bank was not always hospitable to the idea of regional development banks; ILO saw no need for UNIDO; the specialized agencies for the most part opposed the merger that brought the UN Development Program into being.

The greater the number of international organizations the more hazardous it is to generalize about them. Exceptions can be cited, but the most noteworthy features of the organizational situation today, as compared with the situation ten or fifteen years ago, seem to me as follows:

1) The less developed countries have a much stronger voice in the policymaking bodies, often at the cost of transforming those bodies into organs too unwieldy to make policy. The less developed countries (like the Communist countries) are also more strongly represented in international secretariats. The obligation to distribute appointments over a wider geographic area has, at least for the time being, lowered the average technical competence of the secretariats and in some cases made them more partisan in their work.

2) Understandably enough, there continues to be enthusiasm among the less developed countries for machinery that can provide aid or strengthen the case for material assistance, and resistance to machinery geared to enforce standards or criticize poor performance. The history of the rise and fall of the Panel of Experts of the Alliance for Progress (the Nine Wise Men) and the subsequent effort to create a strong Inter-American Committee on the Alliance for Progress (CIAP) show how unwilling the Latin Americans have been to commit themselves to multilateral decisions on the allocation of aid among competing claimants.[5]

3) Regional machinery is sprouting up on every continent, much of it outside the UN framework, and regional economic integration is beginning to replace investment in human resources as the latest panacea for development. Insufficient attention, it can be argued, is being given to potential conflicts between the goals of regional and global integration.

4) The original notion under which within the UN framework certain broad fields of functional or technical specialization could be assigned to permanent, global specialized agencies related to the central political agency (the United Nations) but operating under their own constitutions and charters has been further eroded. The shortcomings of

---

[5] See the essay by Raúl Sáez elsewhere in this volume. Nevertheless, by comparison with present arrangements in Asia, Africa, or the Middle East the Alliance for Progress constitutes a long step toward a multilateral approach to development.

the functional approach (particularly its deleterious effects on development programming and execution at the country level) and the current tension between the functionalism of ILO, UNESCO, and FAO and the newer functionalism of UNCTAD or UNIDO are well brought out in Robert W. Cox's perceptive contribution to this symposium. UNCTAD and UNIDO are specialized agencies in everything but name, with charters that deliberately overlap those of older organs but with less protection from the political winds that rock the General Assembly.

5) The expenditures of international agencies for development purposes are still rising, but no progress has been made in endowing them with independent sources of revenue. Nongovernmental groups periodically pass resolutions urging that the United Nations be given title to the mineral resources of the oceans and ocean beds or the right to levy a surcharge on postage or a tax on international trade, but governments are not that eager to build a financially strong UN. The result has been a significant increase in the number of programs to be financed, like the budget of UNDP, by voluntary pledges with all the uncertainty inherent in that procedure.

6) The whole picture is a lot untidier than it used to be and no one is really minding the store. There once was a hope—it never was more than a hope—that the Economic and Social Council would become the economic and social "general staff" of the United Nations and that economic analysis of the kind not done by the secretariats of the specialized agencies would be provided by the Department of Economic and Social Affairs (of which the secretariats of the regional economic commissions were integral parts). The Economic and Social Council has been enlarged, as a result of a 1963 amendment to the UN Charter, from eighteen to 27 members, thereby giving the less developed countries a comfortable majority. In the Council representatives of the less developed countries have cooperated encouragingly in refurbishing its image as a coordinator and supervisor but in the General Assembly and elsewhere have furthered the fragmentation and decentralization that make orderly supervision by either the Council or the UN Secretary-General impossible.[6]

7) The novelty of the commitment to development, the complexity of the process, and the fact that there is no one best way to develop provide justification for a variety of functional and geographic approaches and for agencies of different size, scope, ideology, and autonomy. A real directorate-general for international economic affairs is not in the cards

---

[6] Walter M. Kotschnig in his essay calls attention to the newly revived and strengthened Committee for Program and Coordination and strikes a more hopeful note concerning the prospects for coordination.

within the foreseeable future. The sense of international community is too feeble, understanding of the strategy of development is too rudimentary, and revolutions, whether of rising expectations or rising frustrations, are too disorderly.

IV

There are several reasons for caution in speaking of the accomplishments and shortcomings of multilateral efforts. The word "multilateral" itself has come to embrace very much more than a project, program, or research undertaking directed, financed, and executed by a single intergovernmental agency. Distinctions between multilateral and bilateral, and national and international, have been blurred as a result of experiments in cooperation and conscious efforts to take advantage of the favorable connotations of the term "multilateral." In consequence the multilateral effort is sometimes only the wagging tail of a bilateral dog. Sometimes it is the dog, but with a bilateral tail and more bark than bite. Occasionally, it reveals itself as a pedigreed thoroughbred.

This study is replete with examples difficult to classify. The World Bank convenes government representatives from selected countries in consortia and consultative groups to review the development prospects and aid requirements of designated nations and to see what can be done about meeting agreed needs. Although a portion of the necessary financing will be provided multilaterally by the World Bank family, another, usually larger portion, will be provided by participating governments in accordance with arrangements worked out bilaterally between lender and borrower.[7] The Inter-American Development Bank, a multilateral institution with its ordinary capital resources subscribed to by all of its members, now finances social development projects from its expanded Fund for Special Operations but previously financed them from a separate Social Progress Trust Fund of more than $500 million contributed entirely by the United States.

The United States Agency for International Development (AID) on occasion joins the World Bank and the Inter-American Development Bank in financing a Latin American project. Private foundations and corporations may also participate in the effort. At other times two or more aid-giving governments join in financing a project in an aid-receiving country and refer to the undertaking as multilateral, even though no intergovernmental agency is involved.

[7] For perceptive accounts of the problem of aid coordination see Michael L. Hoffman, "The Co-ordination of Aid," in *Effective Aid* (London: Overseas Development Institute, 1967), pp. 65–84; and Seymour J. Rubin, *The Conscience of the Rich Nations: The Development Assistance Committee and the Common Aid Effort* (New York: Harper & Row [for the Council on Foreign Relations], 1966), especially pp. 12–20.

A further ground for caution is that even when the multilateral agencies appear to be operating independently, they are not autonomous forces divorced from the governments that create and maintain them. What Roger Revelle refers to as the "dismal record" of the World Health Organization (WHO) in family planning is not in any real sense a commentary on the efficacy of the agency, as he would be the first to admit, but a reflection on the state of public and governmental opinion in different areas of the world. In malaria control the record of WHO is excellent.

Bearing in mind these caveats and turning now to the substantive side of development, we may ask: What problems have been tackled multilaterally? What are the principal successes and failures of the multilateral approach? What has it contributed to popular and expert understanding of the problems of development and to the resolution of recognized problems?

The publications of international organizations and *ad hoc* expert groups have contributed significantly to the slowly emerging, as yet far from complete comprehension of the process of development. The annual *World Economic Report* and regional economic surveys, the biennial *Report on the World Social Situation,* published by the UN, the annual review of *International Trade* by GATT, the *State of Food and Agriculture* by FAO, the annual reports of the IMF and IBRD, the reports of the UN and OECD on the flow of financial resources to the less developed countries, and innumerable special reports on land reform, community development, commodity problems, and human rights provide essential basic data and interpretive analyses of recent trends. Various experts' reports—such as the 1951 report by a panel of experts appointed by the UN Secretary-General, *Measures for the Economic Development of Under-Developed Countries, Trends in International Trade* published by a GATT panel of experts, *Towards a New Trade Policy for Development* by the Secretary-General of UNCTAD, and *Development Assistance Efforts and Policies* by DAC's Chairman—have also been influential and in some cases are virtually classics.

Reports by international agencies and international committees tend to stress the need for international measures. It can be argued that debate and discussion have "overinternationalized" the development problem and exaggerated the degree to which success depends on international action, especially on more liberal trade, aid, and investment policies on the part of the industrialized, high-income countries.

With due allowance for agency loyalties and the primacy each professional accords to his profession as compared with all other professions a slowly growing consensus about the nature of the revolution politely called "development" or "modernization" is detectable. Development is not a stage reached when per capita incomes attain some specified level or after a particular list of "obstacles" has been overcome. It is a process—dynamic, pervasive, never ending, destructive as well as constructive. The essence of the process is the inculcation of new attitudes and ideas, of states of mind eager for progress, hospitable to change, and capable of applying scientific approaches to an ever wider range of problems.

The rapidity with which the process unfolds depends on the will and capacity of the people of the underdeveloped country far more than on natural resources or imported equipment and supplies. It depends on leaders who educate as well as agitate and on followers who teach as well as learn. Communication between them needs to be a two-way exchange with a meaningful feedback from the people to their leaders. Popular participation in development programs appears to be essential to facilitate the learning process, to prevent unbridgeable urban-rural gaps, and to enable inherited institutions to be transformed rather than to be replaced abruptly by unfamiliar, and therefore perhaps unworkable, transplanted institutions. As yet the wish to develop is more widespread than the will, and not enough is known about how to translate the wish into the will.

Although gross national product (per capita as well as total), savings and investment rates, earnings from exports, and other economic indexes should move upward, modernization consists of more than maximizing these. A decent sharing of the increased wealth, the elimination of discrimination based on race, color, or creed, higher literacy rates, broader and better-informed participation in political life, and efficient and humane administration—these, too, are vitally important objectives of development.

The term "economic development" is therefore being superseded by the more generic term "development" (without any qualifying adjectives) or "modernization" and is understood to mean economic, social, and political growth. For countries in the very early stages of development—traditional societies where more than 70 percent of the people are still on the land, where fewer than 30 percent are literate, where the birth rate runs from 40 to 50 births per 1,000 inhabitants per year, where life is truly at the margin of subsistence and man is at the mercy of the elements—modernization involves a top-to-bottom transformation of society. It means fundamental changes in traditional values, motivations, institutions, and patterns of behavior. It is a long-term job. At best it will be an erratic, two-steps-forward, one-step-backward, one-step-sideways movement.

Nevertheless, the journey toward self-sustaining growth need not be as drawn-out and costly in human terms as was the comparable journey for the now high-income, better-integrated nations of Western Europe and North America. Their experience, some of their resources, and other more recent experiences can be drawn on to shorten the time span. On the other hand, higher rates of population increase, greater difficulty in favoring investment over consumption, rising aspirations, and better-equipped competitors make the job more difficult than it was a century ago. Political exigencies demand speed, but how rapid the modernization process can become without destroying its organic nature and internal balance remains unknown. It will differ from area to area.

In addition to increased consensus regarding the general nature of the modernization process there is greater understanding than there was in 1950 of the vast differences between the 80-odd less developed countries. Each nation is to an important extent in a class by itself, dubiously aided by broad-brush policy prescriptions designed to cover simultaneously Brazil and Burundi, Costa Rica and Nepal, Libya and India.

Many new techniques have been devised in the economic and social field during the last two decades. It is easy to forget that in the early 1950's the World Bank was firmly opposed to soft lending, that in the late 1950's a publicly financed preinvestment fund seemed to many a questionable way to promote investment, and that until UNCTAD I non-discriminatory treatment in international trade was an overriding objective of international trade policy. Today, soft lending, like technical assistance or national banks for industrial and agricultural development, is an established technique for promoting growth in the low-income world. A preinvestment fund for financing resource surveys, training institutes, and market analyses, it is readily admitted, can evoke substantial sums for subsequent productive investment. In trade policy, discrimination in favor of the less developed countries is openly advocated by most of the developed countries and is being seriously considered by the rest.

Development planning, like development lending, has been made respectable. Low-income countries have been helped to formulate national development plans and 50 or more countries now have partial or comprehensive programs.

> Some of this planning has been faulty and, at times, even useless. But behind these weaknesses lies a truly remarkable phenomenon—the acceptance of the planning technique.[8]

[8] Irving S. Friedman, *International Problems of Economic Development,* Address to the Canadian Political Science Association, Ottawa, Canada, June 7, 1967 (Washington: International Bank for Reconstruction and Development, 1967), p. 8. Mr. Friedman goes on to say,

> By planning technique . . . I do not mean a detailed control and regulation of economic activity. Rather, it is the method by which governments make commitments to future actions and policies, thus extending the time horizons within which economic calculations

The effective execution of a few fundamental policies and programs is at least as important as the preparation of an elaborate, internally consistent, five-year plan based—all too frequently—on statistical data of doubtful validity and in any event unlikely to be carried out because of the absence of machinery and procedures linking the plan to the actual investment decisions of the government and the private sector. More attention is consequently being given to 1) better sector programming and project preparation in agriculture, education, transportation, and other fields; and 2) the formulation of integrated regional or area development schemes which seek to direct all the necessary inputs simultaneously (so that they will reinforce each other) into a single, manageable, geographic region within a developing country.

International agencies have been helpful in selecting promising regions, providing teachers and supplies, and, at the national level, advising on policies, assisting in the drafting of sectoral as well as overall development programs, and making long-range supply-and-demand projections for particular commodities. FAO is engaged in drawing up an ambitious Indicative World Plan for Agriculture. Jan Tinbergen looks forward to the day when there will also be an indicative overall economic plan for the world and in his essay suggests both a rationale and some guidelines for the undertaking.[9]

The key role of the agricultural sector is currently better appreciated, thanks in part to FAO. Increased food production in developing countries is at last beginning to receive the priority it deserves. Whether large-scale famines during the 1970's and 1980's can be averted remains questionable, but the Secretary-General of the United Nations, without being accused of seeking to keep the less developed countries in rustic subservience, can now warn that:

> Unless production on the farms . . . begins to go up, there is no surplus for saving, no surplus to feed the towns, no surplus to keep pace with rising population and keep down costly imports of food, no agricultural raw materials to feed into industry and, above all, no rise in farm income to provide an expanding market for the nascent industrial system. There is no conflict between the priorities of farming and industry, and the need to re-emphasize farming springs not from any desire to "keep developing economies dependent" but simply to counteract the glamour of factory chimneys which may all too often be smoking above products which no one in the community can afford to buy.[10]

based on objective criteria can play a greater part. The planning technique then becomes an important instrument for coordinating development activity on a number of different fronts, and for maintaining some sort of continuity in the pace of development.

[9] See Jan Tinbergen, "Wanted: A World Development Plan," elsewhere in this volume.

[10] "The United Nations Development Decade at Mid-Point: An appraisal by the Secretary-General" (UN Document E/4071, June 11, 1965), p. 32.

The distinguished UN Advisory Committee on the Application of Science and Technology to Development has identified a number of problems that merit concerted attack by means of scientific research and has made recommendations for mounting the attack. The provision of adequate food supplies heads its list of problems.

Doctrinal fights over the role of private foreign investment are being resolved pragmatically. Endless hours have been spent in futile efforts to develop acceptable multilateral codes for the treatment of private foreign investment. Meanwhile, unilaterally adopted investment guaranty schemes have been successful in safeguarding and perhaps enlarging the flow. There is a possibility that these will be complemented and supplemented by a multilateral scheme.[11] Nevertheless, the flow remains modest (only about half the level of public grants and loans) and is heavily concentrated on extractive industries in a handful of countries. The line between public and private, like the distinction between multilateral and bilateral, is not always clear. The World Bank engages in joint operations with investment banking houses, floats bond issues in the capital markets of industrialized countries to obtain resources for its public loans, and sells to institutional investors the early-maturity portions of previously made loans.

Recognition of the complexity of the development process should not obscure the elemental fact that an inflow of capital for investment purposes remains immensely important. The flow of public grants and loans to less developed countries rose encouragingly during the last half of the 1950's but stabilized in the early 1960's at a level considered grossly inadequate by the less developed countries and by most of the contributors to this volume. The stable absolute level of total aid since 1961 has in reality been a declining level because: 1) In the receiving countries population growth has reduced the amount available per inhabitant while in the donor countries rising incomes have reduced the fraction of the gross national product devoted to economic aid; 2) the terms of aid have been hardening and increasing sums have been needed by the less developed countries to pay interest charges on loans already received; 3) the cost of every kind of assistance has been rising; and 4) the proportion of aid tied to particular sources of supply and therefore not available for purchases wherever the goods are cheapest has also been climbing. The proportion of public grants and loans moving through multilateral channels has risen slightly but remains less than 15 percent of the total.

The population explosion, like the weather, is a phenomenon everyone talks about, but the international agencies are well behind the procession in doing anything about it. The private foundations and some of the

[11] See Stanley D. Metzger's trenchant analysis of investment issues elsewhere in this volume.

smaller bilateral programs (e.g., that of Sweden) have pioneered. The United States aid program has recently overcome its taboos, but the World Health Organization has been prevented by certain of its members from playing an effective role.[12]

The role of international trade in development, skillfully summarized by Isaiah Frank for readers of this symposium, is now much better understood by the international community than it was a decade ago. The focus has shifted from import substitution (i.e., producing at home, almost regardless of cost, items that previously were purchased abroad) to export promotion.

> The shift of focus from imports to exports as the important trade factor in economic development has occasioned a parallel policy shift from measures applied by an individual country to international action. There is a new general awareness that the problems of expanding exports of developing countries, except for temporary and unusual circumstances, can be tackled only as a cooperative venture. . . . [13]

About 85 percent of the export earnings of the less developed countries still comes from primary products. With some exceptions among the minerals and metals, however, the market for these exports is sluggish and subject to considerable price fluctuations. Moreover, most of the primary products exported by the low-income countries must compete with commodities produced and exported by the rich countries.

Agriculture in the developed countries until quite recently has been virtually exempt from the trade liberalization movement of the postwar years. Domestic producers of sugar beets and sugar cane, cereals, and many other primary products are sheltered from foreign competition. Elimination of agricultural protection in the highly developed countries could be an enormous stimulant to the exports of the less developed countries. Full elimination during the foreseeable future is unlikely, but a prompt follow-up on the beginning made in connection with the Kennedy Round would be helpful.

Pending genuine diversification of production and exports by the less developed countries—i.e., pending development—one of the remedies they have sought most persistently is a series of international commodity agreements to stabilize and step up earnings from those primary products that they do export in quantity—coffee, cocoa, tea, bananas, rubber, tin, copper, lead, and zinc, among others. The list of commodity agreements in

---

[12] Richard N. Gardner finds "the ratio of talk to action . . . still distressingly high" and concedes that the UN got off to a slow start insofar as family planning assistance is concerned. He regards 1962–1967 as the years of the breakthrough, however, and calls attention to the record of the UN Children's Fund (UNICEF) and agencies bolder than WHO. See his essay "Toward a World Population Program" elsewhere in this volume.

[13] Margaret G. de Vries, "Trade and Exchange Policies for Economic Development," *Finance and Development,* June 1967 (Vol. 4, No. 2), p. 116.

operation is very short; sensible arrangements are inordinately hard to work out and seldom very successful after having been put into effect. The difficulties and divergencies of interest are distressingly formidable. The International Coffee Agreement with its proposed fund for diversification does represent something of a breakthrough, however. (The International Cotton Textiles Arrangement, negotiated to prevent "market disruption" from imports in countries such as the United States, is a backward step, disadvantageous to the developing countries that export textiles and to consumers in the importing countries. At the same time it is illustrative of the fact that many inherent technical difficulties in working out agreements vanish when powerful countries are determined to surmount them.[14])

The limited role for commodity agreements has underscored the need to move ahead in other ways to promote the export earnings of less developed countries. Pursuant to a request made by the 1964 UNCTAD the staff of the World Bank devised a scheme that would help to relieve commodity agreements of the responsibility they have been least successful in meeting, namely, the maintenance of the total export earnings of producing nations. The scheme, subsequently reviewed by an intergovernmental group of experts, would provide less developed countries with an accessible source of assistance to enable them to maintain internationally approved development programs in the face of unforeseen adverse export movements that are beyond their control and beyond their ability to offset from reserves or to finance on a short-term repayable basis. The plan is predicated on the vital assumption that it would be supplementary to, and not a substitute for, existing forms of aid.

The less developed countries are determined not to be confined to the role of producing and exporting primary products. They want to get into the manufacturing business. Their comparative advantage, initially at least, lies in industries requiring relatively large amounts of unskilled labor and relatively little capital or highly skilled labor.[15] Japan and Italy among the developed countries and Hong Kong, the Republic of China (Nationalist China), and the Republic of Korea (South Korea) among the developing areas have already shown the way.

However, the present tariff structure of the United States and of most other nations as well is rigged against the labor-intensive manufactures that less developed countries are or can become best equipped to supply.

---

[14] Because it deals with processed rather than primary products, the Cotton Textiles Arrangement is not a commodity agreement in the usual sense of the term.

[15] This should not be construed as an argument against the establishment of heavy industries. A number of less developed countries have passed the "initially at least" stage to which I refer or can justify capital-intensive undertakings on other grounds. See, for example, Hla Myint, *The Economics of the Developing Countries* (New York: Frederick A. Praeger, 1965), pp. 136–142, 157–159.

Tariffs generally escalate in accordance with the amount of processing done abroad. Noncompetitive raw materials get the best treatment, semi-manufactures the second best, while manufactured products pay the highest duties. Those particularly discriminated against include not only textiles, carpets, clothing, and accessories but also footwear, glassware, china, and pottery; toys, sporting goods, and bicycles; various processed foodstuffs; and furniture and other simple wood products.

As a result of protracted tariff negotiations held under the auspices of GATT tariffs on manufactured goods have been reduced enormously since 1947. The average nominal or legal tariff in now somewhere between 10 and 15 percent, depending upon how it is calculated. Publicizing the average, however, tends to conceal the fact that many individual rates, including those in which the less developed countries are particularly interested, are well above the average. Moreover, the nominal tariff rates usually understate substantially the true protective effect of the tariff structure.

Zealous protection of labor-intensive lines of production from foreign competition is both a disservice to the less developed countries and to the general public in the industrialized countries. Development means a steady rise in average labor income and should be accompanied by a gradual transfer of resources out of the less sophisticated, low-income-yielding lines. In an economy willing to use adjustment assistance to facilitate the transfer process and enjoying relatively full employment the hardships should be few and the benefits many. The low-cost producers in less developed countries could fill the resulting breach.[16]

In summary, as aid has leveled off, pressure for fresh action on the trade front has increased. Changes that will allow the less developed countries to earn from exports more of the foreign exchange that they need will affect their self-respect, their need for foreign aid, and their integration into the international community. The trade proposal that has evoked the most enthusiasm in the low-income world is for temporary tariff preferences in the industrialized countries for manufactured products from less developed countries. If, for example, the duty on bicycles were 10 percent, it might for a decade be reduced, for less developed countries only, to half of the regular rate or to zero.

A scheme of generalized preferences for less developed countries would sanction a form of discrimination but in my view would not constitute a retrograde or disastrous step. The path to a policy goal like nondiscrimination is usually a zigzag course. Nevertheless, a preference scheme for less developed countries could at best make only a modest contribution

[16] See Harry G. Johnson, *Economic Policies Toward Less Developed Countries* (Washington: Brookings Institution, 1967), especially pp. 78–110.

to a new international division of labor. The greatest potential trade contribution to a better-integrated world enocomy would be much easier access for everyone to the rich markets of the high-income countries. If the low-income countries in turn maintained realistic exchange rates and otherwise equipped themselves to take advantage of the enlarged opportunity, the potential benefit would become real.

V

Judged by historical standards the progress of the less developed countries since the close of World War II has been quite remarkable. But man does not live by historical standards alone. Frustration and foreboding are rife.

India, the largest less developed nation in the non-Communist world, has suffered from two years of unprecedented drought, from tired and undynamic leadership, and from centrifugal forces of ominous strength. The People's Republic of China (Communist China) has been a threat, and the peace with Pakistan is fragile. Nigeria, most populous of the African countries and groomed to be a showcase of purposeful development on that restive continent, has been rent by civil war. The Democratic Republic of the Congo, site of a heroic effort by the international community to build in short order the foundations for a sovereign state, is foundering. Indonesia took itself to the very brink of disaster, hovered, and seems at last to be turning around. In the western hemisphere Brazil and Argentina—for all their promise—have performed indifferently.

The smaller nations are in many cases too small to survive as sovereign entities, yet federations embracing several such states have so far proved unviable. The future of Hong Kong, a genuine success story, has been placed in jeopardy by externally inspired rioting and nearby hostile forces. With one or two exceptions the members of the Arab League have devoted more energy to seeking the destruction of Israel than to emulating the Israeli record in building a nation and making the desert bloom. Everywhere, armaments exact their unholy toll on available resources.

The behavior of the so-called "more developed" or "advanced" countries offers little inspiration to the less developed countries. Their grand designs are petty, self-serving, or nonexistent. Their economies exhibit signs of slowdown. Their commitment to help develop other continents is wavering. Their preoccupation with domestic problems—and, in the case of the United States, with a costly, divisive, interminable war in Vietnam—is all too apparent. Indications that the Union of Soviet Socialist Republics will cooperate in making the world "safe for diversity" are hard to find.

The list of portents could be lengthened and the reasons for disenchantment—which include totally unrealistic expectations in both developed and less developed countries—could be dealt with in more detail. International machinery draws attention to disasters and quite properly removes from its agenda problems that no longer cry for action. Crop failures or falling raw material prices trigger debate; rising earnings and dramatic agricultural achievements such as the increase in the Mexican wheat yield and the phenomenally productive rice strains developed at the International Rice Research Institute receive, at most, two brief cheers.

The postwar record itself consequently deserves mention, if only to offset the widespread impression of stagnation, disintegration, and worse.

In terms of gross domestic product the less developed countries have been growing at a respectable rate since 1950. The rate exceeds the growth rate of the more developed countries during the same period as well as for earlier periods of comparable duration. However, because of the much faster rates of population growth in the less developed countries—almost twice those of the developed countries—the rate of improvement per person has been less in the low-income part of the world than in the high-income part despite the fact that its overall rate of growth has been slightly greater. Moreover, because of the low level from which they started, per capita incomes in the less developed countries in dollar terms have risen only modestly. Although the average rise in per capita income has been small for the less developed world as a whole, there are a number of areas with records that are distinctly encouraging—for example, Israel, Nationalist China, South Korea, Hong Kong, Malaysia, Mexico, Peru, Jamaica, Central America, Tunisia, Ivory Coast, and Pakistan. Some of the current pessimism about India is as naïve as was the optimism of the early 1950's; India has made measurable progress without sacrificing its democratic institutions and has laid a foundation for better-balanced growth in the years to come.

The export earnings of less developed countries grew slowly during the 1950's. But they were in reality high to begin with, partly because of the Korean War boom. Their slow expansion was responsible for much of the gloom about trade prospects during the 1960's. The export proceeds of the developing countries, however, rose at an impressive annual rate of 6 percent during the first half of the Development Decade. Exports of manufactured products, despite the obstacles they encounter, grew at a thumping 14 percent per year—from an admittedly low base.

Significant social progress has also been made, particularly in the fields of education and health, where the payoff is slow but cumulative. School enrollment has risen spectacularly at every level. Literacy rates are up significantly. Maternal and child mortality have been reduced. Successful campaigns against malaria, yaws, smallpox, tuberculosis, and other scourges have been conducted. In the field of health the gap between the more developed and the less developed countries has probably narrowed.[17] Housing has remained thoroughly inadequate, urban problems are accumulating, and industrial production, though it has doubled in the last decade, has provided far fewer jobs than had been expected of it.

There is no UN report on the world political situation and, as yet, we know even less about political development than about economic and social development. Furthermore, the political record of the last quarter century has not been adequately appraised. In many respects the liquidation of vast colonial empires has been astonishingly orderly. The number of nation-states is about two and one-half times what it was in 1945. The new nations have produced a respectable number of remarkable leaders. Heartening examples of democratic development at the grass roots can be cited, but democracy, alas, is not a form of government acquired automatically as levels of living improve; military take-overs, coups, and revolutions continue to occur. The foreign policies pursued by the less developed countries are, except for a few cases of rampant nationalism, readily understandable from the point of view of their own immediate interests and least threatening to the rest of the international community where development itself is most obviously taking root. The new states have hastened to join the United Nations and other international organizations and on the whole have played responsible roles in them.[18]

One can concede that significant progress has been made by the less developed countries since the end of World War II while wondering how much, if any of it, should be attributed to multilateral efforts. Unfortunately, the multilateral contribution to the substantial but unevenly distributed gains noted above cannot be isolated and measured. It has assuredly been important and, equally assuredly I suspect, been minor for most of the major countries though major perhaps for some of the minor countries.

Instructive and influential as the publications of international agencies have been, they constitute a small segment of the burgeoning literature on development. Much appreciated as the multilateral technical assistance programs are, they are not demonstrably superior to bilateral programs and they probably account for less than 10 percent of the technical as-

[17] *1963 report on the World Social Situation* (United Nations Publication Sales No: 63.IV.4 [UN Document E/CN.5/375/Rev.1]) (United Nations, 1963), Chapter I.

[18] This summary of the postwar record of the less developed countries draws heavily on Robert E. Asher, *International Development and the U.S. National Interest* (Washington: National Planning Association, 1967), pp. 21–24.

sistance provided. As already noted, only a small fraction of the capital assistance comes directly through multilateral channels, though the indirect total is considerably larger. The improved export earnings of the less developed countries are attributable to a much greater extent to full employment policies and attendant higher levels of demand in the high-income countries than to the trade programs of multilateral agencies.

Had there been no United Nations, the formation of a political bloc of less developed countries might have been delayed a few more years. Pressures to pursue sensible economic and social policies would have been weaker and more intermittent. Progressive forces in less developed countries would have felt more isolated and ignorant. Without the United Nations and related agencies the emphasis given to the special difficulties of the less developed countries would have been less universal, the analysis less searching, and the incentives to action less compelling. The problems would nevertheless have worked their way to the center of the world stage, for their solution is by almost any standard the major economic and social challenge of the day.

VI

The foundations for more rapid growth in the 1970's are present if governments have the wit and the will to build upon them. National integration, I think, is almost a prerequisite for regional or global integration, and many of the new nations have a long way to go before achieving a genuine sense of national identity and mission, a fusion of tribal and parochial loyalties, and a lasting measure of internal social integration. Backsliding and disorder are to be expected. They will more often reflect differences of opinion about the pace of progress than about the need for modernization.

As the nations of the world modernize and more of them move into a middle-income group, interdependence will assume new meaning. Foreign trade will grow, people will immigrate to as well as emigrate from developing areas, ideas will circulate more readily, and technology will be more easily shared. "The very process of modernization within societies tends to foster international integration without the assistance of formal outside institutions."[19] Nevertheless, international institutions and the consultations, confrontations, and cooperative practices that they institutionalize can speed the process.

International integration can be regional or global. Greater integration at the regional level, now being pursued with enthusiasm, may be a

[19] C. E. Black, *The Dynamics of Modernization: A Study in Comparative History* (New York: Harper & Row, 1966), p. 154.

prerequisite for integration on a wider scale. The larger the number of countries involved and the greater their differences in size, wealth, history, and cultural heritage the harder it is to weld effective international machinery. Concentration on the creation of regional machinery without a concurrent strengthening of interregional bonds, however, can produce powerful, intransigent regional blocs that will make integration on a wider scale, or even peaceful coexistence, much more difficult.

The nations of the world have had very little experience in seeking accommodation on the basis of the welfare of all. They cling tenaciously to obsolescent concepts and tend to support international programs only if they can explain to their inhabitants that national sovereignty remains unimpaired. The building of international community must be, so to speak, undetectable to those involved. A gossamer net of imperceptible weight has to be woven a thread at a time.

Weaving without a master pattern on looms at different locations, with numerous hands on each shuttle, is not conducive to efficiency. During the immediate future the increased political strength of the less developed countries is likely to be reflected in more machinery to deal with specific problems and to overlap or submerge machinery in which the less developed countries lack confidence. A good deal of it will be outside of the universal framework of the United Nations. Some of the industrialized nations that have been the major providers of development assistance may decide to rely more heavily on multilateral machinery. Their motive will be to limit their bilateral commitments rather than to fortify the multilateral approach.

So long as the international machinery remains dependent on voluntary contributions and pass-the-hat exercises, its capacity to mobilize resources and promulgate policies favoring development will be limited. International ownership of a revenue-producing resource or possession of the power to tax would represent a real breakthrough in national versus international relations. Such authority is more likely to develop as a corollary than as a forerunner of unremitting commitment to the brotherhood of man.

In the perspective of human experience the twenty-odd years since the end of World War II constitute a fleeting moment. One hundred years from now, if nuclear holocaust has been avoided, people everywhere may look with pride upon the sturdy, flexible, efficient network of international institutions catering to their needs. Ignorant of the patchwork of yesteryear, forgetting how wary and recalcitrant they were at every turning point, they may, with their customary disdain for history, say in all sincerity, "We planned it that way."

Selected Bibliography

GENERAL REVIEW OF TRADE AND ECONOMIC DEVELOPMENT

Asher, Robert E. and others. *The United Nations and Promotion of the General Welfare.* Washington: Brookings Institution, 1957. xvi + 1216 pp.

Balassa, Bela. *Trade Liberalization Among Industrial Countries: Objectives and Alternatives.* New York: McGraw-Hill (for the Council on Foreign Relations), 1967. xvi + 251 pp.

———. *Trade Prospects for Developing Countries.* Homewood, Ill: Richard D. Irwin, Inc., 1964. 450 pp.

Balassa, Bela and associates. *Studies in Trade Liberalization: Problems and Prospects for the Industrial Countries.* Baltimore, Md: Johns Hopkins Press, 1967. 346 pp.

Bhagwati, Jagdish. *The Economics of Underdeveloped Countries.* London: Weidenfeld and Nicolson, 1966. 252 pp.

Brendel, Gerhard. "The Developing Countries and World Trade." *German Foreign Policy,* 1965 (Vol. 4, No. 6), pp. 443–451.

Broches, Aron. "Le financement du développement économique: Aspects politiques, juridiques, et économiques." *Chronique de Politique Etrangère,* July 1967 (Vol. 20, No. 4), pp. 401–417.

Butler, William. "Trade and the Less Developed Areas." *Foreign Affairs,* January 1963 (Vol. 41, No. 2), pp. 372–383.

Cooper, C. A. and B. F. Massell. *Toward a General Theory of Customs Unions for Developing Countries.* (RAND Corporation paper P-2919-1.) Santa Monica, Calif: RAND Corporation, 1965. 27 pp.

Davis, Frederick. "The Regulation and Control of Foreign Trade." *Columbia Law Review,* December 1966 (Vol. 66, No. 8), pp. 1428–1460.

Delaume, Georges R. *Legal Aspects of International Lending and Economic Development Financing.* Dobbs Ferry, N.Y: Oceana Publications, 1967. 371 pp.

De Vries, Margaret G. "Trade and Exchange Policy and Economic Development: Two Decades of Evolving Views." *Oxford Economic Papers,* March 1966 (Vol. 18, No. 1), pp. 19–44.

Diebold, William, Jr. "New Horizons in Foreign Trade." *Foreign Affairs,* January 1967 (Vol. 45, No. 2), pp. 291–303.

Ebb, Lawrence F. *Regulation and Protection of International Business: Cases, Comments and Materials.* St. Paul, Minn: West Publishing Co., 1964. See especially Part III, "National and International Regulation of Government Barriers to International Trade," pp. 679–876.

"The Encouragement and Protection of Investment in Developing Countries." A report of a conference held on September 28–29, 1961, under the joint auspices of The Federal Trust for Education and Research, The British Institute of International and Comparative Law, and The Institute of Advanced Legal Studies. *International and Comparative Law Quarterly* (London), 1962 (Supplementary Publication No. 3).

Evans, John W. *U.S. Trade Policy: New Legislation for the Next Round.* New York: Harper & Row (for the Council on Foreign Relations), 1967. 105 pp.

Falk, Richard A. and Saul H. Mendlovitz (ed.). *The Strategy of World Order.* Vol. 4: *Disarmament and Economic Development.* New York: World Law Fund, 1966. xv + 672 pp.

Fatouros, A. A. "Comments on International Law and Economic Development." *Proceedings of the American Society of International Law,* 60th annual meeting, Washington, April 28–30, 1966, pp. 18–28.

Feliciano, Florentino P. "Comments on 'The Relevance of International Law to the Development Process.'" *Proceedings of the American Society of International Law,* 60th annual meeting, Washington, April 28–30, 1966, pp. 15–17.

459

Frank, Isaiah. "New Perspectives on Trade and Development." *Foreign Affairs*, April 1967 (Vol. 45, No. 3), pp. 520–540.

Friedman, Irving S. "In defence of development." *World Today*, April 1966 (Vol. 22, No. 4), pp. 142–151.

Friedmann, Wolfgang G. "The Relevance of International Law to the Processes of Economic and Social Development." *Proceedings of the American Society of International Law*, 60th annual meeting, Washington, April 28–30, 1966, pp. 8–15.

Friedmann, Wolfgang G., George Kalmanoff, and Robert F. Meagher. *International Financial Aid*. New York: Columbia University Press, 1966. 498 pp.

Galbraith, Virginia L. *World Trade in Transition*. Washington: Public Affairs Press, 1965. 104 pp.

Gardiner, R. K. A. "Development and Trade in Africa." *African Affairs*, January 1966 (Vol. 65, No. 258), pp. 1–14.

Gardner, Richard N. (ed.) *Blueprint for Peace*. New York: McGraw-Hill, 1966. vi + 404 pp.

———. *In Pursuit of World Order: U.S. Foreign Policy and International Organizations*. 2nd ed. revised. New York: Frederick A. Praeger, 1966.

———. "Legal-economic Problems of International Trade." *Columbia Law Review*, March 1961 (Vol. 61, No. 3), pp. 313–321.

———. "World Trade in Crisis: Legal and Policy Issues," in *The Rule of Law at the International Level*. St. Louis: Bar Association of St. Louis, 1965, pp. 12–25.

Higgins, Benjamin. *Economic Development: Principles, Problems, and Policies*. New York: W. W. Norton & Company, 1959. 803 pp.

Horowitz, Irving Louis. *Three Worlds of Development: The Theory and Practice of International Stratification*. New York: Oxford University Press, 1966. xiv + 475 pp.

Howell, David. "New Paths for World Trade." *Journal of Common Market Studies*, July 1965 (Vol. 3, No. 3), pp. 293–301.

"Informe de Raul Prebisch, Secretario General de la Conferencia de las Naciones Unidas sobre Comercio y Desarrollo." *Revista de Economía Política*, January–April 1964 (No. 36), pp. 205–354.

International Association of Legal Sciences. *Les Aspects Juridiques du Développement Economique. Legal Aspects of Economic Development*. Etudes préparées à la requête de l'Unesco sous la direction de Andre Tunc. Paris: Librairie Dalloz, 1966. 206 pp.

International Financing and Investment. Proceedings of the Second Conference on International Trade and Investment, Yale University Law School, 1962. Edited by John F. McDaniels. Dobbs Ferry, N.Y: Oceana Publications (for the World Community Association), 1964. 738 pp.

Jacobson, Harold Karan. *The USSR and the UN's Economic and Social Activities*. Notre Dame, Ind: University of Notre Dame Press, 1963. xviii + 309 pp.

Johnson, Harry G. *Economic Policies Toward Less Developed Countries*. Washington: Brookings Institution, 1967. 279 pp.

———. *The World Economy at the Crossroads: A Survey of Current Problems of Money, Trade, and Economic Development*. New York: Oxford University Press, 1966. 106 pp.

Joyce, James Avery. *Decade of Development: The Challenge of the Underdeveloped Nations*. New York: Coward-McCann, Inc., 1967. 121 pp.

Kaldor, Nicholas. "International Trade and Economic Development." *Journal of Modern African Studies*, December 1964 (Vol. 2, No. 4), pp. 491–511.

Kirdar, Üner. *The Structure of United Nations Economic Aid to Underdeveloped Countries*. The Hague: Martinus Nijhoff, 1966. xxiv + 361 pp.

Kitamura, Hiroshi. "Foreign Trade: Foreign Trade Problems in Planned Economic Development," in *Economic Development: With Special Reference to East Asia*. Proceedings of a Conference held by the International Economic Association. Edited by Kenneth Berrill. New York: St. Martin's Press, 1964, pp. 191–211.

Krivine, David (ed.). *Fiscal and Monetary Problems in Developing States*. Proceedings of the Third Rehovath Conference. New York: Frederick A. Praeger, 1967. 404 pp.

Lacharriere, Guy de. *Commerce Extérieur et Sous-Développement*. Paris: Presses Universitaires de France, 1964. 279 pp.

Lakdawala, D. T. "Commercial Policy and Economic Growth," in *Trade Theory and Commercial Policy in Relation to Underdeveloped Countries*. Proceedings of the seminar on international trade held under the auspices of the Indian School of International Studies in March 1963. Edited by A. K. Das Gupta. London: Asia Publishing House, 1965. pp. 29–41.

Lasswell, Harold D. "The Relevance of International Law to the Development Process." *Proceedings of the American Society of International Law*, 60th annual meeting, Washington, April 28–30, 1966, pp. 1–8.

Lewis, W. Arthur. "Economic Development and World Trade," in *Problems in Economic Development*. Proceedings of a conference held by the International Economic Association. Edited by E. A. G. Robinson. London: Macmillan, 1965, pp. 483–497.

Little, I. M. and J. M. Clifford. *International Aid: A discussion of the flow of public resources from rich to poor countries, with particular reference to British policy*. London: George Allen and Unwin Ltd., 1966. 302 pp.

Mangone, Gerard J. (ed.) *UN Administration of Economic and Social Programs*. (Columbia University Studies in International Organization, No. 3.) New York: Columbia University Press, 1966. xxii + 291 pp.

Marcus, Edward and Mildred Rendl Marcus. *International Trade and Finance*. New York: Pitman Publishing Corporation, 1965. 616 pp.

Meier, Gerald M. *International Trade and Development*. New York: Harper & Row, 1963. 208 pp.

Metzger, Stanley D. "Development of Rules Relating to International Trade." *Proceedings of the American Society of International Law*, 59th annual meeting, Washington, April 22–24, 1965, pp. 28–33.

————. *International Law, Trade and Finance: Realities and Prospects*. Dobbs Ferry, N.Y: Oceana Publications, 1962. 184 pp.

————. *Law of International Trade: Documents and Readings*. 2 vols. Washington: Lerner Law Book Company, 1966. 1753 pp.

Millikan, Max F. (ed.) *National Economic Planning*. New York: National Bureau of Economic Research, 1967. 413 pp.

Montgomery, John D. *Foreign Aid in International Politics*. Englewood Cliffs, N.J: Prentice Hall, 1967.

Nwogugu, E. I. *The Legal Problems of Foreign Investment in Developing Countries*. Dobbs Ferry, N.Y: Oceana Publications, 1965. 320 pp.

Onitiri, H. M. A. "The Terms of Trade," in *Problems in Economic Development*. Proceedings of a conference held by the International Economic Association. Edited by E. A. G. Robinson. London: Macmillan, 1965, pp. 510–529.

Parthasarathy, G. "The Rich and the Poor Nations and International Economic Co-operation," in *The Indian Yearbook of International Affairs, 1963*. Madras: Diocesan Press, 1963. pp. 465–486.

Patterson, Gardner. *Discrimination in International Trade: The Policy Issues: 1945–1965*. Princeton, N.J: Princeton University Press, 1966. 414 pp.

Paul, Arthur. "The Role of Trade in Development Program," in *Developmental Revolution: North Africa, Middle East, South Asia*. Washington: Middle East Institute, 1963. pp. 226–236.

Pincus, John A. *Trade, Aid, and Development: The Rich and Poor Nations*. New York: McGraw-Hill (for the Council on Foreign Relations), 1967. 400 pp.

Prebisch, Raúl. "Some Fundamental Problems of World Trade." *UN Monthly Chronicle*, February 1966 (Vol. 3, No. 2), pp. 44–52.

Pryor, Frederic L. "Economic Growth and the Terms of Trade." *Oxford Economic Papers*, March 1966 (Vol. 18, No. 1), pp. 45–57.

Re Qua, Eloise G. and Jane Statham. *The Developing Nations: A Guide to Information Sources Concerning Their Economic, Political, Technical and Social Problems*. (Management Information Guide: 5.) Detroit: Gale Research Company, 1965. 339 pp.

Robinson, Austin. "Foreign Trade: Foreign Trade in a Developing Economy," in *Economic Development: With Special Reference to East Asia*. Proceedings of a Conference held by the International Economic Association. Edited by Kenneth Berrill. New York: St. Martin's Press, 1964, pp. 212–227.

Sarre, David A. Godwin. "The Law of International Trade and the Developing Countries," in *Journal of Business Law: 1963.* Edited by Clive M. Schmitthoff. London: Stevens & Sons Limited, 1963. pp. 108–118.

Seers, Dudley. "International Trade and Development—The Special Interests of Africa," in *African Primary Products & International Trade.* Papers delivered at an international seminar in the University of Edinburgh, September 1964. Edited by I. G. Stewart and H. W. Ord. Edinburgh: Edinburgh University Press, 1965. pp. 19–25.

Seidman, Robert B. "Law and Economic Development in Independent English-speaking Sub-Saharan Africa." *Wisconsin Law Review,* Fall 1966 (Vol. 1966, No. 4), pp. 999–1070.

Sewell, J. P. *Functionalism and World Politics: A Study Based on United Nations Programs Financing Economic Development.* London: Oxford University Press, 1966. 359 pp.

Shonfield, Andrew. *The Attack on World Poverty.* New York: Random House, 1962. 269 pp.

Society for International Development. *International Development: 1965.* Edited by Stefan H. Rabock and Leo M. Solomon. Dobbs Ferry, N.Y: Oceana Publications, 1966. 197 pp.

Stanovnik, Janez. "Aid, Trade and Economic Development: The Changing Political Context." *Foreign Affairs,* January 1964 (Vol. 42, No. 2), pp. 242–254.

Stern, Robert M. "Policies for Trade and Development." *International Conciliation,* May 1964 (No. 548).

Stewart, Charles F. and George B. Simmons (comp.). *A Bibliography of International Business.* New York: Columbia University Press, 1964. 603 pp.

Sufrin, Sidney C. *Technical Assistance—Theory and Guidelines.* Syracuse, N.Y: Syracuse University Press, 1966. 160 pp.

Thompson, Dennis (ed.). *Expansion of World Trade: Legal Problems and Techniques.* A conference report published under the auspices of the British Institute of International and Comparative Law. London: Stevens & Sons Limited, 1965. 81 pp.

"Trade Problems between Countries having Different Economic and Social Systems." *Economic Bulletin for Europe,* November 1964 (Vol. 16, No. 2), pp. 31–87.

Trade Theory and Commercial Policy in Relation to Underdeveloped Countries. Proceedings of the seminar on international trade held under the auspices of the Indian School of International Studies in March 1963. Edited by A. K. Gupta. London: Asia Publishing House, 1965. 108 pp.

United Nations Department of Economic and Social Affairs. *Trade and Development: Trends, Needs and Policies.* Part I: *World Economic Survey: 1963.* (UN Documents ST/ECA/84, E/3408.) New York: United Nations, 1964. 306 pp.

United States Tariff Commission. *List of Selected Publications Relating to United States Tariff and Commercial Policy and to the General Agreement on Tariffs and Trade.* (Tariff Commission Publication No. 83.) 7th edition. Washington: U.S. Government Printing Office, March 1963. 181 pp.

U.S. Congress, Senate, Committee on Foreign Relations, Subcommittee on the United Nations Charter. *The United Nations and the Specialized Agencies.* (Staff Study No. 10.) Washington: U.S. Government Printing Office, 1955. 37 pp.

Vartikar, V. S. "The Role of Commercial Policy in the Development of a Subsistence Economy." *Weltwirtschaftliches Archiv,* 1966 (Vol. 95, No. 1), pp. 102–125.

Ward, Barbara. *The Decade of Development: A Study in Frustration?* (Occasional Paper 9.) London: Institute of Economic Affairs, 1966. 58 pp.

Weintraub, Sidney. *The Foreign-Exchange Gap of the Developing Countries.* (Essays in International Finance, No. 48.) Princeton, N.J: International Finance Section, Department of Economics, Princeton University, September 1965. 27 pp.

Woods, George D. "The Development Decade in the Balance." *Foreign Affairs,* January 1966 (Vol. 44, No. 2), pp. 206–215.

TRADE EXPANSION ACT OF 1962 AND THE KENNEDY ROUND

(See also the listings under the General Agreement on Tariffs and Trade)

Ball, George W. "Major Aspects of the Trade Expansion Act." Department of State *Bulletin,* April 9, 1962 (Vol. 46, No. 1189), pp. 597–605.

Blumenthal, W. Michael. "The Kennedy Round." Department of State *Bulletin*, April 26, 1965 (Vol. 52, No. 1348), pp. 628–635.

Brainard, Harry G. "The Trade Expansion Act—1962." *Business Topics*, Winter 1963 (Vol. 11, No. 1), pp. 7–19.

Camps, Miriam. "The Kennedy Round." *World Today*, May 1964 (Vol. 20, No. 5), pp. 215–222.

Clubb, Bruce E. "Dismantling Trade Barriers: Implementation of the Trade Expansion Act." *University of Illinois Law Forum*, Fall 1965 (Vol. 1965), pp. 366–398.

———. "Dismantling Trade Barriers: Implementation of the Trade Expansion Act," in *International Trade, Investment, and Organization*. Edited by Wayne R. LaFave and Peter Hay. Urbana: University of Illinois Press, 1967. pp. 32–64.

Coppock, Joseph D. "Trade Policy Choices Facing the United States." Department of State *Bulletin*, June 25, 1962 (Vol. 46, No. 1200), pp. 1027–1031.

Dale, William B. "United States Programs to Expand International Trade." *The Patent, Trademark, and Copyright Journal of Research and Education*, 1962 (Vol. 6, Conference Number), pp. 132–138.

Dugimont, Jacques. "Les Négociations du Kennedy Round." *Etudes Economiques*, April 1966 (Nos. 127–128), pp. 85–104.

General Agreement on Tariffs and Trade. "Obstacles to the Trade of Less-Developed Countries," in *Proceedings of the Meeting of Ministers (27–30 November 1961)*. Geneva, 1962. pp. 89–170.

Givens, Richard A. "The Search for an Alternative to Protection." *Fordham Law Review*, 1961 (Vol. 30), pp. 17–58.

Gossett, William T. "The Kennedy Round—Progress and Promise." Department of State *Bulletin*, August 19, 1963 (Vol. 49, No. 1260), pp. 291–296.

Greggersen, Joachim. *Trade Agreements Program und Trade Expansion Act of 1962 der Vereingten Staaten von Amerika*. Köln: Bundesstelle für Aussenhandels-information, 1964. 76 pp.

Herter, Christian A. "The Kennedy Round: A Progress Report." Department of State *Bulletin*, July 5, 1965 (Vol. 53, No. 1358), pp. 31–34.

———. "U.S. Aims in the Kennedy Round." *Atlantic Community Quarterly*, Summer 1964 (Vol. 2, No. 2), pp. 240–246.

Johnson, Harry G. "The Kennedy Round." *World Today*, August 1967 (Vol. 23, No. 8), pp. 326–333.

Kenen, Peter B. "The Trade Expansion Act of 1962 and U.S. Tariff Policy." *American Review* (Bologna), December 1962 (Vol. 2, No. 3), pp. 118–147.

Kennedy, John F. "A New Foreign Trade Program." Department of State *Bulletin*, February 12, 1962 (Vol. 46, No. 1181), pp. 231–238.

"La loi Américaine 'd'expansion du commerce': Réflexions sur quelques problèmes futurs." *Revue du Marché Commun*, February 1963 (No. 55), pp. 67–71.

"La 'longue marche' du Kennedy Round." *Revue du Marché Commun*, November 1964 (No. 74), pp. 480–485.

Mathews, Craig. "Non-tariff Import Barriers and the Kennedy Round." *Common Market Law Review*, 1965 (Vol. 11), pp. 403–419.

Metzger, Stanley D. "The Prospects for the Kennedy Round," in *Journal of Business Law: 1965*. Edited by Clive M. Schmitthoff. London: Stevens & Sons Limited, 1965. pp. 103–113.

———. *Trade Agreements and the Kennedy Round: An analysis of the economic, legal and political aspects of the Trade Expansion Act of 1962 and the prospects for the Kennedy Round of negotiations*. Fairfax, Va: Coiner Publications, Ltd., 1964. 119 pp.

———. "The Trade Expansion Act of 1962." *Georgetown Law Journal*, Spring 1963 (Vol. 51, No. 3), pp. 425–469.

"La négociation Kennedy. Quelques points d'interrogation." *Revue du Marché Commun*, July–August 1966 (No. 93), pp. 633–637.

Reischer, Otto Richard. *Trade Adjustment in Theory and Practice*. Prepared for the Subcommittee on Foreign Economic Policy of the Joint Economic Committee, Congress of the United States. Washington: U.S. Government Printing Office, 1961. 98 pp.

Robertson, James. "Adjustment Assistance under the Trade Expansion Act of 1962: A Will-o-the-Wisp." *George Washington Law Review*, June 1965 (Vol. 33, No. 5), pp. 1088–1107.

Roussakis, Emmanuel N. "Les négociations Kennedy et la politique commerciale des États-Unis d'Amerique." *Revue du Marché Commun*, April 1964 (No. 68), pp. 168–173.

Sonderegger, Fritz. "Die Kennedy-Runde als Integrationsinstrument." *Europa-Archiv*, May 25, 1966 (21st Year, No. 10), pp. 377–382.

Surrey, Walter Sterling. "Legal Problems to be Encountered in the Operation of the Trade Expansion Act of 1962." *North Carolina Law Review*, 1963 (Vol. 41), pp. 389–400.

"Trade Expansion Act of 1962." *International Legal Materials*, August 1962 (Vol. 1, No. 1), pp. 340–371.

Weiss, Leonard W. *The New Trade Expansion Act.* (Department of State Publication No. 7372.) Washington: U.S. Government Printing Office, 1962. 18 pp.

Wells, S. J. "The Kennedy Round," in *The Year Book of World Affairs: 1965.* Edited by George W. Keeton and Georg Schwarzenberger. London: Stevens & Sons Limited, 1966. pp. 201–219.

Wilbur, Richard C. "International Aspects of United States Trade Policy." *Notre Dame Lawyer*, 1961 (Vol. 37, No. 1), pp. 98–105.

Wortmann, Herman R. "Is the Kennedy Round a Giant Step Toward Trade Liberalization?" *Business Horizons*, Spring 1965 (Vol. 8, No. 1), pp. 25–34.

UNITED NATIONS CONFERENCE ON TRADE AND DEVELOPMENT

Ali, S. Amjad. "United Nations Conference on Trade and Development." *Pakistan Horizon*, Third Quarter 1964 (Vol. 17, No. 3), pp. 262–271.

Bloch, Henry Simon. *The Challenge of the World Trade Conference.* Occasional Paper of the School of International Affairs, Columbia University. New York: Columbia University Press, 1965. 56 pp.

Bochet, Bernard. "Notes sur l'Organisation et les Travaux de la Conference des Nations Unies sur le Commerce et le Développement." *Tiers-Monde*, October–December 1964 (Vol. 5, No. 20), pp. 865–884.

"La Conférence des Nations-Unies sur le Commerce et le Developpment." *Développement et Civilisations*, September 1964 (No. 19), pp. 20–63.

"La Conférence des Nations unies sur le commerce et le développement. Deux ans d'activité." *Chronique de Politique Étrangère*, March 1967 (Vol. 20, No. 2), pp. 153–226.

Dell, Sidney. "UNCTAD: Retrospect and Prospect," in *Annual Review of United Nations Affairs: 1964–1965.* Edited by Richard N. Swift. Dobbs Ferry, N.Y: Oceana Publications, 1966. pp. 52–85.

Dharma, Kumar. "U.N. Conference on Trade & Development." *India Quarterly*, July–September 1965 (Vol. 21, No. 3), pp. 311–315.

Etra, Aaron. "Time for a Change: the U.N. Conference on Trade and Development." *Revue belge de droit international*, 1966 (Vol. 2, No. 1), pp. 50–67.

Fletcher, Arthur. "What UNCOTAD [*sic*] is About." *Far Eastern Economic Review*, March 26, 1964 (Vol. 43, No. 13), pp. 669–673.

Frank, Isaiah. "Aid, Trade and Economic Development: Issues Before the U.N. Conference." *Foreign Affairs*, January 1964 (Vol. 42, No. 2), pp. 210–226.

Gal-Edd, Israel. "A Framework for Trade between Developed and Less-Developed Countries," in *Proceedings of the United Nations Conference on Trade and Development, Geneva, 23 March–16 July 1964.* Vol. V: *Financing and Invisibles, Institutional Arrangements.* (UN Document E/CONF.46/141/Vol. V.) New York: United Nations, 1964. pp. 493–501.

Gall, Henryk. "Conferencia de las Naciones Unidas sobre Comercio y Desarrollo." *Foro Internacional* (Mexico), July–September 1964 (Vol. 5, No. 1), pp. 99–129.

Gardner, Richard N. "GATT and the United Nations Conference on Trade and Development." *International Organization*, Autumn 1964 (Vol. 18, No. 4), pp. 685–704.

Goodwin, G. L. "The United Nations Conference on Trade and Development: Beginning of a New Era?," in *The Year Book of World Affairs: 1965.* Edited by George W. Keeton and Georg Schwarzenberger. London: Stevens & Sons Limited, 1966. pp. 1–25.

Haelen, A. van. "La première année d'existence de l'U.N.C.T.A.D." *Les Problèmes de l'Europe*, 1965 (No. 30), pp. 27–41.

Hagras, Kamal M. *United Nations Conference on Trade and Development: A Case Study in U.N. Diplomacy.* New York: Frederick A. Praeger, 1965. 184 pp.

Hasselblatt, Waldemar B. "Die Weltkonferenz für Handel und Entwicklung." *Wirtschaftsdienst* (Hamburg), January 1964 (44th Year, No. 1), pp. 25–30.

Hoffman, Michael L. "UNCTAD and the Businessman." *International Development Review*, September 1965 (Vol. 7, No. 3), pp. 11–14.

"International Monetary Issues and the Developing Countries: Report of the Group of Experts" (UN Documents TD/B/32, TD/B/C.3/6, November 1, 1965).

Jeftić, Bora. "Consultations of the 77 Developing Countries." *Review of International Affairs* (Belgrade), April 20, 1966 (Vol. 17, No. 385), pp. 18–20.

Johnson, G. Griffith. "A Perspective on the United Nations Conference on Trade and Development." Department of State *Bulletin*, March 16, 1964 (Vol. 50, No. 1290), pp. 410–415.

Lacharrière, Guy de. "La Conférence des Nations Unies sur le commerce et le Développement. Bilans et perspectives." *Revue du Marché Commun*, October 1964 (No. 73), pp. 438–443.

Maes, Albert. "La signification de la conférence des Nations Unies sur le commerce et le développement." *Chronique de Politique Etrangère*, January 1965 (Vol. 18, No. 1), pp. 31–49.

New Directions for World Trade. Proceedings of a Chatham House Conference, Bellagio, September 16–24, 1963. New York: Oxford University Press, 1964. 241 pp.

Prebisch, Raúl. "Portée de la Conférence des Nations Unies sur le Commerce et le Développement: Rapport adressé au Secrétaire général des Nations Unies par le Secrétaire général de la Conférence." *Tiers-Monde*, July–September 1964 (Supplement, Vol. 5, No. 19). 16 pp.

―――. "Spirit of Conciliation." *UN Monthly Chronicle*, July 1964 (Vol. 1, No. 3), pp. 71–77.

Proehl, Paul O. "The Geneva Proposals to Reform International Trade: 'A Clear Convergence of Responsibilities'?" *George Washington Law Review*, June 1965 (Vol. 33, No. 5), pp. 1031–1066.

Shonfield, Andrew. "Trade as a Tool of Development—The Issues at Geneva." *International Affairs*, April 1964 (Vol. 40, No. 2), pp. 219–231.

"The Significance of the United Nations Conference on Trade and Development: Report to the Secretary-General" (UN Document E/CONF.46/140, July 9, 1964). 15 pp.

Silva, G. R. W. de. "Problems of trade promotion of developing countries." *International Trade Forum* (Geneva), December 1964 (Vol. 1, No. 1), pp. 10–14.

Singer, H. W. "The Geneva Conference on Trade and Development," in *Annual Review of United Nations Affairs: 1963–1964.* Edited by Richard N. Swift. Dobbs Ferry, N.Y: Oceana Publications, 1965. pp. 47–79.

Subham, Malcolm. "UNCOTAD [*sic*] at Work." *Far Eastern Economic Review*, April 30, 1964 (Vol. 44, No. 5), pp. 257–259.

"Tough Issues for New UN Trade Board." *The Banker* (London), April 1965 (Vol. 115, No. 470), pp. 230–235.

Towards a New Trade Policy for Development: Report by the Secretary-General of the United Nations Conference on Trade and Development. (UN Document E/CONF.46/3.) New York: United Nations, February 1964. 125 pp.

United Nations Trade and Development Board. *Report of the Trade and Development Board 1 January–29 October 1965.* (General Assembly *Official Records* [20th session], Supplement No. 15.) New York: United Nations, 1965. 79 pp.

United Nations Trade and Development Board, Committee on Invisibles and Financing Related to Trade. "Consideration of the Adequacy of the Rates of Growth Achieved by the Developing Countries: Problems and Issues: Note by the Secretary-General of UNCTAD" (UN Document TD/B/C.3/4, October 1965).

Ward, Barbara. "The United Nations and the Decade of Development." *World Justice*, March 1966 (Vol. 7, No. 3), pp. 308–335.

Weintraub, Sidney. "After the U.N. Trade Conference: Lessons and Portents." *Foreign Affairs*, October 1964 (Vol. 43, No. 1), pp. 37–50.

Worsnop, Richard L. "World Trade Parleys." *Editorial Research Reports*, March 11, 1964 (No. 10).

COMMODITY AGREEMENTS

"Action by Governments to Stabilise Primary Commodity Prices." *International Labor Review*, March 1962 (Vol. 85, No. 3), pp. 207–233.

Aubrey, Henry G. "International Commodity Markets as a Factor in Development Planning," in *Science, Technology, and Development*. Vol. 8: *Organization, Planning, and Programming for Economic Development*. United States papers prepared for the United Nations Conference on the Application of Science and Technology for the Benefit of the Less Developed Areas. Washington: U.S. Government Printing Office, 1963, pp. 55–67.

Baranyai, L. and J. C. Mills. *International Commodity Agreements*. Mexico City: Centro de Estudios Monetarios Latinoamericanos, 1963. 190 pp.

Bauer, P. T. and B. S. Yamey. "Organized Commodity Stabilization with Voluntary Participation." *Oxford Economic Papers*, March 1964 (Vol. 16, No. 1), pp. 105–113.

Benoit, Emile. "Purchase Guaranties as a Means of Reducing Instability of Commodity Export Proceeds of Underdeveloped Countries." *Kyklos*, 1959 (Vol. 12, No. 3), pp. 300–306.

Bilder, Richard B. "The International Coffee Agreement: A Case History in Negotiation." *Law and Contemporary Problems*, Spring 1963 (Vol. 28, No. 2), pp. 328–391.

Black, John D. and Stanley S. Tsou. "International Commodity Arrangements." *Quarterly Journal of Economics*, August 1944 (Vol. 53, No. 4), pp. 521–552.

Blau, Gerda. "International Commodity Arrangements and Policies." *Monthly Bulletin of Agricultural Economics and Statistics* (Food and Agriculture Organization of the United Nations), September 1963 (Vol. 12, No. 9), pp. 1–9.

———. "International Commodity Arrangements and Policies—II: Commodity Export Earnings and Economic Growth." *Monthly Bulletin of Agricultural Economics and Statistics* (Food and Agriculture Organization of the United Nations), December 1963 (Vol. 12, No. 12), pp. 1–19.

———. *International Commodity Arrangements and Policies*. (Special Studies Program No. 1.) Rome: Food and Agriculture Organization of the United Nations, 1964. 52 pp.

———. "International Commodity Arrangements," in *Problems in Economic Development*. Proceedings of a conference held by the International Economic Association. Edited by E. A. G. Robinson. London: Macmillan, 1965. pp. 553–573.

Blau, Gerda and D. A. Music. *Agricultural Commodity Trade and Development Prospects, Problems and Policies: A reference paper*. (Special Studies Program No. 2.) Rome: Food and Agriculture Organization of the United Nations, 1964. 117 pp.

Blumenthal, W. Michael. "Commodity Trade and Economic Development." Department of State *Bulletin*, May 27, 1963 (Vol. 48, No. 1248), pp. 844–848.

———. "International Commodity Problems." Department of State *Bulletin*, June 18, 1962 (Vol. 46, No. 1199), pp. 997–1002.

Brodie, Henry. "Commodity Agreements—A Partial Answer to the Trade Problems of Developing Countries." Department of State *Bulletin*, July 19, 1965 (Vol. 53, No. 1360), pp. 111–117.

Caine, Sydney. "Commodity Agreements—A New Look. *Lloyds Bank Review*, January 1963, (No. 67), pp. 14–29.

Chamber of Commerce of the United States. *Commodity Agreements—Their Role in the World Economy*. Report of the Committee on Economic Policy. Washington: U.S. Government Printing Office, 1963. 46 pp.

"Commodities and the Underdeveloped Countries." *Westminster Bank Review*, August 1963, pp. 27–37.

Dantwala, M. L. "Commodity Terms of Trade of Primary Producing Countries," in *Problems in Economic Development*. Proceedings of a conference held by the International Economic Association. Edited by E. A. G. Robinson. London: Macmillan, 1965. pp. 498–509.

Dupriez, Léon H. "Commodity and Trade Policy in Africa: The Terms of Trade of African Producers," in *Economic Development for Africa South of the Sahara*. Proceedings of a conference held by the International Economic Association. Edited by E. A. G. Robinson. London: Macmillan, 1964. pp. 503–531.

Ferrero, Romulo. "Trade of the LDC's: No Dead End for Primary Producers." *Columbia Journal of World Business*, Summer 1966 (Vol. 1, No. 3), pp. 51–62.

Gerhard, Hans W. "Commodity Trade Stabilization Through International Agreements." *Law and Contemporary Problems*, Spring 1963 (Vol. 28, No. 2), pp. 276–293.

Hanson, Simon G. "The Experience with the International Coffee Agreement." *Inter-American Economic Affairs*, Winter 1965 (Vol. 19, No. 3), pp. 27–65.

——. "The International Coffee Agreement." *Inter-American Economic Affairs*, Autumn 1963 (Vol. 17, No. 2), pp. 75–94.

Harbury, C. D. "An Experiment in Commodity Control: The International Wheat Agreement, 1949–1953." *Oxford Economic Papers*, February 1954 (Vol. 6, No. 1), pp. 82–97.

Haviland, William E. *International Commodity Agreements*. Montreal: Canadian Trade Committee, Private Planning Association of Canada, 1963. 79 pp.

Hemmi, Kenzō. "International Commodity Agreements: Reality and the Future." *The Developing Economies*, December 1964 (Vol. 2, No. 4), pp. 358–372.

Heymann, H. "The International Tin Scheme," in *Problems in Economic Development*. Proceedings of a conference held by the International Economic Association. Edited by E. A. G. Robinson. London: Macmillan, 1965. pp. 599–616.

Hooft-Welvaars, M. J. "The Organization of International Markets for Primary Commodities," in *Proceedings of the United Nations Conference on Trade and Development, Geneva, 23 March–16 July 1964*. Vol. III: *Commodity Trade*. (UN Document E/CONF.46/141/Vol. III.) New York. United Nations, 1964. pp. 458–521.

Hudson, S. C. and Randolph Gherson. "Trading Problems in International Markets: Competition in International Trade with Particular Reference to Agricultural Commodities." *Journal of Farm Economics–Canadian Journal of Agricultural Economics* (Proceedings of the joint annual meeting, August 20–22, 1958, Winnipeg, Canada, issued as December 1958 [Vol. 40, No. 5] issue of the *Journal of Farm Economics* and 1958 [Vol. 6, No. 2] issue of the *Canadian Journal of Agricultural Economics*), pp. 1717–1728.

"International Organization of Commodity Trade." *Monthly Bulletin of Agricultural Economics and Statistics* (Food and Agriculture Organization of the United Nations), February 1966 (Vol. 15, No. 2), pp. 1–8.

Janton, Henri. "L'organisation du marché des produits de base." *Développement et Civilisations*, December 1965 (No. 24), pp. 19–24.

Krumme, Robert D. "International Commodity Agreements: Purpose, Policy, and Procedure." *George Washington Law Review*, April 1963 (Vol. 31, No. 4), pp. 784–811.

Lacarte, Julio A. "The Problem of Primary Commodity Exports," in *International Development: 1965*. Edited by Stefan H. Rabock and Leo M. Solomon. Dobbs Ferry, N.Y: Oceana Publications, 1966. pp. 167–173.

Liaqat, Ali. "Principle of Buffer Stock and its Mechanism and Operation in the International Tin Agreement." *Weltwirtschaftliches Archiv*, 1966 (Vol. 95, No. 2), pp. 141–187.

MacBean, Alasdair I. *Export Instability and Economic Development*. Cambridge, Mass: Harvard University Press, 1967. 367 pp.

Meade, J. E. "International Commodity Agreements." *Lloyds Bank Review*, July 1964 (No. 73), pp. 28–42.

——. "International Commodity Agreements," in *Proceedings of the United Nations Conference on Trade and Development, Geneva, 23 March–16 July 1964*. Vol. III: *Commodity Trade*. (UN Document E/CONF.46/141/Vol. III.) New York: United Nations, 1964. pp. 451–457.

Mikesell, Raymond F. "Commodity Agreements and Aid to Developing Countries." *Law and Contemporary Problems*, Spring 1963 (Vol. 28, No. 2), pp. 294–312.

——. "Commodity agreements and aid to developing countries," in *Law of International Trade: Documents and Readings*. Edited by Stanley D. Metzger. 2 vols. Washington: Lerner Law Book Company, 1966. Vol. II, pp. 1178–1201.

Nichols, Clarence W. "Policy Problems in International Trade of Agricultural Products." Department of State *Bulletin*, March 16, 1964 (Vol. 50, No. 1290), pp. 416–423.

Onitiri, H. M. A. "The Role of International Organizations in Developing African Primary Products," in *African Primary Products & International Trade*. Papers delivered at an international seminar in the University of Edinburgh, September 1964. Edited by I. G. Stewart and H. W. Ord. Edinburgh: Edinburgh University Press, 1965. pp. 8–18.

Pincus, John A. "Aid, Trade and Economic Development: What Policy for Commodities?" *Foreign Affairs,* January 1964 (Vol. 42, No. 2), pp. 227–241.

———. "Commodity Agreements: Bonanza or Illusion?" *Columbia Journal of World Business,* January–February 1967 (Vol. 2, No. 1), pp. 41–50.

Richter, John Hans. *Agricultural Protection and Trade: Proposals for an International Policy.* New York: Frederick A. Praeger, 1964. xi + 148 pp.

Rowe, J. W. F. *Primary Commodities in International Trade.* London: Cambridge University Press, 1965. 223 pp.

Schmidt, Wilson E. "The Case Against Commodity Agreements." *Law and Contemporary Problems,* Spring 1963 (Vol. 28, No. 2), pp. 313–327.

Swerling, Boris C. *Current Issues in Commodity Policy.* (Essays in International Finance No. 38.) Princeton, N.J: International Finance Section, Department of Economics, Princeton University, 1962. 41 pp.

———. "Financial Alternatives to International Commodity Stabilization." *Canadian Journal of Economics and Political Science,* November 1964 (Vol. 30, No. 4), pp. 526–537.

———. "Principles of Economic Policy, Consistent and Inconsistent: International Commodity Stabilization: Problems of International Commodity Stabilization." *American Economic Review,* May 1963 (Vol. 53, No. 2), pp. 65–111.

Tarr, R. "Bibliographie commentée sur le commerce international des produits de base et la stabilisation de leurs prix." *Les Problèmes de l'Europe,* 1961 (No. 14), pp. 179–189.

United Nations Cocoa Conference. "Preparation of Draft International Cocoa Agreement" (UN Document TD/COCOA.1/3, April 18, 1966).

United Nations Economic Commission for Africa. "International Action for Commodity Stabilization and the Role of Africa" (UN Document E/CN.14/68, November 5, 1960).

Walker, Herman. "The International Law of Commodity Agreements." *Law and Contemporary Problems,* Spring 1963 (Vol. 28, No. 2), pp. 392–415.

COMPENSATORY FINANCING

"Compensatory financing of export fluctuations." Central Bank of Egypt *Economic Review,* 1963 (Vol. 3, No. 1), pp. 1–13.

"Fund Policies and Procedures in Relation to the Compensatory Financing of Commodity Fluctuations." *International Monetary Fund Staff Papers,* 1960 (Vol. 8), pp. 1–76.

Grubel, Herbert G. "The Case against an International Commodity Reserve Currency." *Oxford Economic Papers,* March 1965 (Vol. 17, No. 1), pp. 130–135.

Hart, Albert G. "Monetary Reform to Further Economic Development." *Political Science Quarterly,* September 1964 (Vol. 79, No. 3), pp. 360–377.

International Bank for Reconstruction and Development. *Supplementary Financial Measures. A Study Requested by the United Nations Conference on Trade and Development, 1964.* Washington, 1965. 125 pp.

International Monetary Fund. *Compensatory Financing of Export Fluctuations: A Report by the International Monetary Fund on Compensatory Financing of the Fluctuations in Exports of Primary Exporting Countries.* Washington, 1963. 27 pp.

Kindleberger, Charles P. "Terms of Trade for Primary Products," in *Natural Resources and International Development.* Edited by Marion Clawson. Baltimore, Md: Johns Hopkins Press, 1964. pp. 339–365.

Kruse-Rodenacker, Albrecht. *Die Organisation der Weltagrarmärkte: Eine gemeinsame Aktion der wirtschaftlich unentwickelten Länder.* (European Economic Community Studies, Agricultural Series No. 15.) Brussels: European Economic Community, 1964. 52 pp.

Lehti, Teuvo. "Liquidity Creation and the Financing of Commodity Arrangements." *Monthly Bulletin of Agricultural Economics and Statistics* (Food and Agriculture Organization of the United Nations), March 1966 (Vol. 15, No. 3), pp. 1–9.

Lovasy, Gertrud. "Survey and Appraisal of Proposed Schemes of Compensatory Financing." *International Monetary Fund Staff Papers,* 1965 (Vol. 12), pp. 189–223.

Morgan, D. J. "International Commodity Problems and Schemes for International Compensatory Financing." Banca Nazionale del Lavoro *Quarterly Review*, December 1962 (Vol. 16, No. 63), pp. 307-331.

————. "International Compensatory Financing Applied to the Federation of Malaya and Singapore." *Malayan Economic Review*, October 1962 (Vol. 7, No. 2), pp. 64-76.

United Nations Commission on International Commodity Trade. "Consideration of Compensatory Financial Measures to Offset Fluctuations in the Export Income of Primary Producing Countries. Stabilization of Export Proceeds through a Development Insurance Fund. A Study by the Secretariat" (UN Document E/CN.13/43, January 18, 1962).

United Nations Department of Economic and Social Affairs. *International Compensation for Fluctuations in Commodity Trade.* (UN Document E/3447.) New York: United Nations, April 1961. xi + 96 pp.

United Nations Secretariat. "International Compensatory Financing in Relation to Fluctuations in the Prices of Primary Commodities: Application to Individual Commodities. A Development Insurance Fund for Single Commodities" (UN Document E/CN.13/45, February 6, 1962).

TARIFF PREFERENCES

Johnson, Harry G. "Trade Preferences and Developing Countries." *Lloyds Bank Review*, April 1966 (No. 80), pp. 1-18.

McNeill, Robert L. "Tariff Preferences for Developing Countries." *Proceedings of the American Society of International Law*, 60th annual meeting, Washington, April 28-30, 1966, pp. 93-102.

Mundell, Robert A. "Tariff Preferences and the Terms of Trade." *The Manchester School of Economics and Social Studies*, January 1964 (Vol. 32, No. 1), pp. 1-13.

Ndegwa, Philip. "Preferential trade arrangements among developing countries." *East African Economics Review*, December 1965 (Vol. 12, No. 2), pp. 1-22.

Patterson, Gardner. "Would Tariff Preferences Help Economic Development?" *Lloyds Bank Review*, April 1965 (No. 76), pp. 18-30.

"Les Préférences: le role qu'elles pourraient jouer dans le cadre d'une politique d'aide à l'expansion commerciale des pays en voie de developpement. Un débat nouveau sur des thèmes anciens." *Revue du Marché Commun*, September 1965 (No. 83), pp. 371-375.

Rom, Michael. "A Suggestion for a Preferential Scheme in the Developed Countries for Imports of Manufactures and Semi-Manufactures from Developing Countries." *Aussenwirtschaft* (Zurich), March 1966 (Vol. 21, No. 1), pp. 43-53.

Sundara Rajan, K. S. "Tariff Preferences and Developing Countries." *Proceedings of the American Society of International Law*, 60th annual meeting, Washington, April 28-30, 1966, pp. 86-93.

REGIONAL ARRANGEMENTS

Anselme-Rabinovitch, Leon. "Les Accords de Coopération: Etape de l'Intégration Africaine." *Genève-Afrique*, 1964 (Vol. 3, No. 2), pp. 243-254.

Balassa, Bela. *Economic Development and Integration.* Mexico City: Centro de Estudios Monetarios Latinoamericanos, 1965. 157 pp.

Balogh, Thomas. "Africa and the Common Market." *Journal of Common Market Studies*, (n.d.) (Vol. 1, No. 1), pp. 79-112.

Botero, Rodrigo. "Una Propuesta para Acelerar la Integración Económica en América Latina." *Revista del Banco de la República* (Bogotá), December 1966 (Vol. 39, No. 470), pp. 1390-1394.

Bruyas, J. "La Convention de Yaoundé: Charte de l'Association conclue entre la C.E.E. et dix-huit États africains et malgache (20 juillet 1963)," in *1965 Annales Africaines*. Prepared under the auspices of the Faculté de Droit et des Sciences Economique de Dakar. Paris: Editions Pédonne, 1965. pp. 129-172.

Cardosi, Gabriella. "Movimenti di Integrazione Economica in Africa." *Rivista Internazionale di Scienze Sociali*, September-October 1964 (72nd Year, No. 5), pp. 473-486.

Dell, Sidney. *Experiencias de la Integración Económica en América Latina.* Mexico City: Centro de Estudios Monetarios Latinoamericanos, 1966. 374 pp.

———. *A Latin American Common Market?* London: Oxford University Press (for the Royal Institute of International Affairs), 1966. 336 pp.

———. *Trade Blocs and Common Markets.* New York: Alfred A. Knopf, 1963. 384 pp.

Diab, Muhammad. "The Arab Common Market." *Journal of Common Market Studies,* May 1966 (Vol. 4, No. 3), pp. 238–250.

Farag, A. A. "Economic Integration in Latin America." *Economia Internazionale,* November 1963 (Vol. 16, No. 4), pp. 714–724.

Fernández-Shaw, F. "Estado Actual de la Integración Económica Centroamericana." *Revista de Política Internacional,* November–December 1964 (No. 59), pp. 76–106.

Gardiner, Robert K. "Integrated Economic Development in Africa: The Role of the Economic Commission." *International Development Review,* June 1965 (Vol. 7, No. 2), pp. 7–10.

Garnick, Daniel H. "Regional Integration and Economic Development in the Middle East." *Middle Eastern Affairs,* December 1961 (Vol. 12, No. 10), pp. 294–300.

Haas, Ernst B. and Philippe C. Schmitter. *The Politics of Economics in Latin American Regionalism: The Latin American Free Trade Association After Four Years of Operation.* Denver, Colo: University of Denver Press, 1965. 78 pp.

Hafez, Hamadi. "The Proposed Arab Common Market." *Scribe,* December 1964 (Vol. 9, No. 5), pp. 37–39.

Harrod, Roy. "Economic Development and Asian Regional Cooperation." *Pakistan Development Review,* Spring 1962 (Vol. 2, No. 1), pp. 1–22.

Harrod, Roy and Douglas C. Hague (ed.). *International Trade Theory in a Developing World.* London: Macmillan, 1963. 571 pp.

Hazlewood, Arthur. "The East African Common Market: Importance and Effects." *Bulletin of the Oxford University Institute of Economics and Statistics,* February 1966 (Vol. 28, No. 1), pp. 1–18.

Herrera, Felipe. *América Latina Integrada.* Buenos Aires: Editorial Losada, S.A., 1964. 240 pp.

———. "Aspectos Políticos e Econômicos de Integração da América Latina." *Revista Brasileira de Política Internacional,* March 1965 (8th Year, No. 29), pp. 22–45.

Herrera, Felipe and others. "Document: Proposals for the Creation of the Latin American Common Market." *Journal of Common Market Studies,* September 1966 (Vol. 5, No. 1), pp. 83–110.

Hirschman, Albert O. (ed.) *Latin American Issues: Essays and Comments.* New York: The Twentieth Century Fund, 1961. 201 pp.

Huelin, David. "Economic Integration in Latin America: Progress and Problems." *International Affairs,* July 1964 (Vol. 40, No. 3), pp. 430–439.

Khan, M. A. "A Plea for an Asian Common Market." *Pakistan Review,* March 1962 (Vol. 10, No. 3), p. 23.

Leduc, Michel. "Note sur les Marchés Communs Africains," in *1962 Annales Africaines.* Vol. 2: *Colloque des Facultés de Droit de Mai 1962.* Prepared under the auspices of the Faculté de Droit et des Sciences Economique de Dakar. Paris: Editions Pédonne, 1963. pp. 370–382.

Manzanares, H. "La Convención de Asociación de los Estados Africanos y Malgache a la C.E.E." *Revista de Política Internacional,* May–June 1965 (No. 63), pp. 91–105.

Mills, Joseph C. "La Política de Desarrollo y los Convenios Regionales de Comercio: El Caso de América Latina." *El Trimestre Económico,* July–September 1963 (Vol. 30 [3], No. 119), pp. 383–396.

Mundell, Robert A. "Tariff Preferences and the Terms of Trade." *The Manchester School of Economic and Social Studies,* January 1964 (Vol. 32, No. 1), pp. 1–13.

Perloff, Harvey S. and Romulo Almeida. "Regional Economic Integration in the Development of Latin America." *Economía Latinoamericana,* November 1963 (Vol. 1, No. 2), pp. 150–179.

Prebisch, Raúl. *Towards a Dynamic Development Policy for Latin America.* (UN Document E/CN.12/680/Rev.1.) New York: United Nations, 1963. 103 pp.

Rifaat, M. A. "Afro-Asian organisation for economic co-operation (AFRASEC)." *Civilisations,* 1965 (Vol. 15, No. 1), pp. 73–78.

Segal, Aaron. "The Integration of Developing Countries: Some Thoughts on East Africa and Central America." *Journal of Common Market Studies*, March 1967 (Vol. 5, No. 3), pp. 252–282.

Shoup, Carl S. (ed.) *Fiscal Harmonization in Common Markets.* New York: Columbia University Press, 1967. 2 vols.

Singh, Lalita Prasad. *The Politics of Economic Cooperation in Asia: A Study of Asian International Organizations.* Columbia: University of Missouri Press, 1966. 271 pp.

Urquidi, Victor L. *Free Trade and Economic Integration in Latin America: Toward a Common Market.* Translated by Marjory M. Urquidi. Berkeley: University of California Press, 1962. 190 pp.

Üstünel, Besim. "Western Regionalism and Developing Countries," in *The Turkish Yearbook of International Relations, 1963.* Ankara: The Institute of International Relations of the Faculty of Political Science, University of Ankara, 1965. pp. 63–80.

Vieira, M. A. "L'Association Latino-Américaine de Libre Commerce (A.L.A.L.C.): Ses Principaux Aspects Juridique." *Journal du Droit International*, July–August–September 1966 (83rd Year, No. 3), pp. 617–621.

Wionczek, Miguel S. (ed.) *Integración de la América Latina: experiencias y perspectivas.* Mexico City: Fondo de Cultura Economica, 1964. 381 pp.

Wood, R. N. "The East African Common Market: A Reassessment." *Bulletin of the Oxford University Institute of Economics and Statistics,* November 1966 (Vol. 28, No. 4), pp. 273–279.

REGIONAL DEVELOPMENT BANKS

"Founding of the Arab Development Bank." *Lands East,* January–February 1959 (Vol. 4, No. 1), pp. 4–7.

Houk, J. T. Dock. *Financing and Problems of Development Banking.* New York: Frederick A. Praeger, 1967.

Parkinson, F. "The Alliance for Progress," in *Year Book of World Affairs: 1964.* Edited by George W. Keeton and Georg Schwarzenberger. London: Stevens & Sons Limited, 1964, pp. 96–127.

United Nations Economic Commission for Africa and the Far East. *Regional economic co-operation in Asia and the Far East: The Asian Development Bank and trade liberalization.* (UN Document E/CN.11/707.) (Regional Economic Co-operation Series No. 2.) New York: United Nations, 1965. 137 pp.

U.S. Congress, Senate, Committee on Foreign Relations, *Hearings, Asian Development Bank Act,* 89th Congress, 2nd session, February 16, 1966.

FOOD AND AGRICULTURE ORGANIZATION

Hambidge, Gove. *The Story of FAO.* New York: D. Van Nostrand Company, Inc., 1955. 303 pp.

GENERAL AGREEMENT ON TARIFFS AND TRADE

Allen, James Jay. "The European Common Market and the General Agreement on Tariffs and Trade: A Study in Compatibility." *Law and Contemporary Problems,* Summer 1961 (Vol. 26, No. 3), pp. 559–571.

Balensi, A. "La technique des négociations au G.A.T.T." *Revue du Marché Commun,* May 1962 (No. 47), pp. 193–198.

Catudal, Honoré M. "The General Agreement on Tariffs and Trade: An Article-by-Article Analysis in Layman's Language." Department of State *Bulletin,* June 26, 1961 (Vol. 44, No. 1148), pp. 1010–1020.

Curzon, Gerard. *Multilateral Commercial Diplomacy: An Examination of the Impact of the General Agreement on Tariffs and Trade on National Commercial Policies and Techniques.* London: Michael Joseph, 1965. 367 pp.

————. *Multilateral Commercial Diplomacy: The General Agreement on Tariffs and Trade and its Impact on National Commercial Policies and Techniques.* New York: Frederick A. Praeger, 1966. xii + 367 pp.

Dam, Kenneth W. "Regional Economic Arrangements and the GATT: The Legacy of a Misconception." *University of Chicago Law Review,* Summer 1963 (Vol. 30, No. 4), pp. 615–655.

The Developing Countries and the GATT: The New Chapter on Trade and Development. Geneva: Secretariat of the General Agreement on Tariffs and Trade, February 1965. 10 pp.

"The Developing Countries in GATT," in *Proceedings of the United Nations Conference on Trade and Development, Geneva, 23 March–16 July 1964.* Vol. V: *Financing and Invisibles, Institutional Arrangements.* (UN Document E/CONF.46/141/Vol. V.) New York: United Nations, 1964. pp. 430–469.

Fisher, M. H. "What Chance of Lower Tariffs?: GATT and the Kennedy Round." *World Today,* May 1963 (Vol. 19, No. 5), pp. 208–212.

Galbraith, Virginia. "The General Agreement on Tariffs and Trade." *Current History,* July 1963 (Vol. 43, No. 25), pp. 23–38.

"GATT and the Developing Countries: Complex Kennedy Round Negotiations at Geneva." *National and Grindlays Review,* April 1965 (Vol. 11, No. 2), pp. 11–17.

GATT Programme for Expansion of International Trade: Trade of Less-Developed Countries: Development Plans. Geneva: The Contracting Parties to the General Agreement on Tariffs and Trade, 1962. 60 pp.

"Haves and Have-Nots." *New Republic,* March 28, 1964 (Vol. 150, No. 13, Issue 2572), pp. 6–7.

Hoffman, M. L. "Can the G.A.T.T. System Survive?" *Lloyds Bank Review,* July 1964 (No. 73), pp. 1–14.

International Trade: 1964. Geneva: The Contracting Parties to the General Agreement on Tariffs and Trade, 1965. 185 pp.

"Issue Facing GATT in the New Trading World." Department of State *Bulletin,* January 1, 1962 (Vol. 46, No. 1175), pp. 3–10.

Kunugi, Tatsuro. "State Succession in the Framework of GATT." *American Journal of International Law,* April 1965 (Vol. 59, No. 2), pp. 268–280.

Linder, Staffan B. "The Significance of GATT for Under-Developed and Less-Developed Countries," in *Proceedings of the United Nations Conference on Trade and Development, Geneva, 23 March–16 July 1964.* Vol. V: *Financing and Invisibles, Institutional Arrangements.* (UN Document E/CONF.46/141/Vol. V.) New York: United Nations, 1964. pp. 502–533.

Ramoin, Raoul. "The General Agreement on Tariffs and Trade (G.A.T.T.)." *Journal du Droit International,* July–August–September 1960 (87th Year, No. 3), pp. 731–760.

The Role of GATT in Relation to Trade and Development. Geneva: The Contracting Parties to the General Agreement on Tariffs and Trade, 1964. 56 pp.

"The Role of GATT in Relation to Trade and Development," in *Proceedings of the United Nations Conference on Trade and Development, Geneva, 23 March–16 July 1964.* Vol. V: *Financing and Invisibles, Institutional Arrangements.* (UN Document E/CONF.46/141/- Vol. V.) New York: United Nations, 1964. pp. 470–492.

Schwenger, Robert B. "Synthesis of Trade and Agricultural Policy in GATT." *Journal of Farm Economics,* May 1958 (Vol. 40, No. 2), pp. 238–248.

"United States Participation in the General Agreement on Tariffs and Trade." *Columbia Law Review,* March 1961 (Vol. 61, No. 3), pp. 505–569.

Vernon, Raymond A. *America's Foreign Trade Policy and the GATT.* (Essays in International Finance No. 21.) Princeton, N.J: International Finance Section, Department of Economics and Sociology, Princeton University, 1954. 25 pp.

Wells, S.J. "The Kennedy Round," in *The Year Book of World Affairs: 1966.* Edited by George W. Keeton and Georg Schwarzenberger. London: Stevens & Sons Limited, 1966, pp. 201–219.

White, Eric Wyndham. *GATT as an International Trade Organization: Some Structural Problems of International Trade.* Geneva: Secretariat of the General Agreement on Tariffs and Trade, 1961. 29 pp.

Willmann, Joachim. "La Négociation Kennedy au G.A.T.T." *Politique Etrangère,* 1964 (29th Year, No. 3), pp. 248–259.

INTERNATIONAL ATOMIC ENERGY AGENCY

Caulfield, Daniel Webster. *The International Atomic Energy Agency and its Relationship to the United Nations.* Regensburg: Walhalla und Praetoria Verlag, [1959]. 121 pp.

Kramish, Arnold. *The Peaceful Atom in Foreign Policy.* New York: Harper & Row (for the Council on Foreign Relations), 1963. 276 pp.

Nieburg, H. L. "The International Atomic Energy Agency: A Critical Appraisal," in *Year Book of World Affairs: 1965.* Edited by George W. Keeton and Georg Schwarzenberger. London: Stevens & Sons Limited, 1965, pp. 47–68.

INTERNATIONAL BANK FOR RECONSTRUCTION AND DEVELOPMENT—INTERNATIONAL DEVELOPMENT ASSOCIATION

Cairncross, Alexander K. *The International Bank for Reconstruction and Development.* (Essays in International Finance, No. 33.) Princeton, N.J.: International Finance Section, Department of Economics and Sociology, Princeton University, 1959. 36 pp.

Morris, James. *The Road to Huddersfield: A Journey to Five Continents.* New York: Pantheon Books, 1963. 235 pp.

Ordoobadi, Abbas. *The Loan Policy of the World Bank Group: IBRD, IFC, and IDA.* New York: Frederick A. Praeger, 1966. 200 pp.

Reid, Escott. *The Future of the World Bank: An Essay.* Washington: International Bank for Reconstruction and Development, 1965. 71 pp.

Weaver, James H. *The International Development Association: A New Approach to Foreign Aid.* New York: Frederick A. Praeger, 1965. 268 pp.

INTERNATIONAL LABOR ORGANIZATION

Roberts, Richard S., Jr. *Economic Development, Human Skills and Technical Assistance: A Study of I.L.O. Technical Assistance in the Field of Productivity and Management Development.* Geneva: Librairie Droz, 1962. 157 pp.

Sulkowski, Joseph. "The Competence of the International Labor Organization Under the United Nations System." *American Journal of International Law,* April 1951 (Vol. 45, No. 2), pp. 286–314.

INTERNATIONAL MONETARY FUND

Ausfricht, Hans. *The International Monetary Fund: Legal Bases, Structure, Functions.* New York: Frederick A. Praeger (for The London Institute of World Affairs), 1964. 125 pp.

Communiqué of Ministers and Governors and Report of Deputies [on improvements needed in the international monetary system]. Communiqué of the Ministerial Meeting of the Group of Ten on July 25–26, 1966, in The Hague. Washington: International Monetary Fund, 1966. 25 pp.

Gardner, Richard N. *Sterling-Dollar Diplomacy: Anglo-American Collaboration in the Reconstruction of Multilateral Trade.* Oxford: Clarendon Press, 1956. 392 pp.

Harrod, Roy F. *Reforming the World's Money.* New York: St. Martin's Press, 1965. viii + 181 pp.

"International Monetary Issues and the Developing Countries: Report of the Group of Experts" (UN Documents TD/B/32, TD/B/C.3/6, November 1, 1965).

Triffin, Robert. *Gold and the Dollar Crisis: The Future of Convertibility.* New Haven, Conn: Yale University Press, 1960. 195 pp.

———. *The World Money Maze: National Currencies in International Payments.* New Haven, Conn: Yale University Press, 1966. xii + 585 pp.

ORGANIZATION FOR ECONOMIC COOPERATION AND DEVELOPMENT

Esman, Milton J. and Daniel S. Cheever. *The Common Aid Effort: The Development Assistance Activities of the Organization for Economic Co-operation and Development.* Columbus: Ohio University Press, 1967. 412 pp.

The OECD at Work. New York: McGraw-Hill, 1964.

UNITED NATIONS CONFERENCE ON THE APPLICATION OF SCIENCE AND TECHNOLOGY FOR THE BENEFIT OF THE LESS DEVELOPED AREAS

Science and Technology for Development: Report on the United Nations Conference on the Application of Science and Technology for the Benefit of the Less Developed Areas. Vol. I: *World of Opportunity* (UN Document E/CONF.39/1, Vol. I) and Vol. VII: *Science and Planning* (UN Document E/CONF.39/1, Vol. VII). New York: United Nations, 1963. 167 pp. and 267 pp., respectively.

UNITED NATIONS DEVELOPMENT PROGRAM

Mangone, Gerard J. (ed.) *UN Administration of Economic and Social Programs.* (Columbia University Studies in International Organization, No. 3.) New York: Columbia University Press, 1966. xxii + 291 pp.

Report of the Economic and Social Council: 1 August 1965–5 August 1966. (General Assembly *Official Records* [21st session], Supplement No. 3.) New York: United Nations, 1966. 122 pp.

United Nations Development Programme: Report of the Governing Council: Second Session (8–24 June 1966). (Economic and Social Council *Official Records* [41st session], Supplement Nos. 11 and 11A.) New York: United Nations, 1966. 82 pp.

UNITED NATIONS EDUCATIONAL, SCIENTIFIC AND CULTURAL ORGANIZATION

Shuster, George N. *UNESCO: Assessment and Promise.* New York: Harper & Row (for the Council on Foreign Relations), 1963. 130 pp.

UNITED NATIONS INDUSTRIAL DEVELOPMENT ORGANIZATION

"Activities in the Field of Industrial Development: Report of the *Ad Hoc* Committee on the United Nations Organization for Industrial Development" (UN Documents A/6229 and E/C.5/145, May 4, 1966).

"Activities in the Field of Industrial Development: Report of the Second Committee" (UN Document A/6508, November 11, 1966).

UNITED NATIONS REGIONAL ECONOMIC COMMISSIONS

Asfour, Edmond Y. "International Co-operation in Africa and the Establishment of the Economic Commission for Africa." *Civilisations,* 1960 (Vol. 10, No. 2), pp. 181–189.

Gregg, Robert W. "The UN Regional Economic Commissions and Integration in the Underdeveloped Regions." *International Organization,* Spring 1966 (Vol. 20, No. 2), pp. 208–232.

Lokanathan, Palamadai Samu. "ECAFE, the Economic Parliament of Asia," in *The Indian Yearbook of International Affairs: 1953.* Edited by Charles Henry Alexandrowicz. Madras: Diocesan Press, 1953, pp. 3–27.

INDEX

INDEX

Abdel-Rahman, Dr. I. H., 437
ACC. *See* Administrative Committee on Coordination
ADB. *See* Asian Development Bank
Addis Ababa, UNESCO Conference (1961) in, 313
Administrative and Budgetary Questions, Advisory Committee (GA) on, 34
Administrative Committee on Coordination (ACC), 34, 128, 329
  population subgroup of, 355
  Science and Technology, Subcommittee on, 395
Administrative Sciences, International Institute of, 205
Advisory Committee (GA) on Administrative and Budgetary Questions. *See* Administrative and Budgetary Questions, Advisory Committee (GA) on
Advisory Committee on the Application of Science and Technology to Development. *See* Application of Science and Technology to Development, Advisory Committee on the
Advisory Social Welfare, 29
Afghanistan in U.N., 19
Africa
  agricultural production in, 333, 364
  development in, 182
  Economic Development and Planning, Institute for (Special Fund), 437
  EEC and, 87, 90, 103, 186, 194
  France and, 218, 280
  GATT in, 83
  IBRD-IDA loans and credits to, 167, 168
  in IMF, 133
  investment (foreign) in, 52
  population growth and family planning, 336, 338, 340, 350, 354, 358, 359

  research center on, 345
  Science and Technology, Regional Center for (UNESCO), 413
  in U.N., 20
  on UNCTAD, 105
  UNESCO, educational goals for, 313
  U.S. aid to, 194, 207, 248
  world protein gap in, 25
  See also African Development Bank, East Africa, North Africa
African Development Bank, 143, 183, 184, 186, 187, 194–96, 201, 203, 272, 437, 443
  ADB and, 194
  EIB and, 106
  IDB and, 194
  loans of, 196
  projects of, 185
  publicly owned development banks, support of, 185
  and SUNFED, 30
  UNDP and, 195
  U.S. and, 279, 387
  World Bank Group and, 195
  Zambian-Tanzanian railway, and, 195–96
Agency for International Development (AID). *See under* United States
Agriculture
  developing countries and, 61, 62, 288, 451
  education for, 373
  food aid and, 368–69
  prices in, 369
  world food production in, 363–66
    capital assistance for, 366–67
    technical assistance for, 370–73, 375–76
  See also Food and Agriculture Organization, World Food Program, *under individual countries*
Agudelo, Hernando, 246, 248, 266–67
Albania in U.N., 20

Alliance for Progress, 5, 219, 380, 436
  AID loans under, 387
  antecedents of, 248–52
  coordinator for, 254, 264
  Inter-American Committee (CIAP) on, 1, 179, 190, 219, 226, 260–67, 443
  IDB and, 183
  multilateralization of, 260–67
  Nine Wise Men, 11, 14, 219, 226, 249, 255, 256–58, 259, 263–67, 268, 443
  IA-ECOSOC, reports to, 248, 254, 256
  Punta del Este, Charter of, 249–61 *passim*, 267, 268
  Twenty-One, Committee of, and, 251
  U.S. and AID, 260
Almeida, Rómulo, 245
American States, First International Conference of (1889-1890), 186, 188, 244
Application of Science and Technology to Development, Advisory Committee on the, 24–25
Apter, David, on development and democracy, 328–39
Arab League, 454
Arab States, Science and Technology, Regional Center for (UNESCO), 413
Argentina
  agricultural production in, 368
  IMF and, 138
  investment (foreign) in, 51
  Kennedy Round and, 90
  Petroleum, National Institute of, 407
  population problems in, 350
  reserves (1946) of, 132
  situation in, 454
Asia
  agricultural production in, 333, 364
  EEC and, 103
  IBRD-IDA loans and credits to, 167
  in IMF, 133
  Institute for Economic Development and Planning (Special Fund), 437
  population growth and family planning in, 336, 338, 340
  U.S. aid for, 358, 359
  research center for, 345
  Science and Technology, Regional Center for (UNESCO), 413
  in U.N., 21
  on UNCTAD, 105

UNESCO, educational goals for, 313
U.S. aid to, 194, 248
world protein gap in, 25
Asian Development Bank (ADB), 43, 183, 184, 190–91, 197, 201, 203, 272, 281, 437, 443
  African Development Bank and, 194
  financing of, 197, 198, 199, 200
  IBRD on, 171
  Japan and, 190–91
  Mekong River development and, 191–93
  SUNFED and, 30
  U.S. and, 188, 190, 279, 387
  voting in, 186, 187, 191
Asian Population Conference (1963), 351
Australia
  ADB and, 198
  agricultural production in, 364, 368
  in DAC (OECD), 232
  GATT's Article XXIII, Chilean case under, 82
  and IBRD, 440
  investment (foreign) in, 51
  Kennedy Round and, 90
  on U.N. economic matters, 17
  UNCTAD Issues, Working Party on (OECD), 240
Austria
  in DAC (OECD), 232
  foreign aid by, 6, 282
  in U.N., 20

Banfield, E. C., on Southern Italy, 330
Bangkok, family planning center (ECAFE) in, 351
Bank for International Settlements, 200
Barbados in U.N., 20
Belgium
  ADB and, 190
  on family planning, 381, 382
  foreign aid by, 6
  in IMF Group of Ten, 132
  and Tripartite Declaration (1936), 131
Berle, Adolf, 188
Birth control. *See* Contraception, Family planning, Population
Black, Eugene, on population growth, 343
Bogotá, Act of (1960), 251, 253, 264
Bogotá, Economic Agreement of (1948), 249
  private foreign investment under, 294

Bogotá, Ninth International Conference at (1948), 246, 291, 294
Bolivia, 189
  IDB loan to, 379–80
Brazil, 454
  GATT's Article XXIII, case under, 82
  growth of, 50
  IBRD and, 165
  IMF and, 138
  import demand of, 60
  Kubitschek, President Juscelino, 250, 251
  Operation Pan America, proposal for, 250, 251
  reserves (1946) of, 132
  U.S. investment in, 51
Bretton Woods Conference, 315. *See also listings under* IBRD and IMF
Bulgaria in U.N., 20
Burma in U.N., 19
Buron, Robert, 233

Cairo Conference of Nonaligned Nations, 115
Calvo Doctrine, 290, 294, 295
Camargo, Alberto Lleras, 263
Cambodia
  Mekong River development and, 191–93
  OECD seminar in, 234
  UNDP/UNESCO project in, 407
Cameroon, OECD seminar in, 234
Canada
  agricultural production in, 364, 368
  in DAC (OECD), 232
  foreign aid by, 282, 285
  and GATT, 88, 97
  IBRD, dollar obligations and, 170
  in IMF Group of Ten, 132
  investment (foreign) in, 51
  investment (private foreign), protection of, 293
  in OECD, 440
  on UNCTAD, 105
Candau, M. G., on family planning, 341, 353
Caribbean nations in U.N., 21
Central America
  GATT and, 83
  income, per capita in, 455
  technical assistance in, 207–8
  telecommunications projects in, 189
Central American Bank for Economic Integration, 189, 201, 272
Central American Common Market, 190
  IDB and, 201

Central American Economic Integration, General Treaty for, 247
Ceylon
  on family planning, 344, 350, 381
  GATT's Article XVIII and, 80, 81
  IMF and, 138
  OECD seminar in, 234
Chandpur Irrigation Project, 379
Chile, 189
  Alliance for Progress and, 260
  GATT's Article XXIII, case against Australia under, 82
  growth in, 50
  IMF and, 138
China, People's Republic of (Communist China)
  birth rate in, 337
  ECOSOC, seating on, 101
  foreign aid by, 278
  India, relations with, 454
  population growth in, 333
China, Republic of (Nationalist China)
  birth rate in, 389
  EPTA aid to, 210
  IMF Executive Board in, 135
  income, per capita in, 455
  industries in, 452
  investment disputes, IBRD arbitration convention and, 299
Civil and Political Rights, International Covenant on private foreign property, expropriation of, 297
Cleveland, Harlan, on less developed countries, 433
Cocoa, 66, 451
  UNCTAD, commodity agreement for, 126
Coffee, 61, 62, 66, 423
  International Coffee Agreement, 370, 452
Cold War, 19, 312, 435
Coleman, James, on educational model and development, 324–25
Colombia
  Alliance for Progress and, 260
  IBRD consultative group and, 178, 189, 229
  IMF and, 138
Colombo Plan, 436
Commission for Social Development. *See* Social Development, Commission for
Commodities
  classification of, 426-28. *See also* International Commodity Agreements, Interim Coordinating Com-

Commodities (*cont.*)
mittee on; International Commodity Trade, Commission on
Commonwealth, UK aid to, 218, 279
Congo, Democratic Republic of, situation in, 454
Consortia, 271, 272, 273, 361, 387, 438, 445
advantages of, 227–28
IBRD organization of, 14
weaknesses of, 223, 227–28
Consultative groups, 272. *See also under* IBRD
Contraception
injectable contraceptive, 332
intrauterine contraceptive device (IUCD), 332, 341, 342, 353, 358, 389
pill, 332, 341, 353, 358, 389
U.N. support of, 349–50
See also Family planning
Convention for the Protection of Private Property. *See* Private Property, Protection of, Convention for the
Convention on the Settlement of Investment Disputes. *See* Investment Disputes, Convention on the Settlement of
Coordination Committee, 34
Cotton and cotton textiles, 53, 55, 82
Cotton Textile Arrangement, 83–84, 92, 111, 452
Council of Europe, 284
Cuba, GATT's Article XVIII and, 81
Cyprus in U.N., 20
Czechoslovakia
GATT and, 94
on UNCTAD, 105

DAC (OECD). *See* Development Assistance Committee
Denmark
in DAC (OECD), 232
foreign aid and multilateral assistance by, 271, 282
on population growth and family planning, 350
on private foreign investment, 304
Desalinization process, 408–9
Development Assistance Committee. *See under* Organization for Economic Cooperation and Development (OECD)
Development Decades. *See* United Nations Development Decades
Development world plan, 421–26, 426–29
Dillon, C. Douglas, 148, 257

Dumbarton Oaks, 17
Draper, General William H., Jr., on family planning, 347

East Africa
in DAC (OECD), 237
GATT and, 83
East African Development Bank, 196
East African Economic Community and Common Market, 196, 201
Eastern Europe
foreign aid by, 278, 287
on UNCTAD, 94
ECA. *See* Economic Commission for Africa (U.N.)
ECAFE. *See* Economic Commission for Asia and the Far East (U.N.)
ECE. *See* Economic Commission for Europe (U.N.)
ECLA. *See* Economic Commission for Latin America (U.N.)
Economic Affairs, Director-General, establishment of, proposal for, 129
Economic Commission for Africa (ECA), 219
Economic Commission for Asia and the Far East (ECAFE), 430
population problems and, 351
survey of progress by, 374
Economic Commission for Europe (ECE), 442
Economic Commission for Latin America (ECLA), 11, 247
import substitution and, 70
Economic Justice, International Court of, 226, 262
Economic and Social Council (ECOSOC), 24, 33, 39, 40, 101, 121, 127, 444
China, People's Republic of, seating on, 101
Coordination, Special Committee on, 128
developed countries and, 18, 100
developing countries' criticism of, 31–32, 101
development
IBRD's President on, 283–84
world plan for, 431
Development Planning, Committee for, 12, 24, 28, 40, 121, 262, 421
EPTA and, 209
financial issues and, 18
functional commissions of, 18, 32
Housing, Building, and Planning, Center for, 437
Housing, Building, and Planning, Committee on, 25

IBRD President on, 167
ITO Charter and, 103
OEEC and, 430
planning, long-range, 24
population problems and, 343, 348–49, 351, 354–55
private foreign investment, protection of, 296
Program and Coordination, Committee for, 34, 40, 128
Soviet bloc's role in debates, 19
U.N. Advisory Committee on Application of Science and Technology and, 396–97, 401–2
UNCTAD and, 104, 122, 123, 125
UNDD and, 13, 28
UNIDO, relation to, 125
ECOSOC. See Economic and Social Council (U.N.)
ECSC. See European Coal and Steel Community
Ecuador
IDB and, 189, 229
OECD seminar in, 234
EDF. See European Development Fund
Education
development and, 9, 317–25
manpower and, 330
EEC. See European Economic Community
EFTA. See European Free Trade Association
Egypt, population growth in, 346
EIB. See European Investment Bank
Eisenhower, Milton, on IDB, 247
Eisenhower, President Dwight D.
on family planning, 346–47
on Latin American development, 251
EPTA. See Expanded Program of Technical Assistance
ERP. See European Recovery Program
Euratom. See European Atomic Energy Community
Europe
agricultural production in, 372
colonies of (former), aid to, 5–6
commitments by agencies in, 156
education in, 325, 373
IBRD, currency obligations, 170
IBRD-IDA loans and credits to, 167, 168
Latin American development and, 245
reserves of, 148
See also Council of Europe, Eastern

Europe, Economic Commission for Europe, European Atomic Energy Community, European Coal and Steel Community, European Economic Community, European Free Trade Association, Organization for Economic Cooperation and Development, Organization for European Economic Cooperation, Western Europe
European Atomic Energy Community (Euratom), 436
European Coal and Steel Community (ECSC), 436
European Development Fund (EDF), 186, 272, 281, 437
European Economic Community (EEC), 110, 189, 272, 436
Africa and, 87, 103, 186, 194
Asia and, 103
in DAC (OECD), 232
developing countries on, 83
EIB and, 186
financial integration in, 183
GATT and, 88, 90, 439
IMF and, 150–51
Latin America and, 103
Soviet Union on, 103
tariffs under GATT's Part IV and, 88
UNCTAD and, 109
European Free Trade Association (EFTA)
GATT's Part IV and, 88
European Investment Bank (EIB), 183, 184, 186, 187, 190, 195, 198, 272
European Recovery Program (ERP), Soviet Union and, 18–19
Expanded Program of Technical Assistance (EPTA), 8, 20, 26, 27, 29, 100, 204, 208–13, 345, 436
AID and, 222
budget of, 22
FAO and, 382
projects of, 210–13, 216, 218
resources, allocation of, 209, 212, 219–20
Special Fund and, 213, 214, 215, 216, 222, 273, 438, 443
TAB and, 209, 211, 212, 217
UNESCO, aid to, 405
See also Special Fund, United Nations Development Program
Export-Import Bank, 246, 379
IBRD and, 174
on U.S., 188

Exports
  developing countries and, 45, 60–
    69, 139–40, 143, 146, 425, 455
    agricultural raw materials, 61,
      66, 422–23, 451–52
    manufactures, 61, 453
    oil, increase in, 61
    shortfalls. *See under* International
      Bank for Reconstruction and
      Development and International
      Monetary Fund
  foreign exchange and, 48–50
  promotion of, 126, 128
  UNCTAD view of, 60–61, 63
  See also under General Agreement
    on Tariffs and Trade, Interna-
    tional Bank for Reconstruction
    and Development, International
    Monetary Fund, Organization of
    American States, United Nations
    Conference on Trade and Devel-
    opment, United Nations Indus-
    trial Development Organization

FAO. *See* Food and Agriculture Or-
  ganization
Family planning, 25, 450–51
  Albert and Mary Lasker Founda-
    tion, 346
  cost of, 367
  foreign aid and, 341–42
  "gap," 335–38, 336–37
  guidelines for action, 338–43
  infant mortality and, 363, 365
  International Planned Parenthood
    Federation, 346, 356, 358
  nutrition and, 363
  Planned Parenthood Federation of
    America, 346, 358
  U.N. and, 343–55
  WHO and, 446
  world development plan and, 423
  See also Contraception, Population
    growth
Famine, 334
Far East
  DAC (OECD) and, 237
  inflation in, 145
Fats and Oils, 61, 370
Federal Reserve Bank of New York,
  131
Fibers, 66, 370
Finances of the United Nations and
  the Specialized Agencies, *Ad Hoc*
  Committee of Experts to Examine
  the, 34
Finland
  EPTA and, 210
  IBRD and, 440

IBRD-IDA loans and credits to, 167
  in U.N., 20
UNCTAD Issues, Working Party
  on (OECD), 240
Food. *See* Agriculture, Food and Agriculture Organization, World Food
  Program
Food and Agriculture Organization
  (FAO), 1, 10, 13, 273, 326, 329,
  403, 430, 442, 444
  agricultural production, in develop-
    ing countries, 25
  Atomic Energy in Agriculture,
    Joint Division of, 409
  budget of, 380, 382–83
  commodities
    projections for agricultural, 24
    study groups for, 370
  education and, 9, 406
  food aid of, 375
  IBRD and, 163, 205, 378
  Indicative World Plan for Agricul-
    tural Development, 24, 384,
    449
  locust control and, 375, 383–84
  Mediterranean Development Proj-
    ect of, 439
  population problems and, 25, 343
  programs of, 376, 383–84
  tsetse fly project of, 409
  World Bank Group and, 438
  world food production and, 333–34
Fowler, Henry H., 149
Ford Foundation, 346, 353, 358, 371,
  372, 376, 382, 387
Foreign aid, 224
  bilateral, 3, 13, 14, 15, 224–26,
    389–91
  family planning and, 341–42
  See also under individual countries;
    Multilateral assistance
France
  Africa and, 218, 280
  in DAC (OECD), 232
  developing countries and, 114
  foreign aid by, 5, 6, 208, 218, 272,
    279, 280, 282, 344
  GATT'S Part IV and, 88
  IBRD and, 199
  in IMF Group of Ten, 132
  and investment (private foreign),
    293
  Kennedy Round and, 90
  OECD and, 231
  on population problems, 350, 382
  Tripartite Declaration (1936) and,
    131
  on UNCTAD, 105, 117
  U.S. and, 103

Fruits, 369, 370, 451
Fulbright, Senator J. William
  on family planning and foreign aid, 357
  on multilateral assistance, 389
Functionalist pluralism, 327–31

GA. *See* General Assembly (U.N.)
Gabon, UNDP railroad project for, 215
GATT. *See* General Agreement on Tariffs and Trade
General Agreement on Tariffs and Trade (GATT), 1, 11, 73–75, 94–95, 101, 102, 127
  action program of, 103
  Article XVIII of, 80, 81, 82
  commodity problems and, 95–96, 126
  cotton textiles under, 83–84
  developing countries on, 72–73, 101–3
  development and, 44, 70
  exports and, 46, 128, 439
  foreign exchange earnings and, 50
  Haberler Report, 84
  as international organization, 102
  International Trade Center, 126, 128, 437
  investment (foreign), and, 53
  ITO and, 75, 102, 436
  Kennedy Round and, 76, 77, 88–90, 96, 91, 126, 439, 451
    food donation program of, 368
    U.S. tariff concessions under, 89
  obligations under, 81, 82–84
  Part IV, 96, 439
    EFTA acceptance of, 88
  regional arrangements and, 83
  Soviet nonparticipation in, 103
  tariff negotiations under, 76–80, 453
  trade, expansion of, 54, 70, 84–88, 93
  Trade and Development Chapter, 103
  UNCTAD and, 34, 35, 70, 71, 86, 109, 124, 127
  U.S. and, 73, 102
  voting in, 96–97
  Western Europe and, 73
General Assembly (GA), 21, 39, 127, 430
  Asia in, 20
  coordination in, 34
  developing countries and, 31, 444
  development and, 418, 419, 420, 431
  Economic and Financial (Second) Committee

developed countries' participation in, 100
family planning programs and, 349–50
trade conference and, 104
EPTA and, 209
Finances of U.N. and Specialized Agencies, *Ad Hoc* Committee of Experts to Examine the, 34
financial issues and, 18
human rights and, 25–26
Institutional Arrangements, Committee on (UNCTAD), 105
investment (private foreign) and, 291, 296–97, 298
planning and policy formulation in, 40
population problems and, 343, 345–46, 347, 348–50, 351, 381
U.N. Advisory Committee on the Application of Science and Technology to Development, 396
UNCTAD and, 104, 118, 123
UNDP and, 216
Germany, Democratic Republic of (East Germany)
  nonrecognition of, 280
Germany, Federal Republic of (West Germany)
  ADB and, 190, 281
  in DAC (OECD), 232
  EDF and, 281
  foreign aid and multilateral assistance by, 175, 218, 272, 279, 280–81, 282, 285
  IBRD and, 199
    currency obligations, 170
  in IMF Group of Ten, 132
  on investment (private foreign), 295, 304
  OECD and, 231
  training activities, government subsidy of, 277
Ghana
  IBRD and, 199
  on population problems, 350
  in U.N., 20
Grains
  protection of, 61
Greece
  desalinization in, 409
  EPTA aid to, 210
  OECD consortium and, 229
  on population problems, 350
Guinea
  OECD seminar in, 234
  on population problems, 350
  in U.N., 20
Guyana in U.N., 20

Haiti
  GATT's Article XVIII and, 80
Hammarskjöld, Dag, 343
Harriman, W. Averell, on private foreign investment and foreign aid, 307
Havana Charter. *See under* International Trade Organization
Hoffman, Paul, 216–17, 442
Holland. *See* Netherlands
Hong Kong
  export market of, 53
  income, per capita in, 455
  industries in, 452
  situation in, 454
Horowitz, Governor David, 172–74, 202, 276
Housing, building, and planning. *See* Housing, Building, and Planning, Committee on, *under* Economic and Social Council; Housing, Building, and Planning, Center for, *under* Economic and Social Council
Human resources, 7, 8–9
Human rights
  GA on, 25–26
Human Rights, Commission on, 32
Human Rights Services, 29
Hungary
  in U.N., 20

IAEA. *See* International Atomic Energy Agency
IA-ECOSOC. *See* Inter-American Economic and Social Council (OAS)
IBRD. *See* International Bank for Reconstruction and Development
Iceland in U.N., 19
IDA. *See* International Development Association (IBRD)
IDB. *See* Inter-American Development Bank
IFC. *See* International Finance Corporation (IBRD)
ILO. *See* International Labor Organization
IMCO. *See* Intergovernmental Maritime Consultative Organization
IMF. *See* International Monetary Fund
Imports
  developing countries and, 58–60, 65
  substitution as means to industrialization, 45
India, 454
  agricultural production in, 366, 367, 371–72, 373
  Intensive District Program, 387

development planning for, 10, 429
growth of, 50
IBRD and, 176, 178, 191, 229, 361, 387
IDA and, 168, 176
IMF and, 138, 146
income, per capita in, 374
Indus Waters Treaty and, 374
leather industry in, 383
population growth and family planning in, 333, 338, 340, 341, 346, 348, 350–54 *passim*, 367, 381
reserves (1946) of, 132
UNESCO science projects in, 407
Indian Ocean expedition, 404
Indonesia, 454
  in ADB, 190
  DᴬC (OECD) and, 237
  IMF and, 138
  population growth and family planning in, 333, 338
  in U.N., 19
Indus River project, 272, 275
  Indus Waters Treaty, 374
Industrial development, 9–10, 45, 288. *See also* United Nations Industrial Development Organization
Industrial raw materials. *See under* Raw materials
Infant mortality, 363, 366
Institution building, 7, 8–9
Inter-American Committee on the Alliance for Progress (CIAP). *See listing under* Alliance for Progress
Inter-American Conferences, 186, 188, 294–95
  Bogotá, Ninth International at (1948), 246, 291, 294
  Buenos Aires Economic Conference (OAS, 1957), 246, 249, 291, 294
  Finance and Economy, meeting of Ministers of, Quitandinha, Brazil, (1954), 246, 249
Inter-American Development Bank (IDB), 183, 184, 186–90, 197, 201, 203, 272, 279, 437
  ADB and, 191
  African Development Bank and, 194
  agricultural development and, 377, 379–80
  Central American Common Market and, 201
  Ecuador consortium and, 229
  financing and, 197, 198, 199, 200
  U.S. and, 200
  Fund for Special Operations, 251, 379, 380, 445

IBRD and, 171, 189
loans of, 185, 189
multilateral characteristics of, 247, 261
Preinvestment Fund for Latin American Integration, 442
publicly-owned development banks, support of, 185
Social Progress Trust Fund, 251, 380, 445
SUNFED and, 30
U.S. and, 197, 307, 387
Inter-American Economic and Social Council (IA-ECOSOC), 256–57
Alliance for Progress and, 252–53, 261
CIAP and, 263, 266
Nine Wise Men and, 248, 254, 256, 267
Inter-American Institute of Agricultural Sciences, 376
Inter-American Treaty of Reciprocal Assistance (Rio Treaty), 246, 261
Intergovernmental Maritime Consultative Organization (IMCO), 435, 436
International Atomic Energy Agency (IAEA), 392, 394, 403, 408, 436
budget of, 16
programs of, 408–11
desalinization and, 393, 408–9
technical assistance under, 410
International Bank for Reconstruction and Development (IBRD), 1, 11, 16, 27, 43, 101, 152–53, 155, 168, 177–78, 179–81, 224, 272, 273–74, 390, 436
on ADB, 171
agricultural development and, 375, 376–79, 387
Alliance for Progress and, 263
Board of Governors, 154, 155, 168
bonds of, 149, 199
Brazil and, 165
Bretton Woods Conference of, 152, 154
capital assistance under, 7
Central America, telecommunications projects of, 189
Charter of, 152–53, 168
amended to permit lending to IFC, 171
CIAP, assistance to, 179
consortia, 14, 229, 273, 361, 387, 438, 445
consultative groups of, 14, 178, 229, 273, 438, 445

credits, terms of, 161–62
criticism of, 171–72, 183, 185
developing countries', 101–2
Latin America's, 188
debts to, 175
development and, 420, 440, 441
Development Advisory Service of, 188
Economic Development Institute, 177
education and, 9, 163, 205, 313–14
Executive Directors of, 154, 155, 186, 305
Export-Import Bank and, 174
exports and, 46, 69, 159, 275–76, 452
FAO, funds for, 383
financial issues and, 18
financing of, 199
funded debt and, 202
funds of, 169–76
Horowitz Plan for IDA soft loans, 172–74, 202, 276
IDB and, 171, 189
India and, 178, 191, 229, 361, 387
Indus River project of, 182, 191, 374
Investment Disputes, Convention on the Settlement of (Arbitration Convention), 53, 291, 299–301, 304, 305, 306
loans, 153, 161, 162–63, 164–66
for agricultural development, 160, 163, 205, 376, 378
for education, 163, 205
for electric power, 160
geographical distribution of, 167–68
to India, 176
for industry, 160
to Latin America, 188, 445
for "maintenance," 159
for manufacturing, 160, 163
for mining, 160, 163
to Pakistan, 176
for postwar reconstruction, 161
program approach to, 158–59, 185–86
project loans, 7, 10, 158, 185–86
for public service, 160
for science and technology, 399
for transportation, 160
membership of, 154, 197
Pakistan and, 178, 191, 229, 361
Pan-American Highway and, 189
policies of, 185, 448
population growth and, 343

International Bank for Reconstruction and Development (IBRD) (*cont.*)
  private foreign investment and, 53, 291, 299–301, 304, 305, 306
  regional development banks and, 185, 443
  regional projects of, 182
  Soviet nonparticipation in, 103
  state-owned development banks and, 166, 185
  state-owned industries and, 166
  SUNFED and, 30, 171
  Switzerland and, 202
  Tanzanian-Zambian railway, and, 196
  technical assistance by, 176–77
  Turkey and, 165
  UK, balance of payments deficit and, 175–76
  UNCTAD and, 71, 109, 124
  U.S. and, 132, 165, 188, 198, 202
    balance of payments deficit and, 175–76
  voting in, 155, 261
  World Bank Group and, 152
International Center for Theoretical Physics (Trieste), 410
International Clearing Union, 132
International commodity agreements, 451–52
  Interim Coordinating Committee on, 126
International Commodity Trade, Commission on, 126
  International Trade, Commission on, transformation into, 105
International Council of Scientific Unions, Indian Ocean expedition, 404
International Court of Economic Justice, 226, 262
International Covenant on Civil and Political Rights, 25–26
International Covenant on Economic, Social, and Cultural Rights, 25–26
International Development Association (IDA), 7, 27, 43, 100, 154, 165, 188, 272–74, 436, 442
  agricultural development and, 376, 377–79
  Charter of, 170–71
  commitments by, 155
  credits of, 162, 164
    for education, 161
    geographical distribution of, 167–68

  income transferred to, 170
  India and, 168
  development funds for, 420
  funds of, 170–76, 271, 274, 279, 280, 281
  loans to, 154, 176, 180, 199–200
    Horowitz Plan for soft loans, 172–74, 202, 276
  membership of, 154
  SUNFED and, 30
  Swiss loan to, 181
International Economic Association, 314
International Finance Corporation (IFC), 7, 27, 43, 154, 196, 272, 436
  Charter of, 168, 171
  commitments by, 155
  development financing companies, of, 166
  funds from, 171
  investment policies of, 168–69
  manufacturing and, 163, 169
  mining projects of, 163
  state-owned development banks and, 185
  SUNFED and, 30
  U.S. and, 188
  World Bank Group and, 152
International Hydrological Decade, 404, 407
  IAEA participation in, 410
International Labor Organization (ILO), 1, 326, 329, 439, 444
  development and, 314, 315, 325, 431
  International Institute for Labor Studies of, 437
  manpower activities of, 9, 310
    trade-union support of, 312
  technical assistance of, 207–8
  UNIDO on, 443
International Monetary Fund (IMF), 1, 11, 101, 124–25, 200
  analysis of, 151
  Board of Governors of, 149
  Bretton Woods Conference, 131–32, 133, 140
  criticism of, developing countries', 101–2
  drawings, special rights of, 150
  exchange standards, developing countries and, 142–44
  Executive Board of, 135–36, 149
  exports and, 46, 69, 139–44, 146, 159, 438–39
  financial issues of, 18

Group of Ten and, 124, 131, 132, 134–35, 148, 149, 440
imports and, 134
inflation and, 144–47, 151
investment (private foreign) and, 293
membership of, 132–33, 154
quotas of, 133–35, 140, 141, 148
reserves of, 134, 147–51
London agreement on, 149
resources, drawings on, 135–39
Soviet nonparticipation in, 103
UK and, 134, 135, 136, 137, 148
UNCTAD and, 71, 109, 124
U.S. and, 148, 149
voting in, 134–35
World Bank Group and, 152
world central bank and, 148
International organizations
analysis of, 443–45
emergence of, 1, 3–4
publications of, 446
International Stabilization Fund, 132
International Telecommunications Union (ITU), 24
International Trade, Commission on, 105
International Trade Organization (ITO), 18, 102
GATT and, 74, 102, 436
Geneva Conference (1947), 291
Havana Charter, 18, 75, 103, 291, 435
investment provisions under, 53, 292–94, 295, 296
UNCTAD and, 105
U.S. and, 75, 102
Inter-Parliamentary Union, 284
Investment (foreign), 50–53
See also Private foreign investment
Investment Disputes, Convention on the Settlement of, 53, 291, 299–301, 304, 305, 306
Iran
ADB and, 191
IMF and, 138
OECD seminar in, 234
Iraq
export growth in, 56
Ireland
on population problems, 344, 350, 381
in U.N., 20
Irrigation, 392–93
Israel
Bank of, 272, 276
desalinization in, 409

EPTA aid to, 210
export growth in, 56
IDB bonds and, 199
income, per capita in, 455
in U.N., 19
on UNCSAT, 395
Italy, 330
ADB and, 190
in DAC (OECD), 232
EPTA and, 210
on family planning, 381
IMF Group of Ten, and, 132
industries in, 452
in U.N., 20
ITO. See International Trade Organization
ITU. See International Telecommunications Union
Ivory Coast
income, per capita in, 455
OECD seminar in, 234

Jamaica
export growth in, 56
GATT and, 97
income, per capita in, 455
in U.N., 20
Japan
ADB and, 183, 198
agricultural production in, 366, 372
cotton textiles, export of, 84
in DAC (OECD), 232
education in, 324, 373
EPTA and, 210
foreign aid, and multilateral assistance by, 272, 279, 281, 282
GATT's Part IV and, 88
IBRD and, 440
in IMF Group of Ten, 132
income, per capita in, 374
industries in, 452
investment (private foreign) in, 304
in OECD, 440
on population growth and family planning, 350
seismology institution in, 407
silk yarn, trade in, 55
Southeast Asian Development Conference and, 281
tariffs under GATT's Part IV, 88
in U.N., 20
Jeanneney report, 6
Johnson, President Lyndon B.
on Alliance for Progress, 267–68
on CIAP, 267
on foreign aid, 279, 388
on multilateral assistance, 387
on population explosion, 347–48

Jordan
export growth in, 56
Jute, 62

Karachi, UNESCO conference in (1960), 313
Kennedy, President John F.
on Alliance for Progress, 252
CIAP, responsibility for, 267
on foreign aid, 4
on population and family planning, 347
on trade, 103
UNDD, proposal for, 22
Kennedy Round. See under General Agreement on Tariffs and Trade
Kenya
African Development Bank and, 196, 201
IAEA project, Lake Chala, 409
Keynes, John Maynard, Clearing Union Proposal, 139–40
Korea, Republic of (South Korea)
birth rate in, 389
IBRD and, 178, 229
income, per capita in, 455
industries in, 452
Korean War, 455
commodity markets and, 64
Kubitschek, Juscelino, 250, 251, 263
Kuwait in U.N., 20

Labouisse, Henry R., on family planning, 352
LAFTA. See Latin American Free Trade Association
Laos, Mekong River development and, 191–93
Latin America
agencies' commitments in, 156
agricultural production in, 333, 364
Center for Application of Science and Technology to Development (UNESCO), 413
DAC (OECD) and, 234
development in, 14, 182, 219
EEC and, 103, 110
GATT and, 83
IBRD and, 167, 168, 188, 445
IDA and, 167, 168
IMF and, 133, 140, 144
inflation in, 145
Institute for Economic Development and Planning (Special Fund), 437
integration (economic) in, 183
investment (foreign) in, 52, 290, 294

Mediterranean Regional Projects and, 234
OEEC and, 249
population growth and family planning in, 333, 336, 338, 340, 343, 346, 350, 354, 382
U.S. aid for, 358, 359
research center on, 345
in U.N., 21
UNCTAD and, 105
unemployment in, 49
UNESCO and, 313, 407
U.S. aid to, investment in, 5, 51, 188, 194, 218, 246, 248, 290, 308
See also Alliance for Progress, Caribbean nations, Central America, Economic Commission for Latin America, Inter-American Development Bank, Inter-American Economic and Social Council, Latin American Common Market, Latin American Free Trade Association, Organization of American States
Latin American Common Market, 219, 266, 268
Latin American Free Trade Association (LAFTA), 1, 247
League of Nations, 11, 268
Covenant and U.N. Charter, compared, 16
Leather, 62, 383
Lebanon
EPTA aid to, 210
Lerma-Chapala-Santiago Basin, 380
Lewis, Oscar, on poverty, 330
Libya
IBRD and, 199
oil in, foreign investment in, 52
in U.N., 20
Linnemann, Hans, on UNDD, 420
Locust control, 375, 383–84
Luxembourg, EPTA and, 210

MacBean, Alastair I., on export instability, 68–69
Macura, Milos, 351
Malaysia
ADB and, 191
IBRD and, 178, 229, 299
income, per capita in, 455
population growth and family planning in, 350
in U.N., 20
Maldive Islands
in U.N., 20
Malta
in U.N., 20

Manpower
  education and, 9, 330
  See also under International Labor Organization
Manufactures, exports from developing countries, 61
Marshall Plan, 19, 226, 231, 262, 263, 266, 268, 281, 312, 429, 440
Mediterranean Development Project (FAO), 439
Mediterranean Regional Project (OECD), 234
Mekong River development scheme, 15, 183, 191–93, 272, 275
Metals, 62, 451. *See also* Ores, *separate listings of metals*
Mexico, 190
  agricultural production in, 277, 371–72, 379, 380, 455
  desalinization in, 409
  IBRD loans to, 168
  IMF and, 138
  income, per capita in, 455
  investment (private foreign) in, 294
  Lerma-Chapala-Santiago Basin and, 380
  oil expropriations by, 290–91
  U.S. investment in, 51, 294
Middle East
  IBRD-IDA loans and credits to, 167
  locust control in, 375, 383–84
  in U.N., 21
  U.S. aid to, 248
Middle Eastern Regional Radiosotope Center for the Arab Countries, 410–11
Minerals, demand for, 62, 66
Mining, U.S. foreign investment in, 51
Mongolia
  in U.N., 20
Monroe Doctrine, 244
Montevideo Treaty, 247
Montgomery, John, on U.S. foreign aid, 388
Morocco
  IBRD and, 178, 199, 229
  in U.N., 20
Multilateral assistance and development, 13, 389–91, 445–52
  family planning and, 342
  See also Foreign aid, *listings of individual countries*
Multilateral Investment Guarantee Scheme (OECD), 53

NATO. *See* North Atlantic Treaty Organization

Nepal on population growth and family planning, 350
Netherlands, 27
  ADB and, 190
  foreign aid and multilateral assistance by, 6, 271, 282, 285
  in IMF Group of Ten, 132
  on investment (private foreign), 293
  Tripartite Declaration (1936) and, 131
New Zealand
  ADB and, 198
  IBRD-IDA loan and credits to, 167
  investment (foreign) in, 51
  Kennedy Round and, 90
  in UNCTAD Issues, Working Party on (OECD), 240
Nicaragua in GATT, 95
Nigeria
  civil war in, 454
  IBRD and, 178, 229
Nine Wise Men. *See under* Alliance for Progress
North Africa, locust control in, 375, 383–84
North Atlantic Treaty Organization (NATO), Parliamentary Assembly, 284
North Carolina State University, 386
Northern Rhodesia
  GATT's Article XVIII and, 80
Norway
  in DAC (OECD), 232
  on family planning, 344, 350, 381
  on investment (private foreign), 304
  multilateral assistance by, 271
Notestein, Frank W., on contraception, 341
Nuclear energy, economic development and, 393
  See also International Atomic Energy Agency

OAS. *See* Organization of American States
OECD. *See* Organization for Economic Cooperation and Development
OEEC. *See* Organization for European Economic Cooperation
Ohly, John H., 206
Oil, 134, 137, 144
  exports from developing countries, 61
  Libyan, foreign investment in, 52
  Mexican expropriations of, 290–91
  U.S. foreign investment in, 51
Oilseeds, 369, 370
Operation Pan America, 250, 251, 253

Ores, 423
Organization of American States (OAS), 1, 205, 246, 248, 253
collective security under, 261
Economic Cooperation, Special Committee to Study the Formulation of New Measures for, 250
exports, compensatory finance for, 140
IA-ECOSOC. *See under* Inter-American Economic and Social Council
IDB and, 279
Twenty-One, Committee of, 250
Organization for Economic Cooperation and Development (OECD), 1, 233, 234, 242–43, 263
aid by, 4
consortia of, 229
developing countries and, 425
DAC and, 11, 14, 225, 226, 232, 235–39, 241, 242–43, 273, 274, 284, 440
Development Assistance, Financial Aspects of, Working Party on, 241
Development Assistance Efforts and Policies, 446
Development Center and, 233, 234
investment guaranties by, 304–6
multilateral assistance funds from, 3, 270–71, 282
UNCTAD and, 237–38, 240–42
Development Assistance Group, 232
Development Center, 233–34, 440
education and economic development under, 314
family planning and, 361
investment (private foreign) and, 53, 291, 295
investment guaranty by, 305–6
Mediterannean Regional Project, 234
Multilateral Investment Guarantee by, 53
OEEC, changed from, 232
Trade Committee of, 240–41, 440
training and research, multinational institutions for, 276
UNCTAD and, 239–41, 243
World Bank Group and, 156
Organization for European Economic Cooperation (OEEC), 226, 231, 262–63, 436
Alliance for Progress and, 265, 266
ECOSOC, example for, 430
Latin America and, 249

Ministerial Council of Economic Advisers, 265
OECD, transformed into, 232, 440
planning of, 429
U.S. aid to, 263
Organization for Trade Cooperation (OTC)
U.S. and, 102
OTC. *See* Organization for Trade Cooperation
Owen, David, 217

Pakistan
agricultural production in, 371, 372, 378, 387
Chandpur Irrigation Project, 379
Indus Plain, irrigation in, 385–86
DAC (OECD) and, 237
IBRD and, 176, 178, 191, 229, 361
IDA and, 176
income, per capita in, 455
India and, 454
Indus Waters Treaty and, 374
population growth and family planning in, 338, 346, 350, 352, 354
in U.N., 19
U.S. assistance to, 386
Paley Commission, 62, 63
Pan-American Highway, 189
Paper, 62
Percy, Senator Charles, on family planning, 357
Peru
agriculture, education for, 386–87
IBRD and, 178, 229
income, per capita in, 455
OECD seminar in, 234
Petroleum. *See* Oil
Philip, André, 234
Philippines
ADB and, 191
education in, 324
rice in, 277
International Rice Research Institute in, 372
Plastics, 62
Point Four Program. *See under* United States
Poland
in GATT, 94
on UNCTAD, 105
UNDP project for, 215
Pope Paul VI, on development, 283
Population, Committee on, 356, 357
Population Commission, 25, 345, 348, 355
Population Council, 341, 346, 358

Population growth, 10, 25, 450–51. *See also* Asian Population Conference, Contraception, Family planning, World Population Conference, *and under individual countries*
Portugal
in DAC (OECD), 232
EPTA aid to, 210
IBRD-IDA loans and credits to, 167
in U.N., 20
Prebisch, Dr. Raúl, 101, 105, 106, 437
on development, 130
on international organization, 127–28
on tariff preferences, 110
UNCTAD and
conciliation, proposal for, 117
Towards a New Trade Policy for Development, 104–5, 107–8, 109, 110
Trade and Development Board of, 113
See also United Nations Conference on Trade and Development
Private foreign investment
Calvo Doctrine and, 290, 294, 295
criticism of, 289
Havana Charter and, 292–94, 295, 296
IBRD arbitration convention on, 299–301, 304, 305, 306
investment guaranty schemes for, 450
protection of, 290–92
U.S. investment guaranty program for, 302–4
Private Property, Protection of, Convention for the (OECD), 53
Protestant and Orthodox World Council of Churches
on development, 283
Puerto Rico, export market, 53
Pye, Lucian, on Burma, 330

Raw materials
agricultural, 61, 62
industrial, 61–62
natural, 62
price changes of, 66
Regional development banks, 7, 43, 182–83, 185, 271
financing of, 196–200
IBRD and, 185
For more specific questions pertaining to, see African Development Bank, Asian Development Bank, Central American Bank, Inter-American Development Bank
Regional economic commissions (U.N.), 18, 121, 430, 431
exports and, 46, 128
technical assistance and, 219
For specific questions pertaining to, see Economic Commission for Africa; Economic Commission for Asia and the Far East; Economic Commission for Europe; Economic Commission for Latin America
Regionalism, 13–14, 54
Resource gap, developing countries and, 49
Rice, 277, 366, 369, 370, 372, 455
International Rice Research Institute, 372, 455
Riddleberger, Ambassador James, 232
Rio Treaty, 246, 261
Rockefeller Foundation, 277, 346, 358, 371–75 *passim,* 382
Roosevelt, President Franklin Delano, 188
Latin American policy of, 245
New Deal, 245
Rosenstein-Rodan, Paul
on Alliance for Progress, 254
on developing countries, 424, 425
Economic Justice, International Court of, 262
Rubber, 62, 66, 370, 423, 451
Rumania
in U.N., 20
Rwanda
UNDP and, 215

Santiago de Chile
UNESCO conference in (1962), 313
Saudi Arabia
EPTA aid to, 210
Savings gap, 12
Scandinavia
on family planning, 343
foreign aid by, 6, 285
Science. *See* International Atomic Energy Association; U.N. Advisory Committee on the Application of Science and Technology to Development; United Nations Educational, Scientific and Cultural Organization
Secretariat (U.N.)
developing countries' criticism of, 101

Secretariat (U.N.) (cont.)
    Economic and Social Affairs, Department of, 18, 42, 101, 121, 122, 124, 129, 444
    population activities of, 343, 345, 351, 353, 361
    UNCTAD Conference and, 57
Secretary General (U.N.)
    on agricultural production, 449
    on development, 444
    economic functions of, 129
    EPTA and, 209
    on population problems, 348, 352, 355, 360, 361
    U.N. Advisory Committee on Application of Science and Technology to Development and, 395
    on UNCTAD, 125–26
    on UNDD, 22–23, 28, 420
    on UNDP, 216
    on UNIDO, 125–26
Sen, B. R., on population growth, 343
Sierra Leone
    African Development Bank and, 196
Silk yarn
    Japanese trade in, 55
    U.S. demand for, 55
Singapore
    ADB and, 191
    in U.N., 20
Sino-Soviet bloc, 4, 5, 9. See also China, People's Republic of; Eastern Europe; Soviet Socialist Republics, Union of
Smelting, U.S. foreign investment in, 51
Smith, Adam, "vent for surplus" theory of, 49
Social Development, Commision for, 40
    developing countries, improvement in, 25
    membership enlarged, 32
Sol, Jorge, on Alliance for Progress, 256–57
South Africa, investment (foreign) in, 51
Southeast Asia, 183
    ADB and, 201
    investment (foreign) in, 52
    rice production in, 372
    Science and Technology, Regional Center for (UNESCO), 413
Southeast Asia
    U.S. aid to, 218
Southeast Asian Development Conference, 281
Soviet Socialist Republics, Union of, 454

agricultural production in, 368
developing countries and, 114
education in, 324
on ECOSOC enlargement, 101
on EEC, 103
on ERP, 18–19
on family planning, 382
foreign aid by, 5, 278, 287
on GATT, 103
on IBRD, 103
industry (heavy), 10
on ILO, 312
on IMF, 103
on investment (private foreign), 290
on ITO, 103
planning of, 429
on UNCTAD, 94, 105
wheat, imports of, 148
Spain
    IBRD-IDA loans and credits to, 167
    IDB bonds purchased by, 199
    in U.N., 20
Special Fund (U.N.), 8, 27, 29, 100, 163, 209, 210, 211, 216, 315–16, 345, 436
    agricultural development and, 378
    AID and, 222
    budget (1962) of, 22
    capital investments resulting from, 38
    contributions to, 26
    Economic Development and Planning, Institutes for, 437
    education and economic development, 313–14
    EPTA and, 213, 214, 215, 216, 222, 273, 438
    FAO and, 382
    FAO/IAEA project on tsetse fly, 409
    locust control project of, 383–84
    Mekong River development of, 192–93
    projects of, 213–16, 218
    UNESCO training of engineers, aid for, 406
    See also Expanded Program of Technical Assistance, United Nations Development Program
Specialized agencies, 18, 24
Special United Nations Fund for Economic Development (SUNFED), 27, 30, 115, 315
    IBRD on, 171
Stalin, Joseph, 103

Sudan
  IBRD and, 178, 229
  in U.N., 20
Sufrin, Sidney C., on technical assistance, 205–6
Sugar, 423, 451
  protection of, 61, 369
SUNFED. *See* Special United Nations Fund for Economic Development
Sweden
  in DAC (OECD), 232
  on family planning, 381
  foreign aid and multilateral assistance by, 271, 282
  in IMF Group of Ten, 132
  in U.N., 19
  UNCTAD, on shortfalls, 109, 279
Switzerland
  IBRD and, 170, 202
  investment (private foreign) in, 295
  Tripartite Declaration (1936) and, 131
Synthetics, 61–62

TAB. *See* Technical Assistance Board
Tanzania
  African Development Bank and, 196
  IAEA project concerning Lake Chala, 409
Tariffs
  GATT and, 76–80, 126–27
  UNCTAD and, 127
  See also General Agreement on Tariffs and Trade
Tea, 66, 370, 451
Technical assistance, 205
  human resources development, 7, 8–9
  institution building, 8
  See also Expanded Program of Technical Assistance, Special Fund, United Nations Development Program, *under* International Bank for Reconstruction and Development
Technology. *See* U.N. Advisory Committee on the Application of Science and Technology to Development
Textiles, 423
  See also Cotton and cotton textiles
Thacker, M. S., 262, 395
Thailand
  DAC (OECD) and, 237
  IBRD and, 178, 229
  Mekong River development and, 191–93

on population growth and family planning, 350
  in U.N., 19
Thorp, Ambassador Willard L., 232, 240
Tobago in U.N., 20
Toynbee, Arnold, 257
Trade, 46–48, 126
  See also European Economic Community; European Free Trade Association; General Agreement on Tariffs and Trade; International Commodity Trade, Commission on; Latin American Common Market; Latin American Free Trade Association; Organization for Economic Cooperation and Development; United Nations Conference on Trade and Development
Trade Agreements Program. *See under* United States
Triffin, Robert, on IMF, as world central bank, 148
Trinidad
  export growth in, 56
  in U.N., 20
Tripartite Declaration (1936), 131
Truman, President Harry S., 8, 20, 312
Trusteeship Council (U.N.), Asia's role in, 20
Tunisia
  desalinization in, 409
  IBRD and, 178, 229
  income, per capita in, 455
  population growth and family planning, 346, 350
  in U.N., 20
Turkey
  family planning and, 350, 355
  growth of, 50
  IBRD and, 165
  OECD consortium for, 229, 361

Uganda
  African Development Bank loan to, 196
  on population growth and family planning, 350
  Technical College, 406
U.N. *See* United Nations
UNCSAT. *See* United Nations Conference on the Application of Science and Technology for the Benefit of the Less Developed Areas

UNCTAD. *See* United Nations Conference on Trade and Development

UNDD. *See* United Nations Development Decades

UNDP. *See* United Nations Development Program

UNESCO. *See* United Nations Educational, Scientific and Cultural Organization

United Arab Republic
African Development Bank and, 194
desalinization in, 409
IMF and, 138
Middle Eastern Regional Radioisotope Center for the Arab Countries, 411
population growth and family planning, 333, 350
Special Fund project in, 407

United Kingdom
ADB and, 190
African Development Bank, special fund for, 195
in DAC (OECD), 232
developing countries and, 114
expenditures (World War II) of, 132
on family planning, 344, 381
foreign aid and multilateral assistance by, 5, 6, 218, 272, 279, 280, 282, 344
GATT
Article XVIII, release for Northern Rhodesia, 80
Part IV, 88
IBRD, balance of payments deficit, 175–76
IDA, 175
balance of payments deficit, 176
IDB bonds and, 198
IMF
balance of payments deficits, 134, 136, 137
Group of Ten, 132
quotas, 135, 148
International Clearing Union, proposal for, 132
on investment (foreign), 51
investment (private foreign) and, 293
on monetary organization, international, 131
OECD and, 231
Overseas Development Institute, 285
reserve and payments position of, 125

technical assistance of, 208
textile industry of, 55
Tripartite Declaration (1936) and, 131
on U.N. economic matters, 17
on UNCSAT, 395
UNCTAD, on shortfalls, 109, 279

United Nations (U.N.)
agencies' commitments to, 156
budget of, 21
Charter, 16, 17, 28–29, 30, 418, 432–33, 444
development and, 457, 458
Development Planning, Projections, and Policies, Center for, 421, 431, 437
economic and social programs, resources for, 16
family planning and, 343–55
Institute for Training and Research, 218–19
membership in, 19–22, 103–4
population, budget for, 356
powers of, reinterpreted, 28–30
publications of, 446
science corps of, 412–16
science and development, 393
Statistical Office of, 18
UNCTAD, trade machinery, 115

United Nations Advisory Committee on the Application of Science and Technology to Development, 392, 396–97, 438
on desalinization, 409
International Center for Theoretical Physics (Trieste), 410
membership of, 396–97
research problems of, 397–98, 450
science corps and, 413, 414
world plan of action of, 398–403

United Nations Capital Development Fund, 42, 165, 438, 442

United Nations Children's Fund (UNICEF), 29
contributions to, 17
education and economic development, 313–14
family planning and, 352, 356, 357, 360
FAO and, 383, 384
food aid and, 375

United Nations Conference on the Application of Science and Technology for the Benefit of the Less Developed Areas (UNCSAT), 9, 275, 393
accomplishments of, 262, 394–95
developing lands and, 24

United Nations Conference on International Organization (UNCIO), 17

United Nations Conference on Trade and Development (UNCTAD), 1, 11, 13, 18, 31, 33, 39, 40, 44, 99, 100, 106, 123, 125, 127–30, 436

Commodities, Committee on, 99, 108, 437

commodity terms of trade, 108–9

conciliation, machinery for, 118

conferences, function of, 123

Geneva Conference (1964), 99, 109, 124–25, 237–38, 239–41, 432, 434, 448

New Delhi Conference (1968), 113, 123, 432

developing countries, 21, 33

capital investments in, 111

coordination in, 120–29

development rate in, 112, 113

obligation of, 29–30

development plans of, 33–34, 431

Economic Affairs, Director-General for, 129

ECOSOC and, 122, 123, 125

exports and, 46, 60–61, 63, 67, 69, 128, 369

GATT, conflict with, 126

IBRD recommendation to, 159

IMF on, 141

shortfalls, 109, 279, 423, 452

foreign exchange earnings and, 50

France and, 117

GATT and, 34, 70, 71, 86, 109, 124

General Assembly and, 118, 123

Horowitz Plan, 172–74, 202, 276

IBRD and, 71, 124

IMF and, 71, 124

International Trade Center and, 128

investment (foreign) and, 53

investment guaranty scheme and, 305

Invisibles and Financing Related to Trade, Committee on, 99, 115, 116, 122, 437

ITO and, 105

Manufactures, Committee on, 99, 437

OECD and, 243

Prebisch, Dr. Raúl and. *See* Prebisch, Dr. Raúl

reserves, 149

secretariat, 42, 99, 106–14, 122, 124, 126, 129, 437

Shipping, Committee on, 99, 437

tariffs and, 127

trade and, 24, 34, 54

Trade and Development Board, 33, 99, 113, 116, 118, 120–21, 122, 123, 124, 437

UNIDO and, 35–36, 128

U.S. and, 117, 122

voting in, 114–20

United Nations Conference on Trade and Employment

GATT drawn up at Preparatory Committee of, 73–74

United Nations Development Decades (UNDD), 4, 12, 13, 22–23, 27–28, 57, 91, 107, 334, 420

criticism of, by developing countries, 27

exports by developing countries, 455

United Nations Development Program (UNDP), 8, 26, 27, 42, 121, 163, 204, 205, 216–22, 272, 275, 308, 438, 443, 444

African Development Bank and, 195

contributions to, 42

coordination in, 34

education and, 9

EPTA and, 217

family planning and, 357

funds-in-trust for, 43

Governing Council of, 32–33, 127, 215, 216, 219

Interagency Consultative Board and, 217

science corps and, 412–13, 415–16

Special Fund projects and, 38

UNESCO and, 407

UNIDO and, 37

World Population Program and, 360

See also Expanded Program of Technical Assistance, Special Fund

United Nations Educational, Scientific and Cultural Organization (UNESCO), 1, 9, 40, 273, 310, 326, 329, 404, 439, 444

development and, 314–15, 316, 325, 430

education and, 313

Educational Planning, International Institute for, 437

IBRD, assistance to, 163, 205

on population growth and family planning, 349, 353

Santiago de Chile Conference (1962) of, 313

science corps and, 412, 415

science programs of, 392, 403–8, 411

regional training centers, 413

World Bank Group and, 438

United Nations Industrial Development Organization (UNIDO), 1, 10, 13, 34, 35, 39, 40, 42, 125, 329, 437, 442, 444
  agroindustries and, 25
  development world plan and, 430
  ECOSOC and, 125
  exports and, 126, 128
  financing of, 37
  Industrial Development Board, 35, 36, 127, 437
  ILO and, 443
  personnel problems, 36–37
  U.N. Secretary General on, 125–26
  UNCTAD and, 35–36, 128
  UNDP and, 37
United Nations Institute for Training and Research (UNITAR), 437
United Nations Monetary and Financial Conference at Bretton Woods. See Bretton Woods Conference, under International Bank for Reconstruction and Development and under International Monetary Fund
United Nations Relief and Works Agency for Palestine Refugees in the Near East (UNRWA), food aid, management of, 375
United Nations Research Institute for Social Development, 437
United Nations Special Fund. See Special Fund (U.N.)
United States
  ADB and, 183, 188, 197, 279
  Africa, aid to, 194, 207
  African Development Bank and, 195, 279
  agricultural production in, 334, 364, 365, 368, 372, 373
  AID and, 196, 206, 211, 222
    agricultural development and, 377, 379, 385–87
    Alliance for Progress and, 260
    family planning and, 346, 347, 348, 355–56, 389
    Latin American projects of, 445
  alien property, expropriation of, 308
  Alliance for Progress, Coordinating Committee for, on, 257
  Asia, aid to, 194, 248
  balance of payments, problems of, 148, 280, 281
  CIAP and, 269
  civil rights in, 434
  on consortia, 229–30
  cotton textiles, 83
  in DAC (OECD), 232

desalinization in, 408–9
Economic Advisers, Council of, 265
on economic cooperation, 433
on education, 325
EEC and, 110
EPTA and, 20, 27, 100
expenditures (World War II) of, 132
on Export-Import Bank, 188
on exports and developing nations, 369
on family planning, 340, 343, 344, 346–48, 356–60, 361, 381, 382
  foreign aid for, 357–60, 361, 451
foreign aid and multilateral assistance by, 4–5, 8, 11, 218, 248, 272, 279–80, 281–82, 344, 368, 376, 387–88, 420, 433
Foreign Assistance Act, 269
Foreign Policy Association, 285
Foreign Relations, Council on, 285
France and, 103
GATT and, 73, 102
  Kennedy Round and, 90, 439
  Part IV and, 88
  automobile free trade and, 97
Group of Ten, 132
IBRD and, 132, 165, 175–76, 188, 198, 202
  capital subscription to, 169–70
  dollar obligations, 170
IDA and, 27, 279, 280
IDB and, 188, 197, 200, 203, 307
IFC and, 27, 188
IMF and, 134, 135, 136, 148
International Development, Society for, 285
International Stabilization Fund, and, 132
investments
  in developing countries, 51
  investments, private, protection of, 294, 295–96, 302
ITO, Havana Charter and, 75, 102
Latin America, aid to, 5, 188, 194, 218, 246, 248, 308
Middle East, aid to, 248
mining, foreign investment in, 51
on monetary organization, 131
National Banking Act, 170
OECD and, 231, 440
oil, foreign investment in, 51
  expropriation, Mexican, 290–91
OTC and, 102
Peace Corps, 208, 222, 384
Point Four Program, 8, 204, 246, 312, 388
population in, 333

public utility industries, 166
reserves and payments, 125, 149
Securities and Exchange Act, 170
Special Fund and, 27, 100
Tariff Commission, 77–78, 79
tariffs, 452
  Kennedy Round, concessions under, 89
  UNCTAD preferences for, 109, 110
on technical assistance, 208
textiles and, 452
trade and, 46
Trade Agreements Program, 73
Trade Expansion Act, 90
Tripartite Declaration (1936), and, 131
U.N. central institutions, powers of, 121
U.N. Charter and, 17
on UNCTAD, 105, 117, 122
on UNDP, 217
Vietnam war and, 279–80, 454
Western Europe, aid to, 248
World Bank Group and, 280
Yugoslavia, aid to, 188
Universal Declaration of Human Rights. See Human Rights, Universal Declaration of
Universal Postal Union, 435
Uruguay
  investment (foreign) in, 51
  Kennedy Round and, 90
U.S.S.R. See Soviet Socialist Republics, Union of

Venezuela
  EPTA aid to, 210
  U.S. investment in, 51
Vietnam, Republic of
  IBRD and, 199
  Mekong River development and, 191–93
  war in, 134, 279–80, 281, 454

West Germany. See Germany, Federal Republic of
Western Europe
  on family planning, 343, 346, 354
  foreign aid by, 5–6
  role in establishment of
    EPTA, 27
    GATT, 73
    IFC, 27
    Special Fund, 27
    UNDP, 27
  in Trade and Development Board (UNCTAD), 33

U.S. aid to, 248
See also Council of Europe, Economic Commission for Europe, Europe, European Atomic Energy Community, European Coal and Steel Community, European Economic Community, European Free Trade Association, North Atlantic Treaty Organization, Organization for Economic Cooperation and Development, Organization for European Economic Cooperation
Wheat, 148, 277, 368, 371–72
WHO. See World Health Organization
Williams, John H., on international monetary cooperation, 131
WMO. See World Meteorological Organization
Woods, George D.
  on development, 283–84, 420, 425
  on state-owned enterprises, 167
World Bank. See International Bank for Reconstruction and Development
World Bank Group, 8, 13, 152, 181, 186, 274
  African Development Bank and, 195
  commitments by, 155, 156
  development financing, 160, 166, 438
  FAO and, 438
  funds, sources of, 169–76
  loans of, 160–61
  policies of, 156–57, 158–69
  President George D. Woods's statements on, 167, 283–84, 420, 425
  UNESCO and, 438
  U.S. and, 280
  See also International Bank for Reconstruction and Development, International Development Association, International Finance Corporation
World Food Program, 17, 25, 398
World Health Organization (WHO), 1, 273, 380, 410
  development world plan and, 430
  FAO and nutrition program, 384
  on population problems and family planning, 25, 341–45 passim, 349, 352–61 passim, 381–82, 446, 451
World Meteorological Organization (WMO), 1, 24
World Population Conferences, 345, 349, 381

World Population Program, 358, 360, 361

World protein gap, 25

Yaoundé Convention of Association, 90

Yemen
 in U.N., 19

Yugoslavia
 in IBRD, 154
 U.N. aid to, 210
 U.S. aid to, 188

Zambia
 African Development Bank, Tanzania, railway to, 195–96